the story of
EGYPT

the story of

EGYPT

THE CIVILIZATION THAT SHAPED THE WORLD

———

JOANN FLETCHER

PEGASUS BOOKS
NEW YORK LONDON

THE STORY OF EGYPT

Pegasus Books, Ltd.
148 West 37th Street, 13th Floor
New York, NY 10018

First Pegasus Books paperback edition August 2017
First Pegasus Books hardcover edition August 2016

ISBN: 978-1-68177-456-5

10 9 8 7 6 5 4

Printed in the United States of America
Distributed by Simon & Schuster
www.pegasusbooks.com

For Stephen and Eleanor

Egypt within the ancient world 3000 BC – 30 BC

Sea

ARMENIA

SYRIA (Mitanni)

ASSYRIA

•Gaugamela

MESOPOTAMIA

PHOENICIA

River Euphrates

BABYLONIA

•Babylon

NABATAEA

ARABIA

•Persepolis

Persian Gulf

GEDROSIA

INDIA

Indian Ocean

IA

Red Sea

SABA

Straits of Mandeb

Blue Nile

PUNT

Muziris•

CILICIA

•Tarsus   •Issus

•Carchemish

•Antioch
Ebla

Ugarit•   R. Orontes   Niy•

SYRIA (Mitanni)

•Qatna

•Kadesh

CYPRUS

Byblos•   AMURRU

•Sidon

•Tyre

Megiddo•   Sea of Galilee

PALESTINE

Joppa•   CANAAN

Gezer•   •Jerusalem

Ashkelon•

•Gaza   Dead Sea

Raphia•   ↑JUDAH

Sharuhen•

Petra•

1 Quban
2 Abu Simbel
3 Faras
4 Qasr Ibrim
5 Buhen
6 Mirgissa
7 Semna
8 Kumma
9 Sai Island
10 Sedeinga

11 Soleb
12 Tombos
13 Kerma
14 Karoy
15 Kurgus
16 Gebel Barkal
17 Napata
18 Nuri
19 el-Kurru

0	500	1000 miles
0	800	1600 km

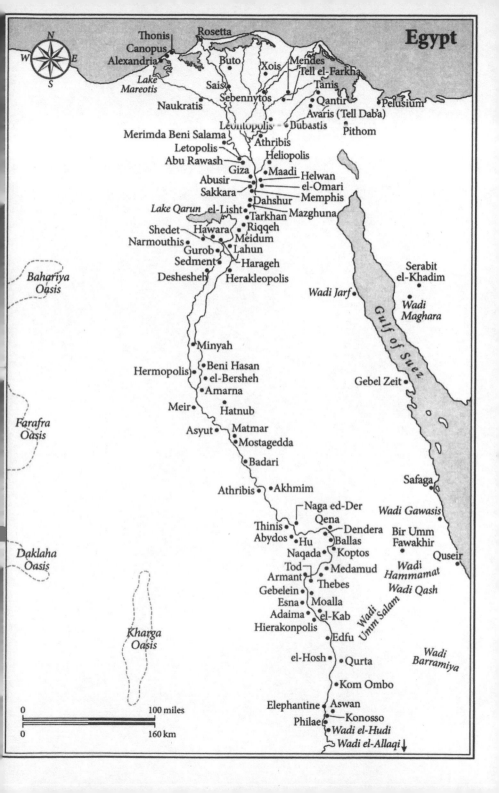

Contents

Introduction   I

1. In the Beginning   5
2. Sahara Savannah: c.55,000–5500 BC   II
3. Seeking the Waters: c.5500–3500 BC   17
4. The North–South Divide: c.3500–3100 BC   30
5. Lords and Ladies of the Two Lands:
   c.3100–2890 BC   39
6. Shifting Focus: c.2890–2686 BC   54
7. The Rise of the Pyramid Age:
   c.2667–2613 BC   60
8. Sons and Daughters of the Sun:
   c.2613–2494 BC   66
9. The Rule of Ra: c.2494–2375 BC   83
10. Clouds Across the Sun: c.2375–2181 BC   96
11. Anarchy in the Two Lands: c.2181–1985 BC   II2
12. Classic Kingdom, Middle Kingdom:
    c.1985–1855 BC   127
13. Proliferate, Disintegrate: c.1855–1650 BC   145
14. Divided and Conquered: c.1650–1550 BC   157
15. Dawn of the Golden Age: c.1550–1425 BC   168
16. Zenith of the Sun: c.1425–1352 BC   196
17. Reflected Glories: c.1352–1295 BC   217
18. Reigns of the Ramessides: c.1295–1069 BC   235
19. Decline, Rise and Fall: c.1069–332 BC   268
20. The Final Flourish: 332–30 BC   304

Chronology   369
Note on Spellings   377

Acknowledgements   379
Notes on Sources   381
Select Bibliography   426
Picture Acknowledgements   461
Index   463

Introduction

This is the story of Egypt – the story of its ancient culture, and how this first came into being, how it developed and flourished, apparently declined, and then finally came to a notional end.

Retold countless times down the centuries, there are as many versions of Egypt's story as there are those to tell it. And so this is simply my version, featuring the people, places and events that have fascinated me my whole life.

And it is fair to say Egypt has pretty much *been* my life. Familiar and accessible through my family's books, photographs and wartime recollections, the ancient Egyptians were, it seems, always around during my childhood, as the inspiration for my earliest drawings, the way I dressed my dolls, the things I read and collected.

The defining moment came in 1972, when the Tutankhamen exhibition arrived in Britain. His beautiful golden face appeared everywhere in the media frenzy for all things pharaonic, and Egyptologists of the day were regularly asked for quotes by the press. The revelation that people actually studied ancient Egypt as their job seemed to me both astonishing and wonderful – so at the age of six, I announced that I was going to do that too.

Admittedly it was not a particularly straightforward career choice for a young girl growing up in the Yorkshire mining town of Barnsley in the 1970s, when ancient Egypt was certainly not on the national curriculum. Assuming I was completely deluded, careers advisors insisted that teaching or nursing were my only realistic alternatives, while letters seeking the advice of curators and academics likewise drew a blank.

Yet my mind was made up. Falling head over heels in love with the country, its people, and its past on my first trip to Egypt at the impressionable age of fifteen, I worked all the harder to gain the required exam results for acceptance on to my dream degree course – Egyptology and ancient history. Initially studying as an undergraduate, then as a postgraduate, I am now lucky enough to teach the subject myself, working with universities, museums, laboratories and television companies, and spending time in Egypt, with my adopted family, with my friends, and with some of my Egyptological heroes.

And this has led to a whole range of fascinating projects I could never have imagined as a child; not only to rediscover the past, but to try to recreate it, to better understand how the Egyptians lived, how they died, and how they then lived on through mummification, preserving themselves for the future.

Work that has taken me all over Egypt, as far afield as Yemen, Sudan and South Africa – not to mention Barnsley, Harrogate and Wigan – the results of diverse projects in diverse places, has certainly caused me to question some long-held notions about Egypt's ancient past and its people, meaning that my story of Egypt inevitably varies from more 'traditional' histories.

For these can sometimes almost suggest that an elite group of men sprang fully formed from the banks of their great river, remaining in splendid isolation for the last three thousand years BC, before apparently disappearing as mysteriously as they had arrived, their exotic and arcane legacy largely impenetrable to the modern west.

Yet for all their esoteric reputation, the Egyptians were actually the most practical and inventive of people, whose view of their world – quite logical when seen through their eyes – is really no more curious than our own.

And certainly all the elements that made up 'ancient Egypt' were already in place far earlier, lasted far longer and covered a much wider area than is generally acknowledged, certainly far beyond the narrow confines of the Nile Valley, and much of traditional Egyptology.

So by pushing back boundaries beyond limited time frames, beyond current borders, and beyond a male elite of kings and priests, there emerges a rather more balanced kind of story.

Spanning millennia, continents and classes, it is a story initiated by climate change and migrating populations, brought together in a very particular environment – a desert irrigated by a single great river, whose fertile banks nurtured the greatest culture the world has ever seen.

Jo Fletcher

Yorkshire

2015

I

In the Beginning

Within their rich body of myth and legend, the Egyptians believed that 'in the beginning' was complete darkness, a darkness made up of the infinite, formless waters from which the very first mound of earth appeared.

Yet creation was no unique event; it reoccurred every single year when the world was created anew from the annual Nile flood, when 'the whole country is converted into a sea', as one ancient eyewitness claimed.

Believed to originate in a cavern in the furthest reaches of southern Egypt, the floodwaters' arrival was heralded by the rising of the Morning Star (Sirius), which the Egyptians identified as the glittering goddess Sothis, 'the most beautiful of all, at the start of a happy year'.

As the Nile's welcome waters began to rise and spill out across the land, they literally brought life, 'hugging the fields, so each is reborn'. As 'the meadows laugh when the riverbanks are flooded', it was said that 'the whole land leaps for joy!' as people threw flowers, offerings and even themselves into the waters.

Just as the rhythms of the river dictated the pace of life as its levels rose and fell each year, so its annual cycle formed a structured calendar of three seasons – the inundation (*akhet*), followed by spring planting (*peret*) and summer harvest (*shemu*). Each year the receding waters would reveal a revitalised land filled with the promise of new life, a layer of rich black wet silt, sparkling in the sunshine, within which bountiful harvests could grow. In fact, the silt was such a stark contrast with the sterile sands of the surrounding deserts that Egypt was very clearly a land of two parts, a dual landscape of Red Land, Black Land: *deshret* and *kemet*.

Since this phenomenon was witnessed along the whole length of the river's course as it flowed its 750 miles from south to north, each separate region of Egypt had its own explanation of these annual events, explanations that took the form of creation sagas in which their own local deity took the starring role.

In Memphis, creation was regarded as the handiwork of Ptah, who had combined masculine and feminine elements within the primeval waters to emerge as the risen land itself. Then, having simply *thought* the world into being, Ptah, 'the Father of the gods' as well as the 'Mother who gave birth to all the gods', summoned up all living things by simply speaking their names, in the earliest known version of the familiar refrain 'In the Beginning was the Word'.

At nearby Sais, a more exuberant variation on this 'word of God' scenario involved the thunderous laughter of Neith 'the Terrifying One', the armed creator goddess who alone gave birth to the sun. And as one who could be both 'the male who acts the female, the female who acts the male', she could at any time make the sky crash down and destroy all she had made, personifying the two extremes of life and death, inherent in the floodwaters and within the sun itself.

Further south, at Hermopolis, it was claimed that life had been created by a cooperative of eight deities, 'the fathers and mothers who were before the original gods'. Taking the form of pairs of male frogs and female snakes, the first creatures seen to emerge from the receding floodwaters, their combined energy was believed to have first sparked life into being, creating the primeval mound, an 'island of flame', from which the sun first burst forth.

But the key creation myth centred on Heliopolis, 'Sun City', where the supreme deity was the sun, 'the mother and father of all' and the 'great He-She'. As the great fiery orb rose up from the primeval mound to create the first spectacular sunrise, its daily journey across the sky thereafter was the constant cycle of renewal that formed the rhythm of an entire culture. For as day followed night followed day, so too did life and death and new life, two states of existence regarded as an eternal continuum – to live was to die, but then to be born again.

And with solar power having initiated this perpetual motion of the universe, it was a process personified by Maat, daughter of the sun. Responsible for everything her single solar parent had created, Maat, the cosmic caretaker, maintained the new universe in perfect balance, with everything countered by its opposite in repeated sets of dualities – day and night, light and dark, fertile and sterile, order and chaos, life and death – each two halves of the same state, and neither able to exist without the other. It was an essential equilibrium obeyed by all, from the living to the dead, and to the very gods themselves, all of whom must 'live by Maat'.

Yet Maat was not an only child. For within a vast body of myth developed over centuries, the androgynous sun produced a plethora of daughters, from the cow goddess Hathor to the lioness Sekhmet and Tefnut, goddess of moisture. Brought forth with her twin brother, Shu, god of the air, the sibling deities were commonly believed to have been brought forth through a sudden expression of body fluid, by 'sneezing out Shu and spitting out Tefnut'; although an alternative version suggested they had been ejaculated into existence via 'the hand of God'.

In turn, male Shu and female Tefnut produced twin children of their own: the laid-back green earth god Geb, usually depicted lying down, and the shimmering sky goddess Nut, arching over him to form the heavens, a celestial powerhouse who physically supported the universe and protected all below her.

Known as 'the great one who bore the gods', Nut's onerous duties also involved daily childbirth, as each day at dawn she gave birth to the sun: a tricky task, given that the sun was technically her grand-parent, but not a problem within Egypt's all-encompassing belief system, which evolved sufficiently over time to synthesise, and indeed rationalise, the most unlikely of divine genealogies.

Nut and Geb were the parents of four more offspring, twin couples Isis and Osiris, Seth and Nephthys. And it was their inter-family feuding that first brought death into the solar saga.

According to myth, Isis and her younger brother Osiris were Egypt's first rulers, joint monarchs presiding over a golden age, until their jealous brother Seth seized power by drowning Osiris, dismembering him and scattering his body parts throughout the Nile Valley.

But Seth's triumph was short-lived. Having first mourned for Osiris, literally crying him a river — her tears caused the Nile's first flood — Isis recovered Osiris's body, which she then reassembled, wrapping the parts together to create the first mummy. Then, using her great magic, she resurrected both his soul and his reproductive powers to conceive their son Horus.

Truly 'more clever than a million gods' and 'craftier than a million men', Isis raised her son in secret to avenge his father and take on his uncle Seth in a series of violent struggles. For Isis was her son's protector, 'more effective than millions of soldiers', whose ability to both nurture and attack was typical of the way the Egyptians never assumed that male and female must necessarily equate simply with the concepts of active and passive.

And while Osiris, his father Geb and fellow deities like fertility god Min were usually portrayed as static and inert, with only their prominent reproductive organ betraying any sign of life, their female counterparts were often seen to be initiating action, from Nut, the 'Great Striding Goddess, sowing precious stones as stars' to her dynamic daughter Isis who, by gradually absorbing the powers of her fellow goddesses, eventually became Egypt's most powerful deity, striding out across the Mediterranean to be worshipped for centuries across three continents.

As the perfectly mummified Osiris took his place as King of the Underworld, bound up tightly in his wrappings to be 'everlasting in perfect condition', he passed, like a parcel, into the permanent care of 'Mighty Isis who protected her brother', and joined him in the night sky; Osiris as the constellation of Orion, guarded by Isis, who absorbed the star qualities of Sothis (Sirius), herald of the Nile flood.

Yet Isis was also present in the land of the living, to protect and guide their son Horus, who had succeeded his father to take the throne of Egypt. Horus came to symbolise the divine nature of kingship, with every subsequent human monarch named 'the Living Horus', and then at death, transformed into 'an Osiris', their souls absorbed into an accumulating underworld power base, reinvigorated each night by the nocturnal visit of the omnipresent sun god.

Although this father–son relationship between Osiris and Horus was the model by which the Egyptians interpreted the transition

8

between monarchs, it was also a three-way relationship, since kingship was very much 'a composite of male and female elements': Isis, whose very name means 'throne', was the vital presence linking the generations together. She was the daughter, sister, wife and mother, whose familial relationships were the foundation of royal continuity.

And this cuts to the very heart of an ancient culture in which female and male, mother and father, sister and brother, daughter and son, were all essential halves of a complete whole. So the modern tendency to focus on the masculine can only ever see half the story. Certainly the Egyptians used the term 'people', featuring both a male and female hieroglyphic determinative sign, while their use of the phrase 'women and men' was similarly balanced with 'mother and father'.

This same notion extended to monarchy's mythical origins, with Isis and Osiris both appearing as rulers in the official king lists, to be succeeded by their son Horus, and then the 'Followers of Horus', the demi-gods, who represented the souls of long-forgotten human monarchs.

For gods and royals dominated the Egyptian worldview, and indeed their history, with humans themselves often something of an afterthought, believed to have been created in a range of different and highly inventive ways.

In the south of Egypt, where the goddess Satet and her ram-headed consort Khnum were believed to regulate the flow of the Nile from their subterranean cave, Khnum was credited with making every human on his potter's wheel. At Sais, it was the goddess Neith who invented birth and is described as 'moulding beings', while at Heliopolis, the androgynous sun, 'Creator of all who makes them live', was 'the beneficent mother of gods and humans'. Mortals were sometimes dubbed 'the cattle of god', although one version of events employed wordplay to claim that they came forth when the sun god wept, the tears (*remyt*) falling to earth as people (*remet*).

And certainly the sun god had plenty of reason to weep, for almost as soon as humans appeared on earth they began to cause trouble.

Deciding to punish them, the sun summoned the gods together and asked which of them would best perform the required cull; their unanimous choice fell on yet another of the sun god's daughters.

Known as 'the Eye of the Sun', this was the cow-like goddess Hathor, the 'Golden One', who wore the sun as a crown and personified love and care for the living and the dead. Yet when roused, she instantly transformed into the lioness Sekhmet, 'the Powerful One', who brought death to all enemies of her sole, solar parent.

And as this uncontrollable force was unleashed upon an unsuspecting world, the treacherous humans ran for their lives and tried to hide in the desert. But the gleeful goddess hunted them down – 'the Eye appears against you, she devours you, she punishes you', wading through their blood to visibly transform into the 'Lady of Bright Red Linen' in her gore-soaked robes.

Her killing spree was only halted when the sun saw the human suffering and relented, devising a plan in which beer was mixed with red ochre and poured out upon the sands. The goddess, assuming it was yet more human blood, gulped it down and was soon too drunk to move, forgetting where she was, and even what she was supposed to be doing, as she fell soundly asleep.

On waking, she was once more gentle Hathor, but imbued with both the powers of primeval Tefnut, goddess of moisture, and the astral goddess Sothis, a supercharged deity whose return to Egypt heralded 'both the coming of the floodwaters and the rejuvenation of the world'.

With the reinvigorated goddess resuming her place as supreme protector of the sun, the remaining humans, spared their fate, returned home to Egypt too, celebrating their deliverance with what would become an annual beer festival, where general inebriation was accompanied by music and dancing to soothe all anger away.

Yet the notion that humans had hidden from the goddess at the desert fringes before migrating back to the Nile Valley does contain a tiny fragment of historical truth, for amidst this mysterious haze of mythic beginnings, it is becoming increasingly clear that key aspects of the Egyptians' true origins did lie far beyond the familiar world of the Nile Valley.

But not in the mystical realm of the gods – in the very heart of the prehistoric Sahara Desert.

2

Sahara Savannah: c.55,000–5500 BC

Today a searing wilderness of barren sands, appropriate to the destructive powers of the sun god's daughter, the Sahara was once a vast, green savannah, stretching right across north Africa from sea to sea.

As a result of the rain belt shifting further north at various times, there was sufficient rainfall to sustain grassy landscapes dotted with acacia and tamarisk trees, and a wide range of wildlife from lions to giraffes, elephants, camels, gazelle, wild cattle and, of course, humans. The earliest human remains from Egypt are – perhaps appropriately – those of a child, who lived around Dendera some 55,000 years ago.

As the Nile Valley was predominantly swamp, these earliest Egyptians inhabited the higher ground on each side, following herds of wild cattle as they wandered the plains in periodic migration. These prehistoric hunter–gatherers also tracked animals along the seasonal, lateral tributaries leading to the Nile. These river valleys (*wadis*), dry beds today, are still dotted with the stone hand axes, flint blades and arrowheads vital to the earliest Egyptians' survival, both in this world and, it seems, the next, since such artefacts were already being placed in graves some 30,000 years ago.

By around 25,000 BC, these early people had established hunting camps at places like Qena, where traces of their cooking fires and the bones of the animals they hunted have been found. Such animals, carved into the sandstone rocks of Qurta near Edfu some 19,000 years ago, form 'the oldest graphic activity ever recorded in the whole of north Africa', this 'Lascaux along the Nile' featuring huge figures of wild cattle, seemingly erupting from the rock face. There are also gazelle, hippos, birds and fish, and the stylised, female figures representing the Egyptians' earliest attempts at self-portraits.

Further traces of these early people have also been found on the high plateau above the West Bank of the Nile at Luxor, where petro-glyphs of cows and stars at the head of one particular *wadi*, now known as the Valley of the Queens, forever mark it out as the home of the goddess Hathor. Believed to give (re)birth to the dead via the womb-like cave at the valley head, the waters of the occasional flash flood gushing forth from here were seen as visible proof that Hathor, later herself known as 'the Great Flood', was surely present.

With such flash floods still capable of 'turning dry *wadis* into raging torrents for a few hours', such conditions were also found in Egypt's Eastern Desert, whose now-arid Wadi Hammamat – the 'Valley of Many Baths' – was a regular thoroughfare 12,000 years ago. Among a number of routes between the Nile and Red Sea, but in places hundreds of miles from either, the rocky terrain nonetheless features repeated rock images of multi-oared ships following the lone star Sirius high above them, while a further image, described as 'the world's oldest map', presumably helped navigate this complex terrain.

Yet the richest source of images in the whole Sahara lies in Egypt's Western Desert, 600 kilometres from the Nile, within the Gilf Kebir 'Great Wall' plateau. Here in the rock shelters of the Wadi Sura, the 'Valley of Pictures', are images of people running, hunting, dancing and drinking milk from the udders of cows, the very origins of ancient Egypt, pictured within 'the earliest sanctuary on the map of Egyptian temple architecture'.

So striking are the images that, looking at them, the eight millennia that separate ancient artist and modern viewer suddenly disappear. For some of these little stick figures can be observed stretching out their arms and legs and swimming! Splashing about in the middle of the desert within their aptly named 'Cave of Swimmers', the people they represent once plied the lake that then existed within Wadi Sura and formed a focus for social gatherings.

More of their swimming companions were discovered in 2002 in the nearby 'Cave of Beasts', in which some 8,000 animals and humans were carved over a background 'wallpaper' made by the artists spitting red paint over their hands. A veritable trail of such handprints overlaid with incised figures have been found at sites further east toward the Nile Valley, both within the Farafra Oasis and in the 'Cave of the Hands' in a *wadi* so remote as to rarely feature on maps. Yet 'the handprint motif in the Cave of Hands is one of the most remarkable and strongest pieces of evidence for connections between early Egyptians and the Sahara/inner Africa'.

Those who inhabited this huge expanse also shared a reliance on cattle, and in south-west Egypt, close to the Sudanese border, summer rains once formed large lakes – *playas* – which attracted both animals and the nomads who followed them. One of the largest was Lake Nabta – Nabta Playa – some sixty miles west of the Nile, where wild cattle were being herded by around 8000 BC. A form of 'walking larder' or 'walking blood banks', such cattle provided milk and blood for protein, as they still do today for the Maasai people; but since the cattle also represented the communities' wealth, most meat was acquired through hunting gazelle, hare and ostrich and, later, the sheep and goats that were introduced from the Near East by about 6000 BC.

By then, previously nomadic herders had set up permanent homes by the lakes in oval houses of tamarisk branches and animal skins. They had hearths for cooking and heating, grinding stones for preparing food, and storage pits which when excavated still contained traces of millet and sorghum, tubers and fruit. There were also ostrich eggs, each huge egg capable of feeding up to eight people and their shells then employed to make beads.

Yet the Neolithic inhabitants of Nabta Playa were still heavily reliant on the annual summer rains, and it was essential for them to be able to predict exactly when these would return to replenish their supplies.

So, drawing on an impressive level of astronomical knowledge acquired over centuries, the same skills that had allowed them to navigate by the stars and create rudimentary rock-carved maps helped them to create a highly innovative piece of time-keeping equipment.

Made up of narrow sandstone blocks set up in a small circle some four metres across, the Stone Circle of Nabta Playa is a far smaller version of Stonehenge. But at more than 2,000 years older, it is the world's oldest known calendar – the first to be created by the sun-fixated Egyptians, who 'by their study of astronomy discovered the solar year . . . in my opinion their method of calculation is better than the Greeks'', admitted a later Greek historian. Indeed, as 'the only rational calendar ever devised', this solar calendar with its origins in the Stone Age Sahara was the way the Egyptians would mark the passing of their entire history; it was adopted by the Romans, and then the papacy, eventually to become the calendar still used in the west today.

The largest of the Nabta calendar stones was aligned to the summer solstice, marking the beginning of the rainy season when people came together at this sacred site to focus on the things 'that would have been of both practical and symbolic importance to the nomads: death, water, cattle, sun and stars'. Close to the calendar site, a high dune, still covered with huge piles of cattle bones, suggests that the beginning of the rainy season was marked by the rare slaughter of precious cattle, both for human consumption and as a sacrificial offering to the unseen forces who brought the rains.

There was also a great slab of sandstone sculpted as a stylised cow, perhaps 'a surrogate sacrificial cow', and the earliest known example of large-scale stonework in the whole of Egypt. There were also mounds topped with stones weighing up to two tons each, possibly marking the burials of Nabta's elite, and some fashioned with anthropomorphic shoulders 'suggesting that they served as stele, perhaps representing the dead.' Like the calendar, they were carefully oriented to the northern hemisphere and the circumpolar stars, the brightest in the sky, which never set and which would later become known as the 'Imperishable Stars'.

Of great importance to the Nabta communities, these monoliths had been transported from a quarry over a mile away, representing a huge investment of time and effort, and an impressive level of organisation and cooperation. And as people began to work together to achieve such tasks by around 6000 BC, those who assembled at Nabta Playa were clearly pooling skills and ideas that in turn triggered other technological developments, from the domestication of cattle to the production of some of the earliest known pottery in Africa.

Yet, by around 5500 BC the rain belt was gradually shifting south, and as the rains began to diminish, so too did the savannah grasslands.

Some of the last Neolithic inhabitants of the remaining savannah can be traced to the lakeside of Gebel Ramlah – 'Sandy Mountain'– only twenty kilometres away from Nabta Playa. This apparently peaceful society, dated to around 5000 BC, was a blend of 'Mediterranean and sub-Saharan' populations whose 'complex and exuberant material culture' is represented by their tools of flint and granite, implements made from animal and fish bones, pottery beakers and bowls, and stone objects ranging from diorite vessels to an exquisite tilapia fish of irridescent mica, pierced for suspension by its female owner.

The fact that such materials were obtained from as far away as Sinai and the Red Sea coast is intriguing, since most were employed purely for personal adornment. As 'remnant vocabulary from a lost language of display', it really is one of the best ways to understand such preliterate cultures. And the striking people of Gebel Ramlah favoured generous quantities of beads in red carnelian, green chalcedony, blue turquoise, black diorite, white limestone and ostrich-egg shell, together with animal teeth, bird bones and shells from the Red Sea, worn as adornments on their arms, wrists, legs and ankles, waists, necks and heads. Noses and lips were enhanced with studs of carnelian, turquoise, shell and bone, and they coloured their faces and bodies with red ochre, yellow limonite and green malachite – mineral pigments from the Eastern Desert crushed up with pebbles on stone palettes.

Even death had little effect on their desire to maintain a well turned-out appearance, personal ornaments being the objects most commonly found with bodies, which were wrapped in mats of fresh green reeds or animal skins and placed within oval pits in the sand. The suggestion that the grave acted as a womb from which the dead could be reborn is further reinforced by the fact that some bodies were 'practically covered' with powdered red ochre – possibly representing the blood of childbirth, with the body itself placed in a contracted foetal postion. Yet this may simply have been a practical decision – allowing for the smallest possible hole to be dug!

Whatever the original motivation, such burials are typical for the men, women and children of fifth-millennium-BC Egypt, whose accompanying possessions strongly suggest a belief that they would still need them after death.

Bodies were arranged in family groups within ancestral burial grounds, presumably representing the social units that had existed in life; this shows genuine care and concern for the dead, since any damage to the existing occupants caused by new interments would be carefully rectified, ornaments repositioned, and stray bones collected and replaced with the correct body, suggesting a need for physical 'completeness'. Nor do the bones reveal any trace of violence; they indicate that the people of Gebel Ramlah were a peaceful community, well nourished, tall in stature and in relatively good health.

But as the rains diminished, these people of the *playas* could not remain in their lakeside idylls. And as the savannah gradually disappeared beneath the encroaching sands, people were eventually forced to migrate ever eastwards, toward the nearest source of water – soon the *only* source of water – the mighty River Nile.

3

Seeking the Waters: c.5500–3500 BC

Driving its course through endless desert, the Nile's bright blue waters, bordered by its lush green banks, form a 'linear oasis', a literal lifeline visible from space.

Yet for all its fame, the Nile's various sources were shrouded in a degree of mystery until the twenty-first century. In the case of the fast-flowing White Nile, long believed to begin at Uganda's Lake Victoria until it was traced to a stream at the base of Burundi's Mount Kikizi in 1937, its furthest tributary, Rwanda's River Kagera, was only identified in 2006. As for the silt-bearing Blue Nile, which begins in Ethiopia and is generally claimed to originate in Lake Tana, it actually issues from a spring at Gish Abay, cared for by the 'Custodians of the Holy Waters' of the Ethiopian Orthodox church.

These two mighty rivers then unite at Khartoum to create the Nile itself, flowing 6,741 kilometres north from the heart of Africa to the Mediterranean Sea. As the world's longest river, it truly deserves its many superlatives, for without the Nile there would be no Egypt.

As the only reliable source of water as the rains continued to decrease throughout the sixth millennium BC, the Nile became a magnet, gradually pulling in those who had once inhabited the plains far beyond.

And it is this transition from savannah-dwelling nomads to Nile-side communities which marked the beginning of the late Neolithic period, Egypt's Predynastic Period — literally 'before the dynasties' of the later, literate culture.

The coming together of people in closer proximity than ever before initiated rapid cultural growth and innovation, for those who came seeking water had little choice but to live along the Nile's narrow banks, whose moist land, heated by the sun, formed the perfect incubator for Egypt's emerging culture.

Blending together the skills of diverse regions east and west of the Nile Valley, from the central African south and the Mediterranean north, this ethnically disparate population had wide variations in their customs and beliefs along the 1,480 km stretch of Egypt's portion of the Nile. And as regional centres polarised over time into a classic north–south divide, this geographical division evoked the concept of dualities, which the Egyptians believed upheld the universe in a state of balance, and which underpinned their entire worldview.

The northern half was known as Lower Egypt and the southern half Upper Egypt, in recognition that the Nile flows from south to north. The names also reflect the very different terrain of the so-called Two Lands, in which the south is made up of the narrow Nile Valley, flanked on each side by desert and mountains, while the north is predominantly the Nile's lush Delta, whose expanse of multiple river channels eventually gives way to the Mediterranean Sea.

Even the climate of the two regions was, and remains, somewhat different, the hotter, drier south again contrasting with the more humid north, where 'a Mediterranean winter rainfall regime continued', and its sedentary population 'followed a more typically Mediterranean path of development'.

This was certainly true of the early inhabitants of the northern Fayum oasis, who lived in wickerwork houses, made pottery and took full advantage of their region's diverse wildlife, particularly the fish, fowl and hippopotami within the Nile-fed Lake Qarun. Each hippo could supply as much meat as five cattle or fifty sheep and goats, together with the pigs kept by these early Fayumi people in Egypt's first farming communities.

Agriculture began here around 5500 BC, somewhat later than in the rest of the Near East, presumably because edible wild plants such as barley-like grasses and carbohydrate-rich sedge roots were easily available. It may also be the case that the women of these early communities were Egypt's first farmers, 'primarily linked with the agricultural settled life in contrast with the males who may have continued at least initially to hunt and perhaps more frequently to herd cattle'.

These first farmers grew wheat and barley, harvested with flint-bladed sickles, threshed with flails and stored their grain within large communal granaries sunk into the dry desert sand. Their interior linings of coiled straw still contain the first traces of cultivated plants in Egypt, which were among the first samples tested by the new technique of radio-carbon dating in 1955 to produce the approximate date of 5145 BC.

Another crop that thrived in the relatively wet and fertile Fayum was flax, from which linen was being manufactured by c.4500 BC. Linen was soon *the* standard clothing textile for simple loincloths and wraparound dresses, complemented by jewellery of turquoise nuggets from the Sinai and the shells of the Mediterranean and Red Seas, acquired from caravan traders who specialised in such items.

North of the Fayum around the Delta, communities established at Maadi by about 4000 BC kept the same livestock as their Fayumi neighbours, consuming pork, mutton and the catfish whose bones they recycled as arrowheads. The people of Maadi hunted ostriches and hippo, domesticated the donkey and were interred with their much loved dogs, as were their neighbours at Heliopolis, buried in the foetal position facing east toward the rising sun.

But what is most striking about these early northern communities is that they buried their dead *beside* the living. At Maadi, the dead were buried beneath the houses in large pots, some thoughtfully provided with holes through which their souls could 'see' out. And at el-Omari, grain storage pits were recycled as graves in which the dead were not only provided with flowers, but also wrapped in the textiles that would become synonymous with Egypt's dead.

The partly subterranean reed houses of Merimda Beni Salama were strengthened by the bones of hippo, whose sturdy tibias were the perfect size for entrance steps. Their severed legs were also set up as totems. Since hippo were quite capable of flattening a home and all within, it is perhaps not surprising that the Egyptians would forever after try to tame such wild animals through magical means, with the hippo made goddess-guardian of the home, the protector of women and children, whose bodies were buried within Merimda's hippo-boned houses.

Grave goods were limited to a single pot or a few flints, since their proximity to the living meant the dead could continue to 'share', and required no separate arrangements.

Yet these were certainly not deprived communities with little material culture. Merimda rapidly grew into a settlement of around 16,000 inhabitants, whose craftspeople exchanged their wares for food and supplies in Egypt's barter economy. There was a flint-knapping workshop and areas for textile production, leather-working and ceramic manufacture, whose output included the earliest known human sculpture from Africa. Dating from around 4500 BC, this small terracotta head, resembling a baked potato, was once painted in red ochre, a large hole in its base allowing it to be fixed atop a pole. It was possibly used as a human proxy in rituals, as this same site also produced Egypt's earliest known stone mace head, a form of weapon that would be employed for the next 5,000 years to bludgeon enemies to death.

The Maadi culture was certainly dynamic. Its northerly location was linked to neighbouring Palestine by sea, and by a 200-kilometre, ten-days'-ride donkey train, along which was transported imports of wine, oil and the conifer resins burned as incense or exported further south. Trade was sufficiently brisk to encourage Palestinian traders to open businesses in Maadi, whose location at the mouth of the *wadi* leading to Sinai gave direct access to basalt. With this stone transformed into fine quality vessels that were exported around the country, the rich copper deposits contained within the basalt were being smelted by 3800 BC, to produce the adzes, chisels, axes and fish-hooks, again exported south upriver, in exchange for the pottery and slate palettes manufactured by their neighbours in Upper Egypt.

The earliest of these southern cultures was centred on Badari, which gives its name to the 'Badarian Culture', traditionally dated to about 5500–4000 BC but recently revised to nearer 4400–3800 BC.

Covering a thirty-kilometre stretch of the Nile Valley from Badari north to Mostagedda and Matmar, relatively little remains of the Badarian settlements strung out along the riverbank, where wheat, barley and flax were cultivated some 600 years later than in the Fayum.

Yet unlike their northern neighbours, the Badarians buried their dead *away* from their limited arable land, in burial grounds at the edge of the desert, whose dry environment has preserved what otherwise would have disappeared. And with these graves effectively acting as time capsules, bringing these most ancient Egyptians into the present, the ancient dead are by far the best way to understand the ancient living.

Again in contrast with the northerners, southern Egyptians tended to face their dead west, toward the setting sun where their souls would be reborn. Yet they were still laid in the same foetal position, in pits in the sand lined with reed mats, their bodies covered with mats or hides like blankets and straw or hide pillows making them comfortable in their final resting place.

The graves were then covered with sand, and as the body fluids that would normally cause decomposition drained away through gravity, the same hot, dry conditions preserved skin, hair, nails and even the internal organs, which, in some cases, still contained a last meal.

Nor were humans the only creatures buried at Badari: cattle, antelope, sheep and dogs were similarly wrapped in matting and placed in pits. Some even shared human graves, including Egypt's earliest known cat, buried with its male owner at Mostagedda around 4000 BC.

The Badarian dead were certainly decked out as elaborately as their near contemporary neighbours at Gebel Ramlah; like them they must have undertaken 'collecting expeditions' through the Eastern Desert to collect stones for adornment, malachite for eye-paint and the greeny-grey slate to make the palettes on which the cosmetic was prepared, sourced exclusively from the Black Mountains of the otherwise beige Wadi Hammamat.

In contrast with the minimal grave goods of Lower Egypt, the Badarians took all their possessions with them for use in an afterlife already regarded as 'earthly life transposed to a less substantial realm'.

Although the names of such preliterate people can never be known, their possessions do give some idea of their lives. The man buried in Badarian Grave 5735 seems to have been something of a Predynastic dandy whose bracelets of seashells were complemented by a black fur pelt over a linen loincloth, overlaid by a nine-metre-long belt of green-glazed beads, wrapped repeatedly round his waist in a fashion known from other burials. A bead and seashell bracelet and matching anklet were worn by his female neighbour in Grave 5738, her beer supply accompanied by a pot of green eye-paint, thoughtfully placed in front of her face in the same way as others had their slate palettes placed beside their hands so they could prepare cosmetics in the next world.

Yet the main type of Badarian grave goods were handmade pots, their characteristic black tops created by placing orangey-red clay vessels upside down in glowing embers to carbonise the top. The resulting black and red combination encapsulated in a simple, yet striking form the Egyptian landscape of Red Land, Black Land. And as black was also the colour of new life, while the red represented chaos and death, 'the two colours were combined to represent the contrast between life and death'.

These two-tone pots contained 'provisions for the dead', but not always the bread and beer claimed. For although empty to the naked eye, enough remains at a molecular level to provide a chemical fingerprint of the original contents: a complex blend of bitumen from the Suez Gulf, a sponge extract from the Mediterranean and a pine resin from the distant shores of southern Turkey.

As evidence that the Egyptians were in contact with a much wider area far earlier than is generally acknowledged, such pots really are a microcosm of the Egyptians' world, with all these exotic and hard-won commodities obtained from far-flung lands brought together inside vessels representing their own red-and-black environment. And if these colours did represent life and death, the pots' contents were equally likely to have played a key role in burial rites.

And this has in fact been confirmed by re-examining material discovered in Badarian burials at Mostagedda. Some of the bodies were partly wrapped in linen coated in a 'toffee-like' substance, which has recently been identified as the same mixture found within the black-topped pots. And quite amazingly, carbon-dating of both the linen and the coating has produced a date of around 4300 BC, not only pre-dating all known embalming in the Old World, but almost 2,000 years earlier than mummification is supposed to have begun in Egypt.

The Badarians' carefully prepared dead were also provided with female figurines, from one 'minimalist' torso with an incised, fan-shaped tattoo believed to have been 'made by a female potter, who knew her craft and her sex', to another woman, carved from bone in such a casual posture that it looks as if 'she has her hands in her pockets'. Because of an emphasis on the breasts and pubic area, such figurines have traditionally been called 'concubines for the dead', although their discovery in the burials of women and children suggests they were actually meant to promote the rebirth of the dead in general.

Similar assumptions have been made about weapons, which are usually assumed to have belonged to men as the only ones thought capable of using them in combat. So the stone mace-heads, 'not rare in the graves of females', are usually dismissed as purely 'votive items' incapable of inflicting much damage, even though recent experimental archaeology has graphically demonstrated their ability to cause serious if not fatal damage – even when wielded by a female Egyptologist of advanced years!

Yet armed conflict did not bring about the end of Badarian culture; it was simply eclipsed by its southern neighbour Naqada. As another site that has given its name to an entire timespan, this was once thought to be a whole millennium, but recent scientific dating techniques have halved this 'to a period of roughly five centuries c.3800–3300 BC'.

With Naqada culture extending from Abydos in the north to Hierakonpolis in the south, Naqada itself lay midway between them, at the mouth of the mineral-rich Wadi Hammamat. Growing rapidly into a large settlement of substantial mud-brick walls, Naqada's cemetery, located in the desert beyond, expanded over some seventeen acres and was the first Predynastic site to be excavated in Egypt in 1895, before which virtually nothing was known about Egypt's earliest past.

Excavating over 2,000 graves in only three months, the early archaeologists reported that 'the bones were stacked up in the courtyard [of the dig house] until we could scarcely get out of our huts, and inside my hut the more perishable and valuable things filled all the spare space – under my bed, on shelves and in heaps'.

With many more burials of Naqada sites excavated in the century since, such bodies were placed in the foetal position and wrapped in reed mats and skins, while some female bodies at Hierakonpolis had their heads and hands wrapped in linen, coated in a similar kind of resin-like mixture to that used in Badarian burials a thousand years earlier. The same continuity included the burial of animals alongside humans, but not only cattle, goats, sheep, dogs and cats, but again, at Hierakonpolis, also baboons, ostrich, hippo, crocodiles, a leopard and even elephants, whose wrapping in linen and matting must have been no small undertaking.

Some of the human burials were sufficiently complete to reveal health problems: almost half of the fifty bodies studied from Gebelein tested positive for malaria; an elderly individual from Adaima was possibly the world's earliest victim of tuberculosis; and Hierakonpolis revealed several examples of achondroplasia, the most common type of dwarfism.

It has even been possible to work out the appearance of these early people, whose hairstyles ranged from short curls to long plaits, and even a well-trimmed beard. While the majority have dark, black-brown hair, the occasional example of ginger and blond suggests such colours 'may originally have been white or grey and had discoloured through the millennia'. Yet the greying hair of one mature lady at Hierakonpolis had been treated with henna, made from the ground-up leaves of a native shrub (*Lawsonia inermis*) that still grows at the site, her reddened hairstyle built up with small, dreadlock-like hair extensions.

As well as the earliest false hair yet found in Egypt, recreated in experimental archaeology to work out how such styles were achieved, so too the perfumes which are also likely to have been manufactured even at this early date. A basket found at Hierakonpolis contained dried fruit, mint, chips of juniper and cypress wood, sedge tubers and 'chunks of resin', a veritable potpourri whose ingredients hint at the earliest version of the later classic fragrance kyphi, with its distinctive, Christmas-pudding-like smell.

The desire of the inhabitants of Hierakonpolis to enhance or transform their appearance included the use of clay masks, with holes for the eyes, mouth and nose. Evidence from Naga ed-Dêr suggests that sandals were worn, along with leather penis sheaths. But most forms of adornment appear to have been stolen by ancient graverobbers, the neck area specifically targeted at Hierakonpolis where its men, women and children, like their Badarian predecessors, had once been buried with their jewellery of steatite and agate, ivory, coral and shells.

The thieves also targeted copper weaponry, including daggers, tied to the left upper arm for rapid access with the right hand. As the weapon apparently used in Egypt's earliest known murder, its victim was none other than 'Gebelein Man', the naturally preserved body of an adult male in the British Museum known to generations of schoolchildren as 'Ginger' on account of his red hair. Acquired by the museum in 1900 and the subject of public scrutiny for more than a century, only in 2012 did curators undertaking CT scans notice that Ginger had literally been stabbed in the back, around 3500 BC.

In fact there is increasing evidence for violent deaths throughout this period, with cut throats, decapitation and smashed skulls found at Adaima, Hierakonpolis and Naga ed-Dêr, together with defence fractures to the arms from warding off blows. And weapons continue to be found in the burials of men and women alike, from bows and arrows to the mace-heads regarded as both 'symbols of authority' and 'symbols of protection'.

Well-used cosmetic palettes were also discovered in the tombs of both sexes. Fashioned into the shapes of stylised animals, some represent deity-like images, from the star-tipped horns of the celestial cow goddess who would come to represent Hathor to the double-barbed arrow of the fertility god Min.

Such palettes also portray hunting scenes in which the hunters wear masks to resemble their prey. The keen vision essential for the hunt was ritually enhanced by the cosmetics prepared on the palettes, emphasising the features and, like ancient sunglasses, reducing the glare of the sun. It also repelled the flies responsible for spreading eye disease, even acting as an antibacterial – the copper content of malachite inhibits *Staphylococcus aureus,* a leading cause of skin infection.

These pigments were also used to outline the eyes of figurines, although one, made of bone around 3800 BC, was provided with separate eyes of lapis lazuli so large she appears to be wearing Jackie O sunglasses. Remarkably, the nearest source of her lapis eyes was 2,000 miles away in Afghanistan, with Egypt already in contact with the western end of the lapis trade route at Byblos on the Levantine coast by the fourth millennium BC.

Other such figurines morph human and animal forms together, their bird-like heads anticipating the way the human spirit, or *ba,* would after death be represented as a bird with a human head, able to flutter around at will. The same figurines sometimes have their arms stretched upwards like a ballerina, so-called 'dancing goddesses', whose pose, still found in modern Sudan, has been described as 'miming cow horns'. The cow would soon become emblematic of Hathor, patron of dance, and as she was also the goddess who cared for dead souls, the clay models of cattle placed in Naqada graves and assumed to sustain the dead as an eternal food source would be equally able to do this as representatives of the bovine divine.

With these same balletic 'cow-dancers' portrayed in rock art, one dominant figure in scenes in the Eastern Desert's Wadi Umm Salam has a crown of tall plumes and a giant erection, key attributes of the fertility god Min. This is perhaps 'the earliest known image of a god in ancient Egyptian religion'. And dating from 4000 BC, the earliest known portrait of a pharaoh-style leader is to be found in the same desert's Wadi Qash, an image which would remain much the same for the next four millennia, with his shepherd's crook sceptre and the same distinctive red crown as found on Naqada pottery.

Such vessels also feature increasing numbers of animals, painted on the surface or added as tiny figurines to the vessel rims to evoke watering holes. The Naqada potters also used imitation stone effects and faience-type glazes to create the huge range of pottery used in life for both practical and ritual purposes. The same pots were also placed in graves according to a set tradition, from the wavy-handled vessels usually placed above the body's head to the large storage jars positioned by the feet. And it is the wide variation in their type, size and colour that formed the very basis on which archaeologists were first able to trace Egypt's preliterate history, using a system of 'sequence dating', in which gradual changes in the style of the pots were plotted chronologically to create a timeframe of relative dates. It was a system used for almost a century, until modern scientific techniques created fixed dates, which continue to be refined and updated as Egypt's early history is pulled into ever-sharper focus.

But not everything the Egyptians took with them into the beyond has a scientific secret or an esoteric meaning. Some things were simply treasured possessions, sufficiently dear for their owners to want to keep for ever. This was surely true of a set of skittles found in Grave 100 at Ballas, each piece carefully retrieved by the archaeologists, who could not resist setting up the game 5,000 years after it had last amused the child it had been buried with.

As studies of grave goods revealed 'the emergence of Homo hierarchicus' by around 3500 BC, 'the tombs of women were larger and contained objects of greater interest than the graves of men'. And, wanting their elevated status to be acknowledged after death, the male and female elite required rather more than the previous hole in the ground. So their grave pits were now enlarged, reinforced with beams, bricks or plaster, and even painted. In the case of Egypt's earliest painted tomb, at Hierakonpolis, its 1.5-metre-high walls were covered with the same red and black images found on pottery and rock art, including boats, and humans engaged in hunting animals and smiting bound enemies with a mace.

The same tomb's dividing wall also reveals that one part was for the body and the other for possessions, from rich jewellery and flawless stone vessels to the costly wines, oils and resins imported from the Levant. Removed from circulation by being buried in the ground like this, such prestige items were soon beyond the reach of most people, since 'the source of materials used to make them had been appropriated by the elite', who had gained control of long-distance trade.

Reflecting a rapid rise in technical ability as much as the social divide were also ivory-handled knives, whose pristine flint blades suggest they were reserved to be worn as a form of adornment or status marker, something that is certainly the case with the Gebel el-Arak knife from Abydos, whose once-gilded, hippo-tooth handle features the image of a bearded man in Mesopotamian dress flanked by two rampant lions.

As the handle is also decorated with the same tall-prowed boats and hand-to-hand conflict found in the rock art of the Eastern Desert, early European Egyptologists assumed this must be evidence of a Mesopotamian 'Master Race', that invaded, via the Red Sea, to bring civilisation to African Egypt. This they rapidly transformed into '*das Volk und das Reich*' – the people and the empire – of the Pharaohs, a once-influential theory reflecting unfortunate attitudes prevalent in 1930s Europe, so later rebranded the 'Dynastic Race'. Yet this is now seriously undermined by the wealth of evidence that the origins of much of Egyptian culture emerged instead from the Western Desert and the Sahara.

And while 'people from Mesopotamia were sailing to the western shore of the Red Sea and entering Egypt via the Wadi Hammamat', they were doing so in order to trade, rather than to conquer, their unmistakable cultural influence on Egypt ranging from mud-brick walls with repeated recesses known as 'palace façade' panelling to the carving of ivory, from furniture legs modelled on bulls' and lions' feet to delicate ivory combs and hairpins.

Beads of garnet, carnelian and lapis were also popular, as, of course, was gold. At first acquired as small nuggets washed down by occasional flash floods into the valleys of the Eastern Desert, Naqada's prime location, close to the gold sources at Bir Umm Fawakhir, explains its ancient name, Nubt – 'Gold Town'. The proximity of Hierakonpolis to the gold within the parallel Wadi Baramiya saw its own sources of wealth increase too, and as gold started to appear in graves, it was already being paired with imported lapis in that classic blue and gold combination, which so well expressed the golden sun against a bright blue sky, reflected in the Nile.

The rarity and value of such aesthetically pleasing combinations also demonstrated to everyone that those in possession of such costly and hard-won materials were special, different and to be held in high regard.

This growing contrast between the haves and have-nots was certainly apparent in the south's regional power centres of Abydos, Naqada and Hierakonpolis, all of which underwent rapid expansion, with fortifications, monumental buildings and imposing cemeteries. Their leaders were buried in ever more elaborate tombs with multiple chambers, surrounded by treasures befitting their status, beneath superstructures of imported cedar. Such tombs were even encircled with fencing, effectively proclaiming 'Keep Out' to the masses.

The emergence of an elite class also spread north into Lower Egypt's power bases at Buto, Harageh and Abusir el-Melek, whose pottery was now made in Upper Egypt. Their former reed-built homes were gradually replaced by the same mud-brick structures as in the south, and their previously low-key burials took on the same characteristics and grave goods as their southern neighbours. Everything was 'associated with the spread, and eventual predominance, of Upper Egyptian social practices and ideology across Egypt'.

For the south would soon come to dominate the north, not only culturally and commercially, but ultimately politically, to create the first nation state anywhere in the world.

4

The North–South Divide:
c. 3500–3100 BC

As Egypt polarised into south and north, into Upper and Lower Egypt, the two halves were eventually subdivided into regional capitals or *nomes*. Each *nome* had its own leaders, its own deities and its own distinctive flag-like standards.

These capitals competed with each other for resources, for influence and ultimately for power. As they did so, they established confederations of allied settlements throughout the Nile Valley, as represented on the so-called 'Towns Palette' portraying seven fortified settlements. Each of the settlements' crenellated walls create the forerunner of the early cartouche, the protective fortress-like shape known as a *serekh*, which surrounded important names, surmounted by a protective deity. And each of the settlements on the Towns Palette is likewise surmounted by a creature: the falcon, scorpion and lion, perhaps representing human leaders. Each also wields a hoe, but it is unclear whether they are founding these settlements or more likely destroying them.

For as territories grew larger, their numbers diminished. And Naqada and its allies were about to be eclipsed by their rivals, Abydos to the north and Hierakonpolis to the south.

As such cities gained a religious as well as a political dimension, Hierakonpolis became the spiritual capital of the south while its northern equivalent was Buto in the Delta. Acquiring their own 'team colours' in the form of crowns, the tall white crown of southern Egypt was pitted against the red crown of the north, with its curling central element 'reminiscent of a bee's proboscis'. It was once assumed that the crowns had originated in Upper and Lower Egypt but, as the earliest images of the red crown appeared in the south, it was probably adopted as a northern emblem only 'when Upper Egypt had come to dominate the north', and typical of the way the Egyptians embellished, if not rewrote, their own history to create a more satisfyingly neat result.

But once the two crowns had become emblems of the two halves of the country, each gained its own heraldic deity. The cobra goddess Wadjet of Buto became the guardian of the north, and the vulture goddess Nekhbet of the Hierakonpolis region became protector of the south. Known as 'The Two Mighty Ones', each was regarded as the king's divine mother, sinuous Wadjet the uraeus (from the ancient Iaret — 'cobra'), rearing up to strike and bring death to royal enemies, whose corpses were then consumed by her vulture sister Nekhbet.

Rather more tranquil were the two lands' floral emblems, the northern papyrus and the southern 'lotus' water-lily, whose variants were the southern sedge plant and the northern bee, specifically the queen bee associated with the creator goddess Neith.

This same duality extended to male gods, with Horus, god of kingship, balanced by Seth, god of chaos. As polar opposites, they were also the heraldic deities of the rival sites Hierakonpolis and Naqada respectively. And brought together within the person of the king, his title 'The Two Lords at Peace Within Him' was balanced by the earlier queen's title 'She Who Sees Horus and Seth', almost in the manner of a split personality.

With all these elements brought together in endless artistic permutations for the next three millennia, from Horus and Seth tying together the heraldic plants of north and south to Wadjet and Nekhbet protecting the royal names, such symbols emphasised the rich diversity of the 'Two Lands', traditionally ruled over by the souls of Buto and Hierakonpolis, who together were known as the 'Followers of Horus'.

Yet far from being simple ciphers representing the disembodied rulers of legendary kingdoms, such forms contain within them long-forgotten aspects of historical truth. For ongoing excavations reveal that Egypt's two mythic capitals, and their equally mythic leaders, really did exist.

Indeed, the legendary capital of the north, Buto, was believed to be fictitious until the original city was discovered in 1983, twenty-three waterlogged feet beneath the modern settlement of Tell el-Fara'in. Here the stratified layers revealed that Buto was originally a place of reed-woven wattle houses, and a temple, made of this same ephemeral material. And it was here amidst the verdant groves of Buto that the goddess Isis was said to have hidden herself following the murder of her brother-husband Osiris by their jealous brother Seth. Her baby son Horus, raised by her to maturity, emerged from Buto to defeat Seth in the so-called 'Butic Cycle', a rich mythical history that spread out beyond Egypt to influence beliefs right along the Levantine coast.

For Buto, located only twenty-four kilometres away from the Mediterranean Sea, not only traded with the Levant and Palestine but had its own Palestinian community, making their distinctive pottery on site, using the potters' wheels that were only adopted by the conservative Egyptians a thousand years later. Links with Syria also brought Buto into contact with distant Mesopotamia, whose niched palace-façade architecture eventually appeared at Buto along with goods from even further east, imported into another important Delta site, Tell el-Farkha, which is only now being fully explored.

As another major settlement, complete with grain silos and a large brewery, the 'administrative-cultic centre' of Tell el-Farkha has recently revealed some spectacular things – figurines of hippo ivory, cosmetic palettes, Red Sea shells and ornaments of gold and semi-precious stones revealing the previously unsuspected wealth and power of Lower Egypt at this time.

Yet the most astonishing of the Tell el-Farkha finds are two gold statuettes thought to represent local rulers, perhaps even a father and son, venerated within the site's temple c.3200 BC. Each wearing a huge vertical penis sheath, both have their eyes and brows inlaid in lapis lazuli imported from Afghanistan.

For Buto, Tell el-Farkha and their Delta hinterland lay 'at the frontier between two traditions, the "African" culture of Upper Egypt and the oriental culture of Palestine'. This was also the case with Buto's southern counterpart, Hierakonpolis.

The subject of much detailed exploration since its discovery in 1897, Hierakonpolis was a city of mud-brick housing stretching over three kilometres along the banks of the Nile. Its farmers grew crops and raised livestock, while its specialised craftspeople transformed into luxury goods the ivory, gold and gems that arrived by boat from both north and south.

It was home to toolmakers, stoneworkers and potters, whose output was so great the site is still littered with the potsherds that inspired the site's current name: Kom el-Ahmar – 'the red mound'. Its ancient name, Hierakonpolis, meaning 'City of the Falcon', honoured Horus, god of kingship, for this was one of the spiritual homes of Egypt's future kings.

It was therefore most convenient that the very first excavations at the site revealed some of the most famous artefacts ever found in Egypt, which had been placed within the earliest temple of Horus. The site is today marked by a series of post-holes in the desert, which once supported four great pillars of cedar imported from the Levant. These fronted a temple with walls of reed matting, set on top of an artificial mound of sand replicating the mound of creation, encircled by blocks of sandstone, limestone and, it seems, 'at least one tall narrow pillar-like human male statue'.

At the front of the temple a large oval courtyard contained a further wooden pillar supporting the cult symbol of the Horus falcon, to which an endless stream of offerings was made; from the luxury goods of the city's workshops to the exotic animals buried in the surrounding cemeteries, and prisoners of war, executed in the divine presence – all appropriate ways to replenish the gods' powers in a reciprocal arrangement in which they would safeguard Egypt and maintain the regular rhythms of the universe.

As the temple filled up, earlier offerings were placed in brick-lined pits, in which the early archaeologists discovered them in 1898. As at Tell el-Farkha, the 'Main Deposit' at Hierakonpolis was made up of similar ivory figurines – bearded men, women with well-dressed long hair, finely attired dwarves and kneeling, bound captives: a range of characters almost suggesting a form of ritual drama played out, chess-style, to determine cosmic events.

Although areas of damp had reduced some of these ivories to the consistency of 'potted salmon', there were also figurines of steatite and lapis lazuli, and weapons on a massive scale – three flint knives almost a metre long, and a trio of huge limestone mace-heads, once displayed on top of stout wooden posts, reflecting the way the mace had come to signify status, power and domination.

All carved with detailed scenes, the so-called 'Scorpion Macehead' is named after the largest figure, who wears the white crown of southern Upper Egypt and a tie-on bull's tail to symbolise his strength. This is 'King' Scorpion, leader of the south, his name written with a small scorpion symbol. In the earliest known representation of artificial irrigation, Scorpion, carrying a hoe, leads the Opening of the Dykes ceremony to let Nile water into the fields via a system of small canals, to bring more of the surrounding land into production. The estimated 16,000km² of land already under cultivation during the Predynastic Period was capable of supporting around 300,000 people, the majority of whom were farmers. Not only did they have to pay part of their grain in taxes, they also had to undertake additional manual labour when required, creating and maintaining the numerous irrigation canals across the country.

With Scorpion's powerful presence guaranteeing the fertility of the land, the women around him are portrayed dancing and clapping, while above them, seated in her carrying chair, is the world's earliest known portrait of a royal woman. Although she is not named, she is most probaby Scorpion's mother or wife, observing events that are both celebratory and sinister. For not only is Scorpion flanked by small male figures who bear fans and the standards of his allies, other regional standards have been transformed into makeshift gibbets, from which swing the bodies of lapwings, symbols of those who had opposed the Ruler in his attempts to unite the south.

But no longer regarded as a fictitious character from Egypt's mythic past, recent discoveries suggest that Scorpion actually existed. Compelling evidence has been found at Abydos, within the 84m² subterranean Tomb U-j, a twelve-roomed palace for the dead. Although it was plundered in ancient times, recent re-excavations have nonetheless uncovered an ivory sceptre and 4,500 litres of imported Levantine wine, stored in 400 pottery vessels, most stamped with an official seal or inscribed with hieroglyphic symbols – including the scorpion.

More of this simple script was found on 164 labels of ivory and bone, once attached to wooden storage chests in the tomb. These list the long-gone contents and their place of origin – bolts of linen cloth, oil and other commodities sent as forms of tax from Buto in the north, Elephantine in the south, and regions to the east and west.

These unassuming little labels, the size of postage stamps, have also been found at sites in the north, and are the earliest evidence for the way in which Egypt's administrative districts (*nomes*) functioned and raised taxes. But what makes them among the most important documents in human history is that they are inscribed with the earliest evidence for writing found anywhere in the world, apparently pre-dating that of Mesopotamia, and proving Egypt had a 'phonetically readable' written script by around 3250 BC.

Marking the beginning of Egypt's historical period, contemporary petroglyphs in the Western Desert likewise form a legible script, in which the combination of scorpion and falcon plus a mace-wielding figure leading a captive has been described as 'a document of the unification of Upper Egypt'. Its location also suggests Scorpion and his forces were using the desert route across the great bend in the Nile at Qena to outflank his rivals at Naqada.

Yet Scorpion is by no means an isolated figure, for the Abydos tomb labels also feature the lion, the elephant, the dog and the seashell. They may be the names of as yet unknown regional leaders – or, they may even be the 'Followers of Horus' listed in the ancient kings lists, for whom Egyptologists have had to create 'Dynasty Zero', preceding the first historical dynasty.

For as well as Scorpion's final resting place, the Abydos cemetery has revealed the subterranean tombs of the last two rulers of this enigmatic dynasty, Iri-hor and Ka. Like Scorpion, they were only ever kings of half a kingdom, the warm-up acts for a successor long credited with finally taking Egypt from prehistory into true history, forever after acknowledged by the Egyptians themselves as the first king of the entire country.

This was the legendary King Narmer, traditionally credited with uniting the two halves of Egypt around 3100 BC to create the world's first nation state and 'the forerunner of all modern countries'.

Although debate continues to rage around Narmer's true identity and the achievements with which he is credited, the moment of unification, however idealised, was forever after regarded as a repeat of the 'First Time', the act of creation itself, when the state of Egypt was born.

This is commemorated on the Narmer Palette, discovered in the main deposit of Hierakonpolis and rightly dubbed 'ancient Egypt's founding monument'.

It certainly is most fitting for a land in which cosmetics played such a key role that its first historical document takes the form of a giant make-up palette, although the circular recess within which the pigments were ground is almost incidental. For the 64-centimetre-high shield-shaped slate palette was not meant for practical use but, like the giant mace-heads, was a ceremonial item, set up vertically within the temple as a means of permanently capturing this key event. It transmits the information on behalf of the ruler in 'classic' Egyptian style, with all the ingredients that would be found in artistic representations for the next three and a half millennia already in place, having been polished and honed over the last few centuries and suddenly pulled into the sharpest focus to best convey all the subtleties and power of royal propaganda.

With the royal name, the so-called 'Horus name', protectively enclosed within the fortified *serekh*, two hieroglyphic symbols spell out the name Narmer: a catfish for *nar* and the chisel for *mer*, literally meaning 'Striking Catfish'. For maximum protection, the royal name is also set between two giant heads of Hathor, below which Narmer himself appears.

Wearing the same southern white crown as Scorpion, and every inch the god-king, Narmer is shown on a huge scale. He wears a tie-on beard as well as a tie-on bull's tail, and a beaded apron adorned with more heads of Hathor, the most appropriate deity to guard this delicate part of the male anatomy and source of royal regeneration.

Kitted out in his protective gear, Narmer holds up his mace to deliver the death blow to the prisoner at his feet, identified as an opponent from the 'Harpoon' region of Lower Egypt, close to Buto. As more unfortunates sprawl out dead below them, the executions are overseen by Horus, perched upon the papyrus emblem of Lower Egypt, whose six blooms each represent one thousand. The ensemble creates a rebus set of hieroglyphs to be read 'The king has defeated 6,000 of the Delta enemy', such scenes now functioning as both an art form and a language.

On the palette's reverse, Narmer wears the red crown, by this time associated with the north, to signify his nationwide takeover. He is preceded by a row of standards topped by falcons, a jackal and the Royal Placenta, part of the 'divine essence passed from ruler to ruler which played an important part in Egyptian kingship ideology from the earliest times'. For these are the standards of the 'the Followers of Horus', the 'souls of the kings of Lower Egypt', whose accumulated powers Narmer now appropriated for himself.

As the king makes formal inspection of the enemy dead, their severed heads, placed between their legs, are each crowned by their own severed penis – a form of ritual dismemberment designed to deprive them of the ability to function fully in the afterlife, in a policy of literal 'divide and conquer'.

Having vanquished all rivals, Narmer underwent a rather more tranquil ceremony, portrayed on one of the large mace-heads from the Hierakonpolis deposit that show him enthroned before an unnamed figure in a carrying chair. Possibly the daughter of a defeated enemy whom he married to legitimise his takeover, the most likely candidate is Neithhotep, who some suggest was 'a descendant of the Predynastic rulers of Naqada'.

So it seems Narmer had extended his dominion over both halves of the land through a combination of diplomatic marriage and military conquest. Having unified Egypt into a single political unit, Narmer and Neithhotep initiated a monarchy that would continue for three millennia, the so-called Dynastic Period named after the thirty successive dynasties of ruling families 'united by kinship or by regional origin or city of residence or both'. And Narmer was forever after named as the very first ruler of the very first dynasty.

5

Lords and Ladies of the Two Lands:
c.3100–2890 BC

At the beginning of official king lists compiled over the next three thousand years, Narmer's name initiated the framework around which the Egyptians calculated their entire history, dating every historical event by the regnal year of each king. And the earliest such list, the Palermo Stone, names the royal mothers alongside their sons.

Having established his own place in history, Narmer took a second name, Menes, based on the epithet *men*, meaning 'to establish' or 'be permanent'. As the name by which he was known in later king lists, these claim that 'in succession to the spirits of the dead and the demigods, the Egyptians reckon the First Dynasty to consist of eight kings. The first of these was Menes [Narmer], who won high renown in the government of his kingdom'.

As the first monarch traditionally credited – albeit retrospectively – with the unification of north and south into a single state, Narmer organised his newly-formed kingdom into forty-two regions (*nomes*), with the help of royal relatives and literate officials, able to utilise an increasingly sophisticated hieroglyphic script to administer the country on his behalf.

Having originally appeared as a means of recording produce, hieroglyphs rapidly became the means by which the state took shape, a way for the expanding civil service of scribes to calculate as taxes the resources required to sustain this state. So however cryptic and speculative, they shed much-needed light on Egypt's shadowy beginnings and its equally shadowy inhabitants, who can now at least be referred to by name.

In the case of the first named woman in history, Narmer's consort Neithhotep, meaning 'Neith (the creator goddess) is satisfied', had her name written within the same protective *serekh* cartouche as her husband the king. This suggests that she held similar status, since 'throughout the whole course of Egyptian iconographical history there is no instance of a *serekh* being used for anyone other than a monarch', their marriage quite possibly undertaken to end long-standing enmity and bring Naqada under Narmer's control.

For although Narmer, like Scorpion, seems to have come from the Abydos area, he was certainly active around the Naqada region, at Koptos, cult centre of Min , whose earliest temple resembled the timber shrine at Hierakonpolis.

And Koptos too yielded spectacular finds, snarling stone lions flanking a ceremonial way leading to three colossal statues of Min, weighing over two tons each. The Victorian archaeologist who uncovered them noted that 'the left hand is in the usual attitude of Min', since the god had originally been grasping his penis firmly in his fist, a large circular hole now representing the location of the vital organ originally formed by a separate piece of stone.

Yet it is certainly tempting to see these holes as emplacements for Min's sacred plant, the conical cos lettuce, which can grow up to a metre in height and exudes a white sap when harvested. Cos lettuces were grown beside the temple to provide the god with a ready supply, the ancient practice of standing the god's portable cult statue upon the lettuce beds to the refrain 'Hail Min placed in the garden' quite possibly dating back to a Predynastic agricultural rite to enhance productivity.

As for the god's monumental limestone statues, they wear only a belt, whose pendant sash is decorated with petrolgyph-like hieroglyphs of lions, cattle, a stork, an elephant, a snake and a gazelle head. Since the same symbols are also found on ivory labels, seal impressions and pottery from the Predynastic tombs at Abydos, some believe that the god's sash is an early king list, on which Narmer's own name has been identified.

Nor were Narmer's embellishments to this temple a coincidence. For Koptos lies at the entrance to the main desert route to the Red Sea, the Wadi Hammamat, along which Narmer's name was inscribed by members of the expeditions he sent out to harvest the region's rich supplies – raw amethysts from its granite cliffs, green malachite from its basalt rocks and the greeny-grey schist slate, sourced exclusively from the *wadi*'s Black Mountains.

The royal couple also extended their reach northward by founding a new city at the apex of the Delta. This was Memphis, forever after Egypt's administrative capital, whose prime location is celebrated in its ancient epithet, 'the Balance of the Two Lands'.

Although the Nile's gradual progress eastwards across its flood plain eventually washed away much of the original city, mighty Memphis was a true metropolis, whose extent was only recently traced many metres below the current water table. By taking geological cores around the area, archaeologists also detected the changes in climate and river levels that had such an impact on every Egyptian, from the farmer in the field to the king and courtiers keeping the state on an even keel. For if the annual flood was too low it caused famine; if too high, it washed away homes and livelihoods.

Even optimum flood levels covered the land for several months each year when, like the primeval waters at the beginning of time 'the whole country is converted into a sea, and the towns, which alone remain above water, look like the islands in the Aegean. At these times water transport is used all over the country, instead of merely along the course of the river'.

The same ancient eyewitness also added that Narmer had created a series of protective canals and dams around his new city, and with the same skill that had created the first calendar several millennia earlier, Egypt's finest minds devised a means of predicting the height of the flood — the Nilometer.

Carved into the quayside waterline at temples along the Nile Valley, it employed calculations using the 'ceremonial cubit', a portable measuring device based on the length of the human forearm. Priests and officials took precise readings from the Nilometers using the cubit, plus their hands and fingers. So a Nile level of 1.92m would be recorded as '3 cubits, 4 hands, 3 fingers' in the royal annals, not only to gauge the amount of land to put under cultivation and then tax, but to predict the final flood height, take any remedial action required and celebrate the appropriate irrigation rites.

Divine intervention would surely be guaranteed in the main

temple of Memphis, which Narmer also founded. Dedicated to the creator god Ptah and his lioness consort Sekhmet, its clergy claimed their temple had been built on the first land to emerge from the floods at the beginning of time. So it is most appropriate that the Memphis temple is the building after which the entire country is named. Known as the 'House of Ptah's Soul' – *Huwt-ka-Ptah*, pronounced *Aigyptos* by later Greek settlers, it validates the claims of the Memphis clergy, who maintained that their temple was the very origin of everything.

But when it came to making plans for death – plans that traditionally began early in life to ensure their completion – Narmer followed his predecessors by choosing burial in the south, back in his homeland Abydos, which would remain the necropolis of kings for the next three centuries.

As the first 'Valley of the Kings', and no less dramatic than its more famous counterpart, the Abydos Royal Cemetery was located at the mouth of a great valley regarded as the entrance to the underworld, where wind-blown sand, funnelled by the cliffs, created a whispering sound believed to emanate from the very dead themselves.

And this cemetery of Egypt's earliest kings was a site of tremendous importance, where the devout came with offerings in such numbers that their pottery vessels still cover a landscape known as Umm el-Qa'ab, 'Mother of Pots'.

It was here in the late nineteenth century that excavations revealed the twinned names of Narmer-Menes on seals, and in the 1970s, Narmer's tomb itself was identified by the small labels and seal impressions, again featuring his name, found in the tomb's subterranean chambers. There were also hundreds of flint arrowheads and ivory inlays from storage boxes, their images of bound captives hinting at military expansion abroad, and the king's name found on pots from as far north as Tell Arad in Palestine and in Nubia, far to the south.

Having established his position as first king of a united Egypt, Narmer apparently met his death in a most unusual manner; the historians of antiquity claimed he was 'carried off by a hippopotamus and perished'. And while this may simply be a euphemism for the forces of chaos the hippo represented, it may possibly have been a historical fact.

Fortunately for the new state, chaos was held at bay by Narmer's heir, whose name, Aha, follows his on early king lists. At the time of his father's death, Aha was still a child, so his mother, Neithhotep, ruled on his behalf as regent, or 'King's Mother'. An official title that appears much earlier than the title 'King's Wife', 'the mother of the royal heir was his official consort' at this time, equated with the goddess Hathor as 'the cow that hath borne the bull', and sufficiently important to be listed alongside the king on the official lists.

Neithhotep's power is certainly reflected in her king-sized tomb. Larger than that of her husband Narmer at Abydos, Neithhotep was laid to rest just south of her probable hometown Naqada, her permanent presence counterbalancing the potent masculinity of the great god Min directly across the river. Within its thick walls, Neithhotep's twenty-one tomb chambers accommodated her burial and such luxurious grave goods as rock-crystal lion gaming pieces, moisturising oils and jewellery, stolen long ago but so precisely recorded on the small labels once attached to her jewel chests that even the beads on her necklaces were numbered.

As for her son Aha, his name, written with the symbols of shield and mace and meaning 'the Fighter', suggests that unification was an ongoing process, perhaps only fully achieved at his accession some time around 3085 BC. He certainly built on father Narmer's achievements, since a small ebony label refers to his southern campaign against Ta-sety, the region bordering Nubia that controlled the lucrative trade routes for ebony, ivory and gold from the mines in the Eastern Desert's Wadi el-Allaqi.

In this most southerly part of Egypt, the Nile's wide flow is broken up by granite outcrops known as cataracts. At the First Cataract, at the border town Aswan, one such outcrop formed the island of Elephantine, where excavations revealed a settlement dating back to this early period. As an important trading post with Nubia – 'the corridor to Africa' – Elephantine was defended against attack by a large fort built on high ground to control river traffic, and by the neighbouring temple dedicated to Satet, goddess-guardian of the frontier, capable of 'killing enemies of the king by her arrows'. Set between the rocks, her temple faced the rising star Sothis (Sirius), Herald of the Flood, whose waters were believed to originate in the cave directly below her temple, and were controlled by Satet's consort, the ram-headed creator god Khnum.

Securing this southern border was an important step in the consolidation of his country, but Aha was also active at the other end of Egypt, at Sais, where he created a new temple to goddess Neith, after whom his mother was named. Then at the apex of the Delta, at the capital Memphis, he built himself a palace whose exterior walls were painted such a dazzling white it was known as Ineb-hedj – 'White Walls'.

The very first 'White House', this palatial centre of government was surrrounded by the villas of the royal relatives and officials who ran the country on Aha's behalf. In Egypt's pre-monetary economy, these homes were supplied by the state, together with tombs in the city's adjoining cemetery Sakkara, named after the local god Sokar, whose imposing location on the high desert escarpment allowed its dead to both overlook and watch over the living below.

Although the houses in the well-watered valley are long gone, the officials' tombs in the high, dry desert remain and are testament to their lavish lifestyles. For their subterranean burials, covered with bench-shaped mud-brick superstructures – *mastabas* – and roofed with imported Lebanese cedar, were surrounded by models of their earthly estates, with granaries, tree-filled gardens and the world's oldest known wooden boats, allowing them to sail the heavens with the gods.

Indeed, the *mastaba* tombs of Aha's courtiers were so imposing that Sakkara was once believed to be the cemetery of Egypt's first kings. Yet Aha and his successors continued to be buried at Abydos in the south. In the same way he had built himself a new royal palace at Memphis, Aha built a duplicate 'Palace of Eternity' at Abydos, a white-painted, mud-brick enclosure, only discovered recently, along with two more created for his mother and his wife. Conceived as a place where their souls could receive offerings after death, or perhaps where their bodies were embalmed prior to burial, the area was surrounded by a fleet of fourteen cedar boats up to twenty-three metres long, and the king's land transport catered for by ten donkeys, buried in a long grave south-west of his enclosure. There were also the burials of seven young lions, raised in captivity, and several royal relatives, although Aha's own body was interred almost a mile further into the desert, to be nearer the cleft in the cliffs marking the entrance to the underworld.

His three-chambered subterranean tomb once contained his body and grave goods, and was covered with a mound of sand coated by white-painted plaster, perhaps to imitate the primeval mound of creation, from which Aha's soul could then arise. All were hidden below the surface of the desert, as were the two adjacent chambers created for Aha's main wife Benerib, whose name, meaning 'Sweetheart', was repeatedly twinned with that of Aha on the ivory artefacts placed in her tomb.

In neat rows beyond were thirty-four individual graves of officials and servants, the royal court accompanying the couple in death as in life. They were previously assumed to have been buried here whenever each of them happened to die, but recent re-examination has revealed an average age of twenty-five, which suggests they may all have died at the same time. Although there are no signs of the neck fracture associated with death by strangulation, poison or stabbing have been put forward as alternatives, both forms of death that are hard to trace through the skeletal fragments which remain. Nonetheless, one of Aha's ivory labels from this very site shows a bound figure being stabbed in the chest, the blood collected in a bowl presumably as an offering to Horus, the god representing the king, portrayed by his nearby standard.

Although some seem unwilling to accept the Egyptians' use of human sacrifice, and regard stabbing with far more revulsion than the standard smiting with a mace, bashing out the brain with a blunt instrument is far more violent than the surgical insertion of a blade. Yet death itself was the most emphatic way for a monarch to demonstrate ultimate power, and Egypt's long-standing trading partners in Mesopotamia were similarly burying hundreds of retainers with their own male and female rulers by 2600 BC; a recent reinvestigation of their assumed 'non-violent' deaths via poison has revealed blunt-force trauma, inflicted by a weighted weapon as part of what can only be described as 'bloody homicidal sacrifice'.

With Aha and Benerib sent off into the afterlife accompanied, it seems, by something of a ceremonial bloodbath, Aha's successor was Djer 'the Strong', his son by wife Khenthap.

Djer may have ruled for as long as fifty years, and as a very active monarch he campaigned against Setchet, located somewhere in modern Sinai or southern Palestine. Djer also initiated a biennial royal progress through his kingdom, which allowed him to see and be seen while his accompanying retinue of officials calculated tax yields, Domesday-style.

He visited Sais and Buto in the north, and in the south built the earliest known temple in Thebes, a small stone sanctuary dedicated to Horus. Only discovered in 1996 at the very top of the Theban mountains on what is known as 'Thoth Hill', its remote location was purposefully selected to give a spectacular view of the Nile Valley, the new temple carefully aligned with the annual rising of the star goddess Sothis (Sirius), whose appearance marked the start of the Nile flood. As part of this same policy of maintaining the floodwaters through divine intervention, Djer acknowledged Sothis's fellow goddess, Satet of Elephantine, whose temple was believed to lie directly over the source of the waters and to whom Djer presented a blue-glazed faience statuette of himself enthroned, the oldest known royal sculpture yet found.

Royal craftspeople certainly produced breathtaking items, some of which were placed in the tombs of Djer's courtiers at Sakkara. This included the massive tomb of his chief wife, Herneith, roofed in stone 'carved with a row of recumbent lions' and containing the queen's guard dog, still curled up across the tomb entrance, to earn Herneith the soubriquet 'the first named dog-lover in history'.

Yet Djer himself planned his own burial at Abydos, with no fewer than 587 of his officials and retainers. Just under half of them were buried around Djer's funerary enclosure, apparently killed to order, and once again portrayed in a scene of the ritual knifing of a bound figure. The remaining courtiers were buried beside Djer's actual tomb, their small grave-stone stelae giving their names and images in profile, people like the long-haired Senba, 'the friend Fed', and the male dwarf, Ded. Here too were buried Djer's wives Nakhtneith and Hetes, whose remains, found within their wooden coffins, had been wrapped in linen 'soaked' in natron, a salty residue obtained from dried-up lake beds by now being used to preserve bodies.

This presumably included their royal husband Djer. As the king buried with the largest number of courtiers in the largest tomb of the First Dynasty, he was accompanied in death by spectacular items, hinted at by fragments the plunderers overlooked, from rock crystal vessels to toilet equipment inscribed 'for the washing of the hands of the double lord', a wooden statue with painted necklaces labelled 'standing image of the *ka* (soul) of King Djer' an insurance policy should his body be damaged or lost.

The single chamber that remained intact when it was found still contained a dozen pottery vessels – a combination of Egyptian jars filled with animal fat, and imported Palestinian pots containing vegetable oil mixed with conifer resin, to create the same fragrant moisturiser used by the living as the antibacterial preservative used for the dead.

Although Djer's missing mummy was at first assumed to have been completely destroyed, the early archaeologists eventually made a surprising discovery in a crevice high in the tomb's northern wall: a mummified arm covered in bracelets of gold, lapis and turquoise. Presumably placed there by the ancient robbers to retrieve later, the jewellery led to the assumption that the arm 'belonged to his queen', although it was most likely the arm of Djer himself, and far more significant than the jewellery found around it. Unfortunately, when it was sent to the Cairo Museum, it was appraised by a curator 'who only cared for display. So from one bracelet he cut away the half that was of plaited gold wire, and he also threw away the arm and linen. A museum is a dangerous place,' concluded the archaeologist who discovered it. But with great foresight he had retained some of the wrappings, and when these came to light again a century later, their golden-brown coating was found to be the same imported conifer resin that had been buried with Djer in the pottery jars, in a continuance of burial practice already dating back one and a half millennia.

Djer was succeeded by his son Wadjet – Djet for short – named after the cobra goddess. He was the first king to fuse the white crown of the south and the red crown of the north, which created the double crown adopted by all subsequent rulers to demonstrate dominion over both halves of the country. Little is known of his reign other than that 'a great famine seized Egypt', the crisis presumably contained through the efforts of experienced officials such as Amka, who had served under Djet's father.

Certainly, many of Djet's courtiers were well rewarded in both life and in death, the contents of some of the 2,000 burials created south of Memphis at Tarkhan, revealing that the 'tombs of women are richer in objects than tombs of men'. With these elite buried in box-like wooden coffins, accompanied by their cosmetic palettes, jewel cases, sandal trays – early shoeboxes – and numerous garments in 'very white, bleached linen', some of these were packed up and sent to museums around the world. One such packing case, opened sixty-five years later, contained the world's oldest dress, a delicate, long-sleeved tunic with a pleated yoke thought to have belonged to a teenage girl who had left it inside out, as it was found, and still, poignantly, with the original creases under the arms.

With Djet's highest-ranking courtiers interred at Sakkara, the massive tomb superstructure of Sekhemkasedj was adorned with three hundred clay cattle heads complete with real horns – a technique long used in shrines at Catal Hüyük in Turkey. An equally impressive tomb, 'Mastaba V', was built just south of Giza, surrounded by fifty-six subsidiary tombs of courtiers and believed to 'represent a lavish burial for the king's mother, constructed in the lifetime of her son' – Djet. Although the name of the occupant is still unknown, as are the reasons for the tomb being located at Giza, it nonetheless set a predecedent, to be followed with spectacular results at the beginning of the so-called Pyramid Age.

As for Djet himself, he followed tradition and was buried at Abydos, where a huge stone stela, bearing the graceful cobra spelling his name, marked the site of his tomb. His rectangular burial chamber, lined with timber, featured the earliest example of a false door, the representation of a real door, through which his soul could come and go between this world and the next.

Djet was also accompanied in death by 335 courtiers, including some of his minor wives. But Djet's chief queen was his sister Merneith, 'beloved of Neith', and, in common with so many royal women, her name was written with the same shield and crossed arrow symbols as used to symbolise the goddess.

Merneith also had a matchless royal pedigree – as a daughter of

Djer, the wife and sister of Djet and the mother of the next king Den, she had 'multigenerational ties to the kingship', and was the ideal candidate to succeed Djet when he died while their son was still in his infancy. So Merneith ruled as regent, and 'may herself have been a reigning monarch', for, like Neithhotep before her, her name was written within the kingly *serekh*. Her name also appears on a king list found at Abydos as recently as 1985, which gives the succession as Narmer, Aha, Djer, Djet and Merneith.

There are official seals marked 'that which is from Merneith's Treasury', while one of her administrators holding 'high fiscal office' was the 'inspector of canals' who oversaw irrigation work, his seal featuring small figures of swimmers performing the front crawl, complete with bubbles.

One hundred and twenty of her courtiers also accompanied Merneith when her time came to cross over to the Land of the Dead, where she too had planned a grand funerary enclosure and tomb at Abydos. Surrounded by these courtiers' small graves, which thoughtfully terminated before her tomb's south-west corner to give her soul direct sight, and indeed access, to the cliffside cleft marking the entrance of the underworld, the size of her tomb befitted her regal credentials. Her multiple tomb chambers were once as well equipped as those of her male predecessors, and like them, she too had monumental stone stelae marking her burial place. These stelae of 'King Merneith' were uncovered in 1900 by archaeologists who claimed 'it can hardly be doubted that Mer-neith (*sic*) was a king', until it was later discovered that *he* was a *she,* and Merneith subtly demoted to the position of 'queen' – a familiar story for Egypt's female rulers.

Yet Merneith had clearly wielded sole power until her son Den came of age, and she had certainly trained him well.

As the best attested First Dynasty ruler, and quite an innovator, Den made a key addition to Memphis's temple of Ptah by installing the god's sacred creature, the Apis bull. The great bull, born to an equally sacred cow, was a symbol of divine and royal might, and believed to carry the god's own spirit within him, would play a key role in state ceremonials for the next three millennia.

Den was the first king to be portrayed with the protective cobra goddess Wadjet adorning his brow, and the first to expand his name with the royal epithet 'He of the Two Ladies', Wadjet and Nekhbet. The second title Den introduced was 'Ruler of Upper and Lower Egypt', the so-called 'Throne-Name', written with the symbols for the sedge plant and the bee. And while the combined red and white dual crown was first portrayed in his father's reign, Den was the first king shown actually wearing it.

For Egypt's king had to dress the part at all times. With his daily, weekly and annual agenda all planned in great detail, together with specific outfits and regalia for each occasion, this was especially important for the coronation, and for the jubilee held after thirty years' rule in order for the king to replenish his powers before the courtiers, before the standards of the gods, and before the ever-watchful souls of his predecessors, the 'Followers of Horus'.

Assisted by officials in his 'robing room', Den put on his diamond-patterned jubilee robe of heavy fabric to perform 'the Procession'. He then disrobed to run the ceremonial race, the first king to be shown sprinting round the sacred track, which may be the 'cultic enclosure' located at Sakkara. He was required to run round two stone markers representing Egypt's boundaries, four circuits as king of the south and four as king of the north, and had to wear the relevant crown for each. He also had to run alongside the Apis bull in order to assimilate its powers, while the spirits of his deceased predecessors were also believed to be present, cheering him on.

Then, having ritually traversed his domain, Den performed 'the Hunt', 'the Sacrifice' and 'the Victory' rites, skewering a hippo with the harpoon of the goddess Neith to restore order over chaos. The event was captured in sculpted form: three gold statues of Den showed him striding forward with the mace, harpooning from a skiff and wrestling a hippo. The statues were created at the Memphis temple workshops, where chief creator deity Ptah was honoured as 'Supreme Craftsman'. The king lists even record the 'birth' of such statuary – duplicates of the real thing capable of housing the souls of those they portrayed, and in Den's case demonstrating his fitness to rule by showing him as the consummate athlete and hunter, whose physical prowess represented Egypt's power and prestige beyond the field of battle.

Yet there too Den was active. In a scene commemorating 'the first time of smiting the Easterners' – carved on an ivory label once attached to a pair of his sandals – he swings back his mace to kill the enemy cowering before him on the sand. Likely to represent one of the local rulers 'who still resided in the Eastern Desert and were strong enough to challenge the developing urban communities in the Nile Valley', the image is accompanied by the simple, chilling statement: 'they shall not exist'. Other captives were led away by the feline goddess Mafdet, another female 'protector of the king' and the 'manifestation of judicial authority', whose standard incorporated an execution blade, symbolising her claws, with which the king decapitated his enemies.

Throughout Egypt, Den honoured his country's many deities, from the sacred ram of Mendes in the Delta to Horus of Hierakonpolis in the south. Inspired by Seshat, goddess of literacy and 'foremost in the library', whose priests were highly active in Den's reign, the king also undertook 'a census of all the people of the north, west and east', assisted by his able chancellor, Hemaka.

Honoured with one of the largest tombs at Sakkara, some fifty-seven metres long, Hemaka's burial within mud-brick walls was fortified with a stone portcullis to protect its rich contents – perfume vessels with gold lids, inlaid stone gaming discs, a wine cellar of 700 vessels and, most appropriately for his role as chief administrator, his circular writing box, which contained blank rolls of papyrus ready for use – the earliest known example of this reed-made paper.

So many officials sought burial at Sakkara during Den's long reign that the site expanded north toward Abu Rawash, to Abusir and to Helwan, where an astonishing 10,000 burials date from this early period. Around fifty of the highest-status tombs were also lined with limestone and, just as funerary architecture continued to develop, so the tombs' contents grew ever more impressive, from full-sized boats to teams of donkeys, the trio buried beside the large Abusir *mastaba* belonging to one of Den's many wives ready to trot off straight into the afterlife after being buried standing up.

But the royal burial ground was still Abydos, where Den's massive tomb was surrounded by 136 graves belonging to his courtiers, his pet lions and his dogs 'Goldie' and Sed – 'the One with the Tail'.

Den himself was eventually interred within the central mud-brick *mastaba*, the timber lining of previous royal burial chambers now replaced by Aswan granite, and an innovative entry staircase blocked by a granite portcullis. A second staircase gave access to a cellar-like chamber, or *serdab*, housing a life-size statue of Den, to which his soul could migrate and receive offerings.

Commemorated long after his death by successors who took objects inscribed with his name into their own graves, Den was a hard act to follow for his shadowy successor Anedjib, who took the throne around 2925 BC.

But regardless of how little is known of Anedjib himself, his architects developed ever more innovative forms of tomb construction, including the first evidence for stepped structures; the Sakkara burial chamber of his official, Nebitka, was topped by a rectilinear stepped superstructure or 'proto-pyramid'. Although concealed beneath its exterior mud-brickwork, Nebitka's tomb certainly eclipsed the king's own burial place at Abydos, which was less than a quarter the size of his predecessor's tomb. And, to bury Anedjib in still greater obscurity, some of the inscribed stone vessels from his tomb were reused by his successor, Semerkhet, who erased Anedjib's names and replaced them with his own. Although this could simply be evidence of pragmatic reuse, the erasing of royal names, effectively removing all trace of an individual, was always significant and may be evidence of some sort of dynastic feud, the details of which are – for now – as obscure as Semerkhet's eight-year reign.

But Semerkhet's burial is most informative; not only did it contain vessels appropriated from his predecessor, its innovative new structure also made retainer sacrifice into an architectural feature. Previously, subsidiary burials had tended to be individual units, but the subsidiary burials of Semerkhet's retainers were all part of the same single building, meaning that those within had to have been buried at the same time – the king's power over life and death permanently enshrined in bricks and mortar by 2900 BC.

Following their slaughter, any hint of decomposition was masked by the perfumed oils poured out around the tomb entrance. For when excavations began here 4,800 years later, the floor was 'saturated with ointment' to a depth of one metre, the archaeologists calculating that 'hundredweights of it must have been poured out here', creating a scent sufficiently strong that it 'could be smelt over the whole tomb'.

This highly fragrant, if bloody, farewell was overseen by Semerkhet's successor Qaa – the 'Arm-raiser' – whose lengthy reign incorporated at least two jubilees. He also undertook numerous progresses around his country as far south as the thriving city of El-Kab, celebrating with his courtiers on the other side of the river at Hierakonpolis. The beer jars found at the site, inscribed with Qaa's name, may well have been supplied by Meriti, 'Director of the Dining Hall and Great Cellar', who was also 'Master Carpenter of Hierakonpolis' and a 'Helping Hand' for his king. The same versatility was demonstrated by Merka, 'Follower of the King', a priest of Neith and, as 'controller of the palace', 'controller of the audience chamber' and 'controller of the royal boat', the head of royal security.

As for the king Merka protected, Qaa himself was eventually buried at Abydos in a tomb whose entrance faced north, toward the circumpolar stars that never set. Otherwise its design followed that of his predecessor, in which twenty-six unfortunate retainers, like Sabef, 'companion of the palace', were slaughtered to join their ruler in death. Yet Sabef and his colleagues seem to have been the last to die with their king; although the royal mace would continue to be used to perform ritual executions, the formalised killing of courtiers, at least in Egypt, ended around 2890 BC with Qaa, who has the distinction of being the very last king of Egypt's very first dynasty.

6

Shifting Focus: c.2890–2686 BC

Marking the beginning of a new era, the first king of the new Second Dynasty, Hetepsekhemwy, broke with three centuries of tradition and abandoned the royal necropolis of Abydos.

Having lived in the palace at Memphis, the new king wished to remain a northern resident for ever and so selected burial in the city's adjoining cemetery Sakkara, where his enormous tomb recreated his palace, complete with bedroom, bathroom and storerooms, cut down into the bedrock for his eternal supplies. His soul was still being sustained with offerings several centuries later by the priest Hetepdief, whose small granite statue, inscribed with his title 'Great of Incense in the Red House' – the royal treasury – is also inscribed with the names of the monarchs whose funerary cults he served – Hetepsekhemwy, and his successors Nebra and Nynetjer. Although these kings of the Second Dynasty are shadowy to say the very least, and evidence for their queens even more sparse, both Hetepsekhemwy and Nebra paid homage to the northern feline goddess Bastet, whose temple 'the House of Bastet' (modern Bubastis), was located in the Delta north of Memphis. Yet another daughter of the sun god, whose name is interpreted 'She of the Perfume Jar', Bastet's rites, like those of all the gods, required ritual purity; King Nebra's daily routine involved ablutions using a large stone bowl inscribed with his name and the words 'washing every day'.

Nebra's successors and the ruling elite followed Hetepsekhemwy's lead in choosing burial at Sakkara, in tombs that, in one case, even featured a model bath. The carefully embalmed bodies of the king's courtiers were also provided with tomb stelae, on which their portraits show immaculately groomed individuals – Lady Heket, 'Funerary

Priestess of the King', or the handsome Neferabu, whose larder-like arrangement of food supplies is duplicated on the stela of Princess Shepsetipet. In her case, however, an actual banquet had been placed beside her coffin – rib of beef, a well-dressed quail, pigeon stew, fish fillets, jars of soft cheese, loaves of bread, stewed figs, cakes and jars of wine, the hot food thoughtfully served on pottery dishes while the cold was set out on platters of stone.

Equally useful stone vessels include the washing bowl of Nebra, inherited by his successor Nynetjer, whose addition of a hieroglyph symbol of a boat meant that 'such objects belonged to the king's travelling outfit'. Nynetjer's royal seals also had his name flanked by the cobra goddess Wadjet, here portrayed as a woman with a tall sceptre, and possibly the source of later records claiming that during Nynetjer's reign 'it was decided that women might hold the kingly office' – a belated point, given the fact that they seemed to have been doing this for well over two centuries already.

The same source added that these Second Dynasty kings continued to honour the sacred animals, including the Apis bull, contemporary records referring to Nynetjer's running with the Apis at Memphis, providing more priests for the cult of Bastet and celebrating the rites of Sokar, god of Sakkara, where Nynetjer was already working on his own galleried tomb.

But despite a reign of at least thirty-five years, his name has not so far been found anywhere outside Memphis. His apparent desire to stay close to the capital may have reflected the need to tackle local unrest, since the ancient records refer to Nynetjer 'hacking up Shemre and the northern lands' of the Delta. There was clearly a serious problem.

Although details are lacking, environmental studies reveal that the summer rains over East Africa 'averaged less from Dynasty II onward than in Dynasty I', and indeed, annual Nilometer readings recorded 'a significant drop in the average height of the annual inundation after the end of the first dynasty'.

This meant that less land could be cultivated, and with fewer crops available to be gathered as the taxes then redistributed to those carrying out state business for the king, the monarchy was in real trouble. Unable to hand out the expected largesse, claims that the king was the bringer of fertility and source of all wealth must have seemed increasingly doubtful. Even the stone vessels inscribed with Nynetjer's name, made to give out to courtiers at his jubilee, remained in storage, as few appreciated such hollow celebrations.

The throne then passed to a series of ephemeral kings based squarely in the north; by around 2700 BC, the south had fallen under the leadership of a very different character.

This was Peribsen, self-styled 'Champion of Maat', although the goddess of universal order was not his only source of divine inspiration.

Although rulers traditionally topped the *serekh* enclosure surrounding their names with the Horus falcon, Peribsen's name was instead surmounted by the Seth animal, a composite mythical creature whose sudden appearance in place of Horus may signify 'some kind of political or religious dispute'. Given that Seth was Horus's murderous adversary in myth, Peribsen was sending out a powerful message. But it was also a subtle message, for Seth was also the god of the vast desert, the patron deity of Naqada and a hugely powerful figure.

Certainly Seth's presence could not have been made more explicit; he sits squarely atop Peribsen's *serekh* inscribed on the black granite stelae he erected at Abydos, the former royal cemetery, now in Peribsen's territory, and now reopened. As a southern ruler, he wanted to be buried in the south's most sacred ground to demonstrate his legitimacy as the successor to the First Dynasty rulers, some of whom are even named on his grave goods. Marked with seal impressions featuring Seth in the white crown of the south, one such impression contains the first complete sentence in Egyptian history – 'the One of Naqada has presented the Two Lands to his son, the King of Lower and Upper Egypt, Peribsen'. As nothing less than an assertion that mighty Seth had given the whole of Egypt back to his faithful devotee Peribsen, this is a very welcome communiqué transmitted from the largely silent Second Dynasty. It announces that Peribsen had begun to pick up the pieces of the Two Lands and put them back together into a single kingdom, a restoration of order that would continue under his successor Khasekhem.

Living up to a name that means 'the Power has Appeared', Khasekhem was a truly transitional figure who propelled Egypt into its first 'classic' phase, now known as the 'Old Kingdom' – a period characterised by tight central control and monumental stone architecture.

Like Peribsen a southerner, Khasekhem was certainly a mighty figure in every sense, apparently standing '5 cubits and 3 palms' high, which would have made him an unlikely eight feet (2.4m) tall when the average height of Egypt's kings was recently calculated at around 5 feet 4' (1.66m). Following his accession around 2686 BC, he undertook campaigns against Ta-sety on the Nubian border, his victory portraits showing him kneeling on a captive, with the inscription 'humbling the foreign lands'. He also replicated the pose within the Horus temple at Hierakonpolis, whose antiquated fixtures and fittings were now rebuilt in stone, including the temple's new door sockets, carved in the shape of bound captives pressed flat to the floor so that each time the doors opened, the pivot, set into their backs, would symbolically grind them down.

Then inside the temple, a pair of statues of Khasekhem were set up, his static pose forming a sharp contrast with the sprawling corpses of the slain carved across his throne base, accompanied by a most precise body count – '47,209 northern enemies', killed during 'the year of fighting the northern enemy'.

Having finally defeated the north to fully reunite Egypt, the triumphant Khasekhem changed his name to Khasekhemwy – 'The Two Powers have appeared'. And with the Horus falcon rejoining Seth atop the royal *serekh* in a divine double act, they formed a new royal epithet: 'The Two Lords are at Peace within Him', the emblematic creatures shown beak to muzzle, as they literally kissed and made up.

Khasekhemwy's name spread as far afield as the Lebanese port of Byblos when he sent a gift to Hathor, the Egyptian goddess worshipped as 'Lady of Byblos' – political recognition that the port was the source of much-needed timber and 'a connecting link' with places as far afield as Crete and Afghanistan.

As trade abroad expanded, so too did the output of the royal workshops, producing at least one life-size standing statue in copper, named 'High is Khasekhemwy'. As the royal architects continued to build in a more permanent medium, the records state that 'the temple called "The-Goddess-Abides" was built of stone', rather than the usual mud-brick, and that Khasekhemwy himself performed its foundation ceremony, 'stretching the cord' to mark its dimensions. The fact that astronomical observations were used to achieve the correct alignment for the building was also reflected in the new religious title 'Chief Observer' or 'Greatest of Seers', awarded to the high priest at Heliopolis, cult centre of the sun god and the sun god's daughter Hathor. As one of 'the divine ancestors of the king', Hathor was also given a new stone shrine at Gebelein, while further south, the el-Kab home of vulture goddess Nekhbet was embellished with the same new-fangled stonework as that used on the temple of Horus across the river at Hierakonpolis.

Stone was again used in Khasekhemwy's burial chamber within his seventy-metre *mastaba* tomb at Abydos, whose additional forty-three storerooms were packed with grave goods. With a small fraction hidden from ancient robbers when the subterranean walls collapsed, there were over 200 stone vessels with gold lids, gold bracelets, the royal sceptre of gold and red sard, ivory chests and furniture, copper axes and Egypt's earliest bronzeware in the form of the king's washing set of jug and basin, carefully wrapped in linen.

Having constructed the largest royal tomb at Abydos, Khasekhemwy also built an accompanying funerary palace that exceeded all others, a hectare of space surrounded by mud-brick walls, still standing, in places, to their original eleven metres height. Plastered and painted white like Khasekhemwy's palace, this funerary version likewise contained 'inner apartments' or storage facilities, known locally as the Shunet es-Zebib – 'the storehouse of the flies'.

Khasekhemwy had already built a half-sized version at Hierakonpolis, described as the world's oldest free-standing brick-built monument, and its walls requiring 'an impressive 4.82 million bricks' to achieve the same eleven-metre high and five-metre thick walls.

This was a means of maintaining Khasekhemwy's eternal presence in Hierakonpolis as the ancient capital of the south, with his desire to be also eternally present in the north represented by a third such enclosure at Sakkara beside the traditional capital Memphis. Today known as the Gisr el-Mudir – 'the Enclosure of the Boss' – it is only fully visible from the air, but its suitably godlike proportions of half a mile long by a quarter of a mile wide (800m × 400m) required no white paint. For this enclosure was built entirely of dazzling white limestone. And although Khasekhemwy died before it was finished and it was never completed, he had nonetheless laid the most solid foundations for his successors of the Third Dynasty and their own massive, stone-built structures – Egypt's first pyramids.

7

The Rise of the Pyramid Age:
c.2667–2613 BC

At the dawn of the Third Dynasty, the key elements that made up the 'classic' culture of ancient Egypt were in place.

King Djoser (c.2667–2648 BC) was a son of Khasekhemwy and his queen Nimaathap, who was 'venerated as the foundress of the IIIrd Dynasty' for over a century after her death.

She was buried in the gargantuan *mastaba* at Beit Khallaf at Abydos, whose eighty-five-metre length exceeded even Khasekhemwy's tomb, and Djoser's name was found within. This suggests that he had interred his mother Nimaathap at Abydos in the same way as he had overseen his father's funeral, to present himself as their true heir.

Yet his parents' burials effectively terminated Abydos's role as Egypt's royal cemetery, for new king Djoser returned north to Memphis, which would now be the centre of royal life and afterlife.

Living in their great white palace amidst the palm groves and vineyards, Djoser and his sister-wife Hetephirnebty were served by an efficient civil service, headed by Hesira, a dapper individual with a pencil moustache, a wig for every occasion and such impressive medical skills he was not only the 'royal dentist' but 'the first authenticated doctor in the world'. But Hesira was only one of the polymaths at court. For he worked alongside the prime minister Imhotep, who was also the royal architect.

Well aware of the grand *mastabas* of past courtiers set high above the city on the desert edge at Sakkara, alongside Khasekhemwy's massive walls, Imhotep and Djoser fully appreciated that monumental architecture was the perfect means of stamping royal authority across large areas of the kingdom. So Djoser's funerary complex would be far more than a grave in which to bury a body – it would be a structure designed to perpetuate his power and keep his soul alive, an aim enhanced by building the entire structure in stone.

With a huge supply of limestone already on site, the dismantling of Khasekhemwy's stone enclosure – which could be seen as simple usurpation – was nonetheless a way of building on the past to make this royal generation even greater than the last, a pattern that would be followed throughout the rest of Egyptian history. Djoser's tomb certainly did this, since his *mastaba*'s stone superstructure was erected directly above the existing chambers of previous kings Hetepsekhemwy and Nynetjer, which were now expanded for Djoser's use.

As Djoser's limestone *mastaba* took shape, so too did his funerary palace enclosure, which for the first time was built not some distance away, but right around the *mastaba* to enclose thirty-seven acres of sacred space.

The only problem was that the tomb itself could no longer be seen from Memphis. So Imhotep decided to build upwards, inspired by the nearby tombs of First Dynasty courtiers with their terraced, stepped superstructures of mud-bricks beneath their outer mud-brick casings. And when three stepped layers of stone were added to Djoser's tomb, the effect was so successful that two more were added, creating a sixty-four-metre-high structure of dazzling white limestone that was visible for miles.

Egypt's very first pyramid was such an extraordinary achievement that Djoser's name was highlighted in red ink in later king lists; and appreciative graffiti 1,400 years later described it as 'the pyramid of Djoser, inventor of stone'. This accolade applied equally to Imhotep, who was allowed to share in his royal master's eternity with his own name and titles set up within this great complex. Indeed, his fame would even outlast that of his king. For Imhotep was ultimately deified as the son of Memphis's creator deity Ptah. Yet even in his lifetime, 'Egypt's Leonardo da Vinci' was not only a brilliant architect and prime minister, but also high priest of Heliopolis, where Djoser built a limestone shrine to the sun god.

The new temple's walls portrayed Djoser enthroned in the company of his wife Hetephirnebty, their daughter Intkaes and his mother Nimaathap, who each appear as minute figures at his feet. Hetephirnebty wears a robe of stiff linen, its shoulders forming two distinctive peaks between which her rounded coiffure would originally have been a bright gold colour. For her attire portrayed the queen as an aspect of the rising sun, most appropriate in a solar temple where mother, wife and daughter each represented the sun god's female protector, the 'Golden One', Hathor-Sekhmet, defenders of the massive male king who sits monolithic and godlike behind them.

Djoser was portrayed in the same way in Egypt's oldest surviving life-size statue, originally set up on the north side of his pyramid inside a small *serdab* chamber, where offerings could be made to his soul. The chamber's walls were also tilted up by 13 degrees to face the northern sky as if preparing for launch, allowing Djoser to gaze directly out through his once-inlaid crystal eyes to the Northern Stars, the so-called Imperishable Stars which never set, which 'know not death', and with which his risen soul would merge.

Yet the *serdab* was only one of many buildings in a complex recreating Djoser's mud-brick palace – but in stone. Although it has been described as 'Sleeping Beauty's palace. Everything is dead, and everything is made for death', everything was actually made to sustain eternal life: there was a robing room and bathroom, together with Egypt's first hypostyle hall featuring stone columns, carved to resemble bunches of reeds. Its walls were carved to look like wooden fencing, and its roof slabs and door frames emulated timber logs, emphasising that while the homes of the living were made of perishable materials, this 'house of eternity' was built to last.

Security was provided by repeated stone heads of the cobra goddess Wadjet projecting from the tops of the walls; and Djoser's commitment to his whole kingdom was also emphasised by two sets of buildings, one for the north and one for the south. Even the layout of the 140-metre ceremonial racecourse, 'the world's oldest sports facility', was specifically positioned on a north–south axis between two markers round which the king must run, an event commemorated in scenes within the pyramid's subterranean chambers.

Again following the interior of the palace, the walls were covered with 36,000 turquoise tiles replicating reeds, some arranged as roll-up blinds to frame a series of 'false doors' through which Djoser's spirit could pass. On each door he performs the ritual race; the same scenes are then repeated in a second, subterranean 'dummy' tomb in the south area of the complex to stress his control of both halves of his kingdom. At only 1.6m², the smaller dimensions of this second burial chamber suggest that the 'South Tomb' contained only part of the royal body – either the placenta or, most likely, the entrails, which may already have been removed during mummification to prevent putrefaction, an assumption based on the additional discovery of a pair of small alabaster embalming tables 'suited to the viscera'.

The rest of Djoser's mummified body was placed twenty-eight metres beneath his pyramid in a red granite burial vault. The human remains found here include a perfectly preserved left foot, carbon-dated to a much later time when burials within such a holy environment attempted to 'tap into' the power of the illustrious past. Additional shafts some thirty metres deep also contained human remains, including a young boy in a rectangular coffin, and parts of a female body carbon-dated to around 2700–2600 BC, who is possibly one of Djoser's daughters.

Inside an additional 400 subterranean storerooms the early archaeologists report being 'ankle deep' in wheat and barley, figs and grapes, while 40,000 stone vessels, many inscribed with the names of predecessors dating back to Djer, allowed Djoser's spirit to absorb their accumulated powers.

Djoser's nineteen-year reign had certainly provided huge inspiration for his own successor, Sekhemkhet (c.2648–2640 BC), who, inheriting the services of his father's architect Imhotep, wasted no time in starting his own copycat complex as soon as he became king, but planned a seventy-metre seven-stepped structure to exceed his predecessor by one layer and ten metres.

But when Sekhemkhet died after a nine-year reign, leaving his pyramid incomplete, his rectangular alabaster sarcophagus, which remained *in situ*, was nonetheless completely empty: the much-decayed 'funerary wreath' atop the sarcophagus turned out to be the remains of a wooden lever with which ancient graverobbers had long ago prised open the original burial.

Unfinished tombs were also the legacy of his two successors, who nonetheless kept trade and taxes flowing, and kept a firm grip on the turquoise and malachite sources of the Sinai and the Nubian goldmines.

The last king of the Third Dynasty, Huni (c.2637–2613 BC), also failed to make much headway on the pyramid tomb he had begun at the new royal burial ground at Meidum, south of Memphis; but he did build seven smaller versions around Egypt.

Standing only twelve metres high, with no internal chambers, these pyramids served a very different purpose from the tombs of his predecessors. These mini-monuments were statements in stone, stamping the king's presence on each administrative region (*nome*) like a territorial marker. The first, named 'Diadem of Huni', was a three-stepped granite pyramid erected on Elephantine, whose adjoining buildings housed the scribes who recorded deliveries of grain. So it seems that these pyramids were collection points for the royal treasury – basically tax offices, which served as permanent reminders of royal power to everyone sailing by along the river. This pattern of pyramids was followed downstream at Edfu, at el-Kula near Hierakonpolis, at Tukh near Naqada, in Abydos, Zawiyet el-Meitin near Minya, at Seila and at Athribis in the Delta – each set within the local administration and its network of officials.

Although such officials generally passed down their titles to their sons, some passed them to their daughters, while others were passed from mother to son or indeed from mother to daughter. Wealth derived from the Crown was also passed down from both parents to their children; this is first expressed in the biography of Metjen, who rose through the ranks from warehouse scribe to royal intimate, and who states that 'there were presented to him the things of his father', and 'there were conveyed to him 50 *aroura* [almost fourteen hectares] of land by his mother Nebsent. She made a will to her children and it was placed in their possession by the king's writings'.

As for his own succession, Huni's queen Djefatnebti had given him a daughter, Hetepheres, while minor wife Meresankh produced his son Snefru. And when 'the majesty of King Huni died, the majesty of King Snefru was now raised up as beneficent king in this entire land'.

Although Huni had died before completing his own eight-stepped pyramid tomb at Meidum, Snefru completed the bulk, if not all, of the structure. Then to further strengthen his claim to the succession, he married his half-sister Hetepheres – 'she whose every command is carried out'. As 'ancestress of the royal family of the IVth dynasty', Hetepheres and her new husband became the first rulers of the Fourth royal Dynasty, whose devotion to the sun would repeatedly be demonstrated in the most dazzling way.

8

Sons and Daughters of the Sun:
c.2613–2494 BC

During Egypt's first 'Golden Age', the sun as the 'Great He-She' was unquestionably its supreme deity.

As 'Daughter of the God', Hetepheres was the earthly embodiment of the sun god's daughters Hathor and Sekhmet, while her husband Snefru (c.2613–2589 BC) honoured the sun god's other daughter Maat by taking the throne-name 'Nebmaat', 'Lord of Truth'. His two names were the first to be written within oval cartouches, rather than the previous rectangular *serekh*.

As the greatest of all Egypt's pyramid-builders, responsible for moving nine million tons of stone to create three pyramids, Snefru was himself a larger-than-life character, long remembered in later folktales. These claim that he created a rowing crew of women 'with the shapeliest bodies, breasts and braids', clothed in dresses of 'fishing net linen' and that as 'they rowed up and down, his majesty's heart was happy to see them row'. But while this could be seen as a lascivious old king seeking dubious amusement, it is in fact a subtle allusion to the king as the sun, propelled across the heavens by representatives of Hathor, whose best-known attributes were her well-groomed hair, notable breasts and ferocious powers of protection.

While Djoser had previously portrayed himself at Heliopolis as a godlike figure surrounded by female relatives, Snefru, as a devotee of Hathor and her alter ego Sekhmet, is represented in one of the most beautiful images to have survived from Egyptian history, a fragmentary wall scene in which Snefru is embraced by the leonine goddess, whose muzzle touches his nose to imbue him with the very breath of life itself.

Ever since Narmer's time, the relationship between king and goddess had run deep. For the name Hathor literally means 'the house/womb of Horus', and when Snefru built Hathor a temple, he added a gold statue of himself as her son, the newborn sun god – 'Horus who came forth from the gold'.

Hathor was described as 'the lady who dwells in a grove at the end of the world' and her sacred sycamores were planted at her temples. For Sekhmet acacia was planted, the tree also featuring in Queen Hetepheres' title 'Leader of Slaughter in the Acacia House'. As the place where meat offerings were presented to Sekhmet at Heliopolis, and dances performed for Hathor, the same ritualised music and dance combined with small-scale animal sacrifice was a feature of Egyptian folk rites into the Twentieth Century AD.

Hathor's priestesses also greeted the sun each dawn with song, while others were 'specifically charged with managing the fields and estates of the goddess'. A whole series of female figures personifying Snefru's royal estates is shown in his funerary temple scenes at Dahshur, expressing a concept previously commemorated by the tiny labels fastened to grave goods. Indeed, few other cultures have turned the 'gathering of taxes into subject matter for sacred art', and yet here they are, each feminised administrative region bearing evocative names such as 'Snefru luscious-of-pastures', 'Dancers of Snefru' and 'Nurse of Snefru', each carrying forth the bounty to sustain his soul.

And there was certainly plenty of wealth within Snefru's kingdom.

With over a hundred cattle farms in the Delta and Middle Egypt alone, Snefru harnessed the techniques of pyramid construction to enhance productivity by creating the world's oldest dam. Located in the Wadi el-Garawi near Helwan, it contained 60,000 tons of rock, measured 320 feet across and was designed to control rare yet dangerous flash floods. Destroyed – ironically – in a particularly catastrophic flood when near completion, it did show that grandiose architecture could have a practical purpose, as the Egyptians continued to redesign their environment to gain maximum returns.

Snefru also undertook a great boat-building programme; the royal shipyards could produce vessels up to fifty metres long, and the king sent forty such ships to Lebanon for cedar, and to Sinai's Wadi Maghara for turquoise. Recent excavations at Wadi Jarf, only fifty kilometres west of Sinai's Red Sea coast, have even located the original harbour, complete with cedarwood boats stored in long stone-cut chambers with stone portcullis doorways.

Snefru also expanded Egyptian power west, sending military expeditions against the Libyans and seizing 11,000 prisoners and 13,100 cattle, while in the south his seizure of 7,000 prisoners and 200,000 cattle was part of 'a deliberate pharaonic policy of discouraging and destroying indigenous settlements in Lower Nubia'. Penetrating as far south as Buhen in modern Sudan to establish an Egyptian colony as a centre for trade, copper production and staging-post for subsequent expeditions, Snefru also secured the gold in Nubia's mines and opened diorite quarries near Abu Simbel.

Such materials were then lavishly deployed throughout Egypt's royal buildings; the exquisite furniture belonging to Hetepheres included golden thrones and a golden bed, surrounded by the finest linen curtains hanging from a gold canopy. A gift from her husband, complete with matching gold storage boxes, the set was 'a portable bed chamber' that 'can be taken down in about fifteen minutes and set up again in about the same time'. The ensemble accompanied Hetepheres as she toured the country with Snefru, at all times shielded from the sun, from insects and from the gaze of mere mortals by fine linen curtains. And within these initimate surroundings Hetepheres and Snefru may well have produced their royal children, Hetepheres Junior – 'eldest daughter whom he loves of his body' – and her chubby-cheeked brother, Khnumkhufu.

Minor wives provided many more royal babies, whose portraits as adults are some of the finest to have survived. A bust of Prince Ankhaf is so lifelike that one museum curator dressed a replica in his own suit, tie and homburg 'to satisfy the writer's curiosity as to what an ancient Egyptian nobleman would look like if living today . . . Discounting the broken nose and the absence of ears, one is struck by the modernity of the face, which might be met with any day in the street', while 'the hat and coat of the writer, who is six feet tall and weighs about 160 pounds, fit the ancient Egyptian perfectly'.

Yet it is the pristine, painted statuary of Snefru's son Prince Rahotep and wife Nofret – 'the most visited pair in Cairo

Museum'– that still excite most reaction from the modern world. With his cropped black hair and a thin moustache, Rahotep's frown lines convey intense concentration when captured by raking light, while Nofret's sullen pout changes to 'pleasant and serene' depending on the time of day one pays them a visit. And while it is a cliché to say that they almost seem alive, the first person to enter their tomb in 1871 fled in terror, claiming that the apparently undead inhabitants 'stared back at him' with their gleaming eyes of quartz-inlaid crystal. Created as a duplicate home for their souls in case their mummified bodies were damaged, it is extraordinary to think that such works of art were never intended to be seen by the living, but to be buried with the dead, the Egyptians' obsession with eternal life once again providing the most magnificent gift to history.

The same artistic standards were also brought to bear in the Meidum tomb Snefru provided for another son, Prince Nefermaat, and his wife Itet. Its walls were embellished with paintings of such quality, best highlighted by the famous 'Meidum Geese', that some academics now claim the paintings to be nineteenth-century forgeries. Their unique colours and proportions are certainly highly innovative, as is the use of inlaid coloured paste from the tomb's other walls, which Prince Nefermaat himself designed, stating that they had been 'made for his gods in writing that cannot be destroyed' by anyone wishing to usurp his final resting place.

Although the *mastabas* of Meidum were all robbed, one still contained its original occupant, royal relative Ranefer, whose body 'lay hitched up against the west wall . . . the head had been broken off by the violators, but carefully replaced, with a stone under it to support its position', according to the archaeologist who entered the tomb in 1890. He also reported the body to be 'marvellously plumped out', for Ranefer had been well mummified. He had been laid full-length to remove his internal organs, which had been dried out, wrapped and buried with him, and the rest of his body had similarly been dried, coated in resins and wrapped in linen that was then painted: his hair in black, his mouth in red and his eyes and eyebrows in green.

As one of the very earliest mummies ever discovered in such an intact state, Ranefer's precious remains were sent to the Royal College of Surgeons in London, where one anatomist used to take the head into lectures 'and shake it so the audience could hear the sound of the dried brain rattling within, a sign it had not been removed as part of the process'. Having survived so much, it is all the more tragic that Ranefer's remains were destroyed in 1941 when the college took a direct hit in the Blitz.

All these people – Ranefer, Nefermaat and Itet, Rahotep and Nofret – had been buried close to the pyramid begun by Huni but certainly completed by Snefru, who filled in its stepped exterior to create the first 'true' pyramid with sloping sides. This was admired for generations, ancient graffiti claiming 'thrice good is the name of king Snefru', at least until the pyramid collapsed into its current, curious, blancmange-like shape.

For his own funeral arrangements, Snefru wanted a completely new burial ground, so moved six miles south of Memphis to Dahshur. Here he began work on the first pyramid built from scratch as a smooth-sided structure. Its design expressed dualities – two separate entrances, two sets of internal chambers and two angles of incline – and the initial 60-degree angle changed to 43 degrees halfway up its 105-metre height, creating what is now known as the 'Bent Pyramid'. Although admittedly it looks rather odd set against the straight lines of later examples, some Egyptologists have suggested its shape intentionally replicates that of the mound of creation, and its two distinct angles represent Upper and Lower Egypt.

Whatever its grand plan, the pyramid was built on a shale bed, and as cracks appeared on the exterior, internal subsidence could no longer be concealed by mere plaster. The king must have been dissatisfied, to say the least; he sent his architects back to the drawing board, and four kilometres north, to begin what must have been the most laborious rebuild in history.

All available manpower was mobilised from a population of around one and a half million; two million tons of stone were laid down over seventeen years by the 'Green Gang', the 'Western Gang' and armies of workmates, whose efforts were finally rewarded with a perfect pyramid. Built at the same 43-degree angle to a height of 104 metres, and model for all subsequent examples, this 'Northern Pyramid' still dominates the Dahshur skyline, true testament to Snefru's vision and the great tenacity of his architects. But this was not just a stairway to climb to the stars; this pyramid was the perfect architectural analogy for the way Snefru's soul would be reborn, its apex topped by a gilded capstone designed to catch the first rays of the sun, whose reviving powers would then be transmitted directly downwards, into the body of the king.

When Snefru died around 2589 BC, his body was mummified by the royal embalmers. Although their highly specialised work was also highly secretive – 'I am one who keeps secrets and I belong to the house of Osiris,' claimed the ancient funerary texts – his remains, found within his Northern Pyramid, reveal that he had been eviscerated and mummified with the same shining golden resins that had been in use for almost two millennia, both to preserve him and to emphasise his solar credentials as his soul rose up to join the sun.

To share in their father's sun-drenched afterlife, more of his children were buried close by, as was his queen, Hetepheres. But she was not to spend eternity with her husband; their son and heir had other plans.

Named after the ram-headed creator god, Khnum-khufu, meaning 'Khnum defends me', but known to history as Khufu (c.2589–2566 BC), the new king built on his father's spectacular legacy to create Egypt's largest, most celebrated monument: the Great Pyramid of Giza.

An empty plateau when Khufu became king, 'the first construction to occur in the east field, to the east of the Great Pyramid' was a tomb for his mother Hetepheres, whose location may have been influenced by the impressive *mastaba* created a mile to the south for the mother of old king Djet.

Cut twenty-seven metres down into bedrock, Hetepheres' tomb had been filled with her possessions, from the bedroom suite given to her by her husband to a gold and ebony carrying chair presented by her son and designed to carry her aloft in the same way Egypt's earliest royal women and gods' statues were conveyed. A most exhilarating, if precarious, way to travel, its gilded surface mirrored the sun travelling through the sky, to emphasise that Hetepheres as 'Daughter of the God' was the earthly embodiment of Hathor 'the Golden One', and thus sufficiently divine to merit the same kind of transport.

Declaring himself the son of Hathor, Khufu required the goddess's presence for his spirit to be reborn. And since his mother Hetepheres was regarded as the goddess incarnate this may explain why Khufu's vast pyramid is directly aligned *behind* the tomb of Hetepheres, which lay closer both to the sunrise and to the Nile, 'in the most important point in his own royal cemetery'.

After her death, Hetepheres was mummified and her internal organs separately preserved in a solution of natron salt within an alabaster chest, still sealed when it was found in her intact Giza tomb in 1925. Yet her matching alabaster sarcophagus was completely empty and the lead archaeologist was obliged to inform an eagerly awaiting crowd, 'I regret Queen Hetepheres is not receiving'. He then theorised that soon after her first burial at Dahshur, her mummy had been destroyed by graverobbers, and when her son Khufu ordered her reburial at Giza to have her body close to his pyramid, no one had dared to tell him, so he unknowingly reburied the empty sarcophagus.

But more recent research suggests Khufu simply adapted his plans. Removing his mother's body from Dahshur to rebury it within the small pyramid he subsequently built beside her Giza shaft tomb, he also provided Hetepheres with the first of Giza's solar boats.

Placed within a huge oval pit sunk into the bedrock, its distinctly elliptical shape with lip-like rim is highly reminiscent of the opening to the birth canal of the sky goddess, through which the sun was reborn each dawn. Indeed, the entire pyramid field was soon punctuated by so many of these distinctly shaped pits that it resembled a vast, esoteric maternity unit. This strong connection between 'birth and boat imagery' also featured in funerary texts, which describe the sun god's journey through the goddess's body in distinctly anatomical terms, the goddess in labour announcing that 'when rage has reached its limit, the Radiant One sails forth'. And, just as the sun was born amidst the red hue of birth-blood, the Giza boat pits were originally sealed with a layer of plaster, mixed with iron oxide to produce a 'rosy pink' hue.

With his mother's burial arrangements carefully planned, Khufu began work on his own tomb, the most famous in human history. Now known as the Great Pyramid of Giza, it was named 'Akhet-Khufu' – Horizon of Khufu.

Khufu's architect was his nephew Hemiunu, who followed the design of his father Snefru's smooth-sided pyramid, but increased its height by forty-two metres.

Hemiunu was also a priest of Thoth, god of learning, and later stories related that the king had discussed his tomb's layout with a magician who 'knew the measures of the chambers of Thoth's sanctuary. For his Majesty Khufu had been spending his time in searching for the chambers of Thoth's sanctuary in order to make a similar one for his pyramid', whose sacred dimensions were apparently stored in a chest in the sun temple at Heliopolis.

Having surveyed the ground, Hemiunu aligned Khufu's pyramid to the cardinal points using the circumpolar stars, calculating which parts of the complex would be in the pyramid's huge shadow at various times of the year.

Although the exact way in which the pyramids were built has long been the subject of debate, not least because each one differs in its plans, materials and methods – not to mention in size and location – the Great Pyramid itself was constructed from 2,300,000 blocks of stone, each weighing an average of two and a half tons. Over Khufu's twenty-three-year reign this required 340 blocks to be moved each ten-hour working day, or thirty-four blocks per hour, roughly equalling one block every two minutes. Although the pyramid was built mainly with limestone from neighbouring quarries, its original white exterior was made of the finest quality Tura limestone, brought over from the east bank of the Nile, while a recent study has revealed that the interior layers were filled with sand.

With the pyramid's 146-metre height unsurpassed until the completion of Lincoln Cathedral spire in AD 1300, it was truly an incredible feat of construction, which 'offered maximum protection for the body buried there'. For beyond a concealed entrance, the only access to the burial chamber was through the ceiling of a descending passage, sealed by three huge blocks of granite. This led to the eight-metre-high Grand Gallery, ascending a further forty-seven metres and again blocked off with a trio of granite portcullises.

At the top of the Grand Gallery, at the very heart of the pyramid, lay its minimalist burial chamber. The most extraordinarily atmospheric place, whose stark, red granite-lined walls still amplify every whisper, this veritable bank vault was created to hold Egypt's greatest treasure, the royal mummy, whose red granite sarcophagus, two and a half centimetres wider than the entrance corridor, was clearly set in place during construction.

A pair of air shafts in the burial chamber and two more in a second chamber far below, were aligned to Orion and the Pole Star, and to Polaris and Sirius, this nocturnal, stellar choice of destination for Khufu's soul paralleled by a solar destination to which he could sail aboard the forty-three-metre-long solar boats that were placed in pits on the pyramid's exterior.

There are two surviving ships, made of Lebanese cedar, caulked with waterproof resin from when they had last plied the Nile, most likely when bringing Khufu's body to his pyramid complex. The best-preserved boat also has a canopy on deck, so similar to Hetepheres' gold canopy that the same craftsmen surely made them both, and perhaps connecting the place in which Khufu was conceived or born to this duplicate structure facilitating his rebirth.

Khufu's need to remain close to his divine mother is also reflected in two large statues of Bastet-Sekhmet, with Khufu as a tiny child at her feet. The royal records also state that two larger-than-life statues were made of the king in both gold and copper, and although it is usually claimed that the only known statue of the builder of Egypt's greatest pyramid is a thumb-sized figurine in ivory, there was in fact large-scale stone statuary that has been identified as Khufu on the basis of his chubby cheeks, as set up throughout his pyramid complex.

This vast complex began at the Nile with the king's valley temple, from which a long causeway 'constructed of polished stone blocks decorated with carvings of animals' originally stretched 825 metres to connect with a funerary temple built behind the tomb of his mother Hetepheres. Its black basalt floor once supported columns of red granite with matching granite dado, a chunk of which the Egyptian government presented to a British diplomat in 1876, and which, set within the walls of the diplomat's local church near Durham, continues to be part of religious architecture to this day.

The white limestone walls of Khufu's funerary temple, carved with offering-bearers, also featured the musical goddess Meret, whose song, rising up through the temple's open roof, 'has caused you to become a transfigured spirit', claimed a later text. It is therefore surely no coincidence that having built the pyramid, its architect Hemiunu was made 'Director of Music in the South and North' in an ancient fusion of Christopher Wren and George Frideric Handel.

Having created Egypt's largest ever pyramid and its musical soundtrack, Hemiunu was rewarded with a fine tomb in the Giza cemetery, where *mastabas*, laid out in streets, created a royal housing estate for the dead. And with Khufu's son Hordjedef, advised to 'beautify your house in the necropolis, the house of death should be for life', it was advice the royal family took seriously.

They were accompanied by the burials of their retainers, from the royal jeweller Werka, 'metalworker of the royal ornaments' to 'the one who delights his lord every day, the dwarf of the king, Periankhu'. For dwarves held a special place at court, where the dwarf Seneb was not only in charge of the royal wardrobe but oversaw Khufu's funerary cult, Seneb's full-sized wife Senetites one of eighty-one Hathor priestesses also buried in the Giza necropolis.

Yet until very recently, all those interred here appeared to exist in splendid isolation, floating in a world of royal privilege seemingly unsupported by the realities of everyday life. The pyramids themselves were assumed to have been built by a vast army of slaves wheeled in, Cecil B. De Mille style, to toil for merciless tyrants before being killed to keep secret the location of the tomb's treasures. Only in 1988 did the discovery of 'Gerget Khufu', the 'settlement of Khufu', reveal the real people behind this legendary site.

Separated from the royal burial ground by the monumental 'Wall of the Crow', a ten-metre-high, twelve-metre-thick barrier dividing the living from the dead, the purpose-built settlement featured detached homes for management and barracks for the builders. They ate in communal dining rooms supplied from on-site warehouses; the bread, beer, meat and fish came from industrial-sized stockyards, breweries and the bakeries that produced dense, high-carbohydrate wheat-and-barley sourdough loaves, baked in chunky pots.

And just as the graves of the Predynastic dead are the best way to understand the Predynastic living, so the six hundred small tombs of the Giza workers similarly preserve a real sense of their original owners. They include the weaver Neferhetpes, mother of eleven children, who had clearly deserved the fourteen types of bread and cakes she requested as offerings in her tomb inscriptions. Such texts also give official titles, from the 'Overseer of Masonry' and 'Director of Draughtsmen' to the 'priestess', the 'weaver', 'baker', 'potter', 'carpenter' and artists like Peteti, protecting his modest tomb with the imaginative curse: 'Listen all of you! The priest of Hathor will beat twice any of you who enters this tomb or does harm to it. The gods will not allow anything to happen to me. Anyone who does anything bad to my tomb, then the crocodile, hippopotamus and lion will eat him'.

In some cases the people are still present too, their skeletal remains unsurprisingly revealing strain-induced health problems. Nearly all the individuals examined showed signs of arthritis and compressed vertebrae; one physical anthropologist was 'surprised to see this kind of arthritis in the women' and added that 'there is more damage to their bones than you would expect from simply doing household chores'.

At least one of Giza's working women was a dwarf, no more than a metre tall, who had died while giving birth to a full-sized foetus.

Yet the bones also showed healed fractures and successful amputations, revealing that the ancient world's largest building site also had medical facilities.

With a 4,000-strong core workforce undertaking much of the work in gangs, their number was greatly increased each summer by farmers. Shipped in from around the country between July and September – when they were unable to work their land while the valley was flooded – they were temporarily redeployed here in a mass effort to propel their god-king Khufu into an afterlife they might just get to share.

When Khufu died around 2566 BC, his body was mummified with no less precision and skill than that employed to create his vast tomb, for his body would be the focus of the entire pyramid complex.

Once embalmed and placed within his coffin, Khufu's body was taken up the causeway to his funerary temple. Standing it upright on the temple's black floor, amidst clouds of thick, sweet incense, the priests performed the Opening of the Mouth ceremony, touching the areas of his mouth, eyes, nose and ears to restore their function and 'switch back on' the soul of Khufu.

Then, entering the pyramid and ascending to its granite-lined burial chamber, the funeral party lowered the coffin into the granite sarcophagus, sealed its heavy lid and took their leave, setting off the portcullis mechanisms to seal the chamber for ever.

Since Khufu had embodied the sun god on earth, his son and successor Djedefra (c.2566–2558 BC) introduced the new title 'Son of Ra' as part of the royal name. And maintaining his family's solar devotion, Djedefra began plans for his own pyramid, but not at Giza. Instead he moved eight kilometres north, to the high desert at Abu Rawash, right opposite the main temple of the sun god at Heliopolis.

At 150 metres above the Nile Valley, almost half the new pyramid's core was formed from a natural promontory of limestone. Requiring far less effort to construct its 200-cubit long sides, its 125-cubit height also appeared greater, by virtue of the site's higher ground.

Djedefra also commissioned over a hundred statues of himself and his family for his pyramid complex, his portraits of red quartzite, with their 'awe-inspiring divine aloofness', balanced by those of his consort and half-sister, Hetepheres II.

Hetepheres II had already been married to Khufu's eldest son Kawab and, at his death, she married his younger brother, Djedefra. Just like her same-named grandmother, she served Sekhmet as 'Overseer of the Butchers of the Acacia House'; and the leonine link extended to her statues, for Hetepheres II, as Hathor-Sekhmet, produced one of the most iconic of all Egyptian images – the sphinx.

Derived from the term *shesep-ankh* – 'living image' – a sculpture of a crouching lioness with Hetepheres II's head was Egypt's first known sphinx, the perfect guardian for Djedefra's Abu Rawash complex.

After a reign of between eight and eleven years, Djedefra was interred here, his funerary cult overseen by his priestess daughter Neferhotpes and his younger brother, Khafra, the new king.

Although Khafra returned to Giza to build his own pyramid tomb beside that of their father, he had nonetheless learned much from his older brother, Djedefra. For he sited his pyramid – called 'Khafra is Great' – on slightly higher ground. So while it may be two metres smaller than Khufu's pyramid, it appears higher, in 'an inspired combination of deference and self-assertion'.

Khafra also utilised the surrounding landscape by transforming the large rocky outcrop in front of the pyramid into an enormous sculpture. Twenty metres high and seventy metres long, it took the form of a protective lion with a human head. Likely inspired by the female prototype of Hetepheres II, the Great Sphinx was itself regarded as female for some two thousand years, when Greek visitors, noticing the red pigment remaining on its massive face, called it *Rhodopis* – 'Rosy-Cheeks'.

But Khafra's sphinx had Khafra's face. Gazing out at every sunrise over the top of the adjoining Sphinx Temple, aligned to the March and September equinoxes, the temple's structure honoured the sun's rising and setting, with two stone pillars in the east and west sanctuaries representing the limbs of the sky goddess, Nut. Female deities also featured on the fifty-metre-wide façade of Khafra's adjoining Valley Temple, whose two doors feature the two deities Bastet-Sekhmet of Lower Egypt, named on its northern entrance, and bovine Hathor of Upper Egypt on its south, each naming Khafra her 'beloved'.

Within this austere temple of red granite, twenty-four life-size statues of Khafra enthroned display the well-developed torso 'of a heavyweight athlete'. His royal headcloth is fronted by Wadjet as the uraeus, and flanked by the protective wings of Horus, who literally watches the king's back while peering over his head, appearing to rise up from the king's body to create 'an unequalled image of the ideal man and of god incarnate in man'.

Of his wives, three were his half-sisters, although the most senior woman at court was still the dowager queen Hetepheres II, whose daughter Meresankh III married Khafra in an uncle–niece marriage.

Although Meresankh and Khafra had five children, Meresankh's most important relationship seems to have been with her mother Hetepheres II, and in Meresankh's tomb, built on her mother's orders, the two women are shown sailing the Nile, tugging riverside reeds in an arcane ritual known as 'Shaking the Papyrus' to recharge their reproductive powers. Meresankh wears a net dress of blue beads in an enduring fashion that is still to be found in Egypt's tourist bazaars. And as the outfits change around the walls, Hetepheres II appears in the same, striking outfit as previous royal women: a stiff white linen robe that features shoulder peaks of such pronounced dimensions they inspired the modern couturier Balmain. Her hair, covered by a wig, retains its original golden yellow colour to emphasise her solar attributes, while the equally chic Meresankh, with her cropped black hair, is now dressed in the leopard-skin robe of a funerary priest. This was a role requiring its holder to be literate, as emphasised by a retainer holding up a document for her appraisal, and by the fact that Meresankh was also a priestess of the literacy god Thoth, a title also held by her mother.

When Meresankh died in her mid-fifties – at a time the average lifespan was around thirty-five – her mummified body was placed in a sarcophagus inscribed 'That which I have given to my daughter' by her grieving mother Hetepheres II, who lived into her seventies, having outlived at least four kings including Khafra, who died around 2532 BC.

Following his mummification, Khafra's body was interred within his pyramid's burial chamber accompanied by traditional rites led by his son and daughter, Menkaura (c.2532–2503 BC) and Khamerernebty, the new royal couple.

In one of a series of superb sculptures, Khamerernebty holds her brother-husband in such a protective embrace that he clearly has no need of the guardian uraeus snake at his brow. With Khamerernebty's presence 'perhaps symbolising her role as royal heiress and "power behind the throne"', the piece was highly influential among their courtiers, whose own sculpted figures also show the wife embracing the husband in an emphatic pose – a pose still to be seen in some formal photographic portraits of Egyptian couples today.

Although Menkaura's eighteen-year reign 'left no significant historical records', his courtiers are rather better attested. The high official Ptahshepses states that he was born in the reign of Menkaura and 'educated among the king's children, in the palace of the king, in the privy chamber, in the royal women's quarters, more honored before the king than any child'.

Equally favoured was Debhen, 'Overseer of the Great Palace', and when his king Menkaura was visiting Giza during the construction of his pyramid, the third to be built at the site, he also gave orders for a tomb to be made for Debhen, for 'when his majesty was upon the road in order to inspect the work upon his pyramid, his majesty commanded the place to be cleared of stone chippings for my tomb'.

Another important presence at court was Abutiyu ('Pointy Ears'), whose Giza tomb inscription calls him 'the dog which was the guard of his majesty. Abutiyu is his name. His majesty ordered that he be buried ceremonially, that he be given a coffin from the royal treasury, fine linen in great quantity, and incense. His majesty also gave perfumed ointment, and ordered that a tomb be built for him by gangs of masons. His majesty did this for him in order that he might be honoured before the great god.'

As the Giza plateau buzzed with crews of builders, including 'Menkaura's Drunkards', his pyramid rapidly took shape – a two-tone structure of white limestone contrasting with the first sixteen courses, which were of the same red granite used for its interior passages. As for the original stone sarcophagus, this is now at the bottom of the Bay of Biscay after the boat carrying it to the British Museum in 1838 sank.

Yet traces of Menkaura's funerary complex do survive, his Valley Temple once housing a series of sculptures 'remarkable in number and quality'. Each featuring a human representative of one of Egypt's forty-two administrative regions (nomes), they accompany the king and Hathor, who, in every case, touches him, holds his hand or puts her arm round him, in one case his mace resting on the side of the goddess's great throne to infuse it with her power.

This same emphasis on the giant female form is found in Queen Khameremebty II's statuary, which includes the earliest colossus of a human, male or female, known from Egypt. It originally stood within the queen's Giza tomb, whose inscriptions reveal that she herself had financed the enterprise.

Yet the grandest tomb for a woman at Giza was the one built for Menkaura's daughter Khentkawes I. Once so huge it is now referred to as the 'Fourth Pyramid of Giza', this huge *mastaba* with vaulted top was erected on an outcrop of bedrock. Khentkawes I was provided with a complex just as elaborate as those of the pyramids of her male predecessors: it included her own funerary temple, causeway, solar boat pit, workers' town – complete with latrines – and, 'quite exceptionally, a Valley Temple and a basin/harbour, which suggests that she reigned as a Pharaoh at the end of the 4th dynasty', according to the archaeologists currently excavating the site.

Khenatkawes I was also shown enthroned at her tomb's granite entrance, wearing the royal cobra at her brow and the tie-on false beard of kingship and accompanied by the inscription 'King of Upper and Lower Egypt, Mother of the King of Upper and Lower Egypt', as translated by the first archaeologist to work there. And although 'an alternative translation which is philologically tenable' later demoted Khentkawes I to 'Mother of Kings', rather than a king herself, many Egyptologists do now believe that Khentkawes I was 'considered a true ruler'. Indeed, 2,000 years after her reign, Classical writers were still claiming that one of the Giza pyramids had indeed been built by a woman: 'this pyramid was erected by the courtesan Rhodopis'; 'this last pyramid, some say, is the tomb of the courtesan Rhodopis', and 'the smallest but most greatly admired of these pyramids was built by Rhodopis'.

As the last major sepulchre to be built on the Giza plateau, Khentkawes I's tomb entrance opened onto the mouth of the *wadi* that formed the main conduit for all the pyramids' construction materials. So 'the channel that gave birth to the Giza necropolis thus became the approach to the tomb of the queen mother, who perhaps gave birth to a new dynasty that moved its necropolis to Saqqara and Abusir'.

Although details are sparse, Khentkawes I married Shepseskaf, perhaps a son of Menkaura, or maybe legitimising his claim through his marriage. Shepseskaf certainly duplicated his wife's style of tomb, but his was located in South Sakkara, where he was buried around 2498 BC as the last king of the Fourth Dynasty.

9

The Rule of Ra: c.2494–2375 BC

The Fifth Dynasty dawned with a trio of kings who were most likely Shepseskaf's sons by Khentkawes I. Their origins were long remembered in popular folk tales in which these future kings of Egypt were born to a character named Ruddedet, who some Egyptologists identify as Khentkawes I herself.

Providing a welcome glimpse into a private world, the story relates that her difficult labour aroused the concern of the sun god. Seeking out the goddesses Isis, Nephthys, Meskhenet and Heket, the god tells them, 'Please go and deliver the three children who are in her womb and who will one day assume the kingship of the whole land'.

As the goddesses set out, disguised as itinerant dancers much like Egypt's *ghawazee*, who until recent times attended births and celebrations, they come upon Ruddedet's husband, Rawoser. So panic-stricken he has his loincloth on upside down, he says to them 'Oh my ladies. See how she is in pain! Her labour is so difficult!' Replying 'Let us see her, because we all understand childbirth', they push past him, taking their places around Ruddedet; Isis in front of her, Nephthys behind her and their companions providing encouragement. As the first royal child slides into Isis' arms, his 'strong bones, gold-covered limbs and a headdress of lapis-lazuli' already in place, they wash him, cut his umbilical cord and lay him on a cushion, as Ruddedet gives birth to two more identical sons. Each is handed to their mother, who names them, as was tradition, and the goddesses give the good news to her husband, who is so delighted he offers them a sack of barley, saying 'Take it as payment for beer'.

It has been suggested that the boys' father Rawoser, 'Ra is great', represented the sun god, who took human form to produce these babies with one of his priestesses. Whatever the historical facts, the Fifth Dynasty certainly increased the already deep devotion to the solar cult; the first Fifth Dynasty king, Userkaf (c.2494–2487 BC), was himself high priest of the sun. Along with Ra, Hathor was the other main beneficiary of his largesse; her 109-strong clergy of eighty-three women and twenty-six men even exceeded the forty-one who served the sun god. Userkaf's palace steward Nika-ankh was also a priest of the goddess at Tehneh in Middle Egypt, a role he passed on to his wife Hedet-heknu and each of their thirteen children, his will stating that each must serve one month a year as Hathor's priest, even if the size of the family did mean some sharing. The income from the temple's land was likewise divided between them, and one of his daughters and one son were so grateful to their fair-minded father they set up a statue of him.

King Userkaf too revered his father, Shepseskaf, and began work on his own tomb directly opposite Shepseskaf's at Sakkara. It was also close to the old pyramid of Djoser and, like it, was built in the form of a pyramid, duplicated on a smaller scale for Userkaf's queen Neferhotpes. Their tombs were then surrounded by the *mastabas* of their officials, like the Treasury Overseer Akhethotep, the Memphis High Priest Ranefer and Ka-aper, whose life-size wooden statue, with inlaid eyes, was so lifelike it was dubbed the 'Sheikh el-Beled' by the locals who found it in 1860, because he so closely resembled their own village headman.

With all such officials wanting burial as close as possible to the royal burial place, now a 'heap of stones flattered by the term pyramid', Userkaf's tomb once stood forty-nine metres high with its funerary temple built on the pyramid's south side to 'ensure that the sun's rays would shine directly into it all year round'. Within its sun-filled interior stood red granite statues of fleshy-nosed Userkaf, three times life size, surrounded by wall scenes of the king hunting by the river, while butterflies, kingfishers, herons and hoopoe flapped above the papyrus groves. The scenes also showed the sailors aboard the royal ship, being ordered to 'sail well like this, hurry up!', and each rower depicted holding his oar at a slightly different angle to suggest one continuous movement. Even the royal troops are shown moving at speed, no doubt inspired by the neighbouring images of old king

Djoser performing his ceremonial race, as they too run swiftly in formation.

These same troops of Userkaf are known to have undertaken a campaign against Nubia, while his officials expanded foreign trade to such an extent that a stone vessel bearing his name eventually reached the Greek island of Cythera.

When Userkaf died after a seven-year reign and was buried in his Sakkara pyramid, his tomb was only part of his plan for immortality. For a short distance north of Sakkara, on the high desert plateau overlooking the Nile at Abusir, he had also built the 'Stronghold of Ra', a huge sun temple, located at the most southerly point from where it was possible to see the wide, gold-tipped obelisk representing the mound of Creation within the illustrious temple of Heliopolis.

And just as at Heliopolis, Userkaf's sun temple also featured open-air altars for daily offerings of oxen and geese, which, having been blessed by the sun's first rays and infused with solar power, were taken by water to Userkaf's pyramid at Sakkara to be presented to his soul. Then, in the 'reversion of offerings', the priests finished off what remained of the well-travelled and by now no-doubt flyblown meat.

The setting of Userkaf's Abusir temple was so spectacular that his successors erected both their tombs and their own sun temples there. Abusir's first three pyramids were built in exactly the same arrangement as the three pyramids of Giza, the diagonal alignments of both sites converging on the obelisk of Heliopolis, which was regarded as the most potent source of solar power on earth.

The best preserved of the Abusir pyramid complexes is the one that belonged to Userkaf's brother Sahura (c.2487–2475 BC), whose reign included quarrying expeditions deep into Nubia for diorite, and military expeditions against both Libya and Sinaii, where rock-cut scenes declared him 'the Great God who smites the Asiatics of all countries'. His scribe Hetep and interpreter Nika-ankh even left graffiti along the Wadi Hamama, which was less well-travelled than the better known Wadi Hammamat but did provide another access route to the Red Sea down which, the royal annals claim, Sahura's expeditions sailed as far as Punt (modern Somalia). They then returned with such exotic produce as monkeys, hunting dogs and '80,000 measures of myrrh' – the fragrant gum resin used in perfume production, in mummification and burned as incense before the sun god.

As the expanding royal treasuries allowed Sahura's generosity to exceed all before him, Nekhbet's daily portions of bread and beer were increased eightyfold, while her northern counterpart Wadjet was each day swamped with 4,800 similar offerings at her cult centre Buto, where she was now worshipped alongside the sun god in an arrangement reflecting the respective roles of Sahura and wife Neferkha-nebty; the word 'Nebty' means 'the Two Ladies' and invokes both Wadjet and Nekhbet.

Yet Abusir was the real focus of Sahura's attention; it was the site of his sun temple and his forty-seven-metre-high pyramid, which lay at the heart of a lavish complex whose 10,000m² of carved wall scenes were so heavily plundered to fuel Egypt's nineteenth-century lime kilns that now only an estimated two per cent survive.

Beginning on the shore of the Nile-fed Lake Abusir, Sahura's Valley Temple was supported by columns of red granite topped by the carved fronds of date palm, the sacred tree of Buto, which appeared to grow from the rich 'Nile mud' represented by the temple's black basalt flooring.

From here a long roofed causeway featured striking images of Sahura as a sphinx, trampling his enemies, as a procession of gods led captured prisoners on ropes. Found only recently are yet more scenes, showing desert-dwelling Bedouin as victims of famine, presumably to contrast with Sahura's well-fed, Nile-side subjects.

At the top of the causeway, the long entrance hall of the walled pyramid enclosure opened out into a court from which stairs led to the flat roof, where astronomer-priests calculated the precise timings of rites, from the monthly lunar festival to the annual festivals of Ra and Hathor. The roof's central section, open to the sky, allowed both moonlight and sunlight to penetrate and highlight walls portraying specific deities, from Seshat, writing down the quantities of captured wealth, to Bastet-Sekhmet, whose image remained the most venerated deity in the entire complex for at least a thousand years, and where early Christians would one day build a chapel.

Yet Sahura was not only shown in close proximity to the great lioness, but was also shown being closely embraced by his wife, Neferkha-nebty, and as an all-action hero who smites Libyans and Nubians, shoots arrows and hunts wildlife, a victorious, sun-fuelled monarch bringing order to chaos.

He was also hugely wealthy, receiving seaborne tribute from as far afield as Syria, whose exotic cargoes included brown bears and foreigners labelled 'interpreters', some offering-bearers labelled 'the Great Green One' – meaning the Mediterranean Sea – in contrast to those bringing forth the home-grown produce of Egypt.

Such bounty was then used in twice-daily rites to feed Sahura's soul as it emerged from his pyramid tomb via his false door, to absorb the food placed upon the altar. Liquid libations were also poured out into copper-lined stone basins, whose copper drains ran for 380 metres throughout the temple, and the same ritual drainage duplicated on high when occasional 'rain falling on the roof was carried off by lion-headed gargoyles, which projected well beyond the eaves, and fell into open channels cut in the pavement'.

Feline protection was also provided within Sahura's palace by his physician Nenekh-sekhmet, named after the lioness goddess. Regarded as the bringer of disease, she was controlled by her priests, who were also doctors. Dr Nenekh-sekhmet was so valued that the king told him 'As these my nostrils enjoy health, as the gods love me, may you depart into the cemetery at an advanced old age as one revered'. Fellow doctor Irenakhty was a court physician, a gastro-enterologist, ophthalmologist and proctologist, literally 'herdsman of the anus', while Lady Peseshat's titles included 'Overseer of Women Physicians', pre-dating the UK law allowing women to practise medicine by 4,000 years.

Yet despite such specialist medical care then available, Sahura died after a twelve-year reign and was buried in his Abusir pyramid, to be succeeded by his youngest brother Neferirkara (c.2475–2455 BC).

Like all Egyptian kings, Neferirkara was awarded the standard five names: 'King of Upper and Lower Egypt', Neferirkara; 'the Son of Ra', Kaikai; 'the Horus', Userkhau; 'He of the Two Ladies', Khaiemnebty; and 'the Golden Horus', Sekhemunebu.

And like all kings, he was served by an army of retainers, although Neferirkara seems to have been a surprisingly humane individual who cared for those who cared for him. When the priest Rawer accidentally made contact with the royal sceptre, a potentially fatal breach of protocol for those without permission, the king dealt with it kindly. As the priest's biographical inscription explains, 'Rawer was following the steps of the king, when the sceptre in the king's hand struck the priest Rawer's foot. The king said "You are safe", and then "it is the king's wish that he be perfectly safe, since I have not struck at him. For he is more worthy before the king than any man".'

Then when Neferirkara's prime minister Weshptah suffered a fatal stroke and died, despite all efforts of the royal physicians and priests, 'the heart of his majesty was exceedingly sad beyond everything . . . and he returned to his private chambers and prayed to Ra', ordering that Weshptah's body was anointed in his presence as part of mummification rites, and placed in a tomb that the king provided.

As for his own afterlife, Neferirkara planned his burial at Abusir within a seventy-metre six-tiered step pyramid. Although he died before its completion, his funerary cult was nonetheless maintained by a clergy that served Ra, Hathor and the 'perfect god' – Neferirkara himself. Exempted from compulsory labour on royal building schemes by a royal decree, a real insight into this clergy's work is contained in a priceless collection of administrative documents, written in a shorthand form of hieroglyphs known as hieratic.

For these are the clergy's original work schedules and duty rosters, accounts and delivery lists, even reminders to restock supplies of ritual ingredients; one note states that they are down to their last pellet of purifying natron salt. There were also royal edicts, and personal correspondence, one disgruntled priest complaining, 'I supplied the foodstuffs but never got any', and invoking 'Ra, Hathor and all the gods' in his official complaint.

There were also records of health and safety checks carried out on Neferirkara's funerary temple, whose partly completed wall scenes portrayed the late king with his wife Khentkawes II. Named 'beloved of Neferirkara', she was also 'Mother of the King of Upper and Lower Egypt (holding office as) the King of Upper and Lower Egypt', just like the first Khentkawes.

Although archaeologists were initially confused by this second Khentkawes, some now believe that Khentkawes II, mother of two successive kings, Raneferef and Niuserra, may also have ruled as pharaoh in her own right. Certainly the stone pillars of her own Abusir pyramid complex portray her with the uraeus cobra at her brow, when the uraeus in this period 'was reserved solely for rulers and divinities'.

And through the documents found in Khentkawes II's Abusir pyramid complex, the Fifth Dynasty court can be repopulated with the names and roles of some of its original personnel – from the library supervisor Kakaiankh and the royal surgeon Nyshepsesnesut to the 'palace official in charge of oil', Ptahhotep. One document even specifies their daily meat rations, from the foreleg allocated to palace hairdresser Userkafankh to the offal for the canal official Neferhotep.

As for Khentkawes II's two sons, the first to be king was Raneferef (c.2448–2445 BC), whose statuary, featuring the Horus falcon cradling the king's head with his wings, was a clear nod to his predecessor Khafra. And in a nod to the more recent past, Raneferef married a woman whose Abusir tomb, only unearthed in 2015, reveals that she too had been called Khentkawes – designated 'the third' to prevent any further confusion with her illustrious, if equally shadowy predecessors.

Although his death in his early twenties meant Raneferef's pyramid was terminated at the first step, his funerary temple, quickly completed in mud-brick by his brother and successor Niuserra (c.2445–2421 BC), is still in existence, standing to its full height in places.

Maintaining Egypt's presence in Sinai and Byblos and active in the quarries of Nubia, Niuserra made offerings to Satis of Elephantine to sustain the annual flood while the king's statue, set up in a shrine to a local war god Montu at Karnak in Thebes, is the earliest object known from this entire site.

But Abusir was still the main focus of royal attention. Having completed his brother's burial here, together with smaller pyramid complexes for his two sisters, dutiful Niuserra also put the finishing touches to the pyramid complexes of his parents Neferirkara and Khentkawes II.

Then, at long last able to embark on his own funerary arrangements, Niuserra built his own fifty-two-metre-high pyramid beside that of his father. His funerary temple, shared with his wife, Repytnub, housed their statues so that their souls would receive offerings of bread, beer, beef and even sweets, provided by Shedu as the temple's 'Chief Confectioner'.

Their temple was thoughtfully built in an L-shape to avoid disturbing existing *mastaba* tombs, which were themselves extended, with a new tomb for Niuserra's prime minister and son-in-law, Ptahshepses. His meteoric rise to power has been described as 'the dazzling career of the royal hairdresser', for Ptahshepses had originally worked in the 'Morning House' within which King Niuserra was washed, shaved, dressed and prepared for his daily duties. He obviously appreciated Ptahhotep, giving him his daughter, Princess Khamerernebty, in marriage, presenting the happy couple with a spectacular tomb complete with double burial chamber and matching sarcophagi.

In common with all the Fifth Dynasty sovereigns, Niuserra created a separate sun temple at Abusir, which he called 'Ra's Delight'. It was modelled on the great sun temple of Heliopolis, and the king personally led the foundation rites, 'stretching the cord, preparing the bricks, chopping the earth, putting sand in the foundation, making works in "Ra's Delight".'

From its intentionally part-submerged valley temple, a causeway led up to a great enclosed terrace that supported a truncated pyramid base topped by a thirty-six-metre-high, thick-set obelisk. The whole complex was focused around a giant alabaster altar for offerings; wine and water were poured out into channels cut into the limestone pavement, flowing out into huge alabaster basins to give a most refreshing effect within the dry desert surroundings.

The south side of the temple also featured a thirty-metre-long solar boat of mud-brick 'inlaid with green stone', with '100 oars of conifer wood', revealing that the sun temple was in fact 'a symbolic port to the world of the gods'.

If Niuserra's sun temple was spectacular enough on the outside, its interior scenes were simply magnificent, its 'Chamber of Seasons' showing nature beneath the beneficent rays of the sun god. As the Nile's blue floodwaters covered the land, chicks emerged from eggs in nests, ducks flapped amidst the vegetation and a range of wildlife flourished, from panthers and gazelles to turtles and hedgehogs. There was even one of the very earliest portrayals of apiculture, in which a bee-keeper blew smoke into a hive, maybe even 'imitating the call of a queen as do beekeepers in Egypt today'.

In the neighbouring Jubilee Chapel, the 'king's children' were shown in their carrying chairs, as their father Niuserra performed the ceremonial race, his post-run wind-down involving refreshing water being poured over the royal feet.

Those allowed to touch the king were obviously his closest retainers. They included the palace manicurists, much appreciated by an elite whose clean nails were compared with those of the working man, who, 'having mixed all kinds of dirt, when he eats bread with his fingers he has washed at the same time' claimed a contemporary satire. In the case of royal manicurists Niankhkhnum and Khnumhotep, their joint *mastaba* at Sakkara is decorated with vignettes of their working lives – an overseer having a manicure, a scribe getting a pedicure and others having their heads, chins and groins shaved. The men's colleagues, Redjy the manicurist and Giyu the barber, are also here, captured in their leisure time enjoying a bout of stick-fighting using the same *nabbut* quarterstaff still used today. The exuberance of this violent sport, as depicted in similar scenes, is reflected by shouts of 'How's that? You're falling!', 'Hack his back!' and 'Open his box for him' – in other words 'Smash his head in!' In calmer scenes, two women bake bread while tending their children, although the prize for multitasking mother has to go to the unnamed woman shown in another Sakkara tomb, breastfeeding her baby while steering a cargo ship, telling the lad who brings her lunch 'Don't obstruct my face with it while I am putting to shore!'

But by far the grandest official's tomb at Sakkara was built for Ty 'the Rich' – another of Niuserra's favourite hairdressers who ended up as 'Overseer of the Sun-Temples of Sahura, Neferirkara, Raneferef and Niuserra'. He was buried here with his priestess wife Neferhotpes;

their services were rewarded with a tomb replicating their swanky villa down in Memphis, with its impressive portico, double courtyard and walls adorned with scenes of their lavish lifestyle. As Ty and Neferhotpes sit within a summer house to watch others work, a group of farmhands are having trouble loading a huge sack of grain onto an uncooperative donkey, while a couple of shifty-looking gents steal milk from a tethered cow – 'Milk, quickly, hurry up, before the boss comes back.' Clearly the tomb owners had a sense of humour to sanction such scenes, particularly in the case of two farmers leading cattle across shallow water, the one bringing up the rear aware of lurking crocodiles, shouting to his oblivious colleague, 'Come on you shit! Drive the cattle forward!'

Yet such tombs are only a few of those which crowd the vast Sakkara cemetery, although many have since been destroyed, their stone burned in local lime kilns, recycled in other buildings or even removed altogether. As one antiquities inspector noted in 1908: 'while searching for a mastaba suitable for sale to one of the great American museums, I was directed by one of our old workmen to a tomb which must once, from the delicacy and firmness of its designs and the massive quality of the blocks on which they were displayed, have been one of the finest in the Saqqara cemetery'. But the inspector's search continued until 1913, when a suitable tomb was finally found, and sold by the Egyptian government, contents included. The original owner, Lord Chamberlain Perneb, then moved with his 'house of eternity' from Sakkara's Fifth Dynasty cemetery to New York's Fifth Avenue, to take up residence in the Metropolitan Museum of Art.

Although most of Niuserra's courtiers were buried at Sakkara while Abusir remained the focus of royal afterlife, things had certainly changed by the time of Djedkara (c.2414–2375 BC). For although Djedkara's name means 'the Soul of Ra endures', it no longer endured at Abusir, where no more sun temples would be built. And it may be that the religious – and perhaps political – focus had gradually begun to shift away from Ra and his powerful priests.

For Djedkara planned his burial at South Sakkara, on an isolated spur of high ground. Although only fifty-two metres high, his pyramid was nevertheless perfectly proportioned for a location that was all about perspective – the closer the pyramid was to the Nile Valley the smaller it could be, for when viewed from the fixed point of Heliopolis they all appeared the same height.

Djedkara also shook up the administration. Making Abydos the administrative capital of the south to balance Memphis in the north, the king sent out his officials to administer the various provinces on a permanent basis, rather than have them pay the occasional visit while still residing at Memphis.

So when former military man Inti was appointed governor of Deshesheh, he and his wife Meretmin relocated themselves and built their tomb there. In addition to the usual snapshot scenes of family life were energetic dancing, bull-wrestling and scenes of Inti's former career as a soldier up in Palestine. Here he and his men had beseiged the 'town of the Sati', whose knife-wielding female inhabitants are portrayed 'fighting Egyptian invaders and Bedawi auxiliaries', in some cases bringing their man to the ground having 'lugged him over by the armpits'.

With Djedkara's reforms implemented by his highest official, his prime minister, those holding this key role during the king's long reign included Senedjemib, who doubled as the king's building manager. Having the texts of royal letters inscribed in his tomb at Giza, letters that Senedjemib describes as those 'his majesty himself wrote with his own fingers in order to praise me', his plans for a giant water feature had certainly met with royal approval. For as Djedkara told him, 'My majesty has seen your ground plan which you sent to be considered for the pool area of this broad court of the palace. How well you know how to express what the king likes above all else – know full well that I love you'.

But the best known of Djedkara's prime ministers was Ptahhotep, who is credited with writing the first surviving book in history, entitled *The Sayings of Ptahhotep*. This self-help manual of moral philosophy, dedicated to goddess Maat, gave advice on everything from correct table manners to marital relations, advising its readers 'not to have sex with a lady-boy' and instead to 'love your wife with ardour, clothe her, while perfume soothes her skin, gladden her heart as long as you live'. And while 'good speech is more hidden than gemstones, it may be found among maids at their grindstones'.

Aided by such counsel, Djedkara sent expeditions to Byblos and despatched Captain Nenekh-Khentikhet to Sinai, where he set up inscriptions naming his king 'Smiter of all Countries'. He also portrayed his king bashing a local in time-honoured fashion, despite the fact that a study of Djedkara's remains reveals he had a 'gracile body-build' and 'somewhat underdeveloped' muscles. Another of Nenekh-Khentikhet's inscriptions reveals that an ancient inscription of old King Snefru had led them directly to the right seam of malachite, while Djedkara's mineral-hunters were also busy around the Ain Sukhna harbour on the Suez Gulf. A staging area for expeditions to Sinai, it was also the starting point for expeditions travelling south to the fabled land of Punt, the destination for Djedkara's seal-bearer Werdjeded, who returned with exotic products, as well as 'a dwarf' – presumably a pygmy – for all of which he was richly rewarded by his king.

Reigning for around four decades, Djedkara celebrated at least one jubilee, and when he died around 2375 BC, aged somewhere in his fifties, his body was mummified, most likely in his pyramid complex at South Sakkara. Although today it resembles a giant reclamation yard, its eastern façade once took the form of a pylon-like gateway, framing the sunrise at dawn, where rites to revive the royal soul within Djedkara's mummified body were followed by burial within his pyramid, where his remains were discovered in 1945.

Yet Djedkara was not alone in his burial site, for there was a second pyramid complex at its north-eastern side with 'smaller scale versions of many of the standard elements of a king's pyramid', including the same wall scenes, multiple columns and storerooms for offerings. Not built for Djedkara's main queen Meresankh IV, who had her own tomb at Sakkara, instead it belonged to another royal consort, whose marriage to Djedkara had apparently 'legitimated his ascent to the throne' – some Egyptologists even suggest that this queen had 'an independent reign' following Djedkara's death.

However, this mystery ruler remains anonymous and forgotten, for not only were parts of her complex reused by a successor who was not her son, when her names were erased and her images destroyed, the 1952 excavation of her complex was never published, so her tomb remains 'the Pyramid of the Unknown Queen' – her fate as mysterious as her identity.

10

Clouds Across the Sun:

c.2375–2181 BC

With the accession of Unas, last king of the Fifth Dynasty, the ruler's name no longer featured the sun god Ra. And as a power struggle between king and clergy now emerged, 'the priesthood of Ra declined in status'.

As the new king promoted Ptah, patron deity of the royal capital Memphis, it was quite possibly Unas who commissioned the so-called 'Memphite Theology', in which Ptah, not Ra, was credited with creating the world.

Unas's plans for his own afterlife were equally innovative, if not radical. He placed his forty-three-metre-high pyramid at Sakkara, beside Djoser's Step Pyramid, and while the loss of its original limestone casing has left little more than a mound of rubble, its interior is a very different matter. In sharp contrast to the stark granite sepulchres of his predecessors, Unas was the first king since Djoser to adorn his burial chamber, the bright blue hieroglyphs set into its white alabaster walls creating the world's oldest body of religious writings.

Now known as the 'Pyramid Texts', liturgies set permanently in stone to replace the none-too-reliable ministrations of an increasingly disaffected priesthood, this compilation of over 700 spells, prayers, hymns and readings, in use for centuries, were now drawn together. Their potency was thought to be such that any hieroglyph taking the form of a snake, lion or similar potential danger was carved in two halves to render them harmless should they reanimate in the world beyond, while concepts both stellar and solar feature a whole cast of deities – as if Unas was throwing everything he had at Death.

The texts begin with an address to the sky goddess Nut, whose children Isis and Osiris make their earliest named appearance in Unas's burial chamber, Osiris's water-filled underworld kingdom the place in which Isis would bring about the king's rebirth. Unas's soul is also required to perform various rites, 'striking the ball in the meadow of the sacred Apis bull' in a game of ritual rounders to assist his passing into the afterlife. And while there are still extensive references to the sun god, the king is now described as the god's secretary, as 'Unas opens his boxes, Unas unseals his documents, Unas seals his dispatches', the king now privy to all Ra's secrets and, presumably, to his power.

This power is most graphically indicated by Unas's choice of the already ancient 'Cannibal Hymn', with its memories of old-style retainer sacrifice; for 'Unas eats men and feeds on the gods, cutting their throats, eating their entrails . . . Unas eats their magic and swallows their spirits . . . He has swallowed the knowledge of every god and their power is in him'. And, as 'sky rains, stars darken, vaults quiver and earth trembles, the planets stand still at seeing Unas rise as power – a god who lives on his fathers and feeds on his mothers!', surely a most unsubtle warning to priests who might wrongly assume that the king served their god, rather than the other way round.

When, at death, Unas's soul rose up to merge with the sun, the Pyramid Texts describe his ascent as a team effort – 'O Nut, take his hand! O Shu, lift him up, lift him up!' The desire to propel his soul skyward was also reflected in the two great solar boats buried at the top of his twisting funeral causeway stretching 750 metres down to the Nile, where all that remains of the original valley temple and harbour is a couple of columns by a bend in the modern road.

Like a modern motorway, this ancient causeway was built through or over the top of any structure in its path, and was once meticulously carved and painted throughout its roofed length. Unas's farmers gathered figs and honey, his goldsmiths fashioned their glittering wares and his stonemasons delivered palm-topped stone columns shipped north from Aswan in a scene captioned 'I brought granite pillars from Elephantine for his majesty Unas within seven days – his majesty praised me for this!'

The obligatory scenes of Unas triumphant, hunting lions, giraffes and enemies, from bearded 'Asiatics' of the Near East to the desert-dwelling Bedouin, echoed earlier scenes from Sahura's causeway, in which men, women and children are portrayed with ribs painfully exposed and their bellies distended. Harrowing images graphically capturing the increasing levels of famine around Egypt's borders, they form a stark and intended contrast to his offering-bearers, processing in eternal formation to sustain the royal soul.

As his pyramid took shape, Unas's two consorts, Nebet and Khenut, were provided with *mastabas*, as was the moustachioed Clark Gable lookalike Irukaptah, 'Butcher of the King's Repast', one of five butchers buried in the Unas cemetery at Sakkara, suggesting beef was very much on the royal menu. Unas's chief farmer, Methethy, was likewise honoured with a tomb and a series of wooden statues, kitted out in beaded collars, belts and necklaces over his plain white kilt.

The same attention to detail is also found in the Sakkara tomb of the prime minister Ptahhotep, grandson and namesake of the famous author, whose wall scenes show him being dressed and groomed, his wig brought from its box as he inhales from a vessel inscribed 'finest perfume for festive-times'. There is even a rare glimpse of the artist responsible for these fine scenes, Niankhptah, whose self-portrait shows him watching a boatmen's jousting match while eating figs and having his beer topped up.

King Unas himself died around 2345 BC and his mummification is alluded to in his Pyramid Texts. First eviscerated to prevent putre-faction, when 'my entrails are washed by Anubis', these were then placed under the care of Horus and his children 'Imsety, Hapy, Duamutef and Qebsenuef', each of whom were reponsible for a specific organ – Imsety protected the liver and Hapy the lungs, Duamutef the stomach and Qebsenuef the intestines.

Then Unas's body was wrapped in finest linen, to become divine – 'O king, this body of yours belongs to a god; it will not grow mouldy, it will not be destroyed, it will not putrefy . . . May your flesh be born to life, and may your life be more than the life of the stars when they live'. As if emerging from a celestial changing room in a new outfit, the mummified king was then greeted by the words 'How fine you look, content, renewed, and rejuvenated'; the rites to reanimate his spirit involved painting his eyes in green and black, and anointing him with 'first-class cedar oil' and 'first-class Libyan oil', the food and drink presented amidst the heady smoke of incense all designed to kick-start the royal senses.

Then, to a rousing chorus of 'Ho, Unas! You have not gone away dead: you have gone away alive,' and 'Spirit – to the sky! Corpse, to the earth!', Unas's body was placed in his text-filled pyramid burial chamber within a huge stone sarcophagus, where some of the royal bones were discovered in 1881.

Yet Unas had left no son as his heir, so the throne passed to his daughter, Princess Iput. She married the non-royal Teti in order to validate his claim to the throne, Teti (c.2345-2323 BC) becoming the first king of the Sixth Dynasty, and Iput yet another royal woman through whom the dynasties were physically connected.

Although Teti's name once more failed to mention the sun god, he was nonetheless still a 'Son of Ra', and embellished the god's temple at Heliopolis with a pair of three-metre-high quartzite obelisks, one of which survived the building of Cairo's vast airport across the ancient site. Teti also rebuilt Bastet's temple at Bubastis, while his gifts to the gods of Memphis included an alabaster sistrum rattle inscribed 'Teti, beloved of Hathor', which was once fitted with copper wires on which small metal plates tinkled when it was shaken. Recreating the act of 'shaking the papyrus' to stimulate fertility, the sistrum was a key part of the sacred song-and-dance routine integral to Hathor's cult, in which the kings themselves were top of the bill – 'it is the king who is the shaker, it is the king who is the chant-ress', as 'the king comes to dance, he comes to sing' when summoned by his 'mother' Hathor.

Teti was actually the son of a woman named Seshseshat, best remembered for her recipe to encourage hair growth based on donkey hoof and date kernels, passed down the generations. Some of her female descendants also shared Seshseshat's name, for Teti followed the usual, if confusing, practice of naming his children after their parents or grandparents, giving all six of his daughters their grandmother's name, thankfully with a distinguishing second name.

And Teti's court was thronged with royal women; in addition to his mother and his six daughters there were his two queens, Unas's daughter Iput and his second queen, Kawit. His appearance in their midst reflected the way the sun god's retinue was likewise composed of female relatives, as all royal males were kept largely in the shadows, to allow the king alone to shine.

Teti selected a small corner of North Sakkara for his own pyramid and the tombs of his wives, and four of the princesses Seshseshat were also buried close by. Married off to members of Teti's court, their tombs were arranged in close-knit family groups in the 'Street of Tombs' around the royal burial site, since 'Teti, apparently more than most other kings, felt the need to be particularly close to a relatively small group of his courtiers'.

With his eldest daughter Seshseshat 'Watet-khethor' married to one Mereruka, whose status as royal son-in-law brought him immediate promotion to chief justice and prime minister, the couple were provided with a splendid tomb whose thirty-two-room layout recreated their villa. Inside, Mereruka's life-size statue still steps forward to greet visitors who once brought him offerings, but today bring only their curiosity, since the tomb is still the most visited place at Sakkara after the Step Pyramid.

Its popularity is certainly well-deserved; in lively scenes that seem to generate an energy all of their own, lads leap high in the air to play *khazza lawizza*, 'jumping the goose', while women honour Hathor with their vigorous, can-can-like dancing. Leaning right back and raising one leg, they expose their sexual organs in the same way the goddess lifted her dress to flash back at the sun, stimulating his waning powers and causing him to laugh and 'stand up' in every sense once revitalised. Their performance is accompanied by the more stately 'Mirror Dance', in which the sun's rays are manipulated through highly reflective polished metal mirrors, a technique still used in Egyptian tombs today as a means of illuminating areas of special interest.

There are also glimpses of Mereruka's working life, including the trial of farmers accused of tax evasion, for which the penalty was a 100-blow beating. Then, in more relaxed mood, Mereruka sits before an easel to paint a scene of the seasons, or sits beside wife Seshseshat within their boudoir, where she sings and plays the harp – *benet* – in a euphemistic scene relying on the wordplay of *benben* – meaning 'to beget' – in place of any more disorderly activity.

Yet however idealised their graceful portraits, the couple's remains were those of 'a large woman, middle-aged at the time of her death', whose husband Mereruka was a middle-aged man with 'a short, wide head and jutting jaw', whose eventual demise was mourned with an excess of fainting and hysteria, brilliantly captured on their tomb walls.

And, just as in life, Seshseshat and Mereruka's neighbours are still Kagemni and his own royal wife a second Princess Seshseshat ('Nebtynubkhet' to her friends), whose marriage again elevated her husband to power as another of Teti's son-in-law prime ministers. Among his fifty or so titles, Kagemni was High Priest of Ra, wise old Teti having appointed his son-in-law to this highest ritual office, presumably to keep his eye on events within Heliopolis.

A third of Teti's prime ministers was Ankhmahor, whose tomb is on the same block as those of Mereruka and Kagemni. Once again the energetic can-can dancers perform upon its walls, where staff perform manicures, pedicures, reflexology and massage in scenes entitled 'making it pleasant'. The therapeutic theme continues with a portrait of the palace physician, named Ankh – meaning simply 'Live!' – and, in a rare scene of male circumcision, a patient undergoing surgery to remove an infected foreskin has his hands over his face, the surgeon saying 'Hold him fast, don't let him faint'.

This emphasis on anatomy also extends to the butchering of Ankhmahor's cattle, for the purposes of both consumption and ritual. Exclaiming 'Hold it fast!', 'Rescue me, this ox is powerful!', the butchers sever the foreleg of a living ox as part of the Opening of the Mouth funeral ceremony, during which the still-twitching, bloody limb was held up to the deceased to allow 'the transmission of the energy of the contracting muscle fibers of the animal into the body of the deceased'. Biomedical research has even demonstrated that such movements can be induced in the limb up to two hours after it has been severed, producing a seemingly magical effect used to great impact in such rituals.

And Ankhmahor himself continues to communicate with the living; his image on his tomb façade addresses passers-by – 'May it be well for you, descendant!' Then, having lifted part of the

'Spell for Protecting the Tomb' from his royal master's Pyramid Texts, he follows his greeting with the warning, 'I was an excellent priest who was learned, never was any true magic hidden from me. So as for those who enter my tomb and have not purified themselves for me as they should, then I shall seize their neck like a bird'.

The same curse was also used by Hermeru, 'Overseer of the guards', although his profession was not restricted to men. The guard Raramu passed his title on to his daughter Theset, while Merinebti, an 'Acquaintance' of King Teti, was also named as a 'Guard' in a role that may well have been more than honorific. For the remains of her 5 foot 2 inches (1.5-metre) body revealed a 'bony scar' down the left side of her ribs, caused by 'cutting with a knife', the fact that 'this damage took place many years before Merinebti died' in her late fifties suggesting she had been attacked by a right-handed person earlier in her life, conceivably when undertaking some form of active service.

For all was not well at the court of King Teti. Later records state that Teti was 'murdered by his bodyguard', and although his cause of death cannot be established from the right arm that alone survived the tomb robbers, Teti's fate is likely to have been part of an ongoing power struggle between the crown and Ra's clergy, for the throne then passed briefly to Userkara (c.2323–2321 BC), whose name again incorporates the sun.

But soon Userkara was replaced by Teti's infant son Pepi (c.2321–2287 BC), or at least by his mother Iput, who became regent, having achieved the hat-trick as the daughter, wife and, most importantly, mother of a king. Iput's *mastaba* tomb was now enlarged to become a pyramid, a form of tomb that was by now provided for all queen mothers, and she was portrayed in its temple wall scenes accepting the tall sceptre Hathor offers her. Nor can it be a coincidence that a pair of sceptre-wielding Sekhmet statues with miniature figures of old king Khufu at her feet were now amended, and one tiny figure renamed Pepi.

And Iput's actual powers seem to have been significant. Excavations close to her tomb at Sakkara have revealed that those officials who had participated in her husband's demise and then gone on to serve

Userkara now had their tomb inscriptions and images defaced. Any reference to former king Userkara was also removed.

Once Pepi I himself became king, mindful of his father's fate he surrounded himself with hand-picked officials, including Weni, Overseer of Palace Guards. So when another conspiracy was uncovered and an undisclosed 'secret charge' brought against one of Pepi's wives, it was Weni who dealt with it. As he himself explains, 'when legal procedure was instituted in private in the palace against the queen Weret-Yamtes, his majesty caused me to enter, in order to hear the case alone. No chief judge and prime minister at all, no prince at all was there, but only I alone, because I was excellent, because his majesty loved me. I alone was the one who put it in writing, together with a single judge. Never before had one like me heard the secret of the royal harem. The king caused me to hear it, because I was more excellent to the heart of his majesty than any official of his'.

Pepi I then threw away the royal rulebook, and for the first time, a king married a commoner. Changing her name to Ankhnespepi – 'Pepi lives for her'– she was the daughter of a powerful family from Abydos, and her mother, Nebet, was made prime minister of the south.

As the role of prime minister was the highest administrative office in the land below that of king, Pepi I's choice of his mother-in-law for this key role was presumably inspired by his own mother Iput's skills in government. And as Prime Minister Nebet relocated south to Abydos, from where she ran Upper Egypt, the tomb she and her husband Khui had begun in Sakkara was abandoned in favour of a new burial place closer to Abydos.

The extraordinary Nebet was also mother of eight children, two of her six sons, Djau and Idi, inheriting her premiership, while her second daughter also married the king, and again adopted the name Ankhnespepi II (the II being a convenient modern distinction). Fortunately, their complex family tree is clarified on the so-called 'Stela of the Two Queens', which Djau set up at Abydos 'in love for the place in which I was born by the favorite of the king, Nebet, to my father, honored by the great god, Khui'.

Meanwhile Pepi I's own pyramid complex was taking shape on

the high desert of Sakkara. Now just a twelve-metre mound of 'unprepossessing ruins', Pepi I's pyramid once rose to a stately fifty-two metres. It was named Men-nefer Pepi – 'Pepi's Beautiful Foundation' – the name, initially covering the surrounding homes of the pyramid's priests eventually applied to the whole of Sakkara and its adjoining city, which is now known by its Greek form 'Memphis'.

After thirty years' reign Pepi I celebrated his first jubilee, and the wish 'may he celebrate very many' was inscribed on gifts given out to courtiers. Perfume pots inscribed with his name have also been found as far north as Ebla in Syria and as far south as Elephantine, where Pepi I is likely to have travelled to placate the gods controlling the Nile. For by around 2300 BC the annual flood levels had become alarmingly low, the failure of the wells serving the diorite quarries of Nubia possibly explaining why the Sixth Dynasty kings switched to more locally sourced alabaster for their sculpture.

Since the jubilee was meant to reinvigorate the king's ability to bring fertility to the land, the festival was now celebrated beyond the capital Memphis, with Pepi visiting sites in the Delta, then going on to Heliopolis where the sun god was honoured, 'even if he was a little out of fashion'. The royal visit continued on south to Abydos, Dendera, and to Koptos, where the royal visit to Min's temple resulted in tax exemptions for its clergy, as Pepi I, 'beloved of the lord of Koptos', celebrated his jubilee before Min's priapic statue.

Further south at Hierakonpolis, Horus was honoured with a superb falcon figure whose gold head was set with piercing eyes of black obsidian. Placing it inside the ancient Horus temple, Pepi I also installed a life-size copper statue of himself, the earliest human figure in metal yet found, and one which held a secret. For inside it, like a Russian doll, was a smaller copper statue of his son and successor, Merenra.

Since Hierakonpolis, the 'City of Horus', was the very home of ancient kingship, this was surely a deliberate act by Pepi I and Ankhnespepi I, determined that their son Merenra would be the next king.

And when Pepi I became 'an Osiris', laid to rest within his pyramid tomb where only a single hand and his well-packaged entrails remained, Merenra (c.2287–2278 BC) did inherit his father's throne, together with his father's second wife Ankhnespepi II – his own aunt – and his administration, including the trustworthy Weni.

Now appointed 'Overseer of the South' and relocated to Abydos, the recent rediscovery of Weni's tomb has identified the costly fittings he claimed as royal gifts in his autobiographical inscription. Weni was also responsible for sourcing the various kinds of stone required for the royal burial plans, from the sarcophagus and false door of the new king to 'the costly, splendid pyramidion for the pyramid of the queen'. All were transported north to Sakkara on a flotilla of ships, a task made easier after his commission to cut a series of channels through the rocky granite cataracts of Aswan to make river communication more efficient. Weni's posting south also allowed him to better monitor the border with Nubia, and it was presumably on Weni's advice that Merenra made a state visit to Aswan, in order to hold a summit meeting with the leaders of Wawat (Lower Nubia), Yam (Sudan) and the Medjai (near Nubia's Red Sea coast).

Following up this meeting, Merenra sent his military commander Harkhuf far to the south into Yam, on three separate occasions, returning with exotic tribute but also with increasingly alarming reports of local unrest, as the various Nubian leaders fought among themselves and then formed a coalition to throw off Egyptian control.

At this crucial time, when strong leadership was required, Merenra died, and was buried in his pyramid deep in the desert at South Sakkara.

With little of his funerary complex completed other than the granite fittings sourced by Weni, the pyramid's internal walls carried sections of Pyramid Text, in which Merenra has become both an Osiris and a Hathor 'with her two faces'. He is described embarking on the sun god's ship, and rising as a star, protected by Isis and Nephthys, who exclaim 'How beautiful to look, how satisfying to gaze at Merenra as he goes forth to the sky among the stars, among the Imperishable Stars, his magic at his feet. He shall go thereby to his mother Nut'.

Aided by the 'spells for entering the womb of Nut' inscribed on his sarcophagus, the goddess did her job supremely well, for Merenra's superbly mummified body was discovered, still inside and largely intact, in 1881.

The throne passed to Pepi II, once thought to be Merenra's half-brother but now believed to be his son. Records also claim that Pepi II 'began his reign at the age of six and continued until his hundredth year', this ninety-four-year reign (c.2278–2184 BC) making him the longest-reigning monarch in history so far.

But as he was only six years old at his accession, the country was actually ruled by his mother, Ankhnespepi II, queen to the last two rulers and now regent 'who all the gods love'. She is shown enthroned in an alabaster figure, wearing the uraeus cobra exclusive to the monarch, her small son Pepi II sitting on her lap, also wearing a uraeus. But since her back was carved flat to be set against a temple wall, young Pepi appeared in profile and so it is she, not he, who faced the viewer as primary subject.

Temples were also embellished with far larger monuments. Aswan governor Sebni was commissioned to produce two great obelisks, cut from the local granite quarries, which he floated downriver to erect at Heliopolis in honour of the sun god, a brilliantly executed exercise achieved 'without the loss of a single sandal', boasts proud Sebni.

Expeditions were also sent to the turquoise mines of Sinai, where the names of mother and son were added to the roll-call of previous rulers at Wadi Maghara, accompanied by her queenly image. There were frequent trade missions up to Byblos and down to Punt, and at one point the long-serving, long-suffering Harkhuf was despatched on his fourth and final mission into Yam in Sudan. Sending reports back to the palace at Memphis describing all the exotic goods he'd obtained, he listed with them a 'dancing dwarf', presumably an African pygmy. This delighted the now-eight-year-old king, who immediately responded with an official thank-you letter, couched in tones of great excitement:

'You have said in your letter that you have brought a dwarf of the god's dances from the land of the horizon dwellers. So come northward to the court at once! Bring this dwarf with you, in order to amuse and gladden the heart of the king of Upper and Lower Egypt, Pepi, who lives forever. But when he goes with you onto the ship, appoint able people to be beside him on each side of the ship so he does not fall into the water. When he sleeps at night appoint able people to sleep beside him in his tent – inspect him ten times a night. For my majesty wants to see this dwarf more than any other gift from Sinai and Punt. Sealed by the king personally'.

With this royal missive carved across the front of Harkhuf's rock-cut tomb in his hometown Aswan, he was a fortunate man. Although advice for foreign travellers was to 'be brave and control your heart, you shall embrace your children and kiss your wife and see your home again', not all were so lucky. A subsequent expedition into Nubia, led by the Aswan governor Mehu, ended in disaster when he was killed by local tribesmen, his body only retrieved after a rescue mission by his son. An earlier team building a ship to sail south to Punt had also been killed by nomads, their bodies recovered by Pepinakht, whose imposing tomb at Aswan became a place of pilgrimage for future expeditions into Nubia and Pepinakht eventually deified, another example of the ultimate in social mobility.

When the regent Ankhnespepi II died and was buried in her pyramid at Sakkara, only discovered in 1998, and the earliest queen's pyramid to feature Pyramid Texts, Pepi II now embarked on his long, long reign as king in his own right.

He was a somewhat colourful character 'with a love of the theatrical'; one story deals with the clandestine affair he had with his general, Sasanet, about whom it was said that 'there was no wife'. The king, 'going out at night all alone, with nobody with him', would throw a brick up at the general's house so a ladder could be let down for him, staying for four hours, and only 'after his Person had done what he desired with him he returned to his palace'.

During the course of his extraordinarily long life, Pepi II also had three principal wives who were also his sisters: Neith, Iput II and Wedjebten, each provided with Pyramid Texts in their 'lavish burial places'. For Pepi II outlived them, and many more minor wives and children, the vast majority of whom predeceased their seemingly immortal father to create a crisis of succession as each heir passed away.

There was certainly a high turnover of officials. With growing numbers of them relocating both their households and their tombs as far south as el-Kab and Aswan, they acquired ever-grander titles, former servants of the crown with ever-decreasing amounts of royal blood in their veins now styling themselves princes and overlords, to whom the king was forced to make ever-increasing concessions in order to keep overall control of his kingdom.

This was also true of the temple hierarchy. Pepi II exempted from taxes those in charge of the cult of Menkaura, now focused on his Giza Valley Temple, into which its priests had moved with their families, building mud-brick walls and granaries close to the innermost shrine to reduce their daily commute to work to the bare minimum. And this same 'villagization of a monument' had also happened in the Valley Temple of Snefru at Dahshur, where fifteen of its functionaries had moved in with their households.

At Min's main cult centre Koptos, Pepi II sent his official Idy to uphold the temple's tax exemptions, a list of which was set up on the temple gateway by royal command, to remind any overly officious tax collector.

Yet some parts of the administration were rather less efficient, as revealed by state papers found within Sakkara's administrative offices, now relocated into the stone chambers of Djoser's pyramid complex. A letter of complaint was written by a 'commander of work troops', who says

'I was brought a letter from the prime minister about bringing the detachment of skilled workers from Tura quarries to get them kitted out in his presence at the Pyramid Enclosure. Now I want to complain about having to come to this out-of-the-way location when you are coming to Tura with the barge anyway. Yours truly has already spent 6 days here in Memphis together with this detachment without getting the clothing. That is what is stopping the work which is the charge of yours truly, since only one day was allowed for this detachment to be clothed. I am telling you this so you are informed'.

The anonymous official was clearly concerned about his overtime, not to mention having his men properly kitted out as part of their wages from the state.

Such dwindling efficiency and declining morale was certainly not helped by the fact that the monarch was becoming increasingly less active. Less able to perform the necessary rites required at his by-now-regular jubilees, which still included the ceremonial race, this was hopefully taken at a more gentle pace as Pepi II grew older, not to mention the accompanying hippo hunting.

For the ageing monarch was clearly not god incarnate. Seriously undermining the last one thousand years of rulers claiming other-wise, Pepi II's role as the bringer of fertility to his land seemed equally risible, as the annual Nile floods continued to fall short, causing widespread drought. With less land under cultivation, crop yields fell, so not only did famine increase but revenues payable to the crown decreased dramatically, and the economy went into meltdown.

Since the king was unable to distribute much to his courtiers beyond his good wishes and the perfume pots given out at his regular jubilees, those who had once craved burial around the bases of royal pyramids were not only dropping titles associating themselves with the king, but also moving away from the increasingly lacklustre and impoverished court. For as everyone knew, even if the Nile level was low for only a single year, 'a year's food supply is lost, the rich man looks concerned, everyone is seen with weapons, friend does not attend friend and want is followed by deceit'.

A spirit of uncertainty certainly pervaded the land when the centenarian monarch finally passed away around 2148 BC. Although his ninety-four-year reign should have given him ample time to build the largest-ever pyramid, his Sakkara tomb rose to a height of only fifty-two metres, presumably due to diminishing royal finances. His mummified body was buried within his sarcophagus, and when the pyramid interior was first cleared in 1881 during excavations funded by the pioneering travel agents Thomas Cook & Son, the surrounding walls of Pyramid Texts were seen to announce that Pepi II had finally boarded the sun god's boat to 'take the hand of the Imperishable Stars' as he rose up to heaven.

Yet those remaining on earth had never known any other king, so the change must have been truly dramatic.

The next monarch, Nemtyemsaf (c.2184 BC), was one of the few surviving sons of Pepi II, born to his sister-wife Neith. An ageing figure himself, able to do little to reignite confidence in the crown, he passed away after only a year in office, to be succeeded by a monarch who ruled for four years (c.2184–2181 BC), but whose chief claim to fame is to have been considered female for the last two and a half thousand years.

This was Neitikrety, better known by the Greek form of the name, Nitocris. As early as the fifth century BC the priests of Thebes were already claiming Nitocris had been their only female ruler, and two centuries later, Egypt's leading historian had stated that Nitocris had been 'the noblest and loveliest of the women of her time, of fair complexion, the builder of the third pyramid'. As her romantic story was embellished ever further, the legendary Nitocris became 'braver than all the men of her time, the most beautiful of all the women, fair-skinned with red cheeks'.

Clearly her legend had been conflated with equally confused references to Khentkawes I, who does indeed seem to have ruled as a king during the Pyramid Age. So it does seem supremely ironic that the same scholar who argued Khentkawes I had not been a king claimed of the mythical Nitocris that 'her historical existence can therefore not be doubted'. He based his reasoning on his painstaking translation of Egypt's main king list, which survives as jigsaw-like fragments of ancient papyrus; but recent microscopic analysis of the relevant fragment naming Neitikrety has revealed that it belongs in a different place. Its repositioning not only brings the number of Sixth Dynasty rulers exactly into line with the other existing king list, but also allows the last piece of the papyrus jigsaw to be fitted into place – a piece that bears the name 'sa Ptah' ('son of Ptah') and which finally demonstrates that the famous female pharaoh Neitikrety was actually a little-known male king, Neitikrety Sa-Ptah, known from other lists to be Nemtyemsaf's successor.

Completely undermining previous claims that the Sixth Dynasty, and indeed the entire Old Kingdom, had collapsed because its last king had been a woman, the end had in fact been a gradual decline, made worse by increasing climate change and an increasingly ageing and ineffectual monarch failing to sufficiently reward those who ran the country on his behalf.

With little need of a king as a figurehead, especially a king who was clearly as human as they were, royal officials had relocated to their hometowns, and as Egypt began to fragment, it was as if the previous millennium of monarchy had never been.

II

Anarchy in the Two Lands:
c.2181-1985 BC

By 2181 BC, Memphis had become so powerless that later records allocated just seventy days for the seventy kings of the Seventh Dynasty.

An effective way of suggesting that there seemed to be a new king every day, it was a hopeless situation for a culture that dated its history by the regnal year of each monarch, making any record-keeping or calendar quite unworkable.

Nor was the Eighth Dynasty much better, when at least seventeen kings ruled from Memphis; the combined Seventh and Eighth Dynasties were allocated the brief timeframe between around 2181–2125 BC, marking the beginning of a so-called Intermediate Period.

From the little known about the Eighth Dynasty rulers, one shadowy king, Neferkauhor, tried to keep hold of the south through his daughter, Princess Nebet, married to the southern prime minister Shemai of Koptos, and the king repeatedly writing to the couple with his many concerns.

With only one Eighth Dynasty ruler, King Ibi, known to have erected a pyramid, it was also the last to feature Pyramid Texts. And as traditional funerary practices came to an end, along with trade with Byblos, the question asked was 'What shall we do for pine trees for our mummies?' as supplies of preservative conifer resins began to run dry.

So too the sixty-five-metre-deep Nile-fed Lake Qarun in the Fayum. And as repeated low Nile flood levels continued to cause famine, the situation was made even worse when a pronounced shift in atmospheric circulation around 2150 BC created 'an abrupt, short-lived cold climate', which led to even less rain in the Ethiopian highlands, the source of the Blue Nile. This in turn saw 'a reduction of water which had catastrophic effects', and no more so than in Egypt.

It must have seemed as if the gods themselves had gone, and with offerings no longer provided, rites were discontinued and buildings left empty. At Edfu, 'the House of Horus was abandoned by him who belonged there', while the hallowed sanctuary of Snefru's pyramid temple at Meidum became a home for herdsmen, their livestock, and certainly their rubbish.

And as the climate continued to deteriorate, even the capital Memphis was gradually engulfed in sand, the people of the Black Land only able to watch as the Red Land, representing all the forces of chaos, literally invaded and overwhelmed them.

This visible breakdown in the rules set down by goddess Maat was perfectly captured in so-called 'Pessimistic Literature', best expressed by a series of verses known as *The Admonitions of Ipuwer*. While perhaps simply the 'distorted vision of a die-hard aristocrat', which claimed that 'necklaces of precious stones are worn by women servants whilst starving noblewomen roam the land dressed in rags', it is indeed hard to feel much sympathy when 'no longer does she know the carrying chair and the butler is lacking . . . for the ladies who suffer like maidservants'.

Yet this revolution in the making genuinely terrified the hierarchically minded Egyptians. And as anarchy really did replace order, Raneferef's Abusir temple was just one of those ransacked as the royal dead themselves were targeted. As Ipuwer claims, 'those buried in tombs are thrown onto high ground, the secrets of the embalmers cast away. Gone is what was here yesterday . . . the king has been robbed by the poor . . . what the pyramid hid is now empty'. This was also the case for many of the smaller, less well constructed and therefore more easily accessible pyramids of the Fifth and Sixth Dynasties.

The royal cemeteries of Sakkara and Abusir certainly provided rich pickings, as did the palaces and state buildings of Memphis. For as Ipuwer continues, 'the children of princes are cast out on the street . . . what belongs to the palace has been stripped . . . the books of the land registry are destroyed, the laws of the chamber thrown out and men walk upon them in the street and beggars tear them up in alleys . . . the secrets of Egypt's kings are laid bare'.

Such destruction of state records certainly explains why this 'is one of the most imperfectly understood eras in ancient Egyptian history'. With Memphis no longer the heart of centralised government and unable to impose state control, the officials who had relocated to their own hometowns now found themselves the rulers of independent petty kingdoms, as had existed before unification a thousand years before. And with no central authority either funding or regulating artistic production, the statues, stelae and tomb scenes produced for these regional leaders, like them, followed no set rules.

Art of the period can therefore appear rather 'idiosyncratic' or indeed rustic; scenes from the Dendera tomb of Sennedjsui, 'brother of the common people', are certainly rustic yet were still expensive, and paid for in kind with 'bread, beer, grain, copper, clothing, oil and honey'.

So most individuals commissioned less costly, small stelae; the Abydos 'Count', Indi, and his priestess wife Mutmuti, are portrayed on their stela in an angular if vigorous fashion. No king is named in the accompanying text, which instead focuses on Indi, described as 'a citizen excellent in combat'.

Reflecting the volatile times, such people required private armies, not only to maintain their borders with their neighbours but also to defend themselves from outside forces against which the government could no longer protect them.

For as Ipuwer claimed, 'foreign peoples are conversant with the livelihood of the Delta', and 'Asiatic' Aamu settlers from Palestine had infiltrated Egypt's north-east border. Libyans and Bedouin posed a threat to the west, Nubia was shaking off Egyptian control in the south, and in Egypt itself 'all is ruin, blood is everywhere, no shortage of dead . . . the lawless despoil the land of the kingship, the tribes of the desert have become Egyptian . . . great and small say "I wish I were dead", little children say "I should not have been born".'

Inscriptions in a tomb at Moalla even state that 'all of Upper Egypt was dying of hunger, everyone eating their children', an extreme claim nonetheless repeated in AD 1200 when eyewitness accounts of serious famine in medieval Cairo similarly stated that 'everyone has come to eating his children'.

But by 2160 BC, the Nile had gradually begun to return to full flow, and a new seat of power emerged close to the Fayum at Henen-nesut. Better known by its Greek title Herakleopolis, 'city of Herakles' – most appropriate for its warlike population – its new rulers were later designated the Ninth and Tenth Dynasties (c.2160–2025 BC), thereby overlapping with the end of the Eighth Dynasty, hanging on to what remained of Memphis.

Later historians claimed that the first Herakleopolitan king, Khety, 'behaving more cruelly than his predecessors, wrought woes for the people of all Egypt'. It is certainly telling that those who served his 'House of Khety' hardly ever mention their monarchs by name, using only their own names and titles in inscriptions and even usurping royal privilege by using the Pyramid Texts. Once the preserve of royalty but now inscribed on officials' coffins, these are now known as the 'Coffin Texts', in what has been described as both 'the democratisation of the afterlife' and 'delusions of grandeur'.

Yet despite his harsh reputation, King Khety did nurture talent. Having any promising children of his officials taught in the palace; one future governor of Asyut recalled that the king 'had me instructed in swimming along with the royal children'. There was also a renewed emphasis on learning, and the next ruler, Khety II, is credited with composing an instruction book for his son and heir Merikara, in which he tells him to 'copy your ancestors, their words endure in books. Open them! Read them! Copy their knowledge. He who is taught will become skilled'. Explaining that 'a tongue is a king's sword and speaking stronger than all fighting', he stressed a king's social obligations and gave moral advice, telling him 'don't be evil, for kindness is good, so make your memorial last through love of you. Life on earth isn't long, and happy is he who is remembered'.

As the new northern kings began to restore Egypt's fortunes, consolidating their borders against further infiltration from Palestine while restarting trade with the Near East, they also resumed large-scale construction projects. Merikara planned a new pyramid complex at Sakkara, and created an eighty-eight-kilometre-long canal linking Herakleopolis with the old capital Memphis, whose former craftsmen were once more employed at a uniform standard.

These new kings were certainly politically astute, making alliances with the regional governors of el-Bersheh, Beni Hasan, Moalla, Akhmim and Asyut, whose leadership congratulated themselves on returning their regions to prosperous times: 'I built a canal for this city . . . I made the Nile flood the barren lands. The goddess was favourable to me . . . I was good with the bow and arrow, I had powerful arms and was much feared by those close to me'. So claimed Asyuti governor Khety, who had inherited his title from his mother Sitra, 'who ruled in Asyut' as 'the worthy stock of her father. The city was satisfied with that which she said. She acted as lord, until her son became strong-armed'. As women could also own property, the soldier Kedes of Gebelein states 'I made a boat of 30 cubits and a small boat that ferried the boatless . . . it was my mother Ibeb who acquired them for me', adding that he was 'the foremost of the whole troop', at a time when such mobile, military men were in great demand throughout the Nile Valley.

Asyut was certainly one of the best-defended regions, its military capability reinforced by the troops of subsequent governor Meseheti. Represented by eighty wooden figurines found in Meseheti's tomb in 1894 – his permanent guards even in death – half were Nubian auxiliaries employed as 'the chief shock troops, bowmen and slingers of the Egyptian armies', while their Egyptian comrades were spear men, whose large black-and-white cowhide shields provided excellent protection against the weapons then available.

Nor was Asyut's increasing wealth only enjoyed by its governors. One woman, buried in a shaft tomb at Matmar, had owned necklaces of gold amulets and a gold seal, and 218 of the 229 seals found at Qau and Badari were recovered from female burials. Lady Khety, 'Countess of the South', based at Beni Hasan, employed her own female seal-bearer, named Tjat.

Seals were used to mark both personal possessions and the letters through which it is possible to tap into conversations of the time – albeit a little one-sidedly, since these are 'letters to the dead', which the bereaved wrote to their late relatives. So a certain Merirtifi asks his late wife Nebitef 'How are you? Is the West taking care of you properly? Please become a spirit before my eyes so I may see you in a dream, and I will then bring offerings for you as soon as the sun has risen'. Other letters were inscribed on bowls for the deceased to read while consuming the offerings within: Shepsi of Qau el-Kebir wrote to his dead mother Iy on such a bowl, reminding her that he had brought the seven quails she had apparently requested; and Merti used the same medium to tell her deceased son Merer that she was sending him bread and beer to enjoy in the company of Hathor.

Similar practices were also found to the south in Waset, a 'one donkey town', better known by its Greek name Thebes (modern Luxor. Like so many others, it was cut in two by the Nile, the river marking the boundary between life and death.

Its West Bank, where the dead were buried, was sacred to Hathor, 'Lady of the Western Mountains', and was dominated by a natural pyramid-shaped peak some 460 metres high. On the opposite East Bank lay the town of Thebes, cult centre of a local war god, Montu, and a Min-like creator deity known as Amen – 'the Hidden One'. Yet the real power lay with the local ruler Montuhotep, his wife Nefru and their son Intef. As a family with their own armed forces – for 'nearly every Theban' owned at least one bow – they were allied with Dendera to the north, although both regions paid lip service to Herakleopolis.

But a shock was in store. Any sense of unity was completely blown apart when Intef (c.2125–2112 BC) declared himself 'Great Overlord of Upper Egypt' and the head of an independent Thebes, his breakaway monarchy, later numbered the Eleventh Dynasty, existing alongside the northern Tenth Dynasty to control a divided Egypt between around 2125 and 2025 BC.

Hoping to split the Thebes–Dendera alliance, the northern kings installed their own men as governors of Koptos, located between the two allies. To keep control of the all-important routes through the Eastern and Western Deserts, the northern kings even built a desert road across the Qena Bend to outflank the Thebans. But Intef gained control of this overland route, constructing his rock-cut tomb where the route began at Dra'Abu el-Naga, on Thebes's West Bank – a prominent site overlooking the Nile, sacred to both Hathor and his father Montuhotep, 'the Ancestor'.

On his death, Intef was succeeded by his son, Intef II (c.2112–2063 BC), who continued the campaign to push north to the border region of Abydos. The Thebans even managed to take the sacred city, but when the northern forces retaliated with a counter-attack, something unthinkable happened – the royal tombs of the First Dynasty kings, including that of Narmer himself, were looted and set on fire, their charred contents obvious when first excavated in modern times.

The destruction of Egypt's earliest royal mummies, believed to house the accumulated royal souls, was a catastrophe of epic proportions. It must have seemed as if the heavens had fallen in, when 'the stars fall upside down on their faces and are unable to raise themselves'. Northern king Khety II would forever regret the desecration, confessing to his son that 'Egypt fought in the graveyard, destroying tombs in vengeful destruction. As I did, so it happened, as is done to one who strays from god's path'.

Intef II wrote to accuse his opponent of failing to protect this most sacred site, while demonstrating his own piety by building a sandstone shrine at Karnak in his hometown Thebes, dedicated to Ra and the local deity Amen.

Then across the river he created a rock-cut tomb at the family burial site Dra Abu el-Naga in the home of Hathor. Its wall inscriptions claimed that 'all rejoice at Hathor's coming and love to see her beauty rise! I let her know, I say at her side that I rejoice in seeing her. My hands do "come to me, come to me", my body says, my lips repeat: holy music for Hathor a million times, because you love music, a million times music!' As lyrics to be sung to summon up Hathor, by one of Intef II's daughters, Ioh, a priestess of the goddess, these were later copied down by subsequent generations who referred to the 'Song in the tomb of King Intef which is in front of the singer with the harp' in order to help visitors locate it. The words inspired a whole genre of funerary songs with the uplifting theme 'O tomb! You were built for festivity! You were founded for happiness!'

When Intef II died after a highly successful, fifty-year reign, during which he had somewhat ambitiously claimed to be 'King of Upper and Lower Egypt', it was announced that the 'Son of Ra, Intef, born of Nefru, who lives like Ra forever, went in peace to his horizon. And his son has taken his place'.

This son, a third Intef (c.2063–2055 BC), expanded even further north to crush the northern kings' allies in Asyut, and he and his sister-wife, Ioh, produced a son they named Montuhotep, appropriately meaning 'the war god Montu is content'. And when young Montuhotep (c.2055–2004 BC) succeeded his father to become the next king of the south, he maintained dynastic tradition by marrying his sister, Nefru.

He also continued the war with the north, finally taking Herakleopolis to defeat the House of Khety around 2025 BC with the help of some sixty battle-scarred veterans, whose remains were discovered in 1923 in a state of 'unpleasant freshness' in their mass war grave at Thebes.

Described by the lead archaeologist as the 'slain soldiers of Montuhotep', most were aged between thirty and forty. One still wore his leather archer's bracer round his wrist, while another had hair extensions at a time when a soldier's hair was the only protection before helmets were introduced. An ebony-tipped arrow was still caught up in the 'bushy' hair of one of the men, the ten killed by such arrows including one arrowhead still *in situ* in the orbit of its victim's eye. Another fourteen men had head injuries probably caused by slingshots or heavy rocks; some of them seemed to have then been 'finished off' by 'storms of furious blows' inflicted by right-handed individuals to the left sides of their heads. Their bodies were then left on the battlefield to be picked at by vultures, before later being gathered together, wrapped in royal linen and brought south to Thebes.

But they had not died in vain. With this final victory making Montuhotep II 'Uniter of the Two lands', Egypt was once more a single political unit, under the sole control of a sole monarch, eulogised by subsequent generations as the one who restored order. And since only political equilibrium enabled full mediation with the gods, Montuhotep II was frequently shown in their company, restoring the perception of a divinely inspired monarchy as both a 'son of Ra' and 'son of Hathor'.

With the defeated rounded up, the king is shown executing northern Egyptians, an accompanying inscription stating that he had 'established Lower Egypt, the Two Banks and the Nine Bows' – the nine traditional enemies of Egypt, which included Nubians, Libyans and Asiatics. Repelled from Egypt's borders by the vigorous campaigning of the 'living god' Montuhotep II, he is shown 'clubbing the Eastern Lands, striking down the Hill Countries, trampling the deserts, enslaving the Nubians, the Libyans, the Asiatics'.

He then consolidated his victories by constructing a series of forts stretching from Hierakonpolis south to Elephantine, invading Lower Nubia (Wawat) and defeating its ruler, who had dared take Egyptian-style royal titles for himself. Thus securing Egypt's access to Nubia's gold, Montuhotep II sent his steward Henenu, 'Overseer of that which is and that which is not', to Aswan for granite and to Syria for timber. There were also royal visits to the quarries of Hatnub and Wadi Hammamat, while the king's son, Crown Prince Intef, made a tour of the south, his father setting out to meet him on his return down the Shatt el-Rigal desert route to the Red Sea, where a fascinating record of the royal progress is preserved on the rock face. It shows the king, the queen mother Ioh, and most of the court, each portrayed by the sculptors who accompanied the royal party in the manner of modern-day official photographers.

With resources now increased, the king could re-employ the craftsmen trained in old-school Memphis traditions; these included Inheretnakht, who had also worked for the northern court at Herakleopolis and was taken on in Thebes as Montuhotep's 'overseer of sculptors, craftsmen and casters of metal'. Among his numerous colleagues was the rather conceited Iritisen, who boasted 'I am indeed an artist wise in his art', and 'I know the making of amulets, there is no man excels by it but I alone and my eldest son – god has decreed him to be excellent in it', a virtual advertisement for 'Iritisen & Son, by royal appointment'.

As building projects resumed, Montuhotep began to repair the ravages inflicted on Abydos during the recent civil war, building throughout the south, although the finest structures were created for Hathor at Gebelein, at Dendera and at Thebes.

The greatest was Montuhotep's own funerary complex, built on Thebes's West Bank at Deir el-Bahari, 'the valley of Montuhotep' and the very home of Hathor. As a natural amphitheatre where the cliffs meet the desert, it was the place where the king's soul would be received by Hathor, who was regarded as his mother, wife and daughter in a cyclic pattern of regeneration. There could be no better place for his soul to dwell than in a tomb that 'was also a womb, set within the mother of mothers, Hathor of the West'.

And Montuhotep was taking no chances. To ensure the permanent protection of the goddess, he married no fewer than five of her priestesses: Henhenet, Kemsit, Kawit, Sadeh and Ashayet, all of whom would eventually be buried close beside him.

Their family burial ground was first explored in 1859 by an aristocrat whose family seat in Ireland still displays chunks of the temple 'embedded in the plaster of the walls of the entrance hall'. Excavations since then have revealed that Montuhotep's unique monument combined aspects of the Theban rock-cut tombs and northern pyramid complexes with some innovative flourishes.

It began with a forty-six-metre-wide causeway, opening out into a forecourt of flower beds and groves of the tamarisk and sycamore trees sacred to Hathor. Their cultivation here, in one of the driest places on earth where temperatures can reach 48°C, demonstrated the king's genuine desire to create a welcome, shady haven for 'Hathor who is under the trees, I tread the stars and climb the sun beams in the retinue of Hathor'.

To enable him to do so, a central ramp rose up from her groves to a great stepped terrace, whose pillars were adorned with huge sandstone figures of Montuhotep. The eighty-pillared hypostyle hall beyond was decorated with scenes of the king hunting hippos, and the enemies he trampled as a sphinx. He also steered the barque of the local god Amen from his home in the temple of Karnak on the East Bank over to the West Bank, to celebrate the newly created 'Festival of the Valley', which would now become an annual event. Then as Montuhotep is embraced by the gods, Hathor tells him 'I have united for you the Two Lands according to the command of the ancient spirits', the souls of all previous kings.

At the back, within the innermost part of the temple, a line of ritual defence was created by the shrine-topped shaft tombs of the bejewelled royal consorts Henhenet, Kemsit, Kawit, Sadeh and Ashayet. With each one 'the king appears as a husband' and 'not even the most prominent figure', as he embraces them and they embrace him, to ensure his soul would be revived, protected and sustained by those best able to care for him.

Two of these tombs were even found intact. Within one, the mummified body of the 'Great Royal Wife', Ashayet, reveals she was a young woman of slight build, her neatly plaited hair set with blobs of resinous fixative, and her henna-coloured fingernails only marred by her habit of biting her thumbnail. Found within her great limestone sarcophagus, she had been buried on her left side to allow her soul to see out through the eyes painted on her wooden coffin, whose lid featured both astronomical calculations and extracts from the Coffin Texts invoking the cooling breeze – 'a living wind is the north wind, through her I am made to live' – and a wise choice, given the stifling heat of her tomb's location. Next to Ashayet's burial was that of the king's six-year-old daughter Mayet, 'Kitten', whose well-wrapped, mummified little body was still adorned with her gold and silver jewelled necklaces within her two wooden coffins and stone sarcophagus.

Beyond the six female burials, an underground passage stretched 150 metres down through the limestone rock, at the end of which the king's vaulted, granite-lined burial chamber held his massive alabaster sarcophagus. It contained only skull fragments and a tibia, but he had nonetheless been eviscerated during his mummification, since there were parts of the so-called Canopic jars that held his entrails, these viscera described as 'the necklace of Hathor' in the Coffin Texts and his remaining linen mummy wrappings, 'the dress' of Hathor.

Maintaining the tradition of dualities, in which the king was ruler of both south and north, his tomb was duplicated beneath the temple forecourt with the Bab el-Hosan – 'Gate of the Horse', named after its discovery by an archaeologist's horse, which literally stumbled into it in 1900. Here another 150-metre-long tunnel led to a chamber directly beneath the temple that contained a statue of the king with the black flesh of Osiris, god of resurrection, whose skin colour of either black or green symbolised the Nile's rich mud and the crops it sustained. The statue was wrapped in linen, presumably as a duplicate for the king's mummy, within this second 'dummy' tomb which acted as a cenotaph.

The temple precincts also contained the tomb of the priestess Amenet, whose mummified body featured the dotted tattoos exclusive to women as permanent talismans against dangers in childbirth. Two further women buried close by were similarly marked, although in their case the absence of any written titles meant that the archaeologists assumed their tattoos must indicate lowly status, dismissing the women as 'dancing girls', even if the location of their burials suggests they were important members of court.

They were certainly buried closer to their king than his male officials, although his much-travelled steward Henenu and his chancellor Akhtoy, general Intef and the sixty royal troops all had impressively located tombs north of the temple.

Within the temple forecourt itself lay the tomb of Montuhotep's sister-wife Queen Nefru, who died early in his reign and was buried beneath an acacia grove sacred to Sekhmet, as 'the one who sweetens the forecourt with the scent of her fragrance'. The scenes in her burial chamber show Nefru's soul making a pilgrimage to Osiris's cult centre at Abydos, being served beer by her butler and attended by her hairdressers, Inu and Henut, who attach hair extensions using hairpins and their own deft fingers. The remains of the queen's burial equipment included fragments of pleated linen robes, a yard-long necklace of amethyst and carnelian, still within the 'swag bag' dropped by the ancient robbers, and some of the earliest known *shabti* figurines – statuettes of servants – who would undertake for her any manual labour required in the afterlife. Although a king's daughter and king's wife, Nefru was never a 'king's mother', an honour that did belong to yet another of Montuhotep II's wives, Queen Temet. It was her son, Sankhkara, who became king after the heir apparent, Prince Inyotef, died, and the mighty Montuhotep II was himself finally taken into Hathor's embrace around 2004 BC.

Having inherited the services of some of his father's capable officials including Henenu, Sankhkara (c.2004–1992 BC) wisely continued his father's policy of strengthening the north-east Delta with fortresses.

Sankhkara also rebuilt the First Dynasty Horus temple at the very top of the Theban mountains after it had collapsed in an earthquake. The original temple had been aligned to the annual rising of Sothis

(Sirius) as the star had appeared a thousand years before; Sankhkara changed its axis by 2°17' to reflect where the star now became visible on the horizon at dawn on 11 July. The temple was also partly rebuilt in limestone, an ambitious project, as the site is so high it takes around three hours to reach on foot. But perhaps it was part of a bigger scheme, for it was at the bottom of these same hills that Sankhkara began his terraced funerary complex, just south of Deir el-Bahari, the necessary stone acquired from Wadi Hammamat by a 3,000-strong expedition led by royal steward Henenu.

The new royal tomb site lay opposite where chancellor Meketre began work on his own rock-cut tomb, which was not entirely pillaged in antiquity. A secret chamber still concealed 'a little world of four thousand years ago', which, much like a long-forgotten and very dusty toyshop, was stuffed full of the wooden models designed to sustain Meketre's soul: female offering-bearers in bead-net dresses; Meketre's villa with its walled garden of trees around a lotus pool of polished metal; his cattle herds, being counted during the two-yearly tax assessment; his workshops with female weavers and male carpenters; male and female brewers and bakers; male butchers, and a flotilla of boats, from Meketre's state vessel with its linen sail and string rigging, to his fishing boats, whose real nets still contain tiny wooden fish.

Another tomb in the vicinity, belonging to prime minister Ipi, had been ransacked of any obvious wealth long ago, but still contained the wooden table on which he was mummified, and the linens, oils and natron salt left over from a process given extra *oomph* by the reading aloud of Coffin Text spells. These included one for 'knocking his blow-fly to the ground', with the deceased told 'Do not putrefy! Do not become maggoty in this your name of "Maggot"! Do not rot, do not drip corruption'.

But the most fascinating texts from Ipi's tomb had been left there quite by accident. They were letters belonging to Hekanakhte, his part-time funerary priest, responsible for making offerings to Ipi's soul. But primarily Hekanakhte was a farmer, frequently travelling away from Thebes on business; he often wrote back to his eldest son Merisu who deputised at Ipi's tomb and also did most of the farming, about which his father sent him endless instruction: 'Hoe every field of mine, keep sieving the seed grain, and hack with your noses into the work. Look here, if you are diligent you shall be thanked and I won't have to make things miserable for you'. Constantly telling him how to do his job, Hekanakhte also moans a lot – 'now what's the idea of sending your brother to me with the old dried-out northern barley instead of giving me sacks of the good new stuff? Fine! As long as you're happy eating good new barley while I'm going without!', the underlining being original to the actual letter.

Hekanakhte was certainly a cantankerous old so-and-so who often repeats himself, starting his sentences 'Now look here!'. Yet the orders fired at his eldest son contrasted sharply with his attitude to his youngest boy Snefru – 'whatever he wants, let him enjoy whatever he wants'. Hekanakhte also tells Merisu to 'greet my mother Ipi a thousand times and a million times', and to take good care of his new wife, who was so unpopular with the rest of the family Hekanakhte had to warn them, 'Do not keep her companions away from her, be it her hairdresser or her servant!'.

Unsurprisingly, some of the papyrus letters were discovered screwed up, and one had never even been opened; poor Merisu must have had quite enough of his father's nagging. But as 'a small window into a timeless world', the letters were so vivid they inspired Agatha Christie, herself the wife of an archaeologist, to write her 1945 novel *Death Comes as the End*.

When King Sankhkara's own end came, his funerary complex was far from being completed; the graffiti of his funerary priests claimed that they officiated on his behalf for the next two centuries while never actually having a proper place in which to perform the necessary ceremonies.

Sankhkara was succeeded by the shadowy and short-lived Montuhotep IV (c.1992–1985 BC). His names appear on inscriptions in the Wadi Hammamat, where he sent 10,000 men to obtain stone for his presumably massive sarcophagus.

This huge expedition was led by the prime minister, Amenemhat, who kept a record of the omens he witnessed en route. A pregnant gazelle apparently led them to the stone required for the sarcophagus lid, on which she then gave birth. And then 'the wonder was repeated as rain was made, the high land was made a lake, the water went to the margin of the stone' – a rare and dramatic rainstorm, regarded as a further omen.

It was certainly the prelude to the dramatic events that then unfolded. For soon after the 10,000-strong expeditionary force returned to Thebes, there was a new king, not coincidentally named Amenemhat. For the former prime minister had seized the throne.

12

Classic Kingdom, Middle Kingdom:
c.1985–1855 BC

When former prime minister Amenemhat took the throne as Amenemhat I (c.1985–1955 BC), his new Twelfth Dynasty marked the beginning of the so-called 'Middle Kingdom'.

As the 'classic' era of Egypt's cultural achievement, this included superbly crafted literary works of political spin, for it had apparently been prophesied that 'a king will come out of the south with the name Ameny . . . the son of a woman from Ta-sety, a child of Upper Egypt. He will seize the White Crown and put on the Red Crown, he will unite the two powers'.

Since Ta-seti was the most southerly region of Egypt, this implies that 'his mother was probably of Nubian descent', and part of the Theban court. Named Nofret, her husband was the priest Sesostris, and their names would be used for the next two centuries, during the dynasty their son created.

His own name, Amenemhat, meant 'Amen is in front', referring to the local god of his hometown Thebes. To this he added the throne-name Wehem-mesut – literally 'the repeater of births' or 'Renaissance Man' – to emphasise his new regime. His accession was also marked by a move back north, for although Amenemhat was a Theban lad, a more strategically placed power base would help keep the country together and maintain its northern borders.

Yet rather than moving back to the old capital Memphis, Amenemhat I wished to distance himself from the city's historical baggage and conflicting loyalties and so created a new city, midway between Meidum and Dahshur, within the Fayum, the wet and fertile region centring on the Nile-fed Lake Qarun.

He named his new city Itj-tawy, meaning 'Seizer of the Two Lands', in reference to his own *coup d'état*. Its new palace, known simply as 'the Residence', was splendidly appointed, 'decked in gold, its ceiling lapis lazuli, walls of silver, floors of acacia, doors of copper, bolts of bronze', and no doubt filled with 'luxuries: a bathroom and mirrors, clothes of royal linen, myrrh and the choice perfumes of the king in every room'.

Here he resided with his sister-wife Dedyt and their daughters, and his second queen Nefer-tatenen, mother of his son and heir Sesostris. Later claiming he had been destined to rule since 'wearing nappies', Sesostris is one of very few royal sons named during their father's reign, when 'apparently they possessed no distinctive titles', held 'no ritual role and rarely appear'. For in marked contrast to the multitudes of royal women surrounding the king, there was only room for one living god.

When planning his home for the afterlife, Amenemhat established a new royal cemetery at Lisht, whose high water table was regarded as tangible proof that the watery underworld kingdom of Osiris and Isis lay close at hand. As work began on the tomb, which would once again be a pyramid, the king restored former glories by taking entire sections from the old pyramid complexes of Dahshur, Giza and Sakkara to reuse at Lisht.

Since the old sites had suffered much damage over the last two centuries, such reuse was inspired as much by piety as the desire to harness some of the greatness of the Pyramid Age.

Having made a particular study of the pyramids at Dahshur and Giza, which had stood the test of time far more successfully than later examples, Amenemhat's architects created him a pyramid standing fifty-eight metres high. Once encased in the limestone carted off to build a bridge in 1837, its form skilfully united the two elements that create life – sun and water. For while its outer triangular structure expressed the continuing desire to rise up to join the sun god, its interior burial chamber was located sufficiently deep to be close to the water table, the kingdom of Osiris, in which the amniotic fluid of Isis reaffirmed 'the tomb being regarded as a uterus in which the mysterious process of rebirth takes place'. The creation of the Aswan Dam in modern times has only raised the water table even further, so that the burial chamber is now completely submerged and remains uninvestigated.

So too its waterlogged valley temple, linked by a causeway up to the base of the pyramid whose funerary temple incorporated recycled blocks from Dahshur, Giza and Sakkara. Other items, brought up from the king's birthplace in the south, related to old king Montuhotep II who 'like Amenemhat I himself, originated from a local family with absolutely no direct links to the Memphite kingship of the Old Kingdom'. So Amenemhat I drew on Montuhotep II's example, styling himself 'beloved of Hathor' and siting the burials of his own wives and daughters, as well as his sisters and mother, within multiple shaft tombs along the western side of his pyramid.

During his three decades as king, Amenemhat I restored the economy to full strength, reintroduced conscription into the army and founded the first of a series of forts in the north-east Delta buffer zone known as the 'Walls of the Ruler'. He sent campaigns into Palestine, where 'fear of the king was throughout the lands like Sekhmet', after he had 'curbed lions, caught crocodiles and made the Asiatics do the dog walk' in subservience, while in Nubia, he 'repressed those of Wawat, and captured the Medjai' to secure access to Nubia's goldmines.

With Egypt's borders secured, Amenemhat I reorganised his administration by appointing his supporters as regional governors.

Yet his most important political move was to make his son Sesostris his co-ruler. Although in direct contradiction of the age-old belief that the living king was Horus and his father the dead king Osiris, in eternal succession, Amenemhat I's own seizing of the throne must have caused him to rethink the inevitable transition, and father and son ruled together prior to Amenemhat's first jubilee around 1955 BC.

But he never got to celebrate the event, for on the seventh day of the third month of his thirtieth year as king, Amenemhat I was assassinated by his bodyguard.

Literature of the time claims that the king's soul left his body and 'flew up to heaven to unite with the sun disc (aten), his divine body merging with the one that made him'. And as 'the Residence was hushed, hearts were in mourning, courtiers crouched head on lap, and grieved', messengers were sent west to inform Sesostris I, then campaigning in Libya.

There was even an 'eyewitness' account from the dead king himself, returning as a ghost to warn his son of traitors. And although an obvious piece of royal propaganda, it nonetheless retains the power to move:

'Listen to what I tell you! Beware of those who are nobodies, whose plots remain hidden. Trust no one, neither a brother nor a friend, have no intimates, they are worthless. It happened after supper when night had come, as I rested peacefully for an hour, weary on my bed, as my heart turned to sleep. But the weapons of my protection were turned against me.

I awoke fighting to find the bodyguard attacking. If only I had been quick enough and seized my weapons I would have made the buggers retreat at once. But none are mighty in the night, and none can stand alone without a helper close beside. And all this happened whilst I was without you, before I had been able to sit with you and tell you of my plans. For I had not prepared for this, had not foreseen the treachery of servants. Had the women marshalled the troops? Were rebels nurtured in the palace? Sesostris my son! I must leave you now and turn away. But you are always in my heart, and my eyes will always see you, my child of a happy hour!'

Sesostris I (c.1965–1921 BC) at least had a trusted confidante in his sister-wife, Neferu IV, writing to one of his officials 'the queen lives and prospers, her head adorned with the kingship of the land'. She also produced the heir, Amenemhat, and five princesses who, like their mother, played their sistrum rattles and jangled their beaded *menat* necklaces in the manner of stage props to help them personify the goddess Hathor.

As the goddess's glittering representatives, the bejewelled royal women accompanied Sesostris I when he appeared enthroned beneath a canopy of gold at royal audiences. On one such occasion he told his courtiers 'I will construct a great house for my father' the sun god, at Heliopolis; his architects duly drew up the plans and 'the king appeared, with all the people following him. The chief lector priest and scribe of the divine books stretched the cord' to map out its foundations, Sesostris I's limestone sun temple finally completed by the erection of two twenty-metre-high red granite obelisks, one of which still stands in the car park of Cairo airport, which today covers the rest of the once vast temple.

Far beyond Heliopolis, Sesostris I was a prolific builder. In the Fayumi capital Shedet (Medinet el-Fayum), the king's statues were set up within his father's temple dedicated to the region's crocodile god, Sobek, the waterborne powerhouse who symbolised royal might, and inspiring Shedet's later Greek name, Krokodilopolis.

At Abydos, Osiris's shrines were demolished and replaced, as at Koptos, where a new temple for Min featured scenes of the king running the jubilee race while holding a ship's steering equipment. Captioned 'hastening by boat to Min, the great god in the midst of his city', Min's fertile form was so shocking for early visitors to the museum where the image ended up that its information label had to act as a fig leaf over his offending feature.

Just south at Thebes, Amen's cult centre at Karnak was expanded with a series of stone shrines, on which Sesostris was shown nose-to-nose with Ra, Horus, Amen and Ptah, the scenes throughout his splendid 'White Chapel' so detailed that even the basket-weave pattern of his red crown is shown.

Then on Egypt's southern border, Sesostris I rebuilt in limestone Satet's Elephantine shrine, from which she could dispense her life-giving Nile waters to Egypt while keeping her arrows trained on the volatile border with Nubia, beyond which the king now launched his campaign.

With his forces including the governor of Beni Hasan, Ameny, who described sailing south 'to reach the ends of the earth' through Lower Nubia, which was now an Egyptian province, Sesostris I continued his father's strategy of building fortresses to house both the Egyptian troops and local Medjai recruited as auxiliaries. Creating the first of his massive mud-brick castles at Buhen, whose inner fort alone was 150 metres by 138 metres, narrow slits in the parapets of its eleven-metre-high crenellated walls allowed arrows to be fired out, while its barbican gates, moats and drawbridge systems remained impervious to human attack, until all were lost for ever beneath the waters of Lake Nasser following the creation of the Aswan Dam in the 1960s.

Sesostris I also sent 3,700 men to the Red Sea harbour of Saww

(Wadi Gawasis), the launching point for seafaring expeditions to Punt, using ships built at Koptos. Dismantled and carried along the Wadi Hammamat for reassembly on the coast, the discovery of some of the original timbers, steering oars, ropes and anchors have recently allowed archaeologists to build and sail a full-scale reconstruction of such a ship.

The king's chilling reputation as 'the throat-slitter of Asia' also went before him when campaigning against the Bedouin of southern Palestine. As the place his official Sinuhe had gone in self-imposed exile after the assassination of Sesostris's father, *The Story of Sinuhe* features the earliest duel in world literature, as Sinuhe, with his bow, dagger, javelin and axe, triumphs over a Palestinian opponent. Yet despite his victory, Sinuhe is well aware that 'there is no bowman that fraternizes with a Delta-dweller. Who can plant a papyrus stalk upon a mountain?' His homesick feelings as a fish out of Nile water are only cured when Sesostris I eventually invites him home to Egypt with an offer he can not refuse – the traditional burial that all Egyptians craved at death – 'think of the day of burial, the passing into reveredness'. Then, describing the deluxe send-off that one day awaits him, featuring a lapis coffin, gilded tomb statue and designer-built tomb in the royal necropolis, the king tells him 'you shall not die abroad, buried by the Asiatics, you shall not be wrapped with sheep skins to serve as your coffin! You have roamed the earth too long, think of your corpse and come home!'

With his own afterlife in mind, Sesostris I had already begun work on his own pyramid complex two kilometres south of his father's at Lisht, where *mastabas* were built close by for the prime minister and the high priest of Heliopolis.

Lisht was also a cemetery for the less wealthy, inscriptions from the site naming those who served officials' households, but who are themselves too often forgotten; a female 'keeper of the dining hall', a housemaid and even a cleaning lady. The site also yielded such everyday objects as a sandstone thimble, a baby's feeding bottle decorated with protective gods and a figurine of a woman breastfeeding her child while having her hair done.

All items found around Lisht's royal cemetery, its focus was Sesostris I's sixty-metre-high pyramid, now just a low mound; its internal granite-lined chambers are only accessible as far as the present level of the groundwater – for like his father, Sesostris wanted a direct route into the underworld kingdom of Osiris, whose waters have only come closer to the living since the pyramid was built.

Amidst a pyramid complex adorned with scenes of battle between Egyptians and 'Asiatic' Palestinians, the king both smiting enemies and embracing goddesses, the presence of Hathor 'residing in the pyramid temple of Sesostris' was guaranteed by the subsidiary pyramids of Queen Neferu III and eight princesses, each interred here when they eventually died, to surround the king in death as they had in life.

When Sesostris I himself died around 1921 BC, after forty-five highly successful years, during which he too had instigated a brief co-regency with his son Amenemhat II (c.1922–1878 BC), the new king took the throne with his sister-wife Neferu V, with whom he produced numerous children.

Amenemhat II's reign was certainly fruitful, relatively peaceful and highly luxurious. A snapshot of royal life is preserved in *The Pleasures of Fishing and Fowling*, in which a courtier exclaims, 'would that I were always in the country! At dawn I would have a bite, then be far away, walking in the place of my heart, down by the river'. His rave reviews inspire the royal family to decamp to their palatial estates in the Fayum and, after prayers to the local crocodile god Sobek, they set about spearing fish and bringing down wildfowl with throwing sticks, assisted by Sekhet, goddess of the hunt.

Following optimum flood levels, hymns of thanks to the Nile reveal that 'at the Residence people feast on the meadows' gifts, decked with lotus for the nose, good things strewn about the houses'. The continuous acquisition of foreign wealth included gold from Nubia, and the silverware and lapis lazuli sent as foreign tribute from Crete, possibly via Byblos, and, like untouched Christmas presents discovered within their original strongboxes, embossed with Amenemhat II's cartouche, after he'd presented them to the temple of war god Montu at Tod, near Thebes.

The same temple also yielded royal 'daybooks' documenting such kingly donations, while another such book, found at Sakkara, records 'the dispatch of the army to the Lebanese coast', returning with

'1,665 units of silver, 4,882 units of gold, 15,961 units of copper', precious stones and gilded weapons – enormous quantities of wealth pouring into Egypt at this time, together with 1,554 Asiatic prisoners of war.

Yet not all contact between Egypt and the Near East was aggressive. With close links between the Delta and Palestine stretching back to the Predynastic age, 'massive immigration at the turn of the 12th and 13th dynasties seems to have consisted of soldiers, sailors and ships' carpenters working on behalf of the Egyptian state', together with the women, destined to become minor wives of the traditionally uxorious Egyptian king.

With Egypt's officials in turn stationed throughout Palestine and Syria, as far afield as central Anatolia and Crete, Amenemhat II's daughters were likewise represented around the Near East. With their statues found as far north as Ugarit, Princess Ita, 'beloved king's daughter of his body', was named on a sphinx found at Qatna, and it may also be Ita, with an expression 'almost light and laughing', who is represented by a stunning sphinx in dark chlorite, thought to have once stood at Heliopolis. A colossal red granite sphinx, possibly made by Snefru, was re-inscribed with the name of Amenemhat II, whose admiration for that giant of the Pyramid Age is reflected in the fact that he returned to Dahshur to begin his own pyramid, near the two built by Snefru 700 years before.

But Amenemhat II made no attempt to replicate such massive monuments. His tomb, now known as the 'White Pyramid' because of the piles of broken limestone rubble that once formed its cladding, contained only the king's empty sarcophagus. Yet excavations in 1894 revealed the subterranean tombs of at least one of his queens, Kemanub, and daughters Sathathormeryt, Itaweret, Khnumet and Ita, whose intact burials revealed some things astounding on many levels.

For Ita's mummified body was adorned with her jewelled collar, bracelets, armlets and a belt to which was attached a spectacular dagger, its pommel a crescent of lapis lazuli, 'probably the largest piece ever worked in Egypt', and its gold hilt, inlaid with lapis and carnelian, holding a bronze blade within its leather sheath. Her sister

Itaweret similarly wore jewellery, while her diadem, mirror and cosmetic chest had been placed in an adjoining chamber with her stone mace, archer's bow and gilded blades.

In a cosy arrangement, their sister Khnumet had been buried in a neighbouring chamber, again provided with a mace, dagger, assorted staffs and a jewel chest containing two crowns. One was a gold diadem featuring the Nekhbet vulture in flight, the second a spun-sugar confection of gold interwoven with tiny jewelled flowers. A set of small gold birds once attached to Khnumet's hair was very similar to Minoan examples found on the island of Aigina, and her gold neckwear of flowers and stars was decorated with tiny gold balls in a technique known as granulation, first developed in Mesopotamia and subsequently common around the Aegean. So Khnumet's jewels were made either on Crete, or by a Cretan craftsman based at the Egyptian court.

Foreign traders and settlers had certainly been entering Egypt for the previous two thousand years from Palestine and the Levant, their regular donkey trains now monitored by Khnumhotep, the 'Overseer of the Eastern Desert'. Khnumhotep was also the governor of Beni Hasan and his tomb here is decorated with vivid scenes of Absha, 'Ruler of the Desert', and his thirty-six-strong retinue of Aamu traders, recognisable as non-Egyptians by their bright dress and colourful sock-like boots. The donkeys in Absha's travelling emporium are bringing supplies of the black lead ore, galena, mined at Gebel Zeit on the Red Sea coast which the Egyptians used to make eye make-up. But they are also carrying with them the bellows they needed for metalworking, and even their small children, representative of the family groups of men, women and children increasingly arriving from Palestine as economic migrants.

The Egyptians were certainly aware of the cultural differences between themselves and such people, and regarded their own personal grooming regimes as next to godliness. So when Sinuhe returned to Egypt after years of living with the 'Sandfarers' of Sinai, he underwent a makeover, bathing in a bathroom, and as he himself describes, 'years were removed from my body. I was shaved and my hair was combed, my squalor returned to the foreign land, my dress to the Sandfarers. I was dressed in fine linen, anointed with fine oil and slept on a bed. I returned the sand to those who dwell in it and the tree oil to those who grease themselves in it'.

The industrious barbers, laundrymen and personal attendants portrayed in the tomb scenes of the elite ensured that their employers would appear eternally pristine, which is certainly the case with Khnumhotep and his fellow governors of Beni Hasan; they are shown enjoying their leisure time watching others exert themselves, from acrobats leaping over bulls to the wrestlers, whose bouts are enlivened by shouts of 'I'm grabbing your leg!', 'I'll make your heart weep and fill with fear!'.

Yet the Beni Hasan cemetery contained many more burials than the thirty-nine rock-cut tombs of the local elite. Up to 800 smaller interments included those of the warrior Userhet, young Seneb with her gold and silver jewellery and even a dog named Heb, who, along with his simple coffin, had pots of provisions for his afterlife.

But Heb, Userhet and Seneb were certainly the exception, since most of those buried at Beni Hasan, as elsewhere throughout Egypt's long history, were anonymous, their modest graves and their sparse contents contrasting sharply with those of the most important courtiers, who still sought burial in the royal cemetery, close to Amenemhat II and his army of daughters.

As for Amenemhat II's son, Sesostris II (c.1880–1874 BC), he had briefly been co-ruler with his elderly father, and at his death became sole king in a seamless transition of power.

He married his sister Nofret II – the 'Lady of the South and North' – and a second wife, Weret, who produced the male heir Sesostris III. And as the royal family grew, the new king extended the same fertility beyond the palace, draining the Fayumi marshes to increase agricultural production. Not only did this swell the royal coffers, it also reduced the incidence of malaria, the dangers of which are hinted at in literature of the time, in the so-called *Satire of the Trades* which claims that in the case of one unfortunate reed-cutter, 'mosquitoes have slain him'.

To capitalise on his public image as bringer of plenty, the second Sesostris moved his funerary complex even nearer the Fayum, to a new site, Lahun. The name means 'mouth of the canal' and it overlooked the channel linking the Fayum to the Nile, where Sesostris

II built his pyramid complex. Surrounded by groves of trees, it was populated by statues of the royal family and served by a clergy described as 'the beautiful girl children of the funerary temple of Sesostris'.

It also incorporated the smaller pyramid of Queen Nofret II and the eight shaft tombs of the royal daughters. Although these were heavily plundered in ancient times, the tomb of Princess Sithathoryunet, elderly by the time she died, had a secret recess in which early archaeologists discovered five wooden boxes holding the princess's jewellery, cosmetics and wig. Although the hair, like the wood, had decayed in the Fayum's damp environment, a mass of gold and gem-encrusted regalia remained – gold and black obsidian pots for perfumes and cosmetics, a silver mirror and a tiny silver compact for her mineral rouge. It is mind-boggling that such consummate crafts-manship and lavish wealth was simply a fraction of only one of the original ten interments.

Yet royal regalia was by no means all that was found at Lahun, where a walled town had been built to house Sesostris II's palace, the 3,000 people who built his pyramid and the priests who then maintained his funerary cult. Named 'Kahun' by its original archae-ologist, its streets were laid out in neat, grid-like rows, with most houses measuring around ten by ten metres in contrast with the veritable mansions built around internal courtyards. A large central area, built atop a rocky outcrop, presumably marked the site of the palace itself.

Sometimes called '*The Marie Celeste* of Ancient Egypt', the town retained its original fixtures, fittings and the possessions of its orig-inal population – tools ranging from a plasterer's float to a midwife's mask, pottery from as far afield as Crete, wooden boxes with sliding lids, baskets, textiles and weaving equipment, metalware, mirrors with Hathor-shaped handles, game boards, balls and spinning tops. There were also the remains of Fayumi foods; not only barley, radishes, beans, peas and dates, but cucumber, watermelon, grapes and figs, juniper and cumin, the safflower and sedge roots used in medicine, dyes and cosmetics, and the flax that produced linen.

Most precious of all were papyrus documents, many relating to the administration, since Kahun had an office for the prime minister to use when he came south from Itj-tawy. There were also business papers from the pyramid complex, including the temple journal, duty rotas and lists of personnel – both Egyptian and Aamu 'Asiatics' – and accounts lists revealing that women received equal pay-rations to men. Medical compendia included the Kahun Veterinary Papyrus dealing with animal diseases, part of which was a 'prescription for a bull suffering from cold fever', while the Kahun Gynaecological Papyrus diagnosed the mysteries of the wandering womb, gave instructions for how to prevent morning sickness, recommended tests to indicate fertility, pregnancy and the sex of a child and provided recipes for contraceptives using crocodile dung, sour milk and a pinch of natron.

Among the private notes and correspondence, someone announced an imminent visit to the presumably messy home of the seal-bearer Neni, telling him 'please let me find the house in very good shape – only after the house has been tidied up shall you have me come there'. There is also a missive from Irer, head weaver and part-time priestess, addressed to none other than the king:

> 'this is a communication to the lord – life, prosperity and health – are you safe and sound? The women weavers are left abandoned, thinking they won't get food provisions inasmuch as not any news has been heard. It is good if the lord takes note. This is [also] a communication about those slave-women who are here unable to weave clothes. Your presence is demanded by those who would work at the warp thread so as to be guided . . . The lord – life, prosperity and health – should spend some time here since not any clothes have been made while my attention is directed to the temple'.

Clearly unimpressed with her foreign workforce, whose productivity went unchecked when she was working at the temple, Irer felt further undermined by a late delivery of ration payments from the royal storehouse and bypassed the mass of officialdom to go straight to the top, although no reply survives to gauge the royal reaction.

Everyday life at Kahun was also represented by the things they took with them into the next world, and although some infants were buried beneath the houses' floors in a practice dating back to Predynastic times, adults were interred in the nearby cemeteries of

Harageh, where modest grave goods were interspersed with greater wealth; the ten-year-old daughter of one well-to-do family was buried with her beads of turquoise, lapis, carnelian and gold, silver cowrie-shell belt and five gold fish amulets.

Such adornments were also popular further south at Meir, whose governor, Ukhhotep IV, had no fewer than twelve wives, something which was most unusual for any man other than the king. And yet Ukhhotep's statues show him flanked by Nubkau, 'his wife whom he loves', and Khnumhotep, who was not only 'his wife whom he loves' but 'his favourite'. They also appear in Ukhhotep's tomb scenes, populated exclusively with female figures, except for him. So as he hunts by the river, one of his wives points out a particularly fine fowl, telling him 'Get me this bird', to which he replies 'I'll do so and get it for you'. The bird was no doubt destined for the same fate as that from another of the Meir tomb scenes, in which a cook, sitting before a fire, exclaims in some exasperation 'I have been roasting this goose since the beginning of time!'

Such well-appointed tombs originally contained great wealth, the largest amount of tomb equipment from the whole Middle Kingdom discovered in the tomb of Djehuti-nakht, governor of Bersheh. Although thieves had taken the best of the jewellery, and had decapitated Djehuti-nakht, whose body was also lost, his detached head at least survived, to reveal that his brain had been removed down his nose as part of the mummification process by this time.

Yet there was still more left of Djehuti-nakht than there was of his king. When Sesostris II died after a brief reign, to be mummified by Lahun's 'embalmers of Anubis' and laid within his pyramid, only his leg bones remained when the pyramid was first entered in 1887, together with the jewelled uraeus once attached to his crown.

His funeral had been led by his son, heir and namesake, Sesostris III (c.1874–1855 BC), whose statues' stern features are assumed to indicate a change in royal policy, and their large ears his ability to hear any plots against him – or he may simply have had large ears. He was certainly an unpopular figure for some, for 'of the forty-some known statues of Sesostris III, all appear to have been intentionally vandalised after his death, as if those who came later wanted revenge on this tyrannical sovereign'. Whatever the truth, the third Sesostris certainly shook things up, both at home and abroad.

Reducing the powers of the hereditary governors (*nomarchs*), which were incompatible with his increasingly centralised government, Sesostris III relied instead on a huge bureaucracy of state-funded pen-pushers, both Egyptians and 'Asiatics' from Palestine, overseen by his new trio of prime ministers, located in the north and south of Egypt and in northern Nubia, where the Nubians were gradually taking back control.

Determined to stop them, Sesostris III ordered a fortified road into Nubia and, by expanding the existing canal channel that had been cut through the First Cataract near Aswan, made the Nile navigable from the Second Cataract all the way north to the Mediterranean, over a thousand miles away.

Once able to move rapidly through his 'sinuous empire', Sesostris III launched a series of brutal invasions against Upper Nubia, which he always referred to as 'vile Kush'. Pushing as far as Semna, where he dammed the Nile to force vessels to pass in single file between Semna and Kumma, he also built eight new forts from Semna up to Buhen. The forts monitored all river and land traffic around the clock, rather like ancient CCTV, producing daily reports known as the 'Semna Despatches', precisely noting the movements of Nubian traders and the Medjai from Nubia's Red Sea coast, some of whom were employed as mercenaries. But with others 'dismissed to their desert', most of the despatches report little more than 'all the affairs of the king's domain are safe and sound', as few dared challenge the military might in their midst.

As Sesostris III also launched a propaganda war, he was described as one 'who shoots the arrow as does Sekhmet', and 'a Sekhmet against his enemies who have trodden on his boundaries'. In Nubia he erected great stone stelae at points along the Nile, flanked by his statues, 'which glowered over the border' at the Nubians, clear warnings to go no further. This was repeated in Palestine, where his stelae were still standing 1,400 years later.

With his borders secured by military means, the king also secured them with magic, employing spells to control all 'who may rebel, who may plot, who may fight, who may think of fighting or who may think of rebelling on this entire earth'. And with Sesostris III's hit list including Ashkelon, Jerusalem, Byblos, the Nubian Medjai and Kush, their names were read aloud as clay or wax statuettes were smashed, burned or buried upside down in an attempt to gain power over regions with which Egypt still traded, but which it nonetheless wished to control.

Then within his expanded kingdom, the king commissioned statues of himself in Aswan granite and the diorite extracted from the newly reconquered quarries of Nubia. Both grim-faced sphinxes and standing figures, they were serenaded with patriotic hymns: 'Hail to you, our Horus, Divine of Form! Land's protector who widens its borders, who smites foreign countries with his crown and holds the two lands in his arms' embrace'.

With particular honour paid to Montu, the war god, whose cult centre Medamud was provided with royal statuary, Sesostris III set up at least seven more of his scowling statues within the Theban funerary temple of Montuhotep II, reunifier of the land. Placing them beside those of the old king to gain reflected glory, Sesostris actively tapped into this past power using a granite blade – inscribed 'King Sesostris made this for his father [i.e. predecessor] Montuhotep' – the same type of blade used in rites to restore the soul of the deceased to both mummies and statues, and yet more evidence for the way in which living kings tried to plug into the power of their ancestors.

But such ancestor worship found its most overt expression at Abydos, cult centre of Osiris, Lord of the Underworld, where Sesostris III not only added yet more granite figures of himself but also commissioned his treasurer, Ikhetnofret, to embellish Osiris's cult statue 'with fine gold which he has let my majesty bring back from Nubia in triumphant victory'. He also ordered a new boat-shaped barque shrine in which the god's statue could be taken from his temple by night and into the desert beyond during the annual 'Mysteries of Osiris' festival.

Since Osiris was regarded as one of Egypt's first rulers, whose successors, Egypt's earliest historical kings, had been buried in the oldest part of the Abydos cemetery, the tomb of King Djer was now identified as the burial place of Osiris himself. After its restoration following the desecration of the First Intermediate Period, a new access stairway was added, to make the old tomb the focal point of the annual Osiris Mysteries procession, when scenes from the god's life, death and resurrection were re-enacted by the faithful until the fifth century AD.

For Osiris was regarded as the salvation of all at death, and as well as burial at Abydos believed to provide a fast track to the afterlife regardless of social status, many people during their lives undertook a pilgrimage, which they commemorated by leaving statues, stelae or *shabti* figures as 'their way of ensuring permanent participation in the sacred rituals of the town'. One of the most endearing aspects of such memorials was the inclusion of family and friends, the most poignant surely the small stela of a singer, a stout, jolly fellow shown reaching forward toward a well-stocked offering-table. The text names him as 'Neferhotep, deceased, born of the housewife Henu. It is his beloved friend, the Carrier of Bricks Nebsumenu, who has done this', referring to the fact that Nebsumenu had commissioned the stela from 'Sonbauf, son of the draughtsman Rensonb'. As an eternal memorial to the friendship of three working men around 1850 BC, 'it is another small reminder that Egypt was not all pyramids and temples, but also people who share with us the pleasures and hurts of this life and the anticipation of the next'.

Foremost among those wanting a place in the sacred necropolis was Sesostris III himself, whose gargantuan cenotaph complex, southeast of the Osiris temple, featured a 270-metre-long subterranean 'dummy' tomb set beneath the cliffs. A 1.5-kilometre roadway stretched down to its associated limestone funerary temple, with those who maintained the royal cult and even the local mayor housed in a nearby settlement covering over six hectares.

Although his spectacular Abydos cenotaph was created to maintain Sesostris III's spirit and bring him nearer to god, his actual tomb was his pyramid, back in the north at Dahshur, where both his grandfather and his ancient predecessor Snefru were buried. The pyramid's seventy-eight-metre-high superstructure of mud-brick was once overlaid in limestone, and its subterranean chambers, smaller than their counterpart at Abydos, were likewise lined in limestone;

his burial chamber had been built of granite, but was found empty, save for a bronze dagger, some pottery, and a dust-filled sarcophagus.

But the old warrior had nonetheless followed tradition and surrounded his Dahshur pyramid with the burials of fourteen of his female relatives, their small pyramids and shaft graves creating 'a vast catacomb of tombs', with their burial chambers connected by passageways.

In much the same way as Khufu had needed the presence of his mother, Hetepheres, in death, so too did Sesostris III, whose own mother, Weret, was buried close to him. The next generations of Hathor's incarnations were represented by Sesostris III's wives Neferhenut and Weret II, his sister Itakayet II and four royal daughters. Although the damp Dahshur environment had reduced their mummified remains to little more than 'resin-treated bones', and their tombs had been ransacked in ancient times, some of their spectacular grave goods had once again missed the robbers' keen eye.

As early as 1894, the lavish jewellery of the king's daughters Mereret and SatHathor were discovered, still inside their gilded wooden jewel chests hidden in secret cavities in the floor. Then a century later, in 1995, archaeologists found the remains of the pyramid of Sesostris III's queen Weret II, its subterranean passage lying beneath the king's pyramid, suggesting that 'she was the king's main consort'.

Although a combination of ancient plundering and ninety-five per cent humidity levels had reduced the queen's mummified body to bones, they reveal a woman of slight build, standing around five feet one inch tall (1.5m), while 'the sharp nasal sills indicate a Caucasoid person'. She was left-handed, undertook little physical activity during her life and, as she had few teeth left and suffered from osteoporosis, was probably well into her seventies at death. She had been buried with all the lavish jewellery she had worn in life, part of which was found, having again been carefully hidden within a sealed niche in her tomb.

According to established practice, the royal family's burial complex was surrounded by the *mastabas* of their state officials, and with similar burials discovered at nearby Riqqeh, near Lake Qarun, the contents of one particular tomb proved most intriguing. Although its roof had collapsed in antiquity, covering the coffin and male mummy, archaeologists discovered a second, unexpected, individual who had 'been suddenly crushed while in a standing, or at least crouching position when the fall occurred'. Since the mummy wrappings were found partly disturbed, exposing an array of jewellery, the evidence suggests that a tomb raider had been stopped in his tracks when the roof fell in and killed him – the ultimate tomb curse in action!

When Sesostris III himself died around 1855 BC, his twenty-year-old son, Amenemhat III, became king and went on to have a long, prosperous and peaceful reign, surrounded by an ever-expanding retinue of wives and daughters, based at the fertile heart of the kingdom, the lush and verdant Fayum.

13

Proliferate, Disintegrate:
c. 1855–1650 BC

When the new king Amenemhat III (c. 1855–1808 BC) was crowned on New Year's Day, 1855 BC, he 'put the Fayum at the centre of his policy', and built new temples here in honour of the local crocodile god Sobek, symbol of royal might, and his female counterpart, the ubiquitous Hathor. Scenes of his coronation were carved on the temple walls in the Fayumi capital, Shedet (Krokodilopolis), where the new king's granite statues portrayed him as 'supreme pontiff' – dressed in the priestly leopard-skin, the beaded *menat* necklace of Hathor and his hair set in thick, dreadlock-like braids.

Just north of Shedet, he erected a colossal pair of eleven-metre-high seated statues of himself in quartzite, raised even higher by 6.5-metre-high pedestals set on the shores of Lake Qarun. When its water level was at its height following the annual Nile flood, Amenemhat III's twin images, surrounded by water, appeared to hover on the surface of the lake – a source of wonder for the next two millennia.

Worshipped in their own right, they emphasised Amenemhat III as the bringer of plenty, in the same way other statues show the king as the androgynous Nile god Hapi. For it was claimed that the king 'makes the land verdant even more than great Hapi', since the annual flood levels remained high for most of his reign.

In temple scenes at Medinet Maadi (Narmouthis), again dedicated to Sobek and Hathor, Amenemhat III was shown with his queen Hetepti and daughter Neferuptah. And as the king worships the omnipresent goddess, the bejewelled Neferuptah shakes her weighty sistrum rattle, beside the caption 'Giving offerings so Neferuptah may live like Ra'. Her status was certainly greater than that of other royal princesses, for Neferuptah was the first woman to have her name enclosed in the oval cartouche until then reserved for ruling monarchs.

She was shown with her father in monuments as far south as Elephantine, including some that portrayed her as a granite sphinx. Amenemhat III's own sphinxes, set up in the north at Bastet's old temple at Bubastis, reflected his status as 'Bastet who guards the Two Lands, and Sekhmet to those who defy him'.

Bubastis was clearly a site of great importance, where the king built an extensive palace in which to celebrate his jubilee. Its Delta location meant close contact with the Mediterranean, and as trade with Byblos continued apace, more sphinxes of the king were set up as far north as Ugarit on the Syrian coast, opposite Cyprus. The king's men were also busy at the Red Sea port of Saww, from which his officials, Nebsu and Amenhotep, led two expeditions to Punt; part of their original cargo has been recently discovered in twenty wooden crates, one still labelled 'the wonderful things of Punt'.

Egypt's quarries at Tura, Wadi Hammamat, Aswan and Nubia were now at their busiest, as was Sinai, where Amenemhat III's Egyptian. and Palestinian officials acquired great quantities of turquoise and malachite when posted here on a 'quasi-permanent basis', founding a temple at Serabit el-Khadim to Hathor, 'Lady of the Turquoise' and the patron of its miners.

With the Sinai still holding King Snefru in godlike esteem, so too did the Middle Kingdom monarchs, Amenemhat III following his father by making his funerary arrangements at Snefru's dual-pyramid site, Dahshur. Building work occupied the first fifteen years of his reign; his completed pyramid was topped with a splendid granite capstone carved with his eyes, to 'behold the perfections of Ra' – 'May the eyes of the king be opened, so he may see Horus-of-the-Horizon, Lord of the Horizon, as he crosses the sky. May he cause the king to shine like a god, and be indestructible'.

The pyramid complex again featured tombs for the royal women and, beyond them, for their courtiers and officials, but those with no direct connection to the administration continued to be buried in their local cemeteries. The inhabitants of Memphis were still buried at Sakkara, while the clergy who maintained the cults of earlier Middle Kingdom rulers around their pyramids at Lisht were buried close to their place of work; these included chief priest Sesenebnef, interred with his insignia and staves.

Another Lisht tomb contained the burial of the fifty-year-old Senebtisi, whose only title was 'Lady of the House' – a housewife – although she was rather a well-off housewife. The region's humidity had been partly held at bay by her costly mummification, the resins poured over her body having hardened to maintain her body's contours, fixing her in place, like a fly in amber, within a nest of three coffins.

Round her neck were necklaces, round her limbs were bracelets and anklets, and round her hips an elaborate beaded 'apron' with a beaded tail suspended at the back. Worn by kings to represent their bull-like strength, they were also worn by women wishing to evoke Shesmetet, an aspect of Sekhmet, whose name derives from *shesmet* – a belt decorated with beads.

But the most intereting thing about this non-royal 'housewife', who stood barely 4 feet 8 inches tall (1.5 metres), were her stone maces, her two bows and arrows, her copper dagger in its gilded sheath and no fewer than ten staves, all placed inside her coffin, beside which was a long box containing yet another set of staffs. As only one of many female burials containing both weapons and jewellery – a combination dating back to Predynastic times – it demonstrates quite forcefully the way in which women were perceived: as both the protective goddess Hathor and her aggressive alter ego Sekhmet.

Yet on a day-to-day basis, most Egyptian housewives seem to have been preoccupied with domestic concerns. In the case of Dedi, married to a priest named Intef, his death was no reason to stop nagging him; Dedi writes to him, 'our servant Imiu, she is ill. Why don't you fight for her night and day with either the man or woman who is doing her harm! If you don't help, the household will simply fall apart!'

In the case of Amenemhat III's own post-mortem domestic arrangements, the numerous wives and daughters who predeceased him continued to be interred around his pyramid. But once again, this particular part of the Dahshur plateau proved unable to cope with the sheer scale of the building work and began to show signs of subsidence and cracking – another, albeit unintentional, link between Amenemhat III and his role model Snefru.

So Amenemhat III's architects went back to the drawing board and designed a new burial structure, making a small-scale stone and wooden model to gain the royal seal of approval before proceeding with the build.

These plans, however, would be implemented at a new site on the eastern edge of the king's beloved Fayum, perhaps as a way for the royal presence to magically reverse the sudden drop in Nile flood levels, which between his thirtieth and fortieth regnal years plummeted dramatically from five to 0.5 metres. Playing havoc with the Egyptian economy, it also caused great hardship in Nubia, where it was reported that 'the desert is dying of hunger' – a major problem for a god-king who styled himself the bringer of plenty.

So the royal cemetery was relocated to the Fayum's Hawara, whose ancient name 'Hut-weret' – great temple – referred to Amenemhat III's huge pyramid temple complex, whose maze-like structure became a true wonder of the ancient world.

Built of white limestone, red granite and yellow sandstone, statues of the king, Hathor and Sobek were set within repeated sets of courts, shrines and crypts to create 'a palace composed of as many smaller palaces as were formerly administrative regions,' stated one ancient visitor. Another claimed there were 3,000 rooms, 'half of which are underground and the other half directly above them', all interconnected by 'winding passageways' to create a complex so elaborate that it eventually became known as 'the Labyrinth'.

Although the complex later became a convenient stone quarry, it was reported as late as 1853 that 'an immense cluster of chambers still remains, and in the centre lies the great square, where the courts once stood, covered with the remains of large monolithic granite columns, and of others of white hard limestone, shining almost like marble . . . At the first superficial survey of the ground, a number of complicated spaces, of true labyrinthine forms, immediately presented themselves, both above and below ground'.

Yet less than forty years later, this had almost all been carted away for reuse, the fabled Labyrinth reduced to little more than scattered blocks around the pyramid's exposed, mud-brick core.

Only below ground did anything remain, with the submerged burial chamber finally located in 1892. Originally sealed by an ingenious sand-lowering portcullis device that the king's architects had added to their scale model (and replicated since in bad Hollywood films), the chamber was 'a technical marvel and completely innovatory', made as it was from a single piece of quartzite weighing over 100 tons.

The chamber held two sarcophagi, one each for Amenemhat III and his daughter Neferuptah, an arrangement echoed in the Coffin Text spells for 'Assembling a family in the realm of the dead: he goes down into the waters seeking his family, seeking his loved ones. I will be in the waters, alive for ever and ever – a spell a million times right!'

When Amenemhat III died after a forty-six-year reign, he was mummified and placed in his stone sarcophagus, where his body remained, albeit in a dissolved state, since the archaeologist reported finding 'bits of bone' in the water. Following his interment, his pyramid's elaborate locking device had been activated to completely seal the whole tomb, in last rites led by Amenemhat III's children, the new king Amenemhat IV and Neferuptah.

Having outlived her father, Neferuptah could no longer be interred within his now-sealed burial chamber, so alternative arrangements were made only two kilometres to the south, where her undisturbed pyramid tomb was finally located in 1956. As in the case of her father, all that remained of her were tiny pieces of resin-coated linen to which skin fragments adhered, for Osiris's watery kingdom had risen up to claim her too, her body, bones and all, disintegrating away within the waterlogged interior of her massive granite sarcophagus.

The archaeologists who discovered Neferuptah's burial noted that, even in antiquity, 'this water used to reach the level of the lid and enter into the sarcophagus during the inundation months'. And while complete submersion was presumably unintentional, the 'Spell for Becoming the Nile' nonetheless declares 'I am the Nile god who comes in joy, dearly beloved, I am the Nile god and I will never grow weary', together with a helpful spell for 'Breathing air among the waters'.

As for Neferuptah's brother, Amenemhat IV (c.1808–1799 BC), who must have been quite old following the lengthy reign of his father, his time as king was recorded at precisely 'nine years, three months and twenty-seven days'.

Although few other details are known, he may have had some power-sharing arrangement with his sister Neferuptah early in his reign, and the new regime simply continued the policies of their father. For 'in spite of a lack of evidence for any brilliant achievements, the reign shows little evidence of any serious decline in Egyptian prosperity and prestige', as their officials continued to be sent out to Sinai, to Wadi Hammamat and to Wadi el-Hudi for supplies of turquoise, slate and amethyst.

As trade with the Levant continued, the fourth Amenemhat sent out gifts of royal favour to the Egyptophile princes of Byblos, whose Egyptian-style tombs contained such gifts, plus copies of Egyptian jewels and a form of local scimitar, the *khopesh*, inlaid with gold and black *niello*, a technique invented in Byblos around 1800 BC.

Within Egypt, Amenemhat IV's courtiers likewise enjoyed an impressive level of wealth; the royal butler Kemuny was the owner of a fine cosmetic chest with pull-out drawer and compartmentalised interior, buried with him in Thebes, where Amenemhat IV seems to have spent some of his time too. Yet at his death around 1799 BC, the king was buried in the north, possibly at Mazghuna, south of Dahshur, in the more northerly of two pyramids.

He was then succeeded by a woman. Another one of his sisters, she was Sobeknefru (c.1799–1795 BC), and was the first female king whose status cannot be argued away, dismissed, played down or ignored. Despite unfounded modern claims that Sobeknefru was 'a usurper', she was regarded as the rightful king both in contemporary king lists and in those composed 1,500 years later. She was 'Mistress of the Two Lands', and took the standard royal titles 'King of Upper and Lower Egypt', Sobekkara; 'Daughter of Ra', Sobeknefru; 'the Horus', She who is beloved of Ra; 'She of the Two Ladies', Powerful Daughter; 'the Golden Horus', Enduring of Appearances.

As the first Egyptian ruler to be named after the crocodile god Sobek, symbol of royal might, in both her birth name, Sobeknefru and her throne-name, Sobekkara, which she adopted at her accession, the new king established her court at the god's cult centre Shedet (Krokodilopolis) in the Fayum.

Like those of Khentkawes I of the Pyramid Age, Sobeknefru's portraits blended male and female attributes, showing her wearing the masculine striped royal headcloth and belted kilt over her otherwise female dress, while in other statuary she is shown in the cloak associated with the coronation.

Her reign happily coincided with a rise in Nile flood levels, an inscription from her third year as ruler, at the Nubian fortress Kumma, recording a height of 1.83 metres. She commissioned new temples at Herakleopolis and at Tell Dab'a, which was also adorned with her life-size basalt statues and at least one sphinx, with more of her statues set up in the Fayum.

And here her name was carved alongside that of her father, Amenemhat III, to present her reign as a co-regency with him, even if this was 'commemorative rather than actual'. The Horus falcons surmounting each of their cartouches were designed to face each other, that of the old king extending the *ankh* sign of life to the Horus falcon that represented his kingly daughter. To further emphasise their relationship, Sobeknefru completed her father's labyrinthine pyramid complex at Hawara, where her names, as well as his, are to be found on its remaining blocks.

Rather less is known about Sobeknefru's plans for her own tomb, however. Although it is most likely the larger of the two pyramids created at Mazghuna, complete with its own portcullis closing-system, work was abandoned mid-build and, as no trace of her burial has yet been found, it is – as in the case of almost every Egyptian ruler – not known exactly when or indeed how she died.

If mentioned at all in standard history books, Sobeknefru is dismissed as the last resort, whose reign 'marks the end of the dynasty and the decline of the Middle Kingdom', since 'so abnormal a situation contained the seeds of disaster'.

Yet despite such unfounded claims, the throne actually passed smoothly to a succession of male kings who made up the Thirteenth Dynasty (c.1795–c.1650 BC), most likely 'descendants of Amenemhat III and/or his predecessors by minor wives', both Egyptian and foreign and of whom there were many. They divided their time between the north and the south to maintain their control over both Upper and Lower Egypt, surviving documents from both Lahun and Thebes revealing the continuity of an administration made up of both Egyptians and growing numbers of Palestinians.

Producing huge amounts of paperwork, 'a mass of documentation on the organisation of the state survives', whereas 'our knowledge of the kings whom these officials served is, in comparison, pitifully small'.

There was certainly a high turnover of kings, with sixty or more named during the 145-year period of the Thirteenth Dynasty, making it pretty impossible to give accurate dates for their reigns. But this does not seem to indicate political decline, and it seems that the Crown was actually part of a 'circulating succession', passed down through a few aristocratic families in a well-ordered power-sharing arrangement.

For these kings continued to send expeditions to Gebel Zeit on the Red Sea and to Semna deep in Nubia, and to plan their burials within the traditional royal cemeteries.

They also followed Sobeknefru's lead by naming themselves after the crocodile god. At least eight were named Sobekhotep, the first of whom chose burial at the ancient royal necropolis, Abydos, where Sobekhotep I's tomb, only discovered in 2013, was constructed from limestone brought south from Tura, and its burial chamber of red quartzite housed the king's *sixty-ton* quartzite sarcophagus.

And as Abydos remained a place of pilgrimage for all classes, from monarchs to 'the washerman Hepet', kings continued to make generous additions to the so-called 'Tomb of Osiris'. Originally the resting place of First Dynasty king Djer, his mummy, lost during the civil war of the First Intermediate Period, was now replaced by a life-size black basalt effigy portraying Osiris as a mummy, laid out on his funerary bed. He is shown with his erect phallus hidden, and indeed protected, by the outstretched wings of Isis in the form of a kite as she magically conceives their son Horus; this somewhat bizarre theme was nonetheless expressed with consummate skill on the orders of Thirteenth-Dynasty king, Khendjer, whose name incorporates that of Djer, but may also suggest Palestinian or Syrian ancestry, making him Egypt's first 'Semitic king'.

Palestinians were also appearing in the households of courtiers in ever-growing numbers; the Abydos priest Amenysonb employed a mixed staff, including the 'Asiatic' brewer Irsi and his countrymen Sobekiry and Senebnebit, whose adoption of Egyptian names was part of their cultural assimilation. As for Amenysonb himself, King Khendjer appointed him to spruce up Abydos and, with the help of prime minister Ankhu, he 'cleansed' Osiris's nearby temple 'on the outside and on the inside', bringing in the painters to enhance the place where the veneration of the royal ancestors, now in the care of Osiris, was a core belief.

As for his own funerary arrangements, Khendjer completed a thirty-seven-metre-high pyramid between those of Pepi II at South Sakkara and Sesostris III at North Dahshur, so he could spend eternity literally in the midst of his ancestors. So too his fellow monarch, Ameny-Qemau, 'the Asiatic', buried in a similar-sized pyramid at Dahshur.

This strong tendency to look back to the past was also found in Thebes, where Sobekhotep II set up his own statue in Karnak's 'Chamber of Ancestors'. And with the court now residing in Thebes for increasing lengths of time, the royal accounts list large numbers of staff, from 'the Department of the Head of the South' to the 'House of the Nurses', the foods they received as daily wages including 2,000 loaves of bread and 300 jugs of beer.

The similarly sizeable entourage of Sobekhotep III was dominated by his two queens and their daughters; one princess's nickname Fendy, meaning 'Nose, or possibly Nosy', was written in the same cartouche as her father the king. Sobekhotep III also portrayed his 'dear mother' Iuhetebu and her husband, whose titles reveal he had not been king himself. Nor had the queen mother's second husband, whose 'lack of titles probably indicates a middle or lower-class origin, and this must have been true of other royal families of that era: they were parvenus', part of the Thirteenth Dynasty's 'circulating succession'.

There was now a fine line between the royals and their courtiers, and as the two groups intermarried, as they had at the end of the Old Kingdom, the Thirteenth Dynasty princess Reniseneb married the mayor of Abydos. The happy couple resided at the mayor's palatial home in South Abydos, where one particular object reveals a most intimate aspect of daily life – a unique 'birth brick', painted with a mother holding her newborn baby, accompanied by Hathor and her fellow deities. As one of the bricks upon which a woman in labour would squat to give birth, 'physically creating a three-dimensional replica of the place of birth of the sun god', the act is referred to in ritual texts – 'Open for me. I am the builder who built the pylon for Hathor, who lifts up in order that she might give birth'.

The successful outcome of birth is represented by another unique find, a bronze statuette of the Thirteenth Dynasty princess Sobeknakht kneeling to breastfeed her small child. The same princess also appears on a stela set up at Edfu, as her dynasty clearly continued to embellish key religious centres with the appropriate imagery.

With statues of the gods and royals manufactured at the royal workshops, the career highlight of Horemkhauf, 'Chief Inspector of the priests of Horus' at Hierakonpolis, was being summoned north to the palace at Itj-tawy 'to fetch Horus of Hierakonpolis together with his mother Isis', whose new statues he 'took up in my arms from the Goods Office of Lisht in the presence of the king' to take back to his city and install in its temple of Horus.

High-quality statues were still being produced by Sobekhotep III's successor, Neferhotep I, who personally oversaw the installation of new cult figures of Osiris and his fellow gods at Abydos, and still received homage from Byblos and its Egyptianised ruler Yantin – 'Jonathan'.

Neferhotep I's name was also found at Buhen, although Nubia, and its rich resources, were now under the control of a confederation of local rulers whose king was based in Upper Nubia ('Kush'), at

Kerma, 'the earliest and largest city in Africa outside Egypt'. Kerma imported pottery from as far afield as the Mediterranean, producing its own local 'Kerma-ware' and items of silver and ivory 'predominantly Egyptian but much modified by African elements'. The huge tumulus tombs of Kerma's kings, complete with sacrificed retainers, also held loot seized from periodic raids up into Egypt. This included granite statues of the beautiful Sennuwy and her husband Hepdjefa, Sesostris I's powerful governor of Asyut, whose joint tomb was breached by the Nubians 300 years after their deaths, and their statues hauled off in triumph to take pride of place as eternal hostages in the tomb of a Nubian king.

Neferhotep I's own centre of power was Thebes, where he and his queen, Senebsen, keen to stress their Theban credentials, set up their statues at Karnak. So too Neferhotep I's brother and successor, Sobekhotep IV, who proudly states that he had actually been born in Thebes. And yet Karnak itself was increasingly becoming the place where the Thirteenth Dynasty came to seek divine intervention.

For although disastrously low Nile floods had hastened the end of the Old Kingdom, equally damaging high floods had been an ongoing problem since the 1770s BC. By the reign of Sobekhotep VIII, the floodwater covered so much of Karnak that it was causing damage, so 'his majesty proceeded to the hall of this temple, Hapi the Great [i.e. the flood] has been seen coming towards his majesty and the hall of this temple, full of water. His majesty was wading in it, together with the workmen', this contemporary report conjuring up an image of a less than majestic majesty.

As the Middle Kingdom 'slipped by stages from prosperity under a strong government into poverty and disorder', the clearest sign of the decline in central authority was the fact that Egypt had once again split into its traditional two lands, Upper and Lower Egypt.

For as the later king lists reveal, a second royal house, under Nehesy 'the Nubian', had set up their power base in the north at Xois (Sakha) in the Delta by around 1750 BC. This Fourteenth Dynasty co-existed with the Thirteenth, which was now based in Thebes, and although there is no evidence of military conflict between the two, Egypt was inevitably weakened by such political division.

And it wasn't long before this political divide would be fully exploited by Egypt's first foreign dynasty.

14

Divided and Conquered:

c. 1650–1550 BC

Although Thirteenth Dynasty Egypt had, apparently, been ruled by at least three monarchs of Palestinian origin, the Palestinian 'Aamu' ('Asiatics') within the Egyptian administration gradually took over government and, eventually, the northern half of the country, marking the beginning of a second Intermediate Period, when there was no single central authority.

The Palestinians' gradual rise to power had certainly been made easier by Egypt's slow fragmentation into its default position of the Two Lands, the Thirteenth Dynasty being now based in Thebes in the south while the co-existent Fourteenth Dynasty held power at Xois in the north.

But a third group of rulers is now known to have emerged between them, based at Abydos, where the recent discovery of the tomb of their previously-unknown ruler Useribra Senebkay provides 'the first material proof of a forgotten Abydos Dynasty, c.1650–1600 BC'.

At the same time, Egyptianised Palestinians living in the Eastern Delta had peacefully taken over the region from within under their leader Salitis, self-styled 'ruler of the uplands' or *heka-hasut*. Better known as the Hyksos in the later king list that numbers these Hyksos rulers as the Fifteenth and Sixteenth Dynasties, the same king list claimed that 'from the regions of the East invaders of obscure race marched in confidence of victory against our land. By main force they easily seized it without striking a blow', adding that they had then burned Egypt's cities, destroyed its temples and massacred or enslaved its people before installing their own ruler.

This vivid account was accepted as fact by early Egyptologists, who believed that a sudden invasion of rampaging Hyksos Palestinians had swept into Egypt in their newfangled war chariots around 1650 BC.

Yet the truth was far less dramatic, though no less destructive or indeed, at times, bloody.

The revision of Hyksos history followed the twentieth-century discovery of their city, Avaris, at Tell Daba in Egypt's north-east Delta. Originally part of the fortified border area between Egypt and Palestine, the region had become home to the 1,554 Asiatic prisoners of war resettled here by Amenemhat II, as well as the Palestinians already working for the Egyptian state as sailors, ships' carpenters, miners and soldiers. As the region continued to develop into a thriving trading centre, Palestinian donkey caravans regularly passed through, while waterborne traffic down the Pelusiac branch of the Nile brought in wine, olive oil and craftspeople from both Crete and Cyprus.

Avaris itself, already settled under Amenemhat III, soon became one of the largest, most cosmopolitan cities in the eastern Mediterranean. And when the royal capital Itj-tawy (Lisht) was abandoned around 1650 BC, Avaris took its place as the home of the new Fifteenth Dynasty of Hyksos kings.

Eventually covering an area of 4km², Avaris's nine-metre-thick fortified walls surrounded housing of Palestinian design. The Hyksos maintained their own funerary customs involving burying their dead close to home, a practice typical of northern burials from Predynastic times. Some even had house extensions built specifically for their dead, who were buried in the foetal position alongside distinctive grave goods, which in the case of deputy treasurer Aamu – 'the Asiatic' – consisted of his chisel-shaped battleaxe and dagger, his pottery and the donkeys he had used in trading expeditions, which were sacrificed and buried with him.

Others preferred Egyptian-style tombs, such as that provided for one nameless nobleman some identify with 'the Biblical Joseph'; his statue was dressed in a multicoloured robe, complemented by his red hair, which was dressed pudding-basin style. Another Egyptian-influenced tomb was built for Sobekemhat, 'Principal of Foreign Lands and Caravan Leader', who had been buried with his Syrian dagger and amethyst scarab, the combinations of Hyksos weapons, Egyptian jewellery and goldware from Crete familiar from other tombs found here.

As Avaris continued to develop trade links with Crete, Byblos, Ugarit and Aleppo, the names of Egypt's Hyksos kings were known as far afield as Knossos, in the Hittite capital Hattusha (Boğazkale in modern Turkey), in Baghdad and, in the case of Hyksos princess Tawa, as far west as Spain.

Within Egypt itself, the Hyksos rulers extended their power to Memphis and eventually as far south as Hermopolis, imposing border controls and taxes on all Nile-going traffic some forty kilometres further to the south at Meir. Their hold over northern Egypt was balanced by an alliance with the Nubian ruler of Kerma, which gave them access to Nubia's gold supplies as well as greater control over southern Egypt, where the old Thirteenth Dynasty, still based at Thebes, was 'keeping alive the embers of Egyptian independence'.

But the Thebans were effectively the filling in a sandwich, surrounded by the Hyksos to the north and their Nubian allies to the south. It was certainly a precarious existence at times, and as sporadic Nubian invasions swept north to seize loot, Thebes's ally Sobeknakht of el-Kab reported that 'Kush came, having stirred up the tribes of Wawat, the land of Punt and the Medjai', and claimed that he and his men had only been able to beat them back with the help of their local goddess Nekhbet, 'strong of heart against the Nubians', as the 'chief of the nomads fell through the blast of her flame'.

But as Egypt's heritage was being carted away by Nubian raiders in the south, similar depredations were taking place in the north, where the Hyksos were removing the ancient monuments across the Delta and Memphis for relocation to Avaris: at least four colossal sphinxes of Amenemhat III were now re-inscribed with the names of the Hyksos king Apophis.

The Egyptians would forever after vilify the Hyksos as brutish and uncultured, but they nonetheless adopted traditional Egyptian titles including 'Son of Ra', and used traditional hieroglyphic script on their own monuments. King Apophis even paid Egyptian scribes to copy out old texts, such as the Rhind Mathematical Papyrus. Originally entitled 'the accurate reckoning for inquiring into things, and the knowledge of all things, mysteries, all secrets', it is a series of mathematical problems featuring equations, fractions and algebra, used for everything from calculating the slope of a pyramid to working out how much grain a captive goose requires as opposed to a free-range bird. Apophis himself would even have been able to read the document, since he claimed to be one who 'reads faithfully all the difficult passages of the writings' as 'a scribe of Ra, taught by Thoth himself'.

For the Hyksos also upheld the cults of Egypt's gods, with Seth their particular favourite. He had been worshipped at Avaris since the Fourteenth-Dynasty ruler Nehesy had called himself 'beloved of Seth, Lord of Avaris', and Apophis 'made Seth his personal lord' and built him a new temple. The Hyksos identified Seth with their own storm god Baal and, with Baal's partner Astarte, 'Lady of Byblos', being simply another form of Hathor, both gained automatic admission into Egypt's highly flexible belief system.

Yet the Hyksos made the greatest impact on Egypt through their technical abilities, introducing advances in metalwork that featured the combined motifs of Syria, Crete and Egypt, and producing military hardware the Egyptians simply did not have – the composite bow, bronze body armour, helmets, smaller, lighter shields and the curved-bladed scimitar – the *khopesh*.

Most prominent of all, however, was the chariot and, to draw it, the horses first introduced by the Hyksos around the same time. Egypt's main forms of transport had previously been boats, donkeys and carrying chairs, so the chariot was revolutionary, not only transforming warfare across the ancient world but, as the status symbol par excellence, also producing a new, elite class of chariot-borne warrior known as the *maryannu* – the 'young heroes'.

Once these military innovations had been introduced into Egypt, it was only a matter of time before the Thebans began to copy the new technology, in what would soon become an ancient-world arms race.

Paying lip service to the Hyksos with whom they were forced to share their country, the Theban Thirteenth Dynasty, retrospectively 'rebranded' the Seventeenth Dynasty, began to portray themselves on the walls of Karnak in the company of their local gods, Amen, Montu and Waset – the personification of Thebes itself – who was now armed with her bow and her curved, Hyksos-style scimitar, as the Thebans bided their time.

For they certainly regarded themselves as the bastions of native tradition. Preserving ancient texts while formulating new ones, the Thebans combined the old Pyramid Texts and Coffin Texts on papyrus to create *The Book of Coming Forth by Day*, the so-called *Book of the Dead*, available to anyone who could afford six months' wages – or three donkeys – to pay for a copy.

The earliest known *Book of the Dead* was made for Montuhotep, wife of the local Theban leader Djehuty around 1650 BC. It was found in her tomb on Thebes's West Bank, where people had been buried for centuries, the majority on the wide plain and their local leaders above them in the rock-cut tombs of the Dra Abu el-Naga cliffs. This was where the later Theban king Sobekemsaf, and his queen Nubkhas, were laid to rest around 1570 BC decked out in crowns, diadems, 'pectorals and jewellery of gold' amounting to some 144 kilograms of bullion, at least according to one of the gang that robbed their tomb some 450 years later.

Sobekemsaf and Nubkhas were succeded by their son, Intef VI, who recognised the political value of maintaining good relations with his region's temples. So when the clergy at Koptos alerted him to the theft of a 'sacred relic' by one of their priests, Intef launched an official investigation, during which time the accused was cast out of the temple and his name removed from temple records.

Intef VI also emphasised Thebes's links with the ancient city of Abydos and its earliest royal necropolis, not only adding to its temple of Osiris but also building the god a new limestone temple nearer Thebes, on the desert road connecting Thebes to Abydos, high in the hills above the Valley of the Kings. Only discovered in 1992, and 'the only major monument uniquely attributable to the Seventeenth Dynasty', Intef VI's new Osiris temple demonstrated that the Thebans' traditional West Bank necropolis was 'considered to be an extension of the Abydene cemetery', which indeed is apparent from their two locations in relation to the pronounced Qena Bend of the Nile.

By doing this, Intef VI was proclaiming himself and his Seventeenth Dynasty as the true heirs of Egypt's earliest kings, so it is appropriate that his tomb at Dra Abu el-Naga was the first of Egypt's royal burials ever discovered in modern times, in 1827. Originally topped by a thirteen-metre-high pyramid, his intact, rock-cut tomb still contained his gold-covered coffin featuring the striped headcloth of kings, although his mummified body within, accompanied by his bows and arrows, was tragically destroyed in the search for valuables.

Another gilded coffin with kingly headcloth found in the Dra Abu el-Naga cemetery contained the body of a woman, buried with a female child, presumably her daughter. Both wore jewellery, the woman decked out in the earliest known 'gold of honour', a necklace of rows of gold beads, traditionally presented by the king, which 'represented an elevation in status when presented to a private person'. Yet, despite her now-anonymous status, she had obviously been a powerful individual, the analysis of her mummified remains also revealing that she had been embalmed in a most unusual manner.

Since the Hyksos controlled trade routes with Lebanon, only the tiniest amount of conifer resin had been available from a dwindling supply, the remaining ninety-nine per cent of her embalming material consisting of purified sheep fat. Almost certainly chosen for its links with the Theban god Amen, whose sacred creature was a ram, this specific post-mortem embalming treatment formed an invisible, yet definite, bond between the deceased woman and her local god.

As a bond only recently revealed by modern science, this has also demonstrated that the Theban elite were developing increasingly sophisticated embalming techniques, carefully selecting ingredients to make powerful, if subtle, statements of political intent. They were also looking back to their past for inspiration, reintroducing the use of natron salt in a solution last employed in the Pyramid Age. For not only did this give the most life-like results as part of the preservation process, the bodies' removal from the natron fluid dramatically re-enacted their rebirth into the next world – in much the same way as Egypt would soon be reborn under the Thebans' leadership.

So successful was this form of mummification that it preserved many members of this most extraordinary Theban family. And although Intef VI's remains were lost, as were those of his successor Tao, the body of Tao's formidable wife, Tetisheri, did survive.

Although not of royal stock – her father was 'the judge' Tjenna and her mother Neferu a housewife – Tetisheri would nonetheless be regarded by succeeding generations as the very founder of their royal line.

As mother of the next royal couple, siblings Seqenra and Ahhotep, 'the Great Ancestress' Tetisheri was worshipped long after her death as 'the bearer of the vital "*ka*" force' – the very soul of the Thebans, which was housed within her mummified body, discovered in 1881.

This had been expertly preserved in the natron solution in a process that now took a standard seventy days – the period for which the brightest star Sothis (Sirius) disappears from the night sky each year. Yet beneath her linen wrappings, the Great Ancestress was in fact a tiny old lady at the time of her death, whose sparse white hair had been interplaited with hair extensions. She also had pronounced maxillary prognathism – buck teeth – a distinctive family trait that would continue down the royal line for several centuries to come.

During their rule over the Theban region, her children Seqenra and Ahhotep produced at least five children, one son and four daughters, all of whom shared the same name – Ahmose, albeit with the addition of second names in the case of the girls. To cater for their expanding family and their expanding ambitions, Seqenra and Ahhotep built a new palace forty kilometres north of Thebes at Deir el-Ballas, a fortified complex with military outposts and an eight-metre-high lookout tower.

Such fortifications were certainly needed when skirmishes began between Thebes and Avaris. As described in the literary tale 'The Quarrel of Apophis and Seqenra', the Hyksos 'chieftain' sent his messenger to the 'prince of the southern city', Seqenra, to demand that he take control of Thebes's hippopotamus pool, whose creatures were making such a noise they kept him awake at night.

Since Thebes and Avaris are 400 miles apart, this curious tale has been subject to many interpretations, but is most likely a veiled allusion to the Theban royal women, whose powers were equated with the pugnacious hippo goddess Taweret. Usually portrayed rearing up on her hind legs and waving knives to protect her offspring, Taweret's image was placed on ceremonial axe-heads; Seqenra's sister-wife Ahhotep not only owned a collection of such weapons, but was also high priestess at Karnak – the so-called 'God's Wife of Amen'. Her role required her to bathe in the temple's sacred lake, possibly the 'hippo pool' referred to in the story, which was originally located in the part of Karnak associated with Taweret, Sekhmet and their fellow goddess Mut. Ahhotep's ritual duties included shooting her arrows at targets of Egypt's enemies and burning their wax effigies in her brazier. Little wonder Apophis felt distinctly ill at ease!

As the war of words between the Hyksos and Thebans escalated into open conflict, Seqenre was killed in violent circumstances as shown by his mummified body: his arms are still in the spasms of death, his lips still drawn back in a grimace and his hair still matted with the blood from the head wounds that killed him. The lack of any additional injuries to his arms and torso suggest that he had not been in a position to fight back, while his head wounds suggest he had either been assassinated in his sleep, killed while unconscious on the battlefield or terminated in a 'ceremonial execution at the hands of an enemy commander, following a Theban defeat'.

Forensic studies have shown the fatal head wounds were made by Hyksos-type blades, specifically a chisel-shaped axe-blow to the forehead revealing the 'typical dimensions of a Palestinian axe-head of the correct date'. A second axe-blow to his left cheek had fractured his jaw, a dagger had been thrust behind his ear and a mace driven down to shatter his cheekbone.

By the time Seqenre's troops had retrieved his battered body it had started to decompose, and when studied in the 1960s it still exuded a 'foul, oily smell', the classic odour of decomposition as the body fats continue to degrade even millennia after death.

Yet the violent fate of Seqenre was not unique, since sixteen severed right hands 'of extraordinary size and robustness' were recently discovered by archaeologists beneath the Hyksos throne room at Avaris. Quite possibly representing the fate of some of Seqenre's fellow Thebans, whose hands were severed as trophies, this soon became a means of counting enemy dead for the Egyptians themselves.

At Seqenre's death his children were still too young to govern, so their mother, Ahhotep, became regent, her powers expressed in texts set up at Karnak:

> 'Give praise to the Lady of the Land, Lady of the shores of the Northern Isles [i.e. the Aegean], her name exalted in every foreign land, the one who governs the multitudes, the king's wife, king's sister, king's daughter and gracious mother of the king, the wise one who cares for Egypt, who cares for its army and protects it, who cares for its fugitives, having gathered together its deserters, having pacified the south, having expelled those who defy her'.

In short, Ahhotep picked up the pieces and continued the fight, in recognition of which she received two sets of Egypt's highest of military decoration, the 'gold flies of valour'. Awarded for bravery in battle, and usually taking the form of small flies – the insect symbolised persistence – Ahhotep's had been supersized into nine-centimetre-long gold pendants, which she presumably wore in life, and which were still around her neck in death.

This was only part of her rich burial, found intact by local people in her tomb at Dra Abu el-Naga in 1859; her huge gilded coffin still contained her mummified body, which was tragically disposed of once it had been relieved of its heavy gold adornments.

Her gold flies had been accompanied by large gold bangles, again awarded for 'military valour', and usually in pairs, although Ahhotep had eight. Further gold bracelets, naming her son Ahmose, were made of precious stones and the earliest known glass in Egypt, while a broad collar of Aegean influence reflects Ahhotep's title 'Lady of the Shores of the Northern Isles' (of the Aegean Sea). Along with her gilded mirror and fan, Ahhotep had also been buried with an arsenal of weapons 'both ceremonial and functional', ranging from an archer's wrist-guard and staff to axes and daggers. One dagger, with a loop for attaching it to clothing, was 'Aegean in form and technique', its inlay of black *niello* portraying a Mycenaean-type lion hunt.

Although the weapons support the bellicose reputation of the Theban queen, and were nothing new in a land where women had been buried with arms for two thousand years, Ahhotep's achievements are still undermined by those who claim that the weapons and military awards were all the property of her male relatives.

One of these, Kamose 'the Brave' (c. 1555-1550 BC), perhaps another of Ahhotep's sons, took on both the Hyksos and their Nubian allies. As revealed in the detailed text from twin stelae later set up at Karnak, his advisors were apparently happy with the status quo, but Kamose was having none of it: 'I would like to know why I have this strength of mine when there is a chief in Avaris and another in Kush, and I sit here, bound to an Asiatic and a Nubian, each with his own slice of Egypt and dividing the land with me. No one can settle when despoiled by the taxes of the Asiatics. So I will grapple with him, so I can slit open his belly! My desire is to save Egypt and to smite the Asiatic!'

So he began by attacking Nubia, securing the old Buhen fort and installing his own man as viceroy of Nubian Kush – 'King's Son of Kush' – to counter the powerful ruler of Kerma further south. He then set out north with his fleet, launching attacks on the most southerly part of Hyksos-held territory and capturing a messenger heading south to Kush with a dispatch from the Hyksos king, Apophis, telling his Nubian ally to come north and help him defeat Kamose.

Undaunted, Kamose pressed on to the walls of Apophis's impenetrable fortress of Avaris, close enough to 'spy his women upon his roof, peering out of their windows toward the harbour, peeping down like little creatures in their holes, the women saying "He is swift!".'

Such a captive audience gave Kamose the perfect stage for some swaggering talk. He shouts out to Apophis: 'Look at me! I am here, successful! I shall not leave you or allow you to tread the fields even when I am gone! Does your heart fail, you vile Asiatic? Look! I'm drinking the wine of your vineyards which the Asiatics who I captured pressed for me. I've smashed up your rest-house, I've cut down your trees, forcing your women into my ships. I have seized your horses and haven't left a single plank of your hundreds of cedar ships which were filled with gold, lapis, silver, turquoise, bronze axes without number. I have confiscated all of it! I haven't left a thing in Avaris!'

Although Kamose failed to take Avaris itself, he secured much of the north before returning south to Thebes in triumph, disembarking at Karnak, where 'Amen grants the scimitar to Kamose, son of Amen'. And with the Hyksos' scimitar now firmly in his grip, together with their horses, such spoils of war allowed Kamose to build up his army for the final push to take back Egypt.

Ordering his staff to 'have everything My Majesty has done in war put upon a stela and have it set in Karnak forever and ever', the so-called Kamose stelae are fitting testament to a ruler whose short, yet dramatic, reign ended with his death around 1550 BC, and with it, the end of the Seventeenth Dynasty.

15

Dawn of the Golden Age:

c. 1550–1425 BC

The beginning of Egypt's Eighteenth Dynasty marked the beginning of the so-called New Kingdom and a true golden age.

Its first monarchs were Ahmose I (c.1550–1525 BC), 'Lord of the Two Lands' and 'Son of Ra', and his sister-wife Ahmose-Nefertari, 'Lady of the Two Lands', 'Daughter of Ra'. And since 'she was heir with her husband to her father Seqenre's holdings', she shared in the decision-making process.

This included plans to honour their joint grandmother Tetisheri with a cenotaph, Ahmose confiding that he 'desires to build for her a pyramid and chapel in the sacred land' of Abydos, part of the last royal pyramid complex to be built in Egypt.

Featuring a terraced temple in the desert cliffs, linked to the pyramid of Tetisheri by a kilometre-long causeway, this terminated with the couple's own fifty-metre-high cenotaph pyramid, whose surrounding complex featured scenes of tightly massed archers, horses, chariots and fallen Asiatics bearing the names of both King Apophis and the city of Avaris itself.

These images documented the last stages of the War of Independence and the siege of Avaris, and were dominated by the five-foot (1.5-metre) king, transformed here into 'superhuman Ahmose'. Seizing both victory and the red crown of the north, which he wears on his triumphal return to Thebes to give thanks to Amen at Karnak, Ahmose succeeded in pushing out the Hyksos in the eleventh year of Apophis's successor Khamudi.

According to an eyewitness account contained in the el-Kab tomb of one of his officers, 'Ahmose son of Ebana' (differentiated from his king by using his mother Ebana's name), officer Ahmose had accompanied his king to Avaris, fighting alongside him in close combat and cutting off the hands of those he killed to keep a tally of his dead. By this late stage of the campaign, the Egyptians had certainly gained the technical advantage, for their sharp weapons of alloyed bronze contrasted with the unalloyed copper available to the Hyksos, whose supplies of imported tin had apparently been cut off.

Following the Egyptian victory, the Hyksos were allowed to leave Egypt and, as evidence from excavations at Avaris supports this 'mass exodus', later historians also refer to the 'departure of the tribe of Shepherds from Egypt to Jerusalem'.

Yet it was no clean break, and King Ahmose's Egyptians pushed north, taking the Hyksos stronghold Sharuhen in Palestine after a lengthy siege. By around 1527 BC, the king had reached Naharin (also known as Mitanni) in Syria, establishing Egypt's border at the River Euphrates. His conquest of the eastern Mediterranean coast-line also led to an alliance with Egypt's long-standing trading part-ners Crete, the foremost sea power of the time.

But tackling the Hyksos was only part of Ahmose's task. For 'when his majesty had slain the nomads of Asia, he sailed south to destroy the Nubian bowmen and made great slaughter among them'. He visited Buhen and its new temple to Horus with his mother Ahhotep and sister-wife Ahmose-Nefertari, and even extended this southern border as far as the Sai Island fortress, where Ahmose's statue was placed permanently on guard.

Finally, with Egypt's boundaries both expanded and secured, Ahmose could focus his attentions on his motherland, starting with rebuilding projects at Memphis and Heliopolis. Having been razed to the ground, Avaris was also rebuilt and reclaimed as part of Egypt under the new name 'Perunefer', its defensive walls and huge grain silos sustaining a population of Egyptian troops, Nubian and Aegean mercenaries, Syrian and Minoan shipwrights and a stockpile of provisions for future campaigns.

Restoration work was also required down in Thebes, after a serious storm damaged Karnak. So Ahmose presented a rich haul of treasure, from vessels of gold and silver that passed down as heirlooms for 500 years, to new gold diadems and necklaces for the temple's statues.

Such regalia was also worn by the royal women; the monarchs' mother Ahhotep, now approaching her eighties, and her daughter

Ahmose-Nefertari, who inherited her mother's role as 'God's Wife of Amen'. This brought massive wealth and prestige, as did her appointment as 'second prophet of Amen' – deputy high priest.

When carrying out her duties at Karnak, Ahmose-Nefertari was, like all clergy, required to bathe in the temple's sacred lake and don pure linen robes. She then led the sacred processions with the king or his deputy, the high priest, the only ones allowed to enter the innermost shrines to give the gods their daily offerings. The role of God's Wife also involved the ritual burning of enemy images, the firing of arrows into ritual targets and the manual stimulation of Amen in her capacity as 'the Hand of God'. For Amen often displayed the same virility as Min, whose erect penis was regularly anointed with Min's favourite, honey-based 'sweet ointment'.

Ahmose-Nefertari's own fertility was impressive too. She had three daughters and at least two sons, one of whom was Amenhotep; his selection as royal heir elevated her own status to 'King's Mother', which, combined with her status as 'King's Daughter', 'King's Sister' and 'King's Wife', imbued her name with great power. Her cartouches were written at either side of those of her brother-husband Ahmose as if to protect it, and this idea was replicated in scenes where Ahmose-Nefertari protectively embraces her husband while her mirror image embraces their son.

When the battle-hardened, if slightly arthritic, King Ahmose died around 1525 BC, aged around thirty-five, his wife oversaw his burial in a rock-cut tomb at Dra Abu el-Naga. His curly hair was thickly coated in the same 'abundant layer' of conifer resin that had been applied to his body, a contemporary medical text even specifying 'the umbrella pine of Byblos'. The use of this deluxe preservative made a permanent statement that Egypt was once more in control of the regions that produced such a substance, with the king literally immersed in the essence of lands he now controlled.

With their son Amenhotep I (c.1525–1504 BC) still a young boy at his father's death, Ahmose-Nefertari ruled as regent and, even when her son was king, married to his sister as per family tradition, his mother remained his co-ruler, as she would for the rest of his reign.

Her power had long been established at Karnak on Thebes's East Bank, while on her personal estates on the West Bank she set up a training college for priestesses. Mother and son were also acknowledged as joint founders of the nearby village of Deir el-Medina, which housed those who built the royal tombs in the Valley of the Kings. The monarchs were more popular here than Amen and their statuettes were the focus of private worship in the houses as well as in the daily rites of the village temple, where the workers consulted them as oracles, asking 'Shall we get our rations?', 'Shall I burn it?', 'Will she get her place?' The villagers even honoured their beloved founders with an annual festival involving 'four solid days of drinking'.

Now the villagers' official role was to build the royal tombs, which were traditionally begun early in the reign to give sufficient time for completion. The advice given by scribe Ani 'of the palace of Queen Ahmose-Nefertari' was to start building a tomb when young – 'Establish your place in the desert as a place to conceal your body, make it your business, a thing of importance . . . Do it and you will be happy'. Since Amenhotep was still a small child at his accession, it is more than probable that his mother, the regent, gave the orders for work to begin on her son's tomb.

Yet in a departure from established practice, this may not have been located in the family plot at Dra Abu el-Naga, but was quite possibly built in the Valley of the Kings, which lay beyond. And the tomb she ordered was most likely the one now designated KV.39 (the thirty-ninth tomb to be discovered here). It is certainly the highest tomb in the valley, lying closest to the pyramid-shaped peak of el-Qurn, the home of Meretseger – 'She who loves silence' – the cobra goddess whose representatives are still very much alive in the form of the snakes that live here.

The tomb was finally excavated in the late twentieth century, when the lead archaeologist claimed it 'was the first to be built in the Valley of the Kings'. The royal architect 'Ineni may have been called to work on the tomb of Amenhotep I, a tomb not yet established with certainty but most likely KV.39', whose chambers were left plain in the style of royal tombs of this time, while its two burial chambers were quite possibly intended for Amenhotep I and either his mother or other family members.

Unlike previous royal tombs, many of which had already been robbed, the entrance to KV.39 was hidden away in an attempt to maintain its secrecy. With no chapels or places for offerings added beside the tomb to draw attention to it, mother and son were the first royals to have a separate funerary temple, built, not coincidentally, directly below the tomb in the bay of Deir el-Bahari, using bricks stamped with Ahmose-Nefertari's name.

The trusted Ineni was also ordered to design scenes at Karnak portraying the mother and son making offerings to Amen with her son and their Eleventh Dynasty Theban predecessors – who had also reunited their country. And, like them keen to demonstrate his military abilities, Amenhotep I led a campaign into Nubia, reinforcing Egypt's boundary at Sai Island in emulation of his father, adding his own statue beside his, before returning home laden with gold and tribute.

But then Amenhotep I died suddenly in his late twenties, his cause of death unknown; the official statement simply claimed that the king, 'having spent a life in happiness and the years in peace, went forth to heaven and joined with the *aten*', a term used since the Old Kingdom to mean circle, and by this time used to describe the sun's disc.

Since Ahmose-Nefertari's son had apparently left no heir, the next king was her son-in-law Tuthmosis (1504–1492 BC), and even though he had married her daughter, yet another Princess Ahmose, his cartouches were nonetheless twinned with those of the ever-present Ahmose-Nefertari, still the most important woman in Egypt.

When she finally passed away, approaching her seventies, it was reported that 'the God's Wife has flown up to heaven'. Her body was mummified in natron solution, and its five-foot two-inch (1.5m) linen-wrapped length placed in a coffin over twelve feet (four metres) long, to emphasise her exceptional status. She was quite possibly placed with her son in KV.39, in the second of the tomb's burial chambers; as, it seems, were some of the other women of their family, whose battered remains, found within, had the same characteristic buck teeth as the late queen.

Posthumously awarded the titles 'Mistress of the Sky', and 'Lady of the West', Ahmose-Nefertari, as 'a goddess of resurrection', was portrayed with the black or blue skin that were 'both colours of resurrection'. With her images on Karnak's walls as potent as the gods' cult statues, they were veiled in the manner of an icon, as revealed by their small surrounding peg holes. And as 'divine patroness of the Theban necropolis', she was the first deity named in the tomb-builders' official reports, and would be featured in the later wall scenes of over fifty Theban tombs.

As their dynasty continued to expand, Tuthmosis I had at least five children by minor wives and by his queen, Ahmose, who, uniquely, is shown pregnant with her eldest daughter. Naming her Hatsheput, meaning 'the foremost noble one', her father Tuthmosis I apparently also named her 'heiress of Horus', announcing before the court that 'she is my successor upon my throne', warning that 'he who does her homage shall live, he who speaks evil in blasphemy of her majesty shall die!'

As 'Egypt's greatest warrior king', Tuthmosis I spent much of his eleven-year reign consolidating the vast empire he'd inherited, both in Syria and in Nubia.

Following rebellion in Nubia early in his reign, the king had set sail south to take on the Kushite king near Kerma. Taking to the field 'furious like a leopard', he immediately killed the enemy king when 'his first arrow pierced the chest of that foe which remained in his fallen body'. And as Kerma was sacked and burned, Tuthmosis commemorated his victory with inscriptions on the new southern border at Tombos, just north of Kerma itself, boasting 'there is not a single survivor among them, the Nubian bowmen have fallen by the sword, gore from their mouths pours down in torrents, the pieces cut from them are too much for the carrion-eaters and their entrails drench their valleys'.

A telling description from a culture that routinely packaged up their own entrails so neatly for the afterlife, the appalling treatment meted out to enemies was much in evidence when the royal fleet sailed back north to Egypt. For 'that wretched Nubian bowman [killed by the king's first arrow] was hanged head downward at the prow of his majesty's ship', the hieroglyphic determinative in the account careful to show Tuthmosis's arrow, still lodged in the enemy king's chest, while his inverted, fly-covered corpse would have been a graphic warning to all who saw its sorry progress.

Launching a second Nubian campaign the following year, Tuthmosis I planned an uninterrupted river journey with a large entourage of soldiers, scribes and priests. So he ordered his Nubian viceroy to dredge the old canal through the First Cataract, for 'his Majesty commanded to dig this canal after he found it stopped up with stones so no ship sailed upon it'.

As the first Egyptian king to sail beyond Tombos, Tuthmosis sailed past Gebel Barkal – 'Pure Mountain' – a spectacular sandstone outcrop, almost a hundred metres high, that his priests identified as the mound of creation, and the primeval home of Theban Amen. Sailing on as far as Kurgus just before the Fifth Cataract, the king had his names inscribed across existing local images on the Hagr el-Merwa, a large rock 'probably of great spiritual significance to the indigenous population'. The inscription also reveals that the king had been accompanied on his epic trip by his wife Queen Ahmose, and apparently their daughter Princess Hatshepsut too, their female presence, as representatives of Hathor-Sekhmet, bringing their own powers of protection to this volatile region.

Another expedition by ship took Tuthmosis I north to Byblos, where a campaign further north not only consolidated Egypt's previous expansion, but exceeded it when the Egyptian forces crossed the Euphrates, its north–south flow so different from their own Nile that the Egyptians named it 'that reversed water which goes downstream in going upstream'.

Tuthmosis set up a stela on the far side of the Euphrates at Carchemish, marking the furthest extent of Egypt's power so far and, not coincidentally, at the crossroads of international trade, for all to see. Celebrating with an elephant hunt in the marshes of Niy, inland from Ugarit, the king rewarded his men, the elderly Ahmose Ebana still sufficiently sprightly to have captured a chariot and its driver, for which he was awarded the gold of valour for a seventh time. As the old soldier returned home in triumph with the army, he finally called it a day, admitting 'I have grown old, reached old age. Favoured as before and loved by my lord, I rest in my tomb'.

Tuthmosis I had not only secured a vast empire stretching from the Euphrates to Sudan, but also all the wealth that accompanied such expansion. So, creating suitably grand monuments to thank the gods for his victories, he also toured northern sites like Heliopolis and Memphis, and at Giza, where tourists already enjoyed 'a pleasure walk' to see its famous tombs, the king focused his attention on the Great Sphinx, an image of Khafra now rebranded Horemakhet – 'Horus in the Horizon', validating his own claim to have 'come from the Aten sun disc', which was now formally recognised as a god in its own right.

The royal quarters at Perunefer (formerly Avaris) were now expanded, perhaps to house a princess sent as part of the continuing Minoan alliance to marry Tuthmosis I. For now its walls were embellished by Minoan artists, brought in to apply the same fresco techniques used at Knossos and Thera, featuring fluid images of spirals, leopards and dogs in 'flying gallop' pose, together with long-haired acrobats leaping over bulls in a sport best known from Knossos, although found earlier in Egypt's Beni Hasan tomb scenes.

Most of Tuthmosis I's royal constructions, however, were focused on the family heartland, Thebes, where the king built a new palace beside Karnak and set his veteran architect Ineni to work on the temple itself. Creating two great pylon gateways flanked by cedarwood flagpoles flying the gods' pennants, reproduced in the hieroglyphic symbol for 'god', he also ordered statues of himself and Ahmose-Nefertari, a hypostyle hall of cedar columns and two twenty-metre-high granite obelisks weighing 140 tons, which Ineni had floated up from the Aswan quarries on purpose-built ships.

Busy Ineni was also ordered to construct the king a 'cliff tomb' (now assumed to be KV.20) on the West Bank, in the Valley of the Kings. In the place where Ineni seems previously to have overseen the burials of Amenhotep I and Ahmose-Nefertari, the new tomb was completed with 'no-one seeing, no-one hearing', since security for the royal burial site remained tight.

And the tomb would soon be needed, as Tuthmosis I died around 1492 BC, Ineni reporting that 'the king rested from life, going forth to heaven, having completed his years in gladness of heart'.

Since his two elder sons had predeceased him, the throne passed to his remaining son, Tuthmosis II (c.1492-1479 BC) and the late king's designated heir, his eldest daughter Hatshepsut. And whereas the new king was born to a minor wife, Hatshepsut was a direct descendant of the 'great ancestress' Tetisheri and Ahmose-Nefertari, whose 'God's Wife' title she had inherited.

Following tradition, Tuthmosis II and Hatshepsut married and had a child, Neferura, although the king, like his father, also produced a son by a minor wife. Also like his father he took action against the Nubians, in response to reports of unrest sending an expedition south to put all male inhabitants of 'vile Kush' to the sword, except a single royal prince who was brought back to Egypt as the first known royal hostage.

The royal family also began plans for their burials at Thebes, where two rock-cut tombs were begun for Hatshepsut and Neferura high in the cliffs in a remote *wadi* south of Deir el-Bahari.

But all this was interrupted when the 'frail' second Tuthmosis died after only a brief reign. His son Tuthmosis III (1479–1425 BC) was still a child, so Hatshepsut became regent. Although she was not 'king's mother', only his stepmother, she was nonetheless the daughter, sister and wife of a king, and 'God's Wife' priestess, like her grandmother Ahmose-Nefertari. She would have been fully aware that her grandmother had also held the titles 'Daughter of Ra' and 'Lady of the Two Lands'.

Hatshepsut must also have known that the epithet 'King of Upper and Lower Egypt' was carved into the granite at Giza for Khentkawes I, and just as Khentkawes II was similarly named at Abusir, official king lists revealed that Sobeknefru too had held full royal titles as 'Horus', 'Lady of the Two Lands, King of Upper and Lower Egypt, and Daughter of Ra'. For Hatshepsut was certainly inspired by Sobeknefru and her father Amenemhat III, whose 300-year-old inscriptions in the Fayum were among those copied verbatim for Hatshepsut.

The copies were probably made by Hatshepsut's archivist Neferkhewet, or her chief steward, Senmut of Armant, who worked on Hatshepsut's titles and even devised new ways of writing them as cryptograms, which he describes as 'images I have made from the devising of my own heart and from my own labour – they have not been found in the writing of the ancestors'.

And with these same ancestral writings having 'decided that women might hold the kingly office' as early as the Second Dynasty, Hatshepsut (c.1473–1458 BC), after seven years as regent, followed in the footsteps of her kingly female predecessors with a coronation on New Year's Day, when she received the crowns of Upper and Lower Egypt, the sceptres, the tie-on bull's tail and the tie-on false beard, as worn by Khentkawes I a thousand years before.

But since such women are usually omitted from accounts of Egypt's history, Hatshepsut is often cited as an exception that proves the rule. For according to one historian, this was 'a wholly new departure for a female to pose and dress as a man . . . flaunting a royal titulary', while another claimed that 'the conventions of the court were all warped and distorted to suit the rule of a woman'. In fact, Hatshepsut has been described as everything from 'this vain, ambitious and unscrupulous woman' to a 'wicked' and 'detested stepmother'.

Although she has more recently been somewhat rehabilitated as 'a resolute and self-controlled woman' and a veritable 'Joan of Arc', the question 'will Hatshepsut become a feminist icon?' is surely a century too late. For her achievements were fully appreciated by the suffragettes, particularly by one late-nineteenth-century vice-president of the Women's Suffrage League, who praised the 'genius and energy of this extraordinary woman', following her lead to create two of the world's leading Egyptological institutions, the Egypt Exploration Society and the UK's first chair in Egyptology at University College London.

But regardless of her mixed press, 'it is generally agreed that, by year 7 of Tuthmosis III, Hatshepsut had adopted her ultimate public guise: she would henceforth be shown as a male king – wearing crowns and clothing typical of male pharaohs and performing all the rituals required of them – but nonetheless be consistently referred to in the accompanying texts by feminine pronouns' – all appropriate for a female king who still fully acknowledged her male co-ruler.

Holding full royal titles, Hatshepsut was 'King of Upper and Lower Egypt', Maatkare ('Maat is the soul of Ra'); 'Daughter of Ra', Khnemet-Amen ('Joined with Amen'); 'the Horus', Weseretkau ('Mighty of souls'); 'She of the Two Ladies', Wadjrenput ('fresh in years'); 'the Golden Horus', Netjeretkhau ('divine of appearances'). And with the feminine ending added to make the son a daughter, the lord a lady and the word 'Majesty' feminine, her advisors coined another useful title – 'the one from the palace' or 'great house', literally *per-aa* and now pronounced 'pharaoh'.

And once crowned pharaoh, she remained pharaoh even when her stepson Tuthmosis III came of age and they ruled together.

During the co-regency, Tuthmosis III led two campaigns through Palestine, and was such an accomplished warrior that 'when he shoots at a copper target, all wood is splintered like a papyrus reed'; and even with 'a target of copper three digits thick, when he had shot his arrow there, it protruded for three palms behind it'.

Hatshepsut too sent 'at least one military expedition into Syria-Palestine', and, presumably inspired by her father, whom she had apparently accompanied all the way to Kurgus, she again went south to Nubia. So despite claims that her reign was 'barren of any military enterprise except an unimportant raid into Nubia', there were in fact up to four such campaigns, her officials stating that she had led her troops against the enemy when 'slaughter was made among them', having 'seized every land with her strong arm', to be known as 'She who will be a Conqueror, flaming against her enemies'.

But as pharaoh, Hatshepsut could no longer function as the necessarily female God's Wife priestess, so handed this hereditary position to her daughter Neferura. She was educated by Senmut, who called himself Neferura's 'father-tutor', and claimed 'I nurtured the king's daughter, I was given to her because of my effectiveness on behalf of the king', her mother. In almost half his statues, Senmut is portrayed with the young Neferura on his lap and eventually, as her chief steward, he accompanied the princess to the Hathor temple of Sinai, where her mother sent expeditions.

Hatshepsut continued to trade with Byblos, exchanging their cedars for Egyptian papyrus, while Egypt's alliance with Crete also brought Minoan tribute into the Nile Valley. Brought by long-haired Cretans in their colourful kilts, as first portrayed in Senmut's tomb, the temple at his hometown, Armant, received Minoan perfume vessels decorated in 'Marine Style', with shells, seaweed and octopuses.

But Crete's prosperity was suddenly destroyed following an

enormous volcanic explosion on Thera, the resulting tsunami destroying Crete's harbours and sweeping around the eastern Mediterranean coastline of Syria, Palestine and Egypt. Analysis of 'many pieces of pumice' discovered in the Eighteenth-Dynasty levels of the Delta reveals that it came from Thera, the cloud of black ash from the eruption covering so much of the ancient world that Egyptian texts would later claim that 'for nine days none could see the face of their fellow'.

Another source of exotic goods was Punt, 'God's Land', located south down the Red Sea and usually assumed to have been what is now Somalia. Yet the 2005 discovery of an Eighteenth-Dynasty Egyptian trading vessel with a cargo from Punt included pottery from both sides of the narrow Straits of Mandeb, which includes both modern Somalia and western Yemen. And since Yemen was home to the same resin-producing shrubs as Somalia, and its terraced temples, hieroglyph-embossed seals and native mummy-making culture all reflect Egyptian influence, it may be that the Egyptians regarded Punt as a widespread region covering both sides of the Red Sea.

It was in Punt that Hatshepsut's expedition traded 'every good thing from the court' in exchange for myrrh, both its resin and the resin-producing shrubs, since Hatshepsut claimed that Amen 'commanded me to plant the trees of God's Land beside his temple in Thebes'. So with much effort, the shrubs were placed in pots and manoeuvred on to the Egyptian ships, with warnings to 'watch out for your feet people! The load is very heavy!'

Their efforts were somewhat hampered by an apparent lack of roots, perhaps the Puntites' attempt to safeguard their lucrative trade, since the Egyptians used huge quantities of their myrrh. Its oil was so favoured by Hatshepsut that the Puntites hailed her as the 'Female Sun who shines like the Aten', appearing with 'the best of myrrh on all her limbs, her skin is gilded, shining as do the stars before the whole land'. Although the use of myrrh was regarded as a form of ritual protection, its protective qualities were a reality; myrrh has been proven to destroy the bacteria *Staphylococcus aureus* and *Bacillus subtilis*, and was appreciated as 'medication' in medical papyri of the time.

Yet most of the myrrh was burned as incense, during noonday rites to connect with the gods, chief among whom was now Hatshepsut's divine 'father', Amen.

The god had certainly come a long way from his supporting role as one of eight creator gods; as patron deity of Thebes, the city's own rise to power had elevated both Amen and his cult temple at Karnak. The temple was now endowed with the increasing wealth of foreign campaigns, which gave great political power to its clergy, and to the female king who had their full support.

As a way of gaining the same support from the northern priest-hood of Ra, both deities were combined to produce the supergod Amen-Ra. He was a deity loved by all; the workman Nebra claimed that 'when I call out to you in distress you come and rescue me. You are Amen-Ra, Lord of Thebes, who comes at the voice of the poor'.

Hatshepsut's own devotion to the god was expressed by her kingly name Khnemet-Amen – 'Joined with Amen' – and her Karnak palace named 'I-am-not-far-from-him'. In fact, Hatshepsut's plans to embellish Karnak were so all-consuming, she claims, 'I did not sleep because of his temple' where she previously served him as 'God's Wife'.

Yet she was also his child, through a piece of political spin that claimed that Amen-Ra had impregnated Queen Ahmes. Having 'found her as she slept in the beauty of her palace, she awoke at the fragrance of the god and he went toward her and lusted after her. He gave her his heart and his love passed through her body. She exclaimed "How splendid it is to see you, you have united me with your favour and your dew is through all my limbs!" And the god did all that he desired with her'.

With their fingers touching in the accompanying temple wall scenes to mark the moment of conception, Hatshepsut was born nine months later, and was regarded as Amen-Ra's daughter 'in very truth'. The ancient term 'Amen's daughter' or '*Amen sat*' in its Greek form '*Amensis*' was the name by which Hatshepsut was still known 1,200 years later.

This meant that Amen-Ra's goddess consort Mut was Hatshepsut's divine mother, so at Karnak the king commissioned 'a monument for her mother Mut, making for her a columned porch of drunkenness anew', since inebriation was a traditional way of communing with the gods. Hatshepsut's 'Chief of All Works', Senmut, was then ordered to link Mut's complex to that of Amen with a pylon gateway, flanked by seated colossi of his female king.

Having 'sat in my palace and thought of my maker' Amen-Ra, Hatshepsut was also inspired to commission a pair of obelisks, whose thirty-metre-high tips, covered in gold, could be seen on both sides of the river, 'illuminating the Two Lands like the Aten' sun god. And her other carefully considered Karnak structure was her 'Red Chapel', whose red quartzite wall scenes, portraying the rites of kingship, featured her centre stage, accompanied by her young male consort Tuthmosis III, and Neferura, carrying out her duties as God's Wife before the gods' statues.

The chapel was essentially a sacred garage, housing the barques on which the statues of Amen, Mut and their fellow gods were carried in procession.

For Karnak lay at the heart of Hatshepsut's plans for an enormous processional way, along which the gods' enthroned statues could be transported at annual ceremonies. This 'Gathering of the Thrones', or 'Ta-ipet-sut, was pronounced in Greek 'Thebes'.

This processional route would link Karnak to a new shrine at Luxor, the venue for the annual Opet festival designed to reinvigorate both gods and royals. The Luxor shrine was then paralleled by a similar structure at Medinet Habu on the West Bank, where the gods' statues travelled over the river from Karnak at a second annual event, the 'Beautiful Festival of the Valley'. The statues were accompanied by the Theban people, who camped out at the tombs of their loved ones and threw parties. The deceased souls, hearing the lively activities above, were said to come 'back up into the world to see the rituals in the west before going back at their pleasure'.

The festival was dedicated to both Amen-Ra and Hathor, with the East Bank the domain of the god while the West Bank belonged to the goddess, whose 'most sacred of sacred places', 'Djeser-djeseru', now known as Deir el-Bahari, was the site of Hatshepsut's funerary temple, built, like almost everything else, by Senmut.

Aligned with Karnak, the site was already home to the temple of Hatshepsut's grandmother Ahmose-Nefertari, the funerary complex of the great Montuhotep II and the subterranean tomb of his sister-wife, Queen Nefru, which was already such a tourist attraction that Senmut left an access tunnel as part of the new temple he was building above. But most important of all was the fact that directly through the cliffs lay the tomb of Hatshepsut's father Tuthmosis I in the Valley of the Kings (KV.20), where Hatshepsut too wanted to be buried; so she abandoned the existing queen's tomb and greatly expanded her father's for their joint interment.

With her builders equally active on both sides of the cliffs, her temple soon dwarfed the smaller complex of Montuhotep II beside it.

Approached by a processional way flanked by multiple sphinxes, her temple's façade was a cascade of colonnades whose multiple Doric columns, pre-dating the supposed invention of this style in seventh-century-BC Greece, were fronted by colossal figures of Hatshepsut as Osiris.

Beyond lay an open-air altar to the sun god, whose presence was reflected in the gold and silver floors. But the temple's uppermost shrine, cut into the cliffs, was by contrast a place of shadow, where Amen-Ra's barque came from Karnak on its annual visit, spending the night surrounded by candles and the bouquets that would later be distributed to the faithful to offer their dead relatives.

Hatshepsut chose to adorn the walls of her temple with key events from her reign, from her father Tuthmosis I declaring her his heir to father and daughter depicted as sphinxes trampling their enemies. There was also her coronation, her expedition to Punt and her divine conception and birth, in which the minuscule Hatshepsut sits in the palm of her divine father Amen-Ra.

Yet perhaps the most intriguing images are those of the temple's creator, Senmut, hidden away within the niches of the temple's chapels almost in the manner of a signature. Senmut, even more lavishly rewarded than fellow courtier, Ineni, who claimed 'her majesty praised me and filled my house with silver and gold and every good thing of the palace', was provided with two tombs; one high in the hills above the temple, in which his sarcophagus was found, and a second, presumably later one, begun beneath the floor of the temple's great court.

With wealth to spare, the unmarried Senmut certainly spoiled his widowed mother Hatnefer, whose mummified body, found in her gold-faced coffin, was that of a pampered old lady. Her fine hair had been filled out with hundreds of plaited extensions, and rings adorned fingers whose nails were coloured red with henna, a fashion copying the king, whose own nails, coloured a fetching combination of red and black, symbolically placed the two halves of Egypt, 'Red Land, Black Land', at her fingertips.

Yet Hatnefer was not alone in her tomb. Her late husband Ramose, their two daughters and *their* children, who had all died before Senmut's rise to power, were now exhumed, rewrapped and reinterred with Hatnefer, close to Senmut's first tomb, as was Senmut's horse, a real status symbol comparable with a modern sports car.

Senmut had certainly deserved his luxuries; the temple he created was simply magnificent. In surroundings created for Hathor's enjoyment, pools of lotus and papyrus were surrounded by groves of persea trees, whose roots are still visible today. A separate chapel for the goddess featured scenes from Hatshepsut's childhood, images of her soldiers, both marching and dancing, and the earliest portrayal of the game-like rite 'Hitting the Ball for Hathor', in which co-ruler Tuthmosis III holds a bat to hit balls, presumably made of clay, which, like curse-figurines, were designed to be hit and destroyed in the earliest version of clay-pigeon shooting.

Hatshepsut's Hathor chapel emphasised the goddess's role not only as a protector, but also as a source of inexhaustible fertility. People came as close to it as possible to pray in the hope of conceiving. They left offerings of wooden phalli, baby clothes and model ears to help the deity 'listen to the petitions of every young girl who trusts in Hathor'. One inscription, addressed to 'noble ladies as well as poor girls, all women who come here at any time', was followed by a pledge that Hathor would help them achieve 'happiness, a child, and a good husband'.

But Hatshepsut by no means focused solely on Thebes; she was active up and down the Nile Valley and inaugurated numerous building projects. On the island of Sai she added her own statue to those of her predecessors, and at Buhen rebuilt Horus's temple with the help of her official Amenemhat, an Egyptianised Nubian. For during her reign 'the Egyptianisation of the Kushite elite in Wawat was rapid', its local leaders 'adopting Egyptian names, working with the vice-regal administration and being buried in Egyptian style tombs'.

Further north she embellished existing buildings at Faras, Qasr Ibrim and Quban, Elephantine, Kom Ombo, el-Kab, Hierakonpolis and Armant. Obtaining alabaster from the quarries of Hatnub for more sphinxes at Memphis, she rebuilt the temples at Meir for Hathor, at Hermpolis for Thoth, and ordered her treasury overseer, Djehuty, to create a rock-cut temple in the Beni Hasan cliffs above 'the Valley of the Knife'. This was a region sacred to the feline deity Pakhet – 'the Scratcher' – who wandered the desert looking for prey but, when pacified, became a protector of motherhood. So Hatshepsut and Neferura honoured Pakhet with a grotto-like temple (*speos*), known by its later Greek name as the *Speos Artemidos*, its façade's inscriptions describing Hatshepsut's mass restoration programme of temples, which had fallen into ruin under the Hyksos some eighty years before:

'The temple of Hathor, Mistress of Cusae [Meir] had begun to fall into ruins, and the earth had swallowed up its august sanctuary so that children played on it. No festival processions took place. So I had it rebuilt and adorned, and had Hathor's statue overlaid in gold in order that she protect the city. I created the temple of Pakhet the Great, its doors of acacia wood fitted with bronze' among a long list of other temples so embellished.

Then Hatshepsut speaks directly: 'Hear me, all you people. I have done all this by the plan in my heart . . . I restored what was ruined, and raised up what had been dismembered since the Asiatics were in the midst of Avaris in the northland, overthrowing what had been created'.

Although her claim was dismissed as 'exaggerated and does scant justice to the merits of her predecessor' by the same scholar who added that the words of her co-ruler Tuthmosis III 'can be accepted with considerable confidence', Hatshepsut had anticipated such scepticism. For she announces to 'all those who see my monuments in future years, beware lest you say "I know not how this has been done", nor shall he who hears of it say it was a boast, but rather "how like her this is, how worthy of her father".'

And recent research has certainly validated Hatshepsut's claims, since 'there is no record of 18th dynasty kings building in Middle Egypt before Hatshepsut', whose monuments reflect her 'preoccupation with a vast project to rebuild Egypt'.

Yet for all her innovations, she was also drawing on the past, and in particular the achievements of Amenemhet III and his own powerful daughter Neferuptah, with whom he had planned to be buried. For it is no coincidence that Neferuptah's sarcophagus inscriptions were added verbatim to Hatshepsut's sarcophagus, placed within the tomb of her father Tuthmosis I (KV.20), to 'be eternal like an undying star', as she says herself, rather poetically.

After more than two decades as pharaoh, Hatshepsut died on the tenth day of the sixth month of her twenty-second regnal year – around 1458 BC. Mummified and laid to rest with her father in accordance with her wishes, she was interred by her sixteen-year-old stepson, nephew and co-ruler Tuthmosis III, who completed her monuments and retained many of her craftsmen, meaning that his sculpted portraits, with their somewhat prominent nose, can be hard to distinguish from those of Hatshepsut.

Yet he was finally sole pharaoh, his prime minister, Rekhmire, announcing that 'I saw his person in his true form, as Ra, Lord of Heaven when he rises, the Aten when he reveals himself'. The king had two 'Great Royal Wives'; the first named Meryetre-Hatshepsut, not of the direct royal line herself, was the mother of the royal heir Amenhotep, while the second 'Great Royal Wife', Satiah, was the daughter of a royal nurse. And with further minor wives and children all requiring suitably regal accommodation, a new palace was built at Miwer (Gurob) in the Fayum, a region the royals had long used as a country retreat.

Finally able to step out of his predecessor's long shadow, the third Tuthmosis had not only inherited the Ahmose family's buck teeth but also their short stature. Yet 'this Napoleonic little man' continued to consolidate Egypt's holdings in Syria-Palestine with no fewer than seventeen campaigns over twenty years.

These began with news that the ruler of Kadesh in Syria was holding a summit meeting with his fellow Levantine leaders, who included the ruler of the old Hyksos stronghold Sharuhen. Tuthmosis

III knew that 'though it had been many years since the Hyksos were pillaging, there had come to be troops who were there in the town of Sharuhen, and from Yaradja to the ends of the earth they had started to defy his majesty'.

So he set out on 'the first campaign of force' around the spring of 1458 BC. After taking Gaza, another three weeks' march brought him to Megiddo, the Biblical Armageddon, where the coalition leaders were waiting for him. As the pharaoh took to the field in his golden chariot, engaging the enemy 'like a terrible lion', their champions soon 'lay like fishes on the ground'. And as the rest retreated into the town, shutting its gates, their leaders were left outside until 'the people hauled them up, pulling them by their clothing'. Although Megiddo then withstood a seven-month seige, the pharaoh finally took the town and its wealth, forcing the leaders within to break up their anti-Egyptian coalition, go back to their own regions and send him tribute.

Keeping the king's diary, scribe Tjennuny states 'I recorded the victories which he won in every land, putting them into writing according to the facts'. And with 'all his majesty did to the enemy recorded day by day on a roll of leather stored in the temple of Amen to this very day', the vast wealth he seized is clearly recorded. That from Megiddo alone is listed as:

'2,500 people including 3 chiefs, 3 charioteers, various women, 87 children and 1,796 male and female servants; 340 prisoners of war; gems, gold, much raw silver; statues of gold, silver, ebony and lapis; much clothing; drinking vessels and 2 great cauldrons; beds and chairs in ivory, gold and wood, plus footstools; 924 chariots, including 2 wrought in gold; 200 suits of armour plus 2 bronze suits of the chiefs of Megiddo and Kadesh; 502 bows; 7 wood and silver poles from the tent of the ruler of Kadesh; staves with human heads; 2,041 mares, 191 foals, 6 stallions; 1,929 cattle; 2,000 goats; 20,500 sheep'.

But the treasures of conquered enemies could also include their most precious possessions: their children. Brought to Egypt as hostages to be educated in the army, in the clergy or in the palaces if deemed 'suitable for wielding sun shades', many were then returned home as Egyptianised client rulers, to govern their home regions on Egypt's behalf.

Less privileged prisoners brought to Egypt were redeployed as 'mercenaries, domestics, quarry workers, artisan and builders', often adopting Egyptian names and taking Egyptian spouses. The royal barber Sabastet, who had fought alongside his king, had taken a Syrian prisoner whom he renamed Iuwyamen, the two men developing such a bond that Sabastet allowed the Syrian to marry his niece, and announced that 'she shall have a share in my inheritance'.

Most marriages, however, involved Syrian women, daughters of local rulers, like Menhet, Menwi and Merti (basically 'Martha'), who all became minor royal wives. When their joint tomb in Thebes was found intact by locals in 1916, periodic flooding had destroyed all trace of the women themselves, but left behind their spectacular jewellery – jewelled head-covers and diadems, collars of gold amulets, gold earrings, bangles, bracelets, belts and finger-rings set with swivelling bezels carved with the names of Tuthmosis III and his predecessor Hatshepsut. There were also jars of perfumes, eye-paint and face cream, and an array of silver and gold-rimmed vessels, including early glass, developed in Mitanni and imported into Egypt, where royal craftsmen would soon elevate it into a breathtaking art form.

Similarly lavish treasures were also awarded the 'Overseer of Northern Foreign Lands', Djehuti, including his bronze dagger, his gold bracelets, rings, perfume vessels, and silver and gold bowls inscribed 'given as a sign of favour by the king to the companion of the king in all foreign lands and on the islands in the middle of the sea, governor of the foreign lands, commander of the army, praised by the king, Djehuti'.

These were all found in 1824 with Djehuti's gold-covered mummy in his tomb at Sakkara. He had served as Tuthmosis III's most outstanding general, whose brilliant military strategies were best demonstrated in his siege of Joppa (Jaffa) on the Palestinian coast.

Having learned that the prince of Joppa wished to see 'the great mace of King Tuthmosis', Djehuti had invited him to his camp outside the town, where he suddenly pulled out the mace, shouting, 'Look at me, Prince of Joppa! This is the mace of King Tuthmosis the fierce lion, son of Sekhmet, and Amen his father has given him strength to wield it'. Then he used it himself, to 'smite the forehead of the Prince of Joppa, and he fell stretched out before him'. Djehuti then put the rest of his plan into action. He hid 200 of his soldiers, Ali-Baba-style, inside baskets, which he sent into Joppa on donkey-back with the claim that they contained tribute. The folk of Joppa, clearly as gullible as their prince, took in the baskets, from which the Egyptian troops emerged to capture their town, anticipating the Greek tale of the Trojan Horse by several centuries.

Around 1451 BC, Tuthmosis III transported his army by sea to Byblos, then took the key Syrian city of Kadesh, returning to the region four years later to engage the powerful yet 'vile' Mitanni. Forcing them back over the Euphrates 'like a herd of mountain goats', he followed them on prefabricated cedar boats, setting up two stelae on the river's eastern bank beside that of his grandfather Tuthmosis I to mark the extent of his conquest. Again like his grandfather, he took part in an elephant hunt in Niy, where his officer Amenemheb was chased by one of the animals, killing it and cutting off its trunk, which was described as its 'hand'.

In recognition of his victory over the Mitanni, the pharaoh received rich gifts from Babylon, from the Hittites and from 'Tanaju', a region including Mycenae, whose envoys presented him with a Minoan-style silver jug and cups of iron – a great rarity in the Bronze Age.

As Tuthmosis III continued his campaigns around Palestine and the Levant, his final campaign took place around 1438 BC in Syria, where he reconquered 'wretched Naharin', the Mitannian-backed region north of Kadesh. Although the Egyptian cavalry were briefly disrupted when the prince of Kadesh sent out a mare to distract the stallions, the horse was caught by Amenemheb, the elephant-slayer, who killed it too and presented its tail to the king.

Such focus on the Near East inevitably meant the pharaoh was less active in Nubia. But he did quell one rebellion, and 'by shooting in the southern land of Taseti', he even captured a live rhinoceros, a prize of such magnitude that it was immortalised in temple scenes back at Armant, where its impressive dimensions were added in a caption beneath. Certainly such exploits made a point, as the tribute sent from Upper and Lower Nubia – Kush and Wawat – included a staggering 794 kilograms of gold over only three years.

With Tuthmosis III's southern boundary Gebel Barkal, boasting a fort named 'Slaughter-of-the-Foreigners' and a temple of Amen and

Mut, Egyptian forts and temples stamped the royal presence all along the Nile up into Egypt. And here the temples received much of the bounty the king obtained from his campaigns and from his own expeditions to Punt. As well as presenting cinnamon perfumes to Min of Koptos, whose temple lay at the start of the desert route to the Red Sea, and ultimately to Punt itself, the king distributed similarly exotic gifts to the Theban people, who sang 'there's perfume of sweet moringa oil! Unguent of myrrh!'

Yet most of the wealth ended up in the city's Karnak temple, since Tuthmosis III credited his victories to Amen-Ra. Accompanying images portrayed the pharaoh as a supersized action man, smiting the massed chiefs of Syria-Palestine with a single blow, while the treasure he took from them was all listed on the temple walls, from the gold used as inlay for the gods' figures to the 1,588 prisoners of war added to the temple personnel. For Karnak had become a mini-city, with its support staff of weavers, artists, butchers and bakers, brewers, florists and perfume-makers – there was even an 'overseer of the wigmakers of Amen of Karnak'.

The temple's gardens were 'planted with every pleasant tree in order to offer vegetables for the divine offerings every day', including the exotic flora and fauna the king brought back from Syria. Portrayed on the walls of Karnak's 'Botanical Gardens' chamber, this included the curious bird that 'lays eggs every day' – the earliest known reference to a chicken. But not only did the garden emphasise Amen's power over all foreign lands, established through the efforts of his son the king, the pharaoh's new-found interest in botany also allowed him to outdo his female predecessor's garden for Amen with its Punt-sourced myrrh shrubs.

Again outdoing Hatshepsut's efforts, the third Tuthmosis erected numerous obelisks, from a pair he set up at Heliopolis to the five he created for Karnak. Building a new sacred lake as the place for ritual ablutions, he also commissioned two new buildings: a festival hall with stone columns in the form of tent supports, reflecting the fact that he had spent much of his life under canvas, and a 'Chamber of Royal Ancestors', whose walls record sixty-one monarchs, from Djoser to Tuthmosis himself.

The next in line for the throne was Tuthmosis's eighteen-year-old son, Amenhotep II (c.1427–1400 BC), who was made co-ruler with the blessing of Amen's priests, both kings adopting Amen's trademark curling rams' horns on their crowns as marks of divine approval. At the same time, Tuthmosis III's former co-ruler, Hatshepsut, began to disappear. Mentioned nowhere in Tuthmosis's ancestral chamber – which does, on the other hand, mention the previous female king Sobeknefru – Hatshepsut's reign was systematically erased from official records in the south.

Since the selective removal of Hatshepsut's names and images occurred twenty-five years after her death, it is clear that this was not an act of random revenge. For her images as a queen were left intact, the targeted erasure focusing only on her time as king. Her names were re-carved as those of her father or brother; this rewriting of history was made easier by the fact that Hatshepsut's regnal years had been shared with Tuthmosis III, who now wanted posterity to see his reign as entirely his – he wanted his years back.

He was probably 'driven by concerns related to the royal succession and ceased once Amenhotep II was securely enthroned'. For both Tuthmosis III and his son came from a minor line of minor wives, whereas Hatshepsut and her relatives represented the main Eighteenth Dynasty. So by removing all trace of her as a king, Tuthmosis III 'disposed of a legitimate alternative to the Tuthmoside line and facilitated his son's succession'.

So Hatshepsut's statues were toppled and her images and names chiselled out, both at Karnak and across the river at Deir el-Bahari, where Tuthmosis III built his own small temple dedicated to Hathor. This was purposefully located right between those of Hatshepsut and Montuhotep II to sever their connection, and provided a new venue for the annual festival procession from Karnak.

His temple's vault-like shrine was cut directly into the cliffs, through which lay the Valley of the Kings, where Tuthmosis III had commissioned work on his tomb (KV.34). As the first in the valley to be decorated, its burial chamber ceiling was painted with the dark blue night sky festooned with stars, while its walls, curved in the form of a protective cartouche, featured sections of the *Amduat* – 'what is in the underworld' funerary scenes. These show the king being suckled by goddess Hathor-Isis in the form of a tree, followed by his three wives and the sun god in various guises, including a rather friendly-looking cat. In the centre of the chamber, Tuthmosis's sarcophagus featured the open-armed figure of 'mother Nut' carved on the underside of the lid so she could lie protectively over his body, which was placed here around 1425 BC after 'completing his lifetime of many years, splendid in valour, in might and in triumph, mounting to heaven and joining the sun'.

The pungent smell of conifer embalming resin still permeated his tomb on its discovery in 1898. His mummified body had originally been buried here with sceptres in his hands, and covered in the usual plethora of amulets and jewellery. But the robbers of antiquity had taken almost everything, even his gold-sandal-shod feet, which reduced his height even further to just under 5 foot 3 inches (1.6 metres).

In the same way as Tuthmosis III had rewritten Hatshepsut's history, he also reorganised her burial arrangements, removing her body and that of her father Tuthmosis I from their joint tomb and reburying Tuthmosis I in a new tomb (KV.38) similar to his own. At some point Hatshepsut's remains were reburied in the small tomb (KV.60) of her old nurse Sitra, where both women's bodies were discovered in 1903, one, with reddish-blond hair once standing around five feet (1.5 metres) tall, tentatively identified as Hatshepsut in 1966, re-examined in 1990 and taken to the Cairo Museum in 2007.

But the Valley of the Kings was not the only royal burial ground at this time. There was also the somewhat-misnamed Valley of the Queens, the resting place of officials like Nebiri, 'Keeper of the Royal Stables'. The special status of horses meant his title was one of great privilege; it had been held by Tuthmosis III's son Amenhotep II when crown prince, and by Nebiri, quite possibly another king's son by a minor wife, or an official raised in the royal nursery. His status was certainly reflected in his costly mummification, which had preserved both his features and his internal organs in such perfect condition that it has been possible to suggest that Nebiri died from a heart attack.

But Nebiri's tomb was just one of many in Thebes, for just like courtiers of the Pyramid Age who sought burial around the pyramids of their rulers, most of Tuthmosis III's officials similarly sought burial close to his, in the Theban hills of Qurna and Dra Abu el-Naga.

The most important such officials were the prime ministers. The staff of prime minister Useramen included his secretary, Amenemhat, who clearly had an interest in ancient monuments. For not only did Amenemhat visit the old tomb of Montuhotep's wife Queen Nefru, leaving his name on the wall, but he also saw the 400-year-old tomb of Lady Senet and, having 'found it like heaven in its interior', copied its scenes of vigorous dancing to recreate in his own tomb.

Useramen was succeeded as prime minister by his nephew Rekhmire, and his tomb is one of the most detailed ever created, its walls containing descriptions of day-to-day government from how much tax each region was paying the crown to Rekhmire's receptions for foreign delegations. And although originally Minoans were depicted here, their characteristic loincloths had been repainted into the dress of the Mycenaeans who had taken over their trade with Egypt following the Thera eruption. There were also envoys from Punt, carrying the eggs and feathers of ostriches, and more myrrh shrubs; and Nubians bringing packs of hounds and a giraffe destined for the royal menagerie, to be joined by the bear and small elephant brought by the Syrian delegates, along with horses and chariots.

Even more informative are the scenes of manufacture, everything from sandals to the statues surrounded by wooden scaffolding, and 'the baking of cakes done safely and well' to create tall, conical confections of ground-up tiger-nuts. As the artists were also experimenting with form and perspective, figures were not only portrayed in profile but from the back as well, including those serving food at Rekhmire's banquet, accompanied by the strains of the popular song 'Put Myrrh upon the hair of Maat' as Rekhmire's daughters play their sistrums to generate a little bit of Hathor's reviving magic.

It was also prime minister Rekhmire who organised the accession of Amenhotep II as sole king and presented him with the 'royal insignia'. He stayed on as prime minister for a time along with the veteran commander and well-documented animal-slayer, Amenemheb.

Inheriting not only his father's military advisors but also his military abilities, twenty-year-old Amenhotep II physically favoured his mother's side, being taller than his father. As Egypt's royal athlete par excellence, he was 'a beautiful youth who was well developed' with 'strong thighs', a swift runner and skilled sailor, who alone rowed the sacred boat at the annual Opet Festival in Thebes. He had gained nautical experience with his responsibility for supervising the Perunefer dockyard at Avaris while he was a prince; and his father had also placed him in charge of the royal stables at Memphis, for 'he loved his horses and took pleasure in them. His heart was steady when he handled them and he knew their characters. He was informed about training them, and became an expert in the matter'.

But the new king was best known for the archery he was taught as a boy by the official Min, who told him 'Draw your bow to your ears! Make strong your two arms! Act with force and strength!' Practising around Giza and Memphis, and regularly demonstrating his skills at public performances, as an 'amusement before the whole land', he would use a bow no one else was strong enough to draw and shoot up to four arrows at a time into copper targets, 'a deed never done before and none had heard of it before'. One arrow even went clean through the copper target to fall out at the other side, 'an impossible feat, except for the king, radiantly mighty', and, of course, outdoing his father Tuthmosis III whose arrow had almost, but not quite, gone through.

Such skills were certainly required very shortly into his sole reign when the Palestinian vassal states exploited the political transition and rebelled. Immediately sailing north to Palestine, Amenhotep II crushed the rebels, hung the twenty severed hands of those he killed 'at the forehead of his horses', and took prisoner '550 enemy charioteers and their 240 wives, 640 Palestinians, 232 male children of princes, 323 female children of princes and 270 female musicians of princes', plus more than 600 kilos of gold.

The pharaoh then celebrated his victory with yet another public archery demonstration, as portrayed on scarabs circulated around the Levant and beyond. Some claim Amenhotep II's archery skills may even have influenced the later Greek poet Homer, whose character Odysseus has a bow that no one else is strong enough to draw, and can shoot through targets made of metal axe heads.

Yet the bow was only one of Amenhotep II's weapons. Having rounded up the seven rebel princes, whom he took back to Egypt, he executed them himself 'with his own mace' – an event immortalised on chunky silver signet rings given out to courtiers. Then in the same way as his great-grandfather Tuthmosis I had hung the body of the Kerma ruler from the prow of his ship, Amenhotep II strung up the seven rebels' corpses at the front of his plunder-laden vessel as he sailed south up the Nile to Thebes, to present these spoils of war to Amen-Ra's priests at Karnak. And as 'his majesty came with his heart rejoicing into the house of his venererable father Amen, his soldiers with him as locusts', six corpses were hung from Thebes's city walls – a gory act that paid homage to Amen-Ra while making a very graphic point to his ambitious clergy. As for the seventh body, it was taken even further south, to Amen's birthplace Gebel Barkal and the city of Napata, 'in order to cause to be seen the victorious might of his majesty for ever and ever'.

Nonetheless, Amenhotep II had to go north again in his seventh year as king to suppress further unrest, sailing up to Byblos and crossing the 'turbulent' waters of the Orontes where 'his majesty turned around to see the ends of the earth'. Marching south through Takhsy and Galilee, he slaughtered rebel enemies 'by shooting arrows', and two years later did the same near Megiddo, when so serious was the threat to Egypt's commercial interests that all the inhabitants of Iturin were slaughtered.

Following this carnage, Egypt's empire for the rest of Amenhotep II's reign was largely peaceful, as Hittite and Babylonian envoys were now joined by the Mitannians, 'who came to him with their tribute upon their backs, seeking peace from his majesty and desiring his sweet breath of life – a notable event!'

The king could now afford to be magnanimous; his personal physician treated a Syrian envoy who had fallen ill at court, and Syrian, Palestinian and Phoenician merchants were now well-established around Memphis. But despite no more public references to 'vile' enemies, the pharaoh still had a dim view of his vassals, and in a letter he wrote from Thebes while 'sitting drinking and making holiday', a slightly inebriated monarch warns his viceroy to beware of Nubians, especially their magicians. Having begun his missive 'this is from the king who is great with the sword stroke', he praises his viceroy as 'a brave one', before contrasting the pair of them with 'the woman from Babylon, the maidservant from Byblos, the little girl of Alalakh, the old woman of Araphka and the people of Takhsy who are nothing at all – really, what use are they?'

Yet, like his father, Amenhotep II appreciated foreign women. Continuing the policy of military conquest followed by diplomatic marriage, the king acquired an extensive retinue of minor wives, with 323 daughters of Palestinian princes being only part of a huge entourage divided between Memphis, Thebes and Gurob.

He had already produced sons when still a prince himself, and five of his boys were placed in the care of the tutor Hekareshu, who ran a school in Karnak's Mut temple. This included the future king, another Tuthmosis, born to Amenhotep II's wife Tia. She was not related to her husband, but inherited from her royal mother-in-law the role of God's Wife at Karnak, whose complex continued to be expanded by the king.

But Amenhotep II's choice of imagery within the temple was most revealing. For not only did he add scenes based on those in the ancient Abusir sun complex of Sahura, the walls of his silver-floored jubilee chapel at Karnak were adorned with images of himself in distinctly solar regalia.

For despite the military abilities and foreign policies he shared with his late father Tuthmosis III, there were already strong signs that Amenhotep II's political agenda was a very different matter.

16

Zenith of the Sun: c.1425–1352 BC

By the reign of Amenhotep II, the Karnak clergy had become so powerful that they even sanctioned the royal succession. So the king seems to have initiated subtle moves to limit their ambitions.

For in a fine retuning of the religious power balance, he made the ancient sun god Ra an increasingly dominant partner in the 'Amen-Ra' brand, in which Ra's clergy in northern Heliopolis proved to be the perfect counterbalance to those of Amen in southern Thebes.

And as Amenhotep II took a new title as 'ruler of Heliopolis', his wife Tia became the first royal woman since the great queens of the Pyramid Age to be named 'Leader of Slaughter in the Acacia House', part of Heliopolis's ancient sun temple where meat and music satisfied the twin natures of the sun god's daughter Hathor-Sekhmet.

Focusing further on the solar powers of the Pyramid Age, Amenhotep II revisited his old stamping-ground Giza, building a rest house by the ancient Sphinx. And taking his chariot for a spin, he would 'drive about and behold the grace of the resting place of blessed Khufu and blessed Khafra', to consciously identify himself with these first 'sons of Ra'.

This attempt to tap into the powers of long-dead kings, and the sun god with whom they merged at death, was now centred on the Great Sphinx. Originally sculpted as an image of Khafra, but given an Eighteenth-Dynasty makeover, complete with appropriate eye make-up, the Sphinx was transformed into Ra-Horakhty, the sun god Ra combined with Horus, god of kingship, to represent all past rulers revived by the powers of the sun. Between its mighty paws, Amenhotep II set up a tall statue of himself; and he built a new temple nearby, honouring not only Khafra, Khufu and the sun god

Sphinx, but the sun disc itself, the Aten. Although it had been a god in its own right since the time of Tuthmosis I, only with Amenhotep II did the Aten gain its characteristic visual form as a disc with human arms.

The king then spread the cult of Ra-Horakhty as far south as the Horus temple at Amada in Nubia and, among his embellishments to Egypt's existing temples, added a shrine to Hermopolis's temple of Thoth, whose new, Nile-fed 'lotus lake' was so impressive the king presented its architect, Kha, with a gold cubit measuring rod. The cubit, inscribed with a statement that the king had personally come to Hermopolis 'and built there a small temple on the second day of the flood, when the river rose in the period of its widening', may even have been used in these flood-related rites.

Like other skilled craftsmen, Kha presumably commuted downriver for the work, for he and wife Meryt lived for much of their lives at Deir el-Medina. A fellow Theban resident was the king's steward and childhood friend Kenamen, whose tomb scenes show him hunting in 'the chariot which his majesty gave as a token of his favour', the very vehicle found in the tomb in the early nineteenth century and sent to Italy with Kenamen's own remains.

Another of the king's childhood companions was Sennefer, mayor of Thebes and 'Overseer of the Granaries and Fields, Gardens and Cattle of Amen' at Karnak. This gave him authority over huge areas of agriculture, and in one of his surviving letters he wrote to one tenant farmer named Baki 'to tell you I am coming to see you after the king has moored at Hutsekhem (Hu) within three days. And don't let me find fault! Pick me many plants, lotus blossoms and other flowers to be made into bouquets fit for presentation. And don't be lazy! For I know you are lazy and like eating in bed!' Sennefer and his wife Sentnay, a royal nurse, were also allowed to erect a statue of themselves in Karnak, while their meteoric rise up the social ladder ultimately allowed them burial in the Valley of the Kings.

As for Amenhotep II's own tomb (KV.35) in the valley, work was again overseen by the talented architect Kha, using the same workmen who had built the last king's tomb. For both burial chambers were covered in similar scenes, in Amenhotep II's case allowing his soul to travel through the underworld with the sun god, who advises those who sail with him to 'draw your bows and be swift with your arrows, punish my enemies as they lurk in the shadows', an ethereal call to arms that would have appealed to this most combative of pharaohs, buried with his favourite longbow beside him around 1400 BC.

His mummification in natron solution caused small bumps beneath his skin, a feature that has commonly been misinterpreted as smallpox, while the golden resins applied to his skin had retained the impression of many of the necklaces, belts and amulets in which his body was once covered. Nor was the king alone in his tomb, which once included the bodies of his mother and one of his sons, Webensenu, 'Overseer of the Horses'.

As for his successor, his teenage son Tuthmosis IV (c.1400-1390 BC), his rise to power is described on the so-called 'Dream Stela' later erected at the feet of the Giza Sphinx. Its text claims that when still 'a stripling like Horus', Prince Tuthmosis, like his father, spent his youth 'enjoying himself on the desert plateau, shooting at targets and hunting lions and wild goats as he flew along in his chariot, with horses swifter than the wind'. But one day, he took a rest, falling asleep in the shadow of the Sphinx, which spoke to him in a dream 'as a father speaks with his son'. It said 'observe me, my son Tuthmosis. I am your father Ra-Horakhty. I shall give you the kingship upon earth and you shall wear its red crown and its white crown. But see how I am in pain and my body in ruins, for the sand of the desert now presses down upon me. I know you are my son and protector so approach me, I am with you, I am your guide'.

So in what is one of the earliest known archaeological excavations, the prince cleared away the sand, while his additional claims to have rebuilt parts of the Sphinx's paws and chest have been verified by modern excavations that discovered bricks stamped with Tuthmosis IV's name, erected as walls to protect from further sand encroachment.

Yet the 'folk tale' that inspired his actions was actually clever propaganda. For Tuthmosis IV's accession marked an important shift in political power and religious allegiance, distancing the new king from the influence of the Karnak clergy who had previously been influential in choosing the heir. And although Amen's clergy remained powerful, Amen himself was nowhere mentioned on the new king's Sphinx Stela, for now the sun god was the 'royal legitimator'.

Following a traditional coronation at Heliopolis, dressed in golden regalia including a sun disc on his head, Tuthmosis IV travelled on to Giza to be acknowledged as the sun god's son at the feet of the Sphinx. Maintaining the same solar focus as his father, he embellished Heliopolis, Abusir and temples throughout Egypt, sailing south with his Great Royal Wife, his sister Iaret. And as the gods' statues were brought out of their temples to greet them as they travelled past, 'men shouted with joy and women danced'.

On reaching Konosso Island, just south of Aswan, the king set up an image of himself striking 'like Sekhmet' in the company of Iaret with her mace, the royal female embodying the protective goddess in these volatile border regions, including an expedition to the turquoise mines of Sinai commemorated with yet more scenes of the king and his sister-wife.

But the woman most often shown with Tuthmosis IV was his mother Queen Tia, depicted as the mace-bearing god's wife at Karnak, where a superb life-size statue of the smiling mother and son embracing was also set up.

For the king was sufficiently astute to keep Amen's priests happy too. Adding a new court to their temple, he finally erected the 105-foot obelisk begun by his grandfather Tuthmosis III, claiming that 'this obelisk had spent 35 years lying on its side on the south side of Karnak. It was commanded I erect it for him since I am his grandson and protector', the erection of an obelisk signalling the reinvigoration of the human or deity to whom it was dedicated.

As for the all-important succession, Tuthmosis IV provided for this with numerous minor wives, from Egyptian women to those acquired from abroad through diplomatic marriage. That which sealed the treaty with Egypt's former enemies the Mitannians was achieved when the pharaoh's 'repeated requests' persuaded the Mitannian king Artatama to send him his daughter, whose dowry included Ugarit, Amurru and control of Kadesh.

And as well as envoys from Nubia bringing gold, ebony, incense and panther skins, they too may have escorted a Nubian princess.

For one of the most fascinating burials in the Valley of the Kings was that of such a woman's son. Named Maiherpera, he was a Nubian, but with the royal family's prominent buck teeth, a 'child of the royal nursery' who had been raised in Egypt, and was later made 'fan bearer on the king's right hand'.

The court was certainly well-populated with up to seventeen royal offspring, although the early death of the eldest boy, Amenemhat, led to the king naming as his heir a younger son Amenhotep, born to minor wife Mutemwia most likely at Gurob. The planned succession had certainly been timely, for after a ten-year reign, Tuthmosis IV died around 1390 BC, the official announcement stating that 'the falcon has flown to heaven and Amenhotep has arisen in his place'.

Mummified with such skill that the handsome king still retains his eyelashes, shoulder-length hair, long fingernails and ears pierced with large holes – the first pharaoh to have such a feature – Tuthmosis IV's body was taken to his tomb in the Valley of the Kings (KV.43), once again created by Kha and his workmen, and which already held the bodies of his eldest son Amenemhat and his daughter Tentamen, who had also predeceased him.

The burial was overseen by new king, Amenhotep III (c.1390–1352 BC), then aged around ten, so it is likely that his mother Mutemwia, who is portrayed literally behind the throne, acted as regent.

At his coronation, the new king took as his throne-name Nebmaatra – 'Ra, lord of truth' – declaring not only the continuing solar agenda, but also the continuing emulation of the past. For 'Nebmaat' had been the throne-name of Snefru and 'Nemaatra' the throne-name of Amenemhat III – two ancient kings whose achievements would be closely studied and emulated by the new monarch.

For just as Hatshepsut had had her Senmut, and Djoser his Imhotep, so Amenhotep III's right-hand man was Amenhotep, son of a couple named Hapu and Yatu. Already a scholar of some reknown, Amenhotep, 'Son of Hapu' was taken on as the king's researcher, scrutinising the ancient records and claiming 'all their mysteries were revealed to me and the king took counsel from them'. The king also sent his officials to study the old temples and tombs of the Fayum, Abusir, Dahshur, Giza, Sakkara and Meidum, where scribe May went 'to see the very great pyramid of the Horus Snefru'.

And soon after his coronation, Amenhotep III would have followed in the footsteps of his father and grandfather to stand before the Great Sphinx at Giza and undergo the transference of accumulated royal power at the feet of the ancient sun god, to become one with Ra-Horakhty, the solar form of Horus.

As a solar king in his golden kingdom, whose glittering reign marked the zenith of Egypt's power, Amenhotep III was already 'the richest man on earth'. And as the most prolific builder in Egyptian history, fully deserving his title 'Menwy' – 'monument man', the equally appropriate epithet 'world's greatest rock star' was plastered across everything from T-shirts to buses to promote a spectacular exhibition of his works in the early 1990s.

When he was still only around thirteen, Amenhotep III married the equally youthful Tiy, who became his Great Royal Wife. She was presumably chosen by Mutemwia, most likely from within her own family. The announcement sent out across the empire stated that 'the Great Royal Wife is Tiy. Her father's name is Yuya, her mother's name is Tuya'. Yuya was possibly of Syrian origin, and lived at Akhmim, a city 'with a high immigrant population' and, like Koptos, a cult centre of the fertility god Min. Yuya was a priest of Min, and his Egyptian wife Tuya was 'Chief of Min's Entertainers', a 'singer of Hathor' and quite possibly part of a minor royal line descended from Ahmose-Nefertari, of which the name Tiy is possibly a shortened form.

At their daughter's marriage, Yuya was promoted to 'Master of the Horse' and Tuya made 'Chief Entertainer of Amen' at Karnak, where their eldest son Anen was made deputy high priest. Their youngest son, Ay, who subsequently inherited his father's role as overseer of the royal stables, eventually rose to the position of Karnak high priest himself.

Yet despite her family's placement within Karnak to represent royal interests, Tiy was the first royal wife in generations not to serve as God's Wife to Amen, the king instead keeping her services for himself. For 'she is in the company of his majesty like Maat is in the company of Ra', goddess-queen to his god-king, and even shown as being a little taller than the king on their colossal statue, which now dominates the Cairo Museum, presumably drawing its inspiration from certain Old Kingdom originals in which the female is portrayed as slightly larger than the male.

Tiy's size here may relate to her role as protector of her husband. Sometimes shown as the pugnacious goddess Taweret, and reflecting Tiy's unique title 'Great of Fearsomeness', the queen was also portrayed as a Sekhmet-like sphinx, guarding her husband's names and trampling his enemies. Yet in the same way Sekhmet could transform into Hathor, so Tiy, as 'the One who fills the palace with love', had hair sufficiently voluminous to evoke Hathor, 'She of the Beautiful Hair'. Even the queen's clothing was carefully selected, one of her robes, made of the iridescent black feathers associated with Nekhbet – the vulture goddess who helped the sun god through the sky – carefully arranged so that the garment's stylised wings protected and supported the queen's abdomen, the home of the next royal generation.

And the royal family soon expanded, as Tiy gave birth to two sons and four daughters. She remained Great Royal Wife even when the same title was awarded retrospectively to the queen mother, Mutemwia, and to the king's two elder daughters; this created three generations of Hathor's representatives to underline the fact that the goddess was simultaneously the mother, wife and daughter of the sun god, embodied by the king.

Part of the king's public image also involved regular displays of strength, so in a world briefly at peace, the third Amenhotep followed his predecessors and turned to big-game hunting, bagging ninety-six bulls over several days in the Wadi Natrun and then 102 'fierce' lions he apparently shot 'with his own arrows' during his first decade as king.

Described as a 'victorious archer', 'a star of electrum when he circles upon his horse', the king was finally able to demonstrate these skills on the battlefield around 1385 BC, following a rebellion by the Nubian chieftain 'Ikheny the Boaster'. In response, the pharaoh 'went forth like Horus, like Montu, a fierce-eyed lion that seized Kush, all chiefs overthrown in their valleys, cast down in their blood, one upon the other', Amenhotep Son of Hapu adding that: 'I saw him fighting hand-to-hand upon the battlefield'.

After crushing the rebellion, Amenhotep III's victory stela was set up on the Aswan to Philae road, showing him standing on the head of a prone Kushite while preparing to smite two more. Following tradition, he then set up statues of himself and Tiy on Sai Island, with the same double act worshipped in two new temples, one at Soleb dedicated to Amenhotep, 'Lord of Nubia', and one at nearby Sedeinga to Tiy, shown here as a 'guardian sphinx', worshipped as the Eye of Ra, Hathor-Sekhmet. Tiy's statue at Mirgissa was even offered libations of red liquid to evoke the dyed beer of the original Eye of Ra legend, its red stains still visible into modern times.

Amenhotep III sailed as far south as Kurgus, where his great-great-great-grandfather, Tuthmosis I, had set up his inscription across the Hagr el-Merwa rock. And with the local Karoy mines supplying huge quantities of gold, even more of this wealth was seized in a second Nubian campaign in the king's twenty-sixth year when Merymose, his viceroy of Nubia, inflicted 'carnage' among the rebels of Ibhet, another key area of gold production far down the Wadi Allaqi.

The accumulation of such wealth allowed the king to exceed even the building programme of Hatshepsut and, like her, Amenhotep III presented himself as the child of Amen-Ra following his own divine conception. But his main emphasis was no longer on Amen but on Ra, and those deities most closely associated with the sun.

Having appointed his eldest son Prince Tuthmosis 'Overseer of all the priests of the north and south', and the royal brother-in-law Anen already second-in-command at Karnak, the king set up a review of the temple's clergy. Headed by Amenhotep, Son of Hapu, who stated that 'the king appointed me to reorganize Amen's temple so I assigned the priests in their places', inscriptions on statues Hapu's son set up around Karnak proclaimed to all who saw them the unprecedented powers given to him by his king. For as the official himself says: 'you people of Upper and Lower Egypt, everyone that sees the Aten sun disc, who comes to Thebes to pray to the lord of gods – come to me, and I shall relay your words to Amen'.

So anyone wishing to reach Amen was now required to go through the king's most trusted official, demonstrating that the balance of power had shifted significantly. The king now named himself 'Amenhotep ruler of Thebes', to emphasise that Thebes was controlled by the northern-born monarch and no one else.

He certainly transformed its landscape like no other king before or since, listing his Theban buildings on a ten-foot stela that claimed that 'it pleased his majesty's heart to make very great monuments, the like of which had not existed since the beginning of the Two Lands'.

The work was carried out by the veteran architect Kha, master sculptor Men and construction overseers, twins Suty and Hor, all managed by the multi-talented 'Overseer of All Works', Amenhotep, Son of Hapu. Declaring 'I did not imitate what had been done before', and working on a scale never equalled, Hapu's son populated Karnak with giants, including one colossus of the king over eighteen metres high, even without its crown – Egypt's largest-ever statue.

But not only did the king dazzle with scale, he also dazzled with gold. Again at Karnak, a pair of obelisks between which the sun rose were set up to flank a new shrine for Maat and Amen, its foundation inscription naming the king as 'the image of Ra who illuminates the two lands like Ra-Horakhty, possessor of sunshine in the face like the sun disc'. Nor did he exaggerate. For Amenhotep III's new shrine was covered in more than five tons of gleaming gold and embellished with almost a ton of lapis lazuli.

Matched with a nearby pylon gateway, again 'worked with gold throughout' and 'inlaid with real lapis-lazuli', a new sacred barque was made in silver and gold to transport the cult statues of Amen and Mut at the annual festivals, when they were carried through the new pylon and down to the Nile to sail in glittering splendour.

These celebrations included the five-kilometre journey upriver for the annual Opet Festival at Luxor Temple, which Amenhotep III greatly expanded from Hatshepsut's original shrine. Its new walls portrayed Amenhotep III kneeling in his rams'-horn crown before Amen-Ra, a spectacular colonnade of columns leading to a solar court open to the sun, beyond which lay a series of dark chambers showing Amenhotep III's immaculate conception. Based on the same scenes as those of Hatshepsut, they show the birth of Amenhotep III, Hathor telling Amen to 'kiss him! Embrace him! Nurse him! For I have loved him more than anything!' When the king himself entered these chambers during the Opet Festival, the potency of such scenes was intended to replenish his powers in secret rites, before the gold-bedecked monarch would then re-emerge into the sunlight, 'his transformations visible to all' as he redirected the powers of god for the benefit of Egypt and its vast empire.

Although this empire had traditionally been ruled from Memphis, where monarchs were still based for much of their reign, other palaces had also accommodated their peripatetic lifestyle.

Yet Amenhotep III eventually relocated permanently to Thebes. Not to the traditional palace attached to Karnak, however, but to a completely new site at the other end of the city, on the opposite bank of the Nile. For on Thebes's West Bank, 'sovereignty was perceived to flow from the inextinguishable fecundity of the mountain goddess' Hathor, so this was the place the king chose to build not only his tomb and funerary temple, but also his new palace, transforming the traditional land of the dead into a land of the living.

As the new permanent home of the head of state, comparable with Versailles or Washington DC, this former backwater was transformed by the development of residential areas, large villas for courtiers, 'rows of small 5-room houses farther to west for minor officials or palace attendants' and smaller quarters for the workers. The old Deir el-Medina village was more than doubled in size, and industrial estates of workshops produced the fixtures and fittings for the splendid new palace.

Covering more than eighty acres, this labyrinthine structure, built of standard mud-brick but with bathrooms augmented with stone, was enhanced with bright paintwork, glazed tiles and gilded inlays, the perfect setting for the god-king to reside in comfort and splendour with his family, and to oversee state business.

The personal items found at the site also explain its Arabic name, *Malkata*, 'the place where things are picked up', for it is still scattered with fragments of court life – rings, bracelets, necklaces, mirror-handles, eye-paint tubes, perfume bottles, cups, amulets and scarabs. Some of these name previous rulers, an interest in the past that is also reflected in the re-use of a 2,000-year-old Predynastic cosmetic palette, re-inscribed with a figure of Queen Tiy. The palace even had its own library, a *per medjat* –'house of books' – whose glazed bookplates inscribed 'Book of the sycamore tree and moringa tree' and 'Book of the pomegranate tree' hint at a royal interest in horti-culture.

And the well-kept royal gardens were indeed 'planted with all flowers', for despite its current desert environment, this was once a lush green landscape intersected with waterways. The largest was a gargantuan T-shaped harbour linked to the Nile and fronting the palace, over two kilometres long and a kilometre wide, requiring the shifting of eleven million cubic metres of soil – equal to the volume of more than four Great Pyramids. This mother of all water features provided mooring for the royal yacht, allowing the king to travel anywhere in his kingdom without ever setting foot on land, although south of the harbour was an additional 'transport' route, a five-kilometre long racetrack along which chariots could achieve speeds of up to forty kilometres an hour. The chariots' golden sides emulated the sun as the vehicles sped along, and the track may have been used for ritual, since it runs directly up to the base of the Theban hills, into which the sun set and where the dead were buried.

The West Bank was certainly a lively place during Amenhotep III's reign, home not only to the royal family, their officials and their servants, but also to 'Syrian settlements inhabited by children of the princes', a reference to all the king's minor wives sent as tribute from across the ancient world.

With Knossos, Rhodes, Phaistos, Troy and Mycenae all ambitiously listed as Egyptian territories by Amenhotep III, his name, with that of Tiy, was found in Mycenae's cult centre, the 'House of Idols'; and Aegean gifts sent to Malkata and Gurob included wine, olive oil, perfume and maybe even women, since some Gurob tombs contained blond-haired individuals.

The king also enjoyed equally good relations with Babylonia, Assyria and Mitanni, with surviving diplomatic correspondence providing a fascinating glimpse into a hidden world of royal protocol.

The king usually began his missives with the lengthy prelude 'so speaks Nibmuarea, great king, the king of Egypt, your brother', 'Nibmuarea' or 'Nimmuaria' being versions of the king's throne-name, Nebmaatra, employed by those outside Egypt. The pharaoh then followed up with an enquiry into the health of his recipients' house-hold, wives, sons, nobles, horses, chariots and countries, telling them that all goes very well for his own versions of the same, but with the subtle additional mention of his 'numerous troops'.

Continuing his father's policy of diplomatic marriage, acquiring a new bride following the accession of each new allied king, Amenhotep III had requested a daughter of the ruler of Arzawa in southern Turkey, and although he was already married to a daughter of the old king of Babylon, he requested another from his successor, new monarch Kadashman-Enlil. When this new Babylonian king tells Amenhotep 'Here you are asking for my daughter in marriage, but my sister who my father gave you was already there with you and no-one has seen her to know if she is alive or dead', the pharaoh asked him 'Have you ever sent here an important man of yours who would know your sister and would be able to speak to her and identify her? The men you've sent here are nobodies – one was a donkey herder!' before assuring him that his sister was fine.

Of course, the Babylonian king shared the common knowledge that in Egypt 'gold is like dust in your country, one simply gathers it up', but seems to have asked for it perhaps once too often. For Amenhotep III tells him 'it's a fine thing to give away your daughters in order to acquire a nugget of gold from your neighbours'. So the Babylonian changed tack and asked for one of the pharaoh's daughters instead, only to be told that 'from time immemorial no daughter of a king of Egypt is given to anyone'. The Babylonian king then replied 'Why not? You are a king; you do as you please', even suggesting 'Send me a beautiful woman as if she were your daughter. Who is going to say 'she is no daughter of a king?' Although Amenhotep III again refused to send a daughter, or any other woman, he at least sent the Babylonian king a housewarming present of new furniture 'overlaid with gold', for 'I have just heard you have built some new quarters'.

Friendly relations with Mitanni had already been sealed when the king's father had married a Mitannian princess and, with the accession of new Mitannian king, Shuttarna, around 1380 BC, the process was repeated when he sent his daughter Kiluhepa to Egypt with her entire entourage of 317 women. Described by the pharaoh as 'a marvel!', the accompanying gifts were displayed for all his courtiers to see, much like a modern wedding reception. Even

Shuttarna's personal statue of the goddess Astarte, the equivalent of Hathor, was sent to bless the marriage. The whole process was then repeated twenty years later with the accession of Shuttarna's son, Tushratta, whose daughter, Taduhepa, duly arrived in Egypt with yet more rich wedding gifts, including presents for the previous bride, her aunt Kiluhepa. And Tushratta again sent the statue of Astarte to make new bride Taduhepa 'the image of my brother's desire', telling the pharaoh 'may our mistress Astarte give both of us great joy. And let us remain friends'.

Such warm words were in marked contrast to the obsequious communications from Egypt's vassal rulers, who told the pharaoh 'I am your servant, the dirt beneath your feet! I send my daughter to the palace, to you the king, my lord, my god, my Sun!' Yet, even with hundreds of foreign women already at court, Amenhotep III told one such vassal, 'I am sending you everything for the acquisition of beautiful female cupbearers. Send extremely beautiful ones in whom there is no defect, so the king your lord will say to you "this is excellent".'

Arriving at court to join their Egyptian counterparts, the women took Egyptian names, which have been translated as 'the Much Sought-After One', 'the Catlike One', 'Hot-tempered like a Leopard' and, in the case of Lady Sati, 'She who strikes with fury for the brilliant Aten'. Although interpreted by some to have meant that she was an ancient 'Miss Whiplash', it is surely another reference to the dual-natured personality of Hathor-Sekhmet, the women's beauty only enhancing the goddess's powers, which sustained and protected the king in rituals such as those carried out within Karnak's Temple of Mut.

For Amenhotep III, 'beloved of Mut', filled her temple with yet more statues, their distinctly feline theme including two smiling monumental sphinxes of himself, claiming to 'strike fear in every foreign land', and eventually taken to St Petersburg in 1820, where they are regularly, if most incongruously, covered in snow. These were once surrounded by no fewer than 365 granite statues of lion-headed Sekhmet, 'the flame of Mut', each weighing over a ton. One for every day of the year, they were designed to give constant protection to the king through generous offerings of red wine and red-dyed beer, recreating the means by which, in myth, the goddess's attempts to destroy humankind had been thwarted.

Since such symbolism was linked directly to the Nile flood, the power of the sun and general fertility, similar rites were played out in temples across Egypt, particularly at Heliopolis, where Sekhmet had been worshipped with Ra almost since the beginning of recorded time. And it was here at Heliopolis where Amenhotep III built the first temple to the Aten sun disc, installing as its high priest the Syrian-born Aper-El, who had been schooled in Egypt.

At nearby Memphis, where the king was hailed as Amenhotep 'United-with-Ptah', the city's creator god, he appointed his eldest son, Tuthmosis, as Ptah's High Priest. This made the young teenager responsible for the god's Apis bull, housed in its golden stall in the temple; when it died, the bull was mummified, its entrails preserved in Canopic jars the size of dustbins and its body interred in the adjoining cemetery at Sakkara in ceremonies led by the king and his son. But Prince Tuthmosis is best known for the Sakkara burial of his cat, Tamiu, the status of this much-loved pet further enhanced by its strong link with the sun god. For a cat's reflective eyes allow it to see in the dark, as recreated in tomb scenes in which the gilded coating of the painted cats' eyes allow them to spy out any evil that might befall their owners' souls.

With Abydos another highly venerated site, whose so-called 'tomb of Osiris' remained a place of pilgrimage, there may well have been plans for a subterranean shrine to Osiris, incorporating the rise and fall of the annual flood levels, since a new shrine to goddess Satet at Elephantine acknowledged her island's role in producing the flood's life-giving waters.

The flood certainly affected Amenhotep III's birthplace, the Fayum, site of the 'Labyrinth' complex of Amenemhat III, whose quartzite colossi by Lake Qarun symbolised the old king as bringer of plenty with all the powers of Sobek.

Inspired by such monumental statements, Amenhotep III built a new temple to Sobek at Sumenu (Dahamsha), where a seven-ton alabaster statue of himself with the god was discovered in 1967 within a vertical, water-filled shaft, 'believed to have been a tank for the

keeping and breeding of Sobek's earthly manifestation – the crocodile'.

The harnessing of the Nile's waters was not only employed to
create the vast harbour at Malkata, but also for 'a lake for Tiy in
her town of Djarukha [Akhmim]', a watery expanse on which to
celebrate the Opening of the Lakes flood festival aboard the royal
yacht. A third such water feature was added in front of Luxor temple,
filled by 'the groundwater, happy in its lake', and the king incorporated this same design in his funerary temple built on Thebes's
West Bank at Kom el-Hetan.

This was the largest royal temple ever created in Egypt – perhaps
anywhere on earth – covering over thirty-six hectares. Plans for
this massive project were again masterminded by the now-elderly
Amenhotep, Son of Hapu. And although the once-vast structure
seemed to have vanished almost completely after an earthquake
that was recently dated to around 1200 BC, followed by the plundering that left only the two so-called 'Colossi of Memnon'
statues of the king, the temple is gradually re-emerging from the
ground as ongoing excavations remove accumulated layers of Nile
mud.

For the temple had been deliberately located at the lowest part
of the flood plain in order to harness the powers of the water that
arrived each July. This was followed a month or so later by a rise in
groundwater – proof, for the Egyptians, of a second Nile under the
earth capable of reviving the dead. And so this was the optimum
location for a temple designed to revive and sustain the king's soul,
a place where the quartzite colossi of Amenemhat III within the
floodwaters of the Fayum were now reproduced 500 years later by
the quartzite colossi of Amenhotep III, erected before his temple's
now long-vanished first pylon, and the flood-filled lake that is believed
to have once lay before it.

Beyond this, two more sets of pylons were flanked by further
colossal seated figures of the king and, like the Memnon colossi,
smaller images of the king's mother, wife and daughters. A hypostyle
hall then gave way to an open solar court whose 166 perimeter
columns were interspersed with seven-metre statues of the king.
Those on the north side, of brown quartzite, represented Lower

Egypt, and those on the south, of red granite, were for Upper Egypt. But unlike those of previous royals, represented in the mummiform wrappings of Osiris, these statues were clad as living beings.

Although the surrounding wall blocks were carted off by later kings, who simply turned them round to create their own scenes on the other sides, this reuse preserved the orginal colours of Amenhotep III's scenes, showing him dressed in various regalia, including as a gold-bedecked, bright yellow-gold solar figure.

Yet the most striking aspect of the temple was its free-standing statuary, as many as a thousand statues erected in what has been described as 'the largest sculptural programme in history'. For as well as the sculpted figures of the royal family were Egypt's sacred creatures – crocodiles, hippos, snakes, scarabs and jackals, and hundreds of life-size images of gods from every part of Egypt.

Presented as a 'three dimensional astronomical calendar to guarantee a propitious festival year' by the queen's brother Anen, an astronomer-priest who knew 'the procession of the sky', the arrangement included 365 more Sekhmet statues, set up behind the columns of the solar court among the shadows to represent each night of the year. Considered to work in tandem with the other 365 in Mut's Karnak complex representing the 365 days, Sekhmet was 'she who his majesty follows, in the number of 730, lady of years, sovereign of months and days', whose rites could now be properly measured. For the sundials – usable only by day – were now joined by a new invention: clepsydra water-clocks, which used the measured flow of water to show the passing of time; the earliest example, in alabaster, featured an image of Amenhotep III, 'beloved of the gods of the sky'.

Although the Sekhmet statues were so numerous they can now be found in museums across the world, other statues are only now being reclaimed from the earth, including a pair of thirteen-metre-high, 110-ton standing colossi of the king himself, recently re-erected as one of the most essential parts of the temple. For as one modern sculptor has perceptively observed, 'sculptures endure, and life dies', and these statues were seen as a means of keeping the king alive. Provided with their own clergy and worshipped by courtiers, they were presented with the offerings that would sustain the soul of

Amenhotep III when it was eventually placed in his tomb, the location of which was again completely innovative.

For Amenhotep III's final resting place would be in the secluded western branch of the Valley of the Kings, which even now retains its tranquil atmosphere, seemingly far away from the land of the living. As work began on its massive, multi-level structure, with three burial chambers for the king, queen and their eldest daughter, the tomb–builders were still overseen by veteran foreman Kha, whose own mummified body reveals that he ended up with four-teen gallstones – maybe from the stress of such a prestigious job. But having created a tomb fit for a god, Kha received rich rewards; the gold cubit given him by the king's grandfather at the start of his long career was now matched by an electrum bowl bearing Amenhotep III's name, no doubt once filled with costly perfume, and accompanied by the gold-of-honour necklace and matching bracelets that Kha still wears. For his mummified body remains as intact as that of his wife Meryt, both discovered in their undisturbed tomb in 1906, their coffins still covered with the dust sheets placed over them at their funeral and their hundreds of possessions preserving a perfect picture of lives as lived in fourteenth-century BC Egypt.

This was also the happy fate of their contemporaries, Queen Tiy's parents Yuya and Tuya, who were discovered just before Kha and Meryt, in 1905, in their own largely intact tomb in the Valley of the Kings (KV.46), which their son–in–law pharaoh had given them. As one of the archaeologists wrote at the time, 'I really nearly fainted . . . the room looked just as a drawing room would look shut up while the people were away for the summer'. For here was Tuya's jewel casket, Yuya's wig chest, feather-stuffed cushions and gilded chairs sufficiently sturdy to take the weight of the French empress, who visited soon after the tomb's discovery. The couple's gilded coffins were so similar to those of Kha and Meryt that they were surely made in the same Malkata workshop, while the couple's mummified bodies are perhaps the finest ever produced; Yuya's chin is still stubbly, Tuya's ears are each pierced twice in the fashion of the day and their hair remains a yellow blond.

As for the king's numerous 'siblings, women and offspring', some were buried elsewhere in the Valley of the Kings, with others interred in the Qurna foothills and in the desert *wadis* far to the west. The king's mother Queen Mutemwiya, who died in the last decade of her son's reign, may have been interred in the Valley of the Queens just north of Malkata; and, as a place where princes and courtiers were also buried, this may have included Prince Tuthmosis, the son and heir whose unexpected death around 1360 BC turned his parents' world upside down.

With the planned succession similarly turned upside down, this now revolved around their remaining son, Amenhotep, who had previously been based at the sun god's cult centre, Heliopolis. His arrival at Malkata coincided with the first of Amenhotep III's spectacular jubilees, traditionally held after 30 years' reign, and Tiy's steward Kheruef noting that 'his majesty did this in accordance with the writings of old. Past generations of people since the time of the ancestors had never celebrated such jubilee rites'. Certainly not on this scale; and as courtiers and foreign delegates arrived from far and wide with gifts, every Theban, from clergy to maidservant, was exempted from tax as part of the great celebrations.

Following a state banquet – the 'king's breakfast' of bread, oxen, fowl and much ale – the royal couple were transported across the palace harbour in their golden ship and then proceeded by carrying chair to the king's funerary temple, where his powers would be reinvigorated in rites involving Hathor, represented by a glittering, glamorous procession of female relatives headed by Queen Tiy, all the 'royal daughters' and those of foreign rulers.

Beside the royal family and select courtiers, by far the largest part of the audience were the spirits of the multitude of gods who resided within their statues, together with the assembled souls of all past kings, the 'Followers of Horus', before whom Amenhotep performed 'the Hunt', 'The Sacrifice', 'the Victory' and the jubilee race.

Then followed a night-long vigil, as female dancers in Old Kingdom outfits performed to the rousing lyrics of 'Come, Golden Goddess': 'the singers are chanting and it is good for the heart to dance! Shine on our feast in the hour of retiring, and enjoy the dance at night! The procession begins at the site of drunkenness, the women rejoice, and the drunkards play tambourines for you in the cool night, and those who waken bless you!'

And having built up the necessary powers, the reinvigorated king rose at dawn to perform his next ritual, the erection of the maypole-like *djed* pillar, representing the backbone of Osiris. It was hauled up with ropes to resurrect the god symbolically and bring the same stability to the land, this test of strength again encouraged by the words and gestures of the king's largely female entourage before he finally took his throne.

And then as Tiy and their daughters offered him their sistrums, telling him 'reach out to the beautiful one, to the ornament of Hathor, lady of heaven', the goddess herself was presumed to appear to oversee the culmination of the proceedings, when the king was rejuvenated as Ra, 'dazzling in the horizon! For you have been reborn as the sun disc in the sky'.

And having been transformed into the 'Dazzling Aten', Amenhotep III was no longer regarded as a representative of the sun, or even a son of the sun, but was, according to official policy, the actual sun god on earth, to be worshipped by all as 'my lord, my god, my Sun!'

As optimum Nile flood levels brought maximum fertility to the land, the new god-king was shown as the plump, androgynous Nile god Hapy. So although once dismissed as a 'pathetically fat old man', an 'effeminate' cross-dresser who 'might easily be taken for a woman', his images intentionally portrayed him as the 'beneficent mother of gods and men', whose elevation as 'the Great He-She' combined the powers of god and goddess.

But since such powers needed regular replenishment, he held a second lavish jubilee around 1357 BC, hopefully remembering to invite King Kadashman-Enlil of Babylon who had previously complained that 'when you celebrated your great festival you did not send me your messenger saying "Come to eat and drink". And you did not send me a gift in accordance with your festival'. Yet perhaps the snub was intended, since the pharaoh told him 'you for your part sent me just one present. Are we to laugh?'

The king's third jubilee, around 1354 BC, featured the usual feats of royal prowess, albeit quite low-key in comparison to the previous events. For the fifty-year-old king's long-denied mortality was moving closer, and a year later, the dazzling Amenhotep III was dead.

When the news reached Syria, the Mitannian king wrote to the widowed Tiy, 'When I heard that my brother had gone to his fate on that day I sat down and wept. On that day I took neither food nor water but simply grieved'.

And yet Amenhotep III continued to be worshipped as the Aten, in death as in life. With his physical body forming the very home of Egypt's greatest god, his mummification was of incalculable importance. So although embalming techniques were now at their most effective, able to produce such lifelike mummies as the royal in-laws Yuya and Tuya, the king had left orders for something very different to both contain and reflect his solar status.

With the process surely taking place within his funerary temple, whose innovative architecture combined the powers of sun and water with those of Osiris, the king's body was eviscerated and coated in a protective golden layer of resins imported from across his vast empire. Then it was submerged in a solution of Nile water and natron salts from northern Wadi Natrun and southern el-Kab, a combination of ritual ingredients that united the Two Lands while optimising preservation with their subtly different chemical qualities.

After thirty days, when the haemoglobin had leached out of his body to create a bright red, amniotic-like fluid, his body was raised up from the waters as he was physically reborn. Following the drying out process amidst clouds of incense to draw down the gods and drive away flies, his body was coated in a second, thicker layer of warmed resins to seal him within, 'so that when set, the members of the mummy consisted of masses of stony hardness with a covering of skin', intentionally transforming him into 'a statue-like mummy' to be venerated in the same manner as his sculpture.

Covered in gold regalia, wrapped in multiple linen layers and topped with a gold death mask, his body, in its nest of gold coffins, was at last ready for the state funeral, led by son and heir Amenhotep and the widowed Tiy.

Finally laid to rest in his vast tomb in the western branch of the Valley of the Kings (WV.22), the tomb-builders blocked up the burial chamber entrance, plastered it over and added more of the same exquisite tomb scenes of the king with the gods they had created elsewhere in the tomb, before backfilling the passageways and sealing the tomb entrance.

And for now the sun king slept.

17

Reflected Glories: c.1352–1295 BC

Although new king Amenhotep IV (c.1352–1336 BC) inherited his father's throne, his wealth, his palaces, his horses, his officials and even his wives, including the Mitannian Tadukhepa, he seems to have inherited few of his father's talents.

So while the modern world continues to credit the fourth Amenhotep with all the innovations of the third, the son was merely a pale imitation of the father he tried so hard to emulate. But with none of the same diplomatic skills, things soon began to unravel.

Although a hopeful Tushratta of Mitanni wrote 'When they told me that the eldest son of Amenhotep and Tiy is king in his place, I said "my brother is not dead! His eldest son is now in his place and nothing whatsoever will be changed from the way it was before",' the new king offended his Mitannian ally by sending him gold-plated statues instead of the solid gold promised.

So, taking over the diplomatic correspondence, Tiy reassured the Mitannian king that 'my husband always showed love to your father and maintained it for you. You must not forget your love for my husband, and increase it for our son! You must keep sending friendly delegations. You must not cut them off!'. Tushratta replied to the new king, 'Your mother knows all the words I spoke to your father. No-one else knows, so you must ask your mother so she can tell you'. As senior royal female, Tiy remained queen beside her son – his early statuary featured her guiding arm round his back – at least until his second year as king, when Amenhotep IV, no doubt with the help of his mother, chose as his great royal wife Nefertiti.

As one of Egypt's most famous faces, Nefertiti's origins are none-theless unknown, although she probably belonged to a minor branch of the royal house, perhaps a descendant of Ahmose-Nefertari, 'whose cult as a Theban divinity had been greatly expanded by one of her descendants Queen Tiy'. It has been suggested that Nefertiti was Tiy's niece, a daughter of Tiy's youngest brother Ay, whose chief wife Ty is known to have been Nefertiti's wet nurse.

There is also the possibility that Nefertiti was a daughter of Amenhotep III by one of his many foreign wives, since one of her titles was 'Heiress' and she and her new husband were portrayed as the divine twins Shu and Tefnut, children of the creator sun god, embodied by Amenhotep III. The couple are routinely shown worshipping the Aten sun god, whom the new king repeatedly addresses as 'my father the Aten', and meaning it quite literally. The couple wrote the Aten's name in the double cartouche of a king and even amended their own names to incorporate his; Nefertiti took the second name 'Neferneferuaten', meaning 'Exquisite perfection of the Aten', and her husband followed her lead by changing his birth name Amenhotep to the more familiar Akhenaten, 'One beneficial to the Aten'.

Although honouring the sun above all else, the couple clearly continued to acknowledge other traditional deities; their officials were still able to report that 'the offerings for all the gods and goddesses have been issued in full' at the great Ptah temple at Memphis, where the new Aten temple was embellished with prominent wall scenes of Nefertiti, and the Aten also actively promoted as far south as Soleb and Kawa in Nubia.

The royal couple's plans for Karnak would follow the lead of their predecessor's bejewelled shrine, although surpassing their predecessor as was traditional would have been difficult since this one shrine alone was covered with six tons of gleaming gold. So instead the couple created something completely original by thinking outside the box, quite literally.

Beyond Karnak's boundary wall on the easternmost edge, closest to where the sun appeared at dawn, their main temple, Gem-pa-aten – 'the Aten is found' – was swiftly given its 610 × 200-metre dimensions by using small stone blocks, which were far easier to handle. Its walls were then carved with scenes of Aten worship, in which Nefertiti appeared twice as often as her husband to lead the open-air sun worship with their infant daughter Meritaten ('the Aten's beloved'). And much like the former God's Wife priestess, Nefertiti would keep the divine spark aroused by 'satisfying him as he rises at dawn'.

Yet the most startling aspect of the new Aten complex was its twenty-eight colossal royal statues created, or at least re-carved, by the royal sculptor, Bek, who called himself 'one whom his Majesty himself instructed'. For it has been suggested that these Karnak statues were 'actually originals of Amenhotep III recut by Amenhotep IV early in his reign', the round face of the sun king narrowed down into a new physiognomy with exaggerated facial features.

Each statue wears a king's crown and false beard, so are generally assumed to represent Akhenaten. Yet some were shown naked and their lack of genitalia has led to all manner of theories claiming that the new king must have been a eunuch, a hermaphrodite, or had suffered from syndromes ranging from Fröhlich's to Marfan's. The idea that half the statues could simply be female seems to have been lost on those who refuse to acknowledge any female pharaoh beyond Hatshepsut. Yet the statues simply represented Akhenaten and Nefertiti in repeated pairs, to represent the aforementioned divine twins of the sun god from whose original stone image they had literally emerged through re-carving.

Such politically charged imagery evidently proved as unsettling for the ancient priests of Amen as for many Egyptologists. And as the clergy began to voice objections, Akhenaten obliquely referred to 'evil words' he overheard. Claiming 'it was worse than those my father heard, worse than those heard by my grandfather and great-grandfather before him', his listing of predecessors extends back to Amenhotep II, the king who first initiated moves to limit the power of Karnak by raising the sun god to prominence and giving physical form to the Aten.

So the couple reacted swiftly. Recalling much of the army from Syria and Palestine, they began to remove all trace of Amen, sending their agents around the country to erase any mention of the god in order to render his clergy impotent. With their censorship centred on his cult centre Thebes, Karnak itself was closed down and its masses of staff made redundant, the nationwide dissolution of Amen's cult depriving settlements of their civic and religious heart and effectively destabilising, if not destroying, much of the country's infrastructure.

The wealth of centuries seized from the temples' treasuries was now laid before the feet of the new gods – the Aten and his divine children, Akhenaten and Nefertiti. They now had the financial means to establish a brand-new city far from Thebes at a remote site in Middle Egypt, which, as the king announced, 'did not belong to any god or goddess, nor to a male ruler nor a female ruler nor to any other people'.

Today known as Tell el-Amarna, the couple named it 'Akhet-Aten' – 'Horizon of the Aten', since the sun rises between a gap in its eastern hills to form the hieroglyph *akhet*, 'horizon'. The name is also likely to have been based on 'Akhet-Khufu' or 'Horizon of Khufu', the original title of the Great Pyramid of Giza that so inspired the solar aspirations of these Eighteenth Dynasty royals.

Its boundaries were marked with a series of sixteen great stelae, whose inscriptions announced that the new city would be a memorial to the Aten, who would be worshipped in a series of vast new temples at the site. There would also be a new Valley of the Kings, not located on Amarna's west bank, where the sun set, but on the east bank.

For this was where the sun rose, above the site of the planned necropolis, where the king decreed that he and Nefertiti and their children would all be buried even if they should die away from their new city. And since they made further plans for a tomb for the sacred Mnevis bull of Heliopolis, believed to house the soul of the sun god, it is even possible that Amenhotep III himself may have been reburied here, perhaps in the valley's longest tomb, which extended forty metres down into the bedrock. For both royals and courtiers were sometimes exhumed for reinterment with family members, and it seems quite possible that having built a city commemorating the Aten, his greatest devotees would have required the Aten's physical body be brought here from Thebes, which no longer benefited from round-the-clock security; even the workers' village of Deir el-Medina had been abandoned by the tomb-builders who had now relocated to the new capital.

Certainly at Amarna the deceased Amenhotep III was portrayed as if alive, in the company of his widow, Tiy, who herself spent time here in the company of their son and Nefertiti and their growing family. When their second daughter, Meketaten, died tragically young, her mummified body was likewise portrayed as if alive, standing upright and dressed in clothes rather than mummy wrappings. Amenhotep III's physical presence at Amarna may even explain the suggestion of a supposed co-regency between father and son, albeit with the senior king very much a sleeping partner, much like the earlier co-regency between Sobeknefru and her dead father Amenemhat III, described as 'commemorative rather than actual'.

So it is perhaps just possible that the reinterred mummy of the self-styled Dazzling Aten was a means of validating the creation of this new city, forming its centrepiece, toward which its main temple buildings were aligned.

It was certainly a rapidly constructed city, whose size was likened by its first archaeologists to Brighton as they mapped its layout in 1892, together with the ancient road system along which the royal family – even the young princesses – drove their chariots. Along with this means of travelling between their four grand palaces, set within landscaped grounds, the addition of a flyover-type footbridge allowed pedestrian access between the Great Palace and the King's House, whose palatial interiors, modelled on Malkata, featured equally naturalistic wall scenes and lavish designs. There were also intimate scenes of family life portraying those who had once lived here, and even contributions by some of the family themselves; the archaeologists identified the royal nursery on the basis of random, childish paint daubs on its lower walls.

But the royal family consisted not only of Nefertiti's six daughters but also their half-brother (or maybe even full brother) Tutankhaten, whose birth-name meant 'living image of the Aten'. Almost certainly born at Amarna, his father was Akhenaten, and although it is still uncertain if his mother was Akhenaten's minor wife Kiya or as some have suggested, Nefertiti herself, the boy was at least partly raised by Lady Maia, who would proudly claim that she had been the one who 'nourished the flesh of the god'.

In addition to their growing family, the royal couple were occupied with the all-consuming Aten cult focused on the new temples,
chief among which was their Great Aten Temple. Specifically aligned
to function in tandem with the landscape, extending back almost
760m toward the royal cemetery and eastern horizon, this vast, open-
air complex was filled with over a thousand offering-tables, altars
and statues of the royal couple holding out stone trays, images
duplicated in the temple's walls, where there are repeated figures of
Akhenaten and Nefertiti making daily offerings of flowers, perfumes,
incense, food and drink. This included the beer produced in Nefertiti's
own breweries, which in 1990 was recreated from remaining residues
and sold in Harrods as a novel means of funding ongoing excavations. Nor were these rites solemn events, but somewhat evangelical
in style, accompanied by the 'singers and musicians who shout out
for joy in all the temples of Akhetaten'.

Beyond its temples and palaces, the city also housed government
buildings, including the Foreign Office or 'Bureau of Correspondence
of Pharaoh', in which much diplomatic correspondence was discovered. There were also the villas of royal officials, like prime minister
Nakht, high priest Panehesy and royal relatives Ay and Ty, many of
whom were also provided with splendid rock-cut tombs in the
adjacent cliffs. There were the homes and workshops of craftsmen
like chief builder Hatiay and royal sculptor Tuthmose, whose wooden
shelves displayed such works of art as the celebrated painted bust of
Nefertiti in her tall blue crown, a timeless masterpiece today housed
in Berlin's Egyptian Museum.

Industrial estates produced glass and ceramics, warehouses and granaries stored food, and pens held cattle, sheep and pigs. There were also
the humble dwellings and recently discovered cemeteries of most of
the 30,000 or so estimated population. Although this was mainly made
up of those who built and maintained the city, there were also large
numbers of troops to guard it, including foreign mercenaries from
Syria and further afield, a fragmentary papyrus found in one house
featuring men in Aegean-style leather armour and boars'-tusk helmets,
identified as Mycenaeans 'in the service of the pharaoh's military'.

For a strong military presence was essential. The royal family,
cocooned in their world of luxury and ritual, were always guarded,

with a 'flying squad', headed by the police chief Mahu and the battalions of guards who ran alongside their royal chariots in the manner of a modern presidential motorcade.

The air of menace that pervades such scenes is also reflected in images of Akhenaten and Nefertiti executing their enemies, identically dressed in masculine attire and in some cases assisted by the Aten, whose multiple arms simultaneously wield both mace and scimitar. For despite his reputation as a peaceful reformer and 'world's first monotheist', Akhenaten's so-called 'religious revolution' was basically the repression of Amen's priests; foreign vassals were warned that all traitors would be sent in fetters to Egypt where they and their families 'shall die by the axe of the king', the Akujati people of Nubia even impaled by royal command following a rebellion around 1340 BC.

Despite such brutal suppression, Egypt's empire was already fragmenting, and with many of its troops recalled to keep order within Egypt vassal rulers had begun to fight among themselves. Ribhadda of Byblos and Queen Ninurmahmes of the Jordan Valley reported serious unrest, asking the pharaoh for reinforcements, as did King Akizzi of Qatna, just before his palace was destroyed. For as the mayor of Qatna reported, lands were being sent 'up in flames' by the advancing Hittites, who now 'seized all the countries that were vassals of the king of Mitanni', Egypt's long-standing ally.

But the royal couple had focused their attentions on a different way of demonstrating power: a grand state reception to be held in their new royal city, dedicated to the greater glory of the Aten and to themselves as his joint representatives.

To this they invited delegates from as far afield as Syria, Palestine and Punt, Nubia, the Aegean and even the problematic Hittites; scenes at Amarna show their arrival with gifts listed as 'the tribute of Syria and the Sudan, and the West and the East, all countries there at one time, and the Islands in the midst of the Great Green Sea', the Mediterranean. Nor did this exaggerate; large quantities of Mycenaean pottery found at Amarna represent only 'one shipment sent directly from the Argolid to the Egyptian court . . . containing perfumed olive oil to Akhetaten as a greeting gift'.

As the city's inhabitants joined in the celebrations, clapping, dancing and jumping up and down with excitement while ogling the exotic arrivals from across the ancient world, courtiers' tomb scenes also show multiple registers of foreign representatives with their arms raised in adoration, falling to the ground and kissing the earth before the royal couple, who required the largest possible audience to witness what seems to have been a very public coronation.

Since Akhenaten had already been king for twelve years, it is not unreasonable to suppose that this grand event marked Nefertiti's own elevation to full co-regent, when she took the new name 'Ankhkheperura Neferneferuaten'. She is shown in the same kingly crown and regalia as her husband, the two of them enthroned beside each other so closely that their profiles almost form a single kingly entity, their hands entwined. The vacancy of queen was now filled by their eldest daughter, following the earlier precedent set by Hatshepsut.

Yet despite the acclamation of the ancient world, this spectacular event failed to halt the increasing anarchy across their empire, and as this continued to fragment, it seems that lavish foreign tribute had not been the only thing to arrive in the midst of the royal city.

For despite every security precaution, a silent killer had arrived.

During the reign of Amenhotep III there had already been diplomatic correspondence warning that 'there is plague in the land!', and he had turned for help to Sekhmet 'Lady of Plague', whose priests, as the ones tasked to placate her, had composed a 'spell for the "Asiatic disease" to be spoken in the language of Crete', most probably to try to tackle specifically bubonic plague.

As the problem reached epidemic proportions throughout the Near East, the ruler of Ugarit asked Akhenaten to send him a physician, while the mayor of Gazru wrote 'My lord, send archers and myrrh for medication' to deal with the combined threat of war and sickness.

In Egypt, where plague had already claimed the life of at least one Babylonian princess sent in marriage, 'conditions were ripe for the spread of epidemic disease' in the overcrowded backstreets of Amarna. Even the royal family were not safe; for the Great Reception turned out to be the last time some members appeared in public. Two possible plague victims were Nefertiti's two youngest daughters, whose tiny bodies would have been placed in the Royal Tomb, like their seven-year-old sister Meketaten, already buried there in a side chamber.

In keeping with the ancient practice of pharaohs burying their female relatives within their own funerary complexes, queen mother Tiy died around 1338 BC and was likewise buried in Amarna's Royal Tomb, as it seems was one of Akhenaten's minor wives, Kiya.

The death of Akhenaten himself followed soon after, his last recorded regnal year his seventeenth, around 1336 BC. Although it is not known exactly when or indeed how he met his death, it may have been through natural causes, or from plague, or as a result of one of the various syndromes that some claim afflicted him throughout his life. There are even suggestions that he shared the fate of several previous kings and was assassinated, for there would certainly have been those wishing the unorthodox pharaoh dead, along with his disastrous policies.

However he died, power now lay firmly in the hands of his existing co-regent, 'Ankhkheperura Neferneferuaten' – Nefertiti – who now took the new name 'Smenkhkara' (c.1338–1336 BC). With her traditional titles written with a female determinative, later dynastic lists indeed acknowledge the existence of a female pharaoh at the end of the Eighteenth Dynasty, a ruler portrayed wearing kingly crowns but with a distinctly female physique.

But in the first half of the twentieth century many Egyptologists still assumed that a king had to be a man, and allowing only Hatshepsut to remain the exception, were reluctant to acknowledge any other female pharaohs. It didn't help that evidence for the elusive 'Smenkhkara' had first appeared while suffragettes were marching on Whitehall, loudly enquiring how it could be that women had held absolute power in ancient Egypt while they themselves didn't even have a vote. So as far as the Establishment were concerned, it seemed best to imagine Smenkhkara as some mysterious, if feminine-looking, prince, who had replaced Nefertiti in Akhenaten's affections, much like 'the Emperor Hadrian and the youth Antinous'. Or, as *The Sunday Times* succinctly put it more recently, 'better gay than female'.

Although there remains no actual evidence for a *male* individual named 'Smenkhkara', Akhenaten's female-looking successor was surely Nefertiti herself, having taken the throne-name 'Smenkhkara'. Her eldest daughter Meritaten continued as queen, while her second surviving daughter, Ankhesenpaaten, was wed to her half-brother Tutankhaten, to weave together all the strands of the remaining royal house into a new-form monarchy.

And as they led Akhenaten's funeral rites, the accompanying spells proclaimed his soul would 'go forth into the sky on the arms of the living Aten. No evil can affect your limbs, you remain whole and your body will never putrefy as you follow the Aten as he rises at daybreak'.

Akhenaten's mummified body was then interred in Amarna's Royal Tomb, inside a sarcophagus carved with his names and those of the Aten, while on each corner stood Nefertiti, stretching out her arms to give maximum protection to the dead pharaoh. Nefertiti's name is the one found most often within the tomb, suggesting that she had been responsible for her husband's burial before embarking on a reign that may have lasted little more than a year or two. One particularly striking sculpted figure of the female monarch, shown rather older than her famous portrait bust, seemingly carries the weight of the world on her slim shoulders.

For Egypt was on its knees following the upheavals of the last seventeen years, its people suffering serious economic hardship and its empire melting away. As the situation was all the more difficult to deal with from such an isolated capital, the pragmatic monarch seems to have instigated a gradual return to the old order to reverse the nation's fortunes, taking advice from her relative, Ay, Queen Tiy's influential younger brother and Tutankhaten's great-uncle.

As Amarna was gradually abandoned, Memphis once more became the administrative capital and, as the royal family divided their time between Memphis and Thebes, it seems the clergy of Karnak were allowed to resume operations. One of the few clues to the events of this turbulent time is contained in graffiti written by the Theban priest Pawah, which begins with the long-banned words 'Praise to Amen!'. Pawah then admits 'it is good to speak your name! It tastes like life! Come back to us! You were here at the beginning before anything else existed, and will be here when all else is gone. Come from afar and allow your servant Pawah to see you again! Oh Amen, great lord, drive away our fear! Fill our hearts with joy!'

It was a genuine cry from the heart, begging Amen to return and restore order. But there had been years of neglect; it was reported that 'the temples of the gods and goddesses from the Delta to Aswan were in ruins. Their shrines had collapsed and were overgrown in weeds, and the buildings a [public] pathway. The gods had turned their back on Egypt. If an army was sent to the Levant they had no success. If anyone prayed to the gods they never came. Hearts were weakened, for what had been had been destroyed'.

As state-funded restoration began, the monarchy 'installed priests from among the children of local officials' and met the shortfall by supplying servants from the royal household. And with former staff also able to resume employment, be they priests or those who worked the gods' fields, the reopening of the old temples marked the beginning of financial recovery.

With both people and gods described as having 'hearts full of joy, with laughter throughout the entire land now that good things have happened', Thebes's great god was once again the state god and the truce between crown and clergy now sealed with the ultimate public gesture.

For Tutankhaten and Ankhesenpaaten officially dropped the Aten in favour of Amen, to become the more familiar Tutankhamen (c.1336–1327 BC) and Ankhesenamen. Their new statues were set up within Karnak's sacred, spruced-up precincts, and earning the new king the epithet 'Tutankhamen, who spent his life fashioning images of the gods', the temples of Egypt and Nubia were repopulated with new images of the traditional deities in the company of the two new monarchs. Work started at Luxor temple under Tutankhamen's grandfather Amenhotep III but abandoned by Akhenaten was now resumed and, as far south as Soleb in Nubia, Tutankhamen added his own embellishments to the monuments of his illustrious grandfather.

With Ay now prime minister as well as Amen's new high priest, it was once again possible to send Egypt's troops abroad to start to win back their former empire, under the capable leadership of General Horemheb.

Born at Herakleopolis, Horemheb was an educated man whose early statues show him as a scribe and follower of the god 'Thoth, lord of writing'. As 'royal spokesman for foreign affairs', who had led a diplomatic mission to Nubia resulting in a reciprocal visit by the Prince of Aniba to Tutankhamen's court, Horemheb was then appointed commander-in-chief of the army, as portrayed in scenes in his tomb, which was provided for him in the most prestigious part of the Sakkara necropolis.

His tomb was initially found beneath its drifting sands in the nineteenth century, but although one of its statues of a married couple ended up in the British Museum, the lack of any inscription or precise findspot meant the pair remained unidentified until the tomb was rediscovered in 1975. With the tomb's owner now identified as Horemheb, a pair of limestone clasped hands found when the tomb was re-excavated fitted the old statue exactly. So the affection Horemheb felt for his first wife Amenia was the means by which their portraits were eventually identified, recalling a popular saying of the time: 'it is joy when your hand is in hers'.

Touching statuary aside, the rest of Horemheb's Sakkara tomb was filled with wall scenes of his military exploits and the decorations awarded him by Tutankhamen and Ankhesenamen following his victories in the Levant, where urgent action had been required to counter the advance of the Hittites under their king Suppiluliumas I. Having taken full advantage of the power vacuum during the Amarna Period, the Hittite king was besieging Carchemish when he had learned of the death of Akhenaten.

It seems that tentative negotiations may then have begun under Akhenaten's successor, since a shipwreck off the coast of the Hittite heartland in southern Turkey was found to contain a cargo accompanied by a single royal name – Nefertiti.

A further tantalising clue, found in the diplomatic archive of the Hittite capital Hattusha, was a copy of a letter sent by an Egyptian named Dahamanzu – Hittite for the Egyptian 'ta hemet nisu', meaning 'the royal wife'. Since the unusual use of 'ta' as 'the' emphasises that this was *the* royal wife, most likely Nefertiti herself, the contents of her letter are absolutely extraordinary. For she tells the enemy king, Suppiluliumas, 'My husband is dead and I have no son. But people say you have many sons. If you give one of your sons to me he would become my husband, because I will never pick out a servant of mine for a husband'.

Now this was simply unprecedented. Not only were Egypt and the Hittites enemies, but Egypt's royal women *never* married foreigners. So, unsurprisingly, the Hittite king was unconvinced. Exclaiming that 'such a thing has never happened before in my life', he was deeply suspicious, and sent a messenger to check its authenticity, much to the annoyance of his correspondent, who asks 'Why did you say I deceived you? If I had a son, would I have written my humiliation to a foreign land? You didn't believe me, and have said so. But my husband has died and I have no son and I will never take a servant of mine for a husband. I have written to no other country but you, and you have many sons. So send one of them to me, to be my husband and be king in Egypt!'.

Finally convinced, presumably by the wealth and prestige the Hittites would gain from such an alliance, the king sent one of his sons, Zannanza. But unfortunately, like the proverbial lamb to the slaughter, Zannanza and his entourage simply disappeared, presumed murdered.

It is impossible to know if this was the intention all along, engineered by Ay, by Horemheb or even by Nefertiti herself. Alternatively, the unfortunate prince may have been killed by Nefertiti's enemies, unwilling to accept such a plan. Maybe Nefertiti even shared her would-be husband's fate, for she too then vanished, and it remains unclear exactly when and how she died, or indeed where she was initially interred.

Most likely this was in Thebes; the Valley of the Kings had been reinstated as the royal burial ground, and one particular tomb (KV.56), begun here in the same architectural style as the Royal Tomb at Amarna, seems to have been created for a royal woman of the late Eighteenth Dynasty. It had been cut into the valley floor very close to several others created at this time, including a recently discovered tomb (KV.63), and the mysterious KV.55.

Each of these tombs contained the remains of funerary equipment made during the Amarna Period, after Amarna's royal dead were exhumed and brought back to Thebes for reburial by Tutankhamen, either as an act of piety or because they were no longer secure back at Amarna – or maybe a combination of both. Their reburials are still a hugely controversial subject, and present a most complicated challenge, not unlike a bizarre game of musical chairs, since the coffins and their original owners had become separated. The recently discovered tomb KV.63 contained empty coffins, while the body of Akhenaten ended up in the bejewelled coffin of his minor wife Kiya, reburied in tomb KV.55 alongside the body of Queen Tiy.

As for his own tomb, Tutankhamen seems to have planned to be buried at the head of the western branch of the Valley of the Kings, a site inaugurated by his grandfather, Amenhotep III. And close to his grandfather's massive funerary temple Tutankhamen began his own counterpart at Medinet Habu, in which he erected two beautiful, colossal quartzite statues of himself.

But when Tutankhamen died, still not quite twenty years old after a ten-year reign, his funerary temple was incomplete, so his body was presumably mummified elsewhere. It had been prepared much like that of his grandfather Amenhotep III; the archaeologists who found it estimated 'two bucketsful' of thick golden resin had been poured over the body, intentionally transforming him into the same kind of statue-like mummy. Once wrapped in linen, he was ready for burial, along with the mummified bodies of his two tiny daughters, presumably born to his half-sister, wife Ankhesenamen, both of them stillborn; their genetic defects included scoliosis and spina bifida, quite likely as a result of the family's inbreeding.

Since Tutankhamen's planned burial place (WV.23) was also unfinished, an already existing tomb (KV.62) was requisitioned in the main valley, close to those of his immediate family. During the standard seventy-day mummification period, the walls of its small burial chamber were painted a yellow-gold and adorned with scenes of his forthcoming funeral and his reception amidst the traditional gods, his somewhat chubby-looking proportions in keeping with his vital statistics, which his surviving clothing reveal to have included a generous hip size of 110 centimetres.

His funerary equipment was quickly pulled together from family members; some still carried their names, from Akhenaten's on the linens wrapping some of the tomb statues, to Nefertiti's, inscribed on some of the boxes, bangles and gilded bows, on the inlaid gold bands placed over Tutankhamen's mummy and within the four small gold coffinettes that held his internal organs.

And among the items that had been made for others was a gold throne, on which the names and figures of the two previous monarchs Akhenaten and Nefertiti beneath the Aten's rays had been altered to portray Tutankhamen and Ankhesenamen. Two gilded figures of kings standing on the backs of leopards, usually assumed to both represent Tutankhamen, are by no means an identical pair. For one king is male, while the other has breasts so prominent they cannot be dismissed as simply a quirk of Amarna art, so yet another image of that elusive female king, who is surely Nefertiti.

Likewise one of the three golden coffins in which Tutankhamen was buried, since 'the physiognomy of the second coffin differs markedly from that of the first and third'. So as one leading expert has pointed out, 'there is every reason to believe that Tutankhamen was not its intended owner', adding that even the gold death mask, the most iconic object in Egyptian history, 'had originally been a Nefertiti piece'. So, either her body was ruthlessly stripped of its wealth only a few years after her death, or she had been buried without it as part of a cut-price funeral in her unfinished tomb (KV.56).

Once his tomb had been hastily made ready, Tutankhamen's funeral was led by his elderly great-uncle, Ay, who was shown on the tomb walls performing the Opening of the Mouth ceremony on the late king's upright mummy.

Ay (c.1327–1323 BC) then became Tutankhamen's successor, maybe even sharing the throne with the widowed Ankhesenamen for a time. Yet Ay's queen was still his wife, Ty, as borne out by the wall scenes he commissioned for his own tomb (WV.23) in the western branch of the Valley of the Kings; this was the tomb begun for Tutankhamen but now completed by Ay. He also seems to have taken over Tutankhamen's Medinet Habu funerary temple and its pair of colossal, and quite beautiful, statues.

Such statuary revived the sumptuous perfection of Amenhotep III's craftsmen and combined it with a new realism honed during the Amarna Period. This is also apparent in the facial features of an eleven-metre-high figure of a royal woman, carved with the names of a subsequent queen, which was discovered in 1981 at Akhmim, Ay's family hometown and one of the cult centres of the fertility god Min.

Having named his handsome son, Nakhtmin, after the ancient deity, Ay had big plans for him – for Nakhtmin seems to have been Ay's chosen successor.

But with the elderly Ay's death around 1323 BC, Nakhtmin disappeared, his statues severely damaged around the nose and mouth, and the throne passed instead to General Horemheb.

Having been in the Levant fighting to restore Egypt's empire at the death of Tutankhamen, Horemheb (c.1323–1295 BC) now took the throne for himself, with the backing of the Egyptian army. Since his first wife Amenia had died some time during Ay's reign, Horemheb linked himself to the remaining royal line through his second marriage, to Nefertiti's sister Mutnodjmet, meaning the goddess 'Mut is sweet'.

The new royal couple were portrayed enthroned in a life-size granite statue, the back inscribed with Horemheb's coronation decree, which claims Horus had singled him out as ruler even before he had been born. At Ay's death, Horus had apparently taken his protégé to Karnak, where his fellow deity Amen immediately recognised Horemheb as the rightful heir and crowned him on the spot.

His coronation in Thebes was also a way of emphasising the return to absolute orthodoxy, focused on Karnak, where Horemheb took over the statues of Tutankhamen for himself and pulled down those of Akhenaten and Nefertiti. He also demolished the couple's Aten complex, recycling its small building stones to use as filling within his own new buildings, unintentionally preserving them into modern times.

Claiming that 'as long as my life on earth remains, it shall be spent making monuments for the gods' in his 'Great Edict', Horemheb also outlined the legal and social reforms with which he intended to re-establish much-needed order. He ordered a pay rise for state employees, and rewarded some in the army by reappointing them as priests whose loyalty could be guaranteed. Yet any soldier found guilty of stealing would receive 100 blows and five open wounds, while anyone seizing any boat used for government service would have his nose cut off and be exiled to the Sinai, the site of the settlement Rhinocolura – 'Amputated-Nose Town'.

His hardline reforms also extended beyond the army, as Horemheb reorganised the law courts and the state workforce, including the tomb-builders' village of Deir el-Medina. Abandoned during the Amarna Period when it suffered fire damage, it was now rebuilt, the original houses refurbished and new ones built within an extended town wall.

For Horemheb needed its residents to build him a tomb in the Valley of the Kings, the spectacular tomb (KV.57) whose superb wall scenes were far more extensive than those of any of his predecessors, and his repeated image, and those of the surrounding gods, seeming to emerge from the grey-blue surface of the walls' raised relief.

Security in the royal valley was also tightened up and previous royal burials, left vulnerable during the move to Amarna, were checked out by the royal official Maya and his assistant, scribe Djhutmose. Making good the damage in the tomb of Tuthmosis IV, the men repaired broken pottery and tidied up the king's mummy. But at some point the reverse occurred in the tomb of the recently interred Ay, whose names and images were chiselled from the walls, his mummy – now missing – was presumably attacked too, and Ay's Medinet Habu funerary temple taken over and expanded for Horemheb's use, including the two colossal quartzite statues that Ay had previously usurped from Tutankhamen.

But while Horemheb's new tomb was being constructed in the Valley of the Kings, his wife Mutnodjmet died, and so she, like his first wife Amenia, was buried in his original tomb at Sakkara. The skeletal remains of Mutnodjmet's once-mummified body reveal that she had been of slender build, not quite five feet (1.5 metres) tall and around thirty-five to forty-five at death. She had lost all her teeth early in life, probably due to severe anaemia, and the archaeologists also recovered the remains of a newborn child, suggesting that the unfortunate queen had died in childbirth while trying to secure an heir for her royal husband.

With no children of his own, Horemheb had to make alternative arrangements, adopting as his heir the officer turned prime minister, Paramessu – 'the sun god Ra is the one who bore him'. As a trustworthy individual hailing from the Eastern Delta, Paramessu was a perfect choice, because he came with his own ready-made dynasty. For unlike Horemheb, he and his wife Satra had not only a son, but a grandson too.

It was a timely arrangement, as Horemheb died sometime around 1295 BC. And although his tomb, like almost every other, was robbed in antiquity and his body never found, he had nonetheless laid the foundations for the next dynasty of militaristic pharaohs, and in his own time was counted as one of them, the first king of the new Nineteenth Dynasty.

18

Reigns of the Ramessides:

c.1295–1069 BC

With Paramessu now credited with initiating the Nineteenth Dynasty, his name was simplified at his accession to Ramessu, or Ramses.

As the first of eleven kings with this name, the fifty-something Ramses I, who had a brief reign of around sixteen months (c.1295–1294 BC), has been dubbed 'the man in the equivalent of the grey suit', continuing his predecessor's legal and social reforms, with which, as the former prime minister, he was already familiar.

He also continued his predecessor's building programme, embellishing Karnak and, over the river in the Valley of the Kings, ordering a fine, if modestly sized, tomb (KV.16), whose walls, adorned with images of himself before the gods, were so similar to those in the neighbouring tomb of his old boss and predecessor Horemheb that they were almost certainly created by the same artists.

At his death, Ramses I was then buried here, in traditional rites led by his son Seti, who had been made co-ruler prior to his father's death to ensure the smooth transition of power.

And new king Seti (c.1294–1279 BC), now in his thirties, was certainly a striking-looking figure, possibly even a redhead. This would certainly explain his name, based on that of the ancient god Seth, who was particularly venerated around the old Hyksos capital Avaris, from where the new royal family originated. And Seth had been long associated with red, the traditional colour of the hostile desert, while his followers, known as 'red-headed forms', had a reputation as unstable misfits. So it seems likely that, given the new king's possible hair colour, any sense of negativity towards Seth and his turbulent nature was now turned into a positive and the god's great strength – used in myth to protect the sun god Ra – turned to the advantage of the new king, who had himself portrayed as a sphinx with the head of Seth, making offerings to Ra at Heliopolis.

Seti I's highly successful reign was certainly based on strong leadership, and military abilities inherited from both sides of his family; his mother, Sitra, was a soldier's daughter and his own wife Tuya the daughter of a lieutenant of the chariot division.

And with plans for military expansion into the Levant, Seti founded a new settlement at Qantir in the Eastern Delta, with a new palace, royal workshops for the manufacture of weaponry and chariots and military barracks housing both Egyptian and foreign troops, including, it seems, Mycenaeans, whose presence is suggested by the discovery of 'part of the famous boar's tusk helmets worn by the Mycenaean elite'.

After Seti I had undertaken successful campaigns against the Shasu Bedouin in southern Palestine, then advanced north against the Hittites to retake the long-fought-over city of Kadesh, he dealt with sporadic invasions by Libyan tribes on his western border. Campaigning in Nubia to secure Egypt's all-important gold supplies, he also needed prisoners to augment the labour force which would be required for his monumental building projects.

Keen to demonstrate his piety toward Egypt's past, Seti returned to Abydos, cult centre of Osiris and the burial ground of Egypt's earliest kings. And here he built his spectacular Osiris temple, whose original small roof lights still allow the sunlight to penetrate at specific points, enhancing the temple's unique and very special atmosphere.

With its interior walls adorned with repeated figures of Seti I in the company of the gods, all rendered in stunning raised relief of the very highest quality, the temple incorporates a 'Chamber of the Ancestors', whose intact walls include a lengthy king list naming all Seti's predecessors since first king, Narmer – or at least, all those considered worthy of inclusion.

For after the cartouche of Amenhotep III is that of Horemheb, the thirty years or so covering the reigns of the missing Akhenaten, Nefertiti, Tutankhamen and Ay all ascribed to Horemheb, giving him a generous, if inaccurate, fifty-nine years. Also missing are the Hyksos, Hatshepsut and all other female pharaohs, and the list ends with the repeated cartouches of Seti himself.

For this is Egyptian history, Nineteenth Dynasty-style.

Yet this rewriting of the past was not simply a vindictive swipe at unpopular predecessors, since the list had a specific purpose in the running of the state. It was a key part of the Ancestor Ritual, when the names of those deemed to have ruled correctly were read aloud, and their powers drawn together and redirected for the benefit of Egypt.

And this process is actually portrayed beside the list, where Seti stands with his young son, Prince Ramses, who was made co-regent while still 'a child in his embrace'. For unlike the last dynasty, where royal sons hardly ever appeared with their kingly fathers, there had been a complete change in policy, with the male heir now a highly visible part of the royal line-up, reading out the names from a roll of papyrus while his father raises his hand towards the accumulated cartouches, as if to say 'One day, son, this will all be yours'.

It was all part of the new dynasty's desire to be seen as fit rulers in their own right, able to maintain the all-important succession, particularly as they were fully aware that they were not of the original royal line. Yet the masculine, militaristic Nineteenth Dynasty clearly had a genuine understanding of the past, and attempted to reconnect with its glories, something that was also reflected in another part of the temple complex, the 'Osireion'.

A hugely important yet deeply mysterious place, once topped by a mound, the Osireion is usually credited to Seti and described as a 'cenotaph'. Built sufficiently low in the desert that it was annually submerged, at its centre 'a pseudo-sarcophagus and canopic chest stood on an island surrounded by groundwater symbolizing the primeval waters of creation'.

Echoing the Middle Kingdom practice of siting royal burial chambers as close as possible to the water table in order for royal souls to be reborn through the rising floodwaters – as had been repeated by Amenhotep III, whose own funerary temple was also sited low down in the flood plain at Thebes – the Abydos Osireion may even have been originally planned by Amenhotep III, since he is known to have built a new Osiris shrine on top of the nearby tomb of Djer as a means of 'tapping into' the powers of Egypt's earliest rulers.

Certainly both the Osireion and the ancestral king list would have worked in tandem, as a place where the new Nineteenth Dynasty kings could access the accumulation of royal power, built up through the generations of pharaohs before them, pharaohs who had died on earth but were regarded as very much alive in the next world, where they were equated with Osiris himself.

Yet Seti's greatest architectural achievement was at Karnak, where he made his devotion to state god Amen quite clear by building its most famous section, the Hypostyle Hall, whose 134 vast stone columns recreate the primeval swamp from which life had first emerged. This was again believed to have been designed originally by Amenhotep III but abandoned under his successor, and it seems that Seti I revived the plans, to create an amazing structure through which Amen's processional rites would have passed.

Surrounded by wall scenes of Seti I and the once-more powerful priests of Amen participating in the sacred rites, its calm and dark interior gives way to contrasting scenes on the hall's exterior walls, where Seti, with the help of Amen, defeats Egypt's enemies from his war chariot, scenes that capture the chaos and cruelty of war and whose exterior location would demonstrate Seti's prowess to the outside world.

Directly opposite Karnak's great hypostyle hall, over the Nile, Seti I began his funerary temple, where offerings would sustain his soul after death.

When this occurred around 1279 BC, his body was transformed into the perfect example of 'manly dignity', claimed the anatomist who first studied it in the early twentieth century. More recent analysis has also revealed that, even in death, the new dynasty wanted to establish a clear break with previous practices; no longer using natron solution, with its direct replication of the birth process, they had reverted to standard, no-nonsense, dry natron to preserve the royal corpse.

Then, once wrapped in linen and covered by a yellow shroud, Seti's shaven-headed body was laid to rest in his great tomb (KV.17), the largest pharaoh's tomb ever created in the Valley of the Kings.

With almost every surface coloured by the artists Pay and Pashedu, whose brushes were still on the ground when the tomb was first discovered in 1817, its ceiling features black and gold astronomical images of the northern sky, where the multitude of deities include Seth, fully rehabilitated as one of the sun god's protectors.

Then below this artful rendition of the heavens was Seti's alabaster sarcophagus, under which, at the back of the burial chamber, lay a secret tunnel, only recently excavated to reveal that the tomb extends a full 174 metres down into Osiris's kingdom, where Seti I's soul could descend at will from his mummified body.

Seti's funeral was led by his son and heir Ramses II (c.1279–1213 BC). Without doubt one of Egypt's best known pharaohs, and described by some as its greatest, he has also been likened to the planet Jupiter – 'brilliant at a distance but is essentially a ball of gas'. For the famous pharaoh's most impressive feat seems to have been to live so long, his reign amounting to most of the thirteenth century BC in fact.

And it is almost impossible to go anywhere in Egypt without bumping into him, since he is credited with all manner of monuments throughout Egypt and Nubia. Yet in many cases he simply added to existing work, either cutting down earlier royal faces into his own, narrower features or simply adding his own cartouches, the endless repetion of Ramses II's names cut deeply into walls contrasting sharply with previous, more time-consuming techniques of raised relief carving.

And while it could be said that the beginning of an economic downturn may have forced him to adapt rather than create, some Egyptologists are of the opinion that 'Ramses' monuments impress more by their size and quantity than by their delicacy and perfection', for 'he is, when all is said, on the side of the cheap and nasty'.

Yet 'good art is not unknown in Ramses' reign, especially in the earlier years when artists from his father's court were still active'. Their work is clearly visible in Ramses's own cenotaph temple at Abydos near that of his father Seti, its colourful walls of attractive design once featuring a duplicate King List, with the same 'banned royals' from female pharaohs to the Amarna Four.

Censorship aside, the Nineteenth Dynasty were well aware of history, and their officials continued to visit ancient sites, both for inspiration and recreation. Prime minister Paser visited the Theban tomb of Kenamen, scribbling 'very beautiful' on its wall scenes, while treasury scribe Hadnakhte added that he had visited the Step Pyramid at Sakkara 'to take a stroll and enjoy himself', even if some deplored such graffiti on the old monuments, claiming 'my heart is sick when I see the work of their hands . . . if only someone could have denounced them before ever they entered'.

Sakkara was certainly a thriving necropolis during Ramses II's reign and, down in the valley below, the temples of Memphis were expanded, statuary erected and the royal name added everywhere. Ramses also took over his father Seti's new settlement at Qantir in the Delta, which he renamed Per-Ramesse – the 'house of Ramses' – thus becoming the first pharaoh to name a city after himself.

Although little remains of Per-Ramesse today, it was soon 'the most important international trade centre and military base in the country'. It had docks and warehouses, residential streets, government offices and large temples, filled with columns, obelisks and the ubiquitous statues of Ramses. His father's palace having been expanded – 'beauteous of balconies, dazzling with halls of lapis and turquoise' – it now featured gardens of exotic apple and olive trees and the royal zoo, housing an imported giraffe and the king's pet lions.

Yet the main creatures at Per-Ramesse were horses, after Ramses added a stable complex with 460 individual stalls and a huge exercise yard. The king was a great horse lover; his favourites, named 'Mut-is-content' and 'Victory-in-Thebes', were apparently fed 'with his own hand'.

And Per-Ramesse was the perfect base from which to monitor the situation in the Near East, where Egypt's interests were still being threatened by the Hittites. When his father Seti had defeated them outright at Kadesh, the fifteen-year-old Ramses had accompanied him; and he took the Hittites on again five years into his own reign around 1274 BC, with the aim of dislodging them from northern Syria.

He set out with four military divisions, but things got off to a bad start when he received falsified reports claiming the Hittites were some 150 kilometres away. Believing the reports, he marched north ahead of the rest of the army with only a single division, through Canaan towards Kadesh, only to discover too late that the Hittites were actually close by. As their chariots attacked, Ramses was seriously outnumbered, although it was later claimed that he 'does not let himself be moved by the millions of foreigners; he observes them as if they are foetuses made of straw'. Even when his men deserted, forcing him to fight virtually single-handed, the gods apparently came to his aid, Sekhmet 'with him on his horses, her hand is with him', as Amen encouraged him 'Forward! I am with you!', helpfully sending in the Egyptian reinforcements, just in time.

And as they managed to turn the battle around, pushing the Hittite forces back to the Orontes, many were 'forced to fling themselves into the river like crocodiles', including the prince of Aleppo. Unable to swim, the prince had to be rescued by his men, who turned him upside down and shook him to expel the water he had swallowed, a detail the Egyptians recorded with not inconsiderable amusement.

Although both sides then regrouped to face each other the following morning, the Egyptian chariotry now outnumbering their Hittite opponents, each side held their ground and the battle ended in stalemate.

With both sides then claiming victory, a formal peace treaty was eventually agreed, around 1259 BC. This was engraved in a combination of hieroglyphs and cuneiform on elaborate silver tablets and further copies were preserved in both Egypt and the Hittite capital Hattusha; a modern copy now hangs in the General Assembly building of the United Nations.

Following the treaty, diplomatic correspondence flowed regularly between the Egyptians and the Hittites. Ramses's mother, dowager queen Tuya, sent her greetings, while his favourite wife Nefertari wrote 'to my sister Puduhepa, the Great Queen of the Hittites', adding 'may the Sun god of Egypt and the Storm God of the Hittites bring you joy and make the peace good . . . I have sent you a gift, in order to greet you, my sister – a necklace of pure gold, composed of 12 bands and weighing 88 shekels, and some coloured linen for a royal robe for the king'.

As the cordial relations continued, Ramses II sent his physicians to treat the Hittite king's eye problems and to help his sister Matanazi conceive, albeit adding somewhat unchivalrously, 'Fifty is she? Never!

She's sixty for sure! No-one can produce medicine for her to have children', so the pharaoh sent an Egyptian magician as back-up.

In return, Hittite experts came to Per-Ramesse to advise on weapons manufacture, although the most important person to make the 800-mile journey from Hattusha to Egypt was the Hittite monarchs' eldest daughter. Today known only by her Egyptian name, Maathorneferura, she formally sealed the treaty in about 1245 BC by marrying Ramses II, although his excessive demands regarding her dowry brought a stern reprimand from the bride's mother, Puduhepa, who told him 'that you my brother should wish to enrich yourself from me is neither friendly nor honourable!'

Yet Maathorneferura herself was apparently 'a very goddess' whom Ramses 'loved more than anything'. She was suitably honoured with the status of Great Royal Wife, one of seven such women to hold this title during Ramses II's long reign; his two principal 'great wives' were Egyptians: Nefertari, who was probably a southerner descended from the Eighteenth Dynasty royal line, and Isetnofret, whose name means 'Isis the beautiful'.

All these women, together with minor wives from Egypt, Babylonia and a second Hittite princess, helped the pharaoh produce some forty-five sons and forty daughters, four of whom were also elevated to the status of Great Royal Wives, following the example of Amenhotep III, whom Ramses often emulated.

With the royal wives supplying the essential feminine element to the king's overtly masculine role in rituals, as portrayed in temple scenes at Luxor, Great Royal Wife Nefertari plays the sistrum rattles and sings before the gods, attending the Festival of the Mast of Min, in which male competitors climb a set of tall wooden poles in the god's honour. As the king and queen oversee the erection of the poles, Nefertari is shown dancing and drawing attention to her chest with her hands, in a pose designed to stimulate the god's virility.

Similar scenes appear on the West Bank, within the so-called Ramesseum funerary temple of Ramses II, which was also home to reused statues of Amenhotep III. The upper half of one such colossus was dragged off by a circus strongman-turned-antiquities hunter in 1816 and ended up in the British Museum, triggering huge public interest in ancient Egypt, while an engraving of one of the remaining figures inspired English poet Percy Shelley to write his famous verses on the nature of absolute kingship. Although the poem's title, 'Ozymandias', is simply the Greek version of Ramses II's throne-name 'Usermaatra', the inspiring sculpture had originally been made by Amenhotep III and only later appropriated by Ramses for his Ramesseum temple.

Covering the equivalent area of around four football pitches, the Ramesseum remains an atmospheric place. It had once housed multiple buildings and there were smaller temples dedicated to three generations of great royal wives – Ramses's mother Tuya, his wife Nefertari and their daughter Meritamun – as well as a palace for the court when it came south.

The Ramesseum also housed Egypt's oldest-known school building, weaving workshops and a series of huge mud-brick storerooms, whose arched construction housed the grain and other commodities needed for the daily temple offerings. Being so well supplied with storage, the Ramesseum complex soon became the administrative centre of Western Thebes, acting as the local bank from which state employees were paid their wages in the form of food rations.

This included the workers of nearby Deir el-Medina, now expanded to seventy houses within the town wall and another forty in the suburbs beyond, effectively creating the site that remains today.

A dozen or so occupants were named on their door frames – the painter Prahotep, the workman Khabekhnet and their neighbours, foreman Sennedjem and his wife Iyneferti. This couple's possessions were preserved in their family tomb located just a few metres up the hillside, which was found intact in 1886, still containing the mummified bodies of nine members of the family. Iyneferti, who died in her seventies, still wore a ring inscribed with the name of Amenhotep III, reflecting the affection in which the old king was still held in the region.

Although their tomb is quite small, it was superbly decorated by the villagers, who painted each other's tombs and indeed homes during their days off, two in every ten-day week. For these stone-masons, plasterers, draughtsmen and painters were highly valued workers, who managed to get away with imaginative reasons for absences from work, ranging from the repeated death of the same relative to brewing beer – and even staying home to drink it! Their time off averaged out so that they effectively worked only six months a year and their work days were made up of two four-hour shifts, incorporating a very civilised lunch break at noon.

Given the close proximity in which they worked and lived, there are remarkably few reported cases of violence. There is the occasional fight, like the time the tomb-builder Aonakht was sent off to the stone quarries 'for striking the heads of Djaydjay, Paidehu and Montupahapy'. But one villager, the infamous Paneb, was a repeat offender, whose antisocial behaviour included major theft, affairs with numerous women, mass brawling and, on one occasion, chasing his stepfather down the village street, shouting 'I will kill him in the night'.

Such fascinating details of ancient lives are a direct result of the high levels of literacy among the Deir el-Medina villagers, estimated at as much as forty per cent, against the national average of one per cent at best. There are hundreds of surviving letters and thousands of notes, ranging from Paser, writing to his wife Tutuia 'You sent me a message and I came', to postcard-type missives, letting the family know 'I am faring downstream to Memphis'. Then there is the villager Isis, asking her sister Nebuemnu to 'please weave me the shawl very, very quickly. And make one for my backside'. Similar terms found in the village's laundry lists reveal that such 'bands of the behinds' were probably sanitary towels.

Yet the huge collection of written material from Deir el-Medina actually incorporates everything from self-help manuals to medical texts, ghost stories to action adventures – the scribe Kenhirkhopshef even had his own library – while love poems and songs were so popular in the town that every known example from pharaonic Egypt comes from Deir el-Medina, except a single one found liter-ally down the street at the Ramesseum. One of them, containing such lines as 'You restore her in the night when she says to you "take me in your arms and let us lie like this til dawn",' is credited to 'Tashery from the music room', a woman who has been described as one of the earliest known performing artists.

But far beyond Thebes, Ramses II's subjects were busily engaged

Egypt is a desert bisected by the northward-flowing River Nile. It's narrow banks fan out into the Delta on reaching the Mediterranean Sea, while the Red Dea forms Egypt's other coastline.

Herds of wild cattle carved into the sandstone cliffs of Qurta near Edfu 19,000 years ago form the 'oldest graphic activity ever recorded in the whole of North Africa'.

The small stone circle forms the world's oldest known calendar and the stone 'cow' in the centre background in Egypt's earliest large-scale sculpture. Both are from Nabta Playa c. 5000–4500 BC, now re-erected in Aswan Museum.

The earliest known sculpted human head from Egypt, made of painted terracotta c. 4500 BC, and found at Merimda Beni Salama in the Western Delta.

Female Figurine of painted terracotta with upraised arms described as 'miming cow horns', from burial at el-Mamariya near Edfu, c. 3600–3300 BC.

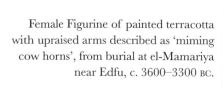

One of two gold-covered male statuettes with lapis-lazuli eyes, possibly representing the younger of two local rulers from c. 3200 bc, and found within the temple area at Tell Farkha in the Delta.

Large ceremonial limestone mace head showing King Scorpion performing irrigation rites, from the temple at Hierakonpolis c. 3150 BC.

Ceremonial slate cosmetic palette of King Narmer commemorating his unification of Egypt into a nation state c. 3100 bc, from the temple at Hierakonpolis

Ivory label portraying the stabbing of a bound figure and the blood collected in a bowl, from the Abydos tomb site of King Aha, c. 3080 BC.

The 'world's oldest dress', a long-sleeved linen tunic of a young woman, found inside out in a tomb at Tarkhan, c. 2950–2800 BC.

The name King Khasekhemwy surmounted by 'kissing' figures of Horus temple at Hierakonpolis, c. 2686 BC.

King Snefru embraced by a lioness deity on a fragment of painted wall scene from the king's Valley Temple at Dahshur, c. 2600 BC.

On the Giza plateau the shadow cast by King Khafra's pyramid in the foreground touches the Great Pyramid of his father King Khufu, surrounded by the small mastaba tombs of courtiers, c. 2580–2530 BC.

Statue group of King Menkaura held by the goddess Hathor, flanked by the personification of the Hermopolis region, from the king's Giza Valley Temple. c. 2500 BC.

Alabaster statuette of the Regent Ankhnespepi II with her infant son King Pepi II on her lap, possibly from a temple in southern Egypt, c. 2278–2270 BC.

Painted wooden models of
Egyptian troops with spears
and large cowhide shields,
found in the Asyut tomb
of local governor Meseheti
c. 2050 BC.

Limestone wall scene
portraying King Sesostris I
performing the ritual race
before the fertility god
Min, from the god's temple
at Koptos, c. 1965–1921 BC.

Granite figure of King Amenemhat III wearing
the menat necklace of Hathor and a hairstyle of
dreadlock-like braids, from the king's temple at
Shedet in the Fayum, c. 1855–1808 BC.

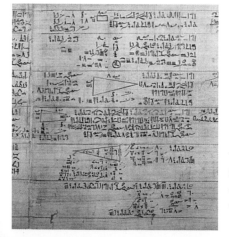

The Rhind Mathematical Papyrus,
featuring equations, fractions, and algebra,
commissioned by Hyksos king Apophis
c. 1542 bc, found at Thebes.

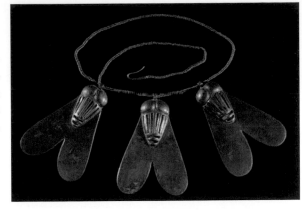

Large gold 'Flies of Valour' military awards worn by Queen Ahhotep and found in her Theban tomb at Dra Abu el-Naga, c. 1560–1530 BC.

Granite statue of King Hatshepsut's daughter Princess Neferura, on the lap of her tutor, the high official Senmut, c. 1470 BC, from Karnak temple, Thebes.

Dier el-Bahari with the temples of kings Montuhotep II (left) and Hatshepsut (right) in the foreground, and the Valley of the Kings royal cemetery located in the desert cliffs behind.

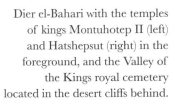

Busy workers casting metal (upper register) and making mud bricks
(lower register), among a wide variety of manufacturing scenes on the
Theban tomb of prime minister Rekhmire, c. 1430–1420 BC.

A cattle herder telling his bowling colleague 'Come on! Get yourself away! Pass on
quietly in order!' from the Theban tomb scenes of scribe Nebamun, c. 1360 BC.

Colossal statue group of King Amenhotep III and Queen Tiy with their daughters by their feet, originally from the king's funerary temple at Kom el-Hetan, c. 1360 BC.

The Colossi of Memnon of Amenhotep III once fronting the king's vast funerary temple of Kom el-Hetan, photographed during one of the last Nile floods in 1965.

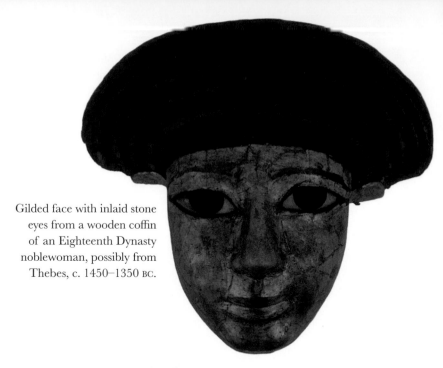

Gilded face with inlaid stone eyes from a wooden coffin of an Eighteenth Dynasty noblewoman, possibly from Thebes, c. 1450–1350 BC.

Gilded statuette of female pharaoh wearing the white crown, from the tomb of Tutankhamen (KV.62) in the Valley of the Kings, c. 1345–1335 BC.

The infant Tutankhaten (later Tutankhamen) on the left lap of Lady Maia (left) who claims to have 'nourished the flesh of the god' in scenes in her tomb at Sakkara, c. 1340–1330 BC.

Limestone statue group of the enthroned god Amen (left) embraced by the smaller figure of King Tutankhamen, later usurped by King Horemheb, from Karnak, c. 1336–1327 BC.

Limestone colossus of a royal woman inscribed with the name of Meritamen, a daughter of Ramses II, from the temple of Akhmim, c. 1327–1295 BC.

The King List from the Chamber of Ancestors in the temple of Seti I at Abydos, with Seti and son Ramses II standing before a selective list of 75 of thier predecessors, c. 1294–1279 BC.

Claiming 'I am a scribe', Queen Nefertari stands before the ibis-headed literacy god Thoth in her tomb (QV.66) in the Valley of the Queens, Thebes, c. 1279–1255 BC.

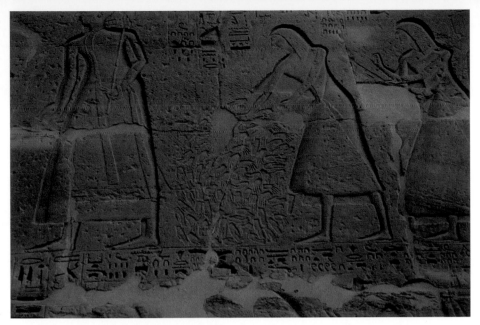

Officials and scribes of King Ramses III count the 12,659 severed hands of enemy dead in the king's funerary temple scenes at Medinet Habu, c. 1180–1153 BC.

Queen Nodjmet and husband Herihor both wearing the royal uraeus, in her Book of the Dead scenes most likely from the Deir el-Bahari cache (DB.320), c. 1070 BC.

Large gilded bronze figure of God's Wife priestess Karomama, daughter of Osorkon II once holding sistrum rattles, possibly from Thebes, c. 874 850 BC.

Gebel Barkal, legendary birthplace of the god Amen, with the pyramids of the successors of the Nubian pharaohs who ruled Egypt between 747–656 BC, Sudan.

Sphinxes of King Nectanebo I (380–362 bc) set up in front of Luxor temple at the beginning of the original Eighteenth Dynasty processional route to Karnak temple.

Alexander the Great with the rams' horns of the god Amen on the obverse of a silver tetradrachm minted by one of his former generals, King Lysimachus of Thrace, c. 305–281 BC.

Colossal statue of Isis 'Pharia' holding a billowing sail beside the Pharos lighthouse of Alexandria on the reverse of a bronze drachm of Antoninus Pius, AD 148.

Painted cartonnage mask of the jackal god Anubis, worn by funerary priest c. 380 BC–AD 100, most likely found in southern Egypt.

The three joint rulers Ptolemy VIII 'Physkon', Kleopatra II 'the sister' and Kleopatra III 'the Wife' standing before the god Horus at Kom Ombo temple, c. 142–116 BC.

The temple of Isis at Philae on the border with Nubia, built between 380 BC–AD 300 and active until the 6th century AD.

A posthumous marble portrait of Kleopatra VII, her head partly veiled by her mantle and ears pierced for earrings, set up in Mauretania (Algeria), c. 20–5 BC.

the length of Egypt and far to the south in Nubia, where the king commissioned seven rock-cut temples. The two most famous, built at Abu Simbel, 250 kilometres south-east of Aswan, were discovered beneath the ever-drifting sands in 1813, one intrepid lady traveller of 1881 not only clearing away the sands again, but staining the newly revealed rock with a solution of coffee to make it blend in with the rest! Then, in 1966, the temples were threatened with water, as the creation of the New Aswan Dam meant that much of Nubia and its many monuments would be permanently submerged beneath the resulting waters of Lake Nasser. So several temples, including the two at Abu Simbel, were painstakingly carved up, moved to higher ground and reassembled by UNESCO, a mammoth undertaking partly funded by sending Tutankhamen's treasures on their first world tour.

And as spectacular feats of ancient engineering alone, they were certainly worth saving.

Carved into a huge sandstone outcrop, the façade of the largest temple featured four seated colossi of Ramses II, one of which had toppled in an earthquake around 1248 BC, only a few years after completion. Each giant figure measured over twenty metres in height and were surrounded by tiny figures of his mother, his wife Nefertari and assorted offspring at the statues' feet. Then within the pillared interior, stretching back fifty metres into the rock, carved scenes portray the ubiquitous Battle of Kadesh and the royal couple, making offerings and executing captives in scenes in which Nefertari, 'united with the king', represents Hathor-Sekhmet. Yet the wow factor is reserved for the inner sanctum, in which a life-size statue of Ramses II sits beside Amen-Ra, Ra-Horakhty and Ptah. No works of art in themselves, they are nonetheless precisely aligned so that twice a year, on 22 February – the king's accession – and 22 October – his birthday – the first, finger-like sun rays light up Ramses's face for twenty minutes in 'a rare astronomical and engineering phenomenon'.

And, echoing the way in which Amenhotep III had built his wife Tiy her own temple in Nubia near his own, Ramses II constructed an accompanying rock-cut temple for Nefertari, 'for whose sake the very sun does shine' as the inscription on her temple's façade announces. Carved into another great sandstone outcrop, there are four more figures of Ramses II, standing around ten metres tall, but flanking two statues of Nefertari. Her distinctive feather crown of Hathor even makes her slightly taller than her husband, albeit in an artistic convention only allowed beyond Egypt's borders in far-flung Nubia, where her two colossal images as Hathor-Sekhmet were on permanent guard in this volatile region.

When the two temples were finally completed, around 1255 BC, inaugural festivities were held in the February, although the 3,000-kilometre round trip seems to have been Nefertari's final public appearance. It is assumed that she was too ill to actually complete the necessary rites; her daughter Meritamen appeared in her place, and Nefertari died some time that same year.

Perfectly mummified and her linen wrappings topped by the red linen shroud of Hathor-Sekhmet, 'Lady of Red Linen', Nefertari was buried in Hathor's sacred Valley of the Queens in a truly spectacular tomb (QV.66). Discovered in 1904, its recently-conserved wall scenes are almost as perfect as the day they were painted, absolute proof that high-quality art 'continued to flourish when not subjected to the dead weight of the king's ego'.

Indeed, husband Ramses is refreshingly conspicuous by his absence, and Nefertari is the central figure, her perfectly groomed appearance enhanced by her gold regalia and silver earrings, which some suggest were sent to her as a greeting gift from the Aegean. Portrayed among the gods, including Hathor, who offers her an ankh to guarantee eternal life, the queen also appears before ibis-headed Thoth, god of literacy, a scribe's palette between them; the accompanying text from the *Book of the Dead* includes the queen's words 'O gods, behold, I am a scribe!' – an intriguing statement, in light of the queen's correspondence with the Hittites.

A fine statuette of Thoth was also discovered among the remains of her original burial equipment, and although her tomb was robbed in antiquity, there were still some of her *shabti* servant figurines, fragments of her clothing and a pair of sandals, parts of wooden storage chests and an enamel knob bearing the name of the Eighteenth Dynasty king Ay, possibly one of Nefertari's ancestors. There were even the remains of some of Nefertari's treasured jewellery: parts of a gold bracelet, a lotus flower earring and two plaques of silver and gold. These were discovered in 1904 and unexpectedly added to in 1988, when one of the conservators working on a section of loose wall plaster discovered behind it another piece of gold, embossed with Nefertari's name. But of the great lady herself, all that remained of her well-mummified body were her knees, amidst the pieces of her pink granite sarcophagus.

At least her tomb fared rather better than the gargantuan 'KV.5', which Ramses either built or at least greatly developed from an existing Eighteenth Dynasty tomb in the Valley of the Kings. Already known in 1825, it is the largest tomb in the entire royal cemetery, and was created to house some of Ramses's many sons. With its multi-level structure of over 120 chambers and corridors, resembling an underground 'multi-storey car park', its rediscovery in 1995 required the removal of tons of stone chippings that had been washed in by repeated flash floods, destroying much of the wall decoration and reducing the once-mummified royal sons to skeletal remains.

For although Nefertari's eldest son Amenhirkhopshef had been made heir apparent, he died before his father, as did the next son, then the next, until Ramses appointed his fourth son, by Great Royal Wife Isetnofret, as his heir.

This was Prince Khamwese. Long remembered as 'a very learned scribe and magician who spent his time in the study of ancient monuments and books', he has also been dubbed 'the first Egyptologist', whose antiquarian interests were in keeping with the spirit of the age.

Unlike his more military-minded father and grandfather, the young Khamwese had chosen a career in the clergy as a priest of Ptah, creator god of Memphis. Taking full advantage of the temple libraries of Memphis and nearby Heliopolis, Khamwese was responsible for organising his father's jubilees, which were traditionally celebrated after thirty years' rule, then at varying intervals thereafter. And since the long-lived Ramses celebrated no fewer than fourteen, each one based on rites dating back to the very first dynasty, Khamwese was kept busy.

He also initiated a restoration programme around Sakkara and Giza, 'because he loved to restore the monuments of kings and make firm again what had fallen into ruin'. So when the work was completed, he had the ancient structures officially inscribed with the name of the monuments' original owners, together with the name of his father, the current pharaoh, and a brief description of the work carried out, inscriptions which have been called 'the biggest museum labels in all history!'

At Sakkara, where one of these inscriptions is still visible on the south side of Unas's pyramid, he also restored the Step Pyramid, the pyramid of Userkaf and the *mastaba* of Fourth Dynasty king Shepseskhaf, adding the old king's previously missing name to his monument. At Abusir he repaired the pyramid of Sahura and Niuserra's sun temple; and at Giza, where Ramses II had requisitioned stone from Khafra's pyramid complex to build a new temple at Heliopolis, Khamwese was doing what he could to preserve what remained. Master builder Maya was appointed as the manager of restorations to the Great Pyramid of Khufu and he and Khamwese's workers unearthed a 1,000-year-old statue of Khufu's son in the process. It was reported that 'Prince Khamwese delighted in this statue of the king's son Kawab which he discovered in the fill of a shaft in the area of the well of his father Khufu'. The prince then placed the antique in a shrine as a kind of museum, 'because he loved the noble ones who dwelt in antiquity before him, and the excellence of all they made'. A very fine sentiment indeed.

By the age of thirty, Prince Khamwese had become Ptah's high priest, responsible for not only Ptah's daily rites in his great Memphis temple, but also the well-being of the god's sacred creature, the Apis bull, 'king of every sacred animal', believed to contain the god's very spirit. Each bull had been mummified at death and buried in Sakkara in a tradition dating back at least to Amenhotep III and his own son, high priest Prince Tuthmosis.

When the Apis bull died around 1263 BC, the funeral procession, led by Khamwese and his father, was accompanied by the same rich funerary goods of jewellery, amulets and *shabti* figures that would have been part of a royal interment. Some were inscribed with Khamwese's name and others with those of courtiers keen to demonstrate their piety, the burial party's footprints still visible in the sandy floor when the tomb was discovered in 1852.

Khamwese also oversaw the funeral of the next bull some fourteen years later, complete with its gilded coffin and gold face mask, but this time he changed the way the creatures were buried.

Rather than placing each one in an individual grave, he repeated the design of his brothers' multiple tomb structure in the Valley of the Kings and initiated the building of a single subterranean catacomb – later known as the Serapeum – with separate side chambers for each bull, and each chamber supplied with a granite sarcophagus weighing up to eighty tons!

He then built a new temple for the Apis cult above the catacomb, inscribed with the words: 'Oh you, who shall enter this temple which I have created for the Apis, and who shall see the things which I have done, engraved on the stone walls as great and effective! Never has the like been done before. It will indeed seem great to you, when you behold the ancestors' poor and ignorant works. So remember my name, when decreeing future works – O Apis, great god, I am the priest Prince Khamwese!'

By around 1229 BC, the fifty-five-year-old Khamwese was finally Crown Prince. But he too died before his father – only five years later, having chosen burial close to the Apis bulls in the region of the Serapeum, where his tomb still lies beneath the drifting sands. Yet he had certainly left his mark. For just as he had wished, he was remembered for more than a thousand years, immortalised in colourful tales in which he wanders around Sakkara, encountering a family of ghosts who guard a secret book of universal wisdom, falling for a beautiful phantom woman and fathering a magical child who turns out to be a famous magician of the past.

As for Khamwese's famous father, Ramses II eventually died in about 1213 BC, somewhere in his eighties, and his body was mummified – as one would expect – to a very high standard. His receding white hair had been touched up with a weak henna rinse to replicate the red hair of his youth, and his prominent nose was packed with resin and peppercorns to retain its distinctive shape beneath the layers of linen wrappings. When these were removed at his official unwrapping before the Egyptian ruler Khedive Tewfiq in 1886, the release of pressure caused Ramses's arms to slowly rise up, much to the temporary alarm of those present.

Like his father Seti I, he was buried in an alabaster sarcophagus in his grand tomb (KV.7) in the Valley of the Kings. The tomb was, like almost every other, robbed in antiquity and its wall decoration destroyed by centuries of flash floods that washed in tons of stone chippings, as was also the case with his children's tomb (KV.5).

The legendary old king was finally succeeded by his thirteenth surviving son Merenptah, a younger brother of Khamwese but already in his fifties. Merenptah's reign was but a decade long (c.1213–1203 BC), and was inevitably spent very much in his father's long shadow.

Merenptah – 'beloved of Ptah' – initially resided in his palace at Memphis, built beside the temple of the creator god after whom he was named. But soon his main residence became Per-Ramesse, in order to be close to rapidly changing events in the Near East.

He honoured his father's peace treaty with the Hittites by sending them food supplies, which had become increasingly necessary as their empire began to fall apart in the widespread chaos that marked the end of the Bronze Age. Part of the same chain of events brought about the collapse of the so-called Palace Culture in mainland Greece, affected the Greek Islands and Ionia and created large numbers of displaced people. And as they began to move east around the Mediterranean down the Levantine coast in search of a better life, the end of the line was Egypt, the fabled land of plenty, on which many of the migrants now set their sights.

With their families in tow, the migrants eventually formed a confederation with the Libyans and attempted to invade Egypt both by land and sea. So the Egyptians referred to them as 'Peoples of the Sea' and named them variously as the 'Sherden', perhaps from modern Sardinia; the 'Ekwesh', identified as Greek Achaeans; the 'Lukka', piratical raiders of Lycia in Asia Minor; the 'Sheklesh', maybe from Sicily; and the 'Teresh', who some claim to be the forerunners of the Etruscans.

As the 16,000-strong coalition force entered the Eastern Delta around 1208 BC, moving south toward Memphis and Heliopolis, Merenptah engaged them in a six-hour battle. His troops killed six thousand and the rest were taken prisoner, and settled in military colonies around the Delta.

Announcing his great victory on a stela, Merenptah claimed that 'all who roamed have been subdued' and Libya destroyed. Adding that he had also dealt with rebellions among Egypt's Palestinian vassals in Canaan, Ashkelon and Gezer, he gives the first known reference to a specific tribe named 'Israel', which Merenptah claimed 'is laid waste, its seed is no more'.

Now known as the 'Israel Stela', this five-ton slab of granite was found at the very back of the huge funerary temple of Amenhotep III where Merenptah had built his own, far smaller, temple almost as an annexe to that of his great predecessor. In his attempt to bask in a little of the sun king's reflected glory, Merenptah, like his father Ramses, had reused much of Amenhotep's original architecture; in fact 'almost all the material used in the construction of his own funerary temple' came from that of Amenhotep.

Yet far from rampant vandalism, recent research has revealed that by around 1200 BC, Amenhotep III's funerary temple had been damaged in an earthquake which cracked the Colossi of Memnon statues and toppled everything else, reducing the once-magnificent monument to little more than a glorified reclamation yard. Merenptah seems to have literally picked up the pieces, turning them round and re-inscribing them on the other side for use in his own adjacent funerary temple.

So his Israel inscription was carved on the back of a stela originally made by Amenhotep III, in much the same way as he built his temple walls from the blocks of the earlier structure after it had collapsed. When excavating Merenptah's temple in the 1990s, archaeologists discovered that it was basically a smaller version of Amenhotep's, effectively turned inside out, the reverse of the recycled blocks covered in stunning images of Amenhotep, whose vivid colours had been preserved through Merenptah's timely appropriations.

With his recycled funerary temple well under way, Merenptah commissioned his tomb (KV.8) in the Valley of the Kings, a massive sepulchre cut down into the bedrock along a straight descending path. A unique side chamber was dedicated to his father Ramses II; its wall scenes were similar to those in his tomb and that of Seti I, with the addition of red-headed deities. Then once the bulk of the work was complete, the king ordered that his funeral equipment should be placed *in situ* well in advance, beginning with statues of the gods, then his four massive stone sarcophagi, whose tricky instal-lation was overseen by prime minister Panehesy. They were placed one within the other; the three outer granite ones had lids carved with effigies of the king, and their undersides with the outstretched figures of goddess Nut to fulfil her eternal promise – 'I have come so I may stretch myself around you, so your heart might live'. The innermost sarcophagus was, like those of his father and grandfather, made of white alabaster, in which Merenptah's gilded cedar coffin would eventually be placed.

As the workers finished off remaining details, the king was so pleased with the results he sent them extra rations of meat, fruit, sesame oil and beer, all much appreciated at a time of growing infla-tion and increasing economic hardship.

When Merenptah died around 1203 BC, his body was mummified so skilfully that it is still possible to see the family resemblance to Ramses II and Seti I. The anatomist who studied his body in 1907 reported it had 'a pleasant odour, like Friar's balsam', while the star-tlingly white appearance of the skin, likely caused by encrustations of the natron salts used as a desiccant, once gave rise to the mistaken assumption that Merenptah must have been the pharaoh of the Exodus who had drowned in the Red Sea!

But the succession was far from straightforward, as the throne was briefly seized by one of Merenptah's younger sons, Amenmesse (c.1203–1200 BC). When it eventually passed to the intended heir, another of Merenptah's sons, Seti II (c.1200–1194 BC), he imme-diately removed all trace of his predecessor, whom he dubbed 'the enemy'.

Already in his mid-fifties at his accession, Seti II was a grandchild of Ramses II, as was his Great Royal Wife, Tawosret, whose name means 'the Mighty One'. The couple were both portrayed in the tomb Seti II was preparing for himself in the Valley of the Kings (KV.14), until the tomb-builders received a surprise visit when 'the chief of police came, saying 'the falcon has flown up to heaven, namely Seti, and another has arisen in his place'.

At the news Seti II had died, the new king was declared to be his red-headed son, Siptah (c.1194–1188 BC), born to a minor Canaanite wife. Young Siptah suffered from polio, and as he was aged only around ten at the time of his accession, his stepmother, Tawosret, became 'great regent of all the land'.

The new royal pair were aided by the Syrian-born scribe Bay, soon made 'Chancellor of the entire land'. He also had a tomb started in the Valley of the Kings (KV.13), and as a self-styled kingmaker, claimed to have 'established the king upon the throne of his father'. As a phrase usually reserved for the gods, this suggests that the ambitious chancellor Bay had begun to overreach himself, so much so that by the time he reached sixteen, Siptah had person-ally ordered Bay's execution, telling the tomb-builders to down their tools as the tomb of the 'great enemy Bay' was no longer required.

But then the teenage Siptah himself died, and Tawosret (c.1188–1186 BC) became pharaoh, taking the new royal names Sitra-meritamen, 'Daughter of Ra, beloved of Amen', 'Chosen one of Mut' and 'Strong Bull, beloved of Maat'. A later historian refers to 'King Thuoris', 'in whose time Troy was taken', an event tradi-tionally dated to the 1180s BC when Tawosret did indeed rule as pharaoh. Her cartouches were modelled on those of her grandfather Ramses II, as were her statues, set up in Heliopolis and Thebes in masculine-style attire.

As a ruler with all the hallmarks of the previous female pharaoh, Nefertiti, it does seem rather coincidental that tomb KV.56 in the Valley of the Kings, believed to have been originally created for Nefertiti by those who re-excavated the site, was now brought back into service.

For when it was first discovered in 1908, it contained so much jewellery that the archaeologists dubbed it the 'Gold Tomb', after the earrings, bracelets, amulets, necklace, sandals and crown-style diadem they found there.

Since some of the pieces named Tawosret and Seti II, it was assumed that the tomb must have been reused to bury Tawosret or one of her children, although the small amounts of gold leaf and stucco are more likely to have come from a jewel casket than a coffin. Close examination of the jewellery itself also reveals that it was not made to be worn, since some of the cartouches in that case would have been upside down. The motifs are equally intriguing:

one pair of bracelets shows Tawosret pouring a drink for the seated Seti II in the same pose adopted by Nefertiti and Akhenaten and a second pair shows Tawosret as the lead figure in front of Seti II. And since Nefertiti may well have been a role model for Tawosret, the jewellery would certainly have been a most fitting votive offering for her female predecessor.

In the turbulent, if poorly documented, times in which Tawosret lived, there is evidence of civil war, and she herself may have been involved in some form of military conflict. A sketch on a large piece of limestone shows a royal woman firing arrows from a chariot at a male opponent, who may perhaps have been her male successor, Sethnakht.

And when Tawosret died around 1186 BC, she was not only the last king of the Nineteenth Dynasty, but the final female pharaoh for almost a thousand years.

Although his origins are unknown, the first king of the new Twentieth Dynasty, Sethnakht (c. 1186–1184 BC), was named after the god Seth, much like the two Seti kings of the previous dynasty from whom he may have been descended.

Plans were under way for Sethnakht's new tomb in the Valley of the Kings (KV. 11), but were abruptly abandoned when his builders accidentally cut through into the tomb of the earlier king Amenmesse. So Sethnakht instead took over and extended the tomb of his predecessor Tawosret (KV. 14), removing both her burial and her names.

Although Sethnakht's reign was as short as Tawosret's had been, later texts claim that he 'set in order the entire land which had been rebellious; he slew the rebels who were in the land of Egypt; he cleansed the great throne of Egypt and was ruler of the Two Lands'. But his greatest contribution to Egypt's history was to produce with his queen Tiy-Mereniset one of its great warrior kings: Ramses III (c. 1184–1153 BC).

The third Ramses certainly enjoyed a far longer reign than his father, but they were years fraught with violence. As the Libyans once more tried to invade Egypt from the west, they again collaborated with the 'Sea Peoples', the Sherden, Sheklesh and Teresh now joined by the Denyen who some identify as the Greek Danaans, the Peleset, possibly the Philistines and the Tjeker and the Weshwesh, most likely from Canaan.

It was reported around 1176 BC that 'suddenly these peoples were on the move, no country able to withstand their arms – the Hittites, Cilicia, Carchemish, Cyprus and other lands' – all fell before the invaders. And now they once more headed for Egypt, when 'their intentions were "Action!", and their wishes filled with wrongdoing and perversion'. But Ramses III was waiting for them on the Delta coast, and believing that the goddesses Anat and Astarte acted as his impenetrable shield, the pharaoh stated that 'their plans were crushed and overturned by the wish of god', since 'I overthrew those who invaded, I slew the Denyen from their islands, the Tjeker were made ashes, the Sherden and the Weshwesh of the sea were made as those who do not exist'.

Enemy casualties were calculated by the piles of body parts severed post-mortem, not only the right hand but also the penis in a form of ritual emasculation dating back to the time of Narmer. Prisoners were then forcibly resettled in the Delta and throughout Egypt's territories in Canaan, soon to be redeployed as the mercenaries who would come to dominate Egypt's army.

With his enemies defeated and Egypt once more secure, Ramses III could not only claim that 'I caused to sit idle the soldiers and chariotry in my time', but also that 'I caused the woman of Egypt to walk freely wheresoever she would, unmolested by others along the road'.

Spending most of his reign in the north, his officials were clearly incredibly busy at Heliopolis, where Ra received no fewer than 2,528,168 floral bouquets during his reign. The king also landscaped the temple grounds, telling Ra, 'I planted olive groves for you in your city of Heliopolis, equipped with gardeners and numerous people to make pure oil, the best of Egypt, in order to light the lamps in your holy dwelling'.

Just north of Heliopolis, at Tell el-Yahudiya, Ramses III built a fine palace, the jewel-like glazed tiles adorning his throne room featuring bound captives from Syria, Nubia and Libya. There to be trampled on whenever he crossed the floor, the same captives were painted on the soles of the royal sandals, no doubt making a real psychological impact whenever foreign envoys paid a visit.

The same style of décor was also employed in the palace Ramses III built in Thebes. Attached to his huge funerary temple at Medinet Habu, his columned throne room, with its adjoining bedroom and limestone-lined en-suite bathroom, led to a 'window of appearances' through which he could watch the rituals in his adjoining temple, which had been completed in only twelve years.

Just like the second Ramses and his son Merenptah, Ramses III took much of the statuary from Amenhotep III's nearby temple ruins for his own at Medinet Habu, whose very name is simply Arabic for 'Hapu's City', in honour of Amenhotep III's great official Amenhotep, Son of Hapu, who had organised this statuary in the first place.

Once fronted by a harbour connected to the Nile, the temple and its original vivid paintwork remains largely intact within its original eighteen-metre-high mud-brick walls. Its unique entrance takes the form of a Syrian-style *migdol* gatehouse, whose upper rooms featured large windows to catch the afternoon breeze, flanked by the sculpted heads of foreign captives.

Beyond the great front pylon, across which Ramses III smites enemies he grasps with a single fist, the temple's interior walls are adorned with detailed scenes of his recent encounters with the Libyans and Sea Peoples. These scenes are of confusion and chaos; one Libyan chief is described as 'slit wide open on the ground', while the royal scribes carefully record the tally of dead: 'hands – 12,659; foreskins – 12,859', as lines of bound captives are led away.

Elsewhere are scenes of stick-fighting and wrestling in which Egyptians tackle competitors from Libya, Syria and Nubia, formalised displays before an invited audience of ambassadors, courtiers and the king himself. As the referee uses a trumpet to start each round, the Egyptian participants proclaim 'My lord the pharaoh is with me and against you!', inevitably emerging victorious as Egypt takes on the world and wins, be it on the sports field or on the field of battle.

As the scenes unfold further, Ramses III himself accompanies the priests, some carrying large cartouches naming thirty previous rulers from Amenhotep III to Tawosret, while his half-Syrian Great Royal Wife Ese performs the ritual fertility dance before the great bull of Min.

The king had an army of minor wives too; they were portrayed in the less formal parts of the temple, playing board games with him while he embraces them and even tickles them under the chin. Yet the sheer number of such women, and all their royal offspring, would ultimately lead to Ramses III's downfall.

For despite his undoubted success in defending Egypt from external threats, he met his end at the hands of his own family.

After some thirty years, at the end of which he celebrated his first jubilee, Ramses III followed the example of Amenhotep III and relocated permanently to Thebes. But his time there was cut short after only a year.

For trial records record that King's Wife Teya wanted one of her sons, Pentawere, to be king, and was unhappy when the son of a rival wife was named heir instead.

With both the motive and opportunity to alter the line of succession, Teya was arrested after 'plotting those matters with the women of the harem, and for making rebellion' with the help of a butler, a cook, the king's personal physician and the court magician, Prekamenef, who, it was alleged, would use his magic and wax images to immobilise the guards and render the king vulnerable.

A total of thirty-eight conspirators were eventually found guilty, including the queen and her son; they died 'of their own accord' apparently in enforced suicide. The other condemned men and women were burned alive just beyond the temple gate, the traditional place of punishment, while three of the judges, who had colluded with the guilty parties, had their ears and noses amputated.

Although state records would never admit that a divine monarch had been killed, couching any sensitive royal matters instead in the most obscure of euphemisms, it seemed that the plot had been discovered in time. For when Ramses III's mummy was partly unwrapped in 1886, no evidence of suspicious death was found, only an unsettling appearance, which inspired the 1932 film *The Mummy*.

But in 2012, CT scans penetrated the remaining wrappings round the king's throat to reveal a serious wound under the larynx, severing all soft tissue down to the bone. He would have died in seconds.

The same scans also revealed that his embalmers had carefully inserted an Eye of Horus amulet into the wound, symbolising whole-ness and health, at least in the next world.

Then Ramses III's body was taken to the Valley of the Kings for burial in his tomb (KV.11). Originally begun by his father Sethnakht until his builders collided with an earlier tomb, Ramses's architects had simply shifted the direction of the entrance corridor, and proceeded to create a cavernous, multi-roomed tomb, on which work was finally halted when its builders received news that 'the hawk has flown to heaven', telling them that Ramses III was dead.

Yet in striking contrast to their usual lengthy work reports, the tomb-builders' laconic statement 'The burial of the coffin took place' may reflect that they had been suffering increasingly from the economic downturn, made worse by administrative incompetence and downright corruption, as deliveries of their food supplies – their wages – had become increasingly erratic. So their foreman Khonsu had lodged an official complaint, which initially produced positive results.

But when the following month's wages again failed to arrive, the workers had downed tools in the first recorded strike in history, which had taken place in Ramses III's twenty-ninth year, around 1155 BC. Marching down towards the Ramesseum with its huge temple granaries, they staged a day-long sit-in, shouting 'We are hungry' and uttering 'great oaths'. The following day, they returned to the Ramesseum and this time stayed all night but, despite them shouting out at passing officials, including the local mayor, they were only paid just prior to Ramses III's jubilee festival, presumably to shut them up.

For the king focused most of his attention on the main temples at Heliopolis, Memphis and Thebes, awarding them land grants so generous that by the end of his reign a third of Egypt's cultivable land belonged to the temples. A staggering seventy-five per cent of this was owned by Karnak, whose priests were now the coun-try's power-brokers. No wonder they named the king 'beloved of Amen' and immortalised him in granite as their god's standard-bearer!

Such largesse obviously had an enormous impact on the balance of state finances and, as food prices continued to increase, the wages of state employees were soon in arrears. So some were forced to seek alternative sources of income through theft – from a copper chisel stolen by the village woman Herya, to the temple gardener Kar peeling off small sections of gilding from temple door jambs. There were even attempts to enter the tombs of Ramses II, Tutankhamen and Yuya and Tuya, in the Valley of the Kings, in search of small items – linen that could be easily traded, metalwork that could be melted down and costly perfumes – those stolen from Tutankhamen's tomb scooped out by someone who left their finger-prints behind.

But heedless of their subjects' continued financial struggles, Ramses III's generous endowments to the gods were lavishly outlined on a forty-one-metre-long illustrated papyrus, created by his son and successor Ramses IV (c.1153–1147 BC), the designated heir and a son of Ramses III's queen Tyti.

And the new king had big plans.

He immediately began work on an ambitious building scheme, expanding his father's temple of Khonsu at Karnak, where Ramses IV's sister-wife, Queen Tentopet, was also the God's Wife priestess.

Ramses IV also commissioned work on his tomb in the Valley of the Kings (KV.2). He had first sent his prime minister to the Valley of the Kings 'to select a spot for cutting out the royal tomb', and now its construction forged ahead by doubling the number of workmen to 120. The plans were drawn up by the Deir el-Medina scribe Amennakht, who used different colours for the proposed sarcophagus of red granite, labelling the burial chamber the 'house of gold', and his papyrus original copied on to a large stone ostracon for use on site.

The king's request for an enormous sarcophagus and his need for large amounts of building stone required a series of quarrying exped-itions, the 8,000 men sent out to the Wadi Hammamat in the Eastern Desert taking with them a detailed map, again produced by Amennakht, who had once more selected different colours for the different rock types, not only to create a highly accurate document, but by far the oldest-known geological map in the world.

He also wrote his name on the back of the map in his charac-teristic handwriting, and even wrote his name on his Deir el-Medina door frame, so it is still possible to visit the very place he undertook his work 3,165 years ago. Perhaps even sitting on the flat roof of his house to benefit from the daylight because of failing eyesight, Amennakht prayed to the local goddess Meretseger, 'You made me see darkness in the day, I shall declare Your power to other people. Be gracious to me in your grace!', with both the deity and her supplicant portrayed on this stela as notably eyeless.

His king, Ramses IV, likewise prayed for 'strength to my limbs', asking Osiris to give him a reign twice as long as his namesake, Ramses II. But clearly the gods were not listening. For after just six years as king, the fourth Ramses was dead.

With 450 people needed to transport his burial equipment to his tomb, including the 120 tomb-builders and sixty police, the work was overseen by the 'Superintendant of All Works' who was also the prime minister – the Karnak High Priest Ramsesnakht.

Ramsesnakht even accompanied state officials when they paid state employees, 'indicating that the temple of Amen, not the state, was now at least partly responsible for their wages'. Ramsesnakht's son, 'Steward of the Estate of Amen', controlled a huge 120-kilometre stretch of prime state-owned farmland in Middle Egypt between the Fayum and Minya, and became 'chief taxing master'.

By now the crown had dwindling influence over the temple's affairs and, indeed, its own, as royal power was not only adversely affected by the unstoppable rise of the Karnak clergy, but by the high turnover of kings, all named Ramses.

Ramses V's brief reign (c.1147–1143 BC) allowed little scope for great deeds, and the grand tomb begun for him in the Valley of the Kings (KV.9) remained unfinished at the time of his death.

Yet this was not owing to any laxity on the part of his tomb-builders, even though their numbers had been cut back to sixty, but because there was serious danger. For as they themselves reported, 'the chief of police came and said to the foremen "do not go up to the valley until you will see what will happen. I will look for you, and I will come and tell you to go up".'

With the builders themselves claiming that they were 'inactive because of the enemy', with sporadic attacks by Libyan raiders, there are also signs that the crown and Karnak clergy were once again at odds.

For the next king, Ramses VI (c.1143–1136 BC), a younger son of Ramses III, took the throne-name 'Nebmaatra' in a direct lift from Amenhotep III. He also took the title 'God ruler of Heliopolis', and may well have begun attempts to reassert royal authority and curb the power of Karnak.

And when it came to the funeral rites of his predecessor Ramses V, Ramses VI certainly ordered that things were done rather differently. For not only was the face of Ramses V 'painted an earthy red colour' to show him newly (re)born, his skin was also covered in tiny lumps, much like that of Amenhotep II. Claimed to be 'highly suggestive of smallpox' by the anatomist who unwrapped the mummy of Ramses V in 1907, this soon became 'the fact that he died from smallpox' and is now completely accepted, even though analysis of skin fragments has found no evidence for the pox virus. In fact, his X-rays reveal that the small pustules are actually natron crystals beneath his skin, because Ramses V had been immersed in a natron solution in a return to the old Eighteenth Dynasty way of doing things.

Yet as the plot thickens further, the perfectly mummified body of Ramses V was not buried for almost two years, perhaps because the Valley of the Kings remained a no-go area. It was finally interred in the king's original tomb (KV.9), by now completed by his successor Ramses VI, who planned to be buried here too. So he had added both their names to its walls, across which 'the god Ra is given greater prominence' in its new-style decoration, the first to differ since the time of Seti I, the burial chamber ceiling now adorned with a fabulous double image of Nut, swallowing the sun to which she then gives birth in an eternal cycle.

But, just as had happened the last time the monarchy had been so focused on internal matters of religion and politics during the Amarna Period, Egypt's remaining empire was dwindling to nothing; its garrisons were abandoned and destroyed, Canaan lost completely and Ramses VI was the last Egyptian king to be named in inscriptions in the Sinai.

Following his death and burial alongside his predecessor Ramses V in their joint tomb (KV.9), Ramses VI was succeeded by his son, Ramses VII (c.1136–1129 BC), who now took power – or what was left of it.

As inflation soared to its highest level, Egypt was on its financial knees. And unable to leave any real mark, Ramses VII was buried in his modest tomb (KV.1), his body never found. Nor was that of his nephew, Ramses VIII (c.1129–1126 BC), the last son of Ramses III, whose tomb has never even been located.

At least Ramses IX (c.1126–1108 BC) gave Egypt some much-needed stability, with the name of this likely grandson of Ramses III found as far north as Gezer in Canaan, as far west as the Daklah Oasis, and as far south as Amara in Nubia, although his ability to exploit the region's goldmines was pretty much non-existent.

As the cash-strapped monarchy was now based largely in the north, Ramses IX focused his attentions on Heliopolis and the sun god, whose high priest was his own son, Prince Nebmaatra.

For southern Karnak was now the priests' domain, a power balance made quite clear in wall scenes showing King Ramses IX presenting honours to Karnak's new high priest Amenhotep, who, quite astonishingly, is shown on the same scale as the pharaoh!

The writing for the monarchy was quite literally on the wall.

Over on the West Bank, the striking tomb-builders were still unhappy at the erratic delivery of their wages, so Herere, wife of high priest Amenhotep, wrote to the troop captain, Peseg, 'What's this about the personnel of the great necropolis concerning whom I wrote to you saying "give them rations" and you haven't yet given them any? As soon as my letter reaches you, you shall look for the grain and give them rations from it. Don't complain to me again!'

But things still didn't improve, and so began wide-scale robberies from the royal tombs themselves.

As revealed by trial records, the stonemason Amenpanufer and his friends broke into the tomb of the Seventeenth Dynasty king Sobekemsaf II and his wife Nubkhas, telling the court that they took treasures amounting to an impressive 144 kilograms of bullion.

Then at some point, the recently sealed tomb of Ramses V and VI (KV.9) was entered and its valuable metals and textiles taken. But financial gain can't have been the only purpose, for the mummified body of Ramses VI was attacked so severely with an axe that it virtually fell apart. Based on the simple laws of physics, this couldn't have been achieved when his body was wrapped, since experiments have demonstrated that a mere three layers of linen are enough to make even the sharpest axe or machete simply bounce off the surface. The damage done to Ramses VI was therefore only possible once his body had been unwrapped, after which his face had been shattered, his mouth broken in and his arms hacked off at the elbows. Even his stone sarcophagus had been laboriously broken up.

This was hardly the random action of furtive tomb-robbers undertaking a smash-and-grab raid in minimal time, well aware that torture and impalement awaited them if caught. So it seems Ramses VI had been specifically targeted, a possibility made all the more likely by the fact that the body of his predecessor Ramses V was left virtually untouched.

There were certainly rumours of official collusion, with the mayor of Western Thebes, Paweraa, accused of failing to maintain security, dismissing the cases put before him and turning a blind eye to activities possibly orchestrated by some of the priests themselves. For they were already reusing royal tombs in the Valley of the Queens and the temples around Deir el-Bahari for their own burials, and perhaps taking the opportunity to settle old scores in the Valley of the Kings.

Such an opportunity seems to have occurred during construction of Ramses IX's tomb (KV.6), when the builders cutting one of its side rooms accidentally broke through into the earlier Amarna tomb KV.55 immediately below it. Calling in the authorities, the official party discovered the mummified body of the 'Great Criminal', Akhenaten, and took the opportunity to rip off the golden face of his coffin and inflict damage to the lower part of his face, making him unable to either breathe or speak in the next world. Having effectively neutralised him, they also removed his names from the tomb, and the body of his mother, Queen Tiy, who lay close by, although their attempts to take out her golden funerary shrines ended in failure when they got stuck in the doorway and were left exactly where they were – much to the curiosity of the archaeologists who found them in 1907, and whose successors have been hotly debating the tomb's remaining contents ever since.

Ramses IX's tomb-builders nonetheless persevered in the tomb above, and when the king died around 1108 BC and was interred in his finished sepulchre in rites led by his obscure successor Ramses X (c.1108–1099 BC), he in turn was buried in the valley in tomb KV.18, although his mummy has never been located.

The very last king of the dynasty was Ramses XI (c.1099–1069 BC). But with even fewer facts available than usual, it is no exaggeration to say that 'the history of this confusing period is still being written'.

The last of the Ramessides ruled for around thirty years, largely from Memphis, since Per-Ramesse was abandoned when its harbour sanded up as the Nile continued to gradually shift east.

In Thebes, Karnak's high priest Amenhotep was not only prime minister but now the self-styled 'Great Confidante of his Master', the king, and was still being portrayed on the same scale.

Even work on Ramses XI's tomb (KV.4) was proving increasingly sporadic, since the tomb-builders were sitting ducks for Libyan raiders and eventually had little choice but to abandon Deir el-Medina, which had been their home for more than 500 years.

As families were scattered, some moved permanently into new housing within the fortified temple complex of Medinet Habu. One of these was the ex-Deir el-Medina scribe Djhutmose, who wrote 'we are now living here in Medinet Habu . . . However, the boys of the tomb [i.e. the workmen] have gone, and are living in Thebes'.

At least Djhutmose had his family, his son and fellow scribe Butehamen and daughter-in-law Ikhtay, a part-time priestess and farmer. Their neighbour, Lady Henuttawy, was the local administrator, receiving and recording grain consignments and organising wage-rations as famine now beset the region. One enterprising farmer claimed that she earned a considerable amount of silver 'in exchange for barley in the year of the hyenas when there was a famine', although the thefts from the tombs of the kings, queens and nobles, from the royal funerary temples and even from their abandoned palaces, only continued.

Direct action was now required, so Ramses XI recalled his Nubian viceroy Panehesy, who came north to Thebes and made himself 'Overseer of Granaries' as well as prime minister to try to control the economic situation.

When this brought him into conflict with Thebes's major land-owner, high priest Amenhotep, the situation deteriorated into 'the war of the high priest', with Amenhotep forced to retreat across the river and take refuge within the fortress-like walls of Medinet Habu.

Under siege from Panehesy, the high priest had little choice but to appeal to the king, who now sent in his army of Libyan merce-naries, led by their no-nonsense Libyan general Piankh.

As the situation spiralled into civil war, with two of the king's men fighting it out between them, Nubian Panehesy was eventually defeated by Libyan Piankh, who took over Panehesy's titles. Then at the death of Amenhotep, General Piankh took over his titles too.

Having started out as the king's man, Piankh now controlled Thebes and the south, and was strong enough to impose a formal power-sharing arrangement that he dubbed a 'Repeating of Births' – a veritable renaissance. For Ramses XI's nineteenth year as king, around 1080 BC, was officially dated 'Year 1' in Thebes, and with the distinction between crown and clergy blurred, Piankh's son could smugly enquire 'Pharaoh? Of whom is he the master these days?'.

Piankh also married the king's daughter, Nodjmet, and she became his deputy, updating him in his absences. After she warns him of traitors, Piankh tells her to interrogate and then kill them: 'Have these two brought to my house, and you should get to the bottom of their words in a good state! And you should kill them and have them thrown [into] the water at night'. He then adopts a softer tone, telling her 'I pray to every god and every goddess whom I pass by to give to you life and health, to let me see you when I return, and fill my eye with the sight of you, every day!'

Although Piankh was now effectively ruler of the south, he nonetheless required serious wealth to maintain his position. But with the errant Panehesy now back in Nubia and in control of its goldmines, Piankh was forced to seek out an alternative source of gold much closer to home – the rich seam of royal gold that ran through the Valley of the Kings.

And this is when tomb robbery became official government policy, as the royal burials were systematically dismantled, their wealth seized and their mummified inhabitants stripped down, rewrapped and moved around for the rest of the eleventh century BC, in what was officially described as 'restoration work'.

Regardless of Egypt's millennia-held belief that the royal mummies were storehouses of ancestral power to be maintained at all costs, the Libyan Piankh clearly thought otherwise.

Writing to scribe Djhutmose and his son Butehamen, Piankh told them to 'go and perform for me a task on which you have never before embarked . . . Uncover a tomb among the tombs of the ancestors'. So Djhutmose accepted, replying 'Please have the men of the tomb who are there in Thebes assembled and send them to me to this side of the river'; he also asked for them to be 'put under the supervision of the scribe Butehamen', his son, now awarded the somewhat euphemistic official title 'Opener of the Gates of the Necropolis'.

The search for royal gold had begun.

From their base at Medinet Habu, Djhutmose, Butehamen and their colleagues regularly travelled the pathways criss-crossing the West Bank hills, marking the location of tombs as they went with their graffiti, 130 of which are in the distinctive handwriting of Butehamen, 'the Opener'.

Among the tombs on his hit list was the tomb of Ramses III and, with the tomb emptied of wealth, Butehamun took the king's mummified body back down to Mēdinet Habu, where it had probably been created. And as the process was now reversed and the body unwrapped, the jewellery and amulets were transferred to Piankh's treasury. Once rewrapped, Butehamen wrote directly onto the king's new linen shroud, 'On this day the high priest gave the order to scribe Butehamen to turn pharaoh Usermaatra Meryamen Ramses into an Osiris, he being made firm again and enduring for eternity', a necessary identification since the original names had been stripped off with the gold removed from the royal coffins.

It was the end of an era, the death of Ramses XI himself around 1069 BC marking the end of the entire New Kingdom.

Although his huge tomb (KV.4) was close to completion, the fate of his fellow pharaohs, escorted from their tombs all around, clearly proved too much. So after five hundred years the Valley of the Kings was finally abandoned as the royal cemetery, and Ramses XI buried elsewhere.

Although his burial place has never been found, it may well have been at Abydos, where excavations in the great desert cemetery in 1859 revealed a large coffin containing a mummy of unspecified sex. As was often the case, the body crumbled to dust at a touch, although the accompanying eighty pieces of jewellery featured the names of Ramses XI. Perhaps a loyal, if very wealthy, courtier, it may even have been the body of the king himself, fulfilling the spirit of the age, the Repeating of Births, by choosing burial among Egypt's earliest kings, in the legendary burial place of Osiris.

19

Decline, Rise and Fall: c.1069–332 BC

As the end of the New Kingdom gave way to a third Intermediate Period, 'a notorious dark age', the country once more split into its default position of two kingdoms, north and south.

In the north, Ramses XI was succeeded by Smendes, first king of the Twenty-first Dynasty (c.1069–1043 BC). Although 'an influential figure of unknown origin', Smendes married Tentamen, likely a princess of the old Ramesside house, and the royal couple were described as 'the pillars which Amen has set up for the north of his land'.

Yet in the south, Amen's high priests were now the undisputed masters. And after Piankh had been succeeded by Herihor, he not only took on Piankh's titles as high priest, prime minister and even viceroy of Nubia, but also married Piankh's widow Nodjmet to cement his power.

For Nodjmet, as a daughter of Ramses XI, was of royal blood, and so Herihor took royal titles too, having his name and that of Nodjmet written in cartouches. Both adopted the royal uraeus cobra in their portraits, and Herihor was even portrayed wearing the double crown. The fears of the Eighteenth Dynasty kings 'which had driven the Amarna revolution had become a reality', as the priests of Amen finally achieved their ultimate goal.

And as king of the gods, Amen now had his name written in a cartouche too, and his cult centre Karnak, which lay at the heart of the theocracy, was still lavishly embellished. Herihor commissioned a new barque for the god's cult statue, and since tradition dictated it should be made of the finest Lebanese cedar, Herihor sent his official Wenamen to Byblos. But whereas the Egyptians once took whatever they wanted from their former vassals, Wenamen now had to wait on the Prince of Byblos, who reminded Amen's envoy, 'I am not your servant nor am I the servant of him who sent you!'.

As for gilding the new barque, Herihor continued Piankh's policy of royal tomb raiding, to the extent that it is claimed that Herihor's tomb contents would make those of 'Tutankhamen look like Woolworths'.

Although neither his tomb nor his body has yet been found, this is not the case with Herihor's wife Nodjmet. Quite old at death, she nonetheless retained some of the same chic glamour of her portraits, her embalmers having effectively rejuvinated her with cosmetics, fillers, false eyebrows and a long plaited wig. Nodjmet's preservation had clearly benefited from 'the striking object-lesson afforded by the handling of these mummies of the 18th, 19th and 20th dynasties' during the so-called 'restoration work'.

This continued under Herihor's successor, priest-king and general Pinudjem I, whose royal pretensions not only involved taking the original coffins of Tuthmosis I for himself, but even a tomb in the Valley of the Kings.

He added his own cartouches to the walls of the unused tomb of Ramses XI (KV.4); this was now transformed into a rewrapping workshop for royal mummies, where gilded fragments naming Tuthmosis III, Hatshepsut and Ramses IV have been found. Gold fragments and huge quantities of wrappings were also found at the valley's oldest tomb, KV.39, where the same work seems to have taken place. As a tomb believed to have been built for Ahmose-Nefertari and her son Amenhotep I, images of 'the Opener' Butehamen making offerings to the two rulers suggest 'that he was involved in the restorations of these earlier burials too'.

Yet even when stripped down and rewrapped, the royal mummies retained their symbolic value, as Pinudjem selected the mummies of Ramses I, Seti I and Ramses II to be buried alongside him, perhaps assuming their presence would give him added legitimacy in the next world.

Pinudjem also enhanced his earthly power through diplomatic marriage to Henuttawy, daughter of the northern pharaoh Smendes. With their union creating harmony between the kings in the north and the priest-kings in the south, the couple's children ruled Egypt between them; two sons followed in their father's footsteps to become successive high priests at Karnak, where their sister inherited many of her mother's titles to become high priestess.

Yet it was their third son, Pasebakhaenniut – 'the Star Appearing in the City', better known by the Greek version of his name, Psusennes (c.1039–991 BC) – who eventually succeeded his grandfather Smendes to rule as pharaoh, alongside his sister-wife Mutnodjmet.

Psusennes and his dynasty took up residence at a new royal capital, Tanis, close to Bubastis in the Eastern Delta. Tanis was created after the old Ramesside capital Per-Ramesse was abandoned, and many of its stone monuments removed to the new city to create gravitas, not to mention a real puzzle for future archaeologists.

Surrounded by fifteen-metre-thick mud-brick walls, Tanis was built as a counterpart to Thebes, complete with a great central temple to Amen and Mut. The temple complex was also the site of the new royal burial ground, as Egypt's pharaohs were now based in the north, both in life and in death.

Having already built a temple at Giza dedicated to Hathor-Isis as 'Mistress of the Pyramids', Psusennes seems to have been influenced by Giza's *mastaba* tombs, which he and his Twenty-first Dynasty successors copied for their own burials within the Tanis temple precincts.

Found largely intact in 1939, their burial chambers were still filled with spectacular treasures to rival those found in the tomb of Tutankhamen, some pieces having clearly been taken from the Valley of the Kings by Psusennes I's father, high priest Pinudjem.

For Psusennes himself had been provided with an amazing gold death mask and silver coffin, both perhaps from one of the Ramesside kings, together with the granite sarcophagus of Merenptah and the gold vessels of Ahmose I.

But despite replicating and recycling parts of the Valley of the Kings, the Tanis pharaohs could not control the regional variations in climate and environment. So whereas Psusennes I's carefully mummified body had been reduced to a skeleton in Tanis's water-logged ground, his priestly siblings, buried in the dry Theban hills, are still as plump and recognisable as the day they died.

Yet the Tanis tombs contained not only the lavish burials of its kings, but also those of its Libyan generals, General Wendjebaendjed was provided with a superb gold mask surely of Nineteenth Dynasty manufacture, a large jewelled scarab inscribed for Ramses VII and a lapis ring naming Ramses IX.

With such military men regarded as sufficiently important to share both the royal resting place and royal wealth, one of Psusennes I's successors was a Libyan himself, Osorkon the Elder (c.984–978 BC). He was followed by his son, Siamen (c.978–959 BC), whose relatively lengthy reign allowed him to expand the temples of Heliopolis, Memphis and at Tanis, where he was portrayed smiting his enemies. Some of these enemies were former Sea Peoples, the Peleset – Philistines – who were threatening Egypt's trade links with Phoenicia. So Siamen undertook a campaign and destroyed the Philistine city of Gezer, allying himself with the Israelite king Solomon, who took over Gezer to secure his southern border, and married Siamen's daughter to seal the alliance.

Good relations were also maintained between Siamen and the Thebans, whose hereditary high priest-king was now Pinudjem I's grandson, Pinudjem II. And it was Pinudjem II who organised the mass reburial of the royal mummies in a series of hidden tombs or caches.

Around forty were reinterred in the priests' family vault at Deir el-Bahari (tomb DB.320), right opposite Karnak, where they remained for 2,855 years. When they were rediscovered in 1871 by a local family, who made a tidy living selling off coffin fragments and smaller items, the appearance of these things on the antiquities market alerted the authorities, who eventually traced the tomb to make the 'official' discovery ten years later. The royal mummies were then swiftly removed, and carried down to the Nile to be sent north to Cairo Museum on a government steamer, 'the largest hearse in history'. As they passed by, the women of the West Bank came out of their homes to watch, and although their dramatic display of mourning was dismissed by some as a reaction to a loss of revenue, it was more likely 'a spontaneous demonstration of traditional grief', as the monarchs who had for so long belonged to them and their special landscape were finally taken from them.

But there were still some royals unaccounted for, at least until 1898, when the tomb of Amenhotep II (KV.35) was first discovered. The pharaoh himself still lay within his sarcophagus, albeit inside a cheap replacement coffin after his gilded ones had been taken by priest-kings; and while they had also stripped away his jewellery, they had at least left his longbow beside him.

Just off his burial chamber was a small side room containing the coffined mummies of Amenhotep II's son Tuthmosis IV, and his son Amenhotep III, together with Merenptah, Seti II, Siptah, Ramses IV, V and VI and an unknown woman some claim to be Tawosret. Their shrouds were even inscribed with the exact date they were all placed here around 966 BC: 'Year 12, fourth month of winter, day six. On this day renewing of the burials by the High Priest of Amen, Pinudjem'.

Although there was still space available in the chamber, three other bodies had been placed separately in a second side room – two adult women and a teenage boy, who had not been rewrapped, had not been given replacement coffins and had not been given back their names. Although rendered anonymous, and kept apart from the others, they were nonetheless Eighteenth Dynasty royals; their bodies had been preserved in the natron solution of the time. Based on accumulated research since the 1970s, they were almost certainly Queen Tiy, her eldest son Prince Tuthmosis and the female pharaoh Nefertiti, an identification that remains controversial but is nonetheless based on facial measurements, which accord, to within a millimetre, with Nefertiti's famous bust. There is also the impression of the exclusively royal brow band at the mummy's forehead, double ear piercings only found during the Amarna period, scattered beads from an Amarna-style collar like the one found on the body of Nefertiti's husband Akhenaten and her right arm, once bent across her chest to hold a sceptre in the pose of a ruling pharaoh.

But her body had certainly suffered desecration. For this right arm had been roughly torn off below the shoulder, and her mouth severely attacked at close quarters with a sharp metal blade. As damage that could only have been inflicted when the body was unwrapped, and not by tomb robbers randomly hacking through wrappings, it most closely resembled the damage done to the mummy of Ramses VI, which lay in the chamber next door.

Indeed, the choice of burial site for all these individuals is intriguing, since tomb KV.35 is neither the largest nor the best hidden. Its selection for these specific individuals seems instead to relate to its original owner, Amenhotep II, the pharaoh who first brought the Aten to the fore and initiated the earliest challenge to the Karnak priests. The side chambers were then used for his immediate successors who had continued to support the Aten – Tuthmosis IV, Amenhotep III, Tiy and Nefertiti and those in the later New Kingdom who had not been particularly Karnak-friendly. So none had been interred within the priest-kings' family vault overlooking Karnak alongside rulers like Tuthmosis III and Ramses III, who had kept the temple coffers full.

Of course it may all be pure coincidence, and the royal mummies simply placed haphazardly in any convenient tomb. But when studied in any detail, a clear picture emerges, and it really does seem that the priests were using the opportunity not just to gain wealth, but in some cases to settle old scores, inflicting specific damage to the bodies of those rulers who had in life undermined their priestly authority. Ultimately, the royal mummies, and all they represented, were still being used to further the political ambitions and status of Karnak's high priest Pinudjem II and his own dynasty.

His power was certainly enhanced when Pinudjem II married Neskhons, daughter of the previous high priest and, like her husband, related to the Tanis kings. Neskhons served alongside her husband at Karnak as the 'Great One of the Harem of Amen-Ra, King of the Gods', and among her plethora of titles was not only 'Overseer of the Southern hill-lands' but also Viceroy of Nubia.

Neskhons' powerful status was reflected in her bejewelled image, even her coffin revealing her penchant for large earrings, which are known to weigh over 100 grams each. But while they may have looked attractive, they stretched the ears so far that Neskhons' lobes became 'long strings', while those of some of her fellow priestesses almost reach their shoulders!

Neskhons' mummified body also reveals that she died soon after the birth of her fourth child, her husband Pinudjem II producing three more offspring with his sister-wife Isimkheb, including Psusennes II (c.959–945 BC), who inherited his father's title of high priest.

Yet Psusennes II's career was not restricted to Karnak, for he was not only supreme military commander, but pharaoh of *all* Egypt.

Although details are sketchy at best, his reign united the land and, aided by his Libyan military advisor General Sheshonq, the general eventually became king himself.

Founding a new Libyan dynasty, the Twenty-second, based at Bubastis in the Delta, Sheshonq I (c.945–924 BC) was a strong leader who kept control of Karnak by making his son Iuput its high priest.

And, securing his control of Egypt by placing trusted family members in key posts, Sheshonq resumed trade with Byblos and mounted campaigns against Israel and Judah around 925 BC. With a force of 1,200 chariots and his Libyan and Nubian mercenaries, Sheshonq won back Gaza and Megiddo, and sacked the temple of Jerusalem. And there, beneath its great gold cherubim – 'the Hebrew name for the winged figure with lion's body and woman's head which the Greeks call a sphinx' – pharaoh Sheshonq 'took all the treasures from the temple of Yahweh and from the royal palace. He took everything', this reference in the Bible naming him 'Shishak, king of Egypt'. On the walls of Karnak too, the mighty figure of Sheshonq I was shown smiting Israel and Judah while Amen looks on, the god's figure now only half the size of the king.

Sheshonq I died soon after his greatest triumph, around 924 BC. His burial place has never been found; nor has that of his son, Osorkon I (c.924–889 BC), although records reveal he was buried somewhere in Thebes, in a tomb which became 'a landmark in the Theban necropolis'.

His successors, however, preferred to embellish the north, his grandson Osorkon II (c.874–850 BC) and his queen, Karomama, building a spectacular red granite temple for the cat goddess Bastet at Bubastis. Surrounded by trees and wide canals, their new temple was the venue for the ancient annual fertility festival, when pilgrims arrived 'by river, men and women together, a great number of each in every boat. Some of the women make a noise with rattles, others play pipes, while the rest of the women, and the men, sing and clap their hands. As they journey by river to Bubastis, whenever they come near any town they bring their boat near the bank. Then some of the women shout mockery to the women of that town, others dance, and the others stand up and expose their persons. But when they have reached Bubastis, more wine is drunk at this feast than in the whole year'.

The temple's 'Festival Hall' was also adorned with scenes of Osorkon II's jubilee, Osorkon himself presiding over a race involving three men, who may be his sons and successors competing for the throne. This recalls the Greek myth of Endymion, whose sons similarly competed in such a race to inherit his territory in Elis, which included the site of the original Olympic games.

And such similarities are intriguing, since their Delta homeland gave the Twenty-second Dynasty easy access to the Mediterranean they referred to as the 'Sea of the Greeks', and to the Greek trading colonies that would soon stretch from Asia Minor to Italy. Dating from the eighth century BC, *The Iliad* and *The Odyssey*, attributed to the Greek poet Homer, mention both Egypt's Mediterranean coastline and 'hundred-gated' Thebes, 'where the houses are furnished in the most sumptuous fashion', at a time when Egyptian bronzes were already being presented as offerings to the Greek goddess Hera on Samos.

If the Greeks were impressed by Egyptian metalwork, the Egyptians themselves were equally impressed by the craftsmanship of the antique metal items taken from the Valley of the Kings, from which they learned much. Soon becoming adept at blending gold with other metals to achieve differing tones, Osorkon II endowed Egypt's temples with superb gold pieces, while his *mastaba* at Tanis still contained fine pieces that the ancient robbers missed.

A high degree of wealth was also available in the south, as reflected in the golden faces of the coffins of Karnak's clergy. Such personnel included a 'Chantress of Amen', Tjentmutengebtiu, whose mummified remains, scanned in a London hospital in 1992, provided the means by which new ultrasound techniques were developed to benefit the living. Chemical analysis also reveals that some of these same individuals had been embalmed with materials obtained from as far away as the Far East; this so-called 'period of decline' may have been rather more dynamic than its usual epithet might suggest.

Among Karnak's highest ranks, the Valley of the Kings was still regarded as the optimum place for burial, a tomb found in 2012, originally created for a daughter of Amenhotep III, having been reused for the 'Chantress of Amen', Nehmes-Bastet, a daughter of Karnak's high priest.

And in the ongoing fusing of crown and clergy, Osorkon II continued to use the temple hierarchy to maintain power, appointing his children to key posts with the proviso that 'brother should not be jealous of brother'. He installed one of his sons as high priest at Memphis, and another high priest at Karnak, where his daughter, Karomama, was also installed as the God's Wife priestess. With her stunning bronze figure, inlaid with pink gold, silver and electrum, commemorating the 'Lady of the Two Lands, divine wife of Amen, daughter of Ra, mistress of crowns', these titles reveal that Karomama was considered the equivalent of a sovereign, and shared many of that post's prerogatives.

But Osorkon II's attempts to bind the country with family ties eventually led to rival princes seeking power for themselves. By around 818 BC, some had even declared themselves, somewhat inaccurately, as 'kings of Upper and Lower Egypt', creating their own petty kingdoms at Leontopolis, Herakleopolis and Hermopolis, which were later accommodated by creating the new Twenty-third Dynasty (c.818–715 BC) to coexist with the Twenty-second (945–715 BC). By 800 BC, 'there were three pharaohs in Egypt', and even the Egyptians themselves were confused, the Karnak clergy admitting that the land 'had sunk into confusion at this time'.

But worse was to come. During the reign of northern king, Osorkon III (c.777–749 BC), whose daughter Shepenwepet I was now God's Wife at Karnak, the temple's traditional rites were severely disrupted when 'the water of Nile rose in this entire land and it reached the two cliffs of the desert as at the beginning of creation. The land was in its power, like the power of the sea. No dyke made by human hand could withstand its force. The water was tremendous, it was high like the sky. All the temples of Thebes resembled a swamp, the people of Amen's city like swimmers in the water'.

Nor were the waters the only unstoppable force sweeping up from the south, for Egypt was about to be engulfed by the mighty Nubians.

Ever since the Nubian Viceroy Panehesy had besieged Thebes in the eleventh century BC and challenged the Egyptian establishment, the rulers of Kush (Upper Nubia, modern Sudan), had been growing in strength from their capital Napata, close to the Fourth Cataract.

So powerful was their king Kashta, his reach extended as far north as Aswan and, claiming himself to be 'King of Upper and Lower Egypt', he had even lined up his daughter Amenirdis – the inspiration for the princess Amneris in Verdi's opera *Aida* – to succeed Osorkon III's daughter Shepenwepet I as God's Wife of Amen at Karnak, to legitimise his claim over Thebes too.

Although Kashta's ambitions were halted by his death, he was succeeded by his son Piye, who had tellingly restored Tuthmosis III's old temple of Amen at Gebel Barkal, the great mountain from which the Egyptians had long claimed Amen had been born. And where the Egyptians had previously claimed the mountain gave them dominion over Nubia, the Nubians now claimed it gave them dominion over Egypt.

Fuelled by a genuine belief in the home-grown power of Amen, Piye now embarked on what he considered to be a holy war. Invading Egypt and taking Thebes with little resistance, he was crowned pharaoh at Karnak, the double uraeus snake on his crown proclaiming his sovereignty over both Egypt and Nubia. He then installed his sister Amenirdis I as the God's Wife priestess at Karnak, her name inscribed on the bronze fittings of new temple doors to announce the new management to the world. And when Piye returned back home to Nubia, she ruled Upper Egypt on his behalf, 'to all intents and purposes the equal of the king'.

To counter the invasion, the Libyan princes of the Delta formed a coalition headed by Tefnakht of Sais, but as he began to extend his reach south down the Nile Valley, Piye returned around 727 BC to take him on.

Stopping off at Karnak to offer sacrifices to Amen, commanding his soldiers to cleanse themselves ritually in the Nile before going to war, Piye and his army then went north 'like a flood of water', Piye apparently 'furious like a leopard' – which is exactly how Tuthmosis I had been described when he had invaded Nubia almost eight centuries earlier.

Taking Memphis by force, the triumphant Piye became the first king of Egypt's Twenty-fifth Dynasty (c.747–656 BC). Erecting his victory proclamation on a stela in Memphis's temple to Ptah, paying homage to the gods of Egypt who were also his, he did the same at Heliopolis after purifying himself 'in the sacred pool'. And as Piye undertook the dawn rites before the ancient sun god, the temple's clergy lay 'stretched out on their bellies before him saying "Live forever, O Horus, Beloved in Heliopolis".'

The same pose was then adopted by the defeated northern princes of Leontopolis, Hermopolis and Tanis, announcing 'Greetings, O Horus, O bull who subdues the other bulls!' The prince of Hermopolis and his wife even sought favour by bringing Piye a gift of horses, only Tefnakht of Sais refusing to attend in person, and instead sending his submission by messenger.

For the rest of his reign Piye retained these Delta princes as his northern vassals, his sister Amenirdis I keeping control of the south and Piye himself returning home to Nubia, where he commemorated his victory with new scenes at Gebel Barkal. At his death around 716 BC, he was mummified and buried beneath his pyramid at the Kushite royal cemetery at el-Kurru, with his chariot team of four favourite horses buried close by.

His brother Shabaqa (c.716–702 BC) then succeeded him, but was forced to go to war soon into his reign when Tefnakht's successor, Bakenrenef, sole king of Egypt's ephemeral Twenty-fourth Dynasty (c.727–715 BC), tried to expand his territory.

So Shabaqa re-invaded Egypt around 715 BC, finally taking the whole of Egypt to gain a kingdom that stretched from modern

Khartoum to the Mediterranean, the entire length of the Nile itself.

Keen to make his mark on his new territory, Shabaqa's most famous contribution to Egypt's ancient culture was to save some of the most important documents in Memphis's temple library, including the age-old Story of Creation. When the original papyrus was found to be damaged, 'this writing was copied out anew by his majesty in the temple of his father Ptah for his majesty found it to be a work of the ancestors which was worm-eaten and could not be understood from beginning to end'; all of this was re-inscribed upon a large slab of basalt now known as the 'Shabaqa Stone'.

And at Karnak, where recent excavations have revealed the remains of Shabaqa's treasury building, his sister Amenirdis remained God's Wife priestess. The Theban mayor, Montuemhat, served as her steward and, having eventually married into the Kushite royal family, his powers were so great he was given a massive fifty-seven-room tomb in front of Deir el-Bahari. Amenirdis herself was buried in a tomb created within the secure walls of Medinet Habu.

When Shabaqa joined his sister in the afterlife, he was buried in a pyramid at the family necropolis el-Kurru, to be succeeded by his nephew, Piye's son, Shabitqa (c.702–690 BC). But it was another of Piye's sons, the mighty Taharqa (690–664 BC), who would be the dynasty's greatest king.

His accession in 690 BC also marks the beginning of certainty, or at least a fixed chronology, in which dates no longer need to be estimated. And new pharaoh Taharqa certainly presided over a new golden age. Crowned in a traditional Egyptian ceremony at Memphis, now his main residence, from which he could best control the north, Taharqa felt genuine affinity with Lower Egypt and its ancient pyramids, which had, after all, inspired those built in his Nubian homeland.

And between Memphis and Nubia lay Karnak, where Taharqa's sister, Shepenwepet II, remained God's Wife priestess for fifty years. With the family's unswerving devotion to Amen also set in stone, Taharqa added a great colonnade of lotus-form columns to Karnak's first courtyard. Then at the temple's sacred lake, he embellished a chapel to Osiris with scenes of himself running the jubilee race while throwing clay balls to the cardinal points, into which God's Wife Shepenwepet II also fires her arrows.

But in 683 BC, Karnak's daily rites were interrupted when the Nile flood reached eighty-four centimetres above the floor of the Hypostyle Hall, something Taharqa claimed to be 'a wondrous thing' that had occurred because 'his Majesty prayed for an abundant Nile and his father Amen-Ra makes it reality. When the time came for the flood of the Nile, it began to increase greatly every day, it flooded the mountains of the southern lands and the low lands of the north. The land was like an inert primordial ocean, the banks could not be distinguished from the river'. Taharqa's prayers were even answered in Nubia, where 'a downpour from the sky made the mountains sparkle as far as their summits. Everyone in Nubia was rich in everything, and Egypt was also plentiful. Everyone thanked the king'.

For although Taharqa spent his life in Egypt, he did not forget his Nubian homeland. He sent his Egyptian builders and craftsmen south to build a temple to Isis on the island of Philae and, as far south as Kawa, erected a temple to Amen-Ra, its walls, carved with copies of Old Kingdom scenes from Sakkara and Abusir, portraying Taharqa as a sphinx trampling his enemies, and accompanying sphinx statues in granite bearing Taharqa's distinctive African features.

But Taharqa's most impressive work was reserved for Nuri and Gebel Barkal. He established a new royal cemetery at Nuri with the largest of all Kushite pyramids, forty-nine metres high; the moat-like corridor of its burial chamber, inspired by Middle Kingdom examples, replicated the underworld kingdom of Osiris. Then across the Nile, Taharqa added greatly to Amen's birthplace, Gebel Barkal itself, adding his four-metre-high granite colossus to the temple of Amen and Mut and setting up a series of red granite lions and grey granite rams brought down from Amenhotep III's Soleb temple further north. The site's emphasis on rebirth and fertility continues to this day as local women still furtively mount the rams when wishing to conceive.

And within the 300-foot high sacred mountain, within the very birthplace of Amen himself, Taharqa created a stunning chapel, its walls showing him before the gods with his mother Abar and his sister-wife Takahatamen. Taharqa's figures, modelled on those of Amenhotep III, were coloured yellow-gold against a blue background, and his crown bears the distinctive rams' horns of Amen.

Having so adorned the interior of the mountain, Taharqa did the same to its exterior, its unusually shaped pinnacle, regarded as a giant uraeus, emphasising that the mountain was the very source of royal power bestowed by Amen. So Taharqa had the pinnacle gilded to catch the rising sun and, like Egypt's traditional obelisks, to act as a brilliant, reflective mirror, casting its light out into the desert to be visible for miles. An inscription carved at the very top of the pinnacle was also covered in gold, but was so inaccessible it could only be seen by the gods – and the brave craftsmen who had risked their lives to erect the scaffolding needed to create the effect.

But beyond such architectural endeavours, the Kushite pharaohs were also keen to defend their borders and allied themselves with Hezekiah, king of Judah, in his struggles to keep down the growing power of Assyria (modern Iraq).

Taharqa himself went to great lengths to keep his army in prime condition. As revealed by the 'Running Stela of Taharqa', the pharaoh instigated regular training runs, on one occasion ordering his army to undertake a 100-kilometre foot race from Memphis to the Fayum and back again. The stela's text even claims that Taharqa not only accompanied his men by chariot to inspire them, but even dismounted to join them, running for an hour during the four-hour outward journey, which was sensibly completed at night to take advantage of the cooler temperatures. On reaching the Fayum they had a two-hour break and then returned to Memphis, a run which – with temperatures rising – took about five hours. At the end, the winners were awarded prizes and everyone who completed the race feasted at royal expense, the king selecting the most promising athletes as shock troops for specific missions.

And these would come soon. For only ten years later, in 674 BC, Assyrian king Esarhaddon, unimpressed with Egypt's interference in the Levant and seeking new sources of wealth, invaded Egypt itself.

Initially defeated by Taharqa and his crack troops, Esarhaddon returned in 671 BC to take Memphis, claiming 'I fought daily very bloody battles against Tarku [sic], king of Egypt and Ethiopia, the one accursed by all the gods. Five times I hit him with my arrows inflicting wounds and then laid siege to Memphis, his royal residence. I destroyed it, tore down its walls and burnt it down'.

Although Esarhaddon failed to capture Taharqa himself, he seized three of the Kushite king's statues as substitutes to take back to his Assyrian capital Nineveh, along with Taharqa's queen, his son and Egypt's finest craftsmen, who would now work for him.

Taharqa himself had fled south, but returned to Memphis to fight on. But although Esarhaddon had died, he was swiftly succeeded by his son Ashurbanipal, who led a second invasion in 667 BC, this time pushing south and forcing Taharqa to flee back to Nubia, where he died in 664 BC and was buried in his pyramid at Nuri.

The Assyrians also executed all Taharqa's Libyan vassals in the north, except for Prince Necho of Sais, whom they retained as client king to rule Egypt on their behalf. According to the Assyrian king, 'I clothed him in coloured garments and a gold necklace, the symbols of his kingship, I made for him; golden rings I placed on his fingers; on an iron dagger, with gold decoration, I wrote my name and gave it to him'.

But the unfortunate Necho didn't last long in his new role, and was killed in 664 BC when Egypt was retaken by Taharqa's nephew and successor, Tantamen (c.664–656 BC). As the Assyrian sources reported, Tantamen 'made Thebes and Heliopolis his fortresses and assembled his armed might'.

But the Assyrians had had enough, and struck back hard. Bringing their full military might to bear, they invaded and plundered Egypt in 663 BC, marching south to Thebes where they sacked the city and even committed the unthinkable – they looted the great temple of Karnak.

Tantamen went back to Nubia, never to return, and with Nubia's control literally in ruins, the Twenty-fifth Dynasty was abruptly terminated.

Although Egypt was now theirs, the Assyrians' moment of glory was fleeting; as serious rebellion broke out in Babylon, their entire focus shifted back east. Appointing Necho's son Psammetichus as their client king in Memphis, they left Egypt, and Psammetichus was left to his own devices.

After he increased his Delta power base by marrying Mehtenweskhet, daughter of the high priest at Heliopolis, Psammetichus was acknowledged as pharaoh, and initiated the extraordinary Twenty-sixth Dynasty (664–525 BC).

Representing over a century of native renaissance centred on their dynastic Delta capital, Sais, the city's massive walls enclosed palaces and a great temple dedicated to the Saite chief deity, Neith. She was hailed as 'her majesty' by the Saite monarchs, who prostrated themselves before her statue. Psammetichus I and Mehtenweskhet even named one of their daughters Nitocris (Neith-ikret) – 'Neith is Excellent' – and the girl became her father's secret weapon to reunite the two lands.

For in 656 BC, with the death of their nominal monarch, Tantamen, in Kush, Thebes felt officially able to recognise Psammetichus as king. To capitalise on this, he sent Nitocris, then ten years old, south to Thebes accompanied by the Saite fleet. They stopped off en route in each region (*nome*) to receive fealty to the king and acquire tribute for Amen.

When Nitocris arrived in great splendour at Karnak, Piye's daughter Shepenwepet II, who was the incumbent God's Wife, and her immediate successor Amenirdis II, Taharqa's daughter, had little choice but to adopt the young Saite princess as their eventual successor. And here Nitocris remained until her death in 585 BC, having lived into her eighties, and having safeguarded Saite interests in the south throughout her long life.

With Egypt united, Psammetichus I took on 30,000 'bronze clad' Greek mercenaries from Ionia and Caria, settling them in camps at Defenneh close to his north-east border, while others were settled closer to Sais at 'Nokratj', the Greek Naukratis, whose prime position on the Canopic branch of the Nile gave easy access to Egypt's main entry point, Thonis, on the coast.

These Greek mercenaries were a key part of the Egyptian army under Psammetichus I's son and successor, Necho II (610–595 BC). Not only providing much-needed protection against the Babylonians, who had taken over from Assyria in the east, they also accompanied Necho II into the Levant to defeat the kingdom of Judah at Megiddo. And by campaigning as far north as Carchemish, Necho II became the first pharaoh since Tuthmosis III to cross the Euphrates, sending the uniform he had worn as a dedication to the Greek god Apollo, equated with the Egyptian Horus, at his temple in Miletus.

Although Necho II's success was short-lived as the Babylonians took back the Levant in 605 BC, their attempts to invade Egypt in 601 BC were repelled by Necho's trusty Greek mercenaries, who established Egypt's borders at Gaza.

Described as 'a man of action from the start, and endowed with an imagination perhaps beyond that of his contemporaries', Necho II also used his Ionian Greek troops to form Egypt's first navy. It was made up of triremes, the most up-to-date warships of their time, which were stationed along Egypt's Mediterranean and Red Sea coastlines.

One ancient Greek source even claims Necho sent out his new ships with a Phoenician crew to circumnavigate Africa. Taking three years to sail down the Red Sea past Punt and southwards down the Indian Ocean coast, they rounded the Cape of Good Hope, noting that they then 'had the sun on their right – to the northward of them', before returning to Egypt via the Straits of Gibraltar. Since this was two thousand years before Vasco da Gama, many have doubted the claim, although previous 'voyages to Punt underline the ancient Egyptians' sea-faring skills and their willingness to travel long distances in search of precious commodities'. And of course Necho's Phoenician crew were purposefully chosen, for, like the Greeks, the Phoenicians had trading posts around the Mediterranean, venturing beyond the Straits of Gibraltar as far as the British Isles.

And recognising the potential of such wide-scale trade, Necho II transformed Egypt's economy by allowing Greek traders to set up shop at Naukratis. He also followed up a Middle Kingdom scheme for a canal to link the Nile and Delta to the Red Sea – anticipating the Suez Canal by a couple of millennia – and a way to import luxury goods from the east. This included myrrh from Saba (Sheba, now in modern Yemen), which was transported north along an overland trade route through Petra. With a Saite statue of a priest of Osiris found in Petra's Temple of the Winged Lions, Egyptian-style mummification was also being employed within the Arabian Peninsula by this time, and is further evidence of long-term contact between the two regions.

Necho II died in 595 BC and he, like his wife Khedebarbenet, was buried within the great temple complex at Sais. Their son and successor, Psammetichus II (595–589 BC), married Takhut, a princess from the Delta city of Athribis, where her intact tomb and treasures were discovered in 1950.

As keen to extend Egypt's reach as his late father, Psammetichus II launched an expedition up to Palestine to initiate a revolt against the Babylonians, although his main focus was to the south, where one of Tantamen's successors had revived Kushite power. Fearing he might re-invade Egypt, and well aware that Tantamen had killed his great-grandfather Necho I, Psammetichus assembled a force of Greek, Egyptian and Jewish troops, and in 592 BC sailed south.

With Psammetichus himself disembarking at Aswan, his capable general Ahmose led the rest of the army south, to the ancient temple of Ramses II at Abu Simbel, where his Greek mercenaries carved graffiti into the leg of one of Ramses's huge statues. Stating that 'when King Psammetichus came to Elephantine this was written by those who went on by boat, Potasimto in command of the foreigners and Ahmose of the Egyptians. Archon and Pelekos wrote these words', this is the oldest Greek inscription in Egypt.

Inspired by their contact with Egypt's past, the army continued south to Napata, fighting pitched battles against the Kushites, in which 'one waded in their blood as in water'. The Kushite capital Napata was sacked, and the survivors eventually moved 185 miles south to a new capital, Meroe.

Psammetichus II then ordered all trace of the Twenty-fifth Dynasty erased from Egypt; he dismantled Taharqa's temple of Isis at Philae, and used its blocks beneath the floor of the site's new temple. He also left a garrison of Jewish troops on Elephantine, where their cedarwood temple to Yahweh functioned beside that of Satis and Khnum for almost 200 years. And he certainly exploited the region's famous granite quarries for his ambitious building schemes.

For despite his brief six-year reign, Psammetichus II was a most prolific builder. As well as erecting granite obelisks at Heliopolis, where his daughter Menekhubaste was a priestess, he also built a granite temple near Sebennytos in the Delta and, out in the Western Desert, founded the temple of Hibis for Amen and Mut in the Kharga Oasis.

At Karnak, he followed tradition and sent his other daughter Ankhnesneferibre south in 594 BC, to be adopted as successor by her aunt Nitocris. Following its sacking by the Assyrians, Karnak had been refitted with new sculpture; a colossal granite figure of the long-dead Amenhotep Son of Hapu stood near the temple entrance, and today performs the same 'meet-and-greet' by the doors of the Cairo Museum. There was also a stunning figure of the ferocious hippo goddess Taweret, with its 'almost too perfect execution', commissioned by Nitocris I's steward Pabasa specifically to protect Nitocris's sacred property.

Beside Karnak was the busy suburb 'House-of-the-Cow', Golden City in Greek, where around a quarter of the houses were owned by women. And here local entrepeneurs Djekhy and his son ran their thriving business, making loans and renting out fields on the West Bank, where they also worked as funeral directors, *choachytes* – literally 'water pourers' – who took offerings to existing burials, helped prepare funerals and transported mummified bodies, which were now subject to tax on entering the necropolis area.

In the case of the Karnak clergy, they were now mainly buried under the floors of Hatshepsut's temple at Deir el-Bahari. This included priest Ankhefenkhonsu, whose wooden funerary stela inspired the famous occultist Aleister Crowley, albeit through its modern registration number '666', given when it was listed in the catalogue of the Cairo Museum. The Theban clergy were also buried with personalised copies of the *Book of the Dead*; the copy made for priest's wife Tasheretenaset was so similar to another made at Memphis that the master copy must have been 'transferred from its Theban workshop to the Memphite area'. This pattern was also repeated when the Memphis-based official Hapimen sent his architects into the tomb of Tuthmosis III in the Valley of the Kings to make an exact replica of the king's stone sarcophagus for Hapimen's own burial.

Such nostalgia for a time when Egypt had been the world's major power was an obvious reaction to recent history, in which foreign invasions had destroyed much of Egypt's ancient heritage, not to mention its pride. So the Saites looked far back into their past; they reproduced excerpts from the ancient Pyramid Texts in their burials and, with 'pyramid-shaped tombs in the Saite period known in the Theban necropolis', courtiers even chose burial close to the original pyramids at Sakkara and Giza.

In some cases the Saites dug down twenty metres to create tombs for themselves in the deepest, most mystical part of this ancient necropolis. One of these early digs at Sakkara discovered the tomb of Imhotep, which they 'reconstituted as his principal sanctuary'. And in their continuing attempts to revive former glories, they entered the pyramids themselves to seek the greats buried within. Remains found in the Step Pyramid of Djoser were rewrapped and reburied in the misguided assumption that they were his, as happened too in the Giza pyramid of Menkaura, where a body was similarly rewrapped and even given a new coffin in the mistaken belief it was the Old Kingdom monarch himself.

Although modern carbon-dating reveals the remains did not date back to the Pyramid Age, this face-to-face contact with long-dead predecessors, regardless of their true identities, clearly inspired the Saites, who transformed mummification practices. In keeping with the way in which arm positions had always been a semaphore-like mark of status when laying out the dead, Saite embalmers revived the ancient practice of crossing the arms on the chest, giving their clients a direct link with their past and, in a democratic move, allowing anyone wealthy enough to afford mummification to be preserved in a pose previously reserved for royalty.

Nor was the procedure restricted to humans; large-scale animal mummification, for which Egypt became famous, began under the Saites. Although specific creatures like the sacred bulls had long been embalmed, with new galleries for the Apis inaugurated under Psammetichus I, the practice now expanded a million-fold, as each deity was honoured with their own sacred creatures. From the hawks sacred to Horus and the ibis of Thoth, cats and dogs, crocodiles and rams, baboons and macaques, shrews, fish and insects – in fact, most of Egypt's fauna were venerated, and at death transformed into linen-wrapped, statue-like, votive offerings.

Created in such numbers that the *theagoi* priests ('bearers of the gods') could no longer proceed along their ceremonial way holding individual creatures, but had to wheel them along in carts, mummified animals were purchased by the devout, who were now able to actually touch an aspect of deity before offering it back to the god to gain their blessing.

For in the Saite spirit of commercialism, everything was for sale, from mummified animals to the amulets mass-produced in moulds, and even the temple walls, whose stone, scraped away as powder, was a most desirable magical commodity.

But the esoteric was not only important for the economy, but was now a graphic means of demonstrating to all foreign outsiders the unique nature of Egypt's special culture. And such arcane rituals certainly impressed some foreign visitors, many of whom believed Egypt was the home of all wisdom. Even the Greeks believed 'it was the Egyptians who originated and taught the Greeks to use ceremonial meetings', a delegation from Olympia (Elis) visiting Psammetichus II in 590 BC to gain a second opinion about the rules of Olympic competition from the Egyptians 'who were the ablest people in the world'. And the pharaonic committee did suggest some reforms based on their own experience. For Egypt's sporting practices were as much bound up in ritual as the Greek Games, the world's first attempt to organise peaceful meetings on an international scale; and, like early drama, considered religious events dedicated to their gods.

During his brief reign, Psammetichus II had become a respected figure on the international stage and, having achieved a great deal both at home and abroad, was succeeded by his son Wahibra, better known by the Greek form of his name, Apries (589-570 BC), who became pharaoh in February 589 BC.

With his new fortified palace at Memphis sited upon a massive thirteen-metre-high mud-brick platform to give panoramic views of the Step Pyramid, Apries also added to the temples of Memphis, Sais and his mother Takhut's hometown Athribis. Down in Karnak his sister Ankhnesneferibre was made God's Wife priestess, her chief steward Shoshenq commissioning a fine statue of Isis that towers over the small figure of Osiris, who she protects in her winged embrace. And as clear testimony to the powers of the God's Wives, Karnak remained firmly under royal control.

For it would be Apries's involvement in matters abroad that would be his undoing.

He had sent his Egyptian and Greek troops into Libya to help its ruler repel large groups of Dorian Greek settlers; but his forces' defeat by the settlers triggered a mutiny among Apries's Egyptian troops, resentful of the influence the Greek mercenaries had over their king.

So Apries sent in his Egyptian general Ahmose, who had previously distinguished himself on the Nubian campaign under Apries's father. But despite Ahmose's best efforts, the rebel troops continued to protest against the king, declaring Ahmose should be their leader. By the time Apries sent a messenger to summon Ahmose back to court the general had clearly warmed to their offer. So remaining on his horse, he 'rose in his saddle, broke wind, and told him to take that back to his master'.

Having lost popular support, Apries was deposed and, although he tried to regain his throne, fell in battle against Ahmose, who buried him with full honour at their dynastic capital Sais. Then he married Apries's daughter.

As a hardened soldier and man of the people, Ahmose was 'fond of his joke and his glass, and never inclined to serious pursuits' – yet by popular demand he was now pharaoh of Egypt – King Ahmose II (570-526 BC).

Some courtiers were initially contemptuous of his humble origins and 'excessive levity', which they felt 'unsuitable for a king'. So to make a point, Ahmose apparently melted down a gold footbath to make a cult statue for Sais's temple. On seeing its veneration by these same courtiers, he 'revealed that the deeply revered statue was once a foot-bath, which they had washed their feet and pissed and vomited in', adding that their attitude to him was much the same 'in that once he had been only an ordinary person and was now their king', whom they must now honour and respect in the same way.

Inheriting Apries's administration, Ahmose II sent the elderly official Peftuaneith south to inspect one of Egypt's most sacred sites, the official duly stating: 'I reported the condition of Abydos to the palace and his majesty's ear, his majesty ordered me to do work in Abydos in order to rebuild Abydos'.

And with building projects from Memphis to Philae, the temple at Sais was greatly expanded in honour of Neith, the Saites' patron deity, who was equated by the Greeks with their own goddess Athena. The priests of Sais were helpful to Greek visitors, especially to Athenians, who were 'in a sense their kinsfolk'.

So Ahmose II sent tasteful gifts to Neith's Greek counterpart Athena at her various cult centres: a gold statue of the goddess and a painting of himself to Cyrene, a basalt figure to Rhodes and to Lindos a four-cubit-high statue in green stone, commissioned from Greece's finest sculptors. Both Lindos and Sparta were also sent spectacular gilded breastplates of resinated linen, the latest in military technology, subsequently developed to great effect by the Greeks for use in the field.

Making alliances sealed with diplomatic marriage, including marriage to the Greek noblewoman Ladice of Cyrene, Ahmose II clearly deserved his epithet, 'the Philhellene'. He also made an alliance with Samos's ruler Polykrates, 'who grew fabulously rich from supplying the Egyptian king with soldiers'; their treaty was sealed when Ahmose sent statues of himself to Samos's temple of the goddess Hera. Ahmose even financed the rebuilding of the temple of Apollo – the Egyptian Horus – at Delphi, one of the four venues for the Olympic Games and home to the first hippodrome for chariot racing. And the sporting link no doubt appealed to a pharaoh better known for his horsemanship than his piety, for beyond their political usefulness 'he had a low opinion of the gods'.

Having built up strong alliances around the Mediterranean, Ahmose II and Egypt benefited from the death of the powerful Babylonian king, Nebuchadnezzar, in 562 BC. For only two years later, Ahmose II took over Cyprus and its fleet, and 'could finally claim to be the dominant power in Palestine and the Levant'.

No longer needing such a strong military presence on his northeast frontier, Ahmose II moved his 30,000 Greek mercenaries from Daphnae to Memphis, where the increasingly cosmopolitan city's great temple of Ptah, or Hut-ka-Ptah – 'the temple of the soul of Ptah' – had long been referred to by the Greeks as *Aigyptos*', the origin of the modern name Egypt.

As trade thrived in the new political stability, international commerce was transformed by the world's first coinage, created in 550 BC by King Croesus of Lydia (western Turkey). Although the Egyptians continued with their traditional, barter-based economy, the new coins were nonetheless used at Naukratis, now a great *emporion* (trading settlement) with a monopoly on imported Greek pottery, silver, wine and olive oil exchanged for Egyptian grain, linen, perfume and papyrus.

Reflecting Naukratis's cosmopolitan blend of Greek and Egyptian cultures, there were also temples to Neith, Amen and Thoth and to the Greek Hera, Apollo and Aphrodite.

Naukratis was also a magnet for poets, historians, courtesans, statesmen and philosophers from all over the Greek world, many of whom learned about Egypt's history from its priests, the custodians of the ancient culture, part of the one per cent literate elite able to interpret the mysterious picture-writing that the Greeks called 'sacred carvings', or 'hieroglyphs'.

Egypt's priests told the visiting Athenian lawgiver Solon that he and his countrymen were as children, since their own history was so short. They also spoke with the Spartan statesman Lycurgus, and the Greek philosopher Thales, who visited during Ahmose II's reign to measure the height of the Great Pyramid 'using a rod and the shadow of the edifice'. Also in Egypt during the sixth century BC was Pythagoras, whose famous theorem regarding the relationship between the three sides of a right-angled triangle was presumably influenced by the way the Egyptians had been calculating the area, height, angles and volumes of pyramids for over a thousand years.

Particularly interested in the phenomenon of the annual Nile flood were fellow Greeks Eudoxos and Anaxagoras and, given their interest in Egypt's great river, it seems appropriate that the Greeks were the ones who named it. Until then it had simply been 'the great river', or 'pa iteru aa', then where the river divided up into smaller branches at the Delta it became na-iteru, 'the rivers'. The 't' was dropped by the sixth century BC and the Egyptian 'r' replaced with the Greek 'l', and the resulting 'Neilos' is the origin of the modern name: the Nile.

But even with the local priests to guide them, the Greeks still found some things completely unfathomable, commenting that 'the Egyptians themselves in their manners and customs seem to have reversed the ordinary practices of mankind'. For in contrast to the serious restrictions imposed on 'respectable' Greek women, who only went out of the house as a last resort, and then fully covered, their Egyptian sisters could 'attend market, and are employed in trade, while men stay at home and do the weaving'. And of course, whereas the Greeks cremated their dead, the Egyptians went to great lengths to preserve theirs.

Similar overtones can be found in some of the Greek descriptions of Egypt's massive monuments, and although genuinely impressed by much of what they saw, they did react with a certain humour when faced with yet another vast tomb, which the Egyptians called 'mer' but which today are better known by the name for a small Greek triangular-shaped cake – the 'pyramis'. Likewise the tapering stone 'tekhen' is now far better known as an 'obelisk', the Greeks' kebab-style roasting skewer.

Yet the special relationship that existed between Egypt and the Greek world would soon be tested to the limit, as they now both faced the full force of the massive Persian Empire, which threatened to engulf them both.

Having effectively replaced Assyria and Babylon in the east, the Persians were inexorably moving westwards, and claiming everything in their path, from Egyptian-held Cyprus to the Lydia of King

Croesus as well as increasing numbers of Greek colonies in Asia Minor. The Greeks' first reaction was to dismiss the well-turned-out Persians as effeminate trouser-wearing cowards, even wheeling out the Trojan War as proof of their own superiority over a weaker Eastern neighbour. Yet the reality was far more serious, as both the Greek-speaking world and Egypt were about to find out.

Having made Egypt the wealthiest power in the region, Ahmose II died in 526 BC, just 'before the storm broke'. Mummified in traditional manner, his linen wrappings were coated in a blend of oils and resins that hardened to create the same impermeable layers used in mummification for the last four millennia and now replicated in cutting-edge linen body armour. Then in time-honoured fashion, Ahmose was buried by his son and successor, Psammetichus III (c.526–525 BC), in his pillared tomb in Sais, 'a great, cloistered building of stone'.

Yet he would not remain at rest here for long.

For the Persian king Cambyses was determined to add Egypt to Persia's portfolio of conquered kingdoms, a determination made all the stronger by Egypt's new naval strength in the eastern Mediterranean.

With Egypt's former allies conquered, or switching sides like Polykrates of Samos, the new king Psammetichus III now faced Cambyses's army on his eastern border at Pelusium. Following the Egyptians' defeat, the pharaoh withdrew to Memphis, while his admiral, Wedjahorresnet, may have defected to the Persian enemy, since their ships 'were able to penetrate the Delta to the very walls of Memphis'.

Despite a ferocious defence, Memphis fell after ten days, Psammetichus III was taken prisoner and Cambyses (525–522 BC) was now 'Great Ruler of Egypt and Great Chief of All Foreign Lands' by right of conquest.

Initiating the Twenty-seventh Dynasty (525–404 BC), he installed a Persian garrision in Memphis and sent 50,000 of his men into the Western Desert to seek legitimisation of his rule from the famously infallible oracle of Amen at Siwa Oasis, although the god was actually never troubled since the men were lost in a sandstorm en route. Cambyses also sent troops south to try to stabilise relations with the king of Kush, that same year marking the mysterious disappearance of the elderly Saite princess Ankhnesneferibre after sixty years as God's Wife of Amen.

With the ancient post abolished, the Persians were presumably reluctant to share their newly acquired power with an individual who traditionally controlled Upper Egypt and was represented on her sarcophagus holding the monarch's crook and flail. It was a reluctance that also extended to the other members of the former royal family.

First executing ex-king Psammetichus III for plotting against his new regime, Cambyses then ordered the body of the previous king Ahmose II to be exhumed and 'punished'. Playing on the Egyptian idea that dead rulers were still regarded as 'alive', Ahmose's body was 'treated with every possible indignity, such as lashing it with whips . . . till the executioners were weary'. But because 'the corpse had been embalmed and would not fall to pieces under the blows, Cambyses ordered it to be burnt', not only to deprive his soul of its physical home, but also to deprive the Egyptians of one of their royal mummies, which could have been a focus of anti-Persian unrest. Nonetheless, there were soon rumours that the body had been substituted for another and Ahmose himself reinterred elsewhere, some even claiming he had been reburied in one of the pyramids of Giza.

Yet Cambyses's purge of rivals continued. For with the loss of their native monarchy, the Egyptians had transferred their devotion to their alternative candidate, the 'king of every sacred animal', the Apis bull, believed to house the soul of Ptah and which now represented the very soul of Egypt. It so happened that a new Apis calf was at that moment being installed at Memphis amidst great celebrations. So Cambyses had it brought before him and, in the presence of its horrified clergy, stabbed it with his dagger to prove it was no deity. Then as the animal bled to death, Cambyses ordered his priests to be flogged, and anyone still celebrating Apis rites executed.

Admittedly the main source for such atrocities was the Greek-born Herodotus of Halicarnassus in Asia Minor, no lover of the Persians. Writing a century after the events, Herodotus's main informants were Egypt's priests, who still resented Cambyses's attempts to reduce revenues to their temples. Yet a Jewish document of 407 BC does refer to 'the destruction of all temples of the Egyptian gods' in the time of Cambyses.

But 'despite the brutality of the initial Persian occupation', Cambyses and his successors are now usually regarded as 'tolerant and respectful rulers of Egypt'. At least they knew how to play the political game with the help of their Egyptian advisors, who knew full well that the written word of official propaganda could cover a multitude of sins. Indeed, it is often pointed out that Cambyses must have honoured the Apis bull, based on inscriptional evidence from the Serapeum catacombs at Sakkara, with 'two of these holy animals being recorded for his reign' – which was all of four years.

Certainly Cambyses benefited greatly from the help of his Egyptian advisors, some of whom adopted the elaborate Persian overgarment, or combined the traditional Egyptian pectoral necklace with new-style Persian torques. Chief among these men was the Saites' former admiral, Wedjahorresnet, who not only retained his naval command but was also made 'royal seal-bearer, chief scribe, administrator of the palace and chief physician', the 'true beloved king's friend', who composed Cambyses's new name as King of Upper and Lower Egypt: 'Mesutira' – 'Offspring of Ra'.

In fact, so useful was his Egyptian advisor that when Cambyses moved back to Persia in 522 BC in response to rebellion, Wedjahorresnet went with him, along with 6,000 of Egypt's finest craftsmen, albeit forcibly deported to Persia, together with thousands of their Greek and Lydian counterparts.

Egypt was now simply another province controlled by military garrisons and a governor, who raised taxes on behalf of the Persian 'Great King', Egypt's absentee pharaoh, now in control of 7,500,000 square kilometres, stretching from the Aegean to the Nubian border, and across to Central Asia.

At his death, Cambyses was succeeded by a courtier, Darius (522–486 BC), whose reign exemplifies the Persian love of refinement and sophistication. For all the fruits of their vast empire were brought together in the monarchs' public image, from the exotic signature fragrance of the king to the numerous shoes of the queen, supplied exclusively by the Egyptian Delta town of Anthylla.

His new capital Persepolis was adorned with multiple images of tribute-bearers from across his vast empire, the same theme repeated in two statues of Darius, carved in Persian style, but made in Egypt. Originally set up at Heliopolis, their bases were carved with small figures representing all the provinces of his empire, their accompanying names written out in the same hieroglyphs which hail Darius as 'the strong Upper Egyptian king, great in his powers, lord of strength, who conquers the Nine Bows, excellent in council, lord of the curved sword, shooting at the target without his arrow missing it, whose strength is like Montu, King of Upper and Lower Egypt, Lord of the Two Lands, Darius, may he live forever!'

Having sent Wedjahorresnet back to Egypt, Darius ordered a commission of Egypt's wisest individuals to set down all Egypt's laws for him, prior to his first visit to the country in 517 BC.

He also completed the Saite canal linking the Nile to the Red Sea at Per-Temu (Pithom), no doubt to take Egypt's tribute to Persepolis all the faster. Trade links were also massively enhanced across Egypt's largely desert landscape when the Persians reintroduced that most Egyptian of beasts, the camel, which had disappeared from the Nile Valley by Predynastic times. Although the Assyrians had apparently brought a small number of them to Egypt in the ninth century BC, it was the Persians who really brought the camel back to Egypt, allowing lucrative trade routes to be developed through the Western Desert oases, including Kharga, where Darius even commissioned a new temple of Amen.

But despite his relatively enlightened rule, Darius's empire was too vast to remain entire for long, and by 499 BC the Greek cities of Ionia had begun to rebel, supported by Athens. And when Athens decisively beat the Persians at the battle of Marathon in 490 BC, it encouraged wide-scale rebellion in Egypt, which only increased with Darius's death in 486 BC.

So his son and successor Xerxes (486–465 BC) 'sent an army against the Egyptian rebels and decisively crushed them, reducing the country to a condition of worse servitude than it had ever been in the previous reign'.

Also retaliating against Egypt's allies, Xerxes invaded the Greek mainland with half a million men, against whom 300 brave Spartans made a vain last stand before Athens was sacked and burned.

But Xerxes did not enjoy his supremacy for long. Within a year he had been decisively defeated twice by the Greeks, by land and sea, and the Greek mainland was now free. Athens was in control of the seas, and Persia's western border pushed back to the Hellespont. Xerxes himself was murdered by his bodyguard in 465 BC, and by 463 BC Egypt had gained sufficient confidence to once more rebel against its Persian overlords.

Led by Inaros of Heliopolis, a prince of the old Saite line, the rebellion quickly spread through the Delta and, with Athenian support, Inaros defeated the Persians and freed Egypt. It was long remembered that 'nobody caused the Persians more trouble and loss than Inaros', an idea immortalised in a series of Homeric-style Egyptian tales of local heroes fighting foreigners.

But Inaros's triumph was short-lived. Persian king Artaxerxes I (465–424 BC) defeated, and apparently crucified, the unfortunate Inaros in 454 BC, after which Egypt was once again reduced to its occupied status.

Although a lack of Egyptian monuments dating from the fifth century BC is assumed to reflect a serious decline of native culture which left few written records, it is fortunate that during that time some Greeks still hopped over 'the frog pond' – as Plato dubbed the Mediterranean – to visit the fabled land of the Nile and write about what they saw.

Chief among them was Herodotus of Halicarnassus, a Greek colony on the coast of Asia Minor, who came to Egypt around 450 BC. He then composed his celebrated *Histories*, which have earned him the reputation as both 'the father of history' and 'the father of lies'. But although often dismissed as unreliable, some of his long-disputed descriptions are now known to be quite accurate, from his 'flying snakes' of Arabia – which do in fact live in (and often fall out of) the region's acacia trees – to much of what he says about Egypt.

Admittedly he did lift some of his best lines from fellow Greek Hekataios of Miletus, who had visited Egypt around 500 BC when researching his own work *Aegyptiaka*. In this Hekataios noted that Egypt's Delta is 'the gift of the river', a statement later copied by Herodotus, whose most famous, if overused, soundbite: 'Egypt is the gift of the Nile' is rarely accurately quoted or indeed, properly credited.

Like Hekataios before him, and so many tourists since, Herodotus was shown many of the same things by his local guides.

Arriving at Naukratis, Herodotus paid a visit to Aphrodite's temple, leaving his name on a Greek cup as an offering, before travelling on through the Delta. At Mendes, famous for its sacred ram, he was told that 'not long ago a goat tupped a woman, in full view of everybody – a most surprising event', even though Athens's queen *archon*-priestess also ritually mated with a bull, believed to represent Dionysos. In myth, a Minoan queen and bull had produced the legendary Minotaur, the Greeks' belief that their gods could transform themselves into animals to impregnate mortal women something with a longer history among the Egyptians, whose ancient *Coffin Texts* do indeed refer to the 'Bull who copulates with fair ladies'.

As an aspect of ritual present at Herodotus's next port of call, Memphis, whose 'large and very remarkable' Ptah temple housed the Apis bull, women would expose themselves en masse to stimulate the animal's powers of fertility. These were obviously still irresistible in 1850, when the archaeologists who discovered a life-size statue of Apis at the Serapeum were soon surprised 'to find several women of the neighbouring Arab village perched on the statue, begging the god to grant them sons'.

Herodotus also visited Heliopolis and the pyramids of Giza, which, he says, he measured himself, describing scenes within the long-vanished funerary temple of Khufu and repeating claims that one of the Giza pyramids had been built by a woman. But surpassing even the Giza pyramids in Herodotus's estimation was his favourite site, the 'Labyrinth' of Amenemhat III; he stated 'I have seen this building and it is beyond my power to describe it'.

Sailing south past Abydos, whose temple of Seti I housed its king list, now surrounded by hundreds of tourists' graffiti in Greek, Phoenician and Persian Aramaic, Herodotus describes the Egyptian 'athletic contests with all the usual events' held at the temple of Min in Akhmim. Then on reaching Thebes and the Karnak temple of Amen who the Greeks equated with Zeus, Herodotus states 'when the historian Hekataios was in Thebes, the priest did to him precisely what they did to me', taking him into the 'hall of statues' and showing him 345 figures of the successive high priests since Narmer.

Yet Herodotus's ultimate goal was Elephantine, the legendary source of the Nile and the limit of the Persian Empire. And as he says himself, 'as far as Elephantine I speak as an eyewitness, but further south only from hearsay'.

Herodotus then went to Athens in 431 BC, at the beginning of the Peloponnesian War when Athens and Sparta slugged it out for nigh on thirty years. But when Persia sided with Sparta to end Athens's imperial ambitions, the end of the war saw increasing rebellions across Persia's empire; as their grip on Egypt weakened, Amyrtaios of Sais once again took back first the Delta, then the rest of the country, to form Amyrtaios's one-man Twenty-eighth Dynasty (404–399 BC).

Although now free of Persian control, the Egyptians fought among themselves and soon another Delta warlord, Nepherites of Mendes, seized the throne to create Egypt's Twenty-ninth Dynasty (399–380 BC).

He and his successor, Hakor, fought off several attacks by an ever-persistent Persia with the help of Greek troops under the Athenian general, Chabrias, whose embarkation point at the Athenian port of Piraeus now had its own temple to Egyptian Isis. The goddess's geographical expansion was also matched by the way in which she continued to absorb the identities of fellow goddesses, even mighty Hathor, to become *myrionymos* – 'the one of countless names'.

Although the Twenty-ninth Dynasty had secured Egypt's independence, its own lifetime was short, ending in 380 BC when its general, Nakhtnebef (Nectanebo) of Sebennytos, declared himself pharaoh. Ruling as Nectanebo I (380–362 BC), he initiated the highly influential Thirtieth Dynasty, true successors to the old kings of nearby Sais, whose creator goddess Neith had chosen Nectanebo and 'appointed him ruler of the Two Lands, placed her uraeus upon his head, captured for him the nobles' hearts and destroyed all his enemies'.

With 'all his enemies' a veiled reference to the Persians, their king Artaxerxes II (405–359 BC) may have had the longest reign of all Persia's kings, but he failed in even his most determined attempts to regain control of Egypt. For the 200,000 men and 500 warships he sent in 373 BC were defeated after a year-long struggle, when Nectanebo I triumphed through a combination of Greek help, Persian infighting and the timely arrival of the Nile flood, which forced a Persian retreat. It also gained Nectanebo I the reputation of 'Mighty Monarch guarding Egypt, Copper Wall enclosing Egypt, Powerful One with active arm and sword master who attacks a host, fiery hearted at seeing his foes, Heart-Gouger of the treason-hearted'.

Nectanebo reinforced his Greek alliance by marrying Ptolemais, a relative of his Athenian general Chabrias, who gave him two sons and a daughter. And with the pharaoh's distinctive, beaked-nose profile and jutting chin reproduced in stone right across the country, he erected Karnak's first great pylon gateway, whose mud-brick construction ramps remain to this day; as too do many of the sphinxes with which he lined the causeway leading south to the Temple of Luxor. And, recreating the same sphinx-lined causeway before the Serapeum of Sakkara, he built a duplicate structure – the 'Bucheum' – for the Buchis bulls of Armant, sacred to the war god Montu.

Not content with promoting the cults of the sacred animals to even greater lengths, Nectanebo also gave tax exemptions to the clergy, from the Horus priests of Edfu to those of Neith at Sais, whom he also awarded a ten per cent cut of all Mediterranean imports.

He was briefly succeeded by his son Djedhor, Greek Teos, (362–360 BC), whose only claim to fame was to be the first Egyptian pharaoh to issue coins. And although the Egyptians themselves regarded gold as too divine a metal to use as mere currency, Teos minted gold coins to pay his Greek mercenaries and his elderly advisor, the Spartan king Agesilaos.

But by taking away the temples' recently awarded financial perks and even imposing a poll tax to fund an ill-advised exped ition up into Palestine, Teos became so unpopular that he was replaced by his nephew Nakhthorheb, better known as Nectanebo II (360–343 BC).

Nectanebo II was also supported by the Spartan Agesilaos, who received a golden handshake of 220 talents, no doubt minted in Egypt's new gold coinage, and at his death, received the extra perk of Egyptian-style mummification before being sent home to Sparta.

And keen to right the religious wrongs of his short-lived prede-cessor, the second Nectanebo led Egypt with a potent combination of piety and self-promotion.

Gaining the full support of the clergy by restoring their finances, he also embarked on the most ambitious building scheme for a thousand years, undertaking building work at over a hundred sites including Philae, Elephantine, Edfu, Armant, Karnak, Koptos, Abydos, Hermopolis, Herakleopolis Magna, el-Kharga, Behbeit el-Hagar, Tanis, Bubastis, Pithom, Sebennytos and Heliopolis; while at Sakkara the site was so full they had to build terraces on the cliffsides to support the new temples.

For Sakkara was the burial ground of the Apis bulls, believed to contain the very soul of Egypt with which Nectanebo II wished to identify. And in the grand tradition of royals choosing burial within the security of temple courtyards, the Serapeum may well have contained the Nectanebo II's own sepulchre, complete with his great green stone sarcophagus, inscribed with finely wrought images of the sun god Ra and his fellow deities.

Nectanebo II was certainly keen to harness the powers of all these gods; he took his duties as Egypt's high priest very seriously and, rather than delegating the role as was usual, personally led key rites invoking the powers of Egypt's glorious past to conjure up a magical defence to maintain independence. .

And this seemed to be working when, in 351 BC, Nectanebo II and his Athenian and Spartan allies fought off a huge invasion force sent by Persian king Artaxerxes III. It immediately transformed the pharaoh into a genuine superhero; he became 'a legend in his own lifetime', worshipped throughout the country as the 'Divine Falcon', the very embodiment of the Living Horus, and Egypt's supreme magician.

Yet for all his tactical planning and ritual protection, Nectanebo II, outnumbered three to one, was ultimately defeated by Artaxerxes III (343–338 BC) at the Battle of Pelusium in 343 BC.

Egypt was taken back into the Persian Empire, which now took its revenge for the last sixty years of freedom.

The Persians targeted the great religious centres of Lower Egypt; Heliopolis and Mendes were sacked and set on fire, and 'Artaxerxes, after taking over all Egypt and demolishing the walls of the most important cities, by plundering the shrines amassed a vast quantitiy of silver and gold and carried off the inscribed records from the ancient temples, which later on were returned to the Egyptian priests on the payment of huge sums'.

As history sadly repeated itself, the tombs of all those who had ruled since Persia was last in control were sacked, although the tomb of Nectanebo II himself remained empty, as the still very much alive monarch escaped south into Nubia. Later making a last-ditch attempt to retake his kingdom with the help of Khabash of Sais, legend would later claim that he then sailed off to the northern Greek kingdom of Macedonia.

Having installed his Persian governor in Memphis, a triumphant Artaxerxes III returned east, 'bearing many possessions and spoils', as well as many of Egypt's troublesome nobility, who were now deported to Persia.

It was left to those who remained to pick up the pieces. The priest Petosiris of Hermopolis speaks of a time when 'nothing was in its former place since fighting had started inside Egypt, the south being in turmoil, the north in revolt. Temples were without their priests who had fled, not knowing what was happening'. Then after restoring the site as best he could, 'I made a solid work of the wall in the temple' to protect it from any future damage.

Yet despite the terrible destruction that marked the Second Persian Period (343–332 BC), the powerful ancient forces invoked by Nectanebo II were clearly still active. For Artaxerxes III was assassinated by a courtier in 338 BC, his son and successor Arses (338–336 BC) killed by the same hand only two years later. And although the assassin bore the Persian name Bagoas, both ancient and modern commentators have nonetheless suggested that he was 'evidently an Egyptian'.

Bagoas even succeeded in placing the last Persian king upon the Persian throne – Darius III (336–332 BC) – whose vast empire still included Egypt. But his reign too would be brief, soon swept away by a power that would transform both Egypt and the entire ancient world for ever.

20

The Final Flourish: 332–30 BC

Although Egypt's last native ruler, Nectanebo II, had tried to retake his kingdom between 338–335 BC, legend claimed that the deposed pharaoh had sailed north to Macedonia, to the court of Philip II.

Located on the Celtic fringe in the far north of Greece, Macedonia was still a monarchy at a time when most of its southern Greek neighbours had adopted forms of democracy. And the Macedonians 'thought about kingship not as the Greeks did but as the Egyptians', its kings equally polygamous, incestuous and so murderous that the succession rate was rapid indeed.

But in 359 BC, Philip II became its ruler, and within twenty years he had single-handedly transformed this feudal, feuding backwater into *the* world superpower through a succession of wars.

Yet his most bitter conflicts were within his own household, for not only did his complex love life involve courtiers both male and female and his cousin, Arsinoe, but seven wives too, including Olympias, the mother of his son Alexander. When the marriage fell apart, the deeply religious Olympias would tell her son that his father had been none other than the king of the Greek gods, Zeus, the Egyptian Amen, while later rumours would even suggest that Olympias's encounter had actually involved Egypt's last pharaoh Nectanebo II, wearing the mask of Zeus-Amen.

Beginning military training by the age of seven, young Prince Alexander was educated by a then little-known Thracian philosopher named Aristotle, who had studied with Plato in Athens. Not only did he teach philosophy and science, encouraging his pupil to read everything from *The Iliad* to the *Histories* of Herodotus, Aristotle also provided a solid background in statecraft, both for Alexander and for his friend Ptolemy, his possible half-brother, the son of Philip's cousin and sometime lover Arsinoe.

By the age of sixteen, Alexander was made regent of Macedon, and father and son fought side by side, extending Macedonian power as far east as the Dardanelles, in preparation for the Greek crusade against Persia.

With everything ready by 336 BC, the big send-off was marked by Philip II's wedding, his eighth, at which he was killed by his bodyguard. As the news spread across Greece, it became imperative that Macedonia had a new king to lead the Persian campaign. The army immediately chose twenty-year-old Alexander.

Having secured all Greece under his sole command with the blessing of the Delphic oracle, Alexander, accompanied by Ptolemy and 46,000 men, set out east in 334 BC and crossed the Hellespont, gateway to the Persian Empire.

A detour to the fabled city of Troy allowed Alexander to exchange his armour for an ancient set used in the Trojan War and place a wreath on the grave of his hero Achilles. He then went on to defeat the massed Persian ranks at the Battle of Granicus, before marching south through the Greek colonies of Asia Minor, who welcomed him as a liberator.

By November 333 BC, Darius III himself was waiting at Issus with 600,000 men, outnumbering Alexander ten to one. But when Darius fled the field, Alexander was victorious, the 110,000 Persians killed that day a figure unmatched 'until the first day of the battle of the Somme'.

Turning down Darius's offer of an alliance, Alexander needed to secure the eastern Mediterranean and Egypt, still under Persian control. So, first knocking out Persian naval capabilities down the Levantine coast, he pressed on to Egypt, and entered Pelusium with no resistance.

Although he was travelling through a landscape familiar to him from descriptions by earlier Greek travellers, Egypt still made an enormous impression on the twenty-four-year-old.

And when the Macedonian army reached the most famous of all the wonders of the ancient world, the pyramids of Giza, Alexander was so impressed he declared he would erect such a monument over Philip's tomb back in Macedonia 'to match the greatest of the pyramids of Egypt'. Yet as he soon discovered, Giza was only the beginning of a pyramid field that stretched for miles to the south, the pyramids of Sakkara perched on the high desert escarpment above Memphis.

And marching into Memphis with his men, Alexander received a rapturous reception from the Egyptians, who hailed him as Saviour and Liberator. Wishful rumour also had it that he was the son of their last native pharaoh, Nectanebo II – the son of Amen himself.

As legitimate pharaoh simply by right of conquest, Alexander was immediately recognised as king by the city's high priest, Egypt's highest surviving aristocrat and spiritual leader. And since the close relationship between the Memphite priests and monarchy was one which wise kings were careful to promote, Alexander was mindful of Plato's advice that 'in Egypt, it is not possible for a king to rule without the help of the priests'.

He was also keen to pay his respects to the city's Apis bull, which at death became an Osiris-Apis, or Serapis, interred within the vast Serapeum beneath Sakkara's sands. Nectanebo II's own tomb here had remained a cenoptaph since his flight into exile, his elaborate yet empty sarcophagus a poignant reminder of Egypt's lost glories.

Wishing to be seen as Nectanebo II's true successor, Alexander was crowned in Memphis in November 332 BC, the Macedonian diadem replaced with the double crown of Egypt. Proclaiming him 'Horus, strong ruler, he who seizes the lands of the foreigners', the high priest named him 'Meryamen Setepenra Aleksandros', the traditional epithets 'beloved of Amen and the chosen one of Ra' no doubt reinforcing his belief in his mother's stories of his apparent divinity.

Alexander held meetings with Egypt's clergy and academics, intrigued by the crossovers of Egyptian and Greek religion in which Zeus was Amen and Dionysos Osiris. The new pharaoh was also fascinated by Egypt's funerary rites and their promise of eternal life and, although Macedonian royals were traditionally cremated, he saw genuine benefits in Egyptian-style mummification, and may even have consulted the embalmers of Sakkara. His respect for Egypt's traditions is certainly preserved in the form of one of the 'keep out' notices his officer Peukestas posted up around the site, which states 'By order of Peukestas: no-one is to pass. The chamber is that of a priest'.

Wanting to view potential sites for a new coastal base to replace those in the Levant, Alexander sailed from Memphis down the Nile's western branch to the coast at Canopus. Named after Menelaus's pilot in Greek legend, Canopus was where the Egyptians worshipped Osiris as a human-headed jar in which Isis had stored the god's dismembered body parts. So the jars used to store mummified entrails were later given the name 'Canopic jars'.

To the west of Canopus, Alexander reached the Egyptian fort of Rhakotis on a narrow isthmus between the sea and Lake Mareotis. Recalling Homer's description of 'an island called Pharos in the rolling seas off the mouth of the Nile', he declared that Homer had been both a great poet and a far-seeing architect, and was 'at once struck by the excellence of the site, and convinced that if a city were built upon it, it would prosper. Such was his enthusiasm that he could not wait to begin the work; he himself designed the general layout of the new town, indicating the position of the market square, the number of temples to be built and which gods they should serve – the gods of Greece and the Egyptian Isis'.

Marking out the city's planned dimensions with barley, a flock of birds suddenly descended and ate all trace of the fledgling city. Alexander's fears of a bad omen were only allayed when his advisors pronounced that it meant the city would flourish and provide abundance for all. Named Alexandria after its founder, it was one of over seventy settlements he created, but it would be his most successful.

While on the coast, news came that much of the Mediterranean had ejected their pro-Persian leaders, who were sent to him for judgement. He despatched them south to the garrison at Aswan, where they were accompanied by Aristotle's nephew Kallisthenes, sent out to investigate his uncle's somewhat revolutionary theory that the annual Nile flood was not summoned up by a subterranean god but caused by rains further south.

Meanwhile Alexander travelled west into the desert, partly to test the viability of ancient caravan routes that passed through the network of oases linking his new coastal city with central Africa, and partly to consult the renowned oracle of Zeus-Amen at the oasis of Siwa.

Set deep in the desert 400 miles west of Thebes, the oracle was regarded as an offshoot of Amen's Karnak temple. Believed infallible, the Siwan oracle had received questions from across the ancient world, the Persian Cambyses losing an entire army in his attempts to gain its word.

Wanting to surpass this failed attempt, Alexander, Ptolemy and a small force set out west in January 331 BC, and he became the first pharaoh ever to complete the journey in person.

The temple's inner sanctuary, which as both pharaoh and high priest he was entitled to enter alone, remains one of very few surviving places where Alexander is known to have stood in person. Presumably he asked the oracle if he really was a son of gods, as claimed by every pharaoh before him, and not uncommon in a world where the line between mortal and divine was at best blurred. And with millions worshipping those who claimed such status, his future plans must have seemed all the more possible.

Apparently more than satisfied by the oracle's pronouncement, Alexander returned to Memphis, where he ordered that Amen's main cult centre Thebes was to be provided with new sanctuaries for the god's cult statue. That in Karnak was to be made of Aswan granite, while the sandstone shrine in Luxor was to be covered in figures of Alexander, as a traditional pharaoh, in the company of his father Amen. Like the earlier images of Amenhotep III on adjoining walls, Alexander would also adopt the rams' horns of Amen, creating the legend of the all-conquering 'Two-horned One', the Arabic *Dhul-Qarnayn*, who even appears in the Koran.

Having appointed Kleomenes of Naukratis to rule Egypt on his behalf, the twenty-five-year-old Alexander left Egypt in spring 331 BC. Having secured the eastern Mediterranean, he now set out after Darius, defeating him a third and final time at Gaugamela later that year to become Great King of the Persian Empire by right of conquest, and taking Darius's daughter as his wife.

He also inherited some five million kilos of Persian gold, much of it transformed into the coinage that changed the entire world economy. As trade flourished across a vast network of new markets, Greek culture and Egyptian religion followed in the wake of a campaign route that extended a further 11,000 miles (almost 18,000 kilometres) east over the next eight years.

As he and his men travelled from the Persian heartlands up to Tajikistan, Alexander acquired a second wife, Roxane. They then crossed the Hindu Kush to reach India, where they fought against rajahs and their fearsome war elephants. Alexander celebrated his victories by adopting the elephant–skin headdress, and the elephants, into his army.

Returning west via the deserts of Gedrosia, and navigating routes through the Indian Ocean and Persian Gulf, Alexander arrived back in Babylon. He made his headquarters on the banks of the River Euphrates in the ancient palace of Nebuchadnezzar, overlooking the Hanging Gardens. And here he received envoys from across the ancient world, planned a campaign into Arabia and contemplated an expedition across north Africa beyond Carthage, as far as the Straits of Gibraltar.

Since setting out from Macedonia in 336 BC, thirteen years of endless campaigning without a single defeat had gained Alexander an empire covering two million square miles (over five million km²) across three continents. Having changed the face of the known world, his reign was a turning point, as the Classical era gave way to the Hellenistic Period, and Greek culture was irrevocably transformed by the many others encountered on his foreign campaigns.

Yet, still only at the beginning of his plans, Alexander the Great was declared dead in Babylon on 10 June 323 BC, aged only thirty-two.

While suffering from a fever made worse by heavy drinking, he had given his signet ring to his highest general Perdikkas, bequeathed 'all his goods to Ptolemy' and left his empire 'to the strongest'. His closest friends held a vigil before a shrine of Serapis, but the Egyptian god was unable to save him and he fell into a fatal coma.

As his men were at a loss to know what to do for the best, his body was left where it lay for almost a week, until Egyptian embalmers arrived at the palace. Yet despite the summer heat, his body had remained in pristine condition, its lifelike complexion, taken as a sign of his divinity, most likely suggesting that he had 'entered a deep, terminal coma due to the onset of cerebral malaria'.

So he was possibly still alive as the embalmers began their work. Removing his brain and major internal organs to prevent the putrefaction that begins immediately at death, they preserved his body with beeswax, 'exotic spices and perfumes', and placed it in an anthropoid coffin made of 200 talents of beaten gold in traditional Egyptian manner. Draped with a Macedonian pall of purple and gold, it was then placed centre stage among his men, to be present as they tried to determine the succession.

Although Alexander's wife Roxane was about to give birth, Alexander also had a half-brother, Philip Arrhidaios, a Macedonian of royal blood but mentally impaired. As the generals were unable to agree between the two candidates, fighting broke out around Alexander's body, but at last they decided to make Arrhidaios king, as Philip III (323–317 BC), along with any future son of Roxane. Yet both kings were mere figureheads, since real power lay with the army and its officers, who dubbed themselves his 'Successors'.

But with none of them capable of replacing Alexander as sole leader, they divided the empire between them, leaving Perdikkas in control of the army. Another general, Antipater, would remain in power in Macedonia; while Lysimachus took Thrace; Antigonas, Asia Minor; Meleagar, Phoenicia; Laomedon, Syria; Seleucus, Babylonia and Ptolemy, probably at his own suggestion, 'was appointed to govern Egypt and Libya and those lands of the Arabs that were contiguous to Egypt'.

As for Alexander's body, it was to be taken from Babylon back to Macedonia in a monumental hearse, a six-by-four-metre golden temple on wheels. Covering only a few miles a day on account of its sheer size and surrounding crowds, the cortege finally reached Syria in winter 322 BC, where the tensions that had been developing between the Successors broke into all-out war.

For Perdikkas now held Alexander's baby son Alexander IV, recently born to Roxane, and was now regent for both the child and his co-ruler, Philip Arrhidaios. Yet with his eyes on the throne himself, Perdikkas needed to bury Alexander's body in the royal cemetery in

Macedonia to be seen as his rightful successor and to claim authority over his many rivals.

Although all were determined to halt Perdikkas's ambitions, Ptolemy seized the initiative by hijacking the coffin at Damascus, bringing Alexander back to Egypt and initiating a war in which Perdikkas and the army, including his Indian war elephants, invaded Egypt in the spring of 321 BC.

Yet once again the Nile came to Egypt's defence, as 2,000 of Perdikkas's men were lost when attempting to cross the Nile at Memphis. Apparently around half fell victim to crocodiles, and Perdikkas was killed in the resulting mutiny. And although his remaining troops offered the regency of Macedonia to Ptolemy, he wisely declined, preferring to keep a firm hold on Egypt and the body of Alexander, which he 'proceeded to bury with Macedonian rites in Memphis'.

Since Alexandria itself was still a building site, the late king was most likely interred in the area of the Serapeum. It has even been suggested that Ptolemy placed Alexander's gold coffin within the unused sarcophagus of Nectanebo II, a powerfully political act that would give physical continuity between Egypt's last native dynasty and the Macedonian Alexander, and may well have prompted the story claiming that Alexander was Nectanebo II's son.

Certainly the Serapeum was redeveloped with an impressive causeway terminating in the so-called 'Philosophers' Circle', a semi-circle of life-size statues of famous Greeks, likely marking the entrance to Alexander's first tomb. Although the eleven remaining figures have been sandblasted to semi-oblivion in Sakkara's windswept desert, such suggested identities as Homer, Pindar, Plato and Aristotle would place Alexander among his favourite poets, philosophers and historians, most appropriate companions while his monumental mausoleum was being constructed in Alexandria, which had become the royal capital by 311 BC.

Ptolemy certainly took his responsibilities to Alexander's memory very seriously. Ruling Egypt as governor on behalf of nominal pharaohs Philip Arrhidaios and Alexander IV, whose names were used on official documents, he alone of all the Successors carried out building work in their names. Much appreciated by the priests, who declared 'this great governor searched for the best thing to do for the gods of Upper and Lower Egypt', Alexander's new shrine for Amen at Karnak was carved in colourful scenes bearing Arrhidaios's name, while down in Aswan the granite temple of Khnum was carved with the names of young Alexander IV.

But the two monarchs never saw the temples created in their names; both continued to be kept hostage in Macedonia as pawns for the Successors' rival ambitions. Arrhidaios was executed in 317 BC, leaving Alexander IV sole king of Macedonia and pharaoh of Egypt. Even when the unfortunate boy was killed in 310 BC, Ptolemy continued to administer Egypt on his behalf for a full five years 'when Pharaoh was ruling under a legal fiction, since he was dead'.

But Governor Ptolemy was very much alive and continued to defend Egypt from the remaining Successors. Seleucus now controlled vast territories from Syria to Afghanistan; while Antigonas's dynasty, which held Macedonia, launched a failed invasion into Egypt in 306 BC. As the ongoing conflicts between the remaining Successors escalated into an arms race involving huge numbers of mercenary troops and fleets of warships, triremes were supersized into quinqueremes with five men to an oar, and Ptolemy even built transport ships known as *elephantagoi*, on which to import his war elephants up the Red Sea from Africa, after Seleucus had cut off their supply from India.

By such means Ptolemy retained the territory of Cyrene (Libya), parts of Phoenicia and Syria, Cyprus and the islands of the Aegean. Yet his masterstroke had been to choose Egypt, a wealthy country that he ruled most successfully with the support of its priests.

Ptolemy was also the last survivor of the Macedonian royal house; his mother Arsinoe had been Philip II's cousin and one-time lover. Indeed, the ancient sources claimed that 'the Macedonians consider Ptolemy to be the son of Philip, asserting that his mother was with child when she was married to Lagus by Philip', and that 'Ptolemy was a blood relative of Alexander'.

Yet only in 305 BC, after eighteen years' rule, did sixty-year-old Governor Ptolemy take the final step and become Pharaoh Ptolemy I (305–282 BC), 'beloved of Amen and the chosen one of Ra'. But as an old-school, no-nonsense Macedonian, he refused divine honours, accepting only the Greek title 'Soter' – 'Saviour' – from the people of Rhodes in gratitude for his help during a siege by rival Successors the Antigonids.

To further counterbalance his rivals, Ptolemy also began to issue his own coinage, on which his 'eagle-like' profile was reflected in his personal badge, the eagle, which became the Ptolemaic royal symbol. A golden eagle is still centrally placed on the Egyptian flag today.

The other image associated with Ptolemy I is Serapis. Although the god had been a favourite of Alexander, it was Ptolemy I who gave the deity his characteristic appearance by blending the existing Egyptian Osiris-Apis with the bearded Greek gods Zeus, Asclepius and Hades, to produce a Greek-looking Egyptian hybrid deity acceptable to all. As a form of Osiris, he was still partnered with Isis, and their twin images as human-headed snakes became Alexandria's guardian spirits.

In order to understand his kingdom's mind-boggling culture, Ptolemy I needed a 'rational synthesis' of Egypt's convoluted religion, so he employed the bilingual high priest of Heliopolis, Merynetjeraa, 'beloved of the great god'. Better known by the Greek version of his name, Manetho, he simplified matters by finding the nearest Greek equivalent to Egypt's numerous gods. So in the same way as Amen was already known as Zeus, Osiris became Dionysos; Hathor, Aphrodite; and Thoth, Hermes, whose sacred animals were honoured with ever-more costly mummification.

Such religious synchronicity was followed up with Manetho's most famous work, a list of all Egypt's known rulers, which he set down in a sequence of thirty dynasties still employed today. And to make the work understandable to his Greek-speaking patrons, Manetho gave the Greek versions of the ancient names, so that Amenhotep became Amenophis, Dhutymose became Tuthmosis and Senwosret, Sesostris. In composing this masterwork, Manetho was able to draw on the ancient king lists located in temples throughout the country, circumventing the rewriting of history in some by cross-referencing with those elsewhere, including the records in temple libraries, the greatest such library within his own workplace at Heliopolis.

No doubt inspired by such storehouses of ancient wisdom, Ptolemy I embarked on plans for a new library to enhance his new city of Alexandria, appointing Aristotle's former student, Demetrius, as its first head librarian.

The new institution was a most fitting addition for a city founded on a literary quote that had also mentioned the island of Pharos. And here in 297 BC, Ptolemy I began work on a great lighthouse. Designed to mark the city's position on a coastline with few discernable features, the lighthouse was connected to the mainland by a causeway that rested on piles driven into the seabed, and effectively divided Alexandria's huge harbour in two. A third harbour, linked to Lake Mareotis by a canal, allowed seaborne traffic direct access to the Nile and the rest of Egypt.

The royal engineers were also active in the Fayum and, by copying land creation schemes from two thousand years earlier, reduced the water flowing into its lake from the Nile by two metres, creating hundreds more square metres of arable land for greater yields, especially of grapes; for although wine had long been produced in Egypt, its increasing Greek population demanded more.

The new farmers were mainly pensioned-off troops settled on reclaimed land around the Fayum in new settlements with Greek-style facilities – gymnasia, theatres and public bathhouses. Their towns' Greek names were based on 'the Hellenic divinity who seemed to fit the local cult best', with the addition of the Greek word *polis* ('city'). So Henen-nesut, for example, became Herakleopolis, 'city of Herakles', and Shedet became Krokodilopolis, reflecting the region's crocodiles, worshipped in the local temples and at death buried in its cemeteries, their funerary expenses met by the Crown as another means of keeping political control.

As for the succession, Ptolemy I had also thought this through with some care. He had produced at least twelve children by three wives and more mistresses, although his eldest son Ptolemy Keraunos – 'Lightning' – was a somewhat unstable character. So his children by his Macedonian wife, Berenike I, would ultimately form the basis of the Ptolemaic dynasty, his son, the future Ptolemy II, born on Kos in 308 BC, made his co-ruler in 285 BC.

When the first Ptolemy finally died in his bed in January 282 BC aged eighty-four, he was the last of the great Successors. After an action-packed life, he had 'played the part of a shrewd, cautious, amiable bourgeois, who in an age of turmoil elevated mediocrity into a saving virtue' – and had lived over half a century longer than Alexander.

Yet whereas Alexander had been embalmed at death, Ptolemy I was cremated according to Macedonian custom in rites led by his successor Ptolemy II. The ancient sources also claim that it was Ptolemy II 'who brought down from Memphis the corpse of Alexander', placing it with his father's ashes in the new tomb that had finally been completed for Alexander in the new city, most probably in a great alabaster sepulchre whose antechamber was discovered within the city's later Catholic cemetery.

When the twenty-eight-year-old Ptolemy II (285–246 BC) was crowned, his late father had ensured he had a queen, Arsinoe I, daughter of his old ally and fellow Successor Lysimachus of Thrace (the modern Balkans). Her dowry brought Egypt territories in the Aegean, and she provided Ptolemy II with three children. Yet the marriage was brought to an end by the unstoppable ambitions of the king's sister, Arsinoe II.

In a game of diplomatic marriage, Ptolemy I and his sixty-year-old colleague Lysimachus had simply swapped their same-named daughters. Ptolemy I had sent his sixteen-year-old daughter Arsinoe II to become Lysimachus's wife and queen of Thrace. She became mother to three sons, then queen of Macedonia, conquered by her elderly husband, just before his death.

As queen of two lands, Arsinoe II was now a powerful woman. So her unstable half-brother, Keraunos, persuaded her to marry him to bolster his own claim to Macedonia – at least until he began to murder her sons, whereupon she fled back home to Egypt.

Taking refuge at the court of her brother Ptolemy II, she was fully aware of her royal status, and intended to join her parents and brother, who were collectively referred to as 'the rulers' – for as one ancient commentator noted, with some understatement, she was 'one to get her own way'.

Certainly laid-back Ptolemy II was no match for his elder sister, who was determined to become monarch for a third time. So with his existing wife sent away to live out her days in Koptos, forty-one-year-old Arsinoe married her thirty-three-year-old brother in 275 BC, to become 'Philadelphus' – 'sibling lover'.

Brother–sister marriage was regular practice among Egyptian and Persian monarchy, and the Macedonian royals also married within their own families. But others in the Greek world were shocked, not only by the marriage but by the fact that Arsinoe II became joint ruler, the first of a succession of Ptolemaic royal women who 'played the same role as kings. Enjoying equal status with males in the eyes of their subjects, they eliminated gender hierarchy for a brief period in Classical antiquity'.

As the first woman in Egypt in almost a thousand years to take equal powers to her male counterpart, the records state that Arsinoe II 'has received the crowns of Upper and Lower Egypt', and as 'Mistress of the Two Lands', she was awarded full kingly titles as 'Arsinoe Philadelphos, King of Upper and Lower Egypt', with her names written in the twin cartouches of a traditional king.

Such ancient titles were a key part of Egyptian culture, and the Ptolemies, as Greek-speaking monarchs, relied heavily on their bilingual Egyptian advisors including Manetho. His king list named pharaonic predecessors both male and female, and Hatshepsut proved a particularly useful precedent, having married her half-brother and ruled as pharaoh. Hailed as 'Daughter of Amen' and 'Daughter of Ra', as Hatshepsut had been, Arsinoe also adopted regal headgear that was 'modelled on the crown of Hatshepsut', in which the red crown of northern Egypt was topped with twin tall feathers, cow horns, solar disc and ram's horns, each relating to a specific deity.

And Arsinoe II underpinned her political position further by playing the goddess too. Representing herself as Egypt's dynamic Isis, who had married her brother Osiris and ruled jointly with him, she sold the idea to the Greeks by comparing herself with Hera, who married her sibling deity Zeus, and with the glamourous, sea-born goddess Aphrodite.

Such comparisons were made at every opportunity by the Greek poets employed as the couple's spin-doctors, who also refer to the couple's shared blond hair. Their portraits show the same wide staring eyes as their putative uncle Alexander, a feature Arsinoe was so keen to exploit that some medical historians have assumed her exaggeratedly large eyes must mean she suffered from an exophthalmic goitre! And she alone of all the Ptolemies, male or female, was portrayed with Alexander's divine ram's horns on her coin images.

Yet big-eyed blonde Arsinoe was far more than a pretty face, and Ptolemy II 'probably owed a good deal of his efficiency in war and in administrative ideas to his sister-wife Arsinoe II'. For it was on her advice that the creation of sufficient defences prevented invasions from Cyrene (Libya) and Nubia, quelled a rebellion by the Crown's Celtic mercenaries and strengthened the Eastern Delta against Seleucid Syria. And Arsinoe II 'reorganized the army; she accompanied it on its campaigns; she won the Syrian war'. She certainly continued the active role played by both Egyptian and Macedonian royal women in military matters, her patronage of Egypt's 4,000-strong fleet demonstrating both her power and that of Egypt wherever it sailed.

Arsinoe II's financial acumen also came to the fore with the creation of a Domesday-style inventory of all Egypt's assets to find out what resources were available. Strict revenue laws then established royal monopolies on everything from linen to oil production, while taxes and import duty were even levied on the slaves from Palestine, Syria and Nubia, required in ever-increasing numbers for rich households and in industry, from the perfume factories around Alexandria to the woollen mills of Memphis.

Swift communication throughout Egypt and abroad was possible due to an incredibly efficient system of royal post, with records kept on an hour-to-hour basis; surviving snippets reveal that on 'the 19th, 11th hour, Nicodemus delivered to Alexander scrolls from King Ptolemy [II] for Antiochous in the Heracleopolite nome; 1 scroll for Demetrius the officer of the Thebaid in charge of the elephant supply'.

Reopening old canal routes to the Red Sea, the couple founded eight new harbour towns down the coast, through which they imported jewels and pearls, silks, spices and incense, 'everything that the king and his beloved royal sister and wife desired'. These were brought in from Arabia, India and the Orient, and regular trade established with southern Arabia carried out by Arab traders who travelled with their precious cargoes; men like Zayd'il bin Zayd, who actually died in Memphis in 264 BC, his coffin inscription revealing that he had 'imported myrrh for the temple of the gods of Egypt'.

Late in his reign Ptolemy II also sent his ambassador to the Mauryan court of the Indian ruler Ashoka; surviving customs documents show that fleets of 120 Ptolemaic ships were sent out to the Indian port of Muziris to import sixty cases of spikenard, five tons of spices, 100 elephant tusks and 135 tons of ebony.

Arsinoe II and Ptolemy II also looked west and, expanding their links with the Greek colonies around Italy, they became the first of Alexander's Successors to make official contact with Rome in 273 BC, the resulting treaty marked by Rome's first silver coins, based on those of Arsinoe II and 'suggesting technical help offered by Egypt to the fledgling Roman mint'.

As the revenue from trade flooded in, the couple displayed their wealth and power at their new Ptolemaia festival and games held every four years. Beginning with a day-long procession, 80,000 troops – 'many chariots, everywhere boots, everywhere men wearing cloaks' – were accompanied by thousands of people in sumptuous costumes. They were followed by the wealth of Africa, Arabia and India, carried by elephants, camels, giraffes and rhinoceros, which were 'objects of amazement'.

As a means of showcasing their divinely inspired dynasty, the procession included golden statues of the gods, great automata that rose up and sat down through a system of siphons and compressed air. There were statues of the Ptolemies' patron deity Dionysos – accompanied by rivers of wine – of the great Alexander, and Ptolemy I and Berenike I, whose gem-encrusted, gold myrtle wreath was an astonishing thirty-five metres in circumference. And with 'myrtle wreath' being contemporary slang for female genitals, it balanced out the twenty-five-metre-long gold penis tipped with a star that emphasised none too subtly the mechanics of the royal succession.

Yet the Ptolemaia procession was only the preamble to the Ptolemaia games. Based on the Olympics, they soon gained equal status after the couple had invited the necessary officials, putting them up in lavish accommodation and even sending them on sight-seeing tours of Egypt's ancient wonders. And having invested huge sums promoting home-grown talent from Alexandria to Thebes, Egypt was soon producing state-funded Olympic victors, both at home and at Olympia itself.

These included the Ptolemaic royals, whose Arab horses, trained in the hippodromes of Alexandria, now dominated Olympic chariot events – half of the fourteen Olympic victors between 296 BC and 244 BC came from Egypt. In this 'sport of kings', which drew strongly on their adopted pharaonic legacy, Ptolemy I was an Olympic victor at Delphi in 314 BC, while his wife Berenike I's team won the chariot race of 284 BC – 'that is great', claimed her proud son Ptolemy II. As for Arsinoe II, her victory in all three races on a single day in 272 BC was commemorated in sculpted form, her victory statue, set up at Olympia with that of her brother-husband, purposefully facing the great temple of Zeus and Hera in a demonstration of shared divinity. Ptolemy II also adopted Arsinoe II's title 'Philadelphus', 'sibling lover', as the couple were worshipped as twin gods *Theoi Adelphoi* around the ancient world.

This of course included Egypt. For 'in their rich house, gold is not heaped up to lie useless, as if the wealth of ever-industrious ants; much is lavished on the shrines of the gods', whose cult statues were now joined by those of Arsinoe II. For Ptolemy II had decreed that 'her statue be set up in all the temples. This pleased their priests for they were aware of her noble attitude toward the gods and of her excellent deeds to the benefit of all people'.

Now that she had become *sunnaos thea*, 'resident goddess' within every temple in Egypt, Arsinoe's ritual duties involved interaction with the temples' sacred animals, as at Mendes, where her powers as a goddess 'Beloved of the Ram' complemented the male fertility of this sacred creature. In Heliopolis and Memphis, which housed the Mnevis and Apis bulls, 'his majesty and his royal sister were together with them'; the same went for the Buchis bull of Armant, which again was worshipped alongside Arsinoe II as his goddess.

The couple's temple-building projects gained them the support of the local clergy, but were also strategically planned. At Koptos, launching point for the couple's trade caravans to their new Red Sea ports, they commissioned a fifty-metre-wide temple to Isis and Min. At Medamud, a new temple of Montu featured some of the last-ever scenes of the ancient jubilee festival, while at Karnak, Arsinoe II, 'Daughter of Amen', was also 'Mistress of the whole circuit of the solar disc', a title last used by the Saite God's Wives priestesses.

Then at the very southern limit of their country, where Isis was worshipped as 'Queen of the South', the couple embellished her temple on Philae with vast funds diverted from the tax revenues of neighbouring Nubia, where they had taken control of the goldmines. The sumptuous temple for the goddess featured images of the couple offering her fine linens, eye-paint and jewellery in exchange for continued life. Ptolemy II was even portrayed worshipping both Isis and his sister-wife together.

The royals' new temple at Philae was a means of demonstrating that they held the entire country, from its furthest southern reaches to their splendid new capital Alexandria, soon to become the most influential city of the ancient world.

After Ptolemy II completed his father's great Pharos lighthouse in 283 BC, the 135-metre limestone tower immediately became one of the wonders of the world. Supporting a blazing beacon reflected, by mirrors of polished metal, for almost fifty miles in all directions, this was regarded as a man-made star through which Isis illuminated the world. She was worshipped as 'Isis Pharia' in her temple beside the lighthouse, where her colossal statue strode forward, her mantle caught in the winds, and inspiring the later, if better-known, 'Winged Victory' statue, set up on Samothrace by the Ptolemies' Antigonid rivals.

The royals also set up their own statuary around their city, along with the statues, obelisks and sphinxes of many of their pharaonic predecessors, brought from sites throughout the Nile Valley to give ancient kudos to their modern city.

The Greek phrase *kosmopolites*, 'citizen of the world', 'might well have had the Ptolemaic capital in mind'. With its constantly expanding 'multi-ethnic, multi-lingual, multi-cultural' population of Greeks, Egyptians and Jews, Persians, Arabs and Celts, Alexandria was the ultimate destination for settlers from across Alexander's former empire and beyond, 'from France, from south Russia, from Italy and Greece, from India and Malta. On the quays at Alexandria, you might meet Buddhist missionaries from India and Sri Lanka, and ships from further east as well. The ancient and mysterious land of Egypt now became a great emporium, and a place to live the good life'.

For this well-planned city has accurately been dubbed 'the New York of the ancient world', with its grid pattern of high-rise buildings, financial houses, passenger terminals, theatres, racetracks, gymnasia, parks and water gardens.

Alexandria's most influential building was the Temple of the Muses ('Museum'), a great research institute with lecture halls, laboratories and observatories, where invited scholars were housed at royal expense. The Museum worked in tandem with the Great Library, established under the couple's father Ptolemy I, and as the twin institutions rapidly acquired legendary status, 'the number of books, the establishing of libraries, and the collection in the Hall of the Muses, why need I even speak, since they are in all men's memories', claimed one ancient commentator.

As the busy scholars invented, experimented, dissected and designed, translating into Greek everything from the Hebrew scriptures to the fabled knowledge of ancient Egypt, it was said that the royal couple 'caused the philosophy of the Egyptians (before alone peculiar to the priests) to be divulged in Greek for the benefit of students'.

For 'in the polyglot land of Egypt many now find pasturage as endowed scribblers, endlessly quarrelling in the Muse's birdcage'. Soon there were 120,000 scrolls of history, rhetoric, philosophy, medicine, law, poetry and miscellaneous material such as *Rules of the House*, written by a famous courtesan on how to behave in her establishment. All carefully catalogued and stored, an eventual collection of almost 500,000 'books' represented the sum of the knowledge of the ancient world, held under the Ptolemies' sole control. Following attempts by their Attalid rivals to set up their own library at their capital Pergamon, the Ptolemies banned the export of Egyptian papyrus, forcing their Attalid rivals to invent parchment (*pergamenon*) as a means of sustaining the race for knowledge, which has always brought power.

Later commentators would remember Ptolemy II as 'the most august of all princes and devoted, if any one was, to culture and learning', and both he and Arsinoe II had been taught as children by Aristotle's successor, Strato. Such tuition would have been relatively straightforward, since the royal Library and Museum were part of the palace complex.

The palace area was located opposite the Pharos lighthouse on the mainland promontory of Lochias, where each monarch built their own quarters as a series of gated communities. Importing huge quantities of marble to create interiors as palatial as those in their Macedonian homeland, the Ptolemies enhanced their Egyptian palaces with indoor fountains, mosaics and statues by the hundred. Walls were hung with tapestries, paintings and portraits, while gilded couches accompanied gold and silver tables, set with tableware 'of gold and studded with gems, wonderful in their workmanship'.

It seems that Arsinoe II made all the decisions relating to décor, displaying her flair at the annual Festival of Adonis, which was held in the public parts of the palace. During the festival there were guided tours, one of which was taken by the inquisitive housewife Gorgo, who told her friend Praxinoa, 'Let's go to the house of the king, rich Ptolemy. I hear the queen has done a beautiful job of decorating it . . . And when you've seen it, what won't you be able to say to someone who hasn't!' But the excessive opulence was not to everyone's taste, one jaded visitor claiming 'everything in Egypt was play-acting and painted scenery', a comment that cut to the heart of this melodramatic monarchy, for whom image was everything.

Certainly Arsinoe II herself used her carefully crafted public image to impress subjects she regarded with near contempt. Sneering at the Alexandrians' 'Flagon-bearing Festival', she dismissed it as 'a very dirty get-together. For the assembly can only be that of a miscellaneous mob who have themselves served with a stale and utterly unseemly feast', although she herself was known to vomit at royal drinking parties.

Having transformed the Ptolemaic house into a dazzling bastion of conspicuous consumption in only seven years, Arsinoe II died at the age of forty-eight at full moon on the night of 16–17 July 268 BC.

The Egyptian records announced that 'this goddess ascended to heaven', and Greek sources claimed her spirit was taken up by Apollo in his golden chariot to reside with his fellow gods on Mount Olympus. There was even an official dirge sung before Ptolemy II: 'They cry for your sister, born of the same womb with you, it is she who has died, and the cities of Egypt, wherever you look, are cloaked in black', the colour of funerals for Europeans, but in Egypt the colour of new life, where Isis herself was 'the black-robed queen'.

With Arsinoe II cremated according to Macedonian custom with funeral games held alongside literary contests, the traditional Egyptian Opening of the Mouth ceremony was performed on her statues in all Egypt's temples. The same rite was then performed every July at the end of the Egyptian year, when the rising of Isis's star Sothis in mid-July marked Arsinoe's soul reappearing in the heavens. This was also celebrated at a new annual festival, the Arsinoeia, at which Arsinoe II's priestess led the Alexandrians through the city to their final destination, the Arsinoeion temple.

Located by the sea, it was marked by an unused stone obelisk Nectanebo II had left at Heliopolis, which Ptolemy II's engineer, Phoinix, had brought to Alexandria. And although it 'cost far more trouble in its carriage and elevation than had been originally expended in quarrying it . . . this obelisk was placed by the king in the Arsinoeion, in testimony of his affection for his wife and sister Arsinoe'. The same source adds that the temple housed a pair of statues of Arsinoe II; a two-metre figure of green peridots from the Red Sea above which an iron statue was magically suspended by the magnetic lodestone roof, so memorable it was still a subject of poetry some 500 years later – true testament to its architect, Dinochares.

Not to be outdone, royal engineer Ktesibius worked his own technical magic in Arsinoe II's second temple on Alexandria's blustery Cape Zephyrion, erecting a great fountain-like cornucopia 'in the form of the Egyptian Bes, who trumpets forth a shrill note when the spout is opened for the flowing wine . . . through the golden mouthpiece there rings a signal for revelling and mirth, like the ancestral melody which Lord Nile produced from the divine waters. So if you will honour this clever device of Ktesibius, come hither young men, to the temple of Arsinoe', where the faithful knew that 'if you pray to her, she will grant fair sailing and make the ocean smooth'.

With streets, cities and entire regions named after her, Arsinoe II was worshipped as far as Cyprus and the Black Sea coast, her cult supported by a special tax levied by the king to keep her spirit alive. For Ptolemy II needed his goddess sister-wife as part of their world-famous double act. For the remaining twenty-two years of his life he never remarried, and still had himself shown with her in his portraits, still added her name to his documents and still minted her coinage. And much like her predecessors, from Amenhotep III to the great Alexander, 'being dead had surprisingly little immediate effect on Arsinoe's career'.

Certainly her physical presence had never been a prerequisite for Ptolemy II, who maintained his relationships with numerous women, and was known as 'the best there is, considerate, a man of wit and taste, partial to the ladies, the height of courtesy, knows who his friends are (and even better, who are not), bestower of much upon many, no denier of favours, as befits a king'. He was also a lover of good living, but increasingly incapacitated by gout, was eventually able to do little more than sit by his palace window, watching his subjects eating picnics on the sands below, gloomily declaring 'Unlucky devil that I am! To think I cannot even be one of those fellows'.

He died aged sixty-two in January 246 BC and, like his sister and parents, was cremated in a Macedonian ceremony, his ashes placed in Alexander's tomb by his thirty-eight-year-old successor, his son Ptolemy III (246–222 BC).

At his accession he married his cousin Berenike, sole ruler of neighbouring Cyrene (Libya). She followed the example of her predecessor Arsinoe II and received full kingly titles as *ta per-aat Bereniga* – 'the pharaoh Berenike' – and 'Female Horus', 'the equivalent of an Egyptian king'. She was clearly her husband's political equal and literally his 'other half'; their union brought two vast territories together, as well as Cyrene's great fleet, which proved decisive in the war against Egypt's Seleucid rivals.

During a five-year campaign when Berenike II ruled Egypt in her husband's absence, she held the title of prime minister last held by a woman two thousand years before.

By 241 BC, the couple had extended their reach as far as Babylonia, finally making peace with their rival Seleucus II and sending him a statue of Isis. This was placed within her own sanctuary at Antioch, from where her cult spread rapidly across the Ptolemies' sphere of influence. They in turn took back Egyptian statues seized a century before by the Persians, a restoration of national pride for which the couple were awarded the title 'Theoi Euergetai', the Benefactor Gods. Their cult was celebrated at the Ptolemaia festival held in both Alexandria and Athens, and at a new festival, the Euergesia, an updated version of the traditional rites of Bastet-Sekhmet.

Capable of harnessing the powers of such ancient, active deities, Berenike II was awarded a unique, if long-winded, Egyptian epithet 'her bravery and strength is that of Neith, her courage that of Bastet-Sekhmet'. And Berenike was certainly a dynamic figure on the world stage, her equestrian abilities as both a rider and breeder reflected in the fact her chariot teams won victories at Nemea, Corinth and Olympia. As eulogised in the 200-verse 'Victory Song for your Horses', she had her own priestess – her 'trophy bearer' – who carried her victors' crowns in annual processions and placed them on her statues.

Like her predecessor Arsinoe II, Berenike II was worshipped as Isis, 'mother of the gods', an epithet she certainly earned by producing six children. Further comparisons with Aphrodite focused on her attractive appearance, which she used to great effect. She carefully matched her regalia to any occasion; the Macedonian diadem was sometimes replaced by an unusual ship's-prow crown to emphasise the couple's naval power, accessorised with an equally unusual anchor-shaped brooch.

She was also a great supporter of Egypt's perfumes industry, taking a great interest in their manufacture; and even Berenike II's hair, worn in corkscrew ringlets around her shoulders, achieved its own immortality after she presented a lock to Arsinoe-Aphrodite-Isis in in the Cape Zephyrion temple, in gratitude for her husband's return from war. And although the lock mysteriously disappeared from the temple overnight, no doubt blown away in the sea breeze, the court astronomer swiftly identified it in the night sky as the constellation Coma Berenikes ('the curl of Berenike'), duly eulogised by the royal poets.

But not all state-funded astronomy was quite so whimsical. In 235 BC, the royal couple appointed Eratosthenes of Cyrene as new director of their Great Library. He was then working on a revolutionary new theory that the earth was round, measuring the distance between Alexandria and Aswan to calculate its circumference to within eighty kilometres. He even calculated the length of the year to establish a reliable calendar of 365¼ days, although his findings were opposed by the Egyptian priests, who preferred their own 360-day year, the remaining five days having long been celebrated as the birthdays of the gods, with an extra day now added for the joint monarchs to make up the leap year.

As the monarchs continued to support scholarship at the Museum, their endowments to the Great Library included not only works obtained from the markets of Athens and Rhodes, but also the original scripts of the great dramatists of Athens. Having taken them out on loan so they could be copied in Alexandria, the couple returned the copies, forfeiting their enormous fifteen-talent deposit in order to keep the priceless originals.

The royal couple also made their mark on their capital's ritual landscape by beginning work on the third and final resting place of Alexander, located near the royal palace, whose subterranean chambers were large enough to house Alexander's mummified body, the ashes of a growing number of Ptolemies and all their funerary equipment.

The city's Serapis temple was also rebuilt, prominently sited on a rocky hill and sheathed in gleaming metal; commentators could only gasp: 'it cannot be done justice with an inadequate description, it is so adorned with great columned halls and statuary which seems almost alive and a great number of other works . . . nothing more magnificent can be seen in the whole world'.

The temple's subterranean chambers housed the cult of Apis, with a priestly decree of 238 BC stressing Ptolemy III and Berenike II's 'constant concern, combined with heavy outlay and expense, for Apis and Mnevis and the other renowned sacred animals in the land'.

As an increasing closeness developed between the crown and the Memphis clergy, high priest Anemho II was often in Alexandria on state business. He helped the royal couple plan a huge new temple of Horus at his cult centre Edfu (Greek Apollinopolis), which would be a shrine to kingship; in the same way as Alexander's powers were drawn down for the benefit of the Ptolemies, so too the accumulated powers of the couple's pharaonic predecessors were channelled through their intermediary Anemho, now designated 'priest of the Royal Ancestors'.

On 23 August 237 BC, Ptolemy and Berenike conducted the temple's foundation ceremony, performing the age-old Stretching the Cord ritual to ensure that it was built 'as the ancestors ordained for it'. And, like the original temple built here in the Old Kingdom, it was aligned to the movement of the sun.

For the sun's rays would highlight different areas of the walls' surface, described as 'beautifully inscribed by the leading craftsmen, all their decorations being carried out according to the ancient records'. The delicate images were accompanied by a new style of hieroglyphs 'with roots firmly in the *Pyramid Texts*, the oldest-known body of religious literature which itself dates back to before 3000 BC'. The addition of some 6,000 new symbols to the standard 800 hieroglyphs was a way for the Egyptian priests to offset the Ptolemies' translations of Egypt's ancient texts into Greek, maintaining their magical nature and adding a further layer of mystery – for even now, 'many Ptolemaic inscriptions remain undeciphered, their secrets yet to be discovered'.

Inaccessible and impenetrable to all but a handful of specialist priests, Edfu's walls were a permanent ritual document whose words created an alliterative effect when read aloud. So of those which have been translated, the phrase 'the Eye of Horus is sound, the Shining One is shining, for Seth no longer exists' would be heard as 'wedjat wedj ti webenet weben ti wehi sep en wenef', and the warning that 'Nekhbet stabs him who violates your inviolable soil' would be vocalised as 'shatat her shemy shash shaw ek shata'.

Accompanied by wall scenes of the king as Horus spearing his enemy Seth, Horus's role as a hunter or *gereg* is believed to be the origin of the name George, and the inspiration of St George spearing the dragon in legend. The scenes are also accompanied by the words 'I hold my harpoon! I drive back the hidden ones, I stab their bodies, I cut them up, I deflect their attack against Horus'. This obsession with spearing, stabbing and generally annihilating the powers of darkness presented the king as defender of the gods, who in turn defended Egypt.

All part of the ancient myth of Horus and Seth, performed as a musical drama, parts of the original script, used by the actors, came from Edfu's temple library, whose niches once contained the sacred books. Another side room, named 'the Chamber of Fabrics', once held sacred vestments, and the walls of 'the Laboratory' were inscribed with the recipes for the ritual perfumes and incense.

In traditional manner, the temple's proportions decrease toward the innermost parts, and there are decreasing levels of light to heighten the sense of mystery. At the heart of the Edfu temple was the stone shrine created by Nectanebo II, now fitted out with an inner shrine of gilded wood housing the god's cult statue and to be seen only by the temple's high priest and the monarchs – a potent link between the Ptolemies and Egypt's last native pharaoh.

In similar vein, Ptolemy and Berenike added to Nectanebo II's other temples, at Karnak creating a series of great stone gateways through which priests like Hornedjitef maintained the same rites that had been practised for centuries. This included the 'reversion of offerings', in which much of the clergy's diet was the meat offerings left uneaten by the gods – but not always cooked too well, judging by the intestinal worms found in the mummies of some of Hornedjitef's colleagues, buried on Thebes's West Bank.

With Thebes as a region now firmly on the tourist trail, Greek graffiti was increasingly appearing in the sepulchres of Western

Thebes, from the Valley of the Kings to the Eighteenth-Dynasty tomb of Sennefer; his figure wears a double heart necklace, which was now embellished with the Greek name 'Alexander', neatly written in hieroglyphs over a thousand years after the original wall scene was painted.

But the biggest attraction were the two massive stone sentinels of Amenhotep III, whose legs were an ancient visitors' book of appreciative grafitti. Not only astonishing in their own right, still standing despite the damage caused by the ancient earthquake, cracks in the northernmost figure emitted a sound each dawn when the stone warmed up. The Ptolemies' historian-priest Manetho, able to read the statues' inscriptions which gave Amenhotep III's throne-name 'Nebmaatra', traditionally pronounced Nimmuria or Mimmuria, had claimed Amenhotep III 'is the king who was reputed to be Memnon and a speaking statue', Memnon being an Ethiopian hero of myth, killed in the Trojan War and mourned by his mother Eos, the dawn.

In another case of cultural fusion, synagogues were built at Athribis, Leontopolis and Alexandria, while relations with Sparta were sufficiently close that its king, Kleomenes III, and his family were given sanctuary at the Alexandrian court. And despite periodic clashes with Syria throughout the reign, Egypt emerged dominant over the former Seleucid Empire, so that Ptolemy III and Berenike II now reigned together over a territory encompassing Egypt, Libya, Israel, Jordan, Syria, Lebanon and Cyprus, Cilicia, Pamphylia, Lycia, Caria, parts of Ionia in modern Turkey, parts of Thrace and the Peloponnese of Greece – the Ptolemaic Empire at its greatest, most powerful extent.

Having lived up to his epithet 'strong protector of the gods and mighty wall for Egypt', sixty-two-year-old Ptolemy III died from illness in the winter of 222 BC and was cremated in ceremonies led by his widow, co-ruler, and now sole pharaoh, Berenike II.

Maintaining the Ptolemaic practice of joint rule, she took as her new co-ruler her twenty-year-old son, Ptolemy IV (221–205 BC). Known as *Philopator*, 'father-loving', he seems to have felt no such attachment to his mother, who was tremendously popular with her Greek and Egyptian subjects, but not with her son's Greek advisor Sosibius or the late king's mistress, Oinanthe.

In a terrifying purge, Sosibius ordered the execution of Berenike II and all her family, except for her fourteen-year-old daughter, Arsinoe III, who was left alive to marry her brother and continue the divine succession. Yet Ptolemy IV's main relationship was with Oinanthe's daughter Agathoklea; the king was remembered as 'a loose, voluptuous, and effeminate prince, under the power of his pleasures and his women and his wine, while the great affairs of state were managed by Agathoklea, the king's mistress, and her mother and pimp Oinanthe'.

As 'an eyewitness of the sickness of the realm', the Spartan king Kleomenes was one of the new king's counsellors whose advice was not wanted by Sosibius either; he had the unfortunate king and his family killed and Kleomenes's flayed body displayed in public.

With the palace in turmoil, Egypt faced crisis point in 217 BC when the Seleucid king Antiochos III brought 70,000 men and 100 Indian war elephants to Egypt's border. Without Kleomenes and his Spartans, Ptolemy IV had little choice but to hastily train up Egyptians in order to field an army of equal strength, backed up by seventy-three somewhat jumpy African elephants.

Eighteen-year-old Arsinoe III also sought divine help, emulating her mother by dedicating a lock of her hair to the goddess Artemis, and joining her brother-husband to lead their forces north to Raphia, where she personally addressed their troops in a tearful yet rousing speech before the two forces clashed.

Much to everyone's surprise the Egyptian forces won the day, and took back lands right up to Cilicia. As the victorious monarchs were welcomed back to Egypt, Arsinoe, the 'heroine of the battle of Raphia', was commemorated on wine vessels, wielding a spear to complement images of her brother on horseback. They sailed on to Memphis, where their victory was commemorated on a great stela with bilingual Greek and Egyptian text, the priests announcing that their statues were to be set up in all the country's temples.

As they continued their progress by river aboard their palatial ship, the couple appeared before their Egyptian subjects whose efforts had brought them victory. Yet as the Egyptians now realised that they themselves had real power, the first serious bouts of internal unrest broke out in Middle Egypt and spread to the Delta. And although they were suppressed, the fuse had been lit.

Things were no easier for the Ptolemies' allies in Rome. Suffering severe grain shortages after Hannibal of Carthage had devastated Italy, in 215 BC they sent a delegation to Alexandria asking for grain, acknowledging Egypt's support with gold coins featuring their war god Mars and the royal eagle of the Ptolemies. Using one north African country to counter the danger still posed by the other in Carthage, a second Roman delegation returned to Egypt in 210 BC 'taking presents to the king and queen to commemorate and renew their friendship', including a smart Roman toga for the king.

But such a sober mode of dress would hardly have appealed to Ptolemy IV, who modelled himself on the god Dionysos. Having taken the title the 'New Dionysos', or 'Dionysos Reborn', he wore the god's sacred ivy leaves as a wreath on his head and even tattooed on his body, leading the wine-fuelled Dionysiac rites, 'carrying a timbrel and taking part in the show'.

He was also inspired to write tragedies based on Dionysos' worship, and the Ptolemies' continuing love of Homer was reflected in the temple the royal couple built for the deified poet. They also embellished their parents' Serapeum, and by 215 BC had completed their parents' great tomb of Alexander, known as the 'Soma'.

Although all trace of the tomb vanished centuries ago, it was said to be 'worthy of the glory of Alexander in size and construction' – a tall, imposing structure topped by a pyramid-shaped edifice, whose subterranean burial chamber housed the cremation chests of the Ptolemies and the mummified body of Alexander, which even had its own priest.

Nor did the couple forget Egypt's sacred city Thebes, creating at Karnak a cavern-like 'tomb of Osiris' and on Thebes's West Bank a gem-like temple beside the ruins of the old workers' village Deir el-Medina, in which Ptolemy IV and Arsinoe III were shown in glorious technicolour, worshipping both the gods and deified individuals from what, to them, was already ancient Egypt.

Further south, the same emphasis on ancestor worship saw the completion of Edfu temple by 207 BC and, even beyond their southern border in Nubia, the couple created a new temple to Horus at Pselchis, in which Arsinoe III was named prominently.

For in October 210 BC, she had fulfilled her expected role and produced a new Horus, a son, inevitably named Ptolemy, the fifth of that name but the first to be born of a full brother-sister marriage.

Yet the fact that he was an only child reflected his parents' estranged relationship; Ptolemy IV spent most of his time with his mistress, or training up his Olympic boxing team. As one Greek visitor observed, the king was 'inattentive and unpleasant to deal with and proved himself negligent and lazy to those conducting foreign affairs . . . due to his shameful philanderings and incoherent and continuous bouts of drunkenness, not surprisingly found in a very short space of time both himself and his kingdom to be the object of a number of conspiracies'.

Indeed, Alexandria was becoming increasingly unstable. And as nationalist riots in Thebes came to a head in 207 BC, the south broke away, declaring independence under self-styled native pharaohs Herwennefer (206–200 BC) and his successor Ankhwennefer (200–186 BC), both named 'beloved of Amen-Ra' by the Theban priests, in direct opposition to the pro-Ptolemaic clergy of Memphis.

At the end of 205 BC, thirty-nine-year-old Ptolemy IV died suddenly. His death was concealed for several months by his courtier Sosibius, buying time to establish himself as regent for the late king's five-year-old son and successor Ptolemy V (205–180 BC); and Arsinoe III, now surplus to requirements, was murdered, like her mother and family before her.

With their deaths only announced *after* their hasty cremation and burial in the tomb of Alexander, their young son was declared king, Sosibius named as his guardian and the child placed in the care of Oinanthe's family.

Following Sosibius's death, Oinanthe held supreme power, at least until her imperious behaviour proved too much for the Alexandrians, still mourning the fate of poor Arsinoe III. Storming the palace, they dragged her out with her family, and as the mob descended, 'some bit them, some stabbed them, others cut out their eyes. Whenever one of them fell, they ripped their limbs apart, until they had in this way mutilated them all. For a terrible savagery accompanies the angry passions of the people who live in Egypt', particularly Arsinoe III's childhood friends, 'young girls', who were especially vicious in the carnage.

As a succession of Greek courtiers vied for control, Alexandria descended into chaos and royal authority in the rest of the country ebbed away, following Thebes's lead. By 200 BC, Syria and much of the eastern Mediterranean had fallen to the Seleucid king Antiochos III, who planned to take over young Ptolemy V's kingdom with the help of his allies in Macedonia. Faced with imminent invasion, young Ptolemy V's ministers asked Rome for help. And having defeated their great enemy Hannibal of Carthage in 202 BC, the Romans' desire to expand their own empire east meant they were only too pleased to assist, attacking Macedonia, which by 197 BC was theirs.

Yet in that same year, the thirteen-year-old pharaoh Ptolemy V celebrated his coming of age festival – his *Anakleteria* – and he started to make decisions for himself.

His first act was to move the royal capital away from volatile Alexandria back to Memphis, no doubt on the advice of its new high priest, Harmakhis, whose clergy were rewarded with generous tax exemptions and allowed to hold their annual synod in Memphis, rather than Alexandria. And with the priests' support, rebels in the Delta were defeated and their ringleaders taken to Memphis, where the king 'had them slain on the wood' in a public execution.

This graphic means of demonstrating royal control over 'enemies of the state' was part of the teenage king's traditional-style coronation, held at Memphis on 26 March 197 BC, a full eight years after his accession, but in a venue that greatly strengthened his position as the rightful ruler of Egypt. And here he received the traditional double crown, in the presence of Egypt's clergy and the all-important priest of Alexander.

The day after the coronation the clergy issued a decree stating that the new king had established order and had spent large sums on the temples. So they now honoured him as 'a god, the son of a god and goddess and being like Horus, son of Isis and Osiris', whose statue would be set up in every temple. Their decree was to be 'written on a stela of hard stone and it should be set up in all temples next to the statue of the king', each stela to be inscribed in 'sacred writing (hieroglyphs), document writing (demotic) and Greek writing' so they could be as widely understood as possible. The most famous surviving example was set up in Neith's temple at Sais, then later transported north to the coast and used as building stone at Rosetta; now known as the 'Rosetta Stone', its Greek and Egyptian inscription was the means by which hieroglyphs were finally translated some 2,000 years later.

Having won back his kingdom with the support of its northern priests, Ptolemy V also benefited from Rome's seizure of Macedonia, which so worried Antiochos III he changed his plans. Instead of invading Egypt, he offered an alliance, to be sealed by a diplomatic marriage between the teenage pharaoh and Antiochos's ten-year-old daughter, Kleopatra, one of thirty-three ancient women known to have held this old Macedonian name.

The young couple married in 194 BC at Raphia, the place where their fathers had fought over twenty years earlier, Egypt once more gaining Syria, but this time as part of the bride's dowry.

As the first Kleopatra to rule Egypt, she took the same kingly titles as her husband, including 'Female Horus', and, like Berenike II, was also appointed prime minister. Popular with the Alexandrians, who called her 'the Syrian', she was a descendant of Alexander's Macedonian general Seleucus and his Persian wife Apama, and her mother was part of the Pontus royal family, although Kleopatra's coin portraits suggest that she had neither her father's sharp features nor the 'ill-favoured looks and boxers' noses' of her mother's side. Fully aware of the power of the image, the first Kleopatra also adopted Berenike II's coiffure of long ringlets, combined with the robes of Isis, for a full goddess ensemble – and like Isis, she was soon a mother, producing a daughter, named Kleopatra, and two sons, both named Ptolemy.

As a genuinely effective double act, the royal couple ended twenty years of anarchy in the south by taking back Thebes. And while the supporters of the rebel pharaoh Ankhwennefer were executed, Ankhwennefer himself was pardoned on the advice of the Memphis priests, to placate local feeling.

The monarchs also maintained their alliance with the Greek states,

Ptolemy V winning the chariot event at the Panathenaic Greek games in 182 BC.

But when he supported Rome's war against Antiochos III, Kleopatra I's father, marital relations must have become strained to say the least. So too the royal finances, the spendthrift Ptolemy V taking back financial concessions he'd made to the Egyptians, and seeking hefty donations from his courtiers. And in the spring of 180 BC, the twenty-nine-year-old pharaoh was poisoned – apparently by his generals.

But unlike his Ptolemaic predecessors, Ptolemy V was not cremated; he became the first Ptolemaic pharaoh to be mummified, in keeping with the Crown's new royal home at Memphis and their increasingly close relations with its increasingly influential priests.

His funerary rites were overseen by his twenty-four-year-old widow Kleopatra I, who maintained the dual monarchy by making her eldest son, six-year-old Ptolemy VI (180–145 BC), her co-regent. Officially known as the 'Pharaohs Kleopatra the mother the manifest goddess and Ptolemy son of Ptolemy the manifest god', the boy king took the additional title Philometor, 'mother-loving'.

During four years' successful rule, Kleopatra I terminated all plans for a campaign against her Seleucid relatives and concentrated on maintaining peace within Egypt. She was a greatly loved figure and her Macedonian name became a popular choice for newborns, one woman writing to her daughter 'Don't hesitate to name the little one "Kleopatra" . . . your little daughter'.

Following her death in April 176 BC, aged only twenty-eight, Kleopatra I was provided with her own clergy, but tellingly only in Thebes. For Alexandria was still controlled by Greek courtiers, ruling in the names of her three royal children: ten-year-old Ptolemy VI, his older sister Kleopatra II and their younger brother, the future Ptolemy VIII, aged about five. The courtiers swiftly married Kleopatra II to her eldest brother to prevent her marriage to any foreign ruler with designs on Egypt.

For the new Seleucid king, Antiochos IV, brother of the late Kleopatra I, used his position as the Egyptian monarchs' uncle as an excuse to invade in 169 BC. Having marched on Memphis, Antiochos IV reminded his nephew Ptolemy VI of his mother's Seleucid origins and, claiming to place the teenage pharaoh under the protection of his Seleucid family, forced the Memphis clergy to crown him as his nephew's co-regent, 'Pharaoh Antiochos', ignoring the existing co-ruler, Kleopatra II.

In retaliation, she formed a rival monarchy with her younger brother, Ptolemy VIII, in Alexandria. They were soon joined by their elder brother and the three monarchs robustly defended their city against Uncle Antiochos until the arrival of the Romans, whose proconsul ordered Antiochos to leave Egypt. And Antiochos had little choice; for the Romans famously drew a circle round him in the sand, and forced him to give his agreement before allowing him to step out.

Egypt was now a virtual protectorate of Rome, and the three young Ptolemies were told that they 'should always consider the trust and good will of the Roman people the supreme defence of their kingdom'.

Having taken the theatrical-sounding epithet 'the Three Philometores', the triple monarchy were now back in Alexandria, where in August 168 BC they gave a joint audience to a priest named Hor. Not only 'feeder of the sacred ibis', Hor was also an interpreter of dreams, and had prophesied Antiochos IV's invasion. As he told the monarchs, 'I dreamt as follows: Isis, the great goddess of Egypt and the land of Syria, is walking on the face of the water of the Syrian Sea. Thoth stands before her and takes her hand, and she has reached the harbour at Alexandria. She says "Alexandria is secure against the enemy".'

Yet it depends on whom this enemy was imagined to be; the most serious threat to Egypt in fact came from within.

With relations between the three monarchs strained at best, famine was once more causing widespread unrest and, as riots broke out in Thebes, Ptolemy VI marched south to deal with the rebels. His younger brother Ptolemy VIII seized his chance, ousting his absent brother with the support of the Alexandrians in the autumn of 164 BC.

Although ex-king Ptolemy VI had gone to Rome to put his case for unfair dismissal before the Senate and had won their backing, the Alexandrians had already deposed the power-mad Ptolemy VIII and asked Ptolemy VI to return immediately and resume his throne.

So the Romans used the opportunity to weaken the Ptolemaic kingdom by dividing it in two, troublesome Ptolemy VIII being given Cyrene (Libya) while his older siblings resumed their joint rule of Egypt as 'pharaohs Ptolemy and Kleopatra'.

Sufficiently astute to spend time in Memphis, they dined with the local elite in their palace beside the Serapeum and paid due homage to the city's Apis bull. They even set up a royal commission to investigate the faking of ibis mummies sold to pilgrims, their rule fully supported by the Memphis priests, whose own statues were now erected within the Serapeum in Alexandria, beside those of the royal family, to present a united front.

Fulfilling another prophecy of priest Hor, which claimed that 'the Queen bears a male child', Ptolemy VI and Kleopatra II did indeed have a son and heir, Ptolemy Eupator ('of distinguished lineage'), followed by a second boy, 'the spare', again named Ptolemy. They also had two daughters – Kleopatra Thea and Kleopatra III – who between them would produce the subsequent monarchs of both the Ptolemaic and Seleucid houses, creating less of a family tree, more a 'genealogical cobweb'.

Ptolemy VI and Kleopatra II were also great builders, improving existing temples and, at Kom Ombo, creating a new one, its decoration part-funded by the local garrison. Such was the couple's popularity that the garrison in Aswan even created an association 'to celebrate the annual festival in honour of the king, queen and their children', whose visits south maintained morale and a secure border with Nubia.

Equally astute was the couple's reinforcement of their north-east border. Following the sacking of the temple at Jersualem by their uncle and former adversary Antiochos IV, who had replaced Yahweh with Zeus, the Ptolemies allowed the Jewish high priest to change the old Ramesside temple of Bastet at Leontopolis into a new temple to Yahweh. This encouraged large numbers of Jewish settlers and guaranteed their military support across this vulnerable region, now known as Tell el-Yahudiya, 'Mound of the Jews'.

The royal couple were popular throughout the Greek world too. They each gained chariot victories in the Greek games of 162 BC, and their military and naval bases around the Aegean kept rich

Cyprus out of the hands of their younger brother Ptolemy VIII, now the ruler of neighbouring Cyrene (Libya).

So Ptolemy VIII made a will leaving all his possessions to Rome, which in return granted *him* control of Cyprus, as a counterbalance to his increasingly powerful siblings in Egypt. Ptolemy VIII even proposed marriage to the wealthy Roman matron Cornelia, daughter of Scipio Africanus, conqueror of Carthage, and although she wisely turned him down, he became a father in 154 BC when his partner Eirene gave birth to his eldest son Ptolemy Apion. Resigned to life in Cyrene, Ptolemy VIII took office as the priest of Apollo, and began work on a great mausoleum for himself in his adopted country.

He was totally written out of the Egyptian succession after his brother and sister made their eldest son, Ptolemy Eupator, their heir. Then at Eupator's premature death, he was simply replaced by his younger brother, known by his modern designation, Ptolemy VII.

When his father, Ptolemy VI, retook Syria, to be awarded the Seleucid diadem at a grand ceremony in Antioch, he established his overall supremacy in summer 145 BC. But at the moment of his greatest triumph, the forty-one-year-old Ptolemy VI was thrown from his horse, which was startled by a war elephant. He sustained severe head wounds and his Egyptian surgeons were unable to save him.

At the news of her brother-husband's sudden death, Kleopatra II immediately took her seventeen-year-old son Ptolemy VII (145 BC) as her co-regent. But the news had already reached Cyrene and Ptolemy VIII, who swiftly invaded Egypt. Promising to spare his nephew's life if Kleopatra II would marry him, he murdered him anyway, 'in his mother's arms', at their wedding.

And this was only the start. For Ptolemy VIII 'murdered many of the Alexandrians; not a few he sent into exile, and filled the islands and towns with men who had grown up with his brother'. Among the exiles were the director of the Great Library and many of its scholars, whose understandably hostile opinion of Ptolemy VIII spread quickly across the ancient world.

He had adopted the name Euergetes, meaning 'benefactor', but the Alexandrians changed it to Kakergetes or 'Malefactor' – but usually called him Physkon, 'Fatty'. For Ptolemy VIII was very short and spectacularly obese, 'with a belly of such size that it would have been hard to measure it with one's arms'. His physique was on full display when in 139 BC he received a Roman delegation. But rather than his fine royal robes impressing them, the transparent linen made them recoil at what lay beneath. Nor was the effect improved when the pharaoh turned down his carrying chair to greet his visitors on foot; the delegates declared that 'already the Alexandrians have derived some fun from our visit – they have seen their king taking a walk!'

Regarded as a monster of epic proportions, Ptolemy VIII was certainly as murderous as many of his predecessors, but was also sufficiently astute to realise that his dynasty's future depended on its Egyptian subjects. He placed them in the highest offices and encouraged racial integration; this culminated in a dynastic marriage between church and state, when Ptolemy VIII married one of his daughters, Berenike, to the son of Memphis's high priest.

After Ptolemy VIII (145–116 BC) was formally crowned at Memphis in 145 BC, his co-ruler and sister-wife Kleopatra II, now in her early forties, had given birth to a son they named Ptolemy 'Memphites', strengthening the ties with Egypt's ancient capital even further. And not only had his older sister produced the heir, she also took her role as one half of 'the Two Horuses' very seriously, re-inscribing a statue of Nefertiti at Karnak with her own names and titles.

So to undermine her power, Ptolemy VIII decided to replace both her and her son Memphites with younger models. In a psychological masterstroke, he chose her daughter Kleopatra III to be the mother of his next batch of children. As uncle and niece produced their first child, in 142 BC, new mother Kleopatra III declared herself the Living Isis to counter any claims of divine associations by her mother. And now that she had produced a new heir to replace Memphites, Ptolemy VIII married her too.

Yet their constant attempts to neutralise Kleopatra II's power proved ineffective, for this 'veritable tigress' was remarkably popular with her subjects, and had the strong military support of her Jewish troops. So Ptolemy VIII and Kleopatra III were forced to accept her as their co-ruler.

Just as before, Egypt had a trio of joint rulers, this time one Ptolemy and two Kleopatras. Differentiated in the ancient records as 'Kleopatra the Sister' and 'Kleopatra the Wife', their serene images across temple walls conveyed absolutely nothing of the reality, from the svelte figure of the famously fat king to the political, if not emotional, maelstrom within which all three were living.

Yet, maintaining a united façade to retain public support, the trio were portrayed in fictitious harmony at Koptos, Gebelein, Kom Ombo, Medamud, Dendera and at Philae, where a triple shrine and pair of seven-metre-high obelisks declared the three co-rulers' names.

On Thebes's West Bank, the innermost part of Hatshepsut's temple at Deir el-Bahari was redeveloped as a healing shrine, where Amenhotep, Son of Hapu, was regularly invoked. Although he had died 1,200 years earlier, his powers remained undiminished and, among a host of testimonials, the Macedonian Polyaratos claimed that his serious illness – a mystery to his doctors – was immediately cured by Hapu's son, who was also thanked by the Greek couple Leon and Lysandra after the birth of a longed-for child.

But in the battle of the royal babies, Kleopatra III needed no divine intervention, and by 135 BC had given birth to five children: the future Ptolemy IX, his younger brother Ptolemy X and their three sisters, each named Kleopatra.

The stage was well and truly set for some serious confrontation, for the ageing Kleopatra II was determined that her one remaining son, Ptolemy Memphites, would be king. Fully aware of her brother's usual murderous modus operandi for dealing with unwanted rivals, she sent her son to Cyrene out of danger, before launching a coup in 132 BC, backed by the Alexandrians and her Jewish troops.

Finally ousting Ptolemy VIII and his brood, they fled to Cyprus. Knowing full well his fourteen-year-old son Memphites was about to be recalled to Alexandria and made king in his place, Ptolemy VIII summoned the boy to Cyprus. Murdering him, and mutilating his body, he sent the pieces back to Kleopatra II in time for her birthday celebrations. Not to be outdone, she had her son's body parts displayed in public, so the Alexandrians could see for themselves what their former king had done.

But despite the support and indeed sympathy of the Alexandrians, the rest of Egypt supported Ptolemy VIII and Kleopatra III, who returned in 130 BC, took back Alexandria by 126 BC and executed all who had opposed them. Kleopatra II herself fled to Antioch, taking the royal treasury with her, a financial loss that placed Egypt in a very weak position. So efforts began to re-establish the lucrative trade links with India – and even further afield; the anchor from an Alexandrian merchant ship of the second century BC has been found off Anglesey, suggesting that the Ptolemies were following the lead of the Phoenicians' trading activities with the remote and mysterious islands of Britannike.

It has been said that the Ptolemies could have achieved even more, had they not spent so much of their time warring against each other – 'but then they would have not been Ptolemies'.

Eventually the three monarchs had little choice but to agree, in 124 BC, to a final reconciliation. Kleopatra II resumed her official role as 'the Sister', alongside her brother and daughter, none of them prepared to give up any of their power to the other.

Having lost three of her children to Ptolemy VIII's ambitions, her two sons murdered by him, and her daughter her deadly rival, Kleopatra II at least had the satisfaction of outliving her detested brother, who died in his bed on 28 June 116 BC. Inevitably she was not mentioned in his will, which left Cyrene to his eldest son Ptolemy Apion, and both Egypt and Cyprus to Kleopatra III 'and whichever of her sons she would make co-regent'.

At the insistence of her mother, the Alexandrians and the army, she had little choice but to accept her eldest son Ptolemy IX (116–107 BC) in a new three-way monarchy. But within a month, the seventy-year-old Kleopatra II was dead.

She left her daughter and her grandson to rule together as 'the Pharaohs Kleopatra and Ptolemy her son'. For Kleopatra III remained in charge, while her son Ptolemy IX, nicknamed *Lathyros* or 'Chickpea', concentrated his efforts on religious duties.

Serving as the priest of Alexander, Ptolemy Chickpea toured his kingdom as far as Elephantine, checking out sites that were also on the itinerary for foreign delegations. For the visit of one Roman senator in 112 BC, officials in the Fayum were instructed 'to make ready guest-chambers and landing-stages and presents, and to take every care that he should be satisfied'. There were even trips laid on to see the famous Labyrinth and sacred crocodiles, which were 'fed on grain and bits of meat and wine, which are always offered by visiting foreigners'.

Gaining Rome's good opinion, Chickpea became increasingly confident and difficult to overrule, so his mother Kleopatra III decided to remove him. Having a couple of her staff beaten up, she claimed they had been injured when her son had tried to kill her, and as the Alexandrian mob went for him, he only just managed to escape with his life to Cyprus. Even there, his mother sent a hit squad, which he only just avoided. The ancient sources admit that 'we know of none of the kings so hated by his mother'.

Kleopatra III now made her favourite, younger son Ptolemy X (107–88 BC) her co-ruler, and he took the official title 'Alexander I'. He also became the priest of Alexander, at least until his mother took this previously male role for herself. Adopting Alexander's elephant-skin headdress, this adoption of male-style attire echoed her pharaonic female predecessors, the desire of such women to be viewed on equal terms with their male counterparts producing some overtly masculine portrayals. Indeed, some of Kleopatra III's powerful images are so far from the feminine ideal they appear decidedly grim.

As her takeover of cherished male roles continued, Kleopatra III was portrayed alone in temple scenes, named 'Female Horus, Lady of Upper and Lower Egypt, Mighty Bull', to become 'both king and queen, both god and goddess'.

Yet her rampant megalomania was not popular with everyone. The Alexandrians gave her the Greek nickname *Kokke*, 'the Scarlet One', which was a slang term for 'vagina' and surely the most unpleasant epithet given to any of the Ptolemies.

Nor had her eldest son Ptolemy IX Chickpea forgotten her attempts to kill him, and in 105 BC he prepared to invade Egypt and take back his throne.

So Kleopatra III packed up all she held dear – her vast treasure and the next generation of Ptolemies, her three grandsons. All sent by ship to Kos, they would remain there for the next fifteen years.

Then she prepared to face her son, Ptolemy IX, in the 'War of the Sceptres', her land forces led by her Jewish generals and the navy by Ptolemy X.

Although her forces resoundingly won the day and Ptolemy IX fled back to Cyprus, the extraordinary Kleopatra III did not live to enjoy her victory for long; only a few months later she was dead, just short of her sixtieth birthday.

She was apparently murdered by her younger son Ptolemy X, who had finally had enough; he replaced her with his niece, Berenike III, who adopted the all-important female ruler's name 'Kleopatra' upon elevation to co-rulership with her thirty-nine-year-old uncle, Ptolemy X 'Alexander'.

Although Ptolemy X obviously wished to emphasise his links with his namesake, beginning his documents 'King Ptolemy who is also Alexander' and even wearing the great man's antique helmet, no amount of wordplay or costume changes could disguise the fact that the tenth Ptolemy was no Alexander. Resembling instead his notorious father, Ptolemy VIII, and so fat he needed two people to support him walking, 'when it came to the rounds of dancing at a drinking party he would jump from a high couch barefoot and perform the figures in a livelier fashion than those who had practiced them'. With such dance skills apparently enhanced by drinking, Ptolemy X's involvement in Dionysos's rites was deliberately misinterpreted by those who simply referred to their king as '*Kokke's* child'.

But the Egyptian clergy were rather more supportive. Since the royal family had become their relatives after Ptolemy VIII married one of his daughters to the Memphis high priest, they had produced a son, Petubastis, who, as a 'half-Ptolemy', combined within himself the DNA of Egypt's two ruling houses.

At his father's death in 103 BC, the seventeen-year-old Petubastis II had become the hereditary high priest. He had crowned his uncle, Ptolemy X, their roles then reversed when Ptolemy X installed his nephew as high priest in a ceremony in Alexandria. And here Petubastis 'drank in the presence of the king. He [the king] handed out to him the golden crook, mace, robe of linen from the southern house and the leather garment according to the ritual of Ptah's festivals and solemn processions. He [the king] placed his golden ornaments on his head according to the custom of his forefathers'.

This extraordinary text reveals the special relationship between the country's secular and religious leaders, who made regular state visits to each other's power bases at Alexandria and Memphis. On one such visit, uncle and niece visited Memphis's Serapeum and received a petition from Peteese, chief embalmer of the sacred bulls, who requested royal protection after being assaulted by his fellow workers. His protected status was thereafter declared on a public notice in Greek and Egyptian, the royals also granting the right of asylum to many of Egypt's temples, continuing tax breaks for their clergy and awarding business contracts to their subjects.

Yet despite such royal attention to domestic detail and the strong leadership of the Memphite clergy in the north, the limited amount of temple-building in the south was insufficient to retain local support. In fact, the south was so out of touch with royal events that local stonemasons preferred to leave cartouches blank, rather than carve the wrong name. And building work was suspended altogether between 91–88 BC, when the south broke away and the country once more fragmented.

And so too did the Ptolemies' empire. The massive territory of Cyrene (Libya) was lost when its ruler, Ptolemy Apion, a son of Ptolemy VIII and the king's half-brother, honoured their father's promise to Rome, bequeathing them Cyrene at his death in 96 BC, not only denying the territory to Egypt but bringing the Romans to its very border.

In 89 BC matters came to a head when Ptolemy X was deposed by the Alexandrians. Raising a mercenary army he was actually unable to pay, he turned to his namesake Alexander for help, repeating the age-old practice of rifling royal tombs and seizing Alexander's gold coffin, melting it down to pay his mercenaries.

On discovering that the burial of their city's founder and figure-head had been desecrated to pay troops to fight against them, the Alexandrians' attempts to lynch their king were only prevented when he escaped by boat. But, pursued by Alexandrian naval squadrons, the tenth Ptolemy drowned in a bitter sea battle off Cyprus.

His younger brother having been killed on his Cypriot doorstep, a delighted Ptolemy IX immediately returned to Egypt and became pharaoh for a second time (88–80 BC). Since his daughter Kleopatra-Berenike III had reigned alongside his late brother, Ptolemy IX simply continued the arrangement, since she was, as even the Romans knew, 'extremely popular with the Alexandrians'.

In Memphis, Ptolemy IX celebrated a second coronation. He also sent his general Hierax to tackle ongoing rebellion around Thebes, one of his officials writing to loyal supporters in Gebelein, 'the greatest god, the king, has reached Memphis, and Hierax has been despatched with considerable forces to bring Thebes under control. We wanted to inform you so that you, knowing this, take courage. Farewell'.

With the rebellion crushed and Thebes sacked, Ptolemy IX's reunited kingdom faced little immediate threat from abroad. Rome was busy with its ongoing war with Pontus (northern Turkey), which had tried to expand its territories in the Mediterranean. These included Kos, where Kleopatra III had sent her treasure some fifteen years earlier together with her three teenage grandsons, all of whom were now taken back to Pontus.

By 84 BC, peace negotiations brought the Romans to Pontus, where one of the Ptolemaic princes, the son of Ptolemy X, went over to the Roman side. Taken back to Rome, he proved a most useful informant regarding the Ptolemaic succession and soon became part of it.

For when Ptolemy IX died in 80 BC, leaving his daughter and co-ruler Berenike III his sole heir, Rome decided to exploit the Ptolemies' tradition of co-rule between a male and female monarch, sending in their protégé, Prince Ptolemy, to become King Ptolemy XI (80 BC).

Although he was, as the son of a king, entitled to the position, the Alexandrians called him *Pareisactus*, 'the Usurper'. After twenty-three years away from court, four of which had been spent in Rome, he was clearly unwilling to be junior partner to his popular – albeit elderly – stepmother and cousin, Kleopatra-Berenike III, and after only eighteen days' co-rule, he murdered her.

Now as any decent advisor could have told him, this was not a wise move. And in time-honoured fashion, the Alexandrians stormed the palace, dragged the king out and tore him to pieces with a violence not seen since they avenged the death of the popular Arsinoe III over a century before.

Although the Romans maintained that Ptolemy XI had left Egypt to them in his will, the Alexandrians were keen to prevent Rome interfering again. So exercising their ancient Macedonian right to select the next king, they sent a delegation to Pontus to offer the crown of Egypt and the crown of Cyprus to the two remaining princes Ptolemy – the 'heir and the spare'.

Both these twenty-something sons of Ptolemy IX 'Chickpea' had a mother or mothers unknown, most likely one or other of the late king's sisters to whom he was married at various times, or perhaps a minor wife, who might have been Syrian, Greek or Egyptian. But Rome's claim that the princes were illegitimate was quite nonsensical in Egypt, where not only did marriage traditionally require little more than 'two people living together', but where legitimacy, as understood in modern terms, was not a prerequisite for royal office. Indeed, many of the greatest pharaohs, from Tuthmosis III to the great sun king Amenhotep III, were born to such 'minor wives'.

So, at the end of 80 BC, the newly appointed King Ptolemy XII (80–58 BC) of Egypt arrived in Alexandria and married Kleopatra V, who was, like him, a child of Ptolemy IX to an unknown mother. The new royal couple took the joint title 'the Father-loving and Brother-and-Sister loving Gods'.

They certainly took their divinity seriously. Whereas previous rulers had been addressed as 'Our Lord the King', the twelfth Ptolemy was 'Our God and Lord the King', taking the name 'New Dionysos', 'Dionysos Reborn'. And dressing the part, he led the obligatory rites with musical performances, playing the pipes (*aulos*) with such skill he was thought 'not a man but a piper (*auletes*) and magician'.

Ptolemy XII became known to the Alexandrians by his cult title Auletes, and his musical talent was much admired among the Greeks, for 'all Spartans learned to play the pipes, as well as the most distinguished Athenians'. But for the Romans, offended by the sight of any man dancing, or being drunk in public, or indeed wearing anything but sober masculine attire, Auletes and the Alexandrians were quite incomprehensible, one Roman historian claiming that '*Macedones in Aegyptios degenerarunt*'.

'Degenerate' musical shows aside, the couple produced their first child, Berenike IV, and when the Memphis high priest Petubastis died and was succeeded by his fourteen-year-old son, Pasherenptah, the lad was invested by his kingly cousin in a grand ceremony in Alexandria.

As Pasherenptah describes, the pharaoh 'appeared solemnly from his palace, to alight at the temple of Isis. Coming forth in procession around the temple of Isis by his war chariot. The king himself halted his war chariot. He arrayed my head for me with the glorious chaplet of gold and all the genuine precious stones, the royal image in its midst. I was made his priest', these references to the king's chariot perhaps alluding to Auletes's victory in the Greek games in the late 70s BC.

High priest Pasherenptah then returned to Memphis for his first major role in office, the official coronation of Auletes, which took place five years after his accession. As the young high priest proudly announced, 'it is me who placed the uraeus upon the king on the day of Uniting-the-Two-Lands for him'.

Pasherenptah's account then reveals that the royal family undertook a progress of their country, as 'the king sailed southward, he sailed northward to inspect the two lands', before returning to Memphis for a state banquet. As a most convivial event, 'his courtiers, his wives, the royal children with his lordly possessions were sitting at meal and were spending a pleasant time while assisting at festivals of all gods and goddesses'.

Yet this apparently standard text is actually of enormous import-ance, because it refers to Auletes's wives – in the plural – and his 'royal children'. So even if Roman sources were adamant that only his eldest child Berenike IV was 'legitimate', the Egyptians officially recognised four more children, two boys (inevitably named Ptolemy) and their two sisters, Arsinoe and Kleopatra, the Kleopatra, surely the most famous woman in history, born in 69 BC and usually designated Kleopatra VII. And although only their father is known by name, all his children were hailed 'Our Lords and Greatest Gods' from birth.

They accompanied their father on such state occasions, and with high priest Pasherenptah now acting as 'the eyes of the king of Upper

Egypt, the ears of the king of Lower Egypt', Auletes began work on a series of magnificent temples throughout Egypt to keep their priests onside too.

At Edfu, a new monumental pylon gateway was decorated with Auletes's huge figures smiting his enemies with a mace in traditional manner and, impressed with the avenues of sphinxes at some of the temples he saw, the king commissioned a series of them for Alexandria, bearing his own features.

But such building projects required significant funds. And despite the depletion of the royal treasury under successive Ptolemies, Auletes had found an alternative source of revenue. For he was once again trading directly with India by sea, instead of the slow overland route, even if it meant appointing extra security to protect his new trade routes from the Nabatean Arabs, whose lucrative role as middleman was no longer needed.

Egypt traded its textiles, wine, glass and slaves from the Horn of Africa for huge quantities of spices, incense, pearls, precious stones, ebony, ivory and silk – all processed in the factories of Alexandria and exported to Rome for huge profits. Yet this direct route to India made the country even more attractive to Rome, which had long coveted Egypt's wealth.

So by 65 BC there were new calls for Egypt's annexation. Only through bribes to the Roman Senate could Auletes keep his kingdom safe from invasion, although it was galling to have to help fund the campaigns of Roman general Pompey 'the Great' – yet another to style himself after Alexander – as he retook Pontus and Judaea, to bring Roman troops permanently to Egypt's north-eastern and western borders. Auletes's kingdom was now surrounded.

And the pharaoh soon began to feel the squeeze. In 60 BC Pompey, Licinius Crassus and Julius Caesar, the effective rulers of Rome, offered Auletes the title 'friend and ally of the Roman people', the closest thing to a guarantee that Egypt would not be taken over. But it would cost 6,000 talents – the equivalent of 1,500,000 gold pieces. A sum that more or less represented Egypt's entire annual revenue, it couldn't all be raised through tax increases, so Auletes had no choice but to borrow vast sums from the phenomenally wealthy Roman banker Rabirius Postumus.

Such financial demands created a dangerous atmosphere in Alexandria. One eyewitness describes the time 'when King Ptolemy had not yet been granted the status of Friend . . . one of the Romans killed a cat and the mob made a rush at his house and neither the officials sent by the king to beg for his release nor the fear which everyone felt for Rome proved powerful enough to save him from their vengeance, even though what he had done was an accident. And I am not relating this from hearsay but it is something I saw with my own eyes during my visit to Egypt'.

Usually cited as proof of how much the Egyptians loved their pets and sacred animals, it was in fact simply one of many flashpoints that finally exploded in 58 BC, when the Romans seized Cyprus.

Claiming that Auletes's brother, Ptolemy of Cyprus, was aiding the pirates disrupting their shipping, the Romans allowed him to remain on the island as high priest of Aphrodite, but, preferring to die a king, Ptolemy of Cyprus took poison as the Romans stripped his palace of its wealth.

Refusing to jeopardise his costly new title 'friend of Rome', Auletes's passive attitude to his brother's fate forced the Alexandrians to exercise their ancient rights, and they deposed him in summer 58 BC. They replaced him with his sister-wife Kleopatra V (58–57 BC) and her daughter 'Kleopatra' Berenike IV (58–55 BC), and their all-female dual monarchy now controlled Egypt.

Leaving his three youngest children in Egypt too, Auletes is believed to have been accompanied by his eleven-year-old daughter, Kleopatra VII. Sailing to Rhodes to meet the Roman statesman Cato, at the time en route to oversee Cyprus's annexation, Auletes summoned the Roman, but was told Cato was receiving medical treatment, so had to go to him instead. Receiving the pharaoh in the latrine as a calculated insult, 'Cato neither went forward to meet him, nor so much as rose up to him, but saluting him as an ordinary person, bade him sit down. This at once threw Ptolemy into some confusion', as Egypt's living god had been reduced to holding royal audience in the toilet.

Father and daughter travelled on to Rome, via Athens. There was really nowhere else to go, since Rome had taken over the rest of the Hellenistic world – Macedonia had fallen in 168 BC, Greece in

146 BC, Cyrene in 96 BC, Asia Minor and Syria in 65 BC and, most recently, Cyprus in 58 BC. And with his kingdom the last one standing, Auletes was determined to get it back – at any price.

So the Egyptian royals travelled on to Rome, which at that time consisted of modest brick-built buildings in contrast to their own marble-clad capital. It nonetheless housed the power-brokers of the ancient world, the Roman Senate. As Auletes bribed his way through their ranks to have them reinstate him as king, endless debates about 'the Egyptian question' achieved nothing.

Auletes and his daughter eventually left Rome for Ephesus, where they received news that Kleopatra V had died, leaving her daughter, Berenike IV, as sole ruler of Egypt.

As she began to seek a husband as co-ruler, there were quite a few candidates from the old Seleucid house, although Auletes's reach was long. Prospective bridegrooms were either killed in mysterious circumstances or their journey to Egypt was blocked by Syria's new and flamboyant Roman governor, Aulus Gabinius – appointed by Pompey, bribed by Auletes and described by his peers as 'a thieving effeminate ballet boy in curlers'.

Not to be outmanoeuvred, the Alexandrians brought forward a Seleucid bridegroom, but after only a week of marriage, his new bride was so unimpressed she had him strangled. Undeterred, they then suggested Archelaos, who claimed to be the son of the late king of Pontus. Having learned from Auletes's own modus operandi, Archelaos bribed Gabinius to reach Egypt, where he married Berenike IV and ruled Egypt with her.

More desperate than ever to take Egypt back, Auletes finally received help from Pompey in return for a massive 10,000-talent bribe. Pompey ordered Gabinius and his Germanic and Gallic cavalry, led by its commander Mark Antony, to accompany a euphoric Auletes and his teenage daughter from Ephesus, through Palestine and into Egypt.

The invaders marched on Alexandria, where Archelaos fell in battle, and Berenike IV was executed on the orders of her father, along with all her supporters. The carnage was only halted by the Roman troops, posted permanently in Egypt by Mark Antony to protect Auletes from the Alexandrians – if not vice versa.

And as these tall, spiky-haired Roman auxiliaries from Gaul and Germany adapted to life in the royal city, they formed a formidable royal bodyguard. Auletes was sufficiently secure in his second term as king (55-51 BC) to clear his huge debts to the Roman banker Rabirius, who had arrived in Egypt looking for his money. So Auletes appointed him minister of finance, allowing him to cream off profits and impose high taxes, until Rabirius got too greedy and had to be placed in protective custody. Managing to escape back to Rome, he was promptly prosecuted for illicit gains, his defence claiming Alexandria to be 'the home of all tricks and deceits'.

Yet for all the corruption and bloodshed, Alexandria was also the home of a cultural renaissance. And with continued royal patronage of the Great Library and Museum, its scholars continued to teach the royal children. In the case of Kleopatra VII, whose handwriting was recently discovered on a piece of papyrus on which she had written 'Let it be done!' in Greek, she was long remembered by Arab historians as 'the virtuous scholar', whose standard Greek was supplemented by her knowledge of eight other languages including Syrian, Hebrew, Parthian, Arabic, Ethiopian and Egyptian.

For Kleopatra was the first of the Ptolemaic house to learn the language of the country they had ruled for three centuries, her linguistic abilities a valuable asset in her father's attempts to retain native support. And as he resumed his temple-building projects around the south, he began a new temple for Hathor-Isis at Dendera on 16 July 54 BC, the most auspicious day of the year when the rising of Isis's star Sirius heralded the start of the Nile flood, presumably in an attempt to try to reverse a run of low Nile floods and boost the failing harvests.

Work on the temple continued at a rapid pace; Kleopatra was portrayed in its wall scenes with her father, although it is he who performs for Hathor, the temple's hymns stating that 'Pharaoh comes to dance, comes to sing! Hathor, see his dancing, see his skipping! O, how fine is the song, which Ra's son sings as the finest singer. He is Horus, a musician! He hates the bright goddess to be sad! Oh beautiful One, Great Cow, Glorious Lady, Queen of Gods! His feet hasten to the Mistress of Music as he dances for her!'

Dendera also had a reputation for the athletic performances of its locals, who dived into the Nile to ride upon the backs of crocodiles. Believing themselves protected by Isis–Hathor, who was able to calm these creatures of Sobek, the Dendera daredevils honed their skills as *sauretai* – the keepers of the sacred crocodiles in temples. So great became their fame among Roman visitors that they even appeared in the arena in Rome in 58 BC, the same year that Auletes and Kleopatra had visited the Italian city, and the resulting marble sculptures of acrobatic Egyptians upon the backs of Nile crocodiles graced many a Roman villa.

Marble was also the medium of choice for the portrait busts Auletes commissioned of his family, whose physical similarities were also reflected in Kleopatra's title 'Image of her Father'. Reinforcing his intentions for the succession at a great ceremony in May 52 BC, the king, now in his mid-fifties, took the sixteen-year-old Kleopatra as his co-ruler, crowning her with the Macedonian diadem and awarding her the title 'Father-loving Goddess'.

In Auletes's will, he decreed that his eldest son Ptolemy XIII (51–47 BC) should rule alongside Kleopatra at his death. But when this occurred less than a year later, Kleopatra VII (51–30 BC) took power into her own hands and, suppressing news of his death for four months, continued to issue official documents in their joint names.

Determined to keep her country independent, she was not prepared to accept the interference of Rome, or the powerful Greek courtiers who already controlled her younger brother. But she needed to be strong. For Kleopatra VII 'did not so much ascend a throne as descend into a snake pit'.

Against such odds, she managed to consolidate her position in Alexandria and, no doubt with the advice of her half-cousin high priest Pasherenptah, embarked on a journey south, fully aware that real power lay at the heart of her antique kingdom. Passing through Memphis, she would have received her official titles: 'Female Horus, the great one, brilliant in counsel' and 'Upper Egyptian King of the land of the white crown, Lower Egyptian King of the land of the red crown', the double crown replacing her Macedonian diadem.

Although she usually wore her hair in a bun secured by hairpins – one Roman portrait even suggested she was a redhead – Egypt's temple scenes portrayed Kleopatra VII in the same traditional long wig worn by both goddesses and female rulers for the last three millennia.

And in the same way as her father had been 'Neos Dionysos', she declared herself *Nea Isis*, 'New Isis' – 'Isis Reborn' – and 'appeared in public dressed in the habit of the goddess Isis, whose 'black raiment' was now worn over the traditional white linen of the Egyptian clergy.

Able to transform herself into a distinctly Egyptian figure, Kleopatra could connect with millions of subjects, speaking to them directly with no need of an interpreter. Fully aware that her personal participation in the rites that had traditionally sustained their country would help secure their loyalty, she became the first monarch in living memory to lead rites for the Buchis bull in person, on 22 March 51 BC. This involved a sacred regatta to transport the bull along the Nile, the ancient texts describing how 'the Lady of the Two Lands, the Goddess, rowed him in the barque of Amen and he reached his temple at Armant'. As a nine-kilometre slog against the prevailing current, it suggests that Kleopatra's role as rower was ceremonial; but her presence as the living embodiment of Hathor-Isis was crucial, balancing the masculinity of the god, and their combined powers sparking the forces of vitality.

Her appearance went down a storm with the public, and as 'Armant and beautiful Thebes were united in drunkenness and the noise was heard in heaven', her participation gained her the backing of the clergy, preventing unrest during eighteen months of continued bad harvests and high taxes. But when the food shortages hit Alexandria, power base of her younger brother Ptolemy XIII, his faction took control, ordering all food cargoes to be diverted to Alexandria 'on pain of death' to deprive Kleopatra's supporters in the rest of Egypt.

Although she was now obliged to share power with her brother, at least the royal pair were temporarily free of Roman interference during the power struggle between Pompey and his rival Julius Caesar. Both monarchs sided with Pompey and sent him the military aid he requested, although Pompey's gratitude to Kleopatra was short-lived. For when Ptolemy XIII's advisors finally managed to oust Kleopatra in summer 49 BC, Pompey recommended that the Senate should recognise Ptolemy XIII as sole ruler.

Leaving Egypt in early 48 BC, Kleopatra retreated to Ashkelon, paying a mercenary army with coins bearing her determined-looking image as she tried to retake her throne. When Julius Caesar finally defeated Pompey to become the most powerful man in the ancient world, she sent him a report of her own situation as she set out to face her brother on Egypt's border.

Hostilities were only suspended by the arrival of Pompey, once more seeking help. But Ptolemy XIII's advisors, wanting nothing more to do with a defeated man, ordered his immediate execution.

When Caesar himself arrived in Alexandria a few days later with a small force, intending to pardon Pompey, he instead received only his embalmed head. Ignoring this most unsubtle message that he should return to Rome, Caesar disembarked, visiting the tomb of his hero Alexander the Great before pointedly taking up residence in the palace.

Declaring himself arbiter of Ptolemy XII Auletes's will and keen to settle the Ptolemies' dynastic dispute to the best advantage of Rome and himself, he ordered brother and sister to appear before him. So Ptolemy XIII breezed in with his advisors to declare Kleopatra a traitor and himself the true heir, until Caesar pointed out that any successor of Auletes still owed him 6,000 talents – money that had presumably been pocketed by Pompey.

Alarmed by such demands, the young king's Greek advisors began to stir up the Alexandrians to surround the palace, meaning that Kleopatra could not reach Caesar by land. So, waiting for nightfall, she took a small boat to the seaward side of the palace and, with the help of her Sicilian courtier, successfully crossed enemy lines.

And she did so with great panache. She is famously claimed to have stretched herself out inside a carpet or bedroll, which her courtier rolled up and carried in to Caesar; but surely no pharaoh, let alone a living goddess, would ever allow themselves to be manhandled in such a manner? And the sudden appearance of a late-night carpet salesman inside a palace on high alert would surely have raised suspicion among the guards.

The most likely reason that this brilliant piece of political daring has been reduced to little more than knockabout comedy seems to be a misunderstanding of the way in which ancient bedlinen doubled as clothing, with the Greek *himation* basically a bedsheet wrapped round the body on waking to form the outer garment. And dressed in such a garment, a heavily swathed Kleopatra would certainly have blended into first-century BC Alexandria, where the prevailing fashion for such drapery formed a perfect disguise when pulled across the face.

For long before it was ever associated with Islam, face-veiling was widespread among elite women in Assyria and the later Greek settlements of Asia Minor, and was also adopted by some elite women in Alexandria. So a similarly attired Kleopatra could easily have entered the labyrinthine palace, her home since birth, and, on reaching Caesar, simply pulled her mantle from her face – a face that has intrigued the world for centuries.

In contrast to recent claims that she was no great beauty based on her deliberately masculine-looking coin portraits, the ancient sources describe the twenty-two-year-old as 'a woman of incomparable beauty and it was incredible when she was young' – something her surviving portraits seem to support.

Yet even this is clearly in the eye of the beholder. For whereas one female historian claims Kleopatra's so-called 'Berlin Head' 'bears a close relationship to the portraits of Alexander' but 'does not flatter her', male commentators believe the same portrait is 'infinitely more beautiful than the unflattering coin portrait', claiming it 'perhaps the finest and most beautiful portrait sculpture' of all the Ptolemies. Yet the world's continuing obsession with this one woman's facial features was best summed up by the seventeeth-century comment: 'the nose of Kleopatra: had it been shorter, the whole face of the earth would have been altered'.

Regardless of Kleopatra VII's physical appearance, the ancient sources agree that it was her character that exterted the real attraction. A modern psychological profile has claimed she had 'a narcissistic personality', but in the context of the time Kleopatra's own belief in her divine status makes this unsurprising. It certainly gave her the supreme self-confidence so admired by Caesar.

For despite a thirty-year age-gap, the twenty-two-year-old pharaoh was not so different from the ambitious fifty-two-year-old general. Both were flamboyant, both pragmatic, and, when necessary, both were completely ruthless. Kleopatra was also one of the very few living descendants of Caesar's hero Alexander, while Caesar's reputation as 'every woman's husband and every man's wife' makes it likely their relationship soon became extremely close.

For, the morning after Kleopatra's veiled arrival, she was reinstated as ruler of Egypt. Her brother was so furious that he rushed from the palace and pulled off his diadem, throwing it to the ground in a dramatic display of teenage rage and shouting that he had been betrayed. The Alexandrians prepared to storm the palace in time-honoured fashion, only halting when Caesar produced Auletes's will, announcing that brother and sister would rule Egypt together.

Caesar certainly took a massive gamble in reinstating her, since Ptolemy XIII's Greek advisors, now deprived of power, were plotting to have both Kleopatra and Caesar assassinated until they were over-heard by Caesar's barber, and were themselves beheaded.

As the situation deteriorated further, the Alexandrians demanded that Ptolemy XIII should rule with his younger sister, Arsinoe IV, rather than with Kleopatra, who they hated as a collaborator. Yet Caesar continued to protect her, even when trapped between the Alexandrians and the sea while awaiting reinforcements. During the ensuing siege and street-to-street fighting, parts of the city were destroyed by fire, including dockside warehouses storing new books awaiting transfer to the Great Library. Even when Caesar's reinforcements did arrive, the Alexandrians continued fighting; the teenage Ptolemy XIII, resplendent in his heavy gold armour, drowned in the Nile during a most determined campaign.

Yet contrary to Roman expectations, Caesar did not annex Egypt but instead kept Kleopatra VII as monarch, with her remaining brother, the twelve-year-old Ptolemy XIV (47–44 BC), as her nominal co-ruler. Early Arab sources also state that she married Caesar in an Egyptian ceremony. So although he was still married to his Roman wife, their polygamous union unrecognised in Rome – as was marriage between a Roman and a foreigner – the fact that Kleopatra was now pregnant offered Caesar the chance of an heir he did not have.

Following Ptolemaic tradition, Kleopatra and Caesar embarked on a Nile cruise, a waterborne Triumph accompanied by 400 Roman warships, to celebrate their victory. It displayed to the Egyptians both the might of Rome and their pregnant monarch as Mother Isis incarnate; and the impact of several million people paying homage as they sailed along must have made a lasting impression on Caesar, who realised he could cultivate his own divine associations in his attempts to bring both Rome and the East under his sole control.

When Caesar eventually left Egypt to take the remainder of the Roman world, he left three legions in Egypt to ensure Kleopatra's safety as she prepared to give birth to her first child on 23 June 47 BC.

Although a pharaoh in labour was no common occurrence, and birth itself fraught with danger, Kleopatra produced a healthy son. As he was the eight-times great-grandson of Ptolemy I, who also 'combined Egypt and Rome in his lineage', she named him 'Ptolemy Caesar', the Alexandrians calling him Caesarion, 'Little Caesar'.

With his small figure added to Horus's large statues at his dynasty's great temple at Edfu, beneath his towering grandfather Auletes smiting his enemies on the front pylon, his mother began work on the Caesarium temple in Alexandria – current home of the grand Hotel Metropole. As part of her plans for the sea-edge temple, she had selected a pair of ancient obelisks from Heliopolis with which she intended to flank its entrance – the one known as 'Kleopatra's Needle' now stands on the Embankment in London, while the other ended up in New York. The Caesarium's original name *Kaisaros Epibaterios*, 'Embarking Caesar', suggests it was the place from which Caesar finally left Egypt, having bestowed on her her throne, her heir and indeed her life.

Kleopatra also began work on her tomb, breaking with tradition as the first of the Ptolemies not to be buried with her predecessors in the dynastic tomb of Alexander. She did, though, require a monument of equal standing – 'of wonderful height and very remarkable', the ancient sources also referring to 'the tomb which she was building in the grounds of the palace', located on Alexandria's Cape Lochias and now beneath the Mediterranean.

While she was busily embellishing her city and making plans for Caesarion's inheritance, by May 46 BC his father had finally returned to Rome, where the Senate made him Dictator for ten years. They also awarded him four Triumphs to celebrate his victories, closely resembling the lavish excess of Ptolemaic processions, and their parade of floats portraying the manner of death of his opponents. His victory against the Alexandrians was marked by models of the pyramids and Pharos lighthouse, and Kleopatra's younger sister Arsinoe IV walking along in gold chains, spared execution and instead exiled to Ephesus.

Caesar now sent for Kleopatra, who arrived amidst yet more great ceremony to be awarded the official title 'friend and ally of the Roman people', the same title that their father Auletes had worked so hard to achieve, now handed over with other 'high titles and rich presents'.

He then installed her in his grand villa in Rome's Trastevere district overlooking the city, where she and their son Caesarion remained European residents for two years. Kleopatra's glamorous public image triggered a real craze for all things Egyptian, and every detail of her appearance was scrutinised and copied, from her hairstyles to her jewellery.

Statues of Kleopatra and Caesar were placed in Rome's temples in a policy of divine self-promotion, the most astonishing erected in the Forum, where Caesar built a new temple to his family's ancestral deity, Venus. At the front, he placed an antique statue of Alexander the Great's horse, with a statue of himself added as the rider to represent himself as Alexander's successor. Then inside, next to the statue of Venus, the great mother, Caesar 'placed a beautiful image of Kleopatra by the side of the goddess' in 'an open acknowledgement of marriage between a descendant of a prestigious dynasty and the daughter of a god'. Although Egyptian monarchs had set up their own statues beside the gods for millennia, living individuals had never been portrayed this way in Republican Rome – so a statue conferring divine power on a woman in the heart of their city was calculated political dynamite.

Alongside a planned building programme that would transform the Eternal City into a marble-clad metropolis modelled on

Alexandria, Caesar was also working on plans to re-route the River Tiber, create a new harbour and drain marshland to increase crop yields, making Rome more self-sufficient.

Having affected Roman culture, religion, politics and even the landscape, Kleopatra even provided Caesar with the means to literally shift time, her astronomer helping him replace the defective Roman lunar calendar with the Egyptian solar-based version, the so-called 'Julian Calendar' still used today.

Yet such rapid and radical changes inevitably triggered rumours that Rome was no longer good enough for Caesar, that he wanted to transfer the government to Alexandria and even create an Alexander-style monarchy with Kleopatra's help. And when the Senate declared him Dictator for Life, king in all but name, sixty die-hard Republicans assumed that their assassination of Caesar in March 44 BC would restore the Republic.

But when their plan failed as Rome descended into chaos, Caesar's deputy and distant cousin, Mark Antony, had to act swiftly to prevent total anarchy.

Focusing on the safety of Caesarion, Kleopatra immediately returned to Egypt and eliminated her remaining brother Ptolemy XIV in order to make her three-year-old son her co-ruler. His name and image represented Caesarion (44–30 BC) as Living Horus to his mother's Living Isis, by extension making the dead Caesar the equivalent of Osiris, who was in legend resurrected by his powerful wife who raised their son to take his place on earth.

And as myth began to become reality, Egypt was drawn into war, as Caesar's chief assassins Brutus and Cassius took on Caesar's deputy Antony, now allied to Caesar's nephew, Octavian, his heir in Roman law.

After the assassins' legions seized part of Egypt's fleet stationed in Cyprus, apparently with the help of the exiled Arsinoe IV in Ephesus, they demanded further ships from Kleopatra, at her refusal preparing to invade Egypt until Antony drew them away to Greece.

Here they were roundly defeated by Antony, and as Octavian claimed the victory on his return west to Rome, Antony went east, to be hailed as the 'New Dionysos' in Athens and reorganising Rome's eastern provinces. Needing Kleopatra's help and Egypt's wealth to achieve his plans, he sent envoys requesting that she came to meet him at Tarsus in Cilicia.

Kleopatra realised the real possibility of forming a new alliance with Rome in the person of Antony, whom she had known for some fourteen years; his desire to emulate both Caesar and Alexander certainly provided useful common ground.

So using the fabled opulence of the Ptolemies to transform a mundane political summit meeting into an unforgettable extravaganza, she matched Antony's 'New Dionysos' persona by dressing as Isis-Aphrodite, so that when her golden ship sailed up the Levantine coast, 'word went round that Aphrodite was coming to revel with Dionysos for the good of Asia'.

Upon her well-publicised arrival, she invited Antony and his officers to dine with her on board her ship, overwhelming him with rich gifts to demonstrate that she had all the resources he needed to take control of Rome. In return, she requested that he terminate her remaining enemies, chief among whom was her sister Arsinoe IV, still claiming to be Egypt's rightful ruler.

Her request was duly carried out and, with the throne of Egypt secured, Kleopatra returned to Alexandria, where Antony joined her.

They spent the winter visiting the sites, the theatre, gaming and hunting, setting up their exclusive dining club 'The Inimitable Livers', whose 'members entertained one another daily in turn, with an extravagance of expenditure beyond measure or belief'. The whole world was searched for exotic produce, from the peacocks and cranes of Samos and Melos to the oysters, pickled in vinegar, from as far afield as Kent and Essex. All was washed down with rivers of wine, imported from Chios, the Rhone Valley, Spain and Cyprus, with that produced closest to the palace around Lake Mareotis described as being 'so good that Maroitic wine is racked off with a view to ageing it'.

Kleopatra discovered she was pregnant at the same time as Antony's supporters took on Octavian and lost, Antony forced to make a speedy return home to Italy, where he had little choice but to agree to a treaty. This was sealed by his marriage to Octavian's sister Octavia, who was soon pregnant too. But in October 40 BC, Kleopatra outdid her rival and gave birth to twins, the third set to be born to one of

Ptolemy VIII's direct line, and who she named Alexander Helios and Kleopatra Selene, 'the Sun' and 'the Moon'.

Although she did not see Antony for three years, during which time he had married and fathered children elsewhere, he once more needed Kleopatra's support when Rome's eastern empire was attacked by the Parthians (fomer Persia), so he made her a very attractive offer.

For when the thirty-one-year-old finally met her forty-six-year-old lover at Antioch in 37 BC, they were married, their joint portraits issued on coins and Kleopatra receiving one of the most generous wedding presents of all time – territories stretching from Cilicia to Syria, Phoenicia, Lebanon and Crete, together with lands in Jordan belonging to the Nabatean Arabs, all of which Antony gave her.

Having regained Egypt's empire at a stroke, the euphoric Kleopatra, soon pregnant again, returned to. Alexandria and gave birth to her fourth child, Ptolemy Philadelphus.

Although Antony's initial invasion of Parthia failed, a second invasion in spring 34 BC seized the Parthians' territory of Armenia and he returned to Egypt for the Triumph-like state celebrations. Riding down the great central highway of Alexandria in a gold chariot, accompanied by Roman troops with Kleopatra's name upon their shields, he presented her with the spoils of a war she had funded at a lavish ceremony at the city's Serapeum temple.

The ceremony – known today as 'The Donations' – was presided over by the youthful high priest Petubastis, who had succeeded his late father Pasherenptah. Kleopatra VII was also accompanied by her four children: her thirteen-year-old co-ruler Caesarion, the six-year-old twins Helios and Selene and two-year-old Ptolemy Philadelphus. And Antony, as commander of the Eastern Provinces, announced the territories he was bestowing on each of them in the name of Rome. He also declared Caesarion sole legitimate heir of the divine Julius Caesar, in order to counter claims by Caesar's nephew Octavian that he himself was 'Commander Caesar, son of the god'.

As battle lines were clearly being drawn, Kleopatra and Antony were supported by both the Greek-speaking nations and considerable numbers of Romans. Antony also divorced Octavia to sever all ties with her brother in preparation for the inevitable war ahead,

Octavian launching a brilliant PR campaign, aided by his spin-doctor poets Horace and Virgil. Throwing every possible allegation at the couple, made all the more plausible in the light of Antony's continuing absence from Rome, Octavian read out what he claimed to be Antony's will, which requested burial with Kleopatra in Alexandria.

Of course, after all the recent civil wars Octavian could not be seen resuming hostilities against a fellow Roman, so he formally declared war on Kleopatra alone as 'enemy of the state'. The thirty-seven-year-old mother of four was clearly a most unnerving opponent, and 'Rome, who had never condescended to fear any nation or people, did in her time fear two human beings; one was Hannibal, and the other was a woman'.

As a majority in the Senate stripped Antony of his official powers, Octavian announced 'let nobody consider him to be a Roman citizen, but rather an Egyptian: let us not call him Antony, but rather Serapis'; he then named the generals they would be fighting as 'Eiras, Kleopatra's hair-dressing girl and Charmion, who were Antony's chief state-councillors'. It was even claimed that Kleopatra wanted to be 'queen of Rome', and as the 'lecherous prostitute queen dared to oppose her yapping Anubis against our Jupiter', the noble, masculine West prepared to take on the corrupt and feminised East in a stereotype that has sadly persisted for over two thousand years.

Yet not everyone was convinced. For almost half the Senate chose to align themselves with Antony, leaving Rome to set up a new senate in Ephesus, where Kleopatra arrived at the head of her 200-strong fleet, then rode around on horseback to oversee the military preparations she was funding.

As the campaign season fast approached, she and Antony travelled to Samos where they summoned their allies for pre-war ceremonials in March 32 BC. Antony, representing Dionysos, ensured that every god received lavish offerings to gain their support, amidst performances by musicians, actors and Anubis-worshipping gladiators, then preparing for imminent victory celebrations.

As the couple's forces then travelled across to the Greek mainland, making camp at Actium on the west coast's Bay of Ambracia, where they moored their 400 great warships, the ships' images were stamped on the silver coins minted on site to pay their troops, from Kleopatra's Egyptian treasury.

She also seems to have employed the same kind of pre-battle protective rites employed by Nectanebo II against the Persians three centuries earlier, although the continued presence of Antony's 'Egyptian wife' apparently shocked their Roman opponents, who referred to her 'monstrous gods and barking Anubis'. One of Antony's most trusted officers now defected to Octavian, claiming Kleopatra had threatened his life and revealing the couple's battle plans, which allowed Octavian's General Agrippa to knock out their supply chain from Alexandria, isolate their position and block their ships in the bay.

With the army sent back to Egypt by land, the fleet broke out of the bay on 2 September 31 BC and, according to a prearranged plan, Kleopatra headed for open sea with a hundred ships. Antony and the rest of their fleet took on Agrippa, with heavy casualties on both sides as they were caught up in rising seas.

Actium was hardly the stuff of legend until elevated by Octavian's eloquent poets, one military historian describing it as 'no heroic battle but a series of skirmishes on land and a few exchanges at sea'. And while Octavian won by default, and indeed in absentia – he was suffering from sea-sickness – the couple had succeeded in their plan of breaking out of the bay and heading south to regroup. Only then did they receive news that their land forces had been intercepted and switched sides.

So, returning swiftly to Alexandria with flags flying to feign victory and buy time, Kleopatra secured her vast treasury. She was still in a strong position since Octavian faced rebellion back in Italy from troops claiming pay that he did not have.

Hailed in hymns as 'the divine protectress of the country', she also had the backing of her existing allies, the Memphite clergy, and the Egyptians, who sent a delegation demonstrating their willingness to bear arms on her behalf. For although Octavian had control of the north and west, the east and south remained free, and this is where Kleopatra planned her next move. She was well aware that the Mediterranean was not Egypt's only coastline, and since the Red Sea was the route to the east, so began a 'most bold and wonderful enterprise' as she followed the ancient Egyptian practice of transporting her remaining fleet overland, to 'set afloat in the Arabian Gulf' – to fight on a different front and, if needs be, escape.

But disaster struck when her ships were destroyed, burned by Nabataen Arab traders who had long resented the Ptolemies' incursions into their territory and were determined to maintain their trade routes around the Red Sea.

And it was this event, not Actium, that determined the fate of Kleopatra VII and Egypt.

In a year-long stalemate, the couple, holed up in Alexandria, renamed their 'Inimitable Livers' dining club 'Those who will die together', a 'Suicide Club', partying each night quite literally as if there were no tomorrow.

Determined to follow the example of her uncle Ptolemy of Cyprus when the Romans took his kingdom from him, rather than walking through Rome as a defeated enemy like her sister Arsinoe, Kleopatra planned an appropriate means of suicide should the need arise. As the sources reveal, she 'was busied in making a collection of all varieties of poisonous drugs and in order to see which of them were the least painful in the operation', including 'venomous animals', discovering a toxin that would supply the perfect means to pass over into the afterlife with the dignity befitting her status.

At the news that Octavian's forces were approaching south through Phoenicia, she stockpiled half 'her gold, silver, emeralds, pearls, ebony, ivory and cinnamon' in her tomb, and put her remaining efforts into the continuity of her dynasty. She sent sixteen-year-old Caesarion with the other half of her treasure to Koptos, from where supporters would take him across the Eastern Desert to the Red Sea to escape by ship; the three youngest royal children were also evacuated, placed in the care of their tutor, who took them south to Thebes.

Their departure cannot have come too soon, as Octavian's forces crossed Egypt's north-eastern border, taking Pelusium with the collusion of the garrison commander and moving swiftly around the Delta coast to Canopus.

As Antony beat them back, the couple received news that their gladiators were already on the march from their base in Cyzicus 'to help their rulers', until they were halted by Octavian's new governor of Syria and eventually executed. The Egyptians too were marching north to fight, until Octavian acted swiftly, eliminating every trace of their figurehead and spiritual leader, the high priest of Memphis, who was also part-Ptolemy. Not only terminating the 3,000-year-old religious post, his men entered the tomb of the last high priest, Pasherenptah, seizing its 'gold and silver ornaments, and all sorts of genuine precious stones', as the current incumbent, sixteen-year-old Petubastis, met his death on 31 July 30 BC, a date so coincidental that he can only have been killed.

For that very same evening in Alexandria, the Suicide Club met for the last time, when it was claimed that an unearthly music could be heard, 'the sound of all sorts of instruments, and voices singing in tune, and the cry of a crowd of people shouting and dancing, like a troop of bacchanals on its way'. As the spectral procession was heard passing through the city and out through the eastern gate, it suddenly grew very loud before disappearing toward the enemy camp, a phenomenon interpreted as Dionysos deserting Antony – yet a far more significant omen for the dynasty the god had once protected.

At dawn on 1 August, Antony led out his troops as the couple's remaining fleet moved out to engage Octavian's ships, only to pull alongside and surrender, as did their remaining land forces. And since Octavian refused to fight him in hand-to-hand combat, suggesting that he found some other way to die, Antony had no choice but to return to the palace.

Assuming Antony dead, Kleopatra had locked herself in her tomb with her maids. But hearing of his attempted suicide, she ordered him brought to her and, despite heavy blood loss, he was helped to the tomb where he died in her arms.

Desperate to prevent her turning her tomb's priceless contents, which he desperately needed, into a funerary pyre, Octavian ordered his men to break in. Seizing the dagger with which Kleopatra tried to kill herself, they 'also shook her dress to see if there were any poisons hid in it'.

Once she had been placed safely under house arrest in her palace, Octavian finally entered the city. Visiting Alexander's tomb to assess the value of its contents, he turned down the offer of viewing the Ptolemies' mummified remains, claiming he did not want to see a row of corpses in much the same way as he refused to honour the Apis bull, claiming 'to worship gods, not cattle'. He then ordered that 'the sarcophagus containing Alexander the Great's mummy was removed from the mausoleum at Alexandria', when it is said he 'actually touched it, with the result that a piece of the nose was broken off'.

Having left his indelible mark on the originator of the Ptolemaic dynasty, Octavian then terminated it altogether by ordering the execution of its fifteenth and final Ptolemy, Caesarion, claiming that 'it is bad to have too many Caesars'. The sixteen-year-old had been captured as he tried to leave the country with half the royal treasury, which was now added to the other half removed from Kleopatra's tomb and sent back to Rome, an amount so huge it caused the interest rate to fall from twelve per cent to four per cent overnight.

He did at least allow Kleopatra to oversee Antony's burial, but her request to be allowed to die too was countered by threats about her remaining children, who had also been seized. For Octavian wanted them all alive for his Triumph in Rome, the crowning moment of a chain of events in a history he had already begun to rewrite amidst the shredding of documents, the toppling of statues and the silencing of all opponents.

Playing along to gain time, Kleopatra withdrew into her private quarters, writing to Octavian to request burial with Antony and knowing she had to act quickly once he had read her letter. She then dismissed all her staff except her maids Eiras and Charmion, the supporting cast in her final performance.

As for what happened next, the ancient sources admit 'what really took place is known to no-one'.

Although her snake-aided suicide is well known, as first made public in the caricature-like effigy with snakes coiling up both arms that later toured Rome, the suggestion that Kleopatra killed herself with the bite of an asp is highly unlikely. For as she knew from her own research, the poison of the asp, the north African viper, caused vomiting and incontinence before death – completely unsuitable for her final plan.

Far more preferable were the results obtained from the Egyptian cobra, whose venom led to drowsiness and gradual paralysis, described as 'a profound natural sleep' – an effect that had long been achieved through mummification.

Although a cobra's venom does not necessarily require the snake to be physically present, the ancient sources assumed that a snake must have been smuggled into the palace inside a basket. But a cobra with sufficient venom to kill a human is around two metres long, and three such creatures would have been needed to kill the three women, since the cobra discharges all its venom in its first bite. Indeed, 'the mind soon begins to boggle at this Medusa-like proliferation of reptiles', not to mention the size of the basket required.

Alternative theories suggested that a snake was already in her quarters, 'kept in a vase, and that she vexed and pricked it with a golden spindle till it seized her arm'. This seems to be an embellishment of the most believable accounts, which state that 'she carried poison in a hollow bodkin about which she wound her hair'. As such hairpins were a vital part of her trademark coiffure, tucked away within her hair, the Roman soldiers who searched her clothing for concealed weapons and poisons may well have failed to find or even notice the bodkin, especially since the bound-up hair of a married woman was regarded as completely inviolable within Roman society.

And of course, she had chosen to die in the company of Eiras, ridiculed by Octavian as 'Kleopatra's hair-dressing girl', incapable of any significant deeds – yet who now may well have helped deprive him of his greatest triumph.

For after Charmion had dressed her in her royal robes, Kleopatra lay on her golden bed, where Eiras perhaps handed over the needle-like hairpin. And as the pharaoh 'made a small scratch in her arm and caused the poison to enter the blood', it swiftly took effect.

Her two servants followed her lead, and the stage-managed tableau was played out to great effect after Octavian read her letter and sent in his guards.

Famously demanding 'Was this well done of your lady, Charmion?', she just managed to reply 'Extremely well done, and as befitting the descendant of so many kings' – the three-thousand-year succession of pharaohs around whom the Egyptians had built their entire history.

And with those three thousand years swiftly brought to their ultimate conclusion on 31 August 30 BC, Egypt was formally annexed by Rome, remaining a part of successive foreign empires until AD 1952, when the story of Egypt would once more be its own.

'Osiris is Yesterday and Ra is tomorrow,
Yesterday belongs to me and I know tomorrow'
(The Book of the Dead)

Chronology

This chronology is based on Shaw & Nicholson 1995 pp.310-12 and Shaw ed. 2000, pp.479-82, with amendments following the recent redating of the Predynastic Period by Dee et al. 2013. It also features women who held kingly titles, and places the 11th Dynasty within the First Intermediate Period, rather than placing the later part within the Middle Kingdom.

As there are no fixed dates before 690 BC, events prior to this are estimated in the text, i.e. 'around 3100 BC', or 'in about 1069 BC'.

Predynastic Period: 5300-3100 BC
Lower Egypt:
Neolithic c.5300-4000 BC
Maadi Culture c.4000-3100 BC

Upper Egypt:
Badarian Period c.4400-3800 BC
Naqada period c.3800-3300 BC

'Dynasty 0': 3300-3100 BC
Rulers including:
Scorpion
Iri-hor
Ka

Early Dynastic Period: 3100-2686 BC
1st Dynasty: 3100-2890 BC
Narmer c.3100 BC
Aha c.3085 BC
Djer c.3040 BC
Djet c.2990 BC

Merneith c.2965 BC
Den c.2960 BC
Anedjib c.2925 BC
Semerkhet c.2900 BC
Qaa c.2890 BC

2nd Dynasty: 2890–2686 BC
Hetepsekhemwy c.2890 BC
Nebra c.2865 BC
Nynetjer
Weneg
Sened
Peribsen c.2700 BC
Khasekhemwy c.2686 BC

Old Kingdom: 2686–2181 BC
3rd Dynasty: 2686–2613 BC
Nebka 2686–2667 BC
Djoser 2667–2648 BC
Sekhemkhet 2648–2640 BC
Khaba 2640–2637 BC
Huni 2637–2613 BC

4th Dynasty: 2613–2494 BC
Snefru 2613–2589 BC
Khufu 2589–2566 BC
Djedefra 2566–2558 BC
Khafra 2558–2532 BC
Menkaura 2532–2503 BC
Khentkawes I c.2503 BC
Shepseskaf 2503–2498 BC

5th Dynasty: 2494–2345 BC
Userkaf 2494–2487 BC
Sahura 2487–2475 BC
Neferirkara 2475–2455 BC
Khentkawes II c.2455 BC
Shepseskara 2455–2448 BC

Raneferef 2448-2445 BC
Niuserra 2445-2421 BC
Menkauhor 2421-2414 BC
Djedkara 2414-2375 BC
Unas 2375-2345 BC

6th Dynasty: 2345-2181 BC
Teti 2345-2323 BC
Userkara 2323-2321 BC
Pepi I 2321-2287 BC
Merenra 2287-2278 BC
Pepy II 2278-2184 BC
Nemtyemsaf 2184 BC
Neitikrety 2184-2181 BC

First Intermediate Period: 2181-2055 BC
7th & 8th Dynasties: 2181-2125 BC
Numerous ephemeral kings including:
Neferkauhor
Ibi

9th & 10th Dynasties (Herakleopolis): 2160-2125 BC
Khety I
Khety II
Merikara

11th Dynasty (Thebes): 2125-2055 BC
Montuhotep I
Intef I 2125-2112 BC
Intef II 2112-2063 BC
Intef III 2063-2055 BC

11th Dynasty (all Egypt): 2055-1985 BC
Montuhotep II 2055-2004 BC
Sankhkara (Montuhotep III) 2004-1992 BC
Montuhotep IV 1992-1985 BC

Middle Kingdom: 1985-1650 BC
12th Dynasty: 1985-1795 BC
Amenemhat I 1985-1955 BC
Sesostris I 1965-1921 BC
Amenemhat II 1922-1878 BC
Sesostris II 1880-1874 BC
Sesostris III 1874-1855 BC
Amenemhat III 1855-1808 BC
Amenemhat IV 1808-1799 BC
Sobeknefru 1799-1795 BC

13th Dynasty: 1795-1650 BC
Up to seventy rulers, including:
Sobekhotep I
Ameny-Qemau
Sobekhotep II
Khendjer
Sobekhotep III
Neferhotep I
Sobekhotep IV
Sobekhotep VIII

14th Dynasty (Xois): c.1750-1650 BC
Kings including:
Nehesy

Second Intermediate Period: c.1650–1550 BC
15th Dynasty (Hyksos): 1650-1550 BC
Salitis
Khyan
Apophis
Khamudi

16th Dynasty: c.1650-1550 BC
Minor rulers contemporary with the 15th Dynasty

17th Dynasty: c.1650-1550 BC
Several rulers based in Thebes, of which the most prominent examples
are listed below:

Sobekemsaf c.1570 BC
Intef VI
Tao I
Seqenra (Tao II) c.1560 BC
Kamose c.1555-1550 BC

New Kingdom: c.1550-1069 BC
18th Dynasty: 1550-1295 BC
Ahmose I 1550-1525 BC
Amenhotep I 1525-1504 BC
Tuthmosis I 1504-1492 BC
Tuthmosis II 1492-1479 BC
Tuthmosis III 1479-1425 BC
Hatshepsut 1473-1458 BC
Amenhotep II 1427-1400 BC
Tuthmosis IV 1400-1390 BC
Amenhotep III 1390-1352 BC
Amenhotep IV/Akhenaten 1352-1336 BC
(Nefernefruaten) Smenkhkara 1338-1336 BC
Tutankhamen 1336-1327 BC
Ay 1327-1323 BC
Horemheb 1323-1295 BC

19th Dynasty: 1295-1186 BC
Ramses I 1295-1294 BC
Seti I 1294-1279 BC
Ramses II 1279-1213 BC
Merenptah 1213-1203 BC
Amenmesse 1203-1200 BC
Seti II 1200-1194 BC
Siptah 1194-1188 BC
Tawosret 1188-1186 BC

20th Dynasty: 1186-1069 BC
Sethnakht 1186-1184 BC
Ramses III 1184-1153 BC
Ramses IV 1153-1147 BC
Ramses V 1147-1143 BC

Ramses VI 1143–1136 BC
Ramses VII 1136–1129 BC
Ramses VIII 1129-1126 BC
Ramses IX 1126-1108 BC
Ramses X 1108-1099 BC
Ramses XI 1099-1069 BC

Third Intermediate Period: 1069-747 BC
21st Dynasty (Tanis): 1069-945 BC
Smendes 1069-1043 BC
Amenemnisu 1043-1039 BC
Psusennes I 1039-991 BC
Amenemope 993-984 BC
Osorkon the Elder 984-978 BC
Siamen 978-959 BC
Psusennes II 959-945 BC

22nd Dynasty (Bubastite/Libyan): 945-715 BC
Sheshonq I 945-924 BC
Osorkon I 924-889 BC
Sheshonq II c.890 BC
Takeloth I 889-874 BC
Osorkon II 874-850 BC
Takelot III 850-825 BC
Sheshonq III 825-773 BC
Pimay 773-767 BC
Sheshonq V 767-730 BC
Osorkon IV 730-715 BC

23rd Dynasty (Tanite/Libyan): 818-715 BC
Several contemporary lines of rulers at Herakleopolis, Hermopolis, Leontopolis and Tanis, including:
Pedubastis I 818-793 BC
Sheshonq IV c.780 BC
Osorkon III 777-749 BC

24th Dynasty: 727-715 BC
Bakenrenef 727-715 BC

Late Period: 747–332 BC
25th Dynasty (Kushite): 747–656 BC
Piye 747–716 BC
Shabaqa 716–702 BC
Shabitqa 702–690 BC
Taharqa 690–664 BC
Tantamen 664–656 BC

26th Dynasty (Saite) 672–525 BC
Necho I 672–664 BC
Psammetichus I 664–610 BC
Necho II 610–595 BC
Psammetichus II 595–589 BC
Apries 589–570 BC
Ahmose II 570–526 BC
Psammetichus III 526–525 BC

27th Dynasty (First Persian Period): 525–404 BC
Cambyses 525–522 BC
Darius I 522–486 BC
Xerxes I 486–465 BC
Artaxerxes I 465–424 BC
Darius II 424–405 BC
Artaxerxes II 405–359 BC

28th Dynasty: 404–399 BC
Amyrtaios 404–399 BC

29th Dynasty: 399–380 BC
Nepherites I 399–393 BC
Hakor 393–380 BC
Nepherites II c.380 BC

30th Dynasty: 380–343 BC
Nectanebo I 380–362 BC
Teos 362–360 BC
Nectanebo II 360–343 BC

Second Persian Period: 343-332 BC
Artaxerxes III 343-338 BC
Arses 338-336 BC
Darius III 336-332 BC

Ptolemaic Period: 332-30 BC
Macedonian Dynasty: 332-305 BC
Alexander the Great 332-323 BC
Philip Arrhidaios 323-317 BC
Alexander IV 323-310 BC

Ptolemaic Dynasty: 305-30 BC
Ptolemy I 305-282 BC
Ptolemy II 285-246 BC
Arsinoe II 275-268 BC
Ptolemy III 246-222 BC
Berenike II 246-221 BC
Ptolemy IV 221-205 BC
Ptolemy V 205-180 BC
Kleopatra I 194-176 BC
Ptolemy VI 180-145 BC
Kleopatra II 176-116 BC
Ptolemy VII 145 BC
Ptolemy VIII 145-116 BC
Kleopatra III 142-101 BC
Ptolemy IX 116-107 BC
Ptolemy X 107-88 BC
Berenike III 101-80 BC
Ptolemy IX 88-80 BC
Ptolemy XI 80 BC
Ptolemy XII (Auletes) 80-58 BC
Kleopatra V 58-57 BC
Berenike IV 58-55 BC
Ptolemy XII (Auletes) 55-51 BC
Kleopatra VII 51-30 BC
Ptolemy XIII 51-47 BC
Ptolemy XIV 47-44 BC
Ptolemy XV (Caesarion) 44-30 BC

Note on Spellings

It must be said that ancient Egyptian names can often appear overwhelmingly confusing. Much of this is due to the way in which the Egyptians based their history around their kings, each of whom had five standard names, which could then change during their lifetime, e.g. Khasekhem rebranding himself Khasekhemwy; or Tutankhaten, Tutankhamen. In some cases the name changes were so frequent it continues to cause great confusion and indeed controversy, e.g. Queen Nefertiti taking an additional name to become Queen Neferneferuaten-Nefertiti; then as co-regent she becomes Ankhkheperura-Neferneferuaten; and eventually as king she is Ankhkheprura-Smenkhkara. And while this is complicated enough, Egyptologists have also changed the way they once read some of these names. So for example, Hatasu became Hashepsowe and is now Hatshepsut; Khuenaten is now Akhenaten; Raneb is now Nebra. Some Egyptologists also prefer different spellings of the same names to others, so that Nefertiti can also be Nofretete, and Tutankhamen Tutenkhamon. This also occurs when writing the names of the Greek-speaking Ptolemies, with the more authentic spellings of Berenike and Kleopatra used in this book, compared to the more common use of Berenice and Cleopatra. And of course under the Ptolemies, their bilingual scholar Manetho produced Greek versions of the ancient Egyptian rulers' names, so for example, Amenhotep became Amenophis; Djhutymose, Tuthmosis; Senwosret, Sesostris, etc.

Place names can be even more confusing, for not only can those with ancient Egyptian names usually have a later Greek version, but a third Arabic version. So for example, Men-nefer which became Memphis is now Mit Rahina. Of those sites known by their Greek names, Thebes for example is derived from the original Egyptian Ta-ipet-sut, and is now the Arabic el-Uksor, or Luxor. Then again, some sites are only known by their Arabic site name, eg. el-Giza, while such Arabic settlement names can also be used for time periods, e.g. el-Badari and the Badarian Period and

377

Badarian Culture, or el–Till and Beni Amra conflated to create Tell el-Amarna, which is both a site and time period.

Clearly the reason why Egyptian names can often appear so confusing is simply because they are – so despite the apparent and inevitable inconsistencies, I have used the names and dates I have always used in order to tell my own version of Egypt's story.

Acknowledgements

Of the many, many people who have provided help, information and support over many, many years I'd particularly like to thank Dr Amr Aboulfath; Dr Assem Allam; Dr Osama Amer; the Beaumont family; Guy de la Bédoyère; Susanne Bell; the Billis family; Richard Bradley; Juliet Brightmore; Rita Britton; Prof. Don Brothwell; Dr Diana Brown; Peter & Tanya Buckley; Kevin Cale; Christine Carruthers; Julie & Adam Chalkley; Prof. Krzysztof Ciałowicz; Maxine Coe; Prof. Matthew Collins; Dr Vanessa Corby; Steve Cross; Linda Dale; Janet Darke; Martin Davidson; Sian Davies; Andrew Dean; Dr David Depraetere; Amber & Simon Dickinson; Dr Sarry el-Dinn; Dr David Dixon; Jackie Dunmore; Mel Dyke; Elaine Edgar; Dr Bill Edwards; Sophie Elwin-Harris; Prof. Earl Ertman; Ceryl Evans; Janice Eyres; Prof. Mahmoud Ezzamel; Mohammed Fekri; Alan & Chris Fildes; Lynne Fletcher; Michael Fletcher; Imogen Forbes; Dr Diane France; Pam Gidney; Anton Gill; Dr Mercedes González; Carrie Gough; Marilyn Griffiths; Janice Hadlow; Prof. Shelley Haley; Julia Hankey; Lynn & Barry Harper; Mohamed Hawash; Kate Hawkins; Pam Hayes; Dr Stan Henrickx; Dr Bernard Hephrun; Kerry Hood; Dr David Howard; Prof. Anthony Humphreys; Ian Hunt; Jeremy Hunt; Sarah Hunt; Dr Dirk Huyge; Lynda Jackson; Duncan James; John & Joan Johnson; Martyn & Christine Johnson; Dr John Kane; Dr Tim Kendall; Leigh Kroeger; Rupert Lancaster; David Langan; Eva Laurie; Duncan Lees; Jackie Ligo; John Livesey; Bill Locke; John Lombard; Mark Lucas; Sarah Lucas; Joan McMahon; Steven & Val McMahon; Claire McNamara; Helen Matthews; Gillian Mosely; Dr Sahar el-Mougy; Natalie Murray; Dr Christopher Naunton; Richard Nelson; Prof. Paul Nicholson; Prof. Terry O'Connor; Geoffrey Oates; Delia Pemberton; Michael & Jane Pickering; Jan Picton; Rod Poole; Maddy Price; Magdy el-Rashidy; Christine Rawson; Ali Reda; Dr Howard Reid; Lisa & Tim Riley; Jennifer Robertson; Bill Rudolph; Filippo Salamone; Dr Ahmed Saleh; Nermine Sami; Julia Samson; Emma Sargeant; Prof. Nick Saunders; Dr Otto Schaden; Dr John Schofield;

ACKNOWLEDGEMENTS

Ian Scorah; Gillian Scott; Phyl & Gordon Semley; Ali Hassan Sheba & family; Alastair Smith; Jean Smith; Dr Hourig Sourouzian; Dr Alice Stevenson; George Stewart; Jackie Teasdale; Angela Thomas; Jean Thompson; 'Tracey'; Caterina Turroni; Dr Eleni Vassilika; Jonathan & Myra Le Vine; David & Carole Walker; Claire Watkins; Ros Watson; Rowena Webb; Dr Andy Wilson; Alison Winfield. But most of all, to Garry & Susan Fletcher, Kate Fletcher, and Stephen, Eleanor, Max & Django, to whom this story is dedicated – with much, much love.

Notes on Sources

1. In the Beginning

'the whole country . . . into a sea', Herodotus II.97, de Selincourt 1954, p.165.

'the most beautiful. . . . a happy year', Papyrus Chester Beatty I, Manniche 1991, p.75.

'hugging the fields is reborn', Famine Stela, based on Lichtheim 1980, p.99.

'the meadows laugh. . . . flooded', Pyramid Texts Spell 581, based on Lichtheim 1975, p.204.

'the whole land leaps for joy!', Hymn to Hapi, Lichtheim 1975, p.208.

'the Father of the gods', Hart 1986, p.174.

'Mother who gave. . . . all the gods', Hart 1986, p.211.

'the Terrifying One', Wilkinson, T. 1999, p.291; 'the Terrible One', Kees 1961, p.28.

'the male who acts the female. . . . the male', Troy 1986, p.18.

'the fathers and mothers. . . . the original gods', Fletcher 2002, p.24.

'the mother and father of all', Peust 2006, p.118.

'great He-She', Hassan 1992, p.317; Troy 1986, pp.2-3, 12-20.

'live by Maat', Hornung 1992, pp.131-2.

'sneezing out Shu. . . . spitting out Tefnut', Fletcher 2002, p.10.

'the great one who bore the gods', Coffin Text Spell 77, Lesko 1999, p.28.

'more clever. . . . million gods', Chester Beatty I Papyrus, Hart 1986, p.104.

'craftier than a million men', Kemp 1991, p.25.

'more effective. . . . millions of soldiers', Lesko 1999, p.156.

'Great Striding. . . . as stars', Pyramid Texts Spell 350, in Lichtheim 1975, p.41.

'everlasting in perfect condition', Hart 1986, p.157.

'Mighty Isis who protected her brother', Lichtheim 1976, p.83.
'a composite. . . . and female elements', Troy 1986, p.3.
'people', Fischer 1989, p.24.
'women and men', Peust 2006, pp.118-19.
'Followers of Horus', McDowell 1999, p.121.
'moulding beings', Hart 1986, p.133.
'Creator of all. . . . gods and humans', BM.EA.826, Lichtheim 1976, p.87.
'the cattle of god', Gordon & Schwabe 2004, p.44.
'*remyt*', '*remet*', Lichtheim 1976, p.199.
'Golden One', Callendar 1994, p.8.
'the Eye appears. . . . punishes you', Pap. Bremner Rhind, Lichtheim 1976, pp.198-9.
'Lady of Bright Red Linen', Hart 1986, p.188.
'both the coming . . . of the world', Darnell, J. 2002, p.143.

2. Sahara Savannah

'the oldest graphic. . . . Lascaux along the Nile', Huyge 2012, p.29.
'turning dry wadis. . . . torrents for a few hours', Bell 1975, p.247.
'Valley of Many Baths',
http://www.eeescience.utoledo.edu/faculty/harrell/egypt/Turin%20Papyrus/
    Harrell_Papyrus_Map_text.htm
'the world's oldest map', Wilkinson, T. 2003, p.50, fig.2.
'the earliest sanctuary. . . . temple architecture', Vörös 2008, p.41.
'wallpaper', Bahn 2014, p.669.
'the handprint motif . . . Sahara/inner Africa', Darnell, D. 2002, p.161.
'walking larder', Wendorf & Schild 2002, p.15.
'walking blood banks', McGregor 2012, pp.41-2.
'by their study of. . . . the Greeks', Herodotus II.3, de Selincourt 1954, p.130.
'the only rational calendar ever devised', Ray 2001, p.83.
'that would have been. . . . cattle, sun and stars', Malville et al. 2007, p.2.
'a surrogate sacrificial cow', Malville et al. 2007, p.4.
'suggesting that they . . . representing the dead', Malville et al. 2007, p.4.
'Mediterranean and sub-Saharan', Malville et al. 2007, p.6.
'complex and exuberant material culture', Wengrow et al. 2014, p.105.
'remnant vocabulary. . . . language of display', Wengrow 2006, p.51.
'practically covered', Kobusiewicz et al. 2009, p.150.

3. Seeking the Waters

'linear oasis', Wilkinson, T. 2010, p.27.

'Custodians of the Holy Waters', Bangs & Scaturro 2005, p.12, pl.1-2.

'ethnically disparate', Kees 1961, p.34.

'a Mediterranean winter. . . . regime continued', Wengrow et al. 2014, p.97.

'followed a more. . . . path of development' , Wengrow et al. 2014, p.96.

'primarily linked with the. . . . herd cattle', Hassan 1992, p.314.

'the first traces of. . . . plants in Egypt', Wendrich & Cappers 2005, pp.12-15.

'collecting expeditions', Majer 1992, p.228.

'earthly life. . . . substantial realm', James 1984, p.20.

'the two colours . . . life and death', Nelson & Khalifa 2011, p.137.

'toffee-like', Jones et al. 2014.

'made by a female. . . . her sex', Petrie Museum UC.9601, Adams 1992, p.13.

'she has her hands in her pockets', BM.EA.59648, Midant-Reynes 2000, p.157, fig.4.a.

'not rare in the graves of females', Cialowicz 1985, p.164.

'to a period of roughly. . . . c.3800–3300 BC', Wengrow et al. 2014, p.102.

'the bones were. . . . in heaps', Petrie & Quibell 1896, p.ix.

'may originally . . . through the millennia', Podzorski 1990, p.85.

'chunks of resin', Fahmy 2003, p.20.

'symbols of authority', Wilkinson, T. 2010, p.49

'symbols of protection', Hassan & Smith 2002, p.63.

'dancing goddesses', Baumgartel 1955, p.64.

'miming cow horns', Hassan 1992, p.314.

'the earliest known. . . Egyptian religion', Wilkinson, T. 2003, p.110, fig.41.

'sequence dating', Petrie 1901, pp.4-12.

'the emergence of Homo hierarchicus', Wengrow 2006, p.173.

'the tombs of women . . . the graves of men', Baumgartel 1970, p.6.

'the source of materials . . . appropriated by the elite', Stevenson 2009.b, p.4.

'Master Race', Adams & Cialowicz 1997, p.53.

'das Volk und das Reich', Wilkinson, T. 2003, pp.25, 30, 84.

'people from Mesopotamia. . . . . Wadi Hammamat', Bomann & Young 1994, pp.31-2.

'associated with the spread. . . . across Egypt', Stevenson 2009.a, p.2.

4. The North-South Divide

For a list of the *nomes* and their standards see Hart 1986, pp.137-42.
'reminiscent of a bee's proboscis', Wilkinson, T. 2010, p.44.
'when Upper Egypt . . . the north', Midant-Reynes 2000, p.183.
'The Two Mighty Ones', Hart 1986, p.134.
'The Two Lords at Peace Within Him', Quibell 1900, pl.II.
'She Who. . . . and Seth'; also 'She Who Sees Horus and Carries Seth',
    Troy 1986, p.189.
'Butic Cycle', Redford 1992, p.47.
'at the frontier between two . . . culture of Palestine', Midant-Reynes 2000,
    pp.218-19.
'at least one tall narrow pillar-like human male statue', Kemp 2000, p.229.
'potted salmon', Annie Quibell in Adams 1990, pp.181-3.
'Opening of the Dykes', Wilkinson, A. 1998, pp.36-7.
'phonetically readable', http://www.dainst.org/en/project/abydos?ft=all
'a document. . . . Upper Egypt', Darnell, J. 2002, p.143.
'the forerunner of all modern countries', Dee et al. 2013, p.2.
'First Time', Aldred 1987, p.84.
'ancient Egypt's founding monument', Wilkinson, T. 2010, p.19.
'the king has . . . the Delta enemy', Midant-Reynes 2000, p.244.
'divine essence . . . the earliest times', Wilkinson, T. 1999, p.199.
'the Followers of Horus', Millet 1990, p.57.
'souls of the kings of Lower Egypt', Millet 1990, p.59.
'a descendant of. . . . rulers of Naqada', Wilkinson, T. 1999, pp.37, 70.
'united by kinship. . . . residence or both', Janosi 2010, p.7.

5. Lords and Ladies of the Two Lands

'to establish', 'be permanent', Spencer 1993, p.63.
'In succession to . . . of his kingdom', Manetho, Waddell ed. 1940, p.33.
'throughout the whole . . . than a monarch', Callender 1992, p.19.
'the left hand. . . . attitude of Min', Petrie 1896, p.7.
'Hail Min placed in the garden', Moens 1985, p.70.
'the Balance of the Two Lands', Uphill 1988, p.47.
'the whole country is . . . the river', Herodotus II.97, de Selincourt 1954,
    p.165.

'ceremonial cubit', Goedicke 1994, p.187.
'3 cubits, 4 hands, 3 fingers', Kemp 1991, p.23.
'carried off and perished', Manetho in Gardiner 1964, p.430.
'the mother of. . . . official consort', Hassan 1992, p.312.
'the cow that hath borne the bull', Gordon & Schwabe 2004, p.44.
'the corridor to Africa', Adams 1977.
'killing enemies. . . . her arrows', Hart 1986, p.191.
'White Walls', Quirke ed. 1997, p.91.
'bloody homicidal sacrifice', Baadsgaard et al. 2012, p.144.
'the Strong', Wilkinson, T. 1999, p.202.
'Thoth Hill', Vörös 2007, pp.82-95.
'carved with a. . . . recumbent lions', Smith 1981, p.436; Emery 1984, pl.32.b.
'the first named. . . . in history', Rice 2006, flyleaf, p.46; Emery 1984, pl.26.
'the friend Fed', Louvre E.21704, Andreu 1997, p.45.
'soaked', Amelineau 1904, pp.227-33.
'for the washing. . . . the double lord', Petrie 1901, p.28.
'standing image of the ka (soul) of King Djer', Petrie 1901, p.28.
'belonged to his queen', Petrie 1901, p.16.
'who only cared for. . . . dangerous place', Petrie 1931, p.174.
'a great famine seized Egypt', Manetho, Waddell ed. 1940, p.29, 31, 33.
'tombs of women. . . . tombs of men', Ellis 1996, http://www.digitalegypt.ucl.ac.uk/tarkhan/gender.html
'very white, bleached linen', Kohler & Jones 2009, p.53, n.131.
'represent a lavish. . . . lifetime of her son', Wilkinson, T. 1999, p.74.
'multigenerational ties to the kingship', Troy 1986, p.139.
'may herself have. . . . reigning monarch', Emery 1984, p.66.
'that which is from Merneith's Treasury', Capel & Markoe eds. 1996, p.28.
'high fiscal office', Petrie 1901, pp.52-3.
'King Merneith', Cairo JE.34550, Petrie 1900, p.26.
'it can hardly be. . . . was a king', Griffith in Petrie 1900.a, p.35.
'robing room', Hassan 1992, p.311.
'cultic enclosure', Wilkinson, T. 1999, p.77.
'Supreme Craftsman', Hart 1986, p.176.
'the first time of. . . . Easterners', BM.EA.55586, Adams & Cialowicz 1997, fig.44.d.
'who still resided . . . in the Nile Valley', Bomann & Young 1994, p.31.

'they shall not exist', McGregor 2008, p.60.

'protector of the king', Petrie 1901, p.25.

'manifestation of judicial authority', Wilkinson, T. 1999, p.290.

'foremost in the library', Hart 1986, p.193.

'a census of all. . . . and east', Breasted 1988 I, p.60.

'Goldie', Rice 2006, p.50.

'the One with the Tail', Louvre E.21702, Louvre 1981, p.10.

'saturated with ointment. . . . the whole tomb', Petrie 1900, p.14.

'Arm-raiser', Wilkinson, T. 1999, p.203.

'Helping Hand', Cairo Inv.4442, Kohler & Jones 2009, pp.154-5.

'Follower of the king. . . . the royal boat', Wilkinson, T. 1999, pp.135-7.

'companion of the palace', Petrie 1900, p.26.

6. Shifting Focus

'Great of Incense. . . . Red House', Cairo CG.1, Saleh & Sourouzian 1987, No.22.

'She of the Perfume Jar', Fletcher 2004, p.238.

'washing every day', Petrie 1901, p.26.

'Funerary Priestess of the King', Cairo Inv. 4446, Kohler & Jones 2009, pp.164-5.

'such objects belonged. . . . travelling outfit', Petrie 1901, p.27.

'it was decided that. . . . kingly office', Manetho in Waddell ed. 1940, pp.37, 39.

'hacking up. . . . northern lands', Palermo Stone, Breasted 1988 I, p.62.

'averaged less from. . . . in Dynasty I', Bell 1970, p.572.

'a significant drop . . . the first dynasty', Wilkinson, T. 1999, p.83.

'some kind of political or religious dispute', Spencer 1993, p.69.

'the One of Naqada . . . Upper Egypt, Peribsen', Petrie 1901, pl.XXVV.190.

'5 cubits and 3 palms', Manetho, Waddell ed. 1940, pp.37, 39.

'humbling the foreign lands', Quibell & Green 1902, p.48.

'47,209 northern enemies', Quibell 1900, pl.XL; Quibell & Green 1902, p.44.

'the year of fighting the northern enemy', Thomas 1995, p.118.

'The Two Lords. . . . Within Him', Petrie 1901, p.31.

'Lady of Byblos', Redford 1992, p.41.

'a connecting link', Smith 1981, p.149.

'high is Khasekhemwy', Sethe 1914.
'the temple called 'The-Goddess . . . of stone', Palermo Stone, Breasted 1988 I, p.64.
'stretching the cord', Brewer et al. 1994, p.17.
'the divine ancestors of the king', Seidlmayer 1996, p.116.
'inner apartments', Hart 1991, p.52.
'an impressive 4.82 million bricks', La Loggia 2012, p.21.

7. The Rise of the Pyramid Age

'venerated as the foundress of the IIIrd Dynasty', Petrie 1901, p.32.
'first authenticated doctor in the world', Nunn 1996, p.124.
'the pyramid of Djoser, inventor of stone', Ray 2001, p.13.
'Egypt's Leonardo da Vinci', Ray 2001, pp.5, 16.
'know not death', Pyramid Texts Spells 570, Faulkner 1969, pp.224-5.
'Sleeping Beauty's. . . . made for death', Vandier in Verner 2001, p.109.
'the world's oldest sport's facility', Decker 1992, fig.5-6, p.29.
'suited to the viscera', Saleh & Sourouzian 1987, No.18.
'ankle deep', Lauer 1976, p.98.
'there were presented . . . the king's writings', Breasted 1988, I, p.79.
'the majesty of King Huni. . . . this entire land', Pap.Prisse II.7, Brunner 1991, p.154.
'She whose every command is carried out', Troy 1986, p.185.
'ancestress of the royal family of the IVth dynasty', Smith 1981, p.87.

8. Sons and Daughters of the Sun

'Great He-She', Hassan 1992, p.317.
'with the shapeliest. . . them row', Papyrus Westcar, P.Berlin 3033, Lichtheim 1975, p.216.
'fishing net linen', e.g.UC.31209, Hall 1986, p.65.
'the house/womb of Horus', Callender 1994, p.8.
'Horus who came forth from the gold', Coffin Texts V.18b, Troy 1986, p.55.
'the lady who dwells . . . end of the world', Hassan & Smith 2002, p.59.
'specifically charged with. . . . of the goddess', Lesko 996, p.38.

'gathering of taxes into. . . . sacred art', Kemp 1991, fig. 40, p.112.

'Snefru luscious. . . . Nurse of Snefru', Lehner 1997, p.228.

'a deliberate pharaonic . . . in Lower Nubia', Smith & Hall, eds. 1983, p.77.

'a portable bed chamber. . . . about the same time', Reisner 1932, p.58.

'to satisfy the writer's . . . Egyptian perfectly', Boston MFA.27442, Dunham 1943, p.2.

'the most visited pair in Cairo Museum', Cairo CG.3&4, Hart 1991, p.79.

'pleasant and serene', Harpur 2001, p.265.

'stared back at him', Reeves 2000, p.58.

'made for his gods. . . . cannot be destroyed', Petrie 1892, pp.24, 39.

'lay hitched up . . . to support its position', Petrie 1892, p.17.

'marvellously plumped out', Petrie in Drower 1985, p.176.

'and shake it so the audience. . . . part of the process', Adams 1988, p.13.

'thrice good . . . king Snefru', Petrie 1892, pp.10, 40-1.

'I am one who . . . house of Osiris', Coffin Texts Spell 155, Faulkner 1973, p.133.

'Khnum defends me', Kees 1961, p.39.

'the first construction . . . the Great Pyramid', Lehner in Münch 2000, pp.898-9.

'in the most important. . . . own royal cemetery', Wheeler 1935, p.181.

'I regret Queen Hetepheres is not receiving', Reisner in Reeves 2000, p.171.

'birth and boat imagery', Troy 1986, p.23.

'when rage has reached its limit, the Radiant One sails forth', Coffin Texts 148.

'rosy pink', Jenkins 1980, p.50.

'knew the measures . . . his pyramid', P.Berlin 3033, based on Kákosy 1989, p.152.

'offered maximum protection. . . . buried there', Kákosy 1989, p.146.

'constructed of polished . . . of animals', Herodotus II.124, de Selincourt 1954, p.179.

'has caused you . . . transfigured spirit', Harris Pap., Troy 1986, p.88.

'Director of Music in the South and North', Wilkinson, T. 2010, p.81.

'beautify your house. . . . should be for life', based on Wente 1982, p.18.

'The one who delights. . . . Periankhu', Cairo JE.98944, Arnold 1999.a, p.53.

'Listen all of you . . . and lion will eat him', Reeves 2000, p.231.

'surprised to see. . . . household chores', Dr Sarry el-Dinn in Morrell 2001.
'awe-inspiring divine aloofness', Louvre E.12626, Arnold 1999.a, p.54.
'an inspired combination . . . and self-assertion', Wilkinson, T. 2010, p.90.
'Rosy-Cheeks', Herodotus II.134, de Selincourt, p.182.
'of a heavyweight athlete', Cairo CG.15, Arnold 1999.a, p.57.
'an unequalled image. . . . incarnate in man', Cairo CG.14, Terrace & Fischer
    1970, pp.41-4.
'Shaking the Papyrus', Troy 1986, p.58.
'that which I have given to my daughter', Reisner 1927, p.78.
'perhaps symbolising . . . "power behind the throne"', Hart 1991, p.143.
'left no significant historical records', Arnold 1999.a, p.67.
'educated among the king's. . . . than any child', Breasted 1988 I, pp.115-18.
'when his majesty was upon . . . for my tomb', based on Breasted 1988 I,
    pp.94-5.
'the dog which was the guard. . . . before the great god', Reisner 1936, p.97.
'Menkaure's Drunkards', Rowe 1961, p.110.
'remarkable in number and quality', Arnold 1999.a, p.67.
'quite exceptionally, a Valley. . . . end of the 4th dynasty', http://www.
    aeraweb.org/blog/a-perfect-start-giza-season-2014/
'King of Upper . . . Lower Egypt', Hassan 1943, p.3; also Junker in Waddell
    ed. 1940, p.55.
'an alternative translation. . . . philologically tenable', Gardiner 1964,
    p.83.
'considered a true ruler', Verner 1994, p.128.
'this pyramid. . . . courtesan Rhodopis', Herodotus, de Selincourt,II.134,
    p.182.
'this last pyramid. . . . Rhodopis', Diodorus, I.64, 14, trans. Oldfather 1936,
    p.223.
'the smallest . . . by Rhodopis', Pliny 36.17, trans. Rackham et al. 1947-63,
    p.65.
'the channel that gave . . . and Abusir', Lehner 1997, p.107.

9. The Rule of Ra

'Please go . . . payment for beer', Westcar Papyrus Berlin 3033, Lichtheim
    1975, pp.220-2.
'heap of stones flattered. . . . term pyramid', Hart 1991, p.145.
'ensure that the sun's. . . . all year round', Lehner 1997, p.141.

'sail well like this, hurry up!', MMA.22.1.13, Arnold 1999.a, p.79.

'the Great God who. . . . all countries', Breasted 1988 I, p.108.

'80,000 measures of myrrh', Palermo Stone, Breasted 1988 I, p.70.

'interpreters', Smith 1981, p.133.

'the Great Green One', Cairo RT.6.12.24.9, Saleh & Sourouzian 1987, No.37.

'rain falling on the roof. . . . in the pavement', Fakhry in Bell 1975, p.247.

'as these my nostrils . . . old age as one revered', Breasted 1988 I, pp.108-9.

'herdsman of the anus', Nunn 1996, pp.126-7.

'Overseer of Women Physicians', Ghalioungui 1975, pp.159-64.

'King of Upper and Lower. . . . Golden Horus', Palermo Stone, Breasted 1988 I, p.70.

'the priest Rawer was following. . . . any man', based on Donadoni ed. 1997, p.288.

'I supplied the foodstuffs . . . never got any', P.Berlin 11301, based on Wente 1990, pp.55-6.

'Khentkawes, beloved of Neferirkare', Posener-Kriéger 1997, p.17.

'Mother of the King of. . . . Upper and Lower Egypt', Verner 1994, p.123.

'was reserved solely for rulers and divinities', Verner 2001, p.299.

'the dazzling career of the royal hairdresser', Verner 1994, p.173.

'stretching the cord. . . . built this temple in stone', http://www.digitalegypt. ucl.ac.uk/abughurab/inscription.html

'inlaid with green stone', '100 oars of conifer wood', Sethe 1914, p.236.

'a symbolic port to the world of the gods', Lehner 1997, p.152.

'imitating the call. . . . beekeepers in Egypt today', Brewer et al. 1994, p.126.

'having mixed all kinds of dirt . . . same time', Satire of the Trades, Lichtheim 1975, p.187.

'How's that? You're falling!' . . . 'open his box for him', Decker 1992, p.102.

'don't obstruct my face. . . . putting to shore!', Fischer 1989, p.20.

'Milk, quickly, hurry up. . . . the boss comes back', based on Houlihan 2001, p.30.

'Come on you shit! Drive the cattle forward!', Houlihan 2001, p.29.

'while searching for a mastaba . . . Saqqara cemetery', Quibell in Harpur 1986, p.114.

'fighting Egyptian invaders and Bedawi auxiliaries', Petrie 1898, p.6, pl.IV.

'lugged him over by the armpits', Petrie 1898, p.7.

'his majesty himself wrote . . . in order to praise me', Breasted 1988 I, p.122.

'My majesty has seen. . . . I love you', based on Wente 1990, p.19.

'not to have sex with a lady-boy', based on Parkinson 1995, p.68.

'love your wife with ardour . . . as long as you live', Lichtheim 1975, p.69.

'good speech is more hidden . . . at their grindstones', Lichtheim 1975, p.63.

'gracile body-build', 'somewhat underdeveloped', Strouhal & Gaballah 1993, pp.108, 117.

'smaller scale versions . . . a king's pyramid', Lehner 1997, p.154.

'legitimated his ascent to the throne', Bauer in Verner 2001, p.332.

'an independent reign', Roth 1999, pp.45; also Roehrig ed. 2005, p.12.

10. Clouds Across the Sun

'the priesthood of Ra declined in status', Kanawati 1990, p.55.

'striking the ball in . . . Apis bull', Pyramid Texts Spell 254, Faulkner 1969, p.63.

'Unas opens his . . . dispatches', Pyramid Texts Spell 309, based on Lichtheim 1975, p.39.

'Unas eats men. . . . their power is in him', Spell 273-4, based on Lichtheim 1975, pp.37-8.

'sky rains, stars darken . . . feeds on his mothers!', Spell 273, Lichtheim 1975, p.36.

'O Nut, take his hand. . . . lift him up!', Spell 253, Lichtheim 1975, p.33.

'I brought granite . . . his majesty praised me for this!', Verner 2001, p.338.

'Butcher of the King's Repast', McFarlane 2000, p.15.

'finest perfume for festive-times', Hart 1991, p.177.

'my entrails are washed by Anubis', Spell 509, Faulkner 1969, p.184.

'Imsety, Hapy, Duamutef and Qebsenuef', Spell 359, Faulkner 1969, p.116.

'O king, this body . . . stars when they live', Spell 723, Faulkner 1969, p.311.

'How fine you look. . . . and rejuvenated', Spell 153, Allen 2005, p.39.

'first-class cedar oil', 'first-class Libyan oil', Allen 2005, p.22.

'Ho, Unas! You have not. . . . gone away alive', Spell 146, Allen 2005, p.31.

'Spirit – to the sky! Corpse, to the earth!', Spell 210, Allen 2005, p.57.

'Teti, beloved of Hathor', MMA.26.7.1450, Hayes 1958 I, fig.76, p.126.

'it is the king who is the shaker . . . the chantress', Pyramid Texts Spell 506, Troy 1986, p.58.

'the king comes to dance, he comes to sing', Lichtheim 1980, p.107.

'jumping the goose' (literally *Katta al wizza*), Lauer 1976, p.60.

'stand up', Troy 1986, p.92.

'to beget', Troy 1986, p.93.

'a large woman. . . . time of her death', Hart 1991, p.206.

'a short, wide head and jutting jaw', Hart 1991, p.210.

'making it pleasant', Nunn 1996, p.133.

'hold him fast, don't let him faint', Kanawati 1997, p.72; Nunn 1996, p.170.

'Hold it fast. . . . ox is powerful!', based on Kanawati 1997, p.70.

'the transmission . . . the deceased', Sanchez & Tismenetsky 2008; Gordon & Schwabe 2004.

'May it be well for you, descendant . . . like a bird', based on Kanawati 1997, p.67.

'Acquaintance', 'Guard', Kanawati 2001, pp.66-7, pl.20.

'cutting with a knife. . . . Merinebti died', Kanawati & Abder-Raziq 2001, pp.66–7, pl.22.b.

'murdered by his bodyguard', Manetho, Waddell 1940, p.53.

'secret charge', Kanawati 1990, p.63.

'when legal procedure. . . . any official of his', based on Breasted 1988 I, p.142.

'Pepi lives for her', Callender 2012.

'in love for the place. . . . great god, Khui', Cairo CG.1431, Breasted 1988 I, pp.157-9.

'unprepossessing ruins', Verner 2001, p.351.

'Memphis', Hayes 1958 I, p.126.

'may he celebrate very many', Hayes 1958 I, p.127.

'even if he was a little out of fashion', Gardiner 1964, p.93.

'the costly, splendid . . . pyramid of the queen', Breasted 1988 I, p.148.

'with her two faces', Spell 506, Faulkner 1969, p.181.

'How beautiful to look . . . to his mother Nut', Spell 261, based on Allen 2005, p.222.

'spells for entering the womb of Nut', Allen 2005, pp.211-5.

'began his reign at the age of six. . . . hundredth year', Manetho, Waddell, ed. 1940, p.55.

'who all the gods love', Breasted 1988 I, p.156.

'without the loss of a single sandal', Habachi 1984, fig.16, pp.40-1.

'You have said. . . . king personally', based on Wente 1990, pp.20-21.

'be brave and . . . home again', Tale of the Shipwrecked Sailor, Lichtheim 1975, p.213.

'with a love of the theatrical', Ray 2002, p.42.

'there was no wife', Parkinson 1995, p.73.

'going out at night. . . . he returned to his palace', Parkinson 1995, p.72.

'lavish burial places', Gillam 1995, p.225.

'villagization of a monument', Kemp 1991, pp.146-8.

'the commander of. . . are informed', based on Kees 1961, pp.167-8; Wente 1990, p.42.

'a year's food supply . . . by deceit', Hymn to Hapi, Lichtheim 1975, pp.207-8.

'take the hand. . . . Imperishable Stars', Spell 67, Allen 2005, p.246.

'the noblest and . . . the third pyramid', Manetho, Waddell, ed. 1940, p.55.

'braver than . . . cheeks', Armenian version of Eusebius' Manetho, Waddell, ed. 1940, p.57.

'her historical existence . . . be doubted', Gardiner 1964, p.102.

'son of Ptah', Ryholt 2000, p.88.

11. Anarchy in the Two Lands

'what shall. . . . mummies?', Admonitions of Ipuwer, Pap.Leiden 344, Lichtheim 1975, p.152.

'an abrupt, short-lived. . . .catastrophic effects', Hassan http://www.bbc.co.uk/history/ancient/egyptians/apocalypse_egypt_01.shtml

'the House of Horus. . . belonged there', Ankhtifi Autobiography, Lichtheim 1975, p.85.

'distorted vision of a die-hard aristocrat', Gardiner 1964, p.110.

'necklaces of precious . . . dressed in rags', Admonitions, based on Lichtheim 1975, p.152; as for its date, content 'clearly points to the period between Pepi II and the rise to power of the 11th dynasty', Redford 1992, p.66.

'no longer does . . . like maidservants', Admonitions, based on Lichtheim 1975, pp.152-3.

'those buried in tombs. . . . now empty', Admonitions, based on Lichtheim 1975, pp.153-6.

'the children of princes . . . laid bare', Admonitions, based on Lichtheim 1975, pp.152-6.

'is one of the most imperfectly. . . . Egyptian history', Robins ed. 1990, p.17.

'bread, beer, grain. . . . oil and honey', Bolton 56.98.36, Bourriau 1988, p.12.

'a citizen excellent in combat', MMA.25.2.3, Lichtheim 1976, p.84.

'foreign peoples. . . . livelihood of the Delta', Admonitions, Redford 1992, p.67.

'all is ruin . . . not have been born', Admonitions, based on Lichtheim 1975, pp.152-3.

'all of Upper Egypt . . . their children', Ankhtifi Autobiography, Shaw ed. 2000, p.129.

'everyone has. . . . eating his children', Abdel-Latif Al-Baghdadi, http://www.bbc.co.uk/history/ancient/egyptians/apocalypse_egypt_01.shtml

'behaving more cruelly . . . people of all Egypt', Manetho, Waddell ed. 1940, p.61.

'the democratisation of the afterlife', Shaw & Nicholson 1995, p.63.

'delusions of grandeur', Lichtheim 1975, p.131.

'had me instructed. . . . with the royal children', Breasted 1988 I, p.190.

'copy your ancestors . . . remembered', Instructions of Merikare, Lichtheim 1975, pp.97-109.

'I built a canal for . . . those close to me', Robins ed. 1990, p.34.

'who ruled in Asyut. . . . strong-armed', Breasted 1988 I, p.191.

'who acted with his arm. . . . whole troop', Berlin 24032, Lichtheim 1975, p.90.

'the chief shock troops. . . . Egyptian armies', Smith & Hall eds. 1983, p.83.

'Countess of the South', Kamrin 1999, p.126.

'How are you?. . . the sun has risen', based on Wente 1990, p.215.

'one donkey town', Ray 2001, p.26.

'nearly every Theban', Hayes 1958 I, p.280.

'the stars fall . . . raise themselves', Book of the Dead Spell 99.III, Faulkner 1985, p.95.

'Egypt fought in . . . god's path', Instructions of Merikara, based on Lichtheim 1975, p.102.

'all rejoice at Hathor's . . . times music!,' MMA.13.182.3, based on Lichtheim 1976, pp.94-5.

'Song in the tomb. . . . singer with the harp', Lichtheim 1945, p.192.

'O tomb! You were . . . founded for happiness!', Lichtheim 1975, p.194.

'King of Upper . . . taken his place', BM.EA.614, based on Lichtheim 1976, p.91.

'unpleasant freshness', Winlock 2007, p.1.

'storms of furious blows', Winlock 2007, p.17.

'established Lower Egypt . . . Nine Bows', Breasted 1988 I, p.204.

'clubbing the Eastern Lands . . . the Asiatics', Hayes 1958 I, p.154.

'Overseer of that. . . . which is not', Hayes 1958 I, p.165.

'overseer of sculptors. . . . of metal', Bourriau 1988, p.10.

'I am indeed an artist . . . excellent in it,' Louvre C.14, Birch ed. 1878, p.2.

'the valley of Montuhotep', Pinch 1993, p.3.

'was also a womb. . . . Hathor of the West', Romer 1984, p.14.

'embedded in the. . . . entrance hall', Edwards 1965, p.21.

'Hathor who is under . . . retinue of Hathor', Coffin Texts Spell 710, Faulkner 1977, p.269.

'Festival of the Valley', Dorman & Bryan eds. 2007, p.7.

'I have united for . . . ancient spirits', MMA.07.230.2, Hayes 1958 I, p.158.

'the king appears. . . . most prominent figure', Bourriau 1988, p.17.

'Great Royal Wife', BM.EA.40855, Troy 1986, p.157.

'a living wind is the. . . . made to live', Nims 1965, p.138.

'my entrails are her necklace', Coffin Texts Spell 334, Faulkner 1973, p.259.

'dress' of Hathor, Coffin Texts VI.53, Troy 1986, p.46.

'dancing girls', Winlock 1942, p.74.

'the one who sweetens. . . . of her fragrance', Troy 1986, p.156.

'a little world of four thousand years ago', Winlock 1975, p.57.

'knocking his blow-fly to the ground', Coffin Texts Spell 766, Faulkner 1977, p.295.

'Do not putrefy . . . drip corruption', Coffin Texts Spell 756, Faulkner 1977, p.289.

'Hoe every field . . . miserable for you', P.Hekanakhte No.2, based on Ray 2001, p.34.

'now what's the idea. . . . going without!', P.Hekanakhte No.1, based on Wente 1999, p.59.

'whatever he wants. . . . he wants', P.Hekanakhte No.2, based on Ray 2001, p.35.

'greet my mother. . . . a million times', P.Hekanakhte No.1, Wente 1999, p.60.

'Do not keep her. . . . her servant!', P.Hekanakhte No.2, based on Wente 1999, p.62.

'a small window into a timeless world', Ray 2001, p.39.
'the wonder was repeated . . . the margin of the stone', Breasted 1988 I,
   p.216.

12. Classic Kingdom, Middle Kingdom

'a king will come . . . two powers', Verner 2001, pp.382-3; Tidyman 1995,
   p.105.
'his mother was probably of Nubian descent', Verner 2001, p.383.
'Seizer of the Two Lands', Tidyman 1995, p.103.
'decked in gold . . . bolts of bronze', Instructions of Amenemhat, Lichtheim
   1976, p.137.
'luxuries: a bathroom. . . . king in every room', Lichtheim 1975, p.233.
'wearing nappies', Pap. Berlin 3029, Parkinson 1991, p.41.
'apparently they. . . . no distinctive titles', Bell 1975, p.265.
'no ritual role and rarely appear', Robins 1987, p.16.
'the tomb being regarded. . . . rebirth takes place', Frandsen 2007, p.103.
'like Amenemhat I . . . kingship of the Old Kingdom', Janosi 2010, p.12.
'beloved of Hathor', Janosi 2010, p.12.
'Walls of the Ruler', Manley 1996, pp.45, 48; Redford 1992, p.80.
'fear of the king. . . . lands like Sekhmet', Lichtheim 1975, p.225.
'curbed lions . . . the dog walk', Instructions of Amenemhat, Redford 1992,
   p.74.
'repressed those of. . . . Medjai', Instructions of Amenemhat, Lichtheim
   1976, p.137.
'flew up to heaven. . . . and grieved', based on Lichtheim 1976, p.223.
'Listen to what . . . happy hour', BM.EA.10182, based on Lichtheim 1976,
   pp.136-8; Parkinson 1991, pp.49-52.
'the queen lives . . . kingship of the land', Lichtheim 1976, Troy 1986, p.157.
'I will construct a great . . . stretched the cord', Pap. Berlin 3029, Lichtheim
   1975, p.115.
'hastening by boat. . . . midst of his city', Petrie Museum UC.14786, Petrie
   1896, p.11.
'to reach the ends of the earth', Breasted 1988 I, p.519.
'the throat-slitter of Asia', Shaw ed. 2000, p.167.
'there is no bowman . . . upon a mountain?', Redford 1992, p.87.
'think of the day of burial. . . . and come home!', Lichtheim 1975, p.230.
'keeper of the dining hall', Ward 1989 pp.33-4.

'residing in the pyramid temple of Sesostris', Janosi 2010, p.12.
'would that I were always. . . . by the river', Parkinson 1991, pp.83-4.
'at the Residence people . . . strewn about the houses', Lichtheim 1975, p.208.
'the dispatch of the army . . . units of copper', Redford 1992, pp.78-9.
'massive immigration. . . . of the Egyptian state', Wendrich ed. 2010, p.157.
'beloved king's daughter of his body', Fay 1996, pp.30-32.
'almost light and laughing', Brooklyn Acc.No.56.85, Smith 1981, p.187.
'probably the largest. . . . worked in Egypt', Müller & Thiem 1999, p.110.
'Ruler of the Desert', Wheeler 1958, p.120; Manley 1986, p.48.
'years were removed . . . grease themselves in it', Lichtheim 1975, p.233.
'I'm grabbing. . . . fill with fear!', Beni Hasan tomb of Khety, Decker 1992, pp.75-6.
'Lady of the South and North', Troy 1986, p.158.
'mosquitoes have slain him', Lichtheim 1975, p.186.
'mouth of the canal', Müller & Thiem 1999, p.114.
'the beautiful girl. . . . temple of Sesostris', P.Berlin 10037, Wente 1990, p.77.
'The Marie Celeste of Ancient Egypt', http://www.museum.manchester. ac.uk/collection/ancientegypt/virtualkahun/
'prescription for a bull suffering from cold fever', UC.32036, Bourriau 1988, p.83.
'please let me find. . . . me come there', P.el-Lahun, Wente 1990, p.79.
'this is a communication. . . . the temple', Pap.Kahun III.3, based on Lesko 1997, pp.94-5.
'his wife whom he loves', 'his favourite', D'Auria et al. 1988, p.122.
'his favourite whom he loves', Boston MFA.1973.87, Boston 1987, p.16; Cairo JE.30965, Saleh & Sourouzian 1987, No.100.
'get me this bird', 'I'll do so and get it for you', Blackman 1953, pl.28.
'I have been roasting. . . . the beginning of time!', Houlihan 2001, p.36.
'embalmers of Anubis', Quirke 1992, p.32.
'of the forty-some known statues . . . tyrannical sovereign', Andreu et al. 1997, p.93.
'sinuous empire', Kozloff 2012, p.8.
'vile Kush', Gardiner 1964, p.135.
'dismissed to their desert. . . . safe and sound', Smithers 1945, pp.4-5.
'who shoots. . . . as does Sekhmet', Pap.Kahun, Lichtheim 1975, p.198.
'a Sekhmet. . . . trodden on his boundaries', Parkinson 1991, p.47.
'which glowered over the border', Manley 1996, p.50.
'who may rebel . . . on this entire earth', Gillam 2005, p.60.

'Hail to you, our Horus. . . . in his arms embrace', Lichtheim 1975, p.198.
'King Sesostris made this. . . . Montuhotep', MMA.24.2.1, Hayes 1958 I, p.182.
'with fine gold. . . . triumphant victory', Berlin stela 1204, Lichtheim 1975, p.124.
'their way of ensuring. . . . rituals of the town', Harvey 2001 http://archive. archaeology.org/online/features/abydos/abydos.html
'Neferhotep, deceased . . . the draughtsman Rensonb', Ward 1977, p.65.
'it is another small reminder. . . . anticipation of the next', Ward 1977, p.66.
'a vast catacomb of tombs', Lesko 1996, p.10.
'she was the king's main consort', Ben-Tor 2004, p.17.
'the sharp nasal sills. . . . Caucasoid person', Brier & Zimmerman 2000, p.24.
'been suddenly crushed. . . . the fall occurred', Englebach 1915, pp.11-13.

13. Proliferate, Disintegrate

'put the Fayum at the centre of his policy', Zecchi 2008, p.383.
'supreme pontiff', Cairo CG.395, Terrace & Fischer 1970, p.85.
'makes the land verdant. . . . great Hapi', Cairo 20538, Lichtheim 1975, p.128.
'giving offerings. . . . may live like Ra', based on Farag & Iskander 1971, p.104.
'Bastet who guards. . . . who defy him', Cairo 20538, Lichtheim 1975, p.128.
'the wonderful things of Punt', Bard 2008, p.172.
'quasi-permanent basis', Callender 20000, p.168.
'Lady of the Turquoise', Wilkinson, R. 2000, p.239.
'May the eyes. . . . and be indestructible', based on Lehner 1997, p.180.
'Lady of the House', Hayes 1958 I, p.306; dated to Amenemhat III in Quirke ed. 1991 p.17.
'our servant Imiu. . . . will simply fall apart!', based on Andreu et al. 1997, p.74.
'the desert is dying of hunger', Wendrich ed. 2010, p.152.
'a palace composed of as many. . . . regions', Strabo in Lehner 1997, p.183.
'half of which. . . . above them', Herodotus II.148, de Selincourt 1954, p.188.
'winding passageways', Strabo in Gardiner 1964, p.140.
'the Labyrinth', Herodotus II.148, de Selincourt 1954, p.188.
'an immense cluster . . . above and below ground', Lepsius in Bell 1975, p.226.

'a technical marvel and completely innovatory', Lehner 1997, p.182.

'Assembling a family. . . . million times right!', Spells 136 & 146, Faulkner 1973, pp.116, 123.

'this water used to reach. . . . inundation months', Farag & Iskander 1971, p.109.

'Spell for becoming the Nile', Coffin Texts Spell 317, Faulkner 1973, p.240.

'I am the Nile god. . . . grow weary', Coffin Texts Spell 321, Faulkner 1973, p.249.

'Breathing air among the waters', Coffin Texts Spell 373, Faulkner 1977, p.9.

'nine years, three. . . . twenty-seven days', Turin Canon, Gardiner 1964, p.140.

'in spite of a lack of evidence . . . prosperity and prestige', Bell 1975, p.262.

'a usurper', Gardiner 1964, p.183.

'the Horus, She who is beloved. . . . Sobeknefru', Capel & Markoe eds. 1996, p.29.

'commemorative rather than actual', Troy 1986, p.140.

'marks the end of the dynasty. . . . Middle Kingdom', Hayes 1958 I, p.196.

'so abnormal. . . . the seeds of disaster', Gardiner 1964, p.141.

'descendants of Amenemhet. . . . predecessors by minor wives', Bell 1975, p.260.

'a mass of documentation. . . . pitifully small', Bourriau 1988, p.53.

'circulating succession', Quirke ed. 1991, pp.123, 138.

'the washerman Hepet', Cairo Museum No.20281, Parkinson 1991, p.128.

'Semitic king', Gardiner 1964, p.153.

'on the outside and on the inside', Louvre C.12, O'Connor 2009, p.88.

'the Asiatic', Bell 1975, p.260, although others now question this translation.

'Chamber of Ancestors', BM.EA.69497, Reeves 1986, pp.165-7.

'the Department of. . . . House of the Nurses', Gardiner 1964, p.152.

'Nose, or possibly Nosy', Louvre C.8, Macadam 1951, p.22.

'dear Mother', Macadam 1951, p.25.

'lack of titles probably. . . . they were parvenus', Macadam 1951, p.27.

'physically creating a three. . . . might give birth', Wendrich ed. 2010, p.130.

'to fetch Horus of Hierakonpolis . . . the king', MMA.35.7.55, based on Hayes 1958 I, p.347.

'Jonathan', Hayes 1958 I, p.342.

'the earliest and largest. . . . Africa outside Egypt', Roehrig ed. 2005, p.49.
'predominantly Egyptian. . . . by African elements', Smith 1981, p.213.
'his majesty proceeded. . . . together with the workmen', Habachi 1974.a, p.210.
'slipped by stages from. . . . into poverty and disorder', Bell 1975 p.260.
'the Nubian', Shaw ed. 2000, p.190.

14. Divided and Conquered

'the first material proof. . . . c.1650–1600 BC', http://www.penn.museum/press-releases/1032-pharaoh-senebkay-discovery-josef-wegner.html
heka-hasut, Shaw ed. 2000, p.192.
'from the regions of the East. . . . striking a blow', Manetho in Waddell ed. 1940, p.79.
'the Asiatic', Bietak 1996, pp.41-2.
'the Biblical Joseph', Reeves 2000, p.225; also 'it was in their time that Joseph appears to have ruled in Egypt', Manetho, in Waddell ed. 1940, p.97.
'Principal of Foreign Lands and Caravan Leader', Bietak 1996, p.26.
'keeping alive the embers of Egyptian independence', Hayes in Bell 1975, p.262.
'Kush came, having stirred. . . . the blast of her flame', Roehrig ed. 2003, p.50.
'Son of Ra', Shaw ed. 2000, p.193.
'the accurate reckoning. . . . all secrets', BM.EA.10057-8, MacGregor 2012, p.92.
'reads faithfully. . . . Thoth himself', Redford 1992, p.122.
'beloved of Seth, Lord of Avaris', Shaw ed. 2000, p.190.
'made Seth his personal lord', Gardiner 1964, p.163.
'young heroes', Shaw 1991, p.41.
'pectorals and jewellery of gold', Wente 1982, p.22.
'sacred relic', Wente 1990, pp.25-6.
'the only major monument. . . . Seventeenth Dynasty', Darnell, J. 2002, p.132.
'considered to be an. . . . of the Abydene cemetery', Darnell, J. 2002, p.132.
'represented an elevation . . . a private person', Johnson 1993, p.231.
'the bearer of the vital "*ka*" force', Lehner 1997, p.191.

'ceremonial execution at. . . . Theban defeat', Shaw 2009, p.45.

'typical dimensions. . . . correct date', Shaw & Nicholson 1995, p.260.

'foul, oily smell', Harris & Weeks 1973, p.123.

'of extraordinary size and robustness', Bietak 2012, p.33.

'Give praise to . . . defy her', Cairo CG.34001 based on Troy 1986, p.135; Janosi 1992, p.99.

'military valour', Andrews 1990, pp.181, 183.

'both ceremonial and functional', Janosi 1992, p.102.

'Aegean in form and technique', Cairo JE.4666, Müller & Thiem 1999, p.140.

'the Brave', Shaw ed. 2000, p.211.

'I would like. . . . smite the Asiatic', based on Forbes & Garner 1982, p.10; Manley 1996, pp.52, 55.

'King's Son of Kush', Morkot 1987, p.30.

'spy his women . . . He is swift!' based on Gardiner 1964, p.167; Forbes & Garner 1982, p.11.

'Look at me . . . thing in Avaris!', based on Gardiner 1964, p.167; Forbes & Garner 1982, p.11.

'Amun grants the scimitar. . . . son of Amun', based on Forbes & Garner 1982, p.12.

'have everything My. . . . forever and ever', based on Forbes & Garner 1982, p.12.

15. Dawn of the Golden Age

'Lady of the Two Lands', Troy 1986, p.162.

'she was heir with. . . . father Seqenre's holdings', Bryan 2003, p.3.

'desires to build . . . the sacred land', Cairo JE.36335, Breasted 1988 II, p.15.

'superhuman Ahmose', O'Connor 2009, p.108.

'mass exodus', Shaw ed. 2000, p.214.

'departure of the tribe. . . . to Jerusalem', Manetho in Waddell ed. 1940, p.101.

'when his majesty had. . . . slaughter among them', based on Lichtheim 1976, p.13.

'Perunefer', Bietak 2005.b, p.17.

'God's Wife of Amen', Troy 1986, p.113.

'the Hand of God', Troy 1986, p.162.

'sweet ointment', Lichtheim 1976, p.220.

'abundant layer', Smith 1912, p.16.

'the umbrella pine of Byblos', Nunn 1996, p.148.

'shall we get our rations. . . . she get her place?' McDowell 1999, pp.109-11.

'four solid days of drinking', McDowell 1999, p.96.

'Establish your place . . . . will be happy', based on Lichtheim 1976, pp.136-8.

'was the first. . . . the Valley of the Kings', Rose 2000, p.147.

'Ineni may have been called. . . . but most likely KV 39', Bradbury 1985, p.87.

'having spent a life . . . joined with the aten', Breasted 1988 II, p.20; for circle see Posener-Krieger & de Cénival 1968, pl.14; Redford 1976, p.47.

'the God's Wife has flown up to heaven', Shaw ed. 2000, p.229.

'a goddess of resurrection', Troy 1986, p.71.

'both colours of resurrection', Shaw ed. 2000, p.223.

'divine patroness of the Theban necropolis', Troy 1986, p.68.

'he who does her homage. . . . majesty shall die!', Breasted 1988 II, p.97.

'Egypt's greatest warrior king', Reeves 2001, p.32.

'furious like a leopard', Breasted 1988 II, p.34 also translated as 'panther'.

'his first arrow pierced. . . . in his fallen body', Breasted 1988 II, p.34.

'there is not a single . . . valleys', based on Breasted 1988 II, p.30; Wilkinson, T. 2010, p.225.

'that wretched Nubian. . . . majesty's ship', Breasted 1988 II, p.34; Lichtheim 1976, p.14.

'his Majesty commanded to dig . . . sailed upon it', Breasted 1988 II, p.32.

'probably of great spiritual . . . indigenous population', Roehrig ed. 2005, p.51.

'that reversed water . . . in going upstream', based on Breasted 1988 II, p.31.

'I have grown old. . . . in my tomb', based on Breasted 1988 II, p.35. Lichtheim 1976, p.14.

'a pleasure walk', Breasted 1988 II, p.321.

'no-one seeing, no-one hearing', Breasted 1988 II, p.43.

'vile Kush', Gardiner 1964, p.180.

'frail', Adams 1998, p.37.

'Daughter of Ra', 'Lady of the Two Lands', Troy 1986, p.162.

'Horus. . . . and Daughter of Ra', Capel & Markoe eds. 1996, p.29.

'images I have. . . . the ancestors', Berlin 2296 & Cairo CG.42114, Roehrig 2005, ed. p.117.

'decided that women. . . . kingly office', Manetho in Waddell ed. 1940, pp.37, 39.

'a wholly new departure. . . . flaunting a royal titulary', Gardiner 1964, pp.183, 184.

'the conventions of the court. . . . rule of a woman', Breasted 1912, p.269.

'this vain. . . . unscrupulous woman', Hayes 1958 II, p.82.

'wicked', 'detested stepmother', Hayes 1958 II, p.114.

'a resolute and self-controlled woman', Roehrig ed. 2005, p.171.

'Joan of Arc', Dorman 2001.

'will Hatshepsut become a feminist icon?' Ray 2001, p.59.

'genius and energy. . . . extraordinary woman', Edwards 1891, p.281.

'it is generally. . . . feminine pronouns', Dorman 2001, pp.5-6; also Hegazy 1999, p.4.

'King of Upper and Lower Egypt' and the following titles, Breasted 1988 II, p.99; Donohoe 1992, p.882.

'pharaoh', Wilkinson, T. 2010, p.231.

'when he shoots at a copper. . . . palms behind it', based on Nederhof 2006.

'at least one military expedition into Syria-Palestine', Roehrig ed. 2005, p.261.

'barren of any military. . . . unimportant raid into Nubia', Gardiner 1964, p.189.

'slaughter was made. . . . strong arm', Redford 1992, p.151; Habachi 1957, pp.99-104.

'She who will be a Conqueror. . . . against her enemies', based on Lesko 1996, p.17.

'father-tutor', Breasted 1988 II, p.152.

'I nurtured the king's. . . . of the king', Roehrig ed. 2005, p.116.

'Marine Style', BM.GR.1890.9-22.1, Collins 2008, p.39.

'many pieces of pumice', Bietak 2005, p.78, pl.34.

'for nine days. . . . face of their fellow', Ptolemaic text based on MacGillivray 2009 p.160.

'every good thing from the court', Forbes & Garner 1982, p.22.

'commanded me to plant . . . in Thebes', based on Wilkinson, A. 1998, pp.83, 86.

'watch out for your feet . . . load is very heavy!' Forbes & Garner 1982, p.23.

'Female Sun who shines like the Aten', Forbes & Garner 1982, p.24.

'the best of myrrh. . . . the whole land', Breasted 1988 II, p.113.

'medication', Moran 1992, p.316.

'when I call. . . . voice of the poor', Berlin Museum 20377, Lichtheim 1976, p.105.

'I-am-not-far-from-him', Roehrig ed. 2005, p.102.

'I did not sleep because of his temple', Lichtheim 1976, p.27.

NOTES ON SOURCES

'found her . . . desired with her', based on Breasted 1988 II, p.80; Manniche 1987.b, pp.59-60.

'Amensis', Manetho in Waddell ed. 1940, p.101.

'a monument for her mother. . . . drunkenness anew', Lilyquist 2012, p.21.

'sat in my palace. . . . of my maker', Habachi 1984, p.66.

'illuminating the. . . . like the Aten', Habachi 1984, p.63.

'Gathering of the Thrones', Kozloff & Bryan 1992, p.93.

'back up into the world . . . back at their pleasure', Wilkinson, C. 1983, p.98.

'her majesty praised. . . . of the palace', based on Breasted 1988 II, p.143.

'listen to the petitions . . . trusts in Hathor', BM.EA.1459, based on Pinch 1993, p.333.

'noble ladies. . . . a good husband', BM.EA.41645, based on Pinch 1994, pp.334-5.

'the Egyptianisation of the Kushite. . . . style tombs', Morkot 1987, p.33.

'the Valley of the Knife', Hegazy 1999, p.14.

'The temple of Hathor . . . been created', based on Lesko 1997, pp.101-2; Ray 2001, p.48.

'exaggerated. . . . merits of her predecessor', Gardiner 1964, p.188.

'can be accepted. . . . considerable confidence', Gardiner 1964, pp.188-9.

'all those who see . . . worthy of her father', Ray 2001, p.55; Breasted 1988 II, pp.132-4.

'there is no record. . . . before Hatshepsut', Shaw ed. 2000, p.239.

'preoccupation with. . . . project to rebuild Egypt', Redford 1992, p.151.

'be eternal like an undying star', Lichtheim 1976, p.28.

'I saw his person. . . . he reveals himself', Aldred 1988, p.239.

'this Napoleonic little man', Hayes in Terrace & Fischer 1970, p.105.

'though it had been many. . . . defy his majesty', based on Roehrig ed. 2005, p.261.

'the first campaign of force', Armant Stela, Roehrig ed. 2005, p.261.

'like a terrible lion', Breasted 1988 II, p.236.

'lay like fishes on the ground', Breasted 1988 II, p.184.

'the people hauled. . . . by their clothing', Breasted 1988 II, p.184.

'I recorded the victories . . . according to the facts', Breasted 1988 II, p.165.

'all his majesty did. . . . Amun to this very day', based on Breasted 1988 II, p.164.

'2,500 people. . . . 20,500 sheep', based on Breasted 1988 II, pp.187-8; Lichtheim 1976, p.34; Forbes & Garner 1982, p.28.

'suitable for wielding sun shades', Redford 1992, p.224.

'mercenaries, domestics. . . . artisan and builders', Roehrig ed. 2005, p.62.
'she shall have a share in my inheritance', based on Cumming 1984 II, p.87.
'given as a sign of favour . . . Djehuti', Louvre N.713, based on Müller & Thiem 1999, p.144.
'the great mace of King Tuthmosis', Pap.Harris, BM.EA.10060, Peet 1925, p.226.
'Look at me, Prince of Joppa . . . given him strength to wield it', Peet 1925, p.226.
'smite the forehead . . . fell stretched out before him', Peet 1925, p.226.
'like a herd of mountain goats', Breasted 1988 II, p.203.
'wretched Naharin', Breasted 1988 II, p.215.
'by shooting. . . . southern land of Taseti', Nederhof 2006; Williams 1936, p.551.
'there's perfume of. . . . Unguent of myrrh!', based on Manniche 1991, p.23.
'overseer of the wigmakers of Amen of Karnak', Manniche 1987.a, p.143.
'planted with every pleasant. . . . offerings every day', Breasted 1988 II, p.225.
'Chamber of Royal Ancestors', Louvre E.13481, Andreu et al. 1997, p.114.
'driven by concerns. . . . was securely enthroned', Roehrig ed. 2005, p.269.
'disposed of a legitimate . . . his son's succession', Roehrig ed. 2005, p.281.
'completing his lifetime. . . . and joining the sun', Breasted 1988 II, p.234.
'Keeper of the Royal Stables', Nerlich et al. 2011, p.22.
'found it like heaven in its interior', Parkinson 1991, p.147.
'the baking of cakes. . . . safely and well', Breasted 1988 II, p.290; Manniche 1989, p.43.
'Put Myrrh upon the hair of Maat', Fletcher 2000, p.66.
'royal insignia', Breasted 1988 II, p.295.
'a beautiful youth. . . . strong thighs', Lichtheim 1976, p.41.
'he loved his horses. . . . expert in the matter', Decker 1992, p.48.
'Draw your bow . . . force and strength!', Decker 1992, p.37.
'amusement before the whole land', Decker 1992, pp.40-41.
'a deed never done. . . . radiantly mighty', Decker 1992, p.38.
'at the forehead of his horses', Gardiner 1964, p.202.
'550 enemy charioteers. . . . musicians of princes', Gardiner 1964, p.202.
'with his own mace', Forbes & Garner 1982, p.37.
'his majesty came with his heart. . . . as locusts', Hall 1928, p.204.

'in order to cause to be seen. . . . for ever and ever', Gardiner 1964, p.200.
'his majesty turned. . . . ends of the earth', Forbes & Garner 1982, p.35.
'by shooting arrows', Cumming 1982 I, p.30.
'who came to him. . . . notable event!', based on Redford 1992, p.164.
'sitting drinking and making holiday', Cumming 1982 I, p.45.
'this is from the king. . . . are they?', based on Wente 1990, p.27; Cumming 1982 I, pp.45-6.

16. Zenith of the Sun

'drive about . . . and blessed Khafra', Decker 1992, p.48.
'lotus lake', Wilkinson, A. 1998, p.97.
'and built there. . . . period of its widening', Schiaparelli 1927, p.169; Hall 1928, p.204.
'the chariot . . . of his favour', Breasted 1988 II, p.316; Betrò 2014, p.21.
'Overseer of the Granaries. . . . of Amun', Brooklyn Acc.No.48.27, Fazzini et al. 1999, p.83.
'to tell you I am coming. . . . eating in bed!' P.Berlin 10463, based on James 1984, p.178.
'draw your bows. . . . lurk in the shadows', The Book of Amduat, based on Hornung 1990, p.144.
'a stripling like Horus', Breasted 1988 II, p.322.
'enjoying himself. . . . speaks with his son', based on Breasted 1988 II, p.323.
'observe me . . . your guide', based on Breasted 1988 II, pp.323-4; Zivie-Coche 2002, p.49.
'folk tale', Breasted 1988 II, p.321.
'royal legitimator', Shaw ed. 2000, p.255.
'men shouted. . . . women danced', based on Forbes & Garner 1982, p.39.
'like Sekhmet', Breasted 1988 II, p.329.
'this obelisk had spent. . . . grandson and protector', Breasted 1988 II, p.330.
'repeated requests', Gardiner 1964, p.208.
'child of the royal nursery', Reeves & Wilkinson 1996, p.179.
'the falcon has flown . . . arisen in his place', Kozloff 2012, p.51.
'all their mysteries . . . counsel from them', Cairo CG.583, based on Breasted 1988 II, p.374.

'to see the very. . . . Horus Snefru', Petrie 1892, p.41.

'the richest man on earth', Kozloff 2012, p.1.

'Menwy', 'monument man', Kozloff 2012, p.61.

'the Great Royal Wife . . . name is Tuya', based on Breasted 988 II, p.345.

'with a high immigrant population', Kozloff 2012, p.103.

'Chief of Min's Entertainers', 'singer of Hathor', Kozloff & Bryan 1992, p.42.

'she is in the company. . . . company of Ra', Troy 1986, pp.57, 166.

'Great of Fearsomeness', Troy 1986, p.166.

'the One who fills the palace with love', Troy 1986, p.166.

'She of the Beautiful Hair', Fletcher 2004, p.236.

'victorious archer', 'a star . . . his horse', Breasted 1988 II, pp.365-6.

'Ikheny the Boaster', Kozloff & Bryan 1992, p.38.

'went forth like Horus. . . . upon the other', Breasted 1988 II, p.336.

'I saw him fighting. . . . the battlefield', Breasted 1988 II, p.376.

'Lord of Nubia', Morkot 1987, p.35.

'guardian sphinx', Kozloff & Bryan 1992, p.443.

'carnage', Goedicke 1992, p.44.

'the king appointed me . . . in their places', Cairo CG.44862, based on Galán 2000.

'you people of Upper . . . words to Amun', Cairo JE.44861, Terrace & Fischer 1970, p.117.

'it pleased his majesty's. . . . Two Lands', Cairo JE.34025, Lichtheim 1976, p.44.

'overseer of all works', Cairo CG.42037, Kozloff & Bryan 1992, p.251.

'I did not imitate. . . . done before', Breasted 1988 II, p.375.

'the image of Ra. . . . like the sun disc', Kozloff & Bryan 1992, p.100.

'worked with gold. . . . with real lapis lazuli', based on Lichtheim 1976, p.46.

'kiss him . . . more than anything!' Davies 1992, p.30.

'his transformations visible to all', Kemp 1991, p.208.

'sovereignty was perceived. . . . mountain goddess', Donohoe 1992, p.882.

'rows of small. . . . palace attendants', Hayes 1951 pp.35-6.

'the place where things are picked up', Hayes 1958 II, p.245.

'book of the sycamore tree and moringa tree', BM.EA.22878, Davies 1992, p.54.

'book of the pomegranate tree', Yale Art Gallery 1936.100, Kozloff & Bryan 1992, p.399.

'planted with all flowers', Breasted 1988 II, pp.358, 377.

'Syrian settlements. . . . the princes', based on Lichtheim 1976, p.44.

'House of Idols', Kelder 2009, pp.346-7.

'So speaks Nibmuarea. . . . your brother', BM.EA.29784: EA.1, based on Moran 1992, p.1.

'Nimmuaria', Gardiner 1961, p.208; also 'Nimudria', Hawkins 2009, p.74.

'here you are asking. . . . donkey herder!', BM.EA.29784: EA.1, based on Moran 1992, p.1.

'gold is like dust. . . . gathers it up', Cairo JE.12209: EA.16, based on Moran 1992, p.39.

'its a fine thing. . . . from your neighbours', BM.EA.29784: EA.1, based on Moran 1992, p.2.

'from time immemorial. . . . given to anyone', Berlin 1657: EA.4, Moran 1992, p.8.

'why not? You are a king. . . . daughter of a king?' Berlin 1657: EA.4, Moran 1992, p.9.

'overlaid with gold . . . some new quarters', BM.EA.29787: EA.5, Moran 1992, p.11.

'a marvel!' Breasted 1988 II, p.348.

'the image . . . desire', BM.EA.29791:EA.19 & Berlin 191: 20, based on Moran 1992, pp.44, 47.

'may our mistress. . . . remain friends', BM.EA.29793:EA.23, based on Moran 1992, pp.61-2.

'I am your servant. . . . god, my Sun!' BM.EA.29860: EA.187, based on Moran 1992, p.269.

'I am sending you. . . . is excellent', Brussels E.6753:EA.369, based on Moran 1992, p.366.

'the Much Sought-After One. . . . like a Leopard', Redford 2002, p.59.

'She who strikes with fury for the brilliant Aten', Manniche 1987.b, p.30.

'Miss Whiplash', Reeves 2001, p.61.

'strike fear in every foreign land', Kozloff 2012, p.138.

'beloved of Mut', Hayes 1958 II, p.255.

'the flame of Mut', Kozloff & Bryan 1992, p.325.

'united-with-Ptah' Morkot, 1990, pp.323-37.

'believed to have been. . . . the crocodile', Reeves 2000, p.211.

'a lake for. . . . town of Djarukha', Breasted 1988 II, p.349; Hayes 1958 II, p.233.

'the groundwater, happy in its lake', based on Lichtheim 1976, p.45.

'the largest sculptural programme in history', Wilkinson R. 2000, p.188.

'three dimensional . . . festival year', Shaw ed. 2000, p.267; Bryan 1997, pp.61, 65.

'the procession of the sky', Turin Inv.No.5484, Fletcher 2000, p.50.
'she who his majesty . . . months and days', Bryan 1997, p.60.
'beloved of the gods of the sky', Cairo JE.37525, Corteggiani 1986, p.99.
'sculptures endure, and life dies', Antony Gormley in McGregor 2012, p.109.
'I really nearly fainted. . . . the summer', Arthur Weigall in Hankey 2001, pp.56-7.
'siblings, women and offspring', Bickel & Paulin-Grothe 2014, p.24, in reference to KV.64.
'his majesty . . . such jubilee rites', based on Kemp 1991, p.216.
'the singers are chanting. . . . bless you!', based on Manniche 1991, p.61.
'reach out to . . . Hathor, lady of heaven', Fletcher 2004, p.233.
'dazzling in the horizon. . . . sun disc in the sky!' based on Wente 1982, p.24.
'my lord, my god, my Sun!', BM.EA.29860: EA.187, Moran 1992, p.269.
'pathetically fat old man', Hayes 1958 II, p.236.
'effeminate', Kozloff 2012, p.226.
'might easily be taken for a woman', Kozloff & Bryan 1992, p.213.
'beneficent mother of gods and men', BM.EA.826, Lichtheim 1976, p.87.
'the Great He-She', Hassan 1992, p.317.
'when you celebrated. . . . your festival' Cairo JE.12210: EA.3, based on Moran 1992, p.7.
'you for your part . . . we to laugh?' BM.EA.29784: EA.1, based on Moran 1992, p.3.
'when I heard that. . . . simply grieved', Berlin 271: EA.29, based on Moran 1992, p.94.
'so that when set . . . covering of skin', Smith 1912, p.49.
'a statue-like mummy', Fletcher 2004, pp.123, 253.

17. Reflected Glories

'when they told me . . . it was before', Berlin 271: EA.29, based on Moran 992, p.94.
'my husband always . . . cut them off!', BM.EA.29794: EA.26, based on Moran 1992, p.84.
'your mother knows . . . can tell you', Berlin 233: EA.27, based on Moran 1992, p.88.
'whose cult as a Theban . . . descendants Queen Tiy', Aldred 1988, p.261.

'Heiress', Davies 1908, p.28.
'the offerings for all . . . issued in full', based on Wente 1990, p.28.
'satisfying him as he rises at dawn', Fletcher 2004, p.261.
'one whom his Majesty himself instructed', Berlin Inv.no.1/63, Fay 1984, p.78.
'actually originals . . . early in his reign', Kozloff 2012, p.141.
'it was worse . . . great-grandfather before him', based on Murnane 1995, p.78.
'did not belong. . . . to any other people', based on Murnane 1995, p.75.
'commemorative rather than actual', Troy 1986, p.140.
'nourished the flesh of the god', Zivie 2007, p.72.
'singers and musicians shout . . . of Akhetaten', based on Lichtheim 1976, p.91.
'in the service of the pharaoh's military', Kelder 2009, p.347.
'shall die by the axe of the king', Berlin 347: EA.162, Moran 1992, p.249.
'up in flames', BM.EA.29820: EA.53, Moran 1992, p.125.
'seized all the countries. . . . king of Mitanni', Cairo JE.12191: EA.75, Moran 1992, p.145.
'the tribute of Syria . . . Great Green Sea', Davies 1905, p.9.
'one shipment sent directly . . . greeting gift', Kelder 2009, pp.345, 347.
'there is plague in the land!', Berlin 151-1878:EA.11, Moran 1992, p.21.
'spell for the 'Asiatic . . . language of Crete', BM.EA.10059, Panagiotakopulu 2004, p.273.
'my lord, send archers. . . . for medication', BM.EA.29846: EA.269, Moran 1992, p.316.
'conditions were ripe. . . . epidemic disease', Panagiotakopulu 2004, p.273.
'Ankhkheperure Smenkhkare', Reeves 2001, p.177.
'the Emperor Hadrian. . . . Antinous', Newberry 1928, p.7.
'better gay than female', Girling 2003, p.34.
'go forth into the sky. . . . at daybreak', Murnane 1995, p.182.
'Praise to Amen. . . . hearts with joy!', based on Reeves 2001, p.164.
'the temples of. . . . destroyed', Cairo CG.34183, based on Gardiner 1964, pp.236-7.
'installed priests. . . . local officials', Cairo CG.34183, based on Reeves 2001, p.183.
'hearts full of joy . . . things have happened', Cairo CG.34183, based on Reeves 2001, p.183.

'Tutankhamen, who spent . . . images of the gods', Reeves 2001, p.183.
'it is joy when your hand is in hers', Lichtheim 1976, p.143.
'ta hemet nisu', Reeves 2001, p.176.
'My husband is dead . . . a husband', based on Reeves 2001, p.175; Lesko 1997, p.105.
'such a thing has never happened before in my life', based on Reeves 2001, p.175.
'Why did you say . . . king in Egypt!', based on Reeves 2001, p.175; Lesko 1997, p.105.
'two bucketsful', Carter 1927, p.87.
'the physiognomy. . . . its intended owner', Reeves 1990, p.109.
'had originally been a Nefertiti piece', Reeves 2014.
'as long as my life . . . monuments for the gods', Ray 2001, p.77.
'Amputated-Nose Town', Redford 2002, p.118.

18. Reigns of the Ramessides

'the man in the equivalent of the grey suit', Ray 2001, p.80.
'part of the famous boar's . . . Mycenaean elite', Kelder 2009, p.347 footnote 61.
'a child in his embrace', Shaw ed. 2000, p.297.
'a pseudo-sarcophagus. . . . waters of creation', Wilkinson, R. 2000, p.148.
'manly dignity', Smith 1912, p.57.
'brilliant at. . . . ball of gas', Ray 2001, p.78.
'Ramses' monuments . . . and perfection', Shaw ed. 2000, p.301.
'he is, when all is said. . . . cheap and nasty', Ray 2001, p.79.
'good art is not unknown . . . court were still active', Ray 2001, p.80.
'very beautiful', Kitchen 1985 p.148.
'to take a stroll. . . . enjoy himself', Kitchen 1985, p.148.
'my heart is sick. . . . ever they entered', Lauer 1976, p.90.
'the most important . . . base in the country', Shaw ed. 2000, p.300.
'beauteous of balconies . . . lapis and turquoise', Kitchen 1985, p.120.
'Mut-is-content', 'Victory-in-Thebes', Lichtheim 1976, p.72.
'with his own hand', Decker 1992, p.50.
'does not let himself . . . made of straw', Abu Simbel inscriptions, Andreu et al. 1997, p.145.
'with him on his horses, her hand is with him', Lichtheim 1976, p.70.
'Forward! I am with you!', Manley 1996, p.92.

'forced to fling. . . . like crocodiles', Abu Simbel inscriptions, Andreu et al. 1997, p.145.

'to my sister Puduhepa. . . . robe for the king', based on Kitchen 1985, p.80.

'Fifty is she . . . her to have children', Kitchen 1985, p.92.

'that you my brother. . . . nor honourable!' Kitchen 1985, p.84.

'a very goddess', 'loved more than anything', Kitchen 1985, p.88.

'for striking the heads . . . Montupahapy', Geneva Pap. MAH.15247, McDowell 1999, p.186.

'I will kill him in the night', Romer 1984, p.64.

'you sent me a message and I came', Wente 1990, p.154.

'I am faring downstream to Memphis', Lesko 1994, p.54.

'please weave me. . . . my backside', O DeM.132, based on McDowell 1999, p.41.

'bands of the behinds', Hall & Janssen 1985, p.23.

'you restore her. . . . like this til dawn', based on Iversen 1979, pp.78-9.

'Tashery from the music room', Iversen 1979, p.88.

'united with the king', Morkot 1986, p.2.

'a rare astronomical and engineering phenomenon', Ahmed Saleh, http://www.sis.gov.eg/En/Templates/Articles/tmpArticles.aspx?ArtID=66857

'for whose sake the very sun does shine', Kitchen 1985, p.99.

'continued to flourish . . . the king's ego', Ray 2001, p.80.

'O gods, behold, I am a scribe!', Chapter 94, Book of the Dead, McDonald 1996, p.76.

'multi-storey car park', Ray 2001, p.93.

'a very learned scribe . . . monuments and books', Pap.Cairo 30646, Lichtheim 1980, p.127.

'the first Egyptologist', Ray 2002, p.82.

'because he loved . . . fallen into ruin', Ray 2001, p.87.

'the biggest museum labels in all history!', Kitchen 1985, p.107.

'Prince Khamwese delighted. . . . excellence of all they made', Ray 2001, p.88.

'king of every sacred animal', Ray 2001, p.88.

'Oh you, who shall enter . . . Khamwese!', based on Kitchen 1985, p.106; Ray 2001, p.90.

'all who roamed have been subdued', Cairo JE.31408, Lichtheim 1976, p.74.

'is laid waste, its seed is no more', Cairo JE.31408, Saleh & Sourouzian 1987, No.212.

'almost all the material. . . . own funerary temple', Saleh & Sourouzian 1987, No.212.

'I have come so I may . . . your heart might live', based on Hayes 1935, pp.57–60.

'a pleasant odour, like Friar's balsam', Smith 1912, p.66.

'the enemy', Shaw ed. 2000, p.303.

'the chief of police came. . . . arisen in his place', Reeves & Wilkinson 1996, p.152.

'established the king. . . . throne of his father', Gardiner 1964, p.277.

'great enemy Bay', Callender 2006, p.54.

'in whose time Troy was taken', Manetho in Waddell, ed. 1940, pp.148–53.

'set in order. . . . the Two Lands', Great Harris Papyrus, Breasted 1988 IV, pp.198–9.

'suddenly these peoples. . . . and other lands', Shaw 1991, p.62.

'their intentions were "Action!". . . . and perversion', Manley 1996, p.96.

'their plans were crushed. . . . by the wish of god', Manley 1996, p.96.

'I overthrew those . . . who do not exist', Pap. Harris I, Sandars 1985, p.133.

'I caused to sit idle. . . . along the road', Gardiner 1964, p.293.

'I planted olive groves . . . holy dwelling', Pap. Harris I, Kelder 2009, p.344.

'slit wide open on the ground', Redford 2002, p.99.

'hands – 12,659; foreskins – 12,859', Redford 2002, p.27.

'my lord the pharaoh is with me and against you!', Decker 1992, p.81.

'plotting those . . . making rebellion', Judicial Pap.5:7, Redford 2002, p.8.

'of their own accord', Gardiner 1964, p.290.

'the hawk has flown to heaven', Redford 2002, p.105.

'the burial of the coffin took place', McDowell 1999, p.225.

'we are hungry', 'great oaths', Romer 1984, p.119.

'to select a spot for cutting out the royal tomb', Donker van Heel 2012, p.167.

'You made me see darkness . . . in your grace!', BM.EA.374, Parkinson 1999, p.72.

'strength to my limbs', Redford 2002, p.137.

'superintendant of all works', Gardiner 1964, p.295.

'indicating that the temple. . . . for their wages', Shaw ed. 2000, p.307.

'chief taxing master', Gardiner 1964, p.297.

'the chief of police . . . because of the enemy', Turin Pap. Cat.2044, McDowell 1999, p.228.

'painted an earthy red colour', Smith 1912, p.91.

'highly suggestive of smallpox', Smith 1912, p.91.

'the fact that he died from smallpox', Gardiner 1964, p.298.

'the god Ra is given greater prominence', Reeves & Wilkinson 1996, p.164.
'what's this about . . . complain to me again!', based on Lesko 1997, p.97.
'the history of this confusing. . . . being written', Reeves & Wilkinson, 1996, p.204.
'we are now living here in Medinet Habu . . . living in Thebes', Černy 1973, p.370.
'in exchange for barley . . . there was a famine', Peet 1930, p.153.
'the war of the high priest', Gardiner 1964, p.301.
'Pharaoh? Of whom is he the master these days', Forman & Quirke 1996, p.138.
'have these two . . . of you, every day!', Pap. Berlin 10489, based on Ridealgh 2011, p.127.
'go and perform for me. . . . of the ancestors', Reeves & Wilkinson 1996, p.205.
'please have the men . . . the scribe Butehamen', Cerny 1973, p.370.
'Opener of the Gates of the Necropolis', Reeves & Wilkinson 1996, p.205.
'on this day the high priest. . . . for eternity', based on Donker van Heel 2012, p.161.

19. Decline, Rise and Fall

'a notorious dark age', Manley 1996, p.106.
'an influential figure of unknown origin', Shaw ed. 2000, p.331.
'the pillars which Amen. . . . north of his land', Shaw ed. 2000, p.333.
'which had driven the Amarna. . . . become a reality', Reeves 2001, p.191.
'I am not your servant. . . . who sent you!', P.Moscow 120, Lichtheim 1976, p.226.
'Tutankhamen look like Woolworths', Romer in Reeves 2000, p.183.
'the striking object-lesson . . . and 20th dynasties', Smith 1912, p.95.
'that he was involved . . . earlier burials too', Reeves & Wilkinson 1996, p.205.
'the largest hearse in history', Mysliwiec 2000, p.37.
'a spontaneous demonstration of traditional grief', James 1988, p.158.
'long strings', Smith 1912, p.109.
'the Hebrew name . . . derived from Egypt', Barnett 1977, p.46.
'took all the treasures. . . . He took everything', 1 Kings 14: 25–6, Manley 1996, p.102.

'a landmark in the Theban necropolis', Donker van Heel 2012, p.27.

'by river, men and women . . . whole year', Herodotus II.58, in Manniche 1987.b, p.10.

'Sea of the Greeks', Lichtheim 1980, p.88.

'where the houses... sumptuous fashion', Odyssey IV.120–37, Rieu trans. pp.66–7.

'chantress of Amen', Bickel & Paulin-Grothe 2012, p.39.

'brother should not be jealous of brother', Shaw ed. 2000, p.337.

'Lady of the Two Lands. . . . mistress of crowns', Louvre N.500, Andreu et al. 1997, p.176.

'there were three pharaohs in Egypt', Kuhrt 1995, p.628.

'had sunk into confusion at this time', Chronicle of Prince Osorkon, Manley 1996, p.104.

'the water of Nile rose in this. . . . in the water', based on Bell 1975 p.244.

'King of Upper and Lower Egypt', Shaw ed. 2000, p.353.

'to all intents and purposes the equal of the king', Gardiner 1964, p.343.

'like a flood of water', Gardiner 1964, p.338.

'in the sacred pool . . . in Heliopolis', Cairo JE.48862, based on Lichtheim 1980, p.77.

'Greetings, O Horus. . . . the other bulls!', Cairo JE.48862, Manley 1996, p.106.

'this writing was copied. . . . beginning to end', BM.EA.498, Parkinson & Quirke 1995, p.75.

'a wondrous thing . . . everyone thanked the king', Bell 1975, p.243.

'I fought daily very bloody. . . . and burnt it down', Gardiner 1964, p.346.

'I clothed him . . . and gave it to him', Kuhrt 1995, p.634.

'made Thebes and Heliopolis . . . his armed might', Gardiner 1964, p.347.

'her majesty', Vatican No.158, Lichtheim 1980, p.38.

'Nokratj', Fabre 2005, p.61.

'a man of action from the start . . . that of his contemporaries', Redford 1992, p.447.

'had the sun. . . . northward of them', Herodotus IV.42, de Selincourt trans. p.284.

'voyages to Punt underline. . . . precious commodities', Wilkinson, T. 2011.

'when King Psammetichus. . . . wrote these words', based on Parkinson 1999, p.46.

'one waded in their blood as in water', Lichtheim 1980, p.85.

'almost too perfect execution', Mariette in Corteggiani 1987, p.159.

'transferred from its Theban. . . . Memphite area', Munro 2010, pp.201–24.

'pyramid-shaped tombs. . . . Theban necropolis', Kákosy 1989, p.158.

'reconstituted as his principal sanctuary', Ray 2001, p.18.

'it was the Egyptians . . . ceremonial meetings', Herodotus, II.60, de Selincourt translation, p.152.

'who were the ablest . . . in the world', Herodotus, II.160, de Selincourt trans. p.193–194.

'rose in his saddle . . . back to his master', Herodotus II.164, de Selincourt trans. p.196.

'fond of his joke . . . pursuits', Herodotus II.174, de Selincourt trans., p.198.

'excessive levity', 'unsuitable for a king', Herodotus II.173, de Selincourt trans. p.198.

'revealed that the deeply. . . . now their king', Herodotus II.172, de Selincourt trans. p.197.

'I reported the condition. . . . rebuild Abydos', Louvre A.93, Lichtheim 1980, pp.34-5.

'in a sense their kinsfolk', Plato, Timaeus 21.e, in Witt 1971, p.67.

'who grew fabulously rich. . . . king with soldiers', Kuhrt 1995, p.645.

'he had a low opinion of the gods', Herodotus II.175, de Selincourt trans. p.198.

'could finally claim . . . Palestine and the Levant', Manley 1996, p.123.

'using a rod and the shadow of the edifice', Kákosy 1989, p.155.

'the Egyptians . . . practices of mankind', Herodotus II.33, de Selincourt trans. p.142.

'attend market. . . . do the weaving', Herodotus II. 33, de Selincourt trans. p.142.

'before the storm broke', Shaw ed. 2000, p.382.

'a great, cloistered building of stone', Herodotus II.171, de Selincourt trans. pp.196-7.

'were able to penetrate . . . walls of Memphis', Collins 2008, p.199.

'Great Ruler of Egypt. . . . All Foreign Lands', Lichtheim 1980, p.37.

'treated with every . . . to be burnt', Herodotus III.16, de Selincourt trans. pp.209-10.

'king of every sacred animal', Ray 2001, p.88.

'the destruction of all. . . . Egyptian gods', Gardiner 1964, p.364.

'despite the brutality. . . . and respectful rulers of Egypt', Manley 1996, p.126.

'two of these holy. . . . recorded for his reign', Gardiner 1964, p.364.

'royal seal-bearer. . . . chief physician', Vatican No.158, Lichtheim 1980, p.37.

'true beloved king's friend. . . . Mesutira', Vatican No.158, Lichtheim 1980, p.38.

'the strong Upper Egyptian. . . . live forever!', Kuhrt 1995, p.668.

'sent an army against. . . . previous reign', Herodotus VII.7, de Selincourt trans. p.443.

'nobody caused . . . and loss than Inaros', Herodotus III.15, de Selincourt trans. p.209.

'frog pond', Plato, Phaedo 109.b, http://classics.mit.edu/Plato/phaedo. html

'the gift of the river', Griffiths 1966, pp.57–61.

'not long ago a goat. . . . most surprising event', Herodotus II.46, de Selincourt trans. p.148.

'Bull who copulates with fair ladies', Spell 420 in Faulkner 1977, p.68.

'large and very remarkable', Herodotus II.100, de Selincourt trans., pp.166.

'to find several women. . . . grant them sons', Andreu et al. 1997, p.201.

'I have seen this building. . . . to describe it', Herodotus II.148, de Selincourt 1954, p.188.

'athletic contests with all the usual events', Herodotus II.91, de Selincourt trans. p.162.

'when the historian Hekataios. . . . did to me', Herodotus II.143, de Selincourt trans. p.186.

'as far as Elephantine. . . . only from hearsay', Herodotus II.29, de Selincourt trans. p.139.

'she appointed him ruler. . . . destroyed all his enemies', Lichtheim 1980, p.87.

'Mighty Monarch guarding.... treason-hearted', Lichtheim 1980, pp.87-8.

'a legend in his own lifetime', Ray 2001, p.119.

'Artaxerxes, after. . . . of huge sums', Diodorus xvi.51, in Gardiner 1964, p.378.

'bearing many possessions and spoils', Diodorus xvi.51, in Gardiner 1964, p.378.

'nothing was in its former. . . . wall in the temple', based on Lichtheim 1980, pp.44-7.

'evidently an Egyptian', Myśliwiec 2000, p.177.

20: The Final Flourish

'thought about kingship. . . . the Egyptians', Witt 1971, p.50.

'until the first day. . . . of the Somme', Levi 1980, p.179.

'to match the greatest. . . . pyramids of Egypt', Hypomnemata in Andronicos 1988, p.229.

'in Egypt, it is not possible. . . . the priests', Plato, Politics 290d in Vasunia 2001, p.266.

'By order of Peukestas. . . . is that of a priest', Bowman 1986, p.57.

'an island called Pharos . . . mouth of the Nile', Odyssey IV, 354-5, Rieu trans. p.73.

'at once struck by . . . Egyptian Isis', Arrian III.2, de Selincourt trans. p.149.

'all his goods to Ptolemy', Alexander Romance, in Chugg 2004, p.52.

'entered a deep, terminal. . . . cerebral malaria', Chugg 2004, p.34.

'exotic spices and perfumes', Curtius 10.10.9 in Chugg 2004, p.16.

'was appointed to govern. . . . contiguous to Egypt', Arrian 156.F1,5 in Walbank 1981, p.100.

'proceeded to bury . . . rites in Memphis', Pausanias 1.6.3, Chugg 2004, p.46.

'this great governor . . . Egypt', Stela of the Satrap, Dunand & Zivie-Coche 2004, p.200.

'when Pharaoh was ruling. . . . since he was dead', Ray 2001, p.42.

'the Macedonians consider.... Lagus by Philip', Pausanias 1.6.2 in Chugg 2004, p.52.

'Ptolemy was a blood.... of Alexander', Curtius 9.8.22 in Chugg 2004, p.52.

'rational synthesis', Witt 1971, p.126.

'beloved of the great god', Redford 1986, p.121.

'the Hellenic divinity. . . . local cult best', Witt 1971, p.125.

'played the part of a shrewd . . . saving virtue', Welles 1962, p.294.

'who brought down from Memphis. . . . Alexander', Pausanias, in Chugg 2004, p.76.

'one to get her own way', Memnon of Heraclea in Thompson 1955, p.200.

'played the same role as kings . . . in Classical antiquity', Pomeroy 1984, pp.xviii-xix.

'has received . . . Lower Egypt', 'Mistress . . . Two Lands', Cairo CG.22181 in Brooklyn 1988, p.43.

'Arsinoe Philadelphos. . . . Lower Egypt', Brooklyn 1988, p.45.

'Daughter of Amen', 'Daughter of Ra', Troy 1986, p.178.

'modelled on the crown of Hatshepsut', Rowlandson ed. 1998, p.29.

'probably owed a good. . . . sister-wife Arsinoe II', Thompson 1973, p.3.

'reorganized the army. . . . the Syrian war', Thompson 1955, p.200.

'the 19th. . . . the elephant supply', P.Hib.110 in Ellis 1992, p.12.

'everything that the king. . . . wife desired', Cairo 22183, Brooklyn 1988, p.47.

'imported myrrh . . . the gods of Egypt', Simpson 2002 ed. 2002, p.91.

'suggesting technical. . . . fledgling Roman mint', Walker & Higgs 2001, p.15.

'so many chariots... wearing cloaks', Theocritus Idyll 15.G, Dunand & Zivie-Coche 2004, p.204.

'objects of amazement', Diodorus III.36.3 Oldfather trans. p.187.

'myrtle wreath', Whitehorne 2001, p.1.

'that is great', Posidippus AB.88, in Carney 2013, p.28.

'in their rich . . . shrines of the gods', Idyll 17, in Dunand & Zivie-Coche 2004, p.204.

'her statue be set. . . . benefit of all people', Cairo CG.22181 in Brooklyn 1988, p.43.

'resident goddess', Brooklyn 1988, p.45.

'Beloved of the Ram', Cairo CG.22181 in Brooklyn 1988, p.43.

'his majesty and . . . together with them', Cairo 22183, Brooklyn 1988, p.47.

'Mistress of the whole circuit of the solar disc', Troy 1986, p.196.

'citizen of the world', 'might well have . . . in mind', Getty 1996, p.4.

'from France. . . . to live the good life', Romer & Romer 1995, p.75.

'the New York of the ancient world', Walker & Higgs, 2001, p.36.

'the number of books . . . men's memories', Athenaeus, Deipnosophists.V.203, trans. pp.420-21.

'caused the philosophy . . . benefit of students', Sandys 1615, p.111.

'in the polyglot land. . . . the Muse's birdcage', Timon of Phlius in Getty 1996, p.19.

'Rules of the House', Davidson 1997, p.104.

'the most august. . . . and learning', Athenaeus, Deipnosophists XII.536, trans. p.425.

'of gold and . . . workmanship', Athenaeus, Deipnosophists V 195-7 trans. pp.386-93.

'Let's go to . . . someone who hasn't!', Theocritus Idyll 15.82-6 in Bowman 1986, p.217.

'everything in Egypt . . . painted scenery', Plutarch Aratus, 15.2 in Walbank 1979, p.182.

'a very dirty. . . . unseemly feast', Athenaeus, Deipnosophists, Wilkins & Hill 2006, p.104.

'this goddess ascended to heaven', Cairo 22183, de Ruiter 2010, p.139.

'they cry for your sister. . . . in black', Callimachus Iamb.16, in Carney 2013, p.104.

'black-robed queen', Witt 1971, p.147.

'cost far more. . . . sister Arsinoe', Pliny Nat.Hist.36.14, trans. Rackham et al. 1947–63, p.53.

'in the form of the . . . of Arsinoe', Athenaeus, Deipnosophists XI.497, trans. p.219.

'if you pray to her. . . . the ocean smooth', Poseidippus, Romer & Romer 1995, p.62.

'being dead had. . . . on Arsinoe's career', Carney 2013, p.106.

'the best there is. . . . as befits a king', Theocritus, Idylls 14.58–68, in Lewis 1986, p.11.

'Unlucky devil that.... those fellows', Athenaeus, Deipnosophists XII.536, trans. p.425.

'the equivalent of an Egyptian king', Tait 2003, p.7.

'her bravery and strength. . . . that of Bastet-Sekhmet', Troy 1986, p.179.

'Victory Song for your Horses', Callimachus in Clayman 2014, p.145.

'it cannot be done justice . . . whole world', Ammianus Marcellinus, in MacLeod 1995, p.71.

'constant concern . . . animals in the land', Canopus Decree, Rowlandson ed. 1998, p.31.

'as the ancestors. . . . ancient records', Edfu Building Texts, Watterson 1998, p.51.

'with roots firmly. . . . yet to be discovered', Watterson 1997, p.138.

'wedjat wedj ti. . . . sep en wenef', Watterson 1979, p.168.

'shatat her shemy. . . . ek shata', Watterson 1979, p.169.

'gereg', Goedicke 1999, p.43.

'I hold my harpoon. . . . against Horus', based on Wilson 1997, p.183.

'is the king who was . . . . speaking statue', Manetho in Waddell, ed. 1940, pp.113–7.

'strong protector.... mighty wall for Egypt', Hölbl 2001, p.80.

'a loose, voluptuous. . . . and pimp Oinanthe', Plutarch, Dryden trans. p.669.

'an eyewitness of the sickness of the realm', Plutarch in Walbank 1979, p.182.

'heroine of the battle of Raphia', Thompson 1973, p.26.

'taking presents. . renew their friendship', Livy 27.44.10 in Maehler 2003, p.203.

'New Dionysos', Hölbl 2001, p.171.

'carrying a timbrel. . . . part in the show', Plutarch, Dryden trans. p.669.

'worthy of the glory. . . . and construction', Diodorus 18.28 in Chugg 2004, p.81.

'inattentive and. . . . conspiracies', Polybius 5.34.4-10 in Walker and Higgs 2001, p.18.

'some bit. . . . who live in Egypt', Polybius XV.27, 29, 33 in Rowlandson ed. 1998, p.34.

'had them slain on the wood', BM.EA.24, Parkinson 1999, p.199.

'a god, the son of a god. . . . Isis and Osiris', Parkinson 1999, p.198.

'written on a stela . . . statue of the king', Parkinson 1999, p.200.

'sacred writing (hieroglyphs). . . and Greek writing', Parkinson 1999, p.200.

'Female Horus', Hölbl 2001, p.167.

'ill-favoured looks and boxers' noses', Whitehorne 2001, p.83.

'Pharaohs Kleopatra. . . . the manifest god', Whitehorne 2001, p.86.

'Don't hesitate. . . . little daughter', P.Münch III.57, Rowlandson ed. 1998, p.292.

'should always consider. . . . of their kingdom', Livy 45.13.7 in Maehler 2003, p.204.

'I dreamt as follows. . . . secure against the enemy', Ray 2001, p.149.

'the Queen bears a male child', Ray 2001, p.149.

'genealogical cobweb', Rice 1999, p.21.

'to celebrate the annual. . . . their children', Dunand & Zivie-Coche 2004, p.249.

'in his mother's arms', Justin 38.8.4, in Hölbl 2001, p.194.

'murdered many.... his brother', Athenaeus, Deipnosophists XII.549, trans. p.493.

'Malefactor', Athenaeus Deipnosophists XII.549, trans. p.493.

'with a belly... one's arms', Diodorus 33.28a in Thompson 1973, p.101.

'already the Alexandrians... taking a walk!', Diodorus 33.28a in Thompson 1973, p.101.

'the Two Horus', Hölbl 2001, p.195.

'veritable tigress', Thompson 1973, p.6.

'but then they would have not been Ptolemies', Skeat 1962, p.105.

'and whichever of her. . . . make co-regent', Maehler 1983, p.1.

'the Pharaohs Kleopatra and Ptolemy her son', Reymond 1973, p.57.

'to make ready . . . should be satisfied', Pap.Tebtunis 33 in Milne 1916, p.78.

'fed on grain. . . . visiting foreigners', Strabo in Lindsay 1963, p.10.

'we know of none. . . . his mother', Pausanias 1.9.1 in Rowlandson ed. 1998, p.35.

'Female Horus. . . . god and goddess', Whitehorne 2001, p.147.

'the Scarlet One', Green 1990, p.877.

'King Ptolemy who is also Alexander', Dunand & Zivie-Coche 2004, pp.209–10.

'when it came. . . . practiced them', Athenaeus Deipnosophists XII.550, trans. pp.495–7.

'Kokke's child', Strabo 17.797C in Whitehorne 2001, p.221.

'drank in the presence. . . . his forefathers', Reymond 1981, pp.132–33.

'extremely popular with the Alexandrians', Cicero in Whitehorne 2001, p.175.

'the greatest god . . . take courage. Farewell', Maehler 1983, p.2.

'two people living together', Rowlandson ed. 1998, p.319.

'not a man . . . and magician', Athenaeus, Deipnosophists V.206.d in Grant 1972, p.21.

'all Spartans. . . . distinguished Athenians', Athenaeus, Deipnosophists IV.184, trans. pp.314–5.

'Macedones in Aegyptios degenerarunt', Livy 38.17.11 in La'da 2003, p.169.

'appeared solemnly. . . . made his priest', BM.EA.886, based on Reymond 1981, p.148.

'it is me who placed. . . . Two-Lands for him', BM.EA.886, based on Reymond 1981, p.148.

'the king sailed southward. . . . and goddesses', BM.886, in Reymond 1981, pp.148–9.

'Our Lords and Greatest Gods', Grant 1972, p.22.

'the eyes of . . . friend of the King', BM.EA.147, in Lichtheim 1980, p.61.

'when King Ptolemy. . . . my visit to Egypt', Diodorus 1.83.8–9 in Whitehorne 2001, p.181.

'Cato neither went . . . into some confusion', Plutarch, Cato, Dryden trans. p.633.

'a thieving effeminate ballet boy in curlers', Cicero in Graves 1968, p.96.

'the home of all tricks and deceits', Cicero in Wyke 2002, p.211.

'Let it be done!', Pap.Berolinensis 25.239, Walker and Higgs eds. 2001, no.188, p.180.

'the virtuous scholar', el-Daly 2005, p.131.

'Pharaoh comes to dance . . . all he does', based on Lichtheim 1980, pp.107-9.

'Image of her Father', Tait 2003, p.4.

'did not so much. . . . a snake pit', Walker and Higgs eds. 2001, p.23.

'Female Horus . . . brilliant in counsel', Tait 2003, p.4.

'Upper Egyptian King. . . . the red crown', Troy 1986, p.179.

'appeared in public . . . goddess Isis', Plutarch, Life of Antony, Dryden trans. p.768.

'black raiment', Plutarch in Witt 1971, p.147.

'the Lady of the Two. . . . temple at Armant', Bucheum Stela 13, Tarn 1936, p.188.

'Armant and beautiful. . . . heard in heaven', Mond & Myers 1934 I, p.13.

'on pain of death', Pap.BGU.1730, in Skeat 1962, p.104.

'a woman of incomparable . . . was young', Cassius Dio, Roman History XLII. 34, Goudchaux 2001, p.211.

'bears a close . . . does not flatter her', Southern 2001, p.121.

'infinitely more beautiful. . . . coin portrait', Maehler 1983, p.8.

'perhaps the finest. . . . portrait sculpture', Maehler in Smith & Hall 1984, p.96.

'the nose of Cleopatra. . . . been altered', Blaise Pascal, in Brooklyn 1988, p.43.

'a narcissistic personality', Orland et. al. 1990, p.174.

'every woman's . . . man's wife', Suetonius, Caesar 52, Graves trans. p.32.

'combined Egypt and Rome in his lineage', Southern 2001, p.123.

'Embarking Caesar', Grimm 2003, p.48.

'of wonderful height. . . . remarkable' Plutarch, Antony, Dryden trans. p.775.

'the tomb which she. . . . the palace', Cassius Dio 51.8, Scott-Kilvert trans. p.69.

'high titles and rich presents', Suetonius, Caesar 52, Graves trans. p.32.

'placed a beautiful.... the goddess', Appian Civil Wars II.102 in Johansen 2003, p.75.

'an open acknowledgement. . . . daughter of a god', Walker and Higgs eds. 2001, p.277.

'word went round... good of Asia', Plutarch, Antony 26-7 in Rowlandson ed. 1998, p.39.

'members entertained... measure or belief', Plutarch, Antony 27, Dryden trans. p.757.

'so good that Maroitic . . . ageing it', Strabo Geography 17, 1.14 in Empereur 1997, p.217.

'the Sun', 'the Moon', Fletcher 2008, p.257.

'Rome, who had never. . . . a woman', Tarn in Cook et al. eds. 1934, p.111.

'let nobody consider . . . rather Serapis', Cassius Dio 50.27, Scott-Kilvert trans. p.54.

'Eiras, Kleopatra's hair-dressing . . . state-councillors', Plutarch, Antony, Dryden trans. p.770.

'lecherous prostitute . . . Jupiter', Propertius III.11, in Maehler 2003, pp.209-10.

'Egyptian wife . . . barking Anubis', Virgil, Aenid VIII.688–700, in Maehler 2003, p.208.

'no heroic battle. . . . few exchanges at sea', Southern 1998, p.137.

'the divine protectress of the country', Brooklyn 1988, p.52.

'most bold and. . . . the Arabian Gulf', Plutarch ,Antony, Dryden trans. p.773.

'Suicide Club', Forster 1982, p.29.

'was busied in. . . . venomous animals', Plutarch, Antony, Dryden trans. p.774.

'her gold, silver. . . . and cinnamon', Plutarch, Antony, Dryden trans. p.775.

'to help their rulers', Cassius Dio, Scott-Kilvert trans. p.68.

'gold and silver. . . . precious stones', BM.EA.188, in Reymond 1981, p.218.

'the sound of all. . . . bacchanals on its way', Plutarch, Antony Dryden trans. p.775.

'also shook her dress. . . . poisons hid in it', Plutarch, Antony, Dryden trans. p.776.

'to worship gods, not cattle', Cassius Dio 51.16, Scott-Kilvert trans. p.77.

'the sarcophagus. . . . at Alexandria', Suetonius, Augustus 18, Graves trans. pp.59–60.

'actually touched. . . . was broken off', Cassius Dio 51.16, Scott-Kilvert trans. p77.

'it is bad to. . . . many Caesars', Plutarch, Antony, in Grant 1972, p.229.

'what really took. . . . to no-one', Plutarch, Antony, Dryden trans. p.779.

'a profound natural sleep', Plutarch, Antony, Dryden trans. p.774.

'the mind soon begins. . . . of reptiles', Whitehorne 2001, p.192.

'kept in a vase. . . . seized her arm', Plutarch, Antony, Dryden trans. p.779.

'she carried poison. . . . wound her hair', Plutarch, Antony, Dryden trans. p.779; also Cassius Dio, 51.14, Scott-Kilvert trans. p.74.

'Kleopatra's hair-dressing girl', Plutarch, Antony, Dryden trans. p.770.

'made a small scratch. . . . enter the blood', Cassius Dio 51.14, Scott-Kilvert trans. p.75.

'was this well done. . . . so many kings', Plutarch, Antony, Dryden trans. p.779.

'Osiris is Yesterday. . . . know tomorrow', Chapter 17, Book of the Dead, Wente 1982, p.23.

Select Bibliography

Adams, B. 1992, Predynastic Figurine Fragment of Human Female from Qau, KMT 3 (1), pp.12-13

Adams, B. 1996, Elite Graves at Hierakonpolis, Aspects of Early Egypt (Spencer, J. ed.), London, pp.1-15

Adams, B. 1998, Egyptian Mummies, Aylesbury

Adams, B. 1999, Unprecedented Discoveries at Hierakonpolis, Egyptian Archaeology 15, pp.29-31

Adams, B. & Ciałowicz, K. 1997, Protodynastic Egypt, Aylesbury

Adams, W.Y. 1977, Nubia: Corridor to Africa, London

Aldred, C. 1963, Valley Tomb No.56 at Thebes, Journal of Egyptian Archaeology 49, pp.176-8

Aldred, C. 1971, Jewels of the Pharaohs: Egyptian Jewelry of the Dynastic Period, London

Aldred, C. 1973, Akhenaten and Nefertiti, London

Aldred, C. 1988, Akhenaten, King of Egypt, London

Aldrete, G., Bartell, S. & Aldrete, A. 2013, Reconstructing Ancient Linen Body Armor: Unraveling the Linothorax Mystery, Baltimore

Allen, J. 2005, The Ancient Egyptian Pyramid Texts, Atlanta

Allen, J. et al. 1994, Further Evidence for the Coregency of Amenhotep III and IV, Amarna Letters 3, pp. 26-31

Amélineau, E. 1904, Les nouvelles fouilles d'Abydos III (1897-1898), Paris

American University in Cairo, 1997, Description de l'Egypte: publiée par les ordres de Napoléon Bonaparte, Cairo

Andreu, G., Rutschowscaya, M. & Ziegler, C. 1997, Ancient Egypt at the Louvre, Paris

Andrews, C. 1990, Ancient Egyptian Jewellery, London

Andronikos, M. 1984, Vergina: the Royal Tombs and the Ancient City, Athens

Anthes, R. 1986, The Head of Queen Nofretete, Berlin

Antiquity 1927, News & Notes: The Tomb Of Queen Hetepheres, Antiquity 1 (2), pp.216-18

Appian, trans. White, H. 1913, Civil Wars III-IV, London

Arnold, D. 1991, Amenemhat I and the Early Twelfth Dynasty at Thebes, Metropolitan Museum Journal 26, pp.5-48

Arnold, D. 1999.a, When the Pyramids were Built: Egyptian Art of the Old Kingdom, New York

Arnold, D. 1999.b, Temples of the Last Pharaohs, London

Arnold, D. et al. 1996, The Royal Women of Amarna: Images of Beauty from Ancient Egypt, New York

Arrian, trans. de Selincourt, A., 1958, The Campaigns of Alexander, Harmondsworth

Arroyo, R. 2003, Egypt: Music in the Age of the Pyramids, Madrid

Ashton, S. 2003, The Last Queens of Egypt, London

Athenaeus (trans. Gulick, C.) 1928-33, The Deipnosophists II & V, London

Aufderheide, A. 2003, The Scientific Study of Mummies, Cambridge

Baadsgaard, A., Monge, J., Cox, S. & Zettler, R. 2012, Bludgeoned, Burned, and Beautified: Re-evaluating Mortuary Practices in the Royal Cemetery of Ur. Sacred killing: the archaeology of sacrifice in the ancient Near East (Porter, A. & Schwartz, G. Eds.), Winona Lake, pp.125-58

Bahn, P. 2014, Review: Wadi Sura – the Cave of Beasts: a rock art site in the Gilf Kebir (SW-Egypt), Antiquity 88 (340), pp.668-70

Baines, J. & Malek, J. 1980, Atlas of Ancient Egypt, Oxford

Bangs, R. & Scaturro, P. 2006, Mystery of the Nile: The Epic Story of the First Descent of the World's Deadliest River, New York

Bard, K. 1994, The Egyptian Predynastic: a review of the evidence, Journal of Field Archaeology 21(3), pp.265-88

Bard, K. 2007, Introduction to the Archaeology of Ancient Egypt, Malden

Barnett, R. 1977, Illustrations of Old Testament History, London

Bates, O. 1914, The Eastern Libyans, London

Baumgartel, E.J. 1955, The Cultures of Prehistoric Egypt, London

Baumgartel, E.J. 1970, Petrie's Naqada Excavation: a Supplement, London

Bell, B. 1970, The Oldest Records of the Nile Floods, The Geographical Journal 136 (4), pp.569-73

Bell, B. 1971, The Dark Ages in Ancient History I: The First Dark Age in Egypt, American Journal of Archaeology 75 (1), pp.1-26

Bell, B. 1975, Climate and the History of Egypt: the Middle Kingdom, American Journal of Archaeology 79 (3), pp.223-69

Bell, L. 1985, Luxor Temple and the Cult of the Royal Ka, Journal of Near Eastern Studies 44 (4), pp.251-94

Bell, M. 1985, Gurob Tomb 605 and Mycenaean chronology, Mélanges Gamal Eddin Mokhtar I, Cairo, pp.61–86

Bennet, C. 2005, Arsinoe and Berenice at the Olympics, Zeitschrift für Papyrologie und Epigraphik Bd. 154, pp.91–96

Benson, M. & Gourlay, J. 1899, The Temple of Mut in Asher, London

ten Berge, R. & van de Goot, F. 2002, Seqenenre Taa II, the violent death of a pharaoh, Journal of Clinical Pathology 55, p.232

Bergstrom, B. 1984, Reflections on the Association between the Sun-God and Divine Kingship in the 18th Dynasty, in Sundries in Honour of Torgny Säve-Söderbergh, Boreas 13, Uppsala, pp.33–42

Berman, L. ed. 1990, The Art of Amenhotep III, Cleveland

Betrò, M. 2014, Kenamen: l'undicesima mummia, Pisa

Bhardwaj, A. 2014, Walking the Nile, High Life (May), pp.36–42

Bianchi, R.S. ed. 1988, Cleopatra's Egypt: The Age of the Ptolemies, New York

Bianchi, R.S. 2003, Images of Cleopatra VII Reconsidered, Cleopatra Reassessed, British Museum Occasional Paper 103, (eds. Walker, S. & Ashton, S.), London, pp.13–23

Bickel, S. & Paulin-Grothe, E. 2012, The Valley of the Kings: two burials in KV.64, Egyptian Archaeology 41, pp.36–40

Bickel, S. & Paulin-Grothe, E. 2014, KV.40: a burial place for the royal entourage, Egyptian Archaeology 45, pp.21–4

Bierbrier, M. 1982, The Tomb-Builders of the Pharaohs, London

Bietak, M. 1996, Avaris, the Capital of the Hyksos: recent excavations at Tell Dab'a, London

Bietak, M. 2005, The Thutmose Stronghold of Perunefer, Egyptian Archaeology 26, pp.13–17

Bietak, M. 2012, The Archaeology of the 'Gold of Valour,' Egyptian Archaeology 42, p.32

Bietak, M. & Lange, E. 2014, Tell Basta: the palace of the Middle Kingdom, Egyptian Archaeology 44, pp.4–7

Bietak, M. & Strouhal, E. 1974, Die Todesumstände des Pharaos Seqenenre (17 Dynastie), Annalen des Naturhistorischen Museums Wien 78, pp.29–52

Bingen, J. 2007, Hellenistic Egypt: monarchy, society, economy, culture, Edinburgh

Birch, S. ed. 1878, Records of the Past being English Translations of the Assyrian and Egyptian Monuments: X: Egyptian Texts, London

Bjorkman, G. 1971, Kings at Karnak: a Study of the Treatment of the Monuments of Royal Predecessors in the Early New Kingdom, Uppsala

Blackman, A. 1953, The Rock Tombs of Meir VI, London

Blankenberg van Delden, C. 1969, The Large Commemorative Scarabs of Amenhotep III, Leiden

Bomann, A. & Young, R. 1994, Preliminary Survey in the Wadi Abu Had, Eastern Desert, 1992, Journal of Egyptian Archaeology 80, pp.23-44

Bosse-Griffiths, K. 2001, Amarna studies and Other Selected Papers, Freiburg

Boston, Museum of Fine Art 1988, Mummies and Magic: The Funerary Arts of Ancient Egypt, Boston

Bothmer, B. 1960, Egyptian Sculpture of the Late Period, 700 BC to AD 100, Brooklyn

Bothmer, B. 1970, A New Fragment of an Old Palette, Journal of the American Research Center in Egypt 8, pp.5-8

Bourriau, J. 1981, Pharaohs & Mortals: Egyptian Art in the Middle Kingdom, Cambridge

Bourriau, J. 1991, Patterns of change in burial customs during the Middle Kingdom, Middle Kingdom Studies (Quirke, S. ed.), New Malden, pp.3-20

Bowman, A. 1986, Egypt after the Pharaohs, 332 BC – AD 642, London

Breasted, J.H. 1988, Ancient Records of Egypt: Historical Documents from the Earliest Times to the Persian Conquest, I-IV, Chicago

Brewer, D., Redford, D. & Redford, S. 1994, Domestic Plants and Animals: the Egyptian Origins, Warminster

Brier, B. & Zimmerman, M. 2000, The Remains of Queen Weret, Chungara: Revista de Antropología Chilena 32 (1), pp.23-6

Brovarski, E., Doll, S. & Freed, R., eds. 1982, Egypt's Golden Age: the art of living in the New Kingdom, Boston

Brunton, G. 1937, Mostagedda and the Tasian culture: British Museum expeditions to Middle Egypt 1928-1929, London

Brunton, G. 1948, Matmar: British Museum expeditions to Middle Egypt, 1929–1931, London

Brunton, G. & Caton-Thompson, G. 1928, The Badarian Civilisation and Predynastic Remains near Badari, London

Bryan, B. 1984, Evidence for Female Literacy from Theban Tombs of the New Kingdom, Bulletin of the Egyptological Seminar 6, pp.17-32

Bryan, B. 1997, The Statue Program for the Mortuary Temple of Amenhotep III, in The Temple in Ancient Egypt: New Discoveries and Recent Research (ed. S. Quirke), London, pp.57-81

Bryan, B. 2003, Property and the God's Wives of Amen, Women and Property (Lyons, D. & Westbrook, R. eds.), Center of Hellenic Studies, Harvard University, Cambridge, pp.1–15.

Buckley, S. 2011, Revisiting the Amarna Royals: Part 2, Shemu: the Egyptian Society of South Africa, http://egyptiansociety.co.za/2012/04/revisiting-the-amarna-royals-part-2/

Buckley, S. & Evershed, R. 2001, The Organic Chemistry of Embalming Agents in Pharaonic and Graeco-Roman Mummies, Nature 413 (6858), pp.837-41

Buckley, S.A., Evershed, R. & Clarke, K. 2004, Complex Organic Chemical Balms of Pharaonic Animal Mummies, Nature 431, pp.294-9

Bunbury, J. 2012, The Mobile Nile, Egyptian Archaeology 41, p.15-17

Buonaventura, W. 1994, Serpent of the Nile: Women and Dance in the Arab World, London

Butzer, K. 1965, Physical conditions in Eastern Europe, Western Asia and Egypt before the period of agricultural and urban settlement, Cambridge

Callender, G. 1988, A Critical Examination of the Reign of Hatshepsut, Ancient History 18 (2), pp.86-102

Callender, G. 1990, Queen Hetepheres I, Bulletin of the Australian Center for Egyptology 1, pp.25-9

Callender, G. 1996, Problems in the Reign of Hatshepsut, KMT 6 (4), pp.16-27, 79-80

Callender, G. 1998, Materials for the Reign of Sebekneferu, Proceedings from the 7th Annual Conference of Egyptologists, ed. C. Eyre, Cambridge, pp.227-36

Callender, G. 2004, Queen Tausert and the End of Dynasty 19, Studien zur altägyptischen Kultur 32, pp.81-104

Callender, G. 2006, The Cripple, the Queen and the Man from the North, KMT 17 (1), pp.49-63

Callender, G. 2010, Queen Neit-ikrety/Nitokris, Abusir & Saqqara 2010 Vol. I (eds. Bárta, M., Coppens, F. & Krejci, J.), Prague, pp.246-60

Callender, G. 2012, Ankhnespepi II, The Encyclopedia of Ancient History, DOI: 10.1002/9781444338386.wbeah15422

Callimachus, trans. Trypanis, C.A. 1968, Callimachus: Fragments, London

Calverley, A. & Broome, M. 1933-58, The Temple of Sethos I at Abydos I-IV, London

Caminos, R. 1964, The Nitocris Adoption Stela, Journal of Egyptian Archaeology 50, pp.71-101

Capel, A. & Markoe, G. eds. 1996, Mistress of the House, Mistress of Heaven: Women in Ancient Egypt, New York

Carnarvon, Earl of & Carter, H. 1912, Five Years' Explorations at Thebes; A Record of Work Done 1907 –1911, New York

Carney, E. 2013, Arsinoe of Egypt and Macedon: a Royal Life, New York

Carter, H. 1917, A Tomb prepared for Queen Hatshepsuit and other recent discoveries at Thebes, Journal of Egyptian Archaeology 4, pp.106-18

Carter, H. 1927-33, The Tomb of Tutankhamen II-III, London

Carter, H. & Gardiner, A. 1917, The Tomb of Ramesses IV and the Turin Plan of a Royal Tomb, Journal of Egyptian Archaeology 4 (2-3), pp.130-58

Carter, H. & Mace, A. 1923, The Tomb of Tutankhamen I, London

Carter, H. & Newberry, P. 1904, The Tomb of Thoutmosis IV, London

Case, H. & Payne, J. 1962, Tomb 100: the Decorated Tomb at Hierakonpolis, Journal of Egyptian Archaeology 48, pp.5-18

Cassius Dio, trans. Scott-Kilvert, I. 1987, The Roman History: the Reign of Augustus, Harmondsworth

Černy, J. 1973, Community of Workmen at Thebes in the Ramesside Period, Cairo

Cesarani, F., Martina, M., Boano, R., Grilletto, R., D'Amicone, E., Venturi, C. & Gandini, G. 2008, Multidetector CT Study of Gallbladder Stones in a Wrapped Egyptian Mummy, Radiographics 29 (4), http://pubs.rsna.org/doi/full/10.1148/rg.294085246

Chaveau, M. 2000, Egypt in the Age of Cleopatra, Ithaca

Chaveau, M. 2002, Cleopatra: Beyond the Myth, Ithaca

Chugg, A.M. 2004, The Lost Tomb of Alexander the Great, London

Ciałowicz, K. 1985, Predynastic Graves with Weapons found in Egypt and Nubia, Fontes Archaeologici Posnanienses 34, pp.157-80

Ciałowicz, K. 2009, The Early Dynastic administrative-cultic centre at Tell el-Farkha, British Museum Studies in Ancient Egypt and Sudan 13, pp.83-123

Cicero, trans. M. Grant, 1960, Selected Works, Harmondsworth

Clayman, D. 2014, Berenice II and the Golden Age of the Ptolemies, New York

Cockburn, A., Cockburn, E. & Reyman, T.A. eds. 1998, Mummies, Disease and Ancient Cultures, Cambridge

Cohen, R. & Westbrook, R. eds. 2000, Amarna Diplomacy: the Beginnings of International Relations, Baltimore

Collins, P. 2008, From Egypt to Babylon: the International Age 1550-500 BC, London

Conrad, N. & Lehner, M. 2001, The 1988/1989 Excavation of Petrie's 'Workmen's Barracks' at Giza, Journal of the American Research Center in Egypt 38, pp.21-60

Cook, R. 1937, Amasis and the Greeks in Egypt, Journal of Hellenic Studies 57 (2), pp.227-37

Cook, S., Adcock, M. & Charlesworth, M. 1934, The Cambridge Ancient History X: the Augustan Empire, 44 BC-AD 70, Cambridge

Corteggiani, J.P. 1986, The Egypt of the Pharaohs at the Cairo Museum, London

Cotterel, A. 2004, Chariot: the Astounding Rise and Fall of the World's First War Machine, London

Cumming, B. 1982-84, Egyptian Historical Records of the later Eighteenth Dynasty I-III, Warminster

Curto, S. 1971, The Military Art of the Ancient Egyptians, Turin

Curto, S. & Mancini, M. 1968, News of Kha and Meryt, Journal of Egyptian Archaeology 54, pp.77-81

el-Daly, O. 2005, Egyptology: the Missing Millennium, London

Darnell, D. 2002, Gravel of the Desert and Broken Pots in the Road, Egypt and Nubia: Gifts of the Desert (Friedman, R. ed.), London, pp.156-77

Darnell, J. 1997, The Apotropaic Goddess in the Eye, Studien zur altägyptischen Kultur 24, pp.25-48

Darnell, J. 2002, Opening the Narrow Doors of the Desert: discoveries of the Theban Desert Road Survey, Egypt and Nubia: Gifts of the Desert (Friedman, R. ed.), London, pp.132-55

Darnell, J. C. & Manassa, C. 2007, Tutankhamen's Armies: Battle and Conquest during Ancient Egypt's Late 18th Dynasty, Hoboken

D'Auria, S., Lacovara, P. & Roehrig, C. 1988, Mummies and Magic: the Funerary Arts of Ancient Egypt, Boston

Davies, B. 1992, Egyptian Historical Records of the later Eighteenth Dynasty IV, Warminster

Davies, N. de G. 1903-08, The Rock Tombs of El-Amarna I-VI, London

Davies, N. de G. 1913, Five Theban Tombs, London

Davies, N. de G. 1939, Research in the Theban Necropolis: 1938-1939, The Metropolitan Museum of Art Bulletin 34 (12), pp.280-84

Davies, N. de G. 1943, The Tomb of Rekh-mi-Re' at Thebes I-II, New York

Davies, N.M. & Gardiner, A. 1915, The Tomb of Amenemhet, London

Davies, S., Smith, H. & Frazer, K. 2006, The Sacred Animal Necropolis at North Saqqara: the Mother of Apis and Baboon Catacombs, Archaeological Report, London

Davies, W. & Friedman, R. 1998, Egypt, London

Davis, T. 1904, The Tomb of Thoutmôsis IV, London

Davis, T. 1907, The Tomb of Iouiya and Touiyou, London

Davis, T. 1912, The Tombs of Harmhabi and Touatânkhamanou, London

Davis, T. 2001, The Tomb of Siptah with The Tomb of Queen Tiyi, London

Davis, W. 1992, Masking the Blow: the Scene of Representation in Late Prehistoric Egyptian Art, Berkeley

Dawson, D., Giles, S. & Ponsford, M. 2002, Horemkenesi: May he Live Forever! The Bristol Mummy Project, Bristol

Dawson, W.R. & Gray, P.H.K. 1968, Catalogue of Egyptian Antiquities in the British Museum I: Mummies and Human Remains, London

Dayagi-Mendels, M. 1989, Perfumes and Cosmetics in the Ancient World, Jerusalem

Decker, W. 1992, Sports and Games of Ancient Egypt, New Haven

Dee, M., Wengrow, D., Shortland, A., Stevenson, A., Brock, F., Flink, L. & Ramsey, C. 2013, An absolute chronology for early Egypt using radiocarbon dating and Bayesian statistical modelling, Proceedings of the Royal Society A. 469 (2159), pp.1-11

Delmas, A. & Casanova, M. 1990, The Lapis-lazuli Sources in the Ancient East, South Asian Archaeology 1987 (1), pp.493-505

Depuydt, L. 1995, Murder in Memphis: the Story of Cambyses's Mortal Wounding of the Apis Bull (C.23 BCE), Journal of Near Eastern Studies 54 (2), pp.119-26

Der Manuelian, P. & Loeben, C. 1993, From Daughter to Father the Recarved Egyptian Sarcophagus of Queen Hatshepsut and King Thutmose I, Journal of the Museum of Fine Arts, Boston 5, pp.24-61

Derry, D. 1942, Mummification II: methods practiced at different periods, Annales du Service des Antiquités de l'Egypte 41, pp.240-69

Desroches-Noblecourt, C. 1963, Tutankhamen: Life and Death of a Pharaoh, London

Desroches-Noblecourt, C. 1990, Le Message de la Grotte Sacrée, Les Dossiers d'Archéologie, 149-50, pp.4-21

DeVries, C. 1969, A Ritual Ball Game? Studies in Honour of J.A. Wilson, Studies in Ancient Oriental Civilisation 35, Chicago, pp.25-35

Diodorus Siculus, trans. Oldfather, C.H. 1933-47, Diodorus of Sicily I-III, London

Diodorus Siculus, trans. Geer, R.M. 1947-54, Diodorus of Sicily IX-X, London

Diodorus Siculus, trans. Walton, F.R. 1957, Diodorus of Sicily XI, London

Dixon, D. 1969, The Transplantation of Punt Incense Trees in Egypt, Journal of Egyptian Archaeology 55, pp.55-65

Donadoni, S. ed. 1997, The Egyptians, Chicago

Donohoe, V. 1992, The Goddess of the Theban mountain, Antiquity 66 (253), pp.871–85

Donker van Heel, K. 2012, Djekhy and Son: Doing Business in Ancient Egypt, Cairo

Dorman, P. 1988, The Monuments of Senenmut: Problems in Historical Methodology, London

Dorman, P. 2001, Hatshepsut: Wicked Stepmother or Joan of Arc? The Oriental Institute News and Notes 168, pp.1-6

Dorman, P. & Bryan, B. eds. 2007, Sacred Space and Sacred Function in Ancient Thebes, Chicago

Drews, R. 2000, Medinet Habu: Oxcarts, Ships, and Migration Theories, Journal of Near Eastern Studies 59 (3), pp.161-190

Drower, M.S. 1985, Flinders Petrie: a Life in Archaeology, London

Dunand, F. & Zivie-Coche, C. 2004, Gods and Men in Egypt: 3000 BCE to 395 CE, London

Dunham, D. 1943, An Experiment with an Egyptian Portrait: Ankh-haf in Modern Dress, Bulletin of the Museum of Fine Arts Boston 41 (243), p.2

Edgerton W.F. 1951 The Strikes in Ramses III's Twenty-Ninth Year Journal of Near Eastern Studies 10 (3), pp.137-45

Edwards, A. 1888, A Thousand Miles up the Nile, London

Edwards, A. 1891, Pharaohs, Fellahs and Explorers, New York

Edwards, A. & O'Neill, P. 2005, The Social and Political Position of Woman in Ancient Egypt, Proceedings of the Modern Language Association 120 (3), pp.843-57

Edwards, D. 2004, The Nubian Past: an Archaeology of the Sudan, London

Edwards, I. 1965, Lord Dufferin's Excavations at Deir El-Baḥri and the Clandeboye Collection, Journal of Egyptian Archaeology 51, pp.16-28

Edwards, I. 1972, Treasures of Tutankhamen, London

Edwards, I. 1985, The Pyramids of Egypt, Harmondsworth

Ellis, S. 1992, Graeco-Roman Egypt, Princes Risborough

Emery, W. 1984, Archaic Egypt, Harmondsworth

Emery, W., Smith, H. & Millard, A. 1979, The Fortress at Buhen: the Archaeological Report, London

Empereur, J. 1998, Alexandria Rediscovered, London

Empereur, J. 2002, Alexandria: Past, Present and Future, London

Evans, P. 2000, The Land that Time Drowned, La Dolce Vita on the Delta Sunday Times Magazine (20.8.00), pp.28-33, 40-43

Fahmy, A. 2003, A Fragrant Mixture: Botanicals from the Basket in B333, Nekhen News 15, p.20

Fairman, H. & Grdseloff, B. 1947, Texts of Hatshepsut and Sethos I inside Speos Artemidos, Journal of Egyptian Archaeology 33, pp.12–33

Fakhry, A. 1943, A Note on the tomb of Kheruef at Thebes, Annales du Service des Antiquités de l'Égypte 42, pp. 449-508

Farag, N. & Iskander, Z. 1971, The Discovery of Neferwptah, Cairo

Fattovich, R. 2012, Egypt's trade with Punt: New discoveries on the Red Sea Coast, British Museum Studies in Ancient Egypt and Sudan 18, pp.1–59

Faulkner, R. 1942, The Battle of Megiddo, Journal of Egyptian Archaeology 28, pp.2-15

Faulkner, R. 1946, The Euphrates Campaign of Tuthmosis III, Journal of Egyptian Archaeology 32, pp.39-42

Faulkner, R. 1946, The Wars of Sethos I, Journal of Egyptian Archaeology 33, pp.34-9

Faulkner, R. 1969, The Pyramid Texts, Warminster

Faulkner, R. 1973-78, The Ancient Egyptian Coffin Texts I-III, Warminster

Faulkner, R. 1985, The Ancient Egyptian Book of the Dead, London

Fay, B. 1984, Egyptian Museum Berlin, Mainz

Fazzini, R., Romano, J. & Cody, M. eds. 1999, Art for Eternity: Masterworks from Ancient Egypt, Brooklyn

Fenwick, H. 2004, Ancient roads and GPS survey: modelling the Amarna Plain, Antiquity 78 (302), pp.880-85

Filce Leek, F. 1972, The Human Remains from the Tomb of Tut`ankhAmen, Oxford

Fildes, A. & Fletcher, J. 2001, Son of the Gods: Alexander the Great, London

Filer, J. 1995, Ancient Egyptian Bookshelf: Disease, London

Fischer, H. 1962, The Cult and Nome of the Goddess Bat, Journal of the American Research Center in Egypt 1, pp.7-18

Fischer, H. 1989, Egyptian Women of the Old Kingdom and Heracleapolitan Period, New York

Fletcher, J. 1997, Marks of Distinction: the Tattooed Mummies of Ancient Egypt, NILE Offerings I, pp.28-30

Fletcher, J. 1998, Oils and Perfumes of Ancient Egypt, London

Fletcher, J. 2000, Egypt's Sun King: Amenhotep III, London

Fletcher, J. 2002, The Egyptian Book of Living and Dying, London

Fletcher, J. 2004, The Search for Nefertiti, London

Fletcher, J. 2008, Cleopatra the Great, London

Fletcher, J. 2011, Revisiting the Amarna Royals: Part 1, Shemu: the Egyptian Society of South Africa, 15 (4,) pp.1-3

Fletcher, J. 2015, The Most Democratic Form of Adornment: Hair and Wigs in ancient Egypt, El-Rawi: Egypt's Heritage Review 7, pp.66-71

Flores, D. 2003, Funerary Sacrifice of Animals in the Egyptian Predynastic Period, Oxford

Forbes, R. 1964, Studies in Ancient Technology IV, Leiden

Forbes, C. & Garner, G. 1982, Documents of the Egyptian Empire, Melbourne

Forman, W. & Quirke, S. 1996, Hieroglyphs and the Afterlife in Ancient Egypt, London

Forster, E.M. 1982, Alexandria: a History and a Guide, London

Francis, E. & Vickers, M. 1984, Green Goddess: a Gift to Lindos from Amasis of Egypt, American Journal of Archaeology 88 (1), pp.68-9

Fraser, P.M. 1972, Ptolemaic Alexandria, Oxford

Freed, R., Markowitz, Y. & D'Auria, S. eds. 1999, Pharaohs of the Sun: Akhenaten, Nefertiti, Tutankhamen, Boston

Friedman, F. 1995, The Underground Relief Panels of King Djoser at the Step Pyramid Complex, Journal of the American Research Center in Egypt 32, pp.1-42

Galán, J.M. 2000, The Ancient Egyptian Sed-Festival and the Exemption from Corvee, Journal of Near Eastern Studies 59 (4), pp.255-64

Galt, C. 1931, Veiled Ladies, American Journal of Archaeology 35 (4), pp.373-93

Gardiner, A. 1916, The Defeat of the Hyksos by Kamose: the Carnarvon Tablet No.1, Journal of Egyptian Archaeology 3, pp.95-116

Gardiner, A. 1936, The Egyptian Origin of Some English Personal Names, Journal of the American Oriental Society 56, pp.189-97

Gardiner, A. 1959, The Royal Canon of Turin, Oxford

Gardiner, A. 1961, The Egyptian Memnon, Journal of Egyptian Archaeology 47, pp.91-9

Gardiner, A. 1964, Egypt of the Pharaohs, London

Garstang, J. 1903, Maḥâsna and Bêt Khallaf, London

Garstang, J. 1907, The Burial Customs of Ancient Egypt as illustrated by tombs of the Middle Kingdom, London

Getty Museum 1996, Alexandria and Alexandrianism: Papers delivered at a Symposium organized by the J.Paul Getty Museum and the Getty Center for the History of Art and Humanities April 22-25, 1993, Malibu

Ghalioungui, P. 1973, The House of Life: Magic and Medical Science in Ancient Egypt, Amsterdam

Gillam, R. 1995, Priestesses of Hathor: their Function, Decline and Disappearance, Journal of the American Research Center in Egypt 32, pp. 211-37

Gillam, R. 2005, Performance and Drama in Ancient Egypt, London

Girling, R. 2003, Identified: Egypt's Holy Grail, The Sunday Times Magazine (8.6.03), pp.20-34

Goedicke, H. 1992, Problems concerning Amenophis III, Baltimore

Goedicke, H. 1994, Water and Tax, Les Problèmes Institutionnels de l'Eau en Égypte ancienne et dans l'Antiquité méditerranéenne (Menu, B. ed.), Cairo, pp.187-94

Goedicke, H. 1999, George, Bulletin of the Australian Center for Egyptology 10, pp.39-45

Goddio, F. ed. 1998, Alexandria: the Submerged Royal Quarters Surveys and Excavations 1992-97, London

Goneim, M.Z. 1956, The Buried Pyramid, London

Gordon, A. & Schwabe, C. 2004, The Quick and the Dead: Biomedical Theory in Ancient Egypt, Leiden

Gosline, S. 1996, Female Priests: a Sacerdotal Precedent from Ancient Egypt, Journal of Feminist Studies in Religion 12 (1), pp.25-39

Goudchaux, G. 2001, Cleopatra's subtle religious strategy, Cleopatra of Egypt (eds. Walker, S. & Higgs, P.) London, pp.128-41

Goudchaux, G. 2003, Cleopatra the Seafarer Queen: Strabo and India, Cleopatra Reassessed, British Museum Occasional Paper 103, (eds. Walker, S. & Ashton, S.), London, pp.109-12

Grajetzki, W. 2003, Burial Customs in Ancient Egypt: Life in Death for Rich and Poor, London

Grajetzki, W. 2005, The Coffin of the 'King's Daughter' Neferuptah and the Sarcophagus of the 'Great King's Wife' Hatshepsut, Göttinger Miszellen 205, pp.55-65

Grant, M. 1972, Cleopatra, London

Gray, P. 1972, Notes concerning the position of the arms and hands of mummies with a view to possible dating of the specimen, Journal of Egyptian Archaeology 58, pp.200-4

Green, P. 1990, Alexander to Actium: The Hellenistic Age, London

Greek Ministry of Culture, 1999, Minoans and Myceneans: Flavours of their Time, Athens

Griffiths, J. 1966, Hecataeus and Herodotus on 'A Gift of the River', Journal of Near Eastern Studies 25 (1), pp.57-61

Griffiths, J. 1970, Plutarch's De Iside et Osiride, Cardiff

Grimm, G. 2003, Alexandria in the time of Cleopatra, Cleopatra Reassessed, British Museum Occasional Paper No.103, (eds. Walker, S. & Ashton, S.), London, pp.45-9

Habachi, L. 1957, Two Graffiti at Sehēl from the Reign of Queen Hatshepsut, Journal of Near Eastern Studies 16 (2), pp.88-104

Habachi, L. 1984, The Obelisks of Egypt: Skyscrapers of the Past, Cairo

Hall, H. 1928, Review: Relazione sui lavori della Missione Archeologica Italiana in Egitto (Anni 1903-1920); II. La tomba intatta dell' architetto Cha by E. Schiaparelli, Journal of Egyptian Archaeology 14 (1-2), pp.203-5

Hall, R. 1986, Egyptian Textiles, Aylesbury

Hall, R. & Janssen, J. 1985, The Egyptian Laundry, Wepwawet 1, p.23

Hanawalt, R. 1998, Did Tut Lie in State? The Akhetaten Sun: Newsletter of the Amarna Research Foundation 3 (2), pp.6-9

Hankey, J. 2001, A Passion for Egypt: Arthur Weigall, Tutankhamen and the 'Curse of the Pharaohs', London

Harpur, Y. 1987, Decoration in Egyptian Tombs of the Old Kingdom, London

Harpur, Y. 2001, The Tombs of Nefermaat and Rahotep at Meidum, Oxford

Harris, J. & Weeks, K. 1973, X-Raying the Pharaohs, London

Harris, J. & Wente, E. eds. 1980, An X-Ray Atlas of the Royal Mummies, Chicago

Harris, J. 1973, Nefertiti Rediviva, Acta Orientalia 35, pp.5-14

Harris, J. 1992, Akhenaten and Neferneferuaten in the tomb of Tut'ankhAmen, in After Tut'ankhAmen: Research and Excavation in the Royal Necropolis at Thebes, (ed. N. Reeves), London, pp.55-72

Harrison, R. 1978, The Tutankhamen Post-Mortem, Chronicle: Essays from Ten Years of Television Archaeology (ed. R. Sutcliffe), London, pp.40-52

Harrison, T. 2003, Upside Down and Back to Front: Herodotus and the Greek Encounter with Egypt, Ancient Perspectives on Egypt (eds. Matthews, R. & Roemer, C.), London, pp.145-55

Hart, G. 1986, A Dictionary of Egyptian Gods and Goddesses, London.

Hart, G. 1990, Egyptian Myths, London

Hart, G. 1991, Pharaohs and Pyramids: a Guide through Old Kingdom Egypt, London

Harvey, S. 2001, Holy Abydos, Tribute to a conquering king, Archaeology 54 (4) http://archive.archaeology.org/online/features/abydos/abydos.html

Harvey, S. 2004, New Evidence at Abydos for Ahmose's Funerary Cult, Egyptian Archaeology 24, pp.3-6

Hassan, A. 1997, The Queens of the Fourth Dynasty, Cairo

Hassan, F. 1992, Primeval Goddess to Divine King: the Mythogenesis of Power in the Early Egyptian State, The Followers of Horus: Studies dedicated to Michael Allen Hoffman (Friedman, R. & Adams, B.), Oxford, pp.307-21

Hassan, F. 2001, The Fall of the Egyptian Old Kingdom, http://www. bbc.co.uk/history/ancient/egyptians/apocalypse_egypt_01.shtml

Hassan, F. & Smith, S. 2002, Soul Birds and Heavenly Cows: Transforming Gender in Predynastic Egypt, In Pursuit of Gender: Worldwide Archaeological Approaches, New York (eds. Nelson, S. & Rosen-Ayalon, M.), pp.43-65

Hassan, S. 1930, Excavations at Gîza IV, 1932–1933, Cairo

Hayes, W. 1935, Royal Sarcophagi of the XVIII Dynasty, Princeton

Hayes, W. 1949, Career of the Great Steward Henenu under Nebhepetre Mentuhotpe, Journal of Egyptian Archaeology 35, pp.43-9

Hayes, W. 1958, The Scepter of Egypt: a Background for the Study of the Egyptian Antiquities in the Metropolitan Museum of Art I-II, New York

Hayes, W. 1977, Most Ancient Egypt, Chicago

Hegazy, el-S. 1999, Hatshepsut: a fairy king or political genius? Cairo

Hepper, F. 1969, Arabian and African frankincense trees, Journal of Egyptian Archaeology 55, pp. 66-7

Herodotus, trans. de Selincourt, A. 1959, The Histories, Harmondsworth

Heuer, K. 1972, City of the Stargazers: the rise and fall of ancient Alexandria, New York

Heyob, S. 1975, The Cult of Isis among Women in the Graeco-Roman World, Leiden

Hill, M. ed. 2007, Gifts for the Gods: Images from Egyptian Temples, New York

Hodges, H. 1974, Technology in the Ancient World, London

Hoffman, M. 1984, Egypt before the Pharaohs, London

Hölbl, G. 2001, A History of the Ptolemaic Empire, London

Holladay, A. 1989, The Hellenic Disaster in Egypt, Journal of Hellenic Studies 109, pp.176-82

Hollis, S. 2000, Goddesses and Sovereignty in Ancient Egypt, Goddesses who Rule (eds. Benard, E. & Moon, B.), Oxford, pp.215-32

Homer, trans. Rieu, E. 1946, The Odyssey, Harmondsworth

Homer, trans. Rieu, E. 1954, The Iliad, Harmondsworth

Hornung, E. 1990, Valley of the Kings: Horizon of Eternity, New York

Hornung, E. 1992, Idea into Image: Essays on Ancient Egyptian Thought, New York

Houlihan, P. 2001, Wit and Humour in Ancient Egypt, London
Hulit, T. & Richardson, T. 2007, The Warriors of Pharaoh: experiments with new Kingdom scale armour, archery and chariots, The Cutting Edge: Studies in Ancient and Medieval Combat (Molloy, B. ed.), Stroud, pp.52-63
Huyge, D. 2012, The Aurochs of Qurta: Egyptian 'Ice Age' Art, Current World Archaeology 53, pp.28-9
Huyge, D., Watchman, A., De Dapper, M. & Marchi, E. 2001, Dating Egypt's oldest 'art': AMS 14C age determinations of rock varnishes covering petroglyphs at El-Hosh (Upper Egypt), Antiquity 75 (287), pp.68-72
James, T. 1953, The Mastaba of Khentika called Ikhekhi, London
James, T. 1972, Gold Technology in Ancient Egypt: Mastery of Metal Working Methods, Gold Bulletin 5 (2), pp.38-42
James, T. 1973, The Archaeology of Ancient Egypt, London
James, T. 1984, Pharaoh's People: scenes from life in Imperial Egypt, London
James, T. 1988, Ancient Egypt: the Land and its Legacy, London
James, T. 2002, Ramses II, Vercelli
Jánosi, P. 1992, The Queens of the Old Kingdom and their Tombs, Bulletin of the Australian Center for Egyptology 3, pp.51-8
Jánosi, P. 1992, The Queens Ahhotep I and Ahhotep II and Egypt's Foreign Relations, Journal of the Ancient Chronology Forum 5, pp.99-105
Jánosi, P. 1993, The Discovery of Queen Ahhotep I, Journal of the Ancient Chronology Forum 6, pp.87-8
Jánosi, P. 2010, Montuhotep-Nebtawyre and Amenemhat I: Observations on the Early Twelfth Dynasty in Egypt, Metropolitan Museum Journal 45, p.7-20
Janssen, J, 1980, Absence from Work by the Necropolis Workmen of Thebes, Studien zur Altägyptischen Kultur 8, pp.127-52
Janssen, J. 1986, A Notable Lady, Wepwawet 2, pp.30-31
Jaritz, H. 1994, What Petrie Missed, Egyptian Archaeology 5, pp. 14-16
Jasnow, R. 1997, The Greek Alexander Romance and Demotic Egyptian Literature, Journal of Near Eastern Studies, 56 (2), pp.95-103
Jenkins, N. 1980, The Boat Beneath the Pyramid: King Cheops' Royal Ship, London
Johnson, J. 2013, The Amarna Boundary Stelae: a translation, Carnmoor
Johnson, J. 1986, The Role of the Egyptian Priesthood in Ptolemaic Egypt, Egyptological Studies in Honor of Richard A. Parker, (L.H. Lesko, ed.) Hanover, pp.70-84

Johnson, S. 1990, The Cobra Goddess of Ancient Egypt, London

Johnson, W. 1996, Amenhotep III & Amarna: some new considerations, Journal of Egyptian Archaeology 82, pp.65-82

Jones, J. 2002, Towards Mummification: new evidence for early developments, Egyptian Archaeology: Bulletin of the Egypt Exploration Society 21, pp.5-7

Jones, J., Higham, T., Oldfield, R., O'Connor, T. & Buckley, S. 2014, Evidence for Prehistoric Origins of Egyptian mummification in Late Neolithic Burials, PloS One 9 (8), e103608. doi:10.1371/journal.pone.0103608

Kákosy, L. 1989, The Plundering of the Pyramid of Cheops, Studien zur Altägyptischen Kultur 16, pp.145-69

Kamish, M. 1985, Foreigners at Memphis in the Middle of the Eighteenth Dynasty, Wepwawet 1, pp.19-21

Kanawati, N. 1990, Saqqara Excavations shed new light on Old Kingdom History, Bulletin of the Australian Center for Egyptology 1, pp.55-67

Kanawati, N. 1997, Ankhmahor, a Vizier of Teti, Bulletin of the Australian Center for Egyptology 8, pp.65-79

Kanawati, N. 2001, A Female Guard buried in the Teti Cemetery, Bulletin of the Australian Center for Egyptology 12, pp.65-70

Kanawati, N. 2003, Nepotism in the Sixth Dynasty, Bulletin of the Australian Center for Egyptology 14, pp.39-59

Kanawati, N. & Abder-Raziq, M. 2001, The Teti Cemetery at Saqqara VII: the Tombs of Shepsiputah, Mereri (Merinebti), Hefi and Others, Warminster

Kees, H. 1961, Ancient Egypt: a cultural topography, London

Kelder, J. 2009, Royal Gift Exchange between Mycenae and Egypt: olives as 'Greeting Gifts' in the Late Bronze Age Eastern Mediterranean, American Journal of Archaeology 113 (3), pp.339-52

Kemp, B. 1966, Abydos and the Royal Tombs of the First Dynasty, Journal of Egyptian Archaeology 52, pp.13-22

Kemp, B. 1991, Ancient Egypt: Anatomy of a Civilization, London

Kemp, B. 2000, The Colossi from the Early Shrine of Coptos in Egypt, Cambridge Archaeological Journal 10 (2), pp.211-42

Kemp, B. 2005, 100 Hieroglyphs: think like an Egyptian, London

Kemp, B. 2007, Notes from the Field: the lives of the have-nots, Horizon 2 (July), pp.2-3

Kemp, B. & O'Connor, D. 1974, An Ancient Nile Harbour: University Museum Excavations at the Birket Habu, International Journal of Nautical Archaeology and Underwater Exploration 3 (1), pp. 101-36

Kendall, T. 1997, Do Ancient Dances Survive in Present-Day Sudan? The Spirit's Dance in Africa (Dagan, E. ed.), Montreal, pp.306-9

Kinney, L. 2007, Dancing on a Time Line, Bulletin of the Australian Center for Egyptology 18, pp.145-59

Kitchen, K. 1985, Pharaoh Triumphant: the life and times of Ramesses II, King of Egypt, Warminster

Kitchen, K. 1996, The Third Intermediate Period in Egypt (1100-650 BC), Warminster

Kitchen, K. 2006, High society and lower ranks in Ramesside Egypt at home and abroad, British Museum Studies in Ancient Egypt and Sudan 6, pp.31-6

Kleiner, D. 2005, Cleopatra and Rome, Cambridge

Kobusiewicz, M., Kabaciński, J., Schild, R., Irish, J. & Wendorf, F. 2009, Burial practices of the Final Neolithic pastoralists at Gebel Ramlah, Western Desert of Egypt, British Museum Studies in Ancient Egypt and Sudan 13, pp.147-74

Köhler, C. & Jones, J. 2009, Helwan II: the Early Dynastic and Old Kingdom Funerary Relief Slabs, Studien zur Archäologie und Geschichte Altägyptens 25, Leidorf

Kozloff, A. 2012, Amenhotep III: Egypt's Radiant Pharaoh, Cambridge

Kozloff, A. & Bryan, B. 1992, Egypt's Dazzling Sun: Amenhotep III and his world, Cleveland

Kuhlmann, K. 1981, Ptolemais: Queen of Nectanebo I. Notes on the Inscription of an Unknown Princess of the XXXth Dynasty, Mitteilungen des Deutschen Archäologischen Instituts Kairo 37, pp.267-79

Kuhrt, A. 1995, The Ancient Near East c.300-330 BC: II, London

Kuper, R. ed. 2013, Wadi Sura – the Cave of Beasts: a rock art site in the Gilf Kebir (SW-Egypt) (Africa Praehistorica 26), Cologne

La Loggia, L. 2009, Egyptian engineering in the Early Dynastic period: The sites of Saqqara and Helwan, British Museum Studies in Ancient Egypt and Sudan 13, pp.175-96

La Loggia, A. 2012, Counting the Costs: a Project Manager's View of the Fort, Nekhen News 24, pp.21-2

La'da, C. 2003, Encounters with Ancient Egypt: the Hellenistic Greek Experience, Ancient Perspectives on Egypt (Matthews, R. & Roemer, C. eds.), London, pp.157-69

Langton, N. & B. 2002, The Cat in Ancient Egypt, London

Lansing, A. 1919, Statues of the Goddess Sekhmet, Bulletin of the Metropolitan Museum of Art 14 (10) II, pp.3-23

Laourdas, B. & Makaronas, C. eds. 1970, Ancient Macedonia: papers read at the first international symposium held in Thessaloniki, 26-29 August 1968, Thessalonika

Lauer, J-P. 1976, Saqqara: the Royal Cemetery of Memphis, London

Leahy, A. 1996, The Adoption of Ankhnesneferibre at Karnak, Journal of Egyptian Archaeology 82, pp.145-65

Lehner, M. 1997, The Complete Pyramids, London

Lenzo, G. 2010, The Two Funerary Papyri of Queen Nedjmet (P. BM EA 10490 and P. BM EA 10541 + Louvre E. 6258), British Museum Studies in Ancient Egypt and Sudan 15, pp.63–83

Lepsius, R. 1852, Discoveries made in Egypt, Ethiopia and the peninsula of Sinaii in the years 1842-1845, London

Lesko, B. 1997, The Rhetoric of Women in Pharaonic Egypt, Listening to their Voices: the Rhetorical Activities of Historical Women (ed. M. Wertheimer), pp.89-110

Lesko, B. 1998, Queen Khamerernebty II and her sculpture, Ancient Egyptian and Mediterranean Studies in Memory of William A. Ward (ed. L. Lesko), Providence, pp.149-62

Lesko, B. 1999, The Great Goddesses of Egypt, Norman

Lesko, L. ed. Pharaoh's Workers: the villagers of Deir el-Medina, Ithaca

Levi, P. 1980, Atlas of the Greek World, Oxford

Lewis, N. 1986, Greeks in Ptolemaic Egypt: case studies in the social history of the Hellenistic world, Oxford

Lichtheim, M. 1945, The Songs of the Harpers, Journal of Near Eastern Studies 4 (3), pp.178-212

Lichtheim, M. 1975, Ancient Egyptian Literature, I: The Old and Middle Kingdoms, Berkeley

Lichtheim, M. 1976, Ancient Egyptian Literature, II: The New Kingdom, Berkeley

Lichtheim, M. 1980, Ancient Egyptian Literature, III: The Late Period, Berkeley

Lilyquist, C. 2003, The Tomb of Three Foreign Wives of Tuthmosis III, New York

Lilyquist, C. 2012, Treasures from Tell Basta: Goddesses, Officials and Artists in an International Age, Metropolitan Museum Journal 47, pp.9-72

Limme, L. 2008, Elkab, 1937-2007: seventy years of Belgian archaeological research', British Museum Studies in Ancient Egypt and Sudan 9, pp.15-50

Lindsay, J. Daily Life in Roman Egypt, London

Lindsay, J. 1970, Cleopatra, London

Lister, R. 1979, The Travels of Herodotus, London

Llewellyn-Jones, L. 2003, Aphrodite's Tortoise: The Veiled Woman of Ancient Greece, Classical Press of Wales

Lloyd, A. 1972, Triremes and the Saïte Navy, Journal of Egyptian Archaeology 58, pp.268-79

Lloyd, A.1976, Herodotus Book II, Commentary 1-98, Leiden

Lloyd, A. 1977, Necho and the Red Sea: Some Considerations, Journal of Egyptian Archaeology 63, pp.142-55

Lloyd, S. & Müller, H.W. 1980, Ancient Architecture, London

Lohwasser, A. 2001, Queenship in Kush: Status, Role and Ideology of Royal Women, Journal of the American Research Center in Egypt 38, pp.61-76

Lopes, M. 2013, The Apries Palace Project, Egyptian Archaeology 42, pp.36-7

Loret, V. 1899.a, Le Tombeau de Thoutmès III a Biban-el-Molouk, Bulletin de L'Institut d'Egypte 9, pp.91-7

Loret, V. 1899.b, Le Tombeau d'Amenophis II et la cachette royale de Biban el-Molouk, Bulletin de L'Institut d'Egypte 9, pp.98-112

Louvre 1981, Un Siècle de Fouilles Françaises en Égypte 1880-1980, Paris

Louvre 1999, L'art Égyptien au temps des pyramides, Paris

Lubec, G., Holaubek, J., Feldl, C., Lubec, B. & Strouhal, E. 1993, Use of Silk in Ancient Egypt, Nature 362, p.25

Lucas, A. (rev. J.R. Harris), 1989, Ancient Egyptian Materials and Industries, London

Luce, J.V. 1963, Cleopatra as Fatale Monstrum (Horace, Carm. 1. 37. 21), The Classical Quarterly 3 (2), pp.251-57

Lunde, P. & Porter, A. eds. 2004, Trade and Travel in the Red Sea Region: Proceedings of Red Sea Project I, Oxford

Lythgoe, A. 1916, The Tomb of Perneb, The Metropolitan Museum of Art Bulletin 11 (2), pp.31-6

McCarthy, H.L. 2002, The Osiris Nefertari: a Case Study of Decorum, Gender, and Regeneration, Journal of the American Research Center in Egypt 39, pp.173-95

McDowell, A.G. 1999, Village Life in Ancient Egypt: Laundry Lists and Love Songs, Oxford

McFarlane, A. 1990, The Cult of Min in the Third Millenium BC, Bulletin of the Australian Center for Egyptology 1, pp.69-75

McFarlane, A. 2000, The Unis Cemetery I: the Tomb of Irukaptah, Warminster

MacGillivray, J. 2009, Thera, Hatshepsut, and the Keftiu: crisis and response, Time's Up! Dating the Minoan eruption of Santorini (Warburton, D. ed.), Monographs of the Danish Institute at Athens 10, Sandbjerg, pp.154-70

MacGregor, N. 2012, A History of the World in 100 Objects, London

MacLeod, R. ed. 2002, The Library of Alexandria: Centre of Learning in the Ancient World, London

Macadam, M. 1951, A royal family of the Thirteenth Dynasty, Journal of Egyptian Archaeology 37, pp.20-8

Mace, A. & Winlock, H. 1916, The Tomb of Senebtisi, New York

Maehler, H. 1983, Egypt under the Last Ptolemies, Institute of Classical Studies Bulletin 30, pp.1-16

Maehler, H. 2003, Roman Poets on Egypt, Ancient Perspectives on Egypt (eds. Matthews, R. & Roemer, C.), London, pp.203-15

Malville, J., Schild, R., Wendorf, F., & Brenmer, R. 2007, Astronomy of Nabta Playa, African Sky 11 (2), pp.2-7.

Mallory-Greenough, L. 2002, The Geographical, Spatial, and Temporal Distribution of Predynastic and First Dynasty Basalt Vessels, Journal of Egyptian Archaeology 88, pp.67-93

Manassa, C. 2008, Sounds of the Underworld, The Tenth International Congress of Egyptologists, Rhodes pp.152-3

Manetho (trans. Waddell, W.G.) 1940, History of Egypt and other works, London

Manley, B. 1996, The Penguin Historical Atlas of Ancient Egypt, Harmondsworth

Manniche, L. 1987.a, City of the Dead: Thebes in Egypt, London

Manniche, L. 1987.b, Sexual Life in Ancient Egypt, London

Manniche, L. 1989, An Ancient Egyptian Herbal, London

Manniche, L. 1991, Music and Musicians in Ancient Egypt, London

Manniche, L. 2006, In the Womb, Bulletin of the Australian Center for Egyptology 17, pp.97-112

Markowitz, Y., Lacovara, P. & Hatchfield, P. 1997, Jewellery Fragments from the Tomb of Nefertari, Chief of Seers: Egyptian Studies in Memory of Cyril Aldred (eds. Goring, E. et al.), London, pp.220-28

Martin, G. 1974, The Royal Tomb at el-Amarna: the Rock Tombs of El-'Amarna VII; I: the objects, London

Martin, G. 1989, The Royal Tomb at el-'Amarna: the Rock Tombs of El-'Amarna VII; II: the reliefs, inscriptions & architecture, London

Martin, G. 1991, The Hidden Tombs of Memphis: new discoveries from the time of Tutankhamen to Ramesses the Great, London

Mattingly, H. 1950, Zephyritis, American Journal of Archaeology 54 (2), pp.126-8

Meza, A. 1995, An Egyptian Statuette in Petra, Journal of the American Research Center in Egypt 32, pp.179-83

Midant-Reynes, B. 2000, The Prehistory of Egypt: from the First Egyptians to the First Pharaohs, Oxford

Miller, E. & Parkinson, R. 2001, Reflections on a Gilded Eye in 'Fowling in the Marshes', Colour and Painting in Ancient Egypt (Davies, W. ed.), London, pp.49-52

Millet, N. 1990, The Narmer Macehead and Related Objects, Journal of the American Research Center in Egypt 27, pp.53-9

Milne, J.G. 1916, Greek and Roman Tourists in Egypt, Journal of Egyptian Archaeology 3, pp.76-80

Milton, J. 1986, Sunrise of Power: Alexander and the World of Hellenism, Boston

Minas-Nerpel, M. & de Meyer, M. 2013, Raising the Pole for Min in the Temple of Isis at Shanhur, Zeitschrift für Ägyptische Sprache und Altertumskunde 140, pp.150-59

van Minnen, P. 2003, A Royal Ordinance of Cleopatra and Related Documents, Cleopatra Reassessed, British Museum Occasional Paper No.103, (eds. Walker, S. & Ashton, S.), London, pp.35-42

Moens, M. 1985, The Procession of the God Min to the ḥtjw-Garden, Studien zur Altägyptischen Kultur 12, pp.61-73

Mohamed, A. & Anderson, J. 2013, Highlights from the Sudan National Museum, Khartoum

Moioli, M. 2000, Inside the Crocodiles: Tebtunis gods were stuffed with ancient documents, Discovering Archaeology 2 (2), p.65

Mond, R. & Myers, O. 1934, The Bucheum I & II, London

Montserrat, D 1996, Sex and Society in Graeco-Roman Egypt, London

Moran, W. L. 1992, The Amarna Letters, Baltimore

Morkot, R. 1986, Violent Images of Queenship & the Royal Cult, Wepwawet 2, pp.1-9

Morkot, R. 1987, Studies in New Kingdom Nubia, I: politics, economics and ideology – Egyptian imperialism in Nubia, Wepwawet 3, pp.29-49

Morkot, R. 1990, Nb-M3't-R'-United-with-Ptah, Journal of Near Eastern Studies 49, pp.323-37

Morkot, R. 2000, The Black Pharaohs, London

Morkot, R. 2010, Divine of Body: The Remains of Egyptian Kings – Preservation, Reverence and Memory in a World without Relics, Past and Present 206, pp.37-55

Morrell, R. 2001, The Pyramid Builders, National Geographic: Online Extra http://ngm.nationalgeographic.com/ngm/data/2001/11/01/html/ ft_20011101.5. fulltext.html

Moyer, I. 2002, Herodotus and an Egyptian Mirage: The Genealogies of the Theban Priests, Journal of Hellenic Studies 122, pp.70-90

Müller, H.W. & Thiem, E. 1999, The Royal Gold of Ancient Egypt, London

Münch, H. 2000, Categorizing archaeological finds: the funerary material of Queen Hetepheres I at Giza, Antiquity 74 (286), pp.898-908

Munro, I. 2010, Evidence of a Master Copy transferred from Thebes to the Memphis area in Dynasty 26, British Museum Studies in Ancient Egypt and Sudan 15, pp.201–24

Murnane, W. 1980, United with Eternity: a concise guide to the monuments of Medinet Habu, Cairo

Murnane, W. 1995, Texts from the Amarna Period in Egypt, Atlanta

Murray, M. 1905, Saqqara Mastabas I, London

Myśliwiec, K. 2000, The Twilight of Ancient Egypt: First Millenium BCE, Ithaca

Nachtergael, G. 1980, Bérénice II, Arsinoé III et l'offrande de la boucle, Chronique d'Égypte 55, pp.240-53

Naville, E. 1891, Bubastis 1887-1889, London

Naville, E. 1898, The Temple of Deir el-Bahari III, London

Naville, E. 1907, The XIth dynasty temple at Deir el-Bahari I, London

Nederhof, M. 2006, Armant stela of Tuthmosis III http://mjn.host. cs.st-andrews.ac.uk/egyptian/texts/corpus/pdf/ ArmantTuthmosisIII.pdf

Nelson, K. & Khalifa, E. 2011, Nabta Playa Black-topped pottery: technological innovation and social change, British Museum Studies in Ancient Egypt and Sudan 16, pp.133-48

Nerlich, A. 2000, Molecular Archaeology and Egyptology, Egyptian Archaeology: Bulletin of the Egypt Exploration Society 17, pp.5-7

Nerlich, A., Buckley, S., Fletcher, J., Caramello, S. & Bianucci, R. 2011, An Interdisciplinary Study of the Mummified Remains of the 18th Dynasty Official Nebiri, PalArch Journal of Archaeology of Egypt 10(1), p.22

Neugebauer, O & Parker, R.A. 1968, Two Demotic Horoscopes, Journal of Egyptian Archaeology 54, pp.231-35

Newberry, P. 1928, Akhenaten's Eldest Son-in-Law 'Ankhkheprurē', Journal of Egyptian Archaeology 14, pp.3-9

Nicholson, P. & Shaw, I. (eds.), 2000, Ancient Egyptian Materials and Technology, Cambridge

Nilsson, M. 2010, The Crown of Arsinoe II: the Creation and Development of an Imagery of Authority, Gothenburg

Nims, C. 1965, Thebes of the Pharaohs: Pattern for Every City, London

Niwinski, A. 1984, The Bab el-Gusus Tomb and the Royal Cache in Deir el-Bahri, Journal of Egyptian Archaeology 70, pp.73-81

Nunn, J. 1996, Ancient Egyptian Medicine, London

O'Connor, D. 2009, Abydos: Egypt's First Pharaohs and the Cult of Osiris, London

Ockinga, B. 1991, The Tomb of Sennedjem at Awlad Azzaz (Sohag), Bulletin of the Australian Center for Egyptology 2, pp.81-9

Ockinga, B. 1995, Hatshepsut's Election to Kingship: the ba and the ka in Egyptian Royal Ideology, Bulletin of the Australian Center for Egyptology 6, pp.89-102

Oppenheim, A. 1996, The Jewellery of Queen Weret, Egyptian Archaeology 9, p.26

Oren, E. ed. 1997, The Hyksos: New Historical and Archaeological Perspectives, Philadelphia

Orland, R., Orland, F. & Orland, P. 1990, Psychiatric assessment of Cleopatra: a challenging evaluation, Psychopathology 23 (3), pp.169-75

Pack, R.A. 1965, The Greek and Latin literary texts from Greco-Roman Egypt, Ann Arbor

Panagiotakopulu, E. 2004, Pharaonic Egypt and the origins of plague, Journal of Biogeography 31, pp.269-75

Parizek, R., Moneim, A., Fantle, M., Westerman, J. and Issawi, B. 2010, Isotopic data: Implications for the source(s) of Osireion groundwater, Abydos, Egypt, Bulletin of the Tethys Geological Society 5 pp.23-34

Parker, G. 2002, Ex Oriente Luxuria: Indian Commodities and Roman Experience, Journal of the Economic and Social History of the Orient 45 (1), pp.40-95(56)

Parker, R. 1950, The Calendars of Ancient Egypt, Studies in Ancient Oriental Civilization 25, Chicago

Parkinson, R. 1991, Voices from Ancient Egypt: an anthology of Middle Kingdom writings, London

Parkinson, R. 1995, 'Homosexual' Desire and Middle Kingdom Literature Journal of Egyptian Archaeology 81, pp.57-76

Parkinson, R. 1999, Cracking Codes: the Rosetta Stone and Decipherment, London

Parkinson, R. & Quirke, S. 1995, Papyrus: Egyptian Bookshelf Series, London

Parkinson, R. & Schofield, L. 1993, Akhenaten's Army? Egyptian Archaeology 3, pp.34-5

Payne, J. 1968, Lapis Lazuli in Ancient Egypt, Iraq 30, pp.58-61

Peacock, D. & Williams, D. eds. 2007, Food for the Gods: new light on the ancient incense trade, Oxford

Peet, T. 1925, The Legend of the Capture of Joppa and the Story of the Foredoomed Prince, Journal of Egyptian Archaeology 11 (3-4), pp.225-9

Peet, T. 1930, The Great Tomb Robberies of the Twentieth Egyptian Dynasty, Oxford

Pendlebury, J. 1933. The City of Akhenaten II, London

Pendlebury, J. et al. 1951, The City of Akhenaten III, London

Petrie, W. 1890, Kahun, Gurob & Hawara, London

Petrie, W. 1892, Medum, London

Petrie, W. 1894, Tell el Amarna, London

Petrie, W. 1896, Koptos, London

Petrie, W. 1898, Deshasheh 1897, London

Petrie, W. 1900, Royal Tombs of the First Dynasty, London

Petrie, W. 1901, Royal Tombs of the Earliest Dynasties, London

Petrie, W. 1931, Seventy Years in Archaeology, London

Petrie, W. & Quibell, J. 1896, Naqada and Ballas, London

Peust, C. 2006, Ladies and Gentlemen or Gentlemen and Ladies? On the Order of Conjoined Gender Nouns in Egyptian, Bulletin of the Australian Center for Egyptology 17, pp.113-21

Pflüger, K. 1946, The Edict of King Haremhab, Journal of Near Eastern Studies 5 (4), pp.260-76

Philips, J. 1996, Aegypto-Aegean Relations up to the 2nd millennium B.C., in Interregional Contacts in the Later Prehistory of Northeastern Africa, Poznan, pp.459-70

Piccione, P. 2003, Pharaoh at the Bat, College of Charleston Magazine 7 (1), p.36

Pinch, G. 1993, Votive Offerings to Hathor, Oxford

Pinch, G. 1994, Magic in Ancient Egypt, London

Pinch, G. 2001, Red things: the symbolism of colour in magic, in Colour and Painting in Ancient Egypt (ed. W. Davies), London, pp.182-85

Pischikova, E. 2009, The early Kushite Tombs of South Asasif, British Museum Studies in Ancient Egypt and Sudan 12, pp.11-30

Pliny, trans. Rackham, H. et al. 1947-63, Natural History, London

Plutarch 1952, The Lives of the Noble Grecians and Romans: the Dryden Translation, Chicago

Podzorski, P. 1990, Their Bones Shall Not Perish: an examination of predynastic human remains from Naga-ed-Dêr in Egypt, New Malden

Pomeroy, S. 1975, Goddesses, Whores, Wives and Slaves: Women in Classical Antiquity, New York

Pomeroy, S. 1984, Women in Hellenistic Egypt, New York

Poo, M. 1995, Wine and Wine Offering in the Religion of Ancient Egypt, London

Posener-Kriéger, P. 1997, News from Abusir, The Temple in Ancient Egypt: New Discoveries and Recent Research (Quirke, S. ed.), London, pp.17-23

Posener-Kriéger P. & de Cénival, J. 1968, Hieratic Papyri in the British Museum V: The Abusir Papyri, London

Postgate, N., Wang, T. & Wilkinson, T., 1995, The evidence for early writing: utilitarian or ceremonial? Antiquity 69 (264), pp.459-80

Prag, J. & Neave, R. 1997, Making Faces: using forensic and archaeological evidence, London

Prag, K. 1986, Byblos and Egypt in the Fourth Millennium BC, Levant 18, pp.59-74

Prahl, R. 2004, The Origin of the Guanches: Parallels with Ancient Egypt? Migration and Diffusion 5 (19), pp.80-92

Priese, K. ed. 1991, Agyptisches Museum, Mainz

Quaegebeur, J. 1971, Documents concerning a Cult of Arsinoe Philadelphos at Memphis, Journal of Near Eastern Studies 30 (4), pp.239-70

Quibell, J. 1898, The Ramesseum, London

Quibell, J., 1900, Hierakonpolis I, London

Quibell, J. 1908, The Tomb of Yuaa and Thuiu, Cairo

Quibell, J. & Green, F. 1902, Hierakonpolis II, London

Quirke, S. 1990, Who Were the Pharaohs: a history of their names with a list of cartouches, London

Quirke, S. 1991, Royal Power in the 13th Dynasty, Middle Kingdom Studies (ed. S. Quirke), New Malden, pp.123-39

Quirke, S. 1992, Ancient Egyptian Religion, London

Quirke, S. ed. 1998, Lahun Studies, Reigate

Rabino Massa, E. et al. 2000, Malaria in Ancient Egypt: Paleoimmunological Investigation on Predynastic Mummified Remains, Chungara: Revista de Antropología Chilena 32 (1), pp.7-9

Raven, M. 1983, Wax in Egyptian magic and symbolism, Oudheidkundige Mededelingen uit het Rijksmuseum van Oudheden te Leiden 64, pp.7-47

Ray, J. 2001, Reflections of Osiris: Lives from Ancient Egypt, London

Ray, J. 2003, Cleopatra in the Temples of Upper Egypt: the evidence of Dendera and Armant, Cleopatra Reassessed, British Museum Occasional Paper 103, (eds. Walker, S. & Ashton, S.), London, pp.9-11

Ray, J. 2007, The Rosetta Stone and the Rebirth of Ancient Egypt, London

Redford, D. 1984, Akhenaten the Heretic King, Princeton

Redford, D. 1986, The Name Manetho, Egyptological Studies in Honor of Richard A. Parker, (Lesko, L. ed.) Hanover, pp.118-21

Redford, D. 1992, Egypt, Palestine and Israel in ancient times, Princeton

Redford, S. 2002, The Harem Conspiracy: the Murder of Ramses III, DeKalb

Reeves, N. 1986, Miscellanea Epigraphica, Studien zur Altägyptischen Kultur 13, pp.165-70

Reeves, N. 1990, Valley of the Kings: the decline of a royal necropolis, London

Reeves, N. 1990, The Complete Tutankhamen, London

Reeves, N. 2000, Ancient Egypt: the Great Discoveries, a year-by-year chronicle, London

Reeves, N. 2001, Akhenaten: Egypt's False Prophet, London

Reeves, N. 2014, TutankhAmen's Gold Mask
http://www.academia.edu/7516977/TutankhAmens_Gold_Mask_2014_

Reeves, N. & Wilkinson, R. 1996, The Complete Valley of the Kings: Tombs and Treasures of Egypt's Greatest Pharaohs, London

Reisner, G. 1927, The Tomb of Meresankh, a Great-Granddaughter of Queen Hetep-Heres I and Sneferuw, Bulletin of the Museum of Fine Arts 25 (151), pp.64-79

Reisner, G. 1932, The Bed Canopy of the Mother of Cheops, Bulletin of the Museum of Fine Arts 30 (180), pp.56-60

Reisner, G. 1936, The Dog that was Honoured by the King of Egypt, Bulletin of the Museum of Fine Arts 34 (206), pp.96-9

Remijsen, S. 2009, Challenged by Egyptians: Greek Sports in the Third Century BC, The International Journal of the History of Sport 26 (2), pp.246-71

Renberg, G. 2008, Review: Deir el-Bahari in the Hellenistic and Roman Periods: a Study of an Egyptian Temple based on Greek Sources (A. Lajtar), Bryn Mawr Classical Review http://bmcr.brynmawr.edu/2008/2008-01-05.html#n5

Reymond, E. 1973, Catalogue of Demotic Papyri in the Ashmolean Museum I: Embalmers' Archives from Hawara including Greek Documents and Subscriptions, Oxford

Reymond, E. 1981, From the Records of a Priestly Family from Memphis I, Wiesbaden

Reymond, E. & Barns, J. 1977, Alexandria and Memphis: Some Historical Observations, Orientalia 46 (1), pp.1-33

Rice, E. 1999, Cleopatra, London

Rice, M. 1990, Egypt's Making: the Origins of Ancient Egypt: 5000-2000 BC, London

Rice, M. 2006, Swifter than the Arrow: the Golden Hunting Hounds of Ancient Egypt, London

Ridealgh, K. 2011, Yes dear! Spousal dynamics in the Late Ramesside Letters, Current Research in Egyptology 2010: Proceedings of the Eleventh Annual Symposium, (Horn, M., Kramer, J., Soliman, D., Staring, N., van den Hoven, C. & Weiss, L. eds.), Oxford, pp.124-30

Ridgway, B. 1990, Hellenistic Sculpture I: the Styles of ca. 331-200 BC, Madison

Roberts, A. 1995, Hathor Rising: the Serpent Power of Ancient Egypt, Rottingdean

Robins, G. 1987, The Role of the Royal Family in the 18th Dynasty up to the end of the reign of Amenhotep III: 2: Royal Children, Wepwawet 3, pp. 15-17

Robins, G. ed. 1990, Beyond the Pyramids, Atlanta

Roehrig, C. ed. 2005, Hatshepsut: from Queen to Pharaoh, New York

Romer, J. 1984, Ancient Lives: the Story of the Pharaoh's Tombmakers, London

Romer, J. & Romer, E. 1995, The Seven Wonders of the World, London

Rose, J. 2000, Tomb KV.39 in the Valley of the Kings: a double archaeological enigma, Bristol

Rostovtzeff, M. 1928, Greek Sightseers in Egypt, Journal of Egyptian Archaeology 14 (1-2), pp.13-15

Roth, A. 1993, Fingers, Stars and the 'Opening of the Mouth': the nature and function of the ntrwj-blades, Journal of Egyptian Archaeology 79, pp.57-79

Roth, A. 1999, The Absent Spouse: Patterns and Taboos in Egyptian Tomb Decoration, Journal of the American Research Center in Egypt 36, pp.37-53

Roth, A. & Roehrig, C. 2002, Magical Bricks and the Bricks of Birth, Journal of Egyptian Archaeology 88, pp.121-39

Rowe, A. 1961, Studies in the Archaeology of the Near East II: Some Facts Concerning the Great Pyramids of El-Gîza and their Royal Constructors, Bulletin of the John Rylands Library 44 (1), pp.100-18

Rowlandson, J. ed. 1998, Women and Society in Greek and Roman Egypt: a sourcebook, Cambridge de Ruiter, B.F. 2010, The Death of Arsinoe Philadelphus: the evidence reconsidered, Zeitschrift für Papyrologie und Epigraphik 174, pp.139–50

Rutherford, I. 2003, Pilgrimage in Greco-Roman Egypt: New Perspectives on Graffiti from the Memnonion at Abydos, Ancient Perspectives on Egypt (eds. Matthews, R. & Roemer, C.), London, pp.171-89

Ryan, D. 1990, Who is Buried in KV.60: a Field Report, KMT 1 (1), pp.34-9, 53-8

Ryholt, K. 2000, The Late Old Kingdom in the Turin King-list and the Identity of Nitocris, Zeitschrift für ägyptische Sprache und Altertumskunde 127, pp.87–100

Saleh, M. & Sourouzian, H. 1987, Official Catalogue of the Egyptian Museum, Cairo, Mainz

Samson, J. 1972, Amarna, City of Akhenaten and Nefertiti: Key Pieces from the Petrie Collection, Guildford

Samson, J. 1977, Nefertiti's Regality, Journal of Egyptian Archaeology 63, pp.88-97

Sandars, N. 1985, The Sea Peoples: warriors of the ancient Mediterranean, London

Sandys, G. 1615, The Relation of a Journey begun an.Dom 1610, in Four Books, London

Saunders, N.J. 2006, Alexander's Tomb: the two thousand year obsession to find the lost conqueror, New York

Sauneron, S. 1980, The Priests of Ancient Egypt, New York

Säve-Söderbergh, T. ed. 1987, Temples and Tombs of Ancient Nubia: the international rescue campaign at Abu Simbel, Philae and other sites, London

Schiaparelli, E. 1927, La Tomb Intatta dell' Architetto Kha nella necropolis di Tebe, Turin

Schulman, A. 1988, Hittites, Helmets and Amarna: Akhenaten's first Hittite War, The Akhenaten Temple Project 2, (Redford, D. ed.), pp.53-80

Seidlmayer, S. 1996, Town and State in the Early Old Kingdom: a View from Elephantine, Aspects of Early Egypt (Spencer, J. ed.), pp.108-27

Seligman, C. & Murray, M. 1911, Note upon an Early Egyptian Standard, Man 11, pp.163-71

Serpico, M. & White, R. 2000, The botanical identity and transport of incense during the Egyptian New Kingdom, Antiquity 74 (286), pp.884-97

Shaw, G. 2009, The Death of King Seqenenre Tao, Journal of the American Research Center in Egypt 45, pp.159-76

Shaw, I. 1991, Egyptian Warfare and Weapons, Princes Risborough

Shaw, I. ed. The Oxford History of Ancient Egypt, Oxford

Shaw, I. & Nicholson, P. 1995, British Museum Dictionary of Ancient Egypt, London

Shortland, A. ed. 2001, The Social Context of Technological Change: Egypt & the Near East 1650-1550 BC, Oxford

Siliotti, A. & Leblanc, C. 1993, Nefertari e la Valle delle Regine, Florence

Simpson, S. ed. 2002, Queen of Sheba: Treasures from Ancient Yemen, London

Simpson, W. 1972, The Literature of Ancient Egypt: an anthology of stories, instructions and poetry, New Haven

Skeat, T. 1962, Notes on Ptolemaic Chronology III, Journal of Egyptian Archaeology 48, pp.100-105

Smith, G. 1912, The Royal Mummies, Catalogue général des antiquités égyptiennes de la musée du Caire, Nos. 61051-61100, Cairo

Smith, H. 1974, A Visit to Ancient Egypt: life at Memphis and Saqqara (c.500-30 BC), Warminster

Smith, H. & Hall, R. 1984, Ancient Centres of Egyptian Civilisation, London

Smith, H. & Jeffreys, D.G. 1986, A Survey of Memphis, Egypt, Antiquity 60 (229), pp.88-95

Smith, W. 1981, The Art and Architecture of Ancient Egypt, London

Smither, P. 1945, The Semnah Despatches, Journal of Egyptian Archaeology 31, pp.3-10

Southern, P. 1998, Mark Antony, Stroud

Southern, P. 2001, Julius Caesar, Stroud

Sowada, K. 1999, Black-topped Ware in Early Dynastic Contexts, Journal of Egyptian Archaeology 85, pp.85-102

Spence, K. 2000, Ancient Egyptian Chronology and the Astronomical Orientation of Pyramids, Nature 408, pp.320-24

Spencer, J. 1993, Early Egypt: the rise of civilization in the Nile valley, London

Spencer, J. 2011, The Egyptian temple and Settlement at Naukratis, British Museum Studies in Ancient Egypt and Sudan, pp.17, 31–49

Springborg, P. 1990, Ptolemaic Queens, Greek daimon, the Roman Emperor and his genius, Royal persons: patriarchal monarchy and the feminine principle, London, pp.194-214

Stadelmann, R. 2000, Kom el-Hetan: the Mortuary Temple of Amenhotep III, Egyptian Archaeology 16, pp.14-15

Stead, M. 1986, Egyptian Life, London

Stevenson, A. 2009.a, Predynastic burials, UCLA Encyclopedia of Egyptology (ed. Wendrich, W.), http://escholarship.org/uc/item/2m3463b2

Stevenson, A. 2009.b, Palettes, UCLA Encyclopedia of Egyptology (ed. Wendrich, W.), http://repositories.cdlib.org/nelc/uee/1069

Stocks, D. 2001, Testing ancient Egyptian granite-working methods in Aswan, Upper Egypt, Antiquity 75 (287), pp.89-94

Stocks, D. 2003, Immutable laws of friction: preparing and fitting stone blocks into the Great Pyramid of Giza, Antiquity 77 (297), pp.572-8

Strouhal, E. & Callender, G. 1992, Profile of Queen Mutnodjmet, Bulletin of the Australian Center for Egyptology 3, pp.67-76

Strouhal, E. & Gaballa, F. 1993, King Djedkara Isesi and his Daughters, Biological Anthropology and the Study of Ancient Egypt, London (eds. Davies, W. & Walker, R.), London, pp.104-118

Strouhal, E., Gaballa, M., Bonani, G., Woelfli, W., Nemeckova, A. & Saunders, S. 1998, Re-Investigation of the Remains thought to be of King Djoser and those of an Unidentified Female from the Step Pyramid at Saqqara, Proceedings of the Seventh International Congress of Egyptologists (ed. C.Eyre), Leuven, pp.1103-7

Suetonius, trans. Graves, R. 1957, The Twelve Caesars, Harmondsworth

Sullivan, E. 2012, Visualizing the size and movement of the portable festival barks at Karnak temple, British Museum Studies in Ancient Egypt and Sudan 19, pp.1-37

Sweeney, D. 2004, Forever Young? The Representation of Older and Ageing Women in Ancient Egyptian Art, Journal of the American Research Center in Egypt 41, pp.67-84

Tait, J. 2003, Cleopatra by Name, Cleopatra Reassessed, British Museum Occasional Paper No.103, (eds. Walker, S. & Ashton, S.), London, pp.3-7

Tarn, W. 1936, The Bucheum Stelae: a Note, Journal of Roman Studies 26 (2), pp.187-89

Taylor, J. 1998, Nodjmet, Payankh and Herihor: the End of the New Kingdom reconsidered, in Proceedings of the Seventh International Congress of Egyptologists (ed. C. Eyre), Leuven, pp.1143-55

Taylor, J. 2001, Death and the Afterlife in Ancient Egypt, London

Terrace, E. & Fischer, H. 1970, Treasures of the Cairo Museum from Predynastic to Roman times, London

Thomas, A. 1981, Gurob: a New Kingdom Town, London

Thomas, E. 1966, The Royal Necropoleis of Thebes, Princeton

Thomas, N. 1995, The American Discovery of Ancient Egypt, Los Angeles

Thomas, R. & Villing, A. 2013, Naukratis revisited 2012: integrating new fieldwork and old research, British Museum Studies in Ancient Egypt and Sudan 20, pp.81–125

Thompson, D. 1955, A Portrait of Arsinoe Philadelphos, American Journal of Archaeology 59 (3), pp.199–206

Thompson, D. 1973, Ptolemaic oinochoai and portraits in faience: aspects of the ruler-cult, Oxford

Tidyman, R. 1995, Further Evidence of a coup d'etat at the end of dynasty 11? Bulletin of the Australian Center for Egyptology 6, pp.103-10

Tiradritti, F. 1998, Isis, the Egyptian Goddess who Conquered Rome, Cairo

Toivari, J. 1998, Marriage at Deir el-Medina, in Proceedings of the Seventh International Congress of Egyptologists (ed. C.Eyre), Leuven, pp.1143-55

Tomber, R. 2000, Indo-Roman trade: the ceramic evidence from Egypt, Antiquity 74 (285), pp.624-31

Tooley, A. 1991, Child's Toy or Ritual Object, Göttinger Miszellen 123, pp.101-11

Török, L. 1997, The Kingdom of Kush: Handbook of the Napatan-Meroitic Civilization, Brill

Trigger, B., Kemp, B., O'Connor, D. & Lloyd, A. 1983, Ancient Egypt: A Social History, London

Troy, L. 1986, Patterns of Queenship in Ancient Egyptian Myth and History, Uppsala

Uphill, E. 1988, Egyptian Towns and Cities, Aylesbury

Uytterhoeven, I. & Blom-Böer, I. 2002, New Light on the Egyptian Labyrinth: Evidence from a Survey at Hawara, Journal of Egyptian Archaeology 88, pp.111-20

van Dijk, J. 1996, Horemheb and the Struggle for the Throne of Tutankhamen, Bulletin of the Australian Center for Egyptology 7, pp.29-42

Vandersleyen, C. 1995, Who was the First King in the Valley of the Kings? Valley of the Sun Kings: New Explorations in the Tombs of the Pharaohs (Wilkinson, R. ed.), Tucson, pp.22-4

Vassilika, E. 2010, The Tomb of Kha, Turin

Vasunia, P. 2001, The Gift of the Nile: Hellenizing Egypt from Aeschylus to Alexander, Berkeley

Veldmeijer, A. J. 2010, Tutankhamen's Footwear: Studies of Ancient Egyptian Footwear, Batinge

Vergnieux, R. & Gondran, M. 1997, Aménophis IV et les pierres du soleil: Akhénaten retrouvé, Paris

Vermeersch, P., Paulissen, E., Van Peer, P., Stokes, S., Charlier, C., Stringer, C. & Lindsay, W. 1998, A Middle Palaeolithic burial of a modern human at Taramsa Hill, Egypt, Antiquity 72 (277), pp.475-84

Verner, M. 1994, Forgotten Pharaohs, Lost Pyramids: Abusir, Prague

Verner, M. 1997, Further Thoughts on the Khentkaus Problem, Discussions in Egyptology 38, pp.109-17

Verner, M. 2001, The Pyramids, New York

Virgil, trans. Dryden, J. 1968, Virgil's Aened, New York

Vogel, C. 2003, Fallen Heroes? Winlock's 'Slain Soldiers' Reconsidered, Journal of Egyptian Archaeology 89, pp.239-45

Vogelsang-Eastwood, G. 1993, Pharaonic Egyptian Clothing, Leiden

Vogelsang-Eastwood, G. 1999, Tutankhamen's Wardrobe, Leiden

Vörös, G. 2007, Egyptian Temple Architecture: 100 Years of Hungarian Excavations in Egypt, 1907-2007, Budapest

Vos, R. 1993, The Apis Embalming Ritual, P.Vindob.3873, Leuven

Wachsmann, S. 1987, Aegeans in the Theban Tombs: Orientalia Lovaniensia Analecta 20, Louvain

Wade, C. 2008, Sarcophagus Circle: the goddesses in the tomb, The Tenth International Congress of Egyptologists, Rhodes pp.269-70

Wainwright, G. 1913, The Keftiu People of the Egyptian Monuments, Annals of Archaeology & Anthropology 6 (1-2), pp.24-83

Wainwright, G. 1923, The Red Crown in Early Prehistoric Times, Journal of Egyptian Archaeology 9, pp.23-33

Walbank, F. 1979, Egypt in Polybius, Glimpses of Ancient Egypt: Studies in Honour of H.W. Fairman (eds. in Ruffle, J., Gaballa, G.A. & Kitchen K.A.), Warminster, pp.180-89

Walbank, F. 1981, The Hellenistic World, London

Walker, S. & Higgs, P. 2001, Cleopatra of Egypt: from History to Myth, London

Ward, W. 1977, Neferhotep and His Friends: a Glimpse at the Lives of Ordinary Men, Journal of Egyptian Archaeology 63, pp.63-6

Ward, C. 2012. Building pharaoh's ships: Cedar, incense and sailing the Great Green, British Museum Studies in Ancient Egypt and Sudan 18, pp.217-32

Warden, M. 2000, Recarving the Namer Palette, Nekhen News 12, pp.26-7

Watterson, B. 1979, The Use of Alliteration in Ptolemaic, Glimpses of Ancient Egypt: Studies in Honour of H.W. Fairman (eds. in Ruffle, J., Gaballa, G. & Kitchen K.), Warminster, pp.167-9

Watterson, B. 1998, The House of Horus at Edfu, Stroud

Weeks, K. 2000, KV.5: a Preliminary Report on the Excavations of the Tomb of the Sons of Ramses II in the Valley of the Kings, Cairo

Weigall, A. 1911, The tomb of Amenhotep, Annales du Service des Antiquités de l'Egypte II, pp.174-75

Weigall, A. 1927, A History of the Pharaohs II, London

Weinstein, J. 1974, A Statuette of the Princess Sobeknefru at Tell Gezer, Bulletin of the American Schools of Oriental Research 213, pp.49-57

Welles, C. 1962, The Discovery of Sarapis and the Foundation of Alexandria, Historia 11, pp.271-89

Wells, R. 1985, Sothis and the Satet Temple on Elephantine: a Direct Connection, Studien zur Altägyptischen Kultur 12, pp.255-302

Welsby, D. 1996, The Kingdom of Kush: the Napatan and Meroitic Empires, London

Wendorf, F. & Schild, R. 2002, Implications of Incipient Social Complexity in the Late Neolithic in the Egyptian Sahara, Gifts of the Desert (Friedman, R. ed.), London, pp.13-20

Wendrich, W. & Cappers, R. 2005, Egypt's Earliest Granaries: evidence from the Fayuum, Egyptian Archaeology 27, pp.12-15

Wengrow, D. 2001, Rethinking Cattle-Cults in Early Egypt: towards a prehistoric perspective on the Narmer Palette, Cambridge Archaeological Journal 11 (1), pp.91-104

Wengrow, D. 2006, The Archaeology of Early Egypt: Social Transformations in North-East Africa, c.10,000 to 2,650 BC, Cambridge

Wengrow, F., Dee, M., Foster, S., Stevenson, A. & Ramsey, C. 2014, Cultural convergence in the Neolithic of the Nile Valley: a prehistoric perspective on Egypt's place in Africa, Antiquity 88 (339), pp.95-111

Wente, E. 1962, Egyptian 'Make Merry' Songs Reconsidered, Journal of Near Eastern Studies 21 (2), pp.118-28

Wente, E.F. 1982, Funerary Beliefs of the Ancient Egyptians, Expedition 24 (2), pp.17-26

Wente, E. 1990, Letters from Ancient Egypt, Atlanta

Wente, E. & Harris, J. 1992, Royal Mummies of the Eighteenth Dynasty: a Biological and Egyptological Approach, After Tut'ankhAmen (ed. N. Reeves), London, pp.2-20

Werner, E. 1979, Identification of Nefertiti in Talatat Reliefs Previously Published as Akhenaten, Orientalia 48, pp.324-31

Wheeler, N. 1935, Pyramids and their Purpose, Antiquity 9 (33-35), pp.5-21, 161-89, 292-304

Whitehorne, J. 2001, Cleopatras, London

Wilding, D. 1977, Egyptian Saints: deification in Pharaonic Egypt, New York

Wilfong, T. 1997, Women and Gender in Ancient Egypt: from Prehistory to Late Antiquity, Ann Arbor

Wilkinson, A. 1998, The Garden in Ancient Egypt, London

Wilkinson, C. 1983, Egyptian Wall Paintings, New York

Wilkinson, R. 2000, The Complete Temples of Ancient Egypt, London

Wilkinson, T. 1999, Early Dynastic Egypt, London

Wilkinson, T. 2003, Genesis of the Pharaohs, London

Wilkinson, T. 2010, The Rise and Fall of Ancient Egypt, London

Wilkinson, T. 2011, Ancient Egypt and Africa, Shemu: the Egyptian Society of South Africa http://egyptiansociety.co.za/2011/01/ancient-egypt-and-africa-2/

Williams, B. 1988, Narmer and the Coptos Colossi, Journal of the American Research Center in Egypt 25, pp.35-59

Williams, C. 1936, The Season of 1935 to 1936 in Egypt, American Journal of Archaeology 40, pp.551-6

Williams, E. 1985, Isis Pelagia and a Roman Marble Matrix from the Athenian Agora, Hesperia 54 (2), pp.109-19

Wilson, J. 1931, Ceremonial Games of the New Kingdom, Journal of Egyptian Archaeology 17, pp.211-20

Wilson, J. 1955, Buto and Hierakonpolis in the Geography of Egypt, Journal of Near Eastern Studies 14 (4), pp.209-36

Wilson, P. 1997, Slaughtering the Crocodile at Edfu and Dendera, The Temple in Ancient Egypt: New Discoveries and Recent Research, (ed. S.Quirke), London, pp.179-203

Winlock, H. 1917, A Restoration of the Reliefs from the Mortuary Temple of Amenhotep I, Journal of Egyptian Archaeology 4, pp.11-15

Winlock, H. 1924, The Tombs of the Kings of the Seventeenth Dynasty at Thebes, Journal of Egyptian Archaeology 10, p.217-277

Winlock, H. 1940, The Court of King Neb-Ḥepet-Rē Mentu-Hotpe at the Shaṭṭ er Rigāl, American Journal of Semitic Languages and Literatures 57 (2), pp.137-61

Winlock, H. 1942, Excavations at Deir el-Bahari 1911-1931, New York

Winlock, H. 1975, Excavating Egypt: Digger's Luck, The Metropolitan Museum of Art Bulletin 33 (2), pp.56-71

Winlock, H. 2007, The Slain Soldiers of Nebhepetre Montuhotep, New York

Witt, R. 1970, The Egyptian Cults in Macedonia, Ancient Macedonia: papers read at the first international symposium held in Thessaloniki,

26-29 August 1968 (ed. Laourdas, B. & Makaronas, C.J.), Thessalonika, pp. 324-33

Witt, R. 1971, Isis in the Graeco-Roman World, London

Yoshimura, S. & Takamiya, I. 1994, A Monument of Khaemwaset at Saqqara, Egyptian Archaeology 5, pp.19-23

Zabkar, L.V. 1963, Herodotus and the Egyptian Idea of Immortality, Journal of Near Eastern Studies 22 (1), pp.57-63

Zecchi, M. 2008, The Monument of Abgig, Studien zur Altägyptischen Kultur 37, pp.373-86

Ziegler, C. 1990, The Louvre: Egyptian Antiquities, Paris

Zivie, A. 1998, The Tomb of Lady Maïa, Wet-nurse of Tutankhamen, Egyptian Archaeology: Bulletin of the Egypt Exploration Society 13, pp.7-8

Zivie, A. 2007, The Lost Tombs of Saqqara, Toulouse

Zivie-Coche, C. 2002, Sphinx: History of a Monument, London

Picture Acknowledgements

Index

1st Dynasty
Narmer 36–42, 118
Aha 43–45
Djer 45–47, 141–42, 152
Djet 47–48
Merneith 48–49
Den 49–52
Anedjib 52
Semerkhet 52–53, 63
Qaa 53
2nd Dynasty 54–59
3rd Dynasty 60–65
4th Dynasty
Snefru 64–71, 94, 108, 134, 146
Khufu 71–77, 248
Djedefra 77–78
Khafra 78–79, 248
Menkaura 79–81
Khentkawes I 81–82, 83, 110, 176
Shepseskhaf 82, 84, 248
5th Dynasty
Userkaf 84–85
Sahura 85–87, 248
Neferirkara 87–88
Khentkawes II 88–89
Raneferef 89
Niuserra 89–92
Djedkara 92–95
Unas 96–99, 248
story of Ruddedet 83–84
6th Dynasty
Teti 99–102

Userkara 102–3
Pepi I 102–4
Merenra 104–6
Pepi II 106–10
Nemtyemsaf 110
Neitikrety 110–11
7th & 8th Dynasties 112–14
9th and 10th Dynasties 114–17, 118, 119
11th Dynasty (all Egypt) 119–125
11th Dynasty (Thebes) 117–19
12th Dynasty
Amenemhat I 125–26, 127–130
Sesostris I 129, 130–33
Amenemhat II 133–36
Sesostris II 136–39
Sesostris III 139–144
Amenemhat III 144–150, 151, 158, 176, 209, 298
Amenemhat IV 150
Sobeknefru 150–52, 176
13th Dynasty 152–55, 157, 159, 160
14th Dynasty 155–56, 157
15th and 16th Dynasties (Hyksos) 157–160, 162, 163–64, 166, 168–69
17th Dynasty 160–67
18th Dynasty
Ahmose I 168–170
Ahmose-Nefertari 168, 169, 170–73, 175, 182, 218
Amenhotep I 170–72
Tuthmosis I 172, 173–75, 182, 191
Tuthmosis II 176

Tuthmosis III   176, 178, 181, 184, 185–191
Hatshepsut *see* Hatshepsut
Amenhotep II   189–190, 191, 192–98, 272, 273
Tuthmosis IV   198–200, 272
Amenhotep III *see* Amenhotep III
Amenhotep IV/Akhenaten *see* Akhenaten/Amenhotep IV
Nefertiti/Smenkhkara *see* Nefertiti/Smenkhkara
Tutankhamen   1, 221, 226, 227–231, 232, 236, 259
Ay   226, 227, 229, 231–32, 233, 236, 246
Horemheb   227–28, 229, 232–34, 236
19th Dynasty
Ramses I   235, 269
Seti I   235–39, 269
Ramses II *see* Ramses II
Merenptah   250–52, 272
Amenmesse   252
Seti II   252, 272
Siptah   252–53, 272
Tawosret   252, 253–54
20th Dynasty
Sethnakht   254
Ramses III   254–59, 266
Ramses IV   259–260, 272
Ramses V   260, 261, 262–63, 272
Ramses VI   261, 262–63, 272
Ramses VII   261–62
Ramses VIII   262
Ramses IX   262–64
Ramses X   264
Ramses XI   264–67
21st Dynasty   268–274
22nd Dynasty   274–76
23rd Dynasty   276
24th Dynasty   278
25th Dynasty   277–283
26th Dynasty   282–293
27th Dynasty   293–300
28th Dynasty   299
29th Dynasty   299
30th Dynasty   299–303, 304, 306, 311

Aamu settlers   114, 138, 157
Abu Rawash   77
Abu Simbel   245–46, 285
Abusir
  restoration   248
  temples   85, 86, 90–91, 248
  tomb robbing   113
  tombs   51, 85, 86, 87, 88–90, 248
Abydos
  Abydos Dynasty   157
  cenotaph complexes   142, 168, 239
  funerary palaces   58
  Gebel el-Arak knife   27–28
  Osireion   237–38
  regional power centre   28, 30, 93, 103
  restoration   120, 152, 290
  stelae   56, 103, 114
  temples   131, 154, 236
  Tomb of Osiris   141–42, 152–53, 209
  tombs
    Early Dynastic period   42, 44–45, 46–47, 48, 49, 51–53, 56, 58, 60
    Middle Kingdom period   142, 152
    New Kingdom period   267
    Predynastic period   34–35, 35–36, 42
Abydos Dynasty   157
The Admonitions of Ipuwer   113
Aegyptiaka (Hekataios)   298
Aha   43–45
Ahhotep   163, 164, 165–66, 169–170
Ahmose I   168–170
Ahmose II   285, 289–293, 294
Ahmose-Nefertari   168, 169, 170–73, 175, 182, 218
Ahmose, queen of Tuthmosis I   173, 174
Akhenaten/Amenhotep IV
  death   225
  desecration of body   263

disappearance 232, 236
father's first jubilee 213
father's funeral 215
funeral and burial 226
incompetence 217
reburial 230
reign with Nefertiti 218–225
Akhmim 201, 210, 232, 299
Alexander Helios 361, 364
Alexander IV 310, 311, 312
Alexander the Great
  body taken to Egypt 311
  body's return to Macedonia 310
  burial 311
  death and embalming 309–10
  as king 305–9
  reburial 315, 326
  robbing of tomb 344
  tomb 315, 326, 331, 365–66
  youth 304–5
Alexandria
  as capital city 311, 320–21
  culture and learning 351
  deposing of Ptolemy X 344
  deposing of Ptolemy XII (Auletes) 349
  fall to Rome 365–66
  fight against Caesar and Kleopatra VII 356
  founding 307
  instability 332, 333
  Library 314, 321–22, 326
  multiculturalism 320–21
  murder of Oinanthe 332–33
  murder of Ptolemy XI 345–46
  Museum 321, 326
  Pharos lighthouse 314, 320
  return of Ptolemy XII (Auletes) 350–51
  royal palace 322
  Serapeum 331, 337, 361
  stelae 323
  temples 323–24, 326–27, 357

tomb of Alexander 326, 331, 344, 365–66
tomb of Kleopatra VII 357
Amen, god
  Amen-Ra 180–81, 189, 194, 196, 203, 280
  oracle at Siwa oasis 293, 308
  removal of 219–220
  return of 226–27
  rise of 180, 268
  temples 188–89, 194, 270, 277, 280–81, 286, 296 see also Karnak
  Zeus-Amen 304, 306, 313
Amen-Ra, god 180–81, 189, 194, 196, 203, 280
Amenemhat I 125–26, 127–130
Amenemhat II 133–36
Amenemhat III 144–150, 151, 158, 176, 185, 209, 298
Amenemhat IV 150
Amenhotep, High Priest 262, 264, 265
Amenhotep I 170–72
Amenhotep II 189–190, 191, 192–98, 272, 273
Amenhotep III
  building projects 203–6, 208–10, 238, 329
  death and burial 215–16
  family 201–2
  foreign relations 206–8
  funerary temple 210–12, 237, 251
  interests 200–201, 202
  jubilees 213–15
  military campaigns 202–3
  plague 224
  reburial 220–21, 272
  reused statues of 242–43, 256, 280
  succession 200
  tomb 212
  wealth 203, 206
Amenhotep IV see Akhenaten/ Amenhotep IV

Amenhotep, son of Hapu 200, 202, 203, 204, 210, 256, 286, 340
Amenirdis I 277, 278, 279
Amenirdis II 283
Amenmesse 252
Ameny-Qemau 153
Amyrtaios 299
Anedjib 52
animal mummies 288, 313
Ankhesenamen/Ankhesenapaaten 226, 227, 230, 231
Ankhnesneferibre 286, 289, 294
Ankhnespepi I 103, 104
Ankhnespepi II 103, 105, 106, 107
Ankhwennefer 332, 334
Antigonas 310, 312
Antioch 325, 338, 341, 361
Antiochos III 330, 333, 334
Antiochos IV 335–36, 337
Antony, Mark 350, 359–365
Apis bull
  Cambyses's killing of 294
  Sakkara burial ground 301
  veneration of 49, 55, 209, 248–49, 295, 298, 306, 337
Apophis 159–160, 163–64, 166
Apries 289
Archelaos 350
Aristotle 304–5
Arses 303
Arsinoe I 315
Arsinoe II 315–321, 322–24
Arsinoe III 330, 331–32
Arsinoe IV 347, 356, 359, 360
Arsinoe, mother of Ptolemy I 305, 312
Artaxerxes I 297
Artaxerxes II 300
Artaxerxes III 301, 302–3
artists and craftsmen
  First Intermediate period 114, 120
  Late period 281, 282, 295
  Minoan 135, 175
  New Kingdom period 185, 187, 192,
    197, 222, 231–32, 235, 238–39, 243–44
  Old Kingdom period 69, 74, 98
  Predynastic period 33
  Ptolemaic period 327
Ashayet 121, 121–22
Asiatics 114, 120, 134, 138 see also Palestine; Palestinians in Egypt
Assyria/Assyrians 206, 281, 282–83, 286, 296
Astarte, goddess 160, 208, 255
Aswan
  canals 105, 140
  Elephantine island see Elephantine
  quarries 106, 120, 141, 146, 175
  temples 312
  tombs 107
Aswan Dam 128, 131, 245
Asyut region 116, 119
Aten sun disc, god 175, 197, 203, 209, 218–19, 220, 221, 222, 273
aten the sun disc 172
Auletes see Ptolemy XII (Auletes)
Avaris 158, 159, 160, 163–64, 166, 168–69, 235 see also Perunefer
Ay 226, 227, 229, 231–32, 233, 236, 246

Babylonia/Babylonians 194, 206, 207, 284, 285, 291, 325
Badarian culture 20–23
Bakenrenef 278
barques, sacred 121, 141, 181, 182, 204, 268–69, 353
Bastet, goddess 54, 55, 99, 146, 274
Bastet-Sekhmet, goddess 74, 78, 86, 325
Bedouin tribes 86, 114, 132, 236
Beni Hasan 116, 135–36, 175, 184
Berenike I 314, 319
Berenike II 324–330
Berenike III 343, 345
Berenike IV 347, 349, 350
boat-building 67–68

Book of the Dead 161, 246, 287, 368

Bubastis 54, 99, 146, 274–75

Bucheum 300

Buchis bull 300, 319, 353

Buhen 68, 131, 140, 154–55, 166, 169, 183–84

burial practices
First Intermediate period 119
Hyksos Palestinians 158–59
Predynastic period 19–20, 20–23, 23–25, 25–28, 28–29
Sahara savannah period 15–16
see also grave goods; tombs

Buto 29, 30, 31, 31–32, 86

Byblos
diplomacy 150, 154, 268–69
military expeditions 94, 141, 174, 188
trade 26, 57, 89, 106, 112, 146, 178, 274
unrest 223

Caesar, Julius 348, 353–57, 358–59

Cambyses 293–95, 308

camels 296

canals 34, 41, 115–16, 136–37, 140, 174, 285, 296, 314, 317

Canopic jars 122, 209, 307

cartouches
Early Dynastic period 39–40
Middle Kingdom period 145–46, 151, 153
New Kingdom period 170, 172, 218, 236, 253, 268
Old Kingdom period 66
Ptolemaic period 316, 344
Third Intermediate period 269

cats 21, 191, 209, 349

cattle 13, 14, 67, 101

cenotaphs 122, 142, 168, 237–38, 239, 306

chariots 160

clergy
under Amenhotep III 203
Cambyses's brutality 294–95
exempt from taxes 104, 108, 300, 333, 344
hieratic documents 88
relations with royals 96, 102, 152, 161, 219–220, 327
wealth and power 258
see also Karnak, clergy

climate change 55, 104, 109, 112–13

clothing 19, 48, 50, 79, 151, 202, 295, 355

Coffin Texts 115, 122, 124, 149, 298

coinage 291, 300–301, 308–9, 313, 318

common people
Akhet-Aten city 222
burials 136, 146–47, 243
communication with the dead 116–17, 147
communication with the king 138
craftsmen 243–44
Deir el-Medina settlement 171, 243–44
farmers 98, 124–25, 125
Gerget Khufu settlement 75–77
Golden City 286
Hekanakhte letters 124–25
housewives 147
immigrants 135
Kahun settlement 137–39
literacy 244
Medinet Habu settlement 262
monuments to Osiris 142
poverty 258–59, 262
property ownership 116
soldiers 119, 232–33
tomb robbing 262–63
weavers 76
workers' strike 258
worship 180, 183
see also royal officials and household

cosmetics 22, 25–26, 36, 135, 137

craftsmen *see* artists and craftsmen

creation sagas 5, 6–8, 9–10

Crete 133, 135, 158, 159, 169, 178–79
crops 5, 18–19, 20, 33, 40, 55
crowns 30–31, 47, 50
Cyprus 158, 291, 337–38, 340, 341, 344,
346, 349, 350
Cyrene *see* Libya/Libyans

Dahshur
funerary temples 67, 108
reuse of materials from 128, 129
subsidence 147–48
tombs 70–71, 72, 134–35, 142–43,
146, 147–48, 153
dams 41, 67, 128, 131, 245
Darius I 295–96
Darius III 303, 305, 308
Deir el-Bahari 120–23, 124, 172, 181,
190, 263, 271, 279, 286, 340
Deir el-Medina 171, 197, 205, 220, 233,
243, 244, 259–260, 264
Den 49–52
Dendera 11, 114, 117, 351–52
diplomacy 115–16, 199, 206–7, 217,
223–24, 228–29, 241–42, 290–91, 334
disease 24, 25, 76, 87, 136, 224–25, 310
Djedefra 77–78
Djedkara 92–95
Djer 45–47, 141–42, 152
Djet 47–48
Djoser 60–63, 248
Dra Abu el-Naga 117, 118, 161, 162,
165, 170, 191
dwarves 24, 46, 75, 76, 94, 106–7
'Dynasty Zero' 35–36

Early Dynastic period
1st Dynasty *see* 1st Dynasty
2nd Dynasty 54–59
Edfu 64, 113, 154, 327–28, 332, 348,
357
Egypt, etymology 291
Elephantine 43–44, 46, 64, 89, 131,
209, 285, 286, 299

Esarhaddon 282
Euphrates river 169, 174, 284, 309

famines 47–48, 109, 112, 114, 148,
262–63, 264, 331, 336, 353
the Fayum
building projects 131, 145, 148–49
Hawara complex 148–49
Labyrinth 209
land reclamation 136, 314
Predynastic period 18–19
tombs 136–38, 149–150
First Intermediate period
7th & 8th Dynasties 112–14
9th and 10th Dynasties 114–17, 118,
119
11th Dynasty (all Egypt) 119–126
11th Dynasty (Thebes) 117–19
anarchy 113–14
art 114
building projects 120–23
civil war 117–18, 118–120
climate change 112–13
communication with the dead 116–17
craftsmen 120
tomb robbing 113, 118
trade 120
foreign tribute 133–34, 188, 194,
199–200, 206
forts 120, 129, 131, 140, 163, 188–89
funerary palaces 44–45, 54, 58–59, 61
funerary temples
First Intermediate period 122–23, 141
Middle Kingdom period 129, 142
New Kingdom period 172, 181–82,
183, 205, 210–11, 231–32, 233, 238,
242–43, 251, 256, 256–57
Old Kingdom period 67, 74–75, 81,
84, 88–89, 89, 90, 113

Geb, god 7, 8
Gebel Barkal 174, 188–89, 194, 277,
278, 280

Gebel el-Arak knife 27–28
Gebel Ramlah community 15
'Gebelein Man' 25
Gerget Khufu 75–77
Giza
  Alexander's visit 305–6
  Great Sphinx 78, 175, 196–97, 198,
    199, 201
  Herodotus' visit 298
  restoration 247–48
  reuse of materials from 128–29
  settlement of Khufu 75–77
  solar boats 72–73
  stelae 198
  temples 78, 80, 108, 270
  tombs
    1st Dynasty 48
    4th Dynasty 71–72, 73–75, 76, 77,
      78, 79, 80, 81, 248
    5th Dynasty 93
graffiti 61, 70, 85, 125, 226–27, 240,
  285, 298–99, 328–29
grave goods
  Early Dynastic period 43, 44–45, 47,
    55, 58
  First Intermediate period 123, 124–25
  Middle Kingdom period 134–35, 137,
    138–39, 143
  New Kingdom period 187, 212,
    230–31, 246–47, 248, 253–54
  Old Kingdom period 63, 71–72, 74
  Predynastic period 20, 21–23, 24–25,
    25–28, 34–35
  Second Intermediate period 158–59,
    161, 162, 165
  Third Intermediate period 270
Great Pyramid 71, 72, 73–75, 77, 2
48
Great Sphinx 78, 175, 196–97, 198,
  199, 201
Greece/Greeks
  admiration of 14, 275, 288, 291–92
  Alexander as ruler 305

blending with Egyptian culture
  290–92, 313
diplomacy 300, 334–35
mercenaries 283–84, 285, 289, 300
Peloponnesian War 299
Persian war 296, 297, 299
Sea Peoples 250, 254–55, 256, 271
settlers 314
trading colonies 275, 285
visits to Egypt 291–92, 297–99
see also Ptolemaic Dynasty

Hagr el-Merwa rock 174, 203
Hakor 299
Hapi, god 145, 155
Hathor, goddess
  clergy 84
  cow symbol 26
  Hathor-Isis 190–91, 270, 351, 352, 353
  Hathor-Sekhmet see Hathor-Sekhmet,
    goddess
  Hyksos belief in 160
  myths 7, 10
  sistrum song-and-dance routine 99,
    130
  temples 57–58, 66–67, 120, 145, 146,
    178, 183, 184, 190, 340
  Thebes' West Bank 12, 117, 118,
    120–21, 181
Hathor-Sekhmet, goddess 62, 77–78,
  147, 174, 196, 208, 245, 246
Hatshepsut
  Arsinoe II's use of 316
  co-regent with Tuthmosis III 178–185
  disappearance 190, 191, 236
  princess 173, 174
  reburial 191
  regent for Tuthmosis III 176–78
Hawara 148–49, 151
Hekanakhte letters 124–25
Hekataios of Miletus 297–98, 299
Heliopolis
  Acacia House 196

burials 19
creation myth 6, 9
gardens 255
Herodotus' visit 298
library 313
Mnevis bull 220, 319
obelisks 85, 99, 106, 189, 286
Persian sacking 302
sphinxes 236
temples 58, 61–62, 67, 130–31, 196,
  209, 258, 271
Hemiunu 73–75
Herakleopolis 115, 117, 119, 120, 151,
  228
Herihor 268–69
Hermopolis 6, 184, 197, 278
Herodotus 294–95, 297–99
Herwennefer 332
Hetepheres (daughter) 68
Hetepheres II (granddaughter) 77–78, 79
Hetepheres (mother) 64, 65, 66, 67, 68,
  71–72
Hetephirnebty 60, 61–62
Hetepsekhemwy 54
Hibis 286
Hierakonpolis
  burials 24–25, 27
  funerary palaces 58
  Narmer Palette 36–37
  Nekhbet, goddess 31
  Qaa's celebration 53
  regional power centre 28, 30, 32–34
  temples 33–34, 36, 57, 104, 154
  wealth 28
hippopotami 18, 19, 42, 163
Histories (Herodotus) 297–99
Hittites 188, 223, 228–29, 236, 240–42,
  250
Homer 193, 275, 307, 331
Hor 336, 337
Horemheb 227–28, 229, 232–34, 236
horses 160, 183, 188, 191, 193, 240,
  278, 319, 358

Horus, god
  creation myth 8, 9
  Hierakonpolis 31, 33, 104
  Ra-Horakhty 196–97, 201
  and Seth 8, 31, 32, 56, 328
  temples 33–34, 36, 46, 57, 104, 113,
    123–24, 154, 169, 183–84, 197,
    327–28, 332, 348, 357
human sacrifice 45
Huni 64–65
hunting 11, 13, 18, 19, 25, 188, 202
Hyksos Palestinians 157–160, 162,
  163–64, 166, 168–69, 185–86, 236

Ibi 112
The Iliad (Homer) 275
Imhotep 60–61, 63
immigration 134, 135, 152
Inaros 297
India 309, 318, 341, 348
Ineni 171, 172, 175
Intef I 117
Intef II 117–18
Intef III 118–19
Intef VI 161–62
invasions see military campaigns/defence
Iput 99, 99–100, 102–3
Ipuwer 113, 114
Iri-hor 35–36
Isis, goddess
  Hathor-Isis 190–91, 270, 351, 352, 353
  myths 7–8, 9, 32, 83, 96–97
  temples 280, 286, 299, 307, 320, 347
Israel 251, 271, 274
Ita 134, 134–35
Itaweret 134–35
Itj-tawy (Lisht) 127–28, 132–33, 147,
  154, 158

jewellery/adornments
  Early Dynastic period 47
  First Intermediate period 116, 122,
    123

Middle Kingdom period 134–35, 137, 143, 147
New Kingdom period 187, 205, 212, 246, 253–54, 267
Predynastic period 15, 19, 21–22, 25
Second Intermediate period 161, 162, 165
Jewish mercenaries 285, 286, 339, 340, 342
Jewish settlers 329, 337
Judah 274, 281, 284

Ka 35–36
Kadashman-Enlil 207, 214
Kahun 137–39
Kamose 166–67
Karnak
  Assyrian invasion 282
  Aten complex 218–19
  Bucheum 300
  building projects 131, 175, 189, 204, 232, 279–280, 286, 328, 331
  Chamber of the Ancestors 153
  clergy 219
    power struggle with king 196, 198–99, 219, 260–61, 262, 273
    reusing royal tombs 263
    tombs 286–87
    war with Panehesy 265
    wealth and power 180, 189, 258, 260, 262, 268–69, 275–76
  closure 219–220
  floods 155, 276–77, 280
  God's Wife rituals 164, 170
  hypostyle halls 175, 238
  Mut's monument 180–81
  obelisks 175, 181, 189, 199, 204
  Palestinian rebel corpses, display of 194
  processional route to Thebes 181
  pylon gateways 175, 204, 300
  Red Chapel 181
  resumption 226–27

sacred barques 121, 181, 268–69
Seti I's funerary temple 238
shrines 89, 118, 131, 204, 308, 312
statues 89, 153, 155, 175, 197, 199, 204, 208, 219, 227, 286, 289
stelae 166, 167
Temple of Khonsu 259
Temple of Mut 208–9, 211
Tomb of Osiris 331
trees and plants 179–180, 189
Kashta 277
Kerma 154–55, 173
Kha 197, 200, 204, 212
Khafra 78–79, 248
Khamerernebty 79–80, 90
Khamudi 168
Khamwese 247–49
Khasekhem/Khasekhemwy 56–59, 61
Khendjer 153
Khentkawes I 81–82, 83, 110, 176
Khentkawes II 88–89
Khety I 115
Khety II 115, 118
Khnum, god 9, 44, 286, 312
Khnumet 134, 135
Khufu 71–77, 248
Kleomenes 308, 330
Kleopatra I 334–35
Kleopatra II 335–341
Kleopatra III 337, 339–343, 345
Kleopatra Selene 361, 364
Kleopatra V 346, 349, 350
Kleopatra VII
  co-ruler with Caesarion 359
  co-ruler with father 352
  co-ruler with Ptolemy XIII 353, 356
  co-ruler with Ptolemy XIV 356–57
  and Julius Caesar 354–55, 356, 358–59
  and Mark Antony 359–365
  ousted by Ptolemy XIII 353–54
  physical appearance and personality 355
  princess 347, 349–350, 351

sole ruler 352–53
suicide 366–67
war with Rome 361–67
Koptos 40, 104, 108, 117, 131, 161, 189, 319–320
el-Kurru 278, 279
Kush *see* Nubia/Nubians

Lahun 136–39, 152
Late period
  25th Dynasty 277–283
  26th Dynasty 282–293
  27th Dynasty 293–99
  28th and 29th Dynasties 299
  30th Dynasty 299–303
  Second Persian period 302–3
the Levant
  military campaigns 188, 228, 236, 284
  trade 26, 27, 32, 33, 35, 135, 150
libraries 205–6, 244, 247, 279, 313–14, 321–22, 326, 328
Libya/Libyans
  22nd Dynasty 274–76
  23rd Dynasty 276
  bequeathed to Rome 344
  Greek settlers 289
  invasions of Egypt 236, 250–51, 254, 256, 262
  mercenaries 265, 271, 274
  military campaigns 68, 85, 120, 129
  pharaohs 271
  under Ptolemies 312, 324–25, 337, 338
linen 19
Lisht (Itj-tawy) 127–28, 132–33, 147, 154, 158
livestock 18, 19, 33, 67, 222
Luxor *see* Karnak; Thebes
Luxor Temple 181, 204, 210, 227, 300, 308
Lysimachus 310, 315

Maadi culture 19–20

Maat, goddess 7, 66, 113, 204
Maathorneferura 242
Macedonia 304, 333, 334
Macedonian Dynasty 310–12 *see also* Alexander the Great
Mafdet, goddess 51
Malkata 205, 210, 212, 213
Manetho 313, 316, 329
mastaba tombs *see* tombs
Medamud 141, 320
medical practice 76, 87, 101, 138, 179
Medinet Habu 181, 230, 231, 233, 256, 264, 265, 266, 279
the Medjai 105, 129, 131, 140, 159
Megiddo 186, 194, 274, 284
Meidum 64, 65, 69–70, 113
Meir 139, 159, 184
Memphis
  Alexander's coronation 306
  Apis bull *see* Apis bull
  building projects 169, 240
  as capital city 60, 93, 96, 205, 226–27, 264, 279, 333, 337
  creation myth 6
  decline 112, 113–14
  foreign invasions 282, 293, 365
  founding 41
  library 247, 279
  palaces 44, 250, 289
  statue workshops 50
  temples 41–42, 49, 218, 248, 258, 278, 291, 298
Mendes 298, 302, 319
Menkaura 79–81, 108
mercenaries 140, 222, 255, 265, 274, 283–84, 285, 286, 289, 291, 300, 344
Merenptah 250–52, 272
Merenra 104–6
Mereruka 100–101
Meresankh III 79
Meretseger, goddess 171, 260
Merikara 115
Merimda Beni Salama 18–19

Merneith 48–49
Middle Kingdom
  12th Dynasty *see* 12th Dynasty
  13th Dynasty 152–55, 157, 159, 160
  14th Dynasty 155–56, 157
military campaigns/defence
  Avaris-Thebes power struggle 163–67,
    168–69
  Early Dynastic period 57
  First Intermediate period civil war
    117–18, 118–120
  Late period 278, 282, 285, 291, 293,
    296, 300, 301–2
  Middle Kingdom period 129, 132,
    133–34, 140
  New Kingdom period 169, 172, 174,
    178, 185–86, 187–88, 193–94, 202–3,
    227–28, 236, 240–41, 250–51,
    254–55
  Old Kingdom period 68, 85, 94, 105
  Ptolemaic period 311, 312, 325, 330,
    342–43, 353, 360–66
  Second Intermediate period 166–67
  Third Intermediate period 271, 274
Min, god 26, 40, 104, 108, 131, 189,
  201, 320
mines 43, 63–64, 68, 106, 129, 135,
  146, 199, 203, 262, 265, 320
Mitanni/Mitannians 169, 187, 188, 194,
  199, 206, 207–8, 215, 217, 223
Mnevis bull 220, 319, 327
Montu, god 89, 117, 133, 141, 160,
  300, 320
Montuhotep I 117, 119
Montuhotep II 119–123, 129, 141, 182
Montuhotep IV 125
Montuhotep, wife of Djehuty 161
mummification
  animal mummies 288, 313
  Late period 287–88
  Middle Kingdom period 139
  New Kingdom period 198, 215, 230,
    252

Old Kingdom period 69, 71, 72, 77,
  98
Predynastic period 22
Second Intermediate period 162–63
Mut, goddess 164, 180–81, 188–89, 204,
  208–9, 211, 270, 286
Mutemwia 200, 201, 202, 213
Mutnodjmet 232, 233
myrrh 86, 179–180, 189, 285, 318
myths 5–10, 83–84, 96–97

Nabta Playa community 13–14
Naqada 31, 40, 43, 56
Naqada culture 23–27, 28
Narmer 36–42, 118
Narmer Palette 36–37
Naukratis 284, 285, 291, 298
Nebra 54
Necho I 282
Necho II 284–85
Nectanebo I 299–300
Nectanebo II 301–2, 304, 306, 311
Neferhotep I 154–55
Neferhotpes 78, 84, 91–92
Neferirkara 87–88
Neferkauhor 112
Nefermaat 69
Nefertari 241, 242, 243, 245–47
Nefertiti/Smenkhkara
  death and burial 229
  disappearance 232, 236
  origins 217–18
  reburial 272–73
  reign with Akhenaten 218–225
  as sole ruler 225–29
Neferuptah 145–46, 149–150, 185
Neferura 176, 178, 181, 184
Nefru 117, 119, 123, 182
Nehesy 155, 160
Neith, goddess 6, 9, 31, 44, 283, 290,
  334
Neithotep 37, 39–40, 43
Neitikrety 110–11

Nekhbet, goddess 31, 50, 58, 86, 159, 202
Nemtyemsaf 110
Nepherites I 299
Nephthys, goddess 7, 83
Neskhons 273–74
New Kingdom period *see* 18th Dynasty; 19th Dynasty; 20th Dynasty
Nile river
  failure to flood 109, 112–13, 148
  floods 5–6, 10, 41, 155, 276–77, 280, 292
  length 17
  Nilometers 41
  settlements, first *see* Predynastic period
  sources 17
Nimaathap 60, 61
Nitocris 110–11, 283
Niuserra 89–92
Nodjmet 265, 268, 269
Nofret II 136, 137
Nofret, mother of Amenemhat 127
Nofret, wife of Rohotep 68–69
Nubia/Nubians
  25th Dynasty 277–283
  Egyptianised 183–84, 200
  famines 148
  Kerma-ware 154–55
  looting of Egyptian tombs 155
  mercenaries 116, 169, 274
  military campaigns/defence
    Early Dynastic period 68
    First Intermediate period 120
    Late period 285
    Middle Kingdom period 131, 140
    New Kingdom period 172, 173–74, 176, 178, 188, 202–3, 236
    Old Kingdom period 85, 105, 107
    Second Intermediate period 159, 166–67
  mines and quarries 64, 68, 85, 89, 129, 141, 146, 159, 320
  temples 197, 227, 245–46, 280, 332

trade 43
Nuri 280, 282
Nut, goddess 7, 8, 78, 96
Nynetjer 54, 55–56

obelisks
  Late period 286, 323
  Middle Kingdom period 130–31
  New Kingdom period 175, 181, 189, 199, 204
  Old Kingdom period 85, 90, 99, 106
  Ptolemaic period 340, 357
Octavian 359, 361–68
The Odyssey (Homer) 275
Oinanthe 332–33
Old Kingdom period 57
  3rd Dynasty 60–65
  4th Dynasty *see* 4th Dynasty
  5th Dynasty *see* 5th Dynasty
  6th Dynasty *see* 6th Dynasty
Opening of the Mouth ceremony 77, 101, 231, 323
Opet Festival 193, 204, 204–5
Osireion 237–38
Osiris, god
  myths 7–8, 32, 96–97
  temples 123, 131, 141–42, 153, 161, 236
  Tomb of Osiris, Abydos 152–53, 209
Osorkon I 274
Osorkon II 274–76
Osorkon III 276
Osorkon the Elder 271

Pakhet, goddess 184
palaces
  Early Dynastic period 44
  Late period 289
  Middle Kingdom period 127–28, 137, 146, 154
  New Kingdom period 175, 180, 185, 205–6, 221, 240, 250, 255–56
  Ptolemaic Dynasty 322

Second Intermediate period 163
Palestine
  military campaigns
    Late period 169
    Middle Kingdom period 129
    New Kingdom period 169, 178,
      186, 187–88, 193–94, 236, 251
    Old Kingdom period 93
  trade 32
Palestinians in Egypt
  Aamu settlers 114
  in administration 138, 140, 152
  Buto community 32
  in households 153
  Hyksos Palestinians 157–160, 162,
    163–64, 166, 168–69
  merchants 194
  royal family 153, 157
  traders 20
Panehesy 264–65
Paramessu 233–34, 235
Pasherenptah 347, 352, 365
Pepi I 102–4
Pepi II 106–10
Per-Ramesse 240, 242, 250, 264, 270
Perdikkas 310–11
perfumes 24, 51–53, 86, 189, 326
Peribsen 56
Persepolis 296
Persians 292–99, 300, 301, 302–3, 305
Perunefer 169, 175, 193 see also Avaris
petroglyphs 11–13
pharaoh, etymology 178
Pharos lighthouse 314, 320
Philae 280, 320, 340
Philip Arrhidaios 310, 311, 312
Philip II of Macedonia 304, 305, 312
Piankh 265–66
Pinudjem I 269–270
Pinudjem II 271–74
Piye 277–78
The Pleasures of Fishing and Fowling 133
Pompey 348, 350, 353–54

Pontus 345, 346
Predynastic period
  'Dynasty Zero' 34–36
  Lower Egypt 18
    agriculture 18–19
    burial practices and grave goods
      19–20
    Buto 31–32
    crown 30–31
    Fayum communities 18–19
    gods 31
    linen 19
    Maadi culture 19–20
    papyrus symbol 31
    technology 20
    Tell el-Farkha 32
    trade 20, 32
  nomes 30
  Towns Palette 30
  transition to Nile-side communities
    17–18
  Two Lands 18, 30–32
  Upper Egypt 18, 30
    Badarian culture 20–23
    burial practices and grave goods
      20–23, 23–27, 28–29
    cosmetics 25–26
    crown 30–31
    figurines 26
    gods 31
    Hierakonpolis 32–33
    Naqada culture 23–27, 28
    pottery 26–27
    rise of 29
    social split in society 28–29
    trade 22, 25–26, 28
    violent deaths 25
priests/priestesses see clergy
prisoners of war 33, 68, 134, 158,
  186–87, 189, 255
Psammetichus I 283–84
Psammetichus II 285–89
Psammetichus III 293

Psusennes I 270–71
Psusennes II 274
Ptah, god
  myths 6
  temples 41–42, 49, 50, 96, 209, 218,
    247, 248, 278, 279, 291, 298
Ptahhotep 89, 93–94
Ptolemaia festival and games 318–19,
  325
Ptolemaic Dynasty
  Ptolemy I 305, 308, 310–15
  Ptolemy II 314, 315–324
  Arsinoe II 315–321, 322–24
  Ptolemy III 324–29
  Berenike II 324–330
  Ptolemy IV 329–332
  Ptolemy V 332–35
  Kleopatra I 334–35
  Ptolemy VI 335–38
  Kleopatra II 335–341
  Ptolemy VII 338
  Ptolemy VIII 335, 336–37, 338–341
  Kleopatra III 337, 339–343, 345
  Ptolemy IX 340, 341–42, 342–43,
    344–45
  Ptolemy X 340, 342, 343, 344
  Berenike III 343, 345
  Ptolemy XI 345–46
  Ptolemy XII (Auletes) 346–352
  Kleopatra V 346, 349, 350
  Berenike IV 347, 349, 350
  Kleopatra VII see Kleopatra VII
  Ptolemy XIII 352, 353–54, 356
  Ptolemy XIV 356, 359
  Ptolemy XV (Caesarion) 357, 358,
    359, 361, 364, 366
  relation with Memphite clergy
    343–44
Ptolemaic period see Macedonian
  Dynasty; Ptolemaic Dynasty
Ptolemy Apion 344
Ptolemy I 305, 308, 310–15
Ptolemy II 314, 315–324

Ptolemy III 324–29
Ptolemy IV 329–332
Ptolemy V 332–35
Ptolemy VI 335–38
Ptolemy VII 338
Ptolemy VIII 335, 336–37, 338–341
Ptolemy IX 340, 341–42, 342–43,
  344–45
Ptolemy X 340, 342, 343, 344
Ptolemy XI 345–46
Ptolemy XII (Auletes) 346–352
Ptolemy XIII 352, 353–54, 356
Ptolemy XIV 356, 359
Ptolemy XV (Caesarion) 357, 358, 359,
  361, 364, 366
Punt 85, 94, 106, 131–32, 146, 179, 189,
  192, 284
Pyramid Texts 96–97, 102, 107, 109,
  112, 115, 287, 327
pyramids see tombs

Qaa 53
Qantir 236, 240
Qarun, Lake 18, 112, 127, 145, 209
'The Quarrel of Apophis and Seqenra'
  163–64
quarries
  First Intermediate period 120
  Late period 286
  Middle Kingdom 141, 146, 184
  New Kingdom period 175, 259
  Old Kingdom period 63–64, 68, 73,
    85, 89, 94, 104, 106
  Predynastic period 14

Ra, god see sun god Ra
Ra-Horakhty, god 196, 197, 201
Rahotep 68–69
Ramesseum 242–43, 258
Ramses I 235, 269
Ramses II
  building projects 239–240, 244–45
  death 249

family 242
Ramesseum 242–43
reburial 269
tomb 247, 249–250
war and diplomacy 240–42
Ramses III 254–59, 266
Ramses IV 259–260, 272
Ramses V 260, 261, 262–63, 272
Ramses VI 261, 262–63, 272
Ramses VII 261–62
Ramses VIII 262
Ramses IX 262–64
Ramses X 264
Ramses XI 264–67
Ranefer 69–70, 84
Raneferef 89
reforms 93, 232–33, 235
Rekhmire 185, 192
Rhind ·Mathematical Papyrus 159–160
rock paintings 26
Rome
  annexation of Egypt 368
  bribes from Egypt 348
  Caesar's building projects 358–59
  Carthaginian war 331
  civil war 353, 359–360
  Cyprus, seizing of 349
  Cyrene bequeathed to 338
  Cyrene bequested to 344
  desire for Egypt 348
  division of Egypt 336–37
  Egypt as protectorate of 336
  Egypt's first contact 318
  Macedonia, taking of 333, 334
  power 349–350
  royal bodyguard in Alexandria
    350–51
  war with Antony and Kleopatra VII
    361–68
  war with Pontus 345
Rosetta Stone 334
Roxane 309, 310
royal officials and household

architects 60–61, 63, 73, 171, 172,
  175, 197, 204
archivists 176
barbers 91, 187
butchers 77, 98
butlers 150
chamberlains 92
chancellors 51, 123, 124, 253
confectioners 90
engineers 323, 324
in exile 132
governors 93, 106, 107, 115, 116, 131,
  135, 136, 139, 155, 184
guards 102, 103, 105, 116, 222–23
hairdressers 89, 90, 91–92, 123
inspectors 49, 154, 290
intermarrying with royals 154
jewellers 75
librarians 89, 314, 326
manicurists 91
mayors 142, 154, 197, 223, 224, 258,
  263, 279
military officers 87, 94, 105, 106–7,
  107, 123, 146, 168–69, 174, 187, 188,
  192, 265, 271, 345
Nubians 183–84
nurses 191, 197, 218, 221
overseers 80, 84, 87, 102, 103, 105,
  120, 184, 187, 187–88, 197, 198, 203,
  204, 264–65, 273
physicians 60, 87, 89, 194
prime ministers 60, 80, 88, 90, 93,
  93–94, 98, 100–102, 103, 112,
  124–25, 125–26, 153, 185, 192, 222,
  227, 233, 239–240, 252, 260, 264,
  325, 334
sacrificed and buried with monarchs
  45, 46, 49, 52–53
scribes 64, 85, 171, 186, 200, 233,
  240, 244, 247, 253, 259–260, 264,
  266, 269
seal-bearers 94, 116, 138
secretaries 192

stables keeper 191, 193, 201
stewards 84, 120, 123, 124, 176, 178, 181, 182–83, 197, 213, 260, 279, 286, 289
turnover 108, 109
tutors 178, 193, 195
versatile roles 53
Ruddedet story 83–84
Rules of the House 321

Sahara savannah period 11–16
Sahura 85–87, 248
Sai Island 169, 172, 183, 203
Sais 6, 9, 44, 282–293, 299, 334
Sakkara
funerary palaces 58–59
Pyramid Texts 96–97
restoration 247–48
reuse of materials from 128, 129
royal daybook 133–34
sacred track 50
Serapeum 209, 249, 295, 298, 300, 301, 306, 311, 337, 344
state papers 108–9
tombs
Early Dynastic period 44, 46, 48, 51, 52, 54, 54–55
First Intermediate period 115
Late period 287, 301
Middle Kingdom period 147
New Kingdom period 187, 228, 233, 240, 249
Old Kingdom period 60–63, 82, 84–85, 91–92, 92–93, 94–95, 96–99, 100–103, 103–4, 105–6, 107, 109
Salitis 157
Sankhkara (Montuhotep III) 123–25
Satet, goddess 9, 43–44, 46, 131, 209
Satire of the Trades 136
Satis, goddess 89, 286
Saww 131–32, 146
The Sayings of Ptahhoptep 93–94
Scorpion 34–35

Sea Peoples 250, 254–55, 256, 271
Second Intermediate period
15th and 16th Dynasties 157–160, 162, 163–64, 166, 168–69
17th Dynasty 160–67
Abydos Dynasty 157
Avaris-Thebes power struggle 163–67, 168–69
split into Upper and Lower Egypt 157
Second Persian period 302–3
Sekhemkhet 63
Sekhmet, goddess
astronomical calendar 211
Bastet-Sekhmet 74, 78, 86
Hathor-Sekhmet 62, 77–78, 147, 174, 196, 208, 245, 246
myths 7, 10
temples 41–42, 67, 209
Seleucids 317, 325, 329, 330, 333, 335–36, 350
Seleucus 312
Semerkhet 52–53, 63
Semna Despatches 140
Senmut of Armant 176, 178, 181, 182–83
Seqenra (Tao II) 163–65
Serapea
Alexandria 337, 361
Sakkara 249, 295, 298, 301, 306, 311, 337, 344
Serapis, god 306, 309, 313, 326–27
Sesostris I 128, 129, 130–33
Sesostris II 136–39
Sesostris III 139–144
Seth, god 7–8, 31, 32, 56, 160, 235–36, 328
Sethnakht 254
Seti I 235–39, 269
Seti II 252, 272
Shabaqa 278–79
Shabitqa 279
shabti figurines 123
Shedet 131, 145, 151

Shepenwepet I 276, 277
Shepenwepet II 279, 280, 283
Shepseskhaf 82, 84, 248
Sheshonq I 274
ships 67–68, 74, 131–32, 284, 312,
  362–63, 364, 365 see also barques, sacred
Shuttarna 207–8
Siamen 271
Sinai
  military campaigns 85, 94
  mines and quarries 64, 67, 106, 146,
    150, 199
  temples 178
Siptah 252–53, 272
sistrum 99
Siwa oasis 293, 308
Smendes 268
Smenkhkara see Nefertiti/Smenkhkara
Snefru 64–71, 94, 108, 134, 146
Sobek, god 131, 145, 148, 151, 152,
  209–10, 352
Sobekemsaf 161
Sobekemsaf II 262
Sobekhotep I 152
Sobekhotep II 153
Sobekhotep III 153–54
Sobekhotep IV 155
Sobekhotep VIII 155
Sobeknefru 150–52, 176
solar boats 72–73, 74, 84, 90, 97
Soleb 203, 227, 280
Sosibius 329–330, 332
Sothis, goddess 5, 8, 10, 43–44, 46,
  123–24
sphinxes
  Late period 280, 300
  Middle Kingdom period 134, 141,
    146, 151, 159
  New Kingdom period 182, 184, 208
  Old Kingdom period 77–78, 86
  Ptolemaic period 320, 348
  see also Great Sphinx
statues

Early Dynastic period 40, 46, 47, 50,
  52, 54, 57
First Intermediate period 121, 122
Late period 280, 286, 289, 296
Middle Kingdom period 131, 137,
  139, 140, 141, 145, 148, 151, 153, 154,
  155, 209
New Kingdom period 169, 172, 181,
  182, 183, 196, 197, 199, 201–2, 203,
  204, 208, 210, 211–12, 219, 230,
  231–32, 242, 242–43, 245–46, 329
Old Kingdom period 62, 67, 74, 77,
  78, 84, 89, 90, 98, 100, 102, 104
Predynastic period 32, 33
Ptolemaic period 308, 311, 318, 319,
  323, 337, 352
Roman 358
stelae
Early Dynastic period 46, 48, 49, 54,
  55, 56
First Intermediate period 114
Late period 278, 281
Middle Kingdom period 140, 154
New Kingdom period 174, 188, 198,
  202–3, 204, 220, 250–51
Old Kingdom period 103
Ptolemaic Dynasty 330, 333–34
Second Intermediate period 166, 167
stellar alignments 74, 123–24
The Story of Sinuhe 132
sun god Ra
  Amen-Ra 180–81, 189, 194, 196, 203,
    280
  decline 92, 96
  Great He-She 6, 66
  king reborn as 214
  myths 6–7, 9–10, 72–73
  Ra-Horakhty 196, 197, 201
  story of Ruddedet 83–84
  supreme deity 66
  temples 6, 58, 61–62, 85, 86, 90–91,
    99, 106, 113, 130–31, 181–82, 196–97,
    209, 248, 255, 262, 278

see also Aten sun disc, god
Syria/Syrians
  dowry of Kleopatra I 334
  military campaigns 169, 178, 185–86,
    188, 317, 338
  prisoners of war 187
  settlers 206
  trade 32, 120, 146
  tribute 87, 192

Taharqa 279–282
Tanis 270–71, 275
Tantamen 282–83, 285
Tao I 163
Taweret, goddess 163–64, 286
Tawosret 252, 253–54
Tefnut, goddess 7, 10
Tell el-Amarna 220–21, 222, 223–24,
  224–25, 226, 229–230
Tell el-Farkha 32
Tell el-Yahudiya 255, 337
temples
  Amen 188–89, 194, 270, 277, 280–81,
    286, 296 *see also* Karnak
  Amen-Ra 280
  Amenhotep III 203
  Apis bull 249
  Arsinoe II 323–24
  Aten sun disc 196–97, 209, 218,
    218–19, 220, 221, 222
Bastet 54, 99, 146, 274–75
Caesarium 357
Hathor 57–58, 66–67, 120, 145, 146,
  178, 183, 184, 190, 340
Hathor-Isis 270, 351–52
Homer 331
Horus 33–34, 36, 46, 57, 104, 113,
  123–24, 154, 169, 183–84, 197,
  327–28, 332, 348, 357
Isis 280, 286, 299, 319–320, 320, 325
Khnum 312
Khonsu 259
Luxor Temple 210, 227, 300, 308

Min 40, 108, 131, 189, 299, 319–320
Montu 133, 141, 320
the Muses 321
Mut 188–89, 208–9, 211, 270, 280–81,
  286
  at Naukratis 291, 298
Neith 44, 283, 290, 334
Nekhbet 58
Osiris 161–62, 236
Pakhet 184
Ptah 41–42, 49, 50, 96, 209, 218, 247,
  248, 278, 279, 291, 298
Ra-Horakhty 196
Ramses II and Nefertari 245–46
Satet 43–44, 46, 131, 209
Sekhmet 209
Serapis 326–27
Seth 160
Sobek 131, 145, 151, 209–10
Sphinx Temple 78
sun god Ra 6, 58, 61–62, 85, 86,
  90–91, 99, 106, 113, 130–31, 181–82,
  196–97, 209, 248, 255, 262, 278
Thoth 184, 197
Tiy 203
Wadjet 86
Yahweh 286, 337
Zeus-Amen 308
see also funerary temples; Valley
  Temples
Teos 300–301
Teti 99–102
Tetisheri 163, 168
Thebes
  Assyrian invasion 282
  building projects 204
  as capital city 117, 155, 161
  control of 203
  Dendera alliance 117
  graffiti 328–29
  Karnak *see* Karnak
  Luxor Temple 181, 204, 210, 227,
    300, 308

Opet Festival 181, 193
palaces 175, 205–6, 256
power struggle with Avaris 163–67,
  168–69
Ptolemaic power struggle 334, 345
Ramesseum 242–43
rise of 117–18
temples 46, 117, 123–24, 331
tombs *see* Deir el-Bahari; Dra Abu
  el-Naga; Valley of the Kings tombs,
  Thebes
war graves 119
Thera eruption 178–79
Third Intermediate period
  21st Dynasty 268–274
  22nd Dynasty 274–76
  23rd Dynasty 276
  24th Dynasty 278
Thoth, god 73, 79, 184, 197, 246
Tia 195, 196, 199
Tiy 201–2, 203, 213, 214, 215, 217, 218,
  221, 225, 263, 272
Tomb of Osiris 152–53, 209
tomb robbing 69, 161, 234, 246, 250,
  262–63, 265–66, 269, 302, 344
tombs
  1st Dynasty 42, 43, 44–45, 46–47, 48,
    49, 51–53
  2nd Dynasty 54–55, 58–59
  3rd Dynasty 60–64, 65, 248
  4th Dynasty 68–75, 76, 77, 78, 79,
    80, 81, 82, 248
  5th Dynasty 84–85, 86, 88–89, 90,
    91–93, 94–95, 96–99, 248
  6th Dynasty 100–102, 102–3, 103–4,
    105–6, 107, 109
  8th Dynasty 112
  9th and 10th Dynasties 115, 116
  11th Dynasty 117, 118, 120–23,
    124–25
  12th Dynasty 128, 132–33, 134–35,
    135–36, 136–37, 138–39, 142–44,
    146–150, 151

13th Dynasty 152, 153
15th Dynasty 158–59
17th Dynasty 161, 162, 165, 168–69
18th Dynasty 170, 171–72, 175, 178,
  182, 183, 187, 190–92, 197–98, 200,
  209, 212–13, 215–16, 220, 222, 225,
  226, 228, 229–231, 233, 272–73
19th Dynasty 235, 238–39, 243,
  246–47, 249–250, 251–52, 253
20th Dynasty 254, 258, 259, 260, 261,
  262–64, 266–67
21st Dynasty 269, 270–71, 271–73,
  273–74
22nd Dynasty 275, 276
25th Dynasty 278, 279, 280, 282
26th Dynasty 285, 286–87, 293
First Intermediate period 114
Macedonian Dynasty 311, 315, 331
Predynastic period 27, 28–29, 34–35,
  35–36, 42
Ptolemaic Dynasty 357
Towns Palette 29
trade
  Early Dynastic period 43, 57
  First Intermediate period 112, 115
  Late period 285, 291, 296
  Macedonian Dynasty 309
  Middle Kingdom period 146, 150
  New Kingdom period 169, 178, 179,
    240
  Old Kingdom period 67–68, 85, 104,
    106
  Predynastic period 20, 22, 25–26, 28,
    32
  Ptolemaic Dynasty 317–18, 320, 341,
    348, 360
  Second Intermediate period 159
  Third Intermediate period 274
Tura 73, 108, 146, 152
Tushratta 208, 217
Tutankhamen/Tutankhaten 1, 221, 226,
  227–231, 232, 236, 259
Tuthmosis I 172, 173–75, 182, 191

Tuthmosis II 176
Tuthmosis III 176, 178, 181, 184,
 185–191
Tuthmosis IV 198–200, 272
Tuthmosis, son of Amenhotep III 203,
 209, 213, 272
Tuya, mother of Ramses II 241, 243
Tuya, mother of Tiy 201, 212, 215
Two Lands 5, 18, 30–32, 41

Unas 96–99, 248
unification 36–37, 39, 43, 56, 57, 119
Useribra Senebkay 157
Userkaf 84–85
Userkara 102–3

Valley of Pictures 9–10
Valley of the Kings, Amarna 220
Valley of the Kings tombs, Thebes
 18th Dynasty 171–72, 175, 182,
  190–91, 197–98, 200, 212–13, 215–16,
  229–231, 231, 233, 272–73
 19th Dynasty 235, 238–39, 247,
  249–250, 251–52, 253–54
 20th Dynasty 254, 258, 259, 260, 261,
  262–64
 21st Dynasty 269
 22nd Dynasty 276
Valley of the Queens 12, 191, 213, 246,
 263
Valley Temples
 Amenemhat's, Lisht 129
 Khentkawes I's, Giza 81
 Khufu's, Giza 74, 78
 Menkaura's, Giza 80
 Pepi II's, Giza 108
 Sahura's, Abusir 86

Snefru's, Dahshur 108
veterinary practice 138

Wadi el-Garawi dam 67
Wadi Hammamat 12, 23, 28, 40, 120,
 124, 125, 146, 150, 259
Wadjet, goddess 31, 49–50, 55, 62, 86
wars see military campaigns/defence
Waset see Thebes
Waset, goddess 160–61
Wawat 105, 120, 129, 184, 188
wealth
 First Intermediate period 116
 Middle Kingdom period 133–34, 137,
  139, 146, 150
 New Kingdom period 169–170, 175,
  180, 186, 201, 203, 220
 Old Kingdom period 67, 87
 Predynastic period 28, 32
 Ptolemaic period 318
weaponry
 Early Dynastic period 42
 Middle Kingdom period 147
 New Kingdom period 169, 193–94
 Predynastic period 20, 23, 25, 34
 Sahara savannah period 11
 Second Intermediate period 160, 164,
  165
Wedjahorresnet 293, 295, 296
writing 35

Xerxes 296–97
Xois 155, 157

Yuya 201, 212, 215

Zeus-Amen, god 304, 306, 308, 313